Global Implications of Modern Enterprise Information Systems:
Technologies and Applications

Angappa Gunasekaran
University of Massachusetts—Dartmouth, USA

INFORMATION SCIENCE REFERENCE

Hershey · New York

Director of Editorial Content: Kristin Klinger
Director of Production: Jennifer Neidig
Managing Editor: Jamie Snavely
Assistant Managing Editor: Carole Coulson
Typesetter: Jeff Ash
Cover Design: Lisa Tosheff
Printed at: Yurchak Printing Inc.

Published in the United States of America by
     Information Science Reference (an imprint of IGI Global)
     701 E. Chocolate Avenue, Suite 200
     Hershey PA 17033
     Tel: 717-533-8845
     Fax: 717-533-8661
     E-mail: cust@igi-global.com
     Web site: http://www.igi-global.com

and in the United Kingdom by
     Information Science Reference (an imprint of IGI Global)
     3 Henrietta Street
     Covent Garden
     London WC2E 8LU
     Tel: 44 20 7240 0856
     Fax: 44 20 7379 0609
     Web site: http://www.eurospanbookstore.com

Library of Congress Cataloging-in-Publication Data

Global implications of modern enterprise information systems : technologies and applications / Angappa Gunasekaran, editor.

p. cm.

Includes bibliographical references and index.

Summary: "This book presents useful strategies, techniques, and tools for the successful design, development, and implementation of enterprise information systems"--Provided by publisher.

ISBN 978-1-60566-146-9 (hbk.) -- ISBN 978-1-60566-147-6 (ebook)

1. Management information systems. 2. Information technology--Management. I. Gunasekaran, A.

HD30.213.G583 2009

658.4'038011--dc22

2008033934

British Cataloguing in Publication Data
A Cataloguing in Publication record for this book is available from the British Library.

All work contributed to this book set is original material. The views expressed in this book are those of the authors, but not necessarily of the publisher.

Global Implications of Modern Enterprise Information Systems: Technologies and Applications is part of the IGI Global series named *Advances in Enterprise Information Systems (AEIS)* Series, ISBN: 1935-3111

Advances in Enterprise Information Systems (AEIS) Series

ISBN: 1935-3111

Editor-in-Chief: Angappa Gunasekaran, University of Massachusetts—Dartmouth, USA

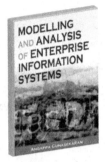

Modelling and Analysis of Enterprise Information Systems

Angappa Gunasekaran, University of Massachusetts—Dartmouth, USA

IGI Publishing * copyright 2007 * 392pp * H/C (ISBN: 978-1-59904-477-4) * US $89.96 (our price)

Insight into issues, challenges, and solutions related to the successful applications and management aspects of enterprise information systems may provide to be a hardship to researchers and practitioners. Modelling Analysis of Enterprise Information Systems presents comprehensive coverage and understanding of the organizational and technological issues of enterprise information systems.

Modelling Analysis of Enterprise Information Systems covers current trends and issues in various enterprise information systems such as enterprise resource planning, electronic commerce, and their implications on supply chain management and organizational competitiveness.

Techniques and Tools for the Design and Implementation of Enterprise Information Systems

Angappa Gunasekaran, University of Massachusetts—Dartmouth, USA

IGI Publishing * copyright 2008 * 303pp * H/C (ISBN: 978-1-59904-826-0) * US $89.96 (our price)

Inter-organizational information systems play a major role in improving communication and integration between partnering firms to achieve an integrated global supply chain. Current research in enterprise resource planning and electronic commerce is crucial to maintaining efficient supply chain management and organizational competitiveness.

Techniques and Tools for the Design & Implementation of Enterprise Information Systems enables libraries to provide an invaluable resource to academicians and practitioners in fields such as operations management, Web engineering, information technology, and management information systems, providing insight into the effective design and implementation of enterprise information systems to improve communication and integration between partnering firms to achieve an integrated global supply chain.

Global Implications of Modern Enterprise Information Systems: Technologies and Applications

Angappa Gunasekaran, University of Massachusetts—Dartmouth, USA

Information Science Reference * copyright 2008 * H/C (ISBN: 978-1-60566-146-9) * US $195.00 (our price)

Many companies have encountered pitfalls in their attempts to successfully implement enterprise resource planning (ERP) that have proven nearly insurmountable, due to lack of techniques and tools for the design and implementation of enterprise information systems (EIS) that are properly aligned with business models and strategic objectives.

Global Implications of Modern Enterprise Information Systems: Technologies and Applications presents useful strategies, techniques, and tools for the successful design, development, and implementation of enterprise information systems (EIS). By assimilating the truly international perspective, this collection constructs on this ascending area of research in an array of related fields will greatly benefit from these cutting-edge findings on modern enterprise information systems.

The Advances in Enterprise Information Systems (AEIS) Book Series aims to expand available literature in support of global markets and the globalized economy surrounding Enterprise Information Systems. The Series provides comprehensive coverage and understanding of the organizational, people and technological issues of EIS. Design, development, justification and implementation of EIS including ERP and EC will be discussed. Global markets and competition have forced companies to operate in a physically distributed environment to take the advantage of benefits of strategic alliances between partnering firms. Earlier, information systems such as Material Requirements Planning (MRP), Computer-Aided Design (CAD) and Computer-Aided Manufacturing (CAM) have widely been used for functional integration within an organization. With global operations in place, there is a need for suitable Enterprise Information Systems (EIS) such as Enterprise Resource Planning (ERP) and E-Commerce (EC) for the integration of extended enterprises along the supply chain with the objective of achieving flexibility and responsiveness. Companies all over the world spend billions of dollars in the design and implementation of EIS in particular ERP systems such as Oracle, Peoplesoft, SAP, JD Edwards and BAAN with the objective of achieving an integrated global supply chain. Inter-organizational information systems play a major role in improving communication and integration between partnering firms to achieve an integrated global supply chain. The Advances in Enterprise Information Systems (AEIS) Book Series endeavors to further this field and address the growing demand for research and applications that will provide insights into issues, challenges, and solutions related to the successful applications and management aspects of EIS.

Hershey · New York

Order online at www.igi-global.com or call 717-533-8845 x 100–

Mon-Fri 8:30 am - 5:00 pm (est) or fax 24 hours a day 717-533-7115

Table of Contents

Detailed Table of Contents

Chapter I

    Emad M. Kamhawi, Zagazig University, Egypt

Responding to the need for a better understanding of the factors that explain ERP systems implementation success, this chapter used a field study to collect data from managers working in Bahraini enterprises that use ERP systems to examine the influence of some selected factors on two perspectives: project and business success of such systems. Results support previous research findings in this area concerning the impact of factors such as project planning, organizational resistance, and ease of use on ERP project success metrics. Also the study results show that project planning; business process reengineering; and organizational fit have significant influence on business success metrics. However, no significant impact was found for some classical success factors such as top management support, technical fit, training, competitive pressure, and strategic fit on both project and business success. The chapter ends with implications for these findings and possible extensions for the study.

Chapter II

    Ronald E. McGaughey, University of Central Arkansas, USA
    Angappa Gunasekaran, University of Massachusetts—Dartmouth, USA

Business needs have driven the design, development, and use of the enterprise-wide information systems we call Enterprise Resource Planning (ERP) systems. Intra enterprise integration was a driving force in the design, development, and use of early ERP systems. Changing business needs have brought about the current business environment, wherein supply chain integration is desirable, if not essential, thus current and evolving ERP systems demonstrate an expanded scope of integration that encompasses limited inter-enterprise integration. This chapter explores the evolution, the current status, and future of ERP, with the objective of promoting relevant future research in this important area. If researchers hope to play a significant role in the design, development, and use of suitable ERP systems to meet evolving business needs, then their research should focus at least in part on the changing business environment, its impact on business needs, and the requirements for enterprise systems that meet those needs.

Chapter III

Purnendu Mandal, Lamar University, USA

Mohan P. Rao, University of Louisiana, USA

The build-up of export-oriented companies since 1990s on the Mexico-USA boarder, and their recent decline, is no surprise to many policy analysts. The focus on the use of low-wage employees, neglecting skills, and infrastructure creation was doomed to fail. Much of the Mexican maquila operations and jobs have gone to China and other low-wage countries. Are maquiladoras technologically competent to ward-off competitive forces from China and other parts of the world? This chapter presents an exploratory study of IT usage and managerial perceptions of IT-related costs and benefits in maquiladoras. The relevant data was gathered through a survey questionnaire. The results show that IT had a positive impact on maquila business performance. These findings will be useful to managers in assessing their organization and taking corrective actions to become further competitive.

Chapter IV

Henk Jonkers, BiZZdesign, The Netherlands

Maria-Eugenia Iacob, Univeristy of Twente, The Netherlands

In this chapter the authors address the integration of functional models with non-functional models in the context of service-oriented architectures. Starting from the observation that current approaches to model-driven development have a strong focus on functionality, we argue the necessity of including non-functional aspects as early as possible in the service design process. We distinguish two modelling spaces, the design space and the analysis space, which can be integrated by means of model transformations. Quantitative results obtained in the analysis space, using special-purpose analysis techniques, can be related back to the design models by means of a reverse transformation. This provides a framework for incorporating non-functional analysis into methodological support for e-service development. While, for detailed design models, quantitative analysis is more or less covered by existing techniques, there is still a gap at the architectural overview level. Therefore, we propose an approach for performance and cost analysis of layered, service-oriented architecture models, which consists of two phases: a "top-down" propagation of workload parameters, and a "bottom-up" propagation of performance or cost measures. By means of an example, the authors demonstrate the application of the approach, and show that a seamless integration with detailed quantitative analysis methods (e.g., queueing analysis for performance predictions) can be achieved.

Chapter V

S. Parthasarathy, Thiagarajar College of Engineering, India

Enterprise Resource Planning (ERP) system is an integrated software system reflecting the business processes of an enterprise. Enterprise Resource Planning (ERP) system is a generic term for integrated systems for corporate computing that supersedes concepts such as Materials Requirements Planning (MRP) of the 1970s and, later, Manufacturing Resource Planning (MRP II) of the 1980s. The objective of customization in ERP implementation is to achieve a fit between the ERP system and the business process that the system supports. A literature review reveals that the customization is the major annoyance in most of the ERP projects. A solution is proposed using a process framework that incorporates participatory learning and decision-making processes based on Nominal Group Technique (NGT) and the evaluation methodology adopting the Analytical Hierarchy Process (AHP). A case study is presented to illustrate its applicability in practice. The upshot of the study is the identification of various customization possibilities for ERP implementation. This study is meant to help managers think about the various feasible customization options available to them. Future research work that can be done in ERP software customization is also indicated.

Chapter VI

Manuel Kolp, Université Catholique de Louvain Place des Doyens, Belgium
Yves Wautelet, Université Catholique de Louvain Place des Doyens, Belgium
Stéphane Faulkner, University of Namur Rempart de la Vierge, Belgium

Organizational Modeling is concerned with analyzing and understanding the organizational context within which a software system will eventually function. This chapter proposes organizational patterns motivated by organizational theories intended to facilitate the construction of organizational models. These patterns are defined from real world organizational settings, modeled in i* and formalized using the Formal Tropos language. Additionally, the chapter evaluates the proposed patterns using desirable qualities such as coordinability and predictability. The research is conducted in the context of Tropos, a comprehensive software system development methodology.

Chapter VII

Piotr Soja, Cracow University of Economics, Poland
Dariusz Put, Cracow University of Economics, Poland

Enterprise resource planning (ERP) systems have been implemented in various and diverse organizations. The size of companies, their industry, the environment, and the number of implemented modules are examples of their heterogeneity. In consequence, a single procedure which leads to the success of implementation does not appear to exist. Therefore, there have been many implementations that have failed during, and also after, the implementation process. As a result, a considerable amount of research has been trying to identify issues influencing ultimate project success and also to recognize the best implementation projects. The aim of this work is to identify the most important characteristics of ERP implementation which affect project success. This study builds on data gathered using a questionnaire directed toward people playing leading roles in ERP implementations in a few dozen companies. Twelve attributes were identified and divided into three sets representing: effort, effect, and the synthetic measure of success calculated on the basis of the obtained data. Two agglomeration methods were employed to identify exemplar and anti-exemplar groups and objects. These elements were thoroughly analyzed, which led to identifying the most and the least desired attributes of an ERP implementation project. The findings are discussed and related with the results of prior research. Finally, implications for practitioners and concluding remarks summarise the chapter.

Other than providing Web services through popular Web browser interfaces, pervasive computing may offer new ways of accessing Internet applications by utilizing various modes of interfaces to interact with their end-users, and its technology could involve new ways of interfacing with various types of gateways to back-end servers from any device, anytime, and anywhere. In this chapter, mobile phone was used as the pervasive device for accessing an Internet application prototype, a voice-enabled Web system (VWS), through voice user interface technology. Today's Web sites are intricate but not intelligent, so finding an efficient method to assist user searching is particularly important. One of these efficient methods is to construct an adaptive Web site. This chapter shows that multimodal user-interface pages can be generated by using XSLT stylesheet which transforms XML documents into various formats including XHTML, WML, and VoiceXML. It also describes how VWS was designed to provide an adaptive voice interface using an Apache Web server, a voice server, a Java servlet engine, and a genetic algorithm based voice Web restructuring mechanism.

Research has showed that social and socio-technical concepts are influenced by culture. The objective of this chapter is to explore how the socio-technical concept of information system success is defined and perceived by a group of French managers. The results show that culture does influence IS success perception. The study has many implications for both academic and practice communities. The results are especially important to multinational organizations that standardize IS in different cultures including France. The research case is a multibillion dollar Canadian multinational organization which decided to standardize an Enterprise Resource Planning (ERP) system in all its worldwide subsidiaries.

Chapter X

Much of the early focus in the area of Semantic Web has been on the development of representation languages for static conceptual information; while there has been less emphasis on how to make Semantic Web applications practically useful in the context of knowledge work. To achieve this, a better coupling is needed between ontology, service descriptions, and workflow modeling, including both traditional production workflow and interactive workflow techniques. This chapter reviews the basic technologies involved in this area to provide system and business interoperability, and outlines what can be achieved by merging them in the context of real-world workflow descriptions.

    Cheng-Yang Cheng, Penn State University, USA
    Vamsi Salaka, Penn State University, USA
    Vittal Prabhu, Penn State University, USA

The success of implementing Enterprise Information System (EIS) depends on exploring and improving the EIS software, and EIS software training. However, the synthesis of the EIS implementation approach has not been investigated. In this chapter, the authors propose an integrated research and training approach for students and employees about enterprise information systems (EIS) that are encountered in an organization. Our integrated approach follows the different stages of a typical EIS project from inception to completion. These stages, as identified, are modeling, planning, simulation, transaction, integration, and control. This ensures that an employee who is trained by this plan has an acquaintance with the typical information systems in an organization. Further, for training and research purposes the authors developed prototype information systems that emulate the ones usually found in organizations. This ensures the EIS software logic is consistent with the business logic. This chapter also discuss some of the case studies conducted with the prototype systems.

    Lea Kutvonen, University of Helsinki, Finland
    Toni Ruokolainen, University of Helsinki, Finland
    Sini Ruohomaa, University of Helsinki, Finland
    Janne Metso, University of Helsinki, Finland

Participation in electronic business networks has become necessary for the success of enterprises. The strategic business needs for participating in multiple networks simultaneously and for managing changes in these networks are reflected as new requirements for the supporting computing facilities. The Pilarcos architecture addresses the needs of managed collaboration and interoperability of autonomous business services in an inter-organisational context. The Pilarcos B2B middleware is designed for lowering the cost and effort of collaboration establishment and to facilitate the management and maintenance of electronic business networks. The approach is a federated one: All business services are developed independently, and the provided B2B middleware services are used to ensure that technical, semantic, and pragmatic interoperability is maintained in the business network. In the architecture and middleware functionality design, attention has been given to the dynamic aspects and evolution of the network. This chapter discusses the concepts provided for application and business network creators, and the supporting middleware-level knowledge repositories for interoperability support.

    Joseph Bradley, University of Idaho, USA
    C. Christopher Lee, Pacific Lutheran University, USA

Training is still a neglected part of most ERP implementation projects. This case study investigates the relation between training satisfaction and the perceptions of ease of use, the perception of usefulness, effectiveness and efficiency in implementing an ERP system at a mid-sized organization. We view training satisfaction as a necessary condition for technology acceptance. Our surrogates for training satisfaction are (1) training level prior to implementation, (2) training level when measured after implementation, (3) understanding of features and functions, and (4) perceived need for more training because these factors contribute to perceived ease of use and usefulness. A survey of 143 employees involved in the implementation of ERP in a mid-sized university was conducted. ANOVA and t-tests were used to explore differences in training satisfaction among groups of users by gender, job type, and education level. We found that training satisfaction differed based on job type and gender but not education level. Multiple regression analysis suggests that (1) post implementation training satisfaction is related to ease of use and (2) current training satisfaction and user participation are related to our variables for usefulness, which are perceived efficiency and effectiveness of the ERP systems in doing respondents' jobs

Chapter XIV

    Diego Milano, Università degli Studi di Roma, Italy
    Monica Scannapieco, Università degli Studi di Roma, Italy
    Tiziana Catarci, Università degli Studi di Roma, Italy

Data quality is a complex concept defined by various dimensions such as accuracy, currency, completeness, and consistency. Recent research has highlighted the importance of data quality issues in various contexts. In particular, in some specific environments characterized by extensive data replication high quality of data is a strict requirement. Among such environments, this article focuses on Cooperative Information Systems.

Chapter XV

    Vipul Jain, Indian Institute of Technology Delhi, India
    S. Wadhwa, Indian Institute of Technology Delhi, India
    S. G. Deshmukh, Indian Institute of Technology Delhi, India

The key part of dynamic supply chain management is negotiating with suppliers and with buyers. Designing efficient business processes throughout the supply chain, and controlling their speed, timing, and interaction with one another, is decisive factors in a competitive and dynamic environment. Coordination is essential for successful supply chain management. Therefore, in this chapter, a novel Negotiation-to-Coordinate (N2C) mechanism is proposed to explore the interactive nature of the buyer-supplier relationships for dynamic environments. The proposed N2C mechanism uses prioritized fuzzy constraints to represent trade-offs among the different probable values associated with the negotiation issues and to signify how agents should make concessions. Supervisor agent in the N2C mechanism takes into account the conflicts of interest of buyer's agent and supplier's agent and the proposal and plan generated by supervisor agents helps in resolving the true and potential conflicts of interests for buyer's agent and supplier's agent. The proposed computational framework based on fuzzy constraints is suited for capturing the dynamics by modeling trade-offs between different attributes of a product leading to a fair and equitable deal for both suppliers and buyers. The proposed approach models the intricacies in the face of the imprecise, uncertain and conflicting nature of objectives. The efficacy of the proposed approach is demonstrated through an illustrative example.

Enterprise Systems are widespread in current organizations and seen as integrating organizational procedures across functional divisions. An Enterprise System, once installed, seems to enable or constrain certain actions by users, which have an impact on organizational operations. Those actions may result in increased organizational control, or may lead to organizational drift. The processes that give rise to such outcomes are investigated in this chapter, which is based on a field study of five companies. By drawing on the theoretical concepts of human and machine agencies, as well as the embedding and disembedding of information in the system, this chapter argues that control and drift arising from the use of an Enterprise System are outcomes of the processes of embedding and disembedding human actions, which are afforded (enabled or constrained) by the Enterprise System.

Preface

Enterprise Information Systems (EIS) such as the Enterprise Resource Planning (ERP), Electronic Data Interchange (EDI), World Wide Web (WWW), E-Commerce (EC) and Radio Frequency Identification (RFID) automate business processes and provide access to data from global operations. These systems have been used to integrate business processes along the supply chain. Technologies such as the Internet, WWW, EDI, and RFID have tremendous applications in the advanced enterprise information systems. In the 21st Century global market, companies heavily rely on global operations which obviously need an advanced enterprise information system such as ERP, EDI, EC, RFID, and WWW. Considering the importance of ERP in operations and competitiveness of companies in global markets, this edited book focuses on the global implications of modern EIS on the physically distributed enterprise environments.

Effective communication along the supply chain is essential to provide a high level of customer service by delivering the right products at the right time, and in the quantity and price. In order to avoid any quality and delivery problems of materials, a real-time and shared enterprise information system such as ERP, EDI, WWW, EC, and RFID are important. The objective of EIS is to facilitate a smooth flow of information along the supply chain. Global supply chain operations, virtual enterprise, outsourcing, and physically distributed enterprise environments force companies to implement modern EIS such as ERP. This edited book presents the global implications of modern EIS and corresponding technologies and applications. It is our hope that both academic researchers and practitioners will benefit from the technology and application strategies, tactics and tools of EIS. An overview of the chapters is presented hereunder.

Chapter I, "Examining the Factors Affecting Project and Business Success of ERP Implementation" by Emad M. Kamhawi responds to the need for a better understanding of the factors that explain ERP systems implementation success. This chapter used a field study to collect data from managers working in Bahraini enterprises that use ERP systems to examine the influence of some selected factors on two perspectives: project and business success of such systems. Results support the impact of factors such as project planning, organizational resistance, and ease of use on ERP project success metrics. Also, this study shows that project planning, business process reengineering, and organizational fit have significant influence on business success metrics. However, no significant impact was found for some classical success factors such as top management support, technical fit, training, competitive pressure, and strategic fit on both project and business success.

Chapter II, "Evolution of Enterprise Resource Planning" by Ronald E. McGaughey and Angappa Gunasekaran, argues that business needs have driven the design, development, and use of the enterprise-wide information systems we call ERP systems. Intra enterprise integration was a driving force in the design, development, and use of early ERP systems. Changing business needs have brought about the current business environment, wherein supply chain integration is desirable if not essential, thus current and evolving ERP systems demonstrate an expanded scope of integration that encompasses limited inter-enterprise integration. This chapter explores the evolution of ERP, the current status of ERP, and future of ERP, with the objective of promoting relevant future research in this important area. If researchers hope to play a significant role in the design, development, and use of suitable ERP systems to meet evolving business needs, then their research should focus at least in part on the changing business environment, its impact on business needs, and the requirements for enterprise systems that meet those needs.

Chapter III, "Information Technology Usage in Maquila Enterprises," by Purnendu Mandal and Mohan P. Rao, claims that much of the Mexican maquila operations and jobs, have gone to China and other low-wage countries. Are maquiladoras technologically competent to ward-off competitive forces from China and other parts of the world? This chapter presents an exploratory study of IT usage and managerial perceptions of IT-related costs and benefits in maquiladoras. The relevant data was gathered through a survey questionnaire. The results show that IT had a positive impact on maquila business performance. These findings will be useful to managers in assessing their organization and taking corrective actions to become further competitive.

Chapter IV, "Performance and Cost Analysis of Service-Oriented Enterprise Architecture," by Henk Jonkers and Maria-Eugenia Iacob, addresses the integration of functional models with non-functional models in the context of service-oriented architectures. Starting from the observation that current approaches, to model-driven development, have a strong focus on functionality; they argue the necessity of including non-functional aspects as early as possible in the service design process. The authors distinguish two modelling spaces, the design space and the analysis space, which can be integrated by means of model transformations. A framework for incorporating non-functional analysis into methodological support for e-service development is presented. Also, they propose an approach for performance and cost analysis of layered, service-oriented architecture models, which consists of two phases: a "top-down" propagation of workload parameters, and a "bottom-up" propagation of performance or cost measures. By means of an example, they demonstrate the application of the approach, and show that a seamless integration with detailed quantitative analysis methods (e.g., queuing analysis for performance predictions) can be achieved.

Chapter V, "Significance of Analytical Hierarchy Process (AHP) and Nominal Group Technique (NGT) in ERP Implementation," by S. Parthasarathy, argues that the objective of customization in ERP implementation is to achieve a fit between the ERP system and the business process that the system supports. Literature review reveals that the customization is the major annoyance in most of the ERP projects. In this chapter, a solution is proposed using a process framework that incorporates participatory learning and decision-making processes based on Nominal Group Technique (NGT) and the evaluation methodology adopting the Analytical Hierarchy Process (AHP). A case study is presented to illustrate its applicability in practice. The main focus of the study is the identification of various customization possibilities for ERP implementation.

Chapter VI, "Specifying Software Models with Organizational Styles" by Manuel Kolp, Yves Wautelet, and Stéphane Faulkner proposes organizational patterns motivated by organizational theories intended to facilitate the construction of organizational models. These patterns are defined from real-world organizational settings, modeled in i* and formalized using the Formal Tropos language. Additionally, the chapter evaluates the proposed patterns using desirable qualities such as coordinability and predictability. The research is conducted in the context of *Tropos*, a comprehensive software system development methodology.

Chapter VII, "Towards Identifying the Most Important Attributes of ERP Implementations," by Piotr Soja and Dariusz Put, identifies the most important characteristics of ERP implementation which affect project success. This study builds on data gathered using a questionnaire directed toward people playing leading roles in ERP implementations in a few dozen companies. Twelve attributes were identified and divided into three sets representing: effort, effect, and the synthetic measure of success calculated on the basis of the obtained data. Two agglomeration methods were employed to identify exemplar and anti-exemplar groups and objects. These elements were thoroughly analysed, which led to identifying the most and the least desired attributes of an ERP implementation project.

Chapter VIII, "A Voice-Enabled Pervasive Web System with Self-Optimization Capability for Supporting Enterprise Applications," by Shuchih Ernest Chang, used mobile phone as the pervasive device for accessing an Internet application prototype, a voice-enabled Web system (VWS), through voice user interface technology. Today's Web sites are intricate but not intelligent, so finding an efficient method to assist user searching is particularly important. One of these efficient methods is to construct an adaptive Web site. This chapter shows that multimodal user-interface pages can be generated by using XSLT stylesheet which transforms XML documents into various formats including XHTML, WML, and VoiceXML. It also describes how VWS was designed to provide an adaptive voice interface using an Apache Web server, a voice server, a Java servlet engine, and a genetic algorithm-based voice Web restructuring mechanism.

Chapter IX, "The Impact of Culture on the Perception of Information System Success," by Dafid Agourram, showed that social and socio-technical concepts are influenced by culture. This study explores how the socio-technical concept of information system success is defined and perceived by a group of French managers. The results show that culture does influence IS success perception. The study has many implications for both academic and practice communities. The results are especially important to multinational organizations that standardize IS in different cultures, including France. The research case is a multibillion dollar Canadian multinational organization which decided to standardize an ERP system in all its worldwide subsidiaries.

Chapter X, "Achieving System and Business Interoperability by Semantic Web Services" by John Krogstie, Csaba Veres, Guttorm Sindre, and Oyvind Skytoen, claims that much of the early focus in the area of Semantic Web has been on the development of representation languages for static conceptual information; while there has been less emphasis on how to make Semantic Web applications practically useful in the context of knowledge work. To achieve this, a better coupling is needed between ontology, service descriptions, and workflow modeling, including both traditional production workflow and interactive workflow techniques. This chapter reviews the basic technologies involved in this area to provide system and business interoperability, and outlines what can be achieved by merging them in the context of real-world workflow descriptions.

Chapter XI, "Integrated Research and Training in Enterprise Information Systems" by Cheng-Yang Cheng, Vamsi Salaka, and Vittal Prabhu, claims that the success of implementing Enterprise Information System (EIS) depends on exploring and improving the EIS software, and EIS software training. However, the synthesis of the EIS implementation approach has not been investigated. They propose an integrated research and training approach for students and employees about enterprise information systems (EIS) that are encountered in an organization. Their integrated approach follows the different stages of a typical EIS project from inception to completion. These stages, as they identified, are modeling, planning, simulation, transaction, integration, and control. This ensures that an employee who's trained by this plan has an acquaintance with the typical information systems in an organization. Further, for training and research purposes they developed prototype information systems that emulate the ones usually found in organizations.

Chapter XII, "Service-Oriented Middleware for Managing Inter-Enterprise Collaborations," by Lea Kutvonen, Toni Ruokolainen, Sini Ruohomaa, and Janne Metso, argues that participation in electronic business networks has become necessary for the success of enterprises. The strategic business needs for participating in multiple networks simultaneously and for managing changes in these networks are rejected as new requirements for the supporting computing facilities. The Pilarcos architecture addresses the needs of managed collaboration and interoperability of autonomous business services in an inter-organizational context. The Pilarcos B2B middleware is designed for lowering the cost and effort of collaboration establishment and to facilitate the management and maintenance of electronic business networks. All business services are developed independently, and the provided B2B middleware services are used to ensure that technical, semantic, and pragmatic interoperability is maintained in the business network. This chapter discusses the concepts provided for application and business network creators, and the supporting middleware-level knowledge repositories for interoperability support.

Chapter XIII, "Training and User Acceptance in a University ERP Implementation: Applying the Technology Acceptance Model," by Joseph Bradley and C. Christopher Lee, investigates the relation between training satisfaction and the perceptions of ease of use, the perception of usefulness, effectiveness, and efficiency in implementing an ERP system at a mid-sized organization. The authors view training satisfaction as a necessary condition for technology acceptance. Their surrogates for training satisfaction are (1) training level prior to implementation, (2) training level when measured after implementation, (3) understanding of features and functions, and (4) perceived need for more training because these factors contribute to perceived ease of use and usefulness. A survey of 143 employees involved in the implementation of ERP in a mid-sized university was conducted. ANOVA and t-tests were used to explore differences in training satisfaction among groups of users by gender, job type, and education level. They found that training satisfaction differed based on job type and gender but not education level. Multiple regression analysis suggests that (1) post implementation training satisfaction is related to ease of use and (2) current training satisfaction and user participation are related to our variables for usefulness, which are perceived efficiency and effectiveness of the ERP systems in doing respondents' jobs.

Chapter XIV, "Measuring and Diffusing Data Quality in a Peer-to-Peer Architecture," by Diego Milano, Monica Scannapieco, and Tiziana Catarci, focuses on Cooperative Information Systems (CISs), for which it is very important to declare and access quality of data. The chapter describes a general methodology for evaluating quality of data, and the design of two architectural components: *(i)* a component named Quality Factory, that implements quality evaluation of XML data; and *(ii)* a component named Object Matcher, that implements object identification of XML data. The detailed design and implementation of a further service, named Data Quality Broker, are presented. The Data Quality Broker accesses data and related quality distributed in the CIS and improves quality of data by comparing different copies present in the system. The Data Quality Broker has been implemented as a peer-to-peer service and a set of experiments on real data show its effectiveness and performance behavior.

Chapter XV, "Modeling Buyer-Supplier Relationships in Dynamic Supply Chains: A Negotiation-to-Coordinate (N2C) Mechanism," by Vipul Jain, S. Wadhwa, and S.G. Deshmukh, presents a novel Negotiation-to-Coordinate (N2C) mechanism to explore the interactive nature of the buyer-supplier relationships for dynamic environments. The proposed N2C mechanism uses prioritized fuzzy constraints to represent trade-offs among the different probable values associated with the negotiation issues and to signify how agents should make concessions. Supervisor agent in the N2C mechanism takes into account the conflicts of interest of buyer's agent and supplier's agent, and the proposal and plan generated by supervisor agents helps in resolving the true and potential conflicts of interests for buyer's agent and supplier's agent. The proposed computational framework based on fuzzy constraints is suited for capturing the dynamics by modeling trade-offs between different attributes of a product, leading to a fair and equitable deal for both suppliers and buyers. The proposed approach models the intricacies in the face of the imprecise, uncertain, and conflicting nature of objectives.

Chapter XVI, "Enterprise Systems, Control and Drift," by Ioannis Ignatiadis and Joe Nadhakumar, argues that an Enterprise System, once installed, seems to enable or constrain certain actions by users, which have an impact on organizational operations. Those actions may result in increased organizational control, or may lead to organizational drift. The processes that give rise to such outcomes are investigated in this chapter, which is based on a field study of five companies. By drawing on the theoretical concepts of human and machine agencies, as well as the embedding and disembedding of information in the system, this chapter agues that control and drift arising from the use of an Enterprise System are outcomes of the processes of embedding and disembedding human actions, which are afforded (enabled or constrained) by the Enterprise System.

Enterprise information systems have become an essential part of global supply chain. Global implications of ERP and other similar systems have tremendous role in the integration of global supply chain operations. An outstanding collection of the latest research associated with the implications of global market, operations, and modern enterprise information systems on technologies and applications, "Advances in Enterprise Information Systems—Volume III on Global Implications of Modern Enterprise Information Systems: Technologies and Applications", provides insight and assistance in learning how to understand and evaluate the global implications of modern enterprise information systems.

My sincere thanks go to all the authors of this edited book whose timely submissions and revisions of chapters have made this book possible. I am thankful to Dr. Medhi Khosrowpour, President of IGI Global, Ms. Kristin Roth, Managing Editor, and Ms. Deborah Yahnke, Editorial Assistant, for their constant support throughout editing the book.

I am grateful to my wife, Latha Parameswari and son, Rangarajan, for their support and understanding during this book project.

Angappa Gunasekaran, PhD
Editor-in-Chief
Advances in Enterprise Information Systems (AEIS) Book Series

Chapter I
Examining the Factors Affecting Project and Business Success of ERP Implementation

Emad M. Kamhawi
Zagazig University, Egypt

ABSTRACT

Responding to the need for a better understanding of the factors that explain ERP systems implementation success, this chapter used a field study to collect data from managers working in Bahraini enterprises that use ERP systems to examine the influence of some selected factors on two perspectives: project and business success of such systems. Results support previous research findings in this area concerning the impact of factors such as project planning, organizational resistance, and ease of use on ERP project success metrics. Also the study results show that project planning; business process reengineering; and organizational fit have significant influence on business success metrics. However, no significant impact was found for some classical success factors such as top management support, technical fit, training, competitive pressure, and strategic fit on both project and business success. The chapter ends with implications for these findings and possible extensions for the study.

INTRODUCTION

ERP systems have drawn much attention of many researchers and practitioners in the last two decades (Wagner *et al.,* 2006; Ehie & Madsen, 2005; Beheshti, 2006). They have been considered as a shift in corporate computing (Sandoe et al., 2001; Davenport, 2000; Turban et al., 2005). The essence of this shift is twofold. Firstly, it helped replacing the firm's many standalone applications that could not communicate with each other within the organization or externally with customers and suppliers, with large systems that facilitate enterprise-wide integration. Secondly, it stimulated organizations' IT strategies to rely more on purchasing large applications software such as ERP systems, instead of in-house-built information systems. These packages offer general or universally applicable solutions that claim to embody "best practices" of business integration.

ERP systems could be defined as comprehensive software packages that seek to integrate the complete range of business processes and functions in order to present a holistic view of the business from a single information and information technology architecture (Gable, 1998). Among the most important attributes of ERP systems are their abilities to: automate and integrate an organization's business processes; share common data and practices across the entire enterprise; and produce and access information in a real-time environment.

Having made substantial progress toward putting these packages in place, organizations began to work on realizing and extending the benefits from these systems. In a field study by Market Data Group, it was found that main perceived benefits of implementing ERP systems are: standardizing or improving business processes; lowering costs; solving Y2K problem of the legacy systems; and accommodating corporate growth or market demand (Connolly, 1999). Tangible benefits included reduction in staff, operational efficiencies, reduction in training, and better inventory management. Also sources of intangible benefits included better compliance with the customer requirements, improved systems reliability, higher data quality, and greater agility in implementing new businesses.

On the other side, the scale and complexity of these systems have proved a challenge to both IS specialists in terms of implementation, and business management in terms of managing business changes essential to gaining benefits from these very expensive investments. In fact, the use of ERP systems has not always led to significant organizational improvements. In many cases, problems in implementing these systems have led to failures. For example a survey of ERP implementers reported that 51% of the ERP systems implementation projects were judged to be unsuccessful by the ERP implementing firms (Aiken, 2002). However as investments in ERP systems continue to increase, implementations problems suggest that causes of these problems or failures need to be understood and solutions leading to success need to be found (Calisir and Calisir, 2004).

Responding to this need, various streams of research have appeared recently. The first and probably the most famous is the one concentrating on identifying ERP systems' critical success factors (Holland et al., 1999 and Bingi et al., 1999). This line of research has its roots in IS success studies in the past two decades (Delone and Mclean, 1992). Somers and Nelson (2004) see that better description of IS implementation success come from understanding the key players and activities associated with ERP implementation. Diffusion of Innovation (DOI) is another important trend used for studying ERP implementation success (Bradford and Florin, 2003). DOI research has evolved from a focus on the organization's innovation, its organizational characteristics, and also its environment as the main groups of variables that affect the diffusion of IT in organizations.

Another important approach for studying ERP implementation is the process approach. By contrast to the previous lines of research in this subject, this approach seeks to explain outcomes by explaining sequences of events overtime, which are classically presented in stages of implementation life cycles (Markus and Tanis, 2000; Rajagopal, 2002). Combining both factors and process views has attracted many researchers, resulting in other frameworks that classify success factors into different stages of ERP implementation life cycle (Nah et al., 2001; Somers and Nelson, 2004). Many other researchers are still trying to use this literature and empirical evidences to group and subgroup critical success factors into frameworks that interpret different ERP problems' settings (Somers and Nelson, 2004; Amoako-Gympah, 2005).

This study tries to extend this literature by suggesting a set of factors that affect success in a developing country setting, namely Bahrain. In the study's theoretical model, we included two separate success metrics: project success and business value metrics. Regression analysis was used, with a sample of Bahraini firms that have adopted ERP systems, to find the different sets of antecedents affecting project success and business success.

THEORETICAL FRAMEWORK AND HYPOTHESES

In spite of their high costs, ERP projects' goals are not easily achieved. Very few companies reported that their initiatives had achieved significant value. Although many companies claimed success, few met their objectives or realized significant financial impact, while some others could have achieved similar value for less money (Buckhout *et al.,* 1999). A study of the Standish Group estimates at 31% the rate of non-succeeding projects; this alarming figure confirms the anxiety underlined by numerous headlines in the computer press (Buckhout *et al.,* 1999). It is clear that things do not come easy with ERP systems' implementations. Some compared ERP adoption with 'unleashing' a beast into the organization that assumes its own authority over things (Nandhakumar *et al.,* 2005).

On the other hand, the meaning of implementation success may differ from one person to another and from one situation to another as well. Moreover, studies examining the different stages of ERP implementation life cycle see that success factors influences on these systems can be temporal, i.e. their relative importance change with the move from one stage to another in the implementation life cycle (Somers and Nelson, 2004).

Also measuring success may differ as well, from one study to another. Many studies used objective organizational measures, such as company cost and/or profits figures as measurement items for IS success (Poston and Grabski, 2001). However, since these types of data items are usually hard to obtain, many researchers use self-reported subjective IS success measures. User satisfaction and intention to use information systems are examples of famous success measures, usually used for studies concentrating on issues related to diffusion of innovation (Bradford and Florin, 2003) and technology acceptance by end users (Amoako-Gympah and Salam, 2004).

Markus and Tanis (2000) distinguish between two types or dimensions of success for ERP systems implementation: project success metrics, in terms of meeting the project due dates, budgets, and scope and performance expected, and business value metrics, in terms of business improvements such as inventory reduction, cycle times reduction, time to market reduction...etc.

In this study we examine the relationships between some selected classical success factors with the two success dimensions suggested by Markus and Tanis (2000). To test these relationships we ran a separate multiple regression analysis for each of the two dependent variables or success dimensions.

The framework suggested in this paper tries to contribute to the studies concentrating on the factors view of ERP implementation success, through two aspects. First, the model reflects a developing country practices. It is thought that the literature of ERP implementation needs to accommodate non-western experiences as viewed by researchers such as Hong and Kim (2002) and Soh et al. (2000) who highlighted the problem of incompatibility of these packages with Asian enterprises. We tried to address the complex adaptation process required for successful implementation of ERP systems by including factors that relate to this issue such as organizational fit, technical fit, strategic fit, and business process reengineering, as discussed shortly. The framework draws on Hong and Kim (2003) and Bradford and Florin (2003) future research suggestions concerning including such variables to reflect different implementation environments for such systems.

Second, the model distinguishes between two important success factors: project metrics and business value metrics, as mentioned above. It tests the suggested success factors against each dimension separately. It is not clear in the literature which success factors might impact differently to these success dimensions. Furthermore, there are no empirical evidences about the possible role that either of the success measures might have in an integrated model.

An extensive review to the related literature was conducted to identify the critical success factors for ERP implementation. What eased this task is that some previous studies have recently done this review before (e.g., Nah et al., 2000; Somers and Nelson, 2004). Based on this desk search, we came up with an initial list of 15 related factors. Three interviews with IT managers with previous experience in managing ERP implementation projects and another interview with a faculty member – with a good background in this subject – were used to refine this list. Our main concern was to include the factors that could be more influential to a developing country setting like Bahrain, and to avoid including unnecessary similar factors. The final list included 10 factors, discussed in turn.

1. **Technical fit:** In an ERP environment, it is likely that certain legacy systems will be retained and consequently need to be integrated with the core ERP technology. In these circumstances, a technical fit is an important requisite for integrating the ERP system with the old remaining systems in the organization. Technical fit then refers to the degree of compatibility with these retained systems, including hardware and software (Delone and Mclean, 1992). Bradford and Florin (2003) in their study of the impact of this factor – as an innovative characteristic – found an evidence of its influence on ERP success.

2. **Organizational fit:** The difference in interests between the organization adopting the ERP system, which desires a unique solution for its organization, and the ERP vendor, who offers a generic solution, applicable to a broad market, creates what is called organizational misfit. Soh et al. (2000) suggested that this difference might be bigger in Asia, because the reference process model underlying most ERP systems is influenced by European or US industry/business practices, which are different from Asian ones. Organizational fit then could be defined according to Hong and Kim (2002) as the congruence between the organizational artifact of ERP and its organizational context. According to the previous arguments, the more compatibility or fitting between the ERP system and its organizational context, the greater chance of implementation success the organization will have.

3. **Strategic fit:** Effective ERP alignment requires a well articulated business vision that charts the way of the ERP system in the organization's competitive strategy. Strategic fit generates clear driver for such expensive and radical projects, and consequently could be considered as a success factor. This factor has been adopted in many previous studies but with different names such as "establishing clear goals and objectives" in Somers and Nelson's study (2004), or "organizational objectives consensus" for Bradford and Florin (2003).

4. **Business process reengineering:** Keeping the ERP package "as is" is always recommended by vendors and even many researchers, for optimal exploitation of the package and for avoiding the technical complexity of customizing the package and the future technical problems in rollouts and

updates, especially in phased implementations of these systems (Sandoe et al., 2001). Preserving the original ERP software usually come on the expense of difficult reengineering process, especially in "big bang" ERP implementation strategies. Therefore, organizations that have better abilities in reengineering their business processes will most likely experience smoother implementation of ERP systems.

5. **Top management support:** Top management support is perhaps the factor that always cited as the most relevant success factor in IS implementation projects (Nah et al., 2002; Slevin and Pinto, 1986). Many studies provided evidences that display how top management support is needed during project implementation and how remained critical for extending and realizing the benefits of the system (Somers and Nelson, 2004; and Bradford and Florin, 2003).

6. **Project planning:** ERP implementations are complicated and risky projects. They require large scale business process reengineering, complex arrangements to adapt with any existing or future software to the core ERP technology, and good management for the different contributions from the functional departments, consultants, business partners, and vendors involved in the project. All these requirements and more, magnify the project management challenges for such undertakings, making them implementation failure-prone (Sandoe et al., 2001). Project planning, which refers to the extent to which timeTables, milestones, workforce, equipments, and budgets are specified, becomes crucial in this type of complicated project environments (Aladwani, 2002).

7. **Training:** Lack of user training has frequently been referred to as a main reason for ERP implementation problems or failures (Al-Mashari & Al-Mudimigh, 2003). Training is essential for complex systems such as ERP, especially with large scale changes in jobs' skills, contents, and computerization. Perhaps what magnify the role of training in these systems is that they do not tolerate errors (Sandoe et al., 2001). Employees should be aware of how their mistakes may escalate and affect what other users doing in different areas of the whole system. Also it was found in previous studies, how training decreases levels of resistance and increases ease of use, which in turn enhance success possibilities of information systems' use (Bradford and Florin, 2003).

8. **Ease of use:** Ease of use is the degree to which a particular system is perceived to be relatively free from physical and mental effort (Davis et al., 1989). A big bulk of research concerning technology acceptance use this parameter as a predicator to the intension to use information systems, which in turn impact success possibilities. Based on different surveys' data, some researchers (Amoako-Gympah and Salam, 2003; Amoako-Gympah, 2005; Calisir and Calisr, 2004) have found that ease of use has an impact on the intensions to use ERP systems.

9. **Resistance:** ERP systems usually introduce large-scale changes that can cause resistance, which may in turn decrease the expected benefits of the system. Previous IS research has made substantial progress in understanding how resistance affect IS success (Cooper and Zmud, 1990) especially from political (Hong and Kim, 2002), and process perspectives (Somers and Nelson, 2004).

10. **Competitive pressures:** Advocates of the resource based view of the firm – as a strategic analysis and formulation approach - see ERP implementation as a catalyst that could be used to enable the firm to better develop unique internal capabilities in order to gain competitive advantages (Sandoe et al., 2001). Also, ERP implementation could be used as a response to level an advantage gained by a competitor, who could successfully implement an ERP system. Therefore it is believed that competitive pressures is one of the motives or drivers that stimulate organizations to implement ERP systems successfully (Bradford and Florin, 2003).

Based on the above arguments and the suggested research model the following hypotheses are postulated:

H1: Technical fit of the retained systems with the new ERP system will have a positive relationship with ERP implementation success.

H2: Organizational fit between the ERP system embedded reference process model and the firm's specific organizational context will have a positive relationship with ERP implementation success.

H3: Strategic fit between the organizations' strategic objectives and the ERP system goals and objectives will have a positive relationship with ERP implementation success.

H4: The degree of business processes reengineering to best of practices of an ERP system will have a positive relationship with ERP implementation success.

H5: Top management support for the ERP system will have a positive relationship with ERP implementation success.

H6: Project planning to best of practices of an ERP system will have a positive relationship with ERP implementation success.

H7: The level of training an organization's employees undergo with respect to ERP systems will have a positive relationship with ERP implementation success.

H8: Perceptions on the ease of use of the ERP system will have a positive relationship with ERP implementation success.

H9: Organizational resistance to ERP system will have a negative relationship with ERP implementation success.

H10: Competitive pressure to adopt an ERP system will have a positive relationship with ERP implementation success.

H11: ERP Project success will have a moderating influence on the relationship between ERP critical success factors with ERP implementation business success.

Since it is not clear which critical success factors might influence differently to the two dimensions of success, project and business, the previous hypotheses did not specify exactly which dimension of success is targeted. Consequently, we first test the effects of the independent variables on each of the success measures separately, then perform a path analysis to test **H11** in order to examine the expected moderating role of the ERP project success variable on business value/success measure.

METHODOLOGY

The study was conducted in the kingdom of Bahrain, which is a small Arabian island, centrally located in the Arabian Gulf, with a monarchy rule form. Its economy depends on oil revenues. Facing declining oil reserves, Bahrain has turned to petroleum processing and refining imported crude. Also it has transformed itself into an international banking center. Other important industries are aluminum smelting and tourism. Current population is approximately 688 thousands residents of whom approximately 235 thousands are not nationals. For more details about the kingdom of Bahrain see for example http://www.odci.gov/cia/publications/factbook/geos/ba.html's web site.

Measures

A Field study was employed for this research. Items used in the operationalization of the constructs were drawn from relevant prior research and provided in appendix A. Specifically items measuring ERP training, competitive pressures, business process reengineering, and technical fit of ERP systems were adapted from Bradford and Florin (2003). The measurement of the business dimension of ERP success was adapted from Bradford and Florin (2003) as well. However, the items for the second dimension of ERP success concerning project success were developed based on previous research on project management (Robey et al., 1993; Aladwani, 2002) and modified to fit the ERP context. The items for measuring organizational fit and organizational resistance to ERP implementation were adapted from Hong and Kim (2002). Items used for measuring ease of use were based on the work of Davis et al. (1989) concerning the Technology Acceptance Model (TAM). The measures for top management support, strategic fit of ERP system, and project planning were self developed relying on related previous research (Nah et al., 2002; Slevin and Pinto, 1986; Aladwani, 2002; Hong and Kim, 2002).

These items were measured with a seven-point likert-scale ranging from 1 = strongly disagree to 7 = strongly agree. The mean of the scores over all questions provided the composite score for each variable.

Sample and Procedure

Only 10 companies were found to have prior experience in ERP implementation in Bahrain. Vendors' web sites (Arabian branches) were surfed and quick telephone interviews were made with their representatives in Bahrain, to come up with this list of companies. The IT manager of each company was contacted, to help us come up with a list of potential interviewees for the study. Our main objective was to identify either IT and/or non IT staff, who are well placed in the ERP system implementation process in their companies, to be aware of the critical factors affecting its success or performance. The list of potential informants had approximately 15 informants for each company. Consequently about 150 copies of the questionnaire were sent to the IT managers of these companies, who forward them to the targeted informants in their companies. Before responding to the questionnaire, respondents expressed being actively involved in their companies' ERP systems, in order to be able to give accurate insight into their firm's ERP implementation process. Only 76 interviewees completed the survey (a response rate of 50%) from 8 companies. Six of the questionnaires were dropped because of incomplete answers to the questions. Table 1 shows the companies participating in the study, while Table two provides a profile of the respondents.

Validity and Reliability

Instrument Validation

Straub's (1989) guidelines to validate the instrument of this research were followed. The content validity of the instrument was established through the adoption of the relevant constructs in the literature. Where necessary, changes were made in the wording of some of the questions to suit the context of the study. The adopted instrument, along with all its items, was discussed with three industry executives from three different organizations experienced with ERP implementation and with one faculty mem-

Table 1. Sample description: Companies profile

Company	ERP Vendor	Use period	No. of employees
Batelco (Bahrain Telecom co)	SAP	3	1600
Asary (Arab Ship-building & Repair Yard)	Oracle	5	1200
Bahrain flour mills	Orion	1	100
Bapco (Bahrain Petroleum)	Oracle	3.5	3000
Aldhaen Craft	Oracle	3	200
GFH (Gulf Financial House)	Oracle	2	100
Alba (Aluminum Bahrain)	SAP	5	3000
Midal Cables	Oracle	4	310

ber. Based on their feedback, minor changes were made in the instructions and wording of some of the items to reflect the research settings. The subjects who had participated in this convenience pre-test were excluded from the final data collection of the study.

Reliability

Reliability is the consistency or precision of a measuring instrument that is the extent to which the respondent can answer the same or approximately the same questions the same way each time (Straub, 1989). The internal consistency reliability was assessed by calculating Cronbach's alpha values. The results of the reliability test conducted for the study's constructs are summarized in the fifth column of

Table 2. Sample description: Respondents profile

	Frequency	*Percentage* [a]
Gender		
Male	51	73
Female	19	27
Department		
IT Department	28	43
Accounting and finance	26	37
Other departments	16	20
Experience in current Job		
Mean = 9.7 years		
SD = 2.3		
Nationality		
Bahraini	36	51.4
Indians	20	28.6
Other nationalities	14	
Respondents from each type of business		
Manufacturing (5 companies)	38	54.2
Oil (1 company)	11	18.6
Telecommunication (1 company)	13	15.7
Banking and finance (1 company)	8	11.4

[a] *Due to rounding the percentage may not add up to 100*

Table 3. The internal consistency (Cronbach's alpha) of the constructs ranged from 0.60 (for technical fit) to 0.88 (for top management support). Given the exploratory nature of the study, the results of these reliability tests seem moderately accepTable (Field, 2000).

Discriminant Validity

Since each variable was measured by multi-item constructs, a discriminant analysis should be employed to check the unidimensionality of the items. Discriminant validity was checked by conducting a factor analysis. In Table 3, discriminant validity was confirmed when items for each variable loaded onto single factors with loadings of greater than 0.5 (Nunnally, 1978). Table 3 provides the loadings of each item on independent and dependent variables. Twelve factors emerged with no-cross construct loadings above 0.5, indicating good discriminant validity (Field, 2000).

Based on these examinations of the psychometric properties of the scales, we conclude that each construct represents a reliable and valid variable (Field, 2000).

RESULTS AND ANALYSIS

Multiple regression analysis was used to test H1 – H10, while path analysis was used for H11. Path analysis is a regression-based technique widely used for studying the direct and indirect effects in models encompassing mediating variables like the research model proposed in this study. The intercorrelation matrix (Table 4) was first examined to assure the validity of the regression analysis looking for possible

Table 3. Summary statistics, and reliability and validity analysis

Measures	Items	Mean	Standard deviation	Reliability: Cronbach's Alpha	Validity: Items loadings on single factors [b]
Technical fit	2	4.5	1.3	0.6	0.92; 0.54
Organizational fit	3	5.2	1	0.83	0.59; 0.34; 0.51
Strategic fit	2	5.3	1	0.62	0.86; 0.51
BPR [a]	2	3.7	1.4	0.7	0.91; 0.76
Top management support	2	5.8	1	0.88	0.87; 0.84
Project Planning	1	5.8	1.2	-	-
Training	2	5.5	1.2	0.77	0.83; 0.79
Ease of use	3	5.2	1	0.83	0.92; 0.74; 0.55
Resistance [a]	2	4	1.3	0.84	0.91; 0.88
Competitive pressures [a]	2	4.8	1.3	.68	0.84; 0.54
ERP Project Success [a]	3	4.3	0.7	0.62	0.85; 0.80; 0.51
ERP Business Success	5	5.2	0.8	0.71	0.85; 0.73; 0.59; 0.77; 0.51

[a] *Reverse score used for one of its items*
[b] *Extraction method: Principal component analysis; rotation method varimax with Kaiser normalization; egienvalue = 1*

Table 4. Correlation matrix between variables

Measures	(1)	(2)	(3)	(4)	(5)	(6)	(7)	(8)	(9)	(10)	(11)	(12)
ERP Business Success (1)	1											
ERP Project Success (2)	.43**	1										
Technical fit (3)	.06	.06	1									
Organizational fit (4)	.47**	.42**	.47**	1								
Strategic fit (5)	.40**	.42**	.32**	.62**	1							
BPR (6)	.10	-.06	-.12	-.27*	-.08	1						
Top management support (7)	.44**	.31**	.29*	.61**	.57**	.02	1					
Project Planning (8)	.53**	.52**	.21	.67**	.6**	-.15	.61**	1				
Training (9)	.29*	.33**	.27*	.53**	.33**	-.18	.34**	.56**	1			
Ease of use (10)	.32**	.15	.37**	.51**	.50**	-.15	.43**	.55**	.49**	1		
Resistance (11)	-.27*	-.35**	-.10	-.21	-.35**	.08	-.24*	-.24*	-.22	-.27*	1	
Competitive pressures (12)	.29*	.16	.35**	.49**	.39**	-.01	.47**	.38**	.37**	.58**	-.09	1

*$p < 0.05$; **$p < 0.01$

multicollinearity problem. All intercorrelations among exogenous variables were reasonably low. Hair et al. (1995) suggest that values of $r > 0.80$ indicate a multicollinearity problem.

Table 3 reports statistics of independent and dependent variables. We first regressed ERP project success on the study's 10 independent variables. Second business success dimension of ERP systems implementation was regressed on the same independent variables. As shown in Table 5, project planning ($B = 0.42, p < 0.01$); ease of use ($B = 0.32, p < 0.05$); and resistance ($B = -0.24, p < 0.05$) are significant predictors of project success of ERP systems' implementation. These variables explain approximately 39.8 percent of the variance in project success, as R^2 parameter shows in Table 5. The results provide support for H6 (project planning – project success relationship); H8 (ease of use – project success relationship); and H9 (employees resistance to ERP systems implementation – project success relationship). The findings however failed to support H1-H5, H7, and H10. They concern the relationships between technical fit; organizational fit; strategic fit; business process reengineering; top management support; training; and competitive pressures with ERP project success.

The results reported in Table 5 further show that project planning ($B = 0.33, p < 0.05$), organizational fit ($B = 0.33, p < 0.05$), and business process reengineering ($B = 0.22, p < 0.05$) have significant direct effects on the business success of ERP system implementation. The antecedent constructs explain approximately 39.4 per cent of the variance in business success. Based on these results, H6 (planning – business success relationship), H2 (organizational fit – business success relationship), and H4 (business process reengineering – business success relationship) are also supported. The analysis failed to support H1, H3, H5, and H7 - H10. They concern the relationships between Technical fit; strategic fit; top management support; training; ease of use; resistance; and competitive pressures, with ERP business success.

Following the suggestions of Cohen and Cohen (1983), hierarchical multiple regression was used to test the mediation hypothesis (H11). We regressed business success on the critical success variables (technical fit, organizational fit, strategic fit, BPR, top management support, project planning, training,

Table 5. Multiple regression results

	Model 1 (Project success) $R^2 = 0.398*$			Model 2 (Business success) $R^2 = 0.394***$		
	Beta	*t*	*p*	*Beta*	*t*	*p*
Technical fit	-0.079	-0.66	0.51	-0.16	-1.38	0.17
Organizational fit	0.18	1.03	0.30	0.33	1.88*	0.05
Strategic fit	0.17	1.22	0.22	0.01	0.05	0.96
BPR	0.04	0.42	0.67	0.22	2.01*	0.04
Top management support	-0.11	-0.79	0.43	0.03	0.19	0.84
Project Planning	0.42	2.63**	0.01	0.33	2.01*	0.04
Training	0.09	0.68	0.49	0.04	0.36	0.71
Ease of use	0.32	2.19*	0.03	0.01	0.01	0.99
Resistance	-0.24	-2.22*	0.03	-0.15	-1.30	0.19
Competitive pressures	0.05	0.42	0.67	0.05	0.37	0.71

* p < 0.05; ** p < 0.01

Table 6. Hierarchical regression results

Regression step 1		Regression step 2		Change in R^2
R^2	*p*	R^2	*p*	
0.394	0.001	0.409	0.001	0.015

ease of use, resistance, and competitive pressures) in the first step, with project success added in step two. I examined the unique contribution of project success (in explaining business success) over and above the critical success factors variables. Table 6 shows that the change in R^2 after introducing project success into the equation is significant (R^2 change = 0.015, p = 0.01), giving support to the proposed mediation hypothesis (H11). Table 7 summarizes hypotheses 11 testing results.

DISCUSSIONS, CONCLUSIONS, AND LIMITATIONS

ERP implementation has been one of the challenges for IS practitioners in the last decade. This study tries to provide an understanding for the factors that influence two main aspects of implementation success of these systems in Bahrain.

The previous section shows that probably not all the factors that were found to be influential in western environment would be so in other countries/areas of the world such as Bahrain or maybe the Arabian Gulf countries in general. The results unexpectedly show that *five* classical success factors, specifically: top management support, strategic fit, technical fit, training, and competitive pressures are not significant predicators to both dimensions of success: project and business success. In the meantime, the correlation analysis shows significant correlations for these variables with one – if not both – success

Table 7. Hypothesis testing results

	Implementation Success Project metrics		Implementation Success Business metrics	
	Number	Support	Number	Support
Technical fit	H1	No	H1	No
Organizational fit	H2	No	H2	Yes
Strategic fit	H3	No	H3	No
BPR	H4	No	H4	Yes
Top management support	H5	No	H5	No
Project Planning	H6	Yes	H6	Yes
Training	H7	No	H7	No
Ease of use	H8	Yes	H8	No
Resistance	H9	Yes	H9	No
Competitive pressures	H10	No	H10	No
Project success (mediating)	---	---	H11	Yes

dimension, as clear in the correlation matrix in Table 4. This contrast in results, may mean that although these *five* factors are related to ERP implementation success, their interaction behavior with the other critical success factors – such as project planning, organizational fit, business process reengineering, resistance and ease of use that were found to be significant predicators – is not significant in relation to success dimensions.

Although the study shows that other factors are significant predicators to ERP implementation success, in the Bahraini business environment, they do not influence both success dimensions together at the same time, except for one of them namely, project planning. Consequently, this suggests that each success dimension has different predicators. The results show that level of organizational resistance to the ERP system and degree of ease of use of the system are significantly related to the project dimension of success. On the other hand, organizational fit and business process reengineering are significantly related to business success.

The study has implications for firms and project mangers in that it shows how assessing employees' resistance is important and how understanding their perception of the degree of ease of use of the ERP package being implemented are critical, for better project management. Obviously, this signifies the role of change management in ERP projects, especially in addressing these issues. Related communications, user involvement, and training schemes are examples of the areas that should be arranged carefully for ERP project success in countries like Bahrain.

On the other hand the results related to the business success dimension draw more attention to the organizational fit factor. Soh et al. (2000) argue that misfit analysis requires both comprehensive understanding of critical organizational processes and detailed knowledge of the ERP package being installed. Before ERP adoption, thorough misfit analysis and resolution plan based on ERP knowledge will help achieve the expected benefits of the system. Also, because BPR was found as a significant predicator, the results suggest that firms embarking on ERP projects should consider changing their business processes than relying on customizing the package to the current processes "as is". Better business results are more probable – as the study suggests – from radical business processes changes.

The only critical success factor that found to be influential on both success dimensions is project planning. This finding comes consistent with the fact that ERP projects are complicated undertakings require proper budgeting, timetabling, monitoring ...etc. skills to deal with these types of projects implementation environments.

The statistical analyses also reveal that project success is a significant mediator of the critical success factors for business success. Meeting ERP project budgets, deadlines, quality standards, systems performance, and management expectations are important for achieving the expected business benefits such as better cash management, reduced cycle times, reduction in inventories ...etc.

Several limitations of this study should be highlighted. One of these limitations is the sample size. This was due to the nature of the small population we are studying. A second limitation is that business metrics and project success dimensions are measured using perceptions of IT and functional managers. This was due to the difficulty in securing the related factual data from the participating organizations.

Many researchers have showed that few empirical studies have examined the impact of ERP on organizations (Bradford and Florin, 2003). Therefore, there are numerous avenues for future research and extensions of this study. Future research could further test and refine constructs and relationships on wider business environment populations. Others could use different methodologies – such as longitudinal and/or case-studies bases methodologies - to explore other factors and or relationships or frameworks. Also in depth treatment could be given to acceptance issues to see the factors that affect ease of use and intentions of using such enterprise-wide systems.

REFERENCES

Aiken, P. (2002). *Enterprise resource planning (ERP) considerations.* VA, Richmod: VCU/Institute for Data Research.

Aladwani, A. M. (2002). IT project uncertainty, planning and success: An empirical investigation from Kuwait. *Information Technology & People, 15*(3), 210-226.

Al-Mashari, M., & Al-Mudimigh, A. (2003). ERP Implementation: lessons from a case study. *Information Technology & People, 16*(1), 21-33.

Amoako-Gympah, K., & Salam, A. M. (2004). An extension of the technology acceptance model in an ERP implementation environment. *Information & Management, 41*(6), 731-745.

Amoako-Gympah, K. (2005). Perceived usefulness, user involvement and behavioral intention: An empirical study of ERP implementation. *Computers in Human Behavior,* Available online January 11, 20005: http://www. sciencedirect.com/science/journal/07475632.

Beheshti, H. M. (2006). What managers should know about ERP/ERP II. *Management Research News, 29*(4), 184-193.

Bingi, P., Sharma, M., & Golda, J. (1999). Critical issues affecting an ERP implementation. *Information Systems Management, 16*(3), 7-14.

Bradford, M., & Florin, J. (2003). Examining the role of innovation diffusion factors on the implementation success of enterprise resource planning systems. *International Journal of Accounting Information Systems, 4*(3), 205-225.

Buckhout, S., Frey, E., & Nemec, J. (1999). Making ERP succeeds: Turning fear into promise. *Strategy + Business magazine, 4*(2), 60-72.

Calisir. F., & Calisir, F. (2004). The relation of interface usability characteristics, perceived usefulness, and perceived ease of use to end-user satisfaction with enterprise resource planning (ERP) systems. *Computers in Human Behavior, 20*(3), 505-515.

Cohen, J., & Cohen, P. (1983). *Applied Multiple Regression/Correlation Analysis for the Behavioral Sciences.* NJ: Lawrence Erlbuam Associates Hillsdale.

Connolly, S. (1999, March 1). ERP: Corporate cleanup. *Computerworld* , 23-26

Cooper, R., & Zmud, R. (1990). Information technology implementation research: a technological diffusion approach. *Management Science, 36*(2), 123-139.

Davenport, T. (2000). *Mission Critical: Realizing the Promise of Enterprise Systems.* MA, Cambridge: Harvard Business School Press.

Davis, F.. Bagozzi, R., & Warshaw, P. (1989). User acceptance of computer technology: A comparison of two theoretical models. *Management Science, 35*(8), 982-1003.

Delone, W., & McLean, E. (1992). Information systems success: the quest for the dependent variable. *Information Systems Research, 3*(1), 60-95.

Ehie, I. C., & Madsen, M. (2005). Identifying critical issues in enterprise resource planning (ERP) implementation. *Computers in Industry, 56*(6), 545-557.

Field, A. (2000). *Discovering Statistics: using SPSS for Windows.* London: SAGE Publications.

Gable, G. (1998). Large package software: A neglected technology. *Journal of Global Information Management, 6*(3), 3-4.

Hair, J., Anderson, R., Tatham, R., & Black, W. (1995). *Multivariate data analysis with readings.* NJ: Prentice-Hall.

Holland, P., Light, B., & Gibson, N. (1999, June 23-25). *A critical success factors model for enterprise resource planning implementation.* Seventh European Conference on Information Systems, Copenhagen.

Holsapple, C., & Sena, M. (2005). ERP plans and decision support benefits. *Decision Support Systems, 38*(4), 575-590.

Hong. K. K., & Kim, Y. G. (2002). The critical success factors for ERP implementation: An organizational fit perspective. *Information & Management, 40*(1), 25-40.

Markus M, L., Tanis, C., & Van Fenema, P. C. (2000). Multisite ERP implementations. *Communications of the ACM, 43*(4), 42-46.

Nandhakumar, J., Rossi, M., & Talvinen, J. (2005). The dynamics of contextual forces of ERP implementation. *Journal of Strategic Information Systems, 14*(2), 221–242.

Nah, F., Lau, J., & Kuang, J. (2001). Critical factors for successful implementation of enterprise systems. *Business Process Management Journal, 7*(3), 285-296.

Nunnally, J.C. (1978). *Psychometric Theory*. New York: McGraw-Hill.

Poston, R., & Grabski, S. (2001). Financial impacts of enterprise resource planning implementations. *International Journal of Accounting Information Systems, 2*(4), 271-294.

Rajagopal, P. (2002). An innovation-diffusion view of implementation of enterprise resource planning (ERP) systems and development of research model. *Information & Management, 40*(2), 87-114.

Robey, D., Smith, L., & Vijayasarathy, L. (1993). Perceptions of conflict and success in information systems development projects'. *Journal of Management Information Systems, 10*(1), 123-39.

Sandoe, K., Corbitt, G., & Boykin, R. (2001). *Enterprise Integration*. NY: Wiley.

Slevin, D., & Pinto, J. (1986). The project implementation profile: new tool for project managers. *Project Management Journal, 17*(4), 57-70.

Soh. C., Kien, S., & Tay-Yap, J. (2000). Cultural fits and misfits: is ERP a universal solution? . *Communication of the ACM, 43*(4), 47-51.

Somers, T., & Nelson, K. (2004). A taxonomy of players and activities across the ERP project life cycle. *Information & Management, 41*(3), 257-278.

Straub, D. (1989). Validating instruments in MIS research. *MIS Quarterly, 13*(2), 147-169.

Turban, E., Aronson, J.& Liang, T. (2005). *Decision Support Systems & Intelligent Systems*. NJ: Prentice Hall.

Wagner, E. L., Scott, S. V., & Galliers, R. D. (2006). The creation of 'best practice' software: Myth, reality and ethics. *Information and Organization, 16*(3), 251-275.

APPENDIX A. SURVEY INSTRUMENT

The different opinions are indicated by the numbers 1: strongly disagree; 2: disagree; 3: somewhat disagree; 4: neutral; 5: somewhat agree; 6: agree; 7: strongly agree.

Dependent Variables: ERP implementation Success
Perceived project success metrics
> The cost of ERP project was significantly higher than the expected budget.
> The ERP project took significantly longer time than expected.
> The system performance of ERP is significantly below the expected level.

Perceived business value metrics
> I believe implementing our ERP system has helped to reduce the company inventorial level.
> I believe implementing our ERP system has helped to reduce the number of employees.
> I believe implementing our ERP system has helped to improve cycle times.
> I believe implementing our ERP system has helped to reduce cost in procurement.
> I believe implementing our ERP system has helped to improve cash management.

Independent Variables: ERP critical success factors

Top management support

> Our ERP system receives strong active support from our top management.
>
> The success of ERP system implementation effort was due to the active championing by key senior management.
>
> ERP alignment

Organizational fit

> I believe that the process built in the ERP system that we implement meet all needs required from organizational process.
>
> The name and meaning of the ERP data items correspond to those of the documents used in our company. (e.g. a sales order sheet, sales report),
>
> User interface structures of our ERP system are well designed to the work structure required for conducting business in our company.

Strategic fit

> When the ERP system initiative began, there was consensus about its specific objectives.
>
> There was clear understanding of how implementing this system will contribute to the company's overall strategies.

Technical fit

> The ERP application was compatible with legacy system software that was retained (minimal interfacing),
>
> The ERP application was compatible with existing hardware.

Business process reengineering

> Our firm tried to customize the ERP package to our business processes with a minimal amount of BPR.
>
> Our firm tried to relay heavily on reengineering its business processes to fit ERP packages.

Competitive pressures

> Our firm experienced competitive pressure to implement an ERP system.
>
> Our firm would have experienced a competitive disadvantage if ERP system had not been adopted.

Project planning

> There was an effective project planning for our ERP system.

Ease of use

> I believe that our firm interaction with ERP system is clear and understandable.
>
> Learning to use the ERP system has been easy for employees.
>
> Overall, the ERP system is easy to use.

Resistance

> There have been many users resisting the ERP system implementation.
>
> There have been many cases blaming occurrence of business problem upon ERP system.

Training

> Our firm provided extensive training with the ERP system.
>
> Our firm is dedicated to making sure employees are very familiar with the ERP system.

Chapter II
Evolution of Enterprise Resource Planning

Ronald E. McGaughey
University of Central Arkansas, USA

Angappa Gunasekaran
University of Massachusetts—Dartmouth, USA

ABSTRACT

Business needs have driven the design, development, and use of the enterprise-wide information systems we call Enterprise Resource Planning (ERP) systems. Intra enterprise integration was a driving force in the design, development, and use of early ERP systems. Changing business needs have brought about the current business environment, wherein supply chain integration is desirable, if not essential, thus current and evolving ERP systems demonstrate an expanded scope of integration that encompasses limited inter-enterprise integration. This chapter explores the evolution, the current status, and future of ERP, with the objective of promoting relevant future research in this important area. If researchers hope to play a significant role in the design, development, and use of suitable ERP systems to meet evolving business needs, then their research should focus at least in part on the changing business environment, its impact on business needs, and the requirements for enterprise systems that meet those needs.

INTRODUCTION

Twenty years ago supplier relationship management was unique to the Japanese (those firms who embraced the JIT philosophy), China was still a slumbering economic giant, the Internet was largely for academics and scientists and certainly not a consideration in business strategy, the very idea of a network of businesses working together as a virtual enterprise was almost like science fiction, and hardly anyone had a cell phone. The world has changed. The cold war is over and economic war is on. We have moved rapidly toward an intensely competitive, global economic environment. Countries like China and India are fast positioning themselves as key players and threatening the economic order that has existed for decades. Information Technology (IT) is more sophisticated than ever, yet we still struggle with how to best use it in business, and on a personal level as well. E-commerce (B2B, B2C, C2C, G2C, B2G) has become commonplace and M-commerce is not far behind, especially in Europe and Japan. In 2007, for the first time, there are more cell phones than tethered phones in the US, and increasingly sophisticated cell phones have capabilities that exceed the capabilities of older PCs. This is the backdrop against which we will discuss the evolving enterprise information system. At this point we will call it ERP, but is should become evident in the course of reading this manuscript that ERP is a label that may no longer be appropriate for evolving enterprise and inter-enterprise systems.

In this paper we define ERP and discuss the evolution of ERP, the current state of ERP and the future of ERP. We will emphasize how the evolution of ERP has been influenced by changing business needs and by evolving technology. We present a simple framework to explain that evolution. Some general directions for future research are indicated by our look at the past, present and particularly the future of ERP.

ERP DEFINED

The ERP system is an information system that integrates business processes with the aim of creating value and reducing costs by making the right information available to the right people at the right time to help them make good decisions in managing resources productively and proactively. An ERP is comprised of multi-module application software packages that serve and support multiple business functions (Sane, 2005). These large automated cross functional systems were designed to bring about improved operational efficiency and effectiveness through integrating, streamlining and improving fundamental back-office business processes. Traditional ERP systems were called back-office systems because they involved activities and processes in which the customer and general public were not typically involved, at least not directly. Functions supported by ERP typically included accounting, manufacturing, human resource management, purchasing, inventory management, inbound and outbound logistics, marketing, finance and to some extent engineering. The objective of traditional ERP systems in general was greater efficiency, and to a lesser extent effectiveness. Contemporary ERP systems have been designed to streamline and integrate operation processes and information flows within a company to promote synergy (Nikolopoulos, Metaxiotis, Lekatis and Assimakopoulos, 2003) and greater organizational effectiveness. These newer ERP systems have moved beyond the back-office to support front-office processes and activities like those fundamental to customer relationship management. The goal of most firms implementing ERP is to replace diverse functional systems with a single integrated system that does it all faster, better, and cheaper. Unfortunately, the "business and technology integration technology in a box" has not entirely met expectations (Koch, 2005). While there are some success stories, many companies devote significant resources to their ERP effort only to find the payoff disappointing (Dalal, Kamath, Kolarik and Sivaraman, 2003; Koch, 2005). Let us examine how we have come to this point in the ERP lifecycle.

THE EVOLUTION OF ERP

The origin of ERP can be traced back to Materials Requirement Planning (MRP). While the concept of MRP was understood conceptually and discussed in the 1960s, it was not practical for commercial use. It was the availability of computing power (processing capability and storage capacity) that made commercial use of MRP possible and practical. While many early MRP systems were built in-house, often at great expense, MRP became one of the first popular off-the-shelf business applications (Orlicky, 1975). In essence, MRP involves taking inventory records, the master production schedule, and bills of materials and calculating time phased material, component and sub-assembly requirements (gross and net), planned orders, delivery dates, and more. Note the term calculating was used rather than forecasting. With a realistic MPS, accurate inventory records, lead times that are known and predictable, and current and correct bills of materials, it is possible to calculate material, component, and assembly requirements rather than forecast them. The shear volume of calculations necessary for MRP with multiple orders for even a few items made the use of computers essential. Initially, batch processing systems were used and regenerative MRP systems were the norm, where the plan would be updated periodically, often weekly. MRP employed a type of backward scheduling wherein lead times were used to work backwards from a due date to an order release date. While the primary objective of MRP was to compute material requirements, the MRP system proved also to be a useful scheduling tool. Order placement and order delivery were planned by the MRP system. Not only were orders for materials and components generated by an MRP system, but also production orders for manufacturing operations that used those materials and components to make higher level items like sub assemblies and finished products. As MRP systems became popular and more and more companies started using them, practitioners, vendors and researchers started to realize that the data and information produced by the MRP system in the course of material requirements planning and production scheduling could be augmented with additional data and used for other purposes. One of the earliest add-ons was the Capacity Requirements Planning module which could be used in developing capacity plans to produce the master production schedule. Manpower planning and support for human resources management were incorporated into MRP. Distribution management capabilities were added. The enhanced MRP and its many modules provided data useful in the financial planning of manufacturing operations, thus financial planning capabilities were added. Business needs, primarily for operational efficiency, and to a lesser extent for greater effectiveness, and advancements in computer processing and storage technology brought about MRP and influenced its evolution. What started as an efficiency oriented tool for production and inventory management was becoming increasingly a cross functional system.

A very important capability to evolve in MRP systems was the ability to close the loop (control loop). This was largely because of the development of real time (closed loop) MRP systems to replace regenerative MRP systems in response to changing business needs and improved computer technology—time-sharing was replacing batch processing as the dominant computer processing mode. With time-sharing mainframe systems the MRP system could run 24/7 and update continuously. Use of the corporate mainframe that performed other important computing task for the organization was not practical for some companies, because MRP consumed too many system resources; subsequently, some companies opted to use mainframes (now growing smaller and cheaper, but increasing in processing speed and storage capability) or mini-computers (could do more, faster than old mainframes) that could be dedicated to MRP. MRP could now respond (update relevant records) to timely data fed into the system and produced by the system. This closed the control loop with timely feedback for decision making by incorporating current data from the factory floor, warehouse, vendors, transportation companies, and other internal and external sources, thus giving the MRP system the capability to provide current (almost real-time) information for better planning and control. These closed loop systems better reflected the realities of the production floor, logistics, inventory, and more. It was this transformation of MRP into a planning and control tool for manufacturing by closing the loop, along with all the additional modules that did more than plan materials—they planned and controlled various manufacturer resources—that led to MRPII. Here too, improved computer technology and the evolving business needs for more accurate and timely information to support decision making and greater organizational effectiveness contributed to the evolution from MRP to MRPII.

The MRP in MRPII stands for Manufacturing Resource Planning rather than materials requirements planning. The MRP system had evolved from a material requirements planning system into a planning and control system for resources in manufacturing operations—an enterprise information system for manufacturing. As time passed, MRPII systems became more widespread, and more sophisticated, particularly when used in manufacturing to support and complement computer integrated manufacturing (CIM). Databases started replacing traditional file systems allowing for better systems integration and greater query capabilities to support decision makers, and the telecommunications network became an integral part of these systems in order to support communications between and coordination among system components that were sometimes geographically distributed, but still within the company. In that context the label CIM II was used for a short time to describe early systems with capabilities now associated with ERP (Lope, 1992). The need for greater efficiency and effectiveness in back-office operations was not unique to manufacturing, but was also common to non-manufacturing operations. Companies in non-manufacturing sectors such as healthcare, financial services, air transportation, and the consumer goods sector (Chung and Snyder, 2000) started to use MRPII-like systems to manage critical resources, thus the M for manufacturing seemed not always to be appropriate. In the early 90s, these increasingly sophisticated back-office systems were more appropriately labeled Enterprise Resource Planning systems (Nikolopoulos, Metaxiotis, Lekatis, and Assimakopoulos, 2003).

MRP II was mostly for automating the business processes within an organization, but ERP, while primarily for support of internal processes, started to support processes that spanned enterprise boundaries (the extended enterprise). While ERP systems originated to serve the information needs of manufacturing companies, their domain was not just manufacturing anymore. Early ERP systems typically ran on mainframes like their predecessors, MRP and MRPII, but many migrated to client/server systems where networks were central and distributed databases more common. The growth of ERP and the migration to client/server systems really got a boost from the Y2K scare. Many companies were convinced of the need to replace older main-frame based systems, some ERP and some not, with the newer client/server architecture. After all, since they were going to have to make so many changes in the old systems to make them Y2K compliant and avoid serious problems—this was what vendors and consultants often told them to create FUD (fear, uncertainty and doubt)--they might as well bite the bullet and upgrade. Vendors and consultants benefited from the Y2K boost to ERP sales, as did some of their customers. Since Y2K, ERP systems have evolved rapidly, bringing us to the ERP systems of today. Present day ERP systems offer more and more capabilities and are becoming more affordable, even for SMEs (Dahlen and Elfsson, 1999).

ERP TODAY

As ERP systems continue to evolve, vendors like PeopleSoft (Conway, 2001) and Oracle (Green, 2003) are moving to an Internet-based architecture, in large part because of the ever-increasing importance of E-commerce and the globalization of business (Abboud and Vara, 2007). Beyond that, perhaps the most salient trend in the continuing evolution of ERP is the focus on front-office applications and inter-organizational business processes, particularly in support of supply chain management (Scheer and Habermann, 2000; Al-Mashari, 2002). ERP is creeping out of the back-office into the front and beyond the enterprise to customers, suppliers and more, in order to meet changing business needs (Burns, 2007). Front-office applications involve interaction with external constituents like customers, suppliers, partners and more—hence the name front-office because they are visible to "outsiders." Key players like Baal, Oracle, PeopleSoft, and SAP have incorporated Advanced Planning and Scheduling (APS), Sales Force Automation (SFA), Customer Relationship Management (CRM), Supply Chain Management (SCM), Business Intelligence, and E-commerce modules/capabilities into their systems, or repositioned their ERP systems as part of broader Enterprise Suites incorporating these and other modules/capabilities. ERP products reflect the evolving business needs of clients and the capabilities of IT, perhaps most notably those related to the Web.

While some companies are expanding their ERP system capabilities (adding modules) and still calling them ERP systems, others have started to use catchy labels like enterprise suite, E-commerce suite, and enterprise solutions to describe their enterprise solution clusters that include ERP among other modules/capabilities. Table 1 lists the various modules/capabilities taken from the product descriptions of vendors like PeopleSoft, Oracle, J.D. Edwards, and SAP, who are major players in the ERP/enterprise systems market.

Perhaps, most notable about ERP today is that it is much more than manufacturing resource planning. ERP and ERP-like systems have become popular with non-manufacturing operations like universities, hospitals, airlines and more, where back-office efficiency is important and so too is front-office efficiency and effectiveness (Chung and Snyder, 2000). In general, it is accurate to state that today's ERP systems, or ERP-like systems, typically include modules/capabilities associated with front-office processes and activities. ERP capabilities are packaged with other modules that support front-office and back-office processes and activities, and nearly anything else that goes on within organizations. ERP proper (the back office system) has not become unimportant because back-office efficiency and effectiveness was, is, and will always be important. Today's focus, however, seems more to be external as organizations look for ways to support and improve relationships and interactions with customers, suppliers, partners and other stakeholders (Knapen, 2007). While integration of internal functions is still important, and in many organizations still has not been achieved to a great extent, external integration is now receiving much attention. Progressive companies desire to do things--all things--faster, better and cheaper (to be agile), and they want systems and tools that will improve competitiveness, increase profits, and help them not just to survive, but to prosper in a dynamic global economy. Today, that means working with suppliers, customers and partners like never before. Vendors are using the latest technology to respond to these evolving business needs, as evidenced in the products and services they now offer or plan to offer their customers. Will ERP be the all-encompassing system comprised of the many modules and capabilities mentioned, or will it be relegated to the status of modules/functionality in all-encompassing systems for the future?

Table 1. Enterprise system modules

Modules
Enterprise Resource Planning (ERP)
Customer Relationship Management (CRM) Sales Management Field Service Management Retail Management
Asset Management Financial Management Yield Management
Business Collaboration
Supplier Relationship Management (SRM)
Inventory Management Order Processing
Business Intelligence Data Warehouse Knowledge Management Analytics and Reporting Online Business Services User Services
E-Commerce M-Commerce
Facilities Management Maintenance Management
Warehouse Management Logistics Management Distribution Management
Project Management
Human Resource Management

ERP AND THE FUTURE

New, multi-enterprise business models like Value Collaboration Networks, customer-centric networks that coordinate all players in the supply chain, are evolving as we enter the 21st century (Nattkemper, 2000). These new business models reflect an increased business focus on external integration. While no one can really predict the future of ERP very far into the future, current management concerns and emphasis, vendor plans, and the changing business and technological environments, provide some clues about the future of ERP. We turn our attention now to evolving business needs and technological changes that should shape the future of ERP.

E-Commerce is arguably one of the most important developments in business in the last 50 years (Jack Welch reportedly called it the "Viagra of business"), and M-Commerce is poised to takes it place along side or within the rapidly growing area of E-Commerce. Internet technology has made E-Commerce in its many forms (B2B, B2C, B2G, G2C, C2C, etc.) possible. Mobile and wireless technology are expected to make "always on" Internet and "anytime/anywhere" location based services (also require global positioning systems) a reality, as well as a host of other capabilities we categorize as M-Business. One can expect to see ERP geared more to the support of both E-Commerce and M-Commerce. Internet, mobile, and wireless technology should figure prominently in new and improved system modules and capabilities (Bhattacharjee, Greenbaum, Johnson, Martin, Reddy, Ryan, White and McKie, 2002; O'Brien, 2002; Sane, 2005). Vendors and their customers will find it necessary to make fairly broad, sweeping infrastructure changes to meet the demands of E-Commerce and M-Commerce (Bhattacharjee, Greenbaum, Johnson, Martin, Reddy, Ryan, White and McKie, 2002; Higgins, 2005). Movement away from client-server systems to Internet based architectures is likely. In fact, it has already started (Scheer and Habermann, 2000; Conway, 2001; Abboud and Vara, 2007). New systems will have to incorporate existing and evolving standards and older systems will have to be adapted to existing and evolving standards, and that may make the transition a little uncomfortable and expensive for vendors and their customers. Perhaps the biggest business challenge with E-Commerce, and even more so with M-Commerce, is understanding how to use these new and evolving capabilities to better serve the customer, work with suppliers and other business partners, and to be generally more efficient and effective. Businesses are just beginning to understand E-Commerce and how it can be used to meet changing business needs as well as how it changes them, and now M-Commerce poses a whole new challenge. E-Commerce and M-Commerce pose challenges for vendors and for their clients. Back-office and front-office processes and activities are being affected by E-Commerce/E-Business and will most certainly be affected by M-Commerce/M-Business.

The current business emphasis on intra and inter organizational process integration and external collaboration should remain a driving force in the evolution of ERP in the foreseeable future. Some businesses are attempting to transform themselves from traditional, vertically integrated organizations into multi-enterprise, "recombinant entities" reliant on core-competency-based strategies (Genovese, Bond, Zrimsek and Frey, 2001). Integrated SCM and business networks will receive great emphasis, reinforcing the importance of IT support for cross enterprise collaboration and inter-enterprise processes (Bhattacharjee, Greenbaum, Johnson, Martin, Reddy, Ryan, White and McKie, 2002; Al-Mashari, 2002). Collaborative commerce (C-commerce) has become not only a popular buzz word, but also a capability businesses desire/need. C-Commerce is label used to describe Internet-based (at least at present) electronic collaboration among businesses, typically supply chain partners, in support of inter-organizational processes that involve not necessarily transactions, but rather information sharing and coordination (Sane, 2005). ERP systems, or their successors will have to support the required interactions and processes among and within business entities, and work with other systems/modules that do the same. The back-office processes and activities of business network partners will not exist in a vacuum--many will overlap. There will be great need for business processes to span organizational boundaries (some do at present), possibly requiring a single shared inter-enterprise system that will do it (we might call it a distributed ERP), or at least ERP systems that can communicate with and co-process (share/divide processing tasks) with other ERP systems—probably the most practical solution, at least in the near future. Middleware, ASPs, and enterprise portal technologies may play an important role in the integration of such modules and systems (Bhattacharjee, Greenbaum, Johnson, Martin, Reddy, Ryan, White and McKie, 2002). Widespread adoption of a single ASP solution among supply chain partners may facilitate interoperability as all supply chain partners essentially use the same system. Could one ASP database serve all supply chain partners? Alternatively, a supply chain portal (vertical portal), jointly owned by supply chain partners or a value added service provider that coordinates the entire supply chain, and powered by a single system serving all participants, could be the model for the future.

Regardless of the means used to achieve greater external integration to complement internal integration, the new focus on supporting/facilitating inter-organizational processes will be important to the future of ERP like systems, whatever they are called! Solution providers and consultants will strive to enable companies to communicate and collaborate with other entities that comprise the extended enterprise (Bhattacharjee, Greenbaum, Johnson, Martin, Reddy, Ryan, White and McKie, 2002; Knapen, 2007). Internet based technologies will unquestionably be key in supporting cross-enterprise ERP in the foreseeable future, and the ASP (also called SAAS—software as a service) model may just be the future of ERP in a business world focused on supply chain management (Burns, 2007). Note that ASP solutions are generally less costly, and consequently, they reduce one particular component of financial risk—the cost of product obsolescence. It is noteworthy also that ASP (SAAS) solutions are moving ERP within reach of SMEs, as it costs much less to "rent" than to "buy." The lower cost of ASPs makes them more attractive to SMEs, increasingly targeted by vendors seeking new customers (Dahlen and Elfsson, 1999; Muscatello, Small and Chen, 2003, Burns, 2007).

Some expect Web services to play a prominent role in the future of ERP (O'Brien, 2002; ACW Team, 2004; Abboud and Vara, 2007). Web Services range from simple to complex, and they can incorporate other Web services. The capability of Web Services to allow businesses to share data, applications, and processes across the Internet (O'Brien, 2002) may result in ERP systems of the future relying heavily on the Service Oriented Architecture (SOA), within which Web Services are created and stored, providing the building blocks for programs and systems. Web Service technology could put the focus where it belongs: on putting together the very best functional solution to automate a business process (Bhattacharjee, Greenbaum, Johnson, Martin, Reddy, Ryan, White and McKie, 2002). The use of "best in breed" Web Service-based solutions might be more palatable to businesses, since it might be easier and less risky to plug-in a new Web Service based solution than replace or add-on a new product module. A greater role for Web Services (the SOA) is expected, and that too would heighten the importance of an Internet Based Architecture to the future of ERP (Abboud and Vara, 2007; Burns, 2007). It should be noted that a Service Oriented Architecture is not incompatible with ASPs, and in fact it should make building, maintaining and providing ASP products/services more efficient and effective.

All from one, or best in breed? Reliance on a single vendor would seem best from a vendor's perspective, but it may not be best from the client's standpoint. While it may be advantageous to have only one proprietary product to install and operate, and a single contact point for problems, there are risks inherent in this approach. Switching cost can be substantial, and if a single vendor does not offer a module/solution needed by the client, then the client must develop it internally, do without it, or purchase it from another vendor. The market is in fact changing in some ways because of this situation. The market was about what a product would do, but it is evolving such that now the focus is on what the product will do in the future (Maguire, 2006). Potential customers are "thinking ahead" and seem better to understand the future consequences of today's system choice. Still, it is not uncommon for a client to be faced with trying to get diverse products to work together, and the problems of doing so are well documented. The single source approach means an organization must place great faith in the vendor, and with the consolidation and changes taking place among enterprise solution providers, that can be risky. Never the less, the "one source" alternative seems most popular at present (Burns, 2007).

So will it be single source, or best in breed? The best in breed approach will be good if greater interoperability/integration among vendor products is achieved (Bhattacharjee, Greenbaum, Johnson, Martin, Reddy, Ryan, White and McKie, 2002). There is a need for greater "out of the box" interoperability, thus a need for standards. Ideally, products will reach a level of standardization where software modules exhibit behavior similar to the plug and play hardware--you just plug in a new module, the system recognizes it, configures itself to accommodate the new module, and eureka, it works! While this is much to hope for, increased standardization brought about by developments like the Service Oriented Architecture, and XML-based XBRL, might make interoperability a reality, though probably not anytime soon. The fact that some are embracing standards for XML (Garbellotto, 2007) and more, does provide some reason for hope, but whether the future of ERP software trends toward the single source or best in breed approach remains to be seen. Regardless of the direction, integration technologies will be important in the new breed of modular, but linked enterprise applications.

Data warehouses, data mining, and various analytic capabilities are needed in support of front office and back office processes and activities involved in CRM, SRM, SCM, Field Service Management, business collaboration and more. Likewise they are important in business intelligence (the process and BI systems) and strategic management. An important trend at present is merging ERP and CRM with BI (Burns, 2007). Data warehouses will play an important role in the future of ERP, because they will require data from ERP and provide data to support decision making in the context of ERP—ERP the process. Ideally, the Data warehouse would be integrated with all front-office, back-office and strategic systems to the extent that it helps close loops by providing accurate and timely data to support decision making in any context, in the form of on-line analytical processing. Knowledge management systems (KMS) endowed with neural networks and expert system capabilities should play a key role in decision making as they will be capable of capturing, modeling and automating decision making processes. Data warehouses and KMS should enable future ERP systems to support more automated business decision making (Bhattacharjee, Greenbaum, Johnson, Martin, Reddy, Ryan, White and McKie, 2002) and they should be helpful in the complex decision making needed in the context of fully integrated supply chain management. More automated decision making in both front-office and back-office systems, should eliminate/minimize human variability and error, greatly increase decision speed, and hopefully improve decision quality. Business Intelligence (BI) tools, which are experiencing a significant growth in popularity, take internal and external data and transform it into information used in building knowledge that helps decision makers to make more "informed" decisions—no pun intended. Current Business Intelligence (BI) tools are largely designed to support strategic planning and control but will likely trickle down to lower level decision makers, where their capabilities will be put to use in tactical and perhaps operational decision contexts. BI tools use data, typically from a data warehouse, along with data mining, analytic, statistical, query, reporting, forecasting and decision support capabilities to support managerial planning and control. The combined capabilities of the data warehouse, KMS and BI should contribute to faster, better, and less costly (in terms of time and effort involved) decisions at all organizational levels. They should be helpful in making decisions in the inter-organizational context of supply chain management, where complexity is increased by the need make decisions involving multiple supply chain partners.

At least in the near future, it appears that greater emphasis will be placed on front-office systems, as opposed to back office systems, and sharing data, applications and processes across the Internet (O'Brien, 2002). Back-office systems will not be unimportant, but they are more mature as a consequence of past emphasis and many work quite well. Emphasis will be on more thorough integration of the modules that comprise back-office systems, integration of back-office systems with front-office and strategic systems, and integration of front-office, back-office and strategic systems with the systems of other organizations, especially within the context of the supply chain (Knapen, 2007). At present greater organizational effectiveness in managing the entire supply chain all the way to the end customer is a priority in business. The greater emphasis on front-office functions and cross enterprise communications and collaboration via the Internet simply reflects changing business needs and priorities. A 2004 ITtoolbox survey of ERP users in Europe, North America, Asia, India and elsewhere showed great interest in improved functionality and ease of integration and implementation (top motives for adding new modules or purchasing new ERP systems). Furthermore the same survey showed greatest interest in modules for CRM, Data Warehousing and SCM (top 3 on list). The demand for specific modules/capabilities in particular shows that businesses are looking beyond the enterprise. This external focus is encouraging vendors to seize the moment by responding with the modules/systems that meet evolving business needs. The need to focus not just on new front office tools but also on strategy will encourage greater vendor emphasis on tools like Data Warehouses and capabilities like Business Intelligence that support strategy development, implementation and control. A CAMagazine enterprise software survey showed that still in 2007, vendors remain focused on providing support for BI and strategic planning and control (Burns, 2007).

The evolving environment of business suggests a direction for these comprehensive enterprise systems that would seem to make ERP an inappropriate label. The Garner group coined the term ERPII to describe their vision of the enterprise system of the future with increased focus on the front office, strategy, and the internet. ERPII was described as a business strategy and a set of collaborative operational and financial processes internally and beyond the enterprise (Zrimsek, 2002). The Gartner Group projected that by 2005 ERPII would replace ERP as the key enabler of internal and inter-enterprise efficiency (Zrimsek, 2002). While not there yet, the systems they described are evolving, but the ERPII label was lost! The name that seems to have stuck, at least for now, is Enterprise Information Systems, or just Enterprise Systems. Wikipedia (2007) describes Enterprise Information Systems as technology platforms that "enable organizations to integrate and coordinate their business processes. They provide a single system that is central to the organization and ensure that information can be shared across all functional levels and management hierarchies. Enterprise systems are invaluable in eliminating the problem of information fragmentation caused by multiple information systems in an organization, by creating a standard data structure."

While the ERP label may linger for a while, ERP will likely be relegated to module(s)/capability status, as a name more fitting for the evolving integrated, inter-enterprise, front office- back office, strategic systems will replace ERP, in much the same way that ERP replaced MRPII.

THE ERP EVOLUTION FRAMEWORK

This framework simply summarizes the evolution of ERP relating the stages in its evolution to business needs driving the evolution, as well as changes in technology. Table 2 presents the framework. As MRP evolved into MRPII, then ERP, and finally to ERPII/Enterprise Information System (present state of ERP), the scope of the system expanded as organizational needs changed, largely in response to the changing dynamics of the competitive environment. As business has become increasingly global in nature and cooperation among enterprises more necessary for competitive reasons, systems have evolved to meet those needs. One can hardly ignore the technological changes that have taken place, because the current state of technology is a limiting factor in the design of systems to meet evolving business needs. From our examination of the evolution of ERP we would conclude that the next stage of the evolution will come about and be shaped by the same forces that have shaped each stage, that being evolving business needs and advances in technology. We expect ERP (the traditional back office system) to take its place along with MRP and MRPII. The functions of ERP will remain important and

Table 2. The evolution of ERP

System	Primary Business Need(s)	Scope	Enabling Technology
MRP	Efficiency	Inventory Management and Production planning and control.	Mainframe computers, batch processing, traditional file systems.
MRPII	Efficiency, Effectiveness and integration of manufacturing systems	Extending to the entire manufacturing firm (becoming cross functional).	Mainframes and Mini computers, realtime (time sharing) processing ,database management systems (relational)
ERP	Efficiency (primarily back office), Effectiveness and integration of all organizational systems.	Entire organization (increasingly cross functional), both manufacturing and non-manufacturing operations	Mainframes, Mini and micro Computers, Client server networks with distributed processing and distributed databases, Data warehousing, and mining, knowledge management.
ERPII	Efficiency, effectiveness and integration within and among enterprises.	Entire organization extending to other organizations (cross functional and cross enterprise--partners, suppliers, customers, etc.)	Mainframes, Client Server systems, distributed computing, knowledge management, internet technology (includes intranets extranets, portals).
Inter-Enterprise Resource Planning, Enterprise Systems, Supply Chain Management, or whatever label gains common acceptance	Efficiency, effectiveness, coordination, and Integration within and among all relevant supply chain members as well as other partners, or stakeholders on a global scale.	Entire organization and its constituents (increasingly global and cross cultural) comprising global supply chain from beginning to end as well as other industry and government constituents	Internet, Service Oriented Architecture, Application Service Providers, wireless networking, mobile wireless, knowledge management, grid computing, artificial intelligence.

necessary, as have the functions of MRP and MRPII, but ERP will likely be absorbed by something bigger, and ERP itself will take its place as an integral part of the Internet based enterprise or inter-enterprise system of the future. Whether that all encompassing system is called Enterprise resource planning, Enterprise suite, Enterprise Information System, or by a label that currently resides in the back of some vendor employee or researchers mind, remains to be seen. One thing seems certain, the next stage in the evolution will hinge on the same forces shaping systems of the past—business need and technological change.

CONCLUSION

ERP has evolved over a long period of time. MRP gave way to MRPII, then MRPII to ERP, ERP to ERPII, and in rather short order ERPII to Enterprise System/Enterprise Information System. It seems that Enterprise system is holding steady for now, but it too may give way to a new label that reflects the "inter-enterprise flavor" of future systems. MRP capabilities still exists as will ERP capabilities, but future systems must provide an increasingly broad set of capabilities and modules that support the back-office, front-office, strategic planning and control, as well as integrating processes and activities across diverse enterprises comprising supply chains and business networks. Whatever the name, current trends suggest certain characteristics which we can reasonably expect. This future system will have to support E-commerce and M-commerce, thus wireless technology, including mobile but not limited to mobile, and the internet will play a role in the evolving architecture. An Internet-based architecture now seems most likely, at least in the near future, and it may be a Service Oriented Architecture wherein Web Services are key. The increased emphasis on front-office systems and strategic planning and control will likely influence new capabilities introduced by vendors for the next few years. Increased automation of decision making is to be expected with contributions from Knowledge Management Systems, Data Warehouses/Data Marts, and Business Intelligence systems fueled by advancements in the field of artificial intelligence. Greater interoperability of diverse systems and more thorough integration within and between enterprise systems is likely to remain a priority. An environment for business applications much like the "plug and play" environment for hardware would make it easier for organizations to integrate their own systems and have their systems integrated with other organizations' systems. Such an environment awaits greater standardization. This ideal "plug and play" environment would make it easier for firms to opt for a "best in breed" strategy for application/module acquisition as opposed to reliance on a single vendor for a complete package of front-office, back-office and strategic systems. At present it seems that selecting a single vendor is preferred (Burns, 2007). Future developments in computer (hardware and software) and telecommunications technology will move us closer to effective inter-organizational system integration and make fully integrated supply chain management a reality. Perhaps we might call the evolving system an Interprise Resource Planning System, Interprise Management System, or Interprise Information System to emphasize the inter-enterprise nature of these systems. Whatever they are called, it seems that what will be required of them goes far beyond what the enterprise resource planning (ERP) label would aptly describe, even with the "II" (ERPII) added!

From the discussion of ERP's future one can extrapolate certain desired capabilities of the interprise/enterprise system of the future. Following is a list of desired/required capabilities:

- Supports interaction of supply chain partners and inter-organizational processes;
- A single corporate database to facilitate true functional system/module integration;
- At some point in time, possibly an inter-organizational database to integrate supply chain partners--maybe supplied by an ASP or some other entity that supports the entire supply chain;
- Any necessary data transfer among/integration of modules is smooth and consistent;
- Possesses flexibility to continuously support agile companies responding to dynamic business environment;
- Employs a fluid yet robust architecture reflective of evolving enterprise models and evolving technology like mobile wireless;
- Utilizes database and data warehouse models/solutions to support transaction intensive applications (front office and back office), query intensive applications, OLAP, and any other necessary internal and/or external interaction with the database or data warehouse;
- Enterprise systems take into account partnering enterprise characteristics like culture, language, technology level, standards, information flows, and provide flexibility to adapt as partnering relationship changes;
- Solution vendors form global alliances with other vendors to better meet needs of clients in any country;
- Solution vendors embrace standards like XML, the Service Oriented Architecture, and evolving wireless standards with due consideration to global business requirements;

For researchers and practitioners the advice is simple. The two primary drivers in the evolution from MRP, to MRPII, to ERP, to ERPII, to Enterprise Systems were business need and technological change. Technological change made possible the development of systems to meet changing business needs. The needs may exist for a while before the technology can help meet them, and the technology can exists for a while before someone recognizes its usefulness in meeting a current or evolving business need. In either case, the focus should be on monitoring business needs and monitoring technological change. Research that does both and is geared towards bringing the two together could make significant contributions to business. The ERP system of the future, whatever it may be called, will be found at the convergence of business need and technological change.

REFERENCES

ACW Team (2004, August 23). SSA Global releases converged ERP with manufacturing capabilities. *Asia Computer Weekly*, 1.

Enterprise Information Systems. A definition from Wikipedia.com http://en.wikipedia.org/wiki/Enterprise_information_systems, accessed 20 November 2007.

Abboud, L., & Vara, V. (2007, January 23). SAP Trails Nimble Start-Ups As Software Market Matures. *Wall Street Journal*, C1.

Al-Mashari, M. (2002). Enterprise resource planning (ERP) systems: A research agenda. *Industrial Management and Data Systems, 102*(3), 165-170.

Arinze, B., & Anandarajan, M. (2003). A framework for using OO mapping methods to rapidly configure ERP systems. Association for Computing Machinery. *Communications of the ACM, 46*(2), 61.

Bhattacharjee, D., Greenbaum, J., Johnson, R., Martin, M., Reddy, R., Ryan, H. L., White, C., & McKie, S. (2002). *Intelligent Enterprise, 5*(6), 28-33.

Burns, M. (2007, September). Work in process: Enterprise software survey 2007. *CAMagazine,* 18-20.

Conway, C. (2001). Top 20 Visionaries. *Comments of Craig Conway, 1724,* 35. *VARbusiness*: Manhassett.

Chung, S., & Snyder, C. (2000). ERP adoption: A technological evolution approach. *International Journal of Agile Management Systems, 2*(1), 24-32.

Dahlen, C., & Elfsson, J. (1999). An analysis of the current and future ERP market. Master's Thesis, Industrial Economics and Management. The Royal Institute of Technology, Stockholm, Sweden.

Dalal, N. P., Kamath, M., Kolarik, W. J., & Sivaraman, E. (2004). Toward an Integrated Framework for Modeling Enterprise Resources. *Communications of the ACM, 47*(3), 83-87.

Davison, R. (2002). Cultural complications of ERP. Association for Computing Machinery. *Communications of the ACM, 45*(7), 109.

Garbellotto, G. (2007, October). The Data Warehousing Disconnect. *Strategic Finance,* 59-61.

Genovese, Y., Bond, B.A., Zrimsek, B., & Frey, N. (2001). The Transition to ERP II: Meeting the Challenges. http://www.gartner.com/DisplayDocument?doc_dc=101237, accessed on 7 July 2005.

Green, J. (2003). Responding to the challenge. *Canadian Transportation Logistics, 106*(8), 20-21.

Higgins, K. (2005, May 23). ERP Goes On The Road. *Information Week, 1040,* 52-53.

ITtoolbox ERP Implementation Survey (2004). Retrieved July 7, 2005, from http://supplychain.ittoolbox.com/research/survey.asp?survey=corioerp_survey&p=2

Lee, J., Siau, K., & Hong, S. (2003). Enterprise integration with ERP and EAI. Association for Computing Machinery. *Communications of the ACM, 46*(2), 54.

Knapen, J. (2007, May 14). SAP Sees Growth Ahead. *The Wall Street Journal Online,* http://online.wsj.article_print/SB11791669268180222214.html accessed 11 November 2007.

Koch, C. (2004). *Koch's IT Strategy: The ERP Pickle.* Retrieved June 16, 2005, from http://www.cio.com/blog_view.html?CID=935

Kremers, M., & Dissel, H. V. (2000). ERP system migrations. Association for Computing Machinery. *Communications of the ACM, 43*(4), 52-56.

Kumar, K., & Hillegersberg, J. V. (2000). ERP experiences and evolution. Association for Computing Machinery. *Communications of the ACM, 43*(4), 22-26.

Letzing, J. (2007, April 25). Big Rivals Move In on Salesforce.com's Turf. *The Wall Street Journal,* B3G.

Lope, P. F. (1992). CIMII: the integrated manufacturing enterprise. *Industrial Engineering, 24,* 43-45.

Markus, M. L., Tanis, C., & van Fenema, P. C. (2000). Multisite ERP implementations. Association for Computing Machinery. *Communications of the ACM, 43*(4), 42-46.

Muscatello, J., Small, M., & Chen, I. (2003). Implementing enterprise resource planning (ERP) systems in small and midsize manufacturing firms. *International Journal of Operations & Production Management, 23*(8), 850-871.

Nattkemper, J. (2000). An ERP evolution. *HP Professional, 14*(8), 12-15.

Nikolopoulos, K., Metaxiotis, K., Lekatis, N., & Assimakopoulos, V. (2003). Integrating industrial maintenance strategy into ERP. *Industrial Management & Data Systems, 103,* 3/4, 184-192.

O'Brien, J. M. (2002). J.D. Edwards follows 5 with ERP upgrade. *Computer Dealer News, 18*(12), 11.

Sane, V. (2005). *Enterprise Resource Planning Overview.* Ezine articles. Retrieved July 2, 2005, from http://ezinearticles.com/?Enterprise-Resource-Planning-Overview&id=37656

Scheer, A.-W., & Habermann, F. (2000). Making ERP a Success. Association for Computing Machinery. *Communications of the ACM, 43*(4), 57-61.

Soh, C., Kien, S. S., & Yap, J. T. (2000). Cultural fits and misfits: Is ERP a universal solution. Association for Computing Machinery. *Communications of the ACM,* 43(4), 47-51.

Willcocks, L. P., & Stykes, R. (2000). The role of the CIO and IT function in ERP. Association for Computing Machinery. *Communications of the ACM, 43,* (4), 32-38.

Zrimsek, B. (2002). *ERPII: The Boxed Set.* Retrieved July 7, 2005, from http://www.gartner.com/pages/story.php.id.2376.s.8.jsp

Chapter III
Information Technology Usage in Maquila Enterprises

Purnendu Mandal
Lamar University, USA

Mohan P. Rao
University of Louisiana, USA

ABSTRACT

The build-up of export-oriented companies since 1990s on the Mexico-USA boarder, and their recent decline, is no surprise to many policy analysts. The focus on the use of low-wage employees, neglecting skills, and infrastructure creation was doomed to fail. Much of the Mexican maquila operations and jobs have gone to China and other low-wage countries. Are maquiladoras technologically competent to ward-off competitive forces from China and other parts of the world? This chapter presents an exploratory study of IT usage and managerial perceptions of IT-related costs and benefits in maquiladoras. The relevant data was gathered through a survey questionnaire. The results show that IT had a positive impact on maquila business performance. These findings will be useful to managers in assessing their organization and taking corrective actions to become further competitive.

INTRODUCTION

In response to competitions, multi-nationals have taken advantages of cheaper labor and government incentives in locating production facilities. Especially, US based multinational companies benefited from NAFTA agreement and moved production from USA to Mexico's maquila region. Mexico's cheap labor market was the main incentive, but recently these companies realized that the availability of IT skills should also have been considered. One should be aware that, at a global level, IT has changed the business perspectives and practices for ever; the manifestation of which is IT-enabled or web-enabled business, e-supply chain, e-collaboration, etc. From policy makers view point, it is imperative to decipher the overall business environment (economic, technical, social and political) in a foreign country before making long term business decisions. Given the IT focus of this chapter, the authors argue that policy makers must understand the complexity in making judgment regarding the IT infrastructure in a given country, and how IT (and its many facets) plays into the overall business decision.

The Global Information Technology Report (Dutta, Lanvin and Paua, 2003) provided a means to combine various facets of IT and building a framework for comprehensive assessment of IT readiness for a country. The report used both quantitative data and qualitative information in measuring a readiness index for each of 82 major economies of the World. As defined in the report, the Networked Readiness Index (NRI) is an aggregated measure of the potential and degree of preparation of a nation within its encompassing environment to participate in the Networked World. Nations could be ranked on the basis of the numerical value of the index, and compared among each other with a view to developing IT policies for the future. The Index is a composite of three components: the *environment* for ICT (information and communication technologies) offered by a given country; the *networked readiness* of stakeholders (individuals, business, and government) to use ICT; and finally, the *network usage* of ICT by the stakeholders. As expected, the ranking between the US and Mexico differs significantly in all indexes (see Table 1). A wide gap that exists between the two countries in IT environment, readiness and usage, and this might indicate that Mexico might not be a place for US companies to develop business ties. In reality, however, US companies established strong presence in Mexico, particularly in the border region. In the past decade Mexico surpassed Japan to become the US's second largest trading partner (Sargent and Matthews, 2003).

As the IT environment, readiness and usage between the US and Mexico businesses differ widely, how Mexico's maquiladoras are managing IT related issues with their business partners in the USA? In the literature, however, very little has been found on the effect of IT on operational, technological and management issues in maquiladoras. Thus, to address this gap in the literature, the main objective of this research has been to study maquiladoras and present a comprehensive view of their IT-enabled operational and business practices, and perceptions of management.

The survey methodology was used in this research. First, an extensive literature review was conducted to identify the factors supporting and inhibiting the growth of maquila businesses. Secondly, based on the literature review and personal experiences of the authors with maquila businesses, a questionnaire was designed and distributed among the maquiladoras. The survey was intended to gather information on such things as plant IT usage, quality and costs of IT, overall IT benefits to plants, etc. Finally, the survey responses were analyzed and presented in this chapter.

Table 1. Network readiness rank (Source: Dutta, Lanvin and Paua, 2003)

	NRI Rank	Environment Component Index	Readiness Component Index	Usage Component Index
USA	2	1	3	4
Mexico	47	60	52	37
Canada	6	4	5	10

SIGNIFICANCE OF MAQUILADORAS

Maquiladoras have been in operation along the U.S.-Mexican border regions for a long time. But their growth accelerated since the mid 1990s mainly due to the North American Free Trade Agreement (NAFTA). Majority of the maquiladoras are owned by American businesses. To secure operational and cost advantages, these companies have set up labor intensive plants in the border region. Maquiladoras are typically assembly plants located in Mexico that receive semi-finished parts/components from American companies, finish the assembly and then export the finished products back to America. The existence of a high labor wage difference between the USA and Mexico has been the primary factor fueling the phenomenal growth of maquiladoras.

Maquiladoras have great political, cultural and economic significance, and many studies focused on such issues (Cravey, 1997; Filippi, 2005; Gruben and Kiser 2001; Karahanna, Evaristo and Srite 2005; Kopinak, 2005; Landau 2005; Quinteros 2005; Young and Fort 1994). However, very little effort has been made to study the effect of IT on operational and management issues in maquiladoras. Maquiladora exports constitute nearly 45 to 50% of the total Mexican exports. Since 1990, the contribution of maquilas in percentage of overall export grew significantly, see Figures 1 and 2.

According to Sargent and Matthews (2004), there are approximately 2500 export processing plants and 90 percent of them are owned by U.S. parent companies. Employment in maquilas grew very fast in the 1990s. It must be recognized, however, that the total employment in maquiladoras now is much less than the peak employment number of year 2000 (see Figure 3).

Though the real income per employee remained nearly constant over the last 15 years or so (see Figure 4), the total remuneration to employees grew significantly (see Figure 5). Maquiladoras played a significant role in economic development and employment situation in the border region between Mexico and USA.

Figure 1. Index of export production volume (Source: INEGI, Banco de Información Económico, Industria Maquiladora de Exportación, www.inegi.gob.mx.)

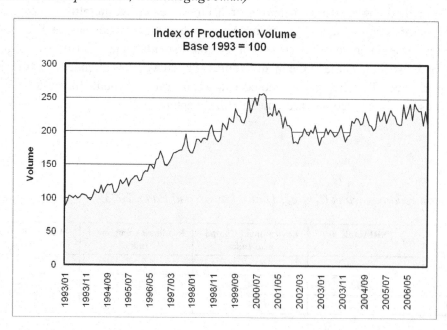

Figure 2. Maquila exports as a percentage of total Mexican exports (Source: INEGI, Banco de Información Económico, Industria Maquiladora de Exportación, www.inegi.gob.mx.)

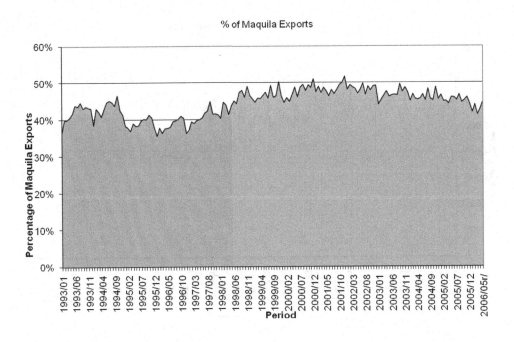

Figure 3. Mexican employment in Maquiladora (Source: INEGI, Banco de Información Económico, Industria Maquiladora de Exportación, www.inegi.gob.mx.)

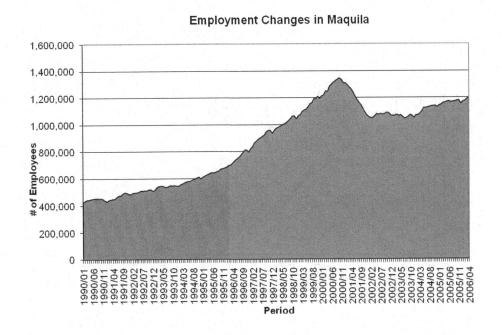

Figure 4. Real income per employee (Source: INEGI, Banco de Información Económico, Industria Maquiladora de Exportación, www.inegi.gob.mx.)

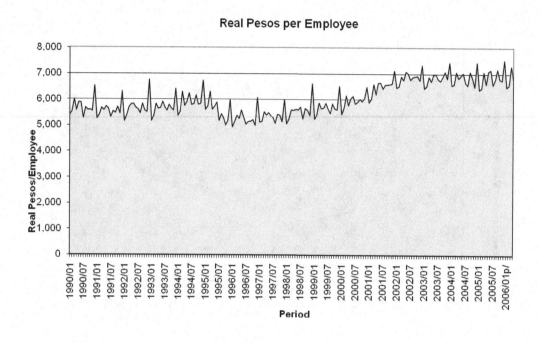

Figure 5. Total remunerations to employees from maquiladoras (Source: INEGI, Banco de Información Económico, Industria Maquiladora de Exportación, www.inegi.gob.mx.)

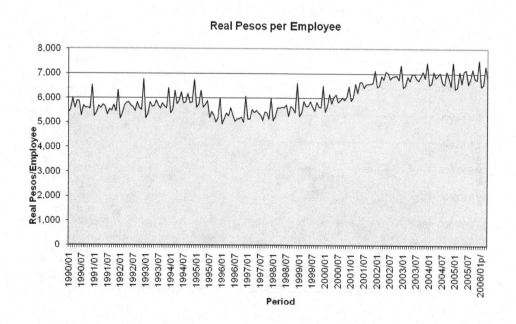

The figures above indicate that the maquiladoras operations reached their peak in year 2000 and since then the assembly operations observed a down turn. During 2001, the total maquila production contracted by 9.2 percent (Sergeant and Matthews, 2003).

PROBLEMS WITH MAQUILAS

To know what has gone wrong with maquila industry one needs to investigate further on maquila environment, industry operations, technology, people and other relevant issues. Some of the industry-wide problems for maquila businesses are discussed below.

Low Local Content in Maquilas

In one of the early studies, Brannon, James and Lucker (1994) found that the Mexican content in maquila operations is less than 2% of value added - Mexico's in-bound assembly operations use very little material inputs that are made in Mexico. Learning from the survey of plant managers and corporate purchasing officers, they suggested that there is a need for a regional focus that concentrates on fostering local technological capacities.

Need for Better Global Chains

Bair and Gereffi (2001) studied the pre-NAFTA and post-NAFTA networks of the blue jeans industry in Torren, a region of 500,000 people in the north Mexican State of Coahuila. Coahuila is about four hours drive by car from US border. Their study focused on how the types of links connecting the local firms to global chains impact upon the development outcomes in export-oriented manufacturing. Bair and Gereffi (2001) advocate establishment of better links than what exists in typical maquila business.

Overseas Competition

A recent report (Fullerton, Barraza & Martha, 2003) indicates that the Mexican in-bound assembly manufacturing sector suffered a business cycle down turn. Apart from the decline in demands from USA's manufacturing sector, the maquiladoras have suffered from the "China Syndrome". In August 2004 *Business Week* reported that "Since maquila employment peaked in October 2000, a quarter-million jobs have been lost. More than 500 maquiladoras have shuttered operations with most production being relocated to China, where factory hands earn one-third what their Mexican counterparts do." (Smith, 2004). China's manufacturing wages are undeniably low which is attracting attention from western businesses. Foreign investments in maquiladora slowed in the early 2000s as it accelerated in China. Many low-wage countries, including China, are attracting out-sourced jobs from the USA.

Need for Reorientation

Sargent and Matthews (2003) provided a good colloquium on what went wrong with Mexico's maquiladoras. Though the maquila industry may not disappear entirely, many maquilas, especially those in the auto parts sector, might make the transition into a higher value-added model. "Our best guess is that these firms will continue to find Mexico an attractive production location, even with a higher cost structure. If nothing else, the advantage of being located next to the largest consumer market in the world is a tremendous benefit for maquila suppliers fully integrated into a coherent JIT, quick-response production model" (Sargent and Matthews, 2003). In recent years, however, there seems to be a little rebound in maquilas; companies which moved to China are thinking to come back to Mexico. Poor customer service and weak protection of intellectual-property rights are main reasons among high-tech companies for remaining in Mexico (Smith, 2004). "People are starting to say: Yeah, China's great for that dollar-a-day labor, but I can't wait 30 days to get my product to a customer" (Smith, 2004).

While overseas competitions and macro economic policy developments are essential for survival of maquiladoras, we also need to consider building business competitiveness. Even when the competitive advantage of the maquila industry is mainly their low labor costs and the proximity with the USA, the adoption of IT is inevitable in order to be in business. The maquila industry could benefit from information technology as an instrument for competitive advantage. As Boynton, Zmud and Jacobs (1994) note, "IT serves an increasingly important role in many organizations in facilitating or enabling the introduction of new products or services and the improvement of operational or managerial work processes. The successful application of IT in such endeavors is inextricably linked with the effective management of number of processes associated with the planning for, acquisition of and implementation of an organization's portfolio." Bakos (1998), stress the important role that IT plays in the normal operation of a plant, such as the exchange of information, good, services, and payments. Use of IT at enterprise level, particularly ERP systems could improve employee productivity. Subramanian and Hoffer (2005) reported increased user productivity and improved job understanding through transition to SAP environment in an organization. Ramaseshan, et al (2006) suggest that investments in Global Customer Relationship Management (GCRM) technologies can be very beneficial to multinational companies. Consequently these companies in developed countries are spending significant amounts in the state-of-the-art technologies and systems. Even with low investments, according to Chung and Sherman (2002), companies in developing countries can have higher returns than their counterparts in the developed countries. Sohal, Moss and Ng (2000) suggest that "all types of organizations can benefit from the adoption of IT. What is needed is a well formulated IT strategy which becomes an integral part of the corporate strategy and hence, contributes to creating and maintaining a competitive advantage." Clearly, there is a need to understand the role of IT and an IT strategy for maquila industry. This study attempts to provide a comprehensive view of IT adoption and benefits to maquila industry.

RESEARCH APPROACH

As there is hardly any information on IT-enabled business operations and IT adoption in maquiladoras, this study is designed to collect data from business managers. A three-page questionnaire was developed to collect the information that covers some aspects based on following theoretical basis:

First, in order to know the overall operation of the maquiladora, general information about the plant and the type of IT used was gathered. Additionally, size of the plant and the extent of export operations are also integrated in the questionnaire. Secondly, based on Levy and Powell (2003) study, questions regarding the level of IT used in the plant and the stages of adoption of IT were included in the questionnaire. Specifically, questions about the time and functional area where IT and e-commerce technologies were installed were included. Thirdly, other research streams focus on benefits on the adoption of IT. For example, Poon and Swatman (1999) propose a model that stress cost reduction and long term business relationships as direct benefits in the implementation of IT. Also, Barney (1991) posits that efficiency and competitiveness is increased by implementing IT in the enterprise. The questionnaire developed includes both advantages and disadvantages to assure validity in the results. And lastly, other data included in the questionnaire is for exploratory purposes. This may help to realize some underlying facts not covered in any previous research.

A five-point Likert scale was used for questions where response was expected in relative term: 1 for very low or totally disagree, to 5 for very high or totally agree. The authors took advantage of local contacts with maquiladora development authorities located at the Mexican side of the border to conduct this survey. Accordingly, McAllen Economic Development Corporation (MEDC) distributed the survey questionnaire via e-mail among their members, roughly 250 companies. Much of McAllen's industrial growth is connected to the maquilas south of the border in Reynosa, Mexico. MEDC has also ties with businesses both sides of the border. A follow up reminder was sent after one month of the initial posting. Altogether 34 responses were received (a response rate of 13.6%) of which 33 responses were used for statistical analysis. As with any survey, there were problem of missing data with this survey. However, the missing data problem was not fixed in order to maintain the originality of the data set.

RESULTS

The data was coded and analyzed using the SPSS statistical software package. Even when the sample size was limited, the data gave high reliabilities in the analysis. Using the sample of 33 responses, we first performed an assessment of reliability to verify the integrity of the measurements using Cronbach's alpha as indicator. Table 2 shows the results of the reliability tests of the four major performance variables. The reliability coefficients of the variables were high enough to be acceptable for an exploratory study (Hair et al, 1998) suggesting that all the items should be retained. The data gathered include maquiladoras from both, Mexico and the USA. A total of 21 (64%) are from Mexico and 12 (36%) are located in the USA.

General Characteristics of Maquiladoras

Many of the maquiladoras were established during mid 1990s. As the survey statistics show, an average maquiladora company is five to ten years old, employs 50 to 200 persons, with the majority of the sample (63%) reported that all their employees are permanent in their positions. The average maquila has between 11 and 50 suppliers. The average company is also new to the use of EDI (four years only) though the company used IT for about nine years (see Table 3).

Businesses being part of a network may enjoy competitive advantage over others. 75% of the respondents reported to be part of a bigger organization. Furthermore, the majority (70%) sends all or part of their production to another part of the company and 82% expect to make profits as a business unit.

Considering the competitiveness aspect of the maquiladoras in our sample, more than half (52%) make at least 50% of their business via e-commerce transactions. This phenomenon can be attributed to the fact that the maquiladoras in both sides of the border use this type of technological advantage for two reasons. One is the pressure of the global competitiveness environment, even when Mexican companies do not report to have the e-commerce transactions to be a great deal of normal activities,

Table 2. Performance factors included in the study

Performance Factors	Alpha
Benefits	.91
Improved quality of information	
Improve competitiveness	
Improve marketing	
Increase sales	
Increase new customers. Markets	
Improve relations with customers	
Improve relations with suppliers	
Increase internal efficiency	
Reduce lead time	
Lower transaction costs	
Lower productions costs	
Disadvantages	.84
Higher costs	
Deteriorated relations with customers	
Deteriorated relations with suppliers/vendors	
Reduced security	
Reduce flexibility in work	
Being forced to double work	
Computer maintenance	
Dependence on E-Commerce	
Costs Related to Competitors	.72
Relative to other domestic competitors	
Relative to other foreign competitors	
Quality related to Competitors	.95
Relative to other domestic competitors	
Relative to other foreign competitors	

Table 3. Statistics of the general data of maquiladoras

	Mean Value		Lowest		Highest	
	Scale	Value	Scale	Value	Scale	Value
Years in Business	3.33	5 to 10 years	2	1 to 5 years	5	> 20 years
Number of Employees	3.73	51 to 200 persons	1	1 to 10 persons	6	>1000 persons
Number of suppliers	2.80	11 to 50 suppliers	1	1 to 10 suppliers	4	> 100 suppliers
No. of Years Using IT	8.69 years		1 year		23 years	
No. of Years Using EDI	4.04 years		1 year		8 years	

and second, because the production and administrative systems of the bigger corporations are adopted in the maquiladoras in the Mexican side.

Maquiladoras in our sample reported also a big confidence in their production process and in the quality of the products they manufacture. More than 90% of our respondents reported to have the same or better quality with respect to both local and foreign competitors.

IT in Functional Areas

One of the primary objectives of this study is to determine the extent of IT adoption in various business functional areas in maquiladoras. Questions were asked to indicate when and in which functional area (manufacturing, sales & marketing, finance, product design, R & D, and administration) IT initiatives were introduced.

Before 1980 only about 18 percent of the respondents were using IT in manufacturing. There has been a steady rise in adoption of IT in manufacturing since then. IT usage in marketing was greater than manufacturing for several years. By year 2000 IT usage in both areas was similar. Before 1980 about 30% of the respondents used IT in marketing, which is much higher than manufacturing. By 2001 most of the companies adopted IT in marketing, which means that they are emphasizing the use of IT in promoting their products and reaching the customers.

It is interesting to note that IT has been more used in finance areas of the companies for a long time. This may be due to the fact that finance systems like payroll and purchasing systems were extensively used in the maquiladoras before the other technologies were available for use in the other areas. As mention before, the area where IT has been used for less time is the manufacturing area.

Impact of Using IT in Different Areas

Table 4 summarizes the impact of IT use in various areas in maquilas. There is a positive relationship between the number of years where IT has been used in product design with some of the benefits that this practice provided. We observed an impact of improve marketing practices and increase the number of customers for the businesses. Also the relationship with customers as well as with suppliers has also been influenced by this practice.

There is a positive relationship between the use of IT in R&D and improvements in marketing and supplier relationships. The usage of IT in finance and administration areas has influence the business in the maquiladoras of our sample. These two areas where IT has been used have improved marketing as a benefit for the company.

Table 4. Impact of using IT in different areas of the company

Number of years	Affect	Correlation factor
Using IT on product design	Improve marketing	.565**
	Increase new customers	.606**
	Improve relations with customers	.311**
	Improve relations with suppliers	.513**
Using IT in R & D	Improve marketing	.698**
	Improve relations with suppliers	.561**
Using IT in Finance	Improve marketing	.449**
Using IT in Administration	Improve marketing	.448**
Using IT overall	Increase sales	.437**
	Increase new customers	.417**

$^*p < 0.10;$ $^{**}p < 0.05;$ $^{***}p < 0.01$

In sum, there have been numerous advantages of using IT in different areas of the company. Furthermore, the overall usage of IT impacts significantly the company. There has been an increase of sales and an increase of new customers.

Impact of Using a Specific IT on the Business

Use of Intranet

There is a positive relationship with the usage of this technology with some benefits related with the business of the companies on our sample. For example, the usage of this technology has increase competitiveness, relation with customers and suppliers, and reduced inventory, among others. Also there is a negative relationship of this practice with some disadvantages reported. This practice had impacted negatively the reduction of the flexibility of work and the practice to double work.

Use of EDI

There is a positive relationship with this practice with some benefits like improve relation with customer. But it has impacted negatively more disadvantages like high costs, reduce flexibility of work, and deterioration elation with vendors, among others.

Use of ERP/SCM Technologies

Again in this case there is an impact of the usage of these technologies with some advantages in the company. They have improved relation with suppliers, reduced inventory, and lower production costs, among others. In the same way there is a negative impact on some disadvantages of the company like higher costs, reduced flexibility of work and being forced to double work. Table 5 shows complete details of this section.

Differences Between the Companies that Use IT

In order to validate if there are differences between the maquiladoras that adopt the usage of the different types of IT, we run independent t-tests. We found important differences in different areas of the business; the differences are listed in Table 6.

Usage of the Intranet

We found important differences between the set of maquiladoras that use this technology against the one that don't use it. For example we found differences in some advantages of the maquiladoras that use this technology over the ones that don't use it. Specifically we found differences in the competitiveness, relations with customers and suppliers, reduce inventory, among others. In the same token, we found differences in some disadvantages that maquiladoras that don't use this technology have over the ones that use it. Among these disadvantages we have high costs, reduce flexibility of work and being forced to double work.

Table 5. The impact on the usage of a specific technology

Usage of the technology	Affect	Correlation factor
Intranet	Improved competitiveness	.395**
	Improved relation with customers	.509***
	Improved relation with suppliers/vendors	.606***
	Reduced inventory	.698***
	Lower transaction costs	.675***
	Lower production costs	.495**
	Reduced flexibility of work	-.751***
	Being forced to double work	-.570***
EDI	Improve relation with customers	.550***
	High costs	-.557***
	Deteriorated relation with vendors	-.479**
	Reduce flexibility in work	-.823***
	Being forced to double work	-.739***
	Computer maintenance	-.462**
ERP/SCM	Improved relation with suppliers	.680**
	Reduced inventory	.508**
	Lower production costs	.519**
	Higher costs	-.707***
	Reduced flexibility in work	-.733***
	Being forced to double work	-.676***
	Computer maintenance	-.574**

$^*p < 0.10;$ $^{**}p < 0.05;$ $^{***}p < 0.01$

Use of EDI

Similarly, we found some advantages of the companies that use this technology over those that don't use it. For example there are differences in competitiveness, relation with customers, and lower transaction costs. In the same way there are some disadvantages of the maquiladoras that don't use this technology over the ones that does use it. For example we found differenced on higher costs, reduce flexibility of work and being forced to double work, among others.

Use of IT Overall

Finally to report the differences of the maquiladoras that use IT overall over the ones that don't use it, we found some important insights. There are some benefits that maquilas using IT overall have over the ones that don't use it. For example we found differences in improved relations with customers and suppliers, reduced lead time, and reduced inventory among others. In the same way, there are disadvantages that the maquiladoras that don't use IT overall have over the ones that do use it. For example we found differences in higher costs, reduced flexibility of work, and being forced to double work, among others.

Table 6. Differences on some aspects on the usage of certain technology

Technology	Benefits	Disadvantages
Intranet	Improve competitiveness**	High costs***
	Improve relations with customers*	Reduced flexibility in work***
	Improve relation with suppliers/vendors**	Being forced to double work***
	Reduced inventory***	
	Lower transaction costs**	
	Lower production costs**	
EDI	Improved competitiveness*	High costs**
	Improve relation with customers*	Reduce flexibility in work**
	Lower transaction costs*	Being forces to double work***
		Computer maintenance**
IT Overall	Improved relation with customers*	Higher costs*
	Improved relation with suppliers**	Reduced flexibility in work*
	Reduced lead time*	Being forced to double work*
	Reduced inventory*	Computer maintenance*
	Lower transaction costs*	
	Lower production costs**	

$^{*}p < 0.10; \ ^{**}p < 0.05; \ ^{***}p < 0.01$

DISCUSSION

The survey provided a much needed understanding of maquiladora industry, in general, and a wealth of IT related information, in particular. Some of the major findings are:

- Most of the maquiladora companies are five to ten years old,
- EDI technology is relatively new to maquiladoras even though some form of IT has been used for long time.
- Both manufacturing and marketing functional areas experienced very high level of IT adoption.
- Benefits from the use of IT increased with the length of IT adoption.
- The use of networks (intranet and extranet) improved customer relations and supplier/vendor relations, reduced inventory and transaction costs.

As predicted by Mercado (2001), this study confirms that the maquila industry was having a tremendous increase in the adoption of IT in the recent years. Some of the factors that might have contributed to this trend are the external pressure and the global environment (Gibbs, Kraemer, and Dedrick, 2003). In the case of the maquiladoras, the external pressure (from the US parent companies) was mainly on conformance of production standards and systems (JIT and TQC). At the individual level, the factor which contributed significantly to the adoption of IT and expansion of e-commerce in the Mexican society is the *level of involvement*. Previous researches stress the importance of involvement as a key element in the adoption of technological innovation (Latour, Hanna, Miller, and Pitts, 2002). Jones and Tollous (2001) established evidence that Mexican nationals have a high level of involvement in the usage of e-commerce and IT in general.

It is interesting to compare the findings of this survey with that of Kuwaiti manufacturing companies as reported in Khalil and Mady (2005): "With the exception of database, e-mail, finance and accounting, and inventory control, the findings suggest a low level of IT adoption in support of internal and external information sharing and in support of the operations function in the investigated companies". In maquilas, both the manufacturing and marketing functional areas showed high level of IT adoption.

As indicated earlier, maquiladoras are an important part of Mexico-USA trade and employment. Maquiladoras, however, have recently suffered production and employment down turn; they are also facing overseas competition. Low-wage countries like China, Honduras, El Salvador or Dominican Republic will seek business out-sourcing from the US and put the maquiladoras in further difficult position. These countries will compete not through IT readiness or IT usage (see Table 7), but primarily through lower local labor costs. It transpires that Mexico's maquiladoras are in a good position to ward-off global competition through effective use of IT.

CONCLUSION

The survey analysis, presented here, shows that IT and B2B e-commerce related IT is in place in maquiladoras and some companies have benefited from the use of IT. Further adoption of IT to become operationally efficient and to closely link electronically with their American partners would be the future developments.

This chapter addressed a major gap in the literature on IT in a special economic and industrial zone. The study of maquiladoras offered a comprehensive view of IT and their variations in maquila industry. To some extent this study presented insights into IT-enabled operations and the benefits of IT to business practices in maquiladoras. This study, however, did not consider behavioral and cultural factors, which should be an important consideration according to Mandal (2006).

This study is significant and timely as maquila-like businesses are growing in various parts of the world. For example, there exists an industrial zone between Hong Kong and China where cheap labor force from China is employed by Hong Kong-owned businesses. The recent migration of US IT jobs to countries such as India, China, Russia, etc., is to some extent related to maquiladoras phenomena.

Table 7. IT readiness and usage in low-wage countries (Source: Dutta, Lanvin and Paua, 2003)

	NRI Rank	Environment Component Index	Readiness Component Index	Usage Component Index
Mexico	47	60	52	37
China	43	51	35	51
Honduras	81	80	78	79
El Salvador	63	66	69	53
Dominican Republic	57	46	56	63

REFERENCES

Bair, J., & Gereffi, G. (2001). Local Clusters in Global Chains: The Causes and Consequences of Export Dynamism in Torreon's Blue Jeans Industry. *World Development, 29*(11), 1185-1903.

Bakos, Y. (1998). The Emerging Role of Electronic Marketplaces on the Internet. *Communications of the ACM, 41*(8), 35-42.

Barney, J. (1991). Firm Resources and Sustained Competitive Advantage. *Journal of Management, 17*(1), 99-120.

Boynton, A. C., Zmud, R. W., & Jacobs, G. C. (1994). The influence of IT management practice on IT use in large organizations. *MIS Quarterly*, September, 299-318.

Brannon, J., James, D., & Lucker, W. (1994). Generating and Sustaining Backward Linkages between Maquiladoras and Local Suppliers in Northern Mexico. *World Development, 22*(12), 1933-1945.

Chung, S., & Sherman, M. (2002). Emerging Marketing. *McKinsey Quarterly, 2*, 62-71.

Cravey, A. (1997). The Politics of Reproduction: Households in the Mexican Industrial Transition. *Economic Geography, 73*(2), 166-186.

Dutta, S., Lanvin, B., & Paua, F. (2003). *The Global Information Technology Report 2002-2003: Readiness for the Networked World*, Oxford University Press.

Filippi, F. (2005). Aspectos Teoricos de las Maquiladoras y la Migración. *Boletin Chiapas al Dia, 485*, 1-5.

Fullerton, T., Barraza de A., & Martha P. (2003). Maquiladoras Prospect in a Global Environment. *Texas Business Review*, October, 1-5.

Gibbs, J., Kreamer, K. L., & Dedrick, J. (2003). Environment and Policy Factors Shaping Global E-Commerce Diffusion: A Cross-Country Comparison. *The Information Society, 19*, 5-18.

Gruben, W., & Kiser, S. (2001). *NAFTA and Maquiladoras: Is the Growth Connected?* Federal Reserve Bank of Dallas. Retrieved from http://www.dallasfed.org/research/border/tbe_gruben.html

Hair, J., Anderson, R., Tatham, T., & Black, W. (1998). *Multivariate Data Analysis*. Fifth Edition, Prentice Hall, New Jersey.

INEGI (Instituto Nacional de Estadistica, Geografia, e Informatica). Retrieved November 2007 from www.inegi.gob.mx.

Jones, K. L., & Tullous, R. (2001). E-Commerce Attitudes and Involvement in the U.S. and Mexico, *Proceedings of the Academy of Business & Administrative Science Conference,* July 2001, Quebec, Canada.

Karahanna, E., Evaristo, J., Srite, M. (2005). Levels of Culture and Individual Behavior: An Integrative Perspective. *Journal of Global Information Management, 13*(2), 1-20.

Khalil, O. E. M., & Mady, T. (2005). IT Adoption and Industry Type: Some Evidence from Kuwaiti Manufacturing Companies. *International Journal of Enterprise Information Systems, 1*(4), 39-55.

Kopinak, B. (2005). The Relationship Between Employment in Maquiladora Industries in Mexico and Labor Migration to the United Status. *The Center for Comparative Immigration Studies, 1-18*. University of California, San Diego.

Landau S. (2005). Globalization, Maquilas, NAFTA and the State. *Journal of Developing Societies, 21*(3/4), 9.

Latour, M. S., Hanna, J. B., Miller, M. D. & Pitts, R. E. (2002). Consumer Involvement with Personal Computer Technology: A Multi-Sample Analysis. *American Business Review*, June, 1-11.

Levy, M., & Powell, P. (2003). Exploring SME Internet Adoption: Towards a Contingent Model. *Electronic Markets, 13*(2), 173-181.

Mandal, P. (2006). Behavioral Factors and Information Technology Infrastructure Considerations in Strategic Alliance Development. *International Journal of Enterprise Information Systems, 2*(4), 77-88.

Mercado, A. (2001). El Comercio Mediante la Red Electronica en Mexico y su Industria Maquiladora, Red de Economia Fronteriza, 1-18. Available at: http://www.nobe-ref.org/Conferences/2001/PANELII_AMERCADO.pdf.

Poon, S., & Swatman, P (1999). An Exploratory Study of Small Business Internet Commerce Issues. *Information and Management, 35*, 9-18.

Quinteros C. (2005). Corporate responsibility and the US–Central America Free Trade Agreement (CAFTA): Are they compatible? *Development in Practice, 15*(3/4), 572-583.

Ramaseshan, B., Bejou, D., Jain, S., Mason, C., & Pancras, J. (2006). Issues and Perspectives in Global Customer Relationship Management. *Journal of Service Research, 9*(2), 195-207.

Sargent, J., & Matthews, L. (2003). Boom or Bust: Is it the end of the Maquiladoras? *Business Horizons*, March-April, 57-64.

Sargent, J., & Matthews, L. (2004). *What Happens When Relative Costs Increase in Export Processing Zones? Technology, Regional Production Networks, and Mexico's Maquiladoras*", Working Paper #2002-19, Center of Border Economic Studies, The University of Texas – Pan American.

Smith G. (2004). Made In The Maquilas -- Again. *Business Week, 3896*, 45.

Sohal, A. S., Moss, S., & Ng, L. (2000). Using information technology productivity: practices and factors that enhance the success of IT. *International Journal of Technology Management, 20*(3/4), 340-353.

Subramanian, G. H., & Hoffer, C. S. (2005) An Exploratory Case Study of Enterprise Resource Planning Implementation. *International Journal of Enterprise Information Systems, 1*(1), 23-38.

Young, G., & Fort, L. (1994). Household Responses to Economic Change: Migration and Maquiladora work in Ciudad Juarez, Mexico. *Social Science Quarterly, 75*(3), 656-670.

ADDITIONAL READINGS

Bair, J., & Gereffi, G. (2003). Upgrading, uneven development, and jobs in the North American apparel industry. *Global Networks, 3*(2), 143-169.

Bates, C. (2007). Intercultural Rhetoric, Technology Transfer, and Writing in U.S.-Mexico Border Maquilas. *Technical Communication, 54*(1), 133-133.

Bellman, M. J. (2004). Rationality And Identity In The Participation Choices Of Female Maquila Workers. *Comparative Political Studies,* 37(5), 563-589.

Bougher, K. (2003). Women's Lives for Sale: Free Trade and Education in El Salvador. *Off Our Backs,* 33(11/12), 15-18.

Delgado-Wise, R., & Humberto, C. M. (2007). The Reshaping of Mexican Labor Exports under NAFTA: Paradoxes and Challenges. *International Migration Review, 41*(3), 656-679.

Jeffcott, B. (2007). Sweat, fire and ethics. *New Internationalist, 399,* 20-21.

Ortez, O. (2004). Spreading manufacturing growth gains through local jobs: lessons from the Guatemalan highlands. *Development in Practice, 14*(½), 163-170.

Pasquarella, J., & Pasquarella, J. (2003). Guatemala: Victory for Maquila Workers. *NACLA Report on the Americas, 37*(3), 5-46.

Prieto, M., & Quinteros, C. (2004). Never the twain shall meet? Women's organizations and trade unions in the maquila industry in Central America. *Development in Practice, 14*(½), 149-157.

Rauch, M., Seffer, K., & Noemi, G-O. (2006). The Great Divide: Structural and Politico-Economic Explanations for the US-Mexican Real Wage Level Gap Revisited. *Conference Papers -- International Studies Association, 1.*

Salas, C. (2005). The Decline of the Decent Job. *NACLA Report on the Americas, 39*(1), 23-39.

Salzinger, L. (2004). From Gender as Object to Gender as Verb: Rethinking how Global Restructuring Happens. *Critical Sociology, 30*(1), 43-62.

Thatcher, B. (2006). Intercultural Rhetoric, Technology Transfer, and Writing in U.S.–Mexico Border Maquilas. *Technical Communication Quarterly, 15*(3), 385-405.

Toledo, E. de la G. (2007). The Crisis of the Maquiladora Model in Mexico. *Work & Occupations* 34(4), 399-429.

Traub-Werner, M. (2006). Worldly Encounters in Free Trade: Export Apparel in the Caribbean Basin. *Antipode, 38*(1), 178-180.

Weiler, S., & Zerlentes, B. (2003). Maquila sunrise or sunset? Evolutions of regional production advantages. *Social Science Journal, 40*(2), 283.

Chapter IV
Performance and Cost Analysis of Service–Oriented Enterprise Architectures

Henk Jonkers
BiZZdesign, The Netherlands

Maria-Eugenia Iacob
University of Twente, The Netherlands

ABSTRACT

In this chapter the authors address the integration of functional models with non-functional models in the context of service-oriented architectures. Starting from the observation that current approaches to model-driven development have a strong focus on functionality, we argue the necessity of including non-functional aspects as early as possible in the service design process. We distinguish two modelling spaces, the design space and the analysis space, which can be integrated by means of model transformations. Quantitative results obtained in the analysis space, using special-purpose analysis techniques, can be related back to the design models by means of a reverse transformation. This provides a framework for incorporating non-functional analysis into methodological support for e-service development. While, for detailed design models, quantitative analysis is more or less covered by existing techniques, there is still a gap at the architectural overview level. Therefore, we propose an approach for performance and cost analysis of layered, service-oriented architecture models, which consists of two phases: a "top-down" propagation of workload parameters, and a "bottom-up" propagation of performance or cost measures. By means of an example, the authors demonstrate the application of the approach, and show that a seamless integration with detailed quantitative analysis methods (e.g., queueing analysis for performance predictions) can be achieved.

INTRODUCTION

Current approaches to model-driven development of applications and services, including OMG's Model Driven Architecture (MDA), have a strong focus on functional properties. Non-functional aspects, such as security, cost and Quality of Service (QoS), are often added as an 'afterthought'. However, it becomes more and more accepted that these aspects should become an integral part of the design process, from the global architectural descriptions, located in the higher layers of the MDA framework (CIM-PIM) to detailed system specifications (PSM).

Architectures describe components, their relations and underlying design principles of a system (IEEE, 2000). Constructing architectures may help to, among others, increase the insight and overview required to successfully align the business and ICT. Architectural descriptions may be used to relate detailed design models to each other (of applications and services, but also of, e.g., business processes or the technical infrastructure). The combination of design models, together the realisations specified by the architectural description, prescribe the realisation of a system.

While existing techniques for quantitative analysis mainly address properties of detailed design models, the quantitative aspects of architectural models have hardly received any attention in literature. Nevertheless, quantitative properties are important also at this architectural level. In the first place, because the quantitative properties of the detailed designs influence each other: for example, business processes imposes performance requirements on the applications and technical infrastructure, while the performance characteristics of systems influence the quantitative behaviour of business processes. Similarly, the total costs for running the business include costs made in the application and infrastructure layers. Moreover, the availability of global performance and cost estimates in the early architectural design stage can provide invaluable support for system design decisions, and prevent the need for expensive redesigns at later stages.

Based on the above observations, we present in this paper our view on how models of functional and non-functional aspects, as well as the analysis of these models, can be considered in an integrated way, through all the MDA layers of models. We show the role of architectural models, and how model transformations can be used to link the different types of design and analysis models. In this context, we propose an approach for the quantification and quantitative analysis of architectural models. This approach is based on the propagation of quantitative input parameters and of calculated performance and cost measures through a layered, service-oriented architectural model. It complements existing detailed performance and cost analysis techniques (e.g., queueing analysis for performance predictions), which can be 'plugged in' to provide the performance results for the model elements.

Through an example, we also show how analysis of non-functional aspects influences the design process, thus corroborating the common claim that non-functional aspects should be integrated in the development process in an early stage.

Non-Functional Properties

While functional aspects describe the functions that a system provides and the way in which it performs these functions, non-functional aspects describe qualities of these functions. This is similar to a (service) contract, which generally specifies the functional characteristics of a service that have been agreed upon, while a Service Level Agreement (SLA) may specify requirements for the delivered QoS.

Some of the non-functional aspects have a qualitative nature, while others are quantifiable (although, for some of the aspects that we classify as qualitative, proposals exists to assign quantitative values to them). Aspects such as security, integrity, trust, flexibility and maintainability, accessibility and scalability, but also the (partly subjective) user's perception of quality (e.g., image quality) belong to the former category. The latter category includes, among others:

1. Performance measures:
    - Timeliness (delay, response time, jitter, latency)
    - Throughput (bandwidth)
    - Resource utilisation
2. Reliability measures
    - Availability (MTBF, percentage of time available)
    - Error rate
3. Cost measures
    - Fixed costs
    - Variable costs

Note that a strict distinction between functional and non-functional aspects is not always possible, and that this separation may depend on a specific application: e.g., for real-time systems, the (maximum) response time (a performance/QoS measure) will often be a functional requirement.

From this brief survey it becomes clear that the main thrust of work on non-functional aspects is the establishment of suitable metrics and of the confidence that system designs meet targets expressed in terms of these metrics. For example, once a design has been produced, performance problems can seldom be fixed by adding functions and generally the solution lies in redesign. It is therefore particularly important here that problems are detected early in the design cycle. This is where the main value of model-driven non-functional analysis lies, which, as we will argue, starts at the level of architectural (computation-independent) models, and propagates through all MDA model layers, using model transformations techniques.

Viewpoints on Performance and Costs

Although the framework we propose for the integration of design and analysis models through transformations applies, in principle, to any kind of (functional or non-functional) aspects, our focus in this paper is on the analysis of performance and cost aspects, in particular in the context of architectural models. Architectures can be described from different viewpoints, which result in different views on architectural models (IEEE, 2000). These views are aimed at different *stakeholders* that have an interest in the modelled system. Also for the performance aspects of a system, a number of viewpoints can be discerned, resulting in different (but related) performance measures:

- **User/customer view** (stakeholders: customer; user of an application/system): *response time*, the time between issuing a request and receiving the result; the response time is the sum of the processing time and waiting times (synchronisation losses); *cost per use* of a service.
- **Process view** (stakeholders: process owner; operational manager): *completion time*, the time required to complete one instance of a process (possibly involving multiple customers, orders, products

etc., as opposed to the response time, which is defined as the time to complete one request); *cost per completion* of a process.

- **Product view** (stakeholders: product manager; operational manager): *processing time*, the amount of time that actual work is performed on the realisation of a certain product or result: the response time without waiting times (this can be an order of magnitude lower than the response time); *cost per completion* of a product.
- **System view** (stakeholders: system owner; system manager): *throughput*, the number of transactions/requests that are completed per time unit; *cost per time unit* of using the system.
- **Resource view** (stakeholder: resource manager; capacity planner): *utilisation*, the percentage of the operational time that a resource is busy. On the one hand, the utilisation is a measure for the effectiveness with which a resource is used. On the other hand, a high utilisation can be an indication of the fact that the resource is a potential bottleneck. *Resource cost* (or *tariff*), the cost per time unit for using the resource.

The performance viewpoints are a refinement of the views mentioned in, e.g., Herzog (2001), which only discerns a user view and a system view. Figure 1 summarises the views on performance.

Paper Outline

The remainder of this paper is organised as follows. In Section 2, we put forward our view on the role of model transformations, analysis and integration in the context of MDA, which form the background of our research. Section 3 summarises the ArchiMate language, which is used to express models at the architectural level. Section 4 presents a short review of related work in two areas related to the topics that we discuss: performance and cost analysis of architectural models, and design model to analysis model transformations. In Section 5 we present our approach for performance and cost analysis of architectural models, which is illustrated by means of an example. Finally, in Section 6, we draw our conclusions and give some pointers to future work.

Figure 1. Performance viewpoints

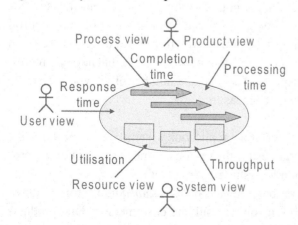

Figure 2. Cost viewpoints

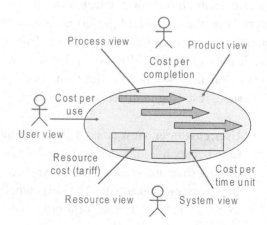

MODEL TRANSFORMATIONS, ANALYSIS AND INTEGRATION

In this section we present our view on model integration, with a focus on the specification and analysis of non-functional aspects, and the role that model transformations play in this. Similar to Skene and Emmerich (2003a, 2003b), we distinguish between models in a design space and in an analysis space, and define transformations between these spaces. However, we explicitly include the whole MDA stack, as well as the integration of heterogeneous design models by means of an integration model at the architectural level. Before we explain our two central ideas - the role of model transformations and analysis and model integration - in more detail, we first summarise the MDA philosophy.

Model Driven Architecture

Model Driven Architecture (MDA) (Miller and Mukerji, 2003; Soley and the OMG Staff Strategy Group, 2000) is a collection of standards that raise the level of abstraction at which software solutions are specified. Typically, MDA results in software development tools that support specification of software in UML instead of in a programming language like Java. Design models at different levels of abstraction are derived from each other through model transformations. More specifically, different platform-specific models (PSMs) can be derived automatically or semi-automatically from the same platform-independent model (PIM), making use of information from a platform model.

More recently, MDA has extended its focus to more business-oriented concepts and languages, reflecting the growing awareness that it is important to take into account business considerations in software development decisions. For this purpose, MDA has been extended with a computation-independent model (CIM) layer. However, we believe that business process models also have correspondents at the platform-independent level (describing the logical structure of the processes) and at the platform-specific level (describing the realisation and/or orchestration of processes in terms of, e.g., BPEL specifications (Andrews *et al.*, 2002) etc.). Also notice that UML is probably not the most suitable language to express business-oriented models; specific business process modelling languages, such as ARIS (Scheer, 1994) or Testbed (Eeertink *et al.* 1999) are better equipped for this purpose.

The Role of Transformations and Analysis

In MDA, model transformations play a central role. Transformations are used to derive, e.g., platform-independent models from computation-independent models and platform-specific models from platform-independent models. The left-hand side of Figure 3 illustrates this. As in these top-down transformations information is added (i.e., the lower-level models are refinements of the higher-level models), it is still unclear to what extent these transformations can be performed fully automatically.

Model analysis is another important activity in the system development process. Analysis can be used in all design stages to check whether the design meets certain requirements or to perform certain optimisations. This includes the analysis of both functional and non-functional properties of a design. Analysis often requires specific analysis models, expressed in a separate formal analysis language. Therefore, we make a distinction in Figure 3 between the design space, with design models expressed in design languages such as UML, business process modelling languages or architectural description languages, and the analysis space, with analysis models expressed in a special-purpose analysis language (cf. Skene and Emmerich, 2003a and 2003b). The derivation of an analysis model from a design model can also be expressed in terms of a model transformation. This will be addressed in more detail in Section 4.2. As the figure shows, there is a strong symmetry between the design space and the analysis space: for any design model, there may be a corresponding analysis model.

In summary, the following types of model transformations are relevant (see Figure 2):

- Vertical model-to-model transformations in the design space: architectural model (CIM) to platform-independent design model (PIM) and platform-independent design model (and platform model) to platform-specific design model (PSM); these are standard transformations identified in the MDA. (Model-to-code transformations in the design space are not shown in this figure.)
- Horizontal model-to-model transformations from the design space to the analysis space, either at the architectural, platform-independent or platform-specific level. In order to relate the analysis results to the original design models, we typically follow a sequence of three steps:
    1. A transformation from a model from the design space to a (formal) model in the analysis space.
    2. The actual analysis of the model, using a proprietary analysis technique, to derive the required (quantitative) properties.
    3. A reverse transformation of the model in the analysis space to a model in the design space, including attributes with the analysis results.
- Vertical model-to-model transformations in the analysis space: platform-independent performance model to platform-specific performance model.

Integration and Refinement

A second central idea, besides, transformation is model integration, in which enterprise architecture models play a crucial role, both as a starting point for model-driven development (i.e. enterprise architecture model roughly covers the CIM level of MDA – see Figure 3) and to keep an overview of the relations between the different types of design models (see Figure 4), possibly expressed in different languages. Since enterprise architecture covers a wide range of aspects - from the technical infrastruc-

Figure 3. Model transformations

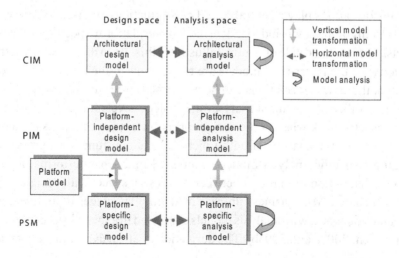

Figure 4. Integration of models

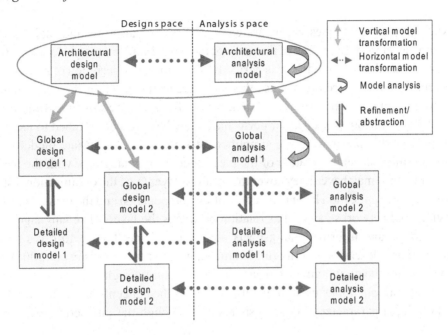

ture layer (e.g., computer hardware and networks), through software applications running on top of the infrastructure, to business processes supported by these applications - it is justified to expect that such an architecture model can form the basis of both conceptual model integration and tool integration. ArchiMate (Jonkers *et al.*, 2004) is an architecture modelling language that has been designed specifi-cally for this purpose (Leeuwen *et al.*, 2004; Steen *et al.*, 2004). In contrast to languages for models within a domain (e.g., the Unified Modelling Language, UML (Scott, 2004) for modelling applications and the technical infrastructure, or the Business Process Modelling Notation BPMN (BPMI, 2003) for modelling business processes), a language for enterprise architecture should describe the elements of an enterprise at a relatively *high level of abstraction*, and should pay particular attention to the *relations* between these elements.

In model integration, model-to-model transformations also play an important role, as is shown in Figure 4. Transformations from the architecture modelling language to specific design languages (e.g., UML or business process modelling languages) and back are required to realise model integration. Thus, an architecture model could act as 'glue' between the other design models. Starting with the global design models, refinement steps can be carried out to describe more detailed designs. Again, the design models at all of these levels may have a counterpart in the analysis space. These may undergo an analysis process. We ultimately also aim for the integration of the quantitative results: the detailed analysis results may be the input for an "architectural" analysis process at the architectural analysis model level (see Figure 4). A prerequisite for this is the compositionality of analysis results. However, techniques that cover quantitative analysis throughout the whole 'stack' of interoperable layers of an architecture model hardly exist. In the remainder of this paper we focus on the transformation and the performance analysis method applicable at the architectural level (see Figure 4). For a detailed discussion and illustration of the whole framework presented in Figure 4, we refer to Jonkers *et al.* (2005).

ARCHITECTURAL MODELLING WITH ARCHIMATE

In the ArchiMate project, techniques for integrated modelling, visualisation and analysis of enterprise architectures were developed. Since one of the goals of the ArchiMate language (Jonkers *et al.*, 2004) is the integration of detailed design models, it is perfectly suited for the description of architectural design models as described above. Therefore, we use this language as the basis for the performance analysis technique we propose in this paper. In this section, we briefly introduce this modelling language, and show how quantitative attributes needed for performance analysis can be attached to its concepts.

For the purpose of this paper we use a simplified version of the ArchiMate modelling language. Figure 5 shows an informal representation of the metamodel of this language with the main concepts and the relations that they may have. They cover the business layer (e.g., the organisational structure and business processes), the application layer (e.g., application components) and the technical infrastructure layer (e.g., devices and networks), as well as relation betweens the layers. The language considers the structural, behavioural and informational aspects within each layer. Figure 10 gives an example of ArchiMate model. For a description of the full language, we refer to Jonkers *et al.* (2004).

In order to allow for the quantitative analysis, the architecture design models (expressed in Archi-Mate) are endowed with *attributes* used to quantify some of the concepts and relations. There can be attributes for both input parameters and analysis results, although the distinction may not always be

Figure 5. The simplified ArchiMate metamodel

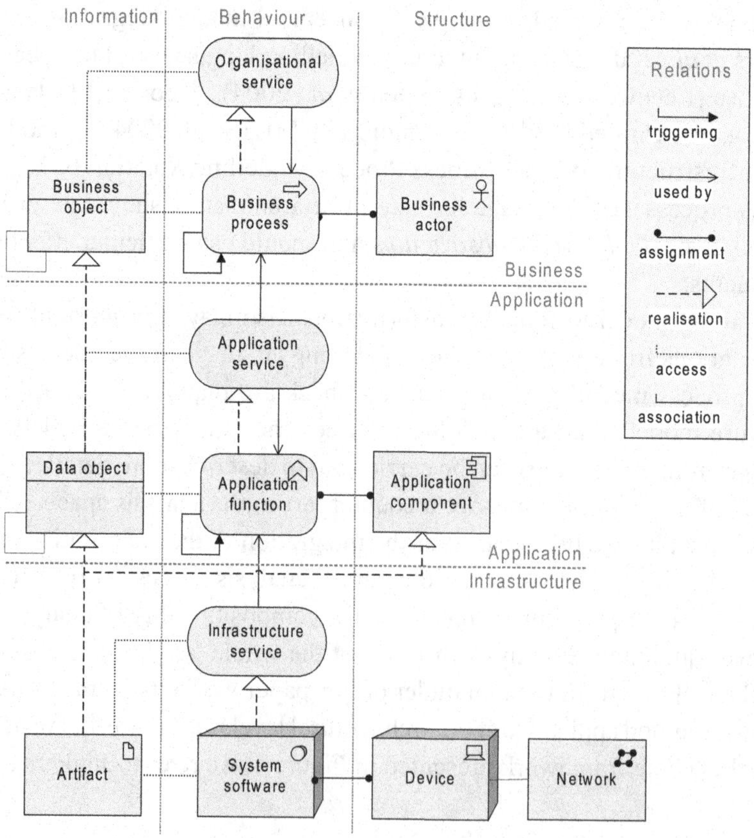

sharp: the result of one analysis phase may be the input of a later analysis phase. In our approach we identify the specific quantitative attributes that we use for ArchiMate models. Also note that before being analysed, ArchiMate models will undergo a transformation process, which we call (in Section 5.2) model normalisation. Normalised models (which are what in Figure 4 we call architectural analysis model), inherit all the quantitative attributes from the ArchiMate source models.

Model Structure

The metamodel of Figure 5 shows that an architecture model displays a regular structure, which may be viewed as a hierarchy of "layers". We can distinguish layers of two types: *service layers* and *realisation layers*. A service layer exposes external functionality that can be used by other layers, while a realisation layer models the implementation of services. Thus, we separate the externally observable behaviour (expressed as services) from the complex internal organisation (contained within the realisation layers). Figure 10 shows an example of a layered view of an ArchiMate model. Looking at the horizontal structure of the metamodel, we notice that realisation layers basically contain three types of elements. They might model some pieces of *internal behaviour* (expressed as processes, functions or system software). Further, each behaviour element can access *objects*, and is assigned to exactly one *resource* (see Figure 6).

Quantitative Input and Output

One of the most difficult tasks related to quantitative analysis is to obtain reliable input data. There are several possible sources for this data. For existing systems, measurement is one of the most reliable methods, although it is not easy to do this in a correct way: e.g., it should be clearly defined what exactly is to be measured, the number of measurements must be sufficient and the measurements must be taken under various circumstances that may occur in practice. If the system or organisation is still

Figure 6. Structural properties of ArchiMate models

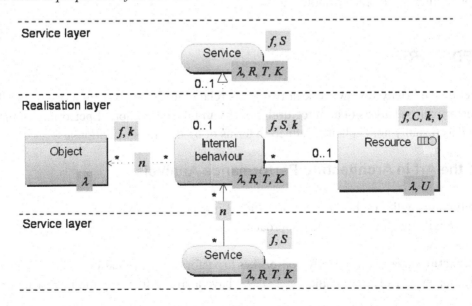

to be developed, measurement is no option. Possible alternatives are then the use of documentation of components to be used, or to use estimates (e.g. based on comparable architectures). However, it often is very difficult to correctly interpret available numerical data, and to evaluate the reliability of the available data. We assume that the following input is provided for analysis (see Figure 6):

- For any 'used by' and 'access' relation e a weight n_e, representing the average number of uses/accesses. For any 'realisation' and 'assignment' relation, we set $n_e = 1$: they represent a 1-to-1 mapping of a behaviour element to a service and to a resource, respectively.
- For any behaviour element a, a service time S_a representing the time spent internally for the realisation of a service (excluding the time spent waiting for supporting services). Since a service represents the externally observable behaviour of a behaviour element a, we may assume that it inherits the service time from the behaviour element that realises it. Therefore, we leave the choice of specifying this input value for either one of these nodes. Also, for any internal behaviour element a, a fixed cost k_a (cost per execution).
- For any resource r a capacity C_r (by default $C_r = 1$), a fixed cost k_r (cost per use) and a variable cost v_r (cost per time unit/tariff). For any object o, a fixed cost k_o per access (we do not specify variable costs for object, because the duration of the access is not known).
- For any node a, an arrival frequency f_a. Typically, arrival frequencies are specified in the top layer of a model, although we do allow for the specification of arrival frequencies for any node in the model.

Given these input values, the goal of our approach is to determine the following performance measures (see Figure 6):

- the workload (arrival rate) λ_a for each node a. (Provided that no resources are overloaded, the throughput for each node is equal to its arrival rate.)
- the processing time T_a, the response time R_a and the total cost K_a, for each behaviour element or each service a.
- the utilisation U_r, for each resource r.

RELATED WORK

In this section we briefly review work in two areas related to the analysis approach described in the sequel: performance analysis of architectural models, and the derivation of performance models from design models (usually not explicitly defined in terms of model transformations).

State of the Art in Architecture Performance Analysis

In this section, we will only be able to give a global impression of existing performance analysis approaches. We will roughly classify the approaches based on the layers of the ArchiMate metamodel that they address.

Infrastructure layer. Traditionally, approaches to performance evaluation of computer systems and communication systems Harrison and Patel (1992) have a strong focus on the infrastructure domain.

Queueing models, for example, describe the characteristics of the (hardware) resources in a system, while the workload imposed by the applications is captured by an abstract stochastic arrival process. Also, a lot of literature exists about performance studies of specific hardware configurations, sometimes extended to the system software and middleware level. Most of these approaches have in common that they are based on detailed models and require detailed input data.

Application layer. Performance engineering of software applications Smith (1990) is a much newer discipline compared to the traditional techniques described above. A number of papers consider performance of software *architectures* at a global level. Bosch and Grahn (1998) present some observations about the performance characteristics of a number of often-occurring architectural styles. Performance issues in the context of the SAAM method (Kazman *et al.*, 1994) for scenario-based analysis are considered in Lung *et al.* (1998).

Another direction of research address the approaches that have been proposed to derive queuing models from a software architecture described in an architecture description language (ADL). The method described by Spitznagel and Garlan (1998) is restricted to a number of popular architectural styles (e.g., the distributed message passing style but not the pipe and filter style). In Di Marco and Inverardi (2004) queueing models are derived from UML 2.0 specifications which, however, in most cases do not have an analytical solution.

Business layer. Several business process modelling tools provide support for quantitative analysis through discrete-event simulation. Also, general-purpose simulation tool, e.g., Arena or ExSpect (based on high-level Petri nets) are often used for this purpose. A drawback of simulation is that it requires detailed input data, and for inexperienced users it may be difficult to use and to correctly interpret the results. BiZZdesigner (BiZZdesign, 2007) offers, in addition to simulation, a number of analytical methods. They include completion time and critical path analysis of business processes (Jonkers *et al.* 1999) and queueing model analysis (Jonkers and van Swelm 1999). Petri nets (and several of its variations) are fairly popular in business process modelling, either to directly model processes or as a semantic foundation. They offer possibilities for performance analysis based on simulation, but they also allow for analytical solutions (which are, however, fairly computation-intensive). Business process analysis with stochastic Petri nets is the subject of, among others, Schomig and Rau (1995).

Design Model to Performance Analysis Model Transformations

Automated derivation of analysis models from design models (most commonly based on the Unified Modelling Language – UML or on business process/workflow modelling languages) and software architecture specifications has received significant attention in the recent years. Such analysis models can subsequently be fed into model solvers and produce, for example, the desired performance estimates. To make this possible, extensions to UML have also been defined that allow for the specification of the required input and output values, most notably using profiles; e.g., the profile for Modelling Quality of Service and Fault Tolerance Characteristics and Mechanisms (OMG, 2004) and the profile for Schedulability, Performance and Time (OMG, 2003). Since UML has become the standard notation for software specification, we have noticed an increasing number of approaches in which we find different types of UML source diagrams. The number and types of diagrams used depend on the intended target analysis model. Typically, these target models fall in one of the following categories:

- Queueing Network Models (QNM) or Layered QNMs (Alsaadi, 2004; Cortellessa *et al.*, 2000, Di Marco and Inverardi, 2004; Gu and Petriu, 2002; Skene and Emmerich, 2003a and 2003b, Smith and Williams, 2000), which can be derived from a combination of annotated diagrams that specify the behaviour aspect (sequence, use-case, activity and/or collaboration diagrams) and the structure aspect (class, component or deployment diagrams)
- Labelled (stochastic) Petri nets (Bernardi *et al.*, 2002; López-Grao *et al.*, 2004), which can be derived from (annotated) diagrams that specify behaviour (e.g. sequence, statechart or activity diagrams)
- Stochastic Process Algebras (SPA) (Canevet *et al.*, 2004) or PEPA nets (Pooley, 1999), also derived from behaviour diagrams such as statechart diagrams, collaboration diagrams or activity diagrams.

We refer to Balsamo and Simeoni (2001a, 2001b) for an extensive analysis and comparison of these approaches.

Next to the above-mentioned transformations that are mostly concerned with the application and technology scope, in the business scope there are also some approaches that are concerned with the derivation of quantitative analysis models from business process models. Many business process modelling tools provide a simulation facility, but analytical solutions are less common. Boekhoudt *et al.* (2000) propose an approach to derive series-parallel (SP) trees from business process models, which can be used to calculate, among others, completion times. In Jonkers *et al.* (1998), a mapping from business process models to stochastic Petri nets and to a combination of task graphs and queueing networks is shown.

Note that the above-mentioned transformation approaches only address a one-way transformation from design model to analysis model. However, a reverse transformation is also essential, in order to match the analysis results with the appropriate elements in the original model.

State of the Art in Architecture Cost Analysis

Model-based cost analysis has received much less attention in the literature than model-based performance analysis.

In his master's thesis, Huang presents a cost model for IT infrastructure (Huang, 2007). At the application layer, some work has been done in the area that is called 'software economics' (Boehm & Sullivan, 2000). However, in these approaches, the role of modelling is very limited.

At the business layer, business process modelling tools such as BiZZdesigner (BiZZdesign, 2007) and ARIS (Misof, 2007) offer some support for business analysis. The *e³value* approach (Gordijn & Akkermans, 2001) is aimed at the modelling and analysis of value flows (including money flows) between organisations, in the context of an e-business setting. However, the approach can also be applied to model and analyse value flows between departments within a single enterprise.

Relation to the ATAM/CBAM Architecture Analysis Methodology

Finally, we would like to position our contribution with respect to the methodological approach for software architecture analysis – ATAM/CBAM, developed at the Software Engineering Institute of Carnegie Mellon University (Kazman, Klein & Clemens, 2000: Kazman, Asundi & Klein, 2002). ATAM and CBAM have been developed to guide architectural decisions during software development by linking these decisions to business goals and quality attributes. We believe that an adaptation of these methods, primarily by redefining and aligning the above mentioned attributes to the specific features of service oriented enterprise architecture, may be used as well to justify and guide architectural decisions during enterprise architecture development.

The Cost Benefit Analysis Method (CBAM) is a quantitative approach for making design decisions. The core of this method consists of an assessment of several quality attributes (such as performance, availability, security, modifiability, and usability) of alternative architectural strategies with respect to the costs involved and the benefits (expressed in terms of ROI) they may have for different stakeholders. This assessment is used to justify the selection of one of the alternatives. We argue that the idea of combining the ArchiMate modelling and analysis approach presented in this paper and (possibly an adaptation of) CBAM/ATAM as analysis and decision support methodology is feasible. More precisely, the ArchiMate approach may cover the activities one has to carry out in Step 5 of CBAM ("Develop architectural strategies") in the following ways: the ArchiMate language can be used to model the several possible architectural strategies, and then the analysis approach proposed in the remainder of this paper can be used to assess these alternatives with respect to the considered quality aspects. It should be noted, however, that our approach only considers quality aspects related to performance and cost (although it is reasonable to expect that the development of analysis algorithms for other types of quality attributes of ArchiMate models may constitute the subject of future research). For the modelling activity there is already a lot of tool support on the market (e.g., commercial tools such as ARIS[1], BiZZdesign Architect (BiZZdesign, 2007), etc. offer support for ArchiMate). Unfortunately, none of the abovementioned vendors have implemented the proposed analysis algorithms yet.

TRANSFORMATION AND ANALYSIS OF ARCHIMATE MODELS

In this section we present our approach for the quantitative analysis of service-oriented models expressed in the ArchiMate language.

Analysis is possible by propagating quantities through the layers. A natural option for this is to first consider workload measures that are imposed as a "demand" to the model elements from the layers that contain the users of the system (e.g., customers). These quantities propagate to the deeper layers of the architecture, yielding the *demands* of each of the model elements. Once the workloads have been determined, we determine the effort these workloads require from the resources and the behaviour elements. This can be expressed in terms of, e.g., performance measures (e.g., utilisations for resources, processing and response times for behaviour elements) or costs. From the 'deepest' layers of the models, these measures propagate to the higher layers. In summary, our analysis approach consists of the following two phases (see Figure 7): a *top-down* calculation and propagation of the workloads imposed by the top layer; this provides input for a *bottom-up* calculation and propagation of performance measures. In the rest of this section we will show how these phases of analysis can be realised in a systematic manner.

However, before we can perform the two above-mentioned analysis steps, we first have to transform the ArchiMate model into a normalised analysis model.

Transformation to a Normalised Model

ArchiMate models often do not display the regular structure of the ArchiMate metamodel. This is due to the fact abstraction rules may be used to create simplified views on the architecture. These abstractions have a formal basis in an operator that has been derived for the composition of relations (for the details

Figure 7. Layers of ArchiMate models

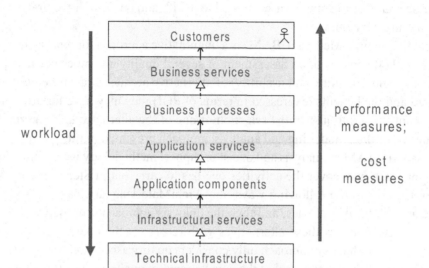

see Buuren *et al.*, 2004). For instance, a 'realisation' relation with a consecutive 'used by' relation may be replaced by a new 'used by' relation that short-circuits a service.

The first step in our approach is a model transformation, deriving a normalised version of the input model, which conforms to the structure described in Figure 6. More precisely, the ArchiMate design model is transformed in an architectural model in the analysis space, expressed in a language that resembles ArchiMate, but can be considered a separate language which: (1) does not contain the concepts that are irrelevant for the analysis; (2) abstracts from the specific layers that the ArchiMate language distinguishes, and (3) only allows for the direct relations between concepts as shown in the metamodel (Figure 5).

Since some concepts and relations are irrelevant for the analysis (e.g., objects and network), these are disregarded in the transformation. The remaining concepts are mapped to generic, layer-independent concepts (cf. Figure 6); e.g., business actors, application components and devices are all mapped onto the generic 'resource' concept, as shown in Figure 8. These generic concepts inherit the quantitative attributes of the source concepts.

Finally, the model will be subjected to a series of transformations rules, an example of which is given in Figure 9. Also in these rules, the quantitative attributes of the concepts are taken into account. There is a limited set of transformation rules, eventually resulting in the normalised model.

As a proof-of-concept, we have implemented the transformation from an ArchiMate model to a normalised model with the graph-based model transformation tool GReAT (Karsai and Agrawal, 2003).

Performance Analysis

Once we have obtained a normalised model through a model transformation, we first determine the workload for each node in the model (top-down). After this, we analyse the required performance measures, based on special-purpose performance analysis techniques, which propagate through the model in a bottom-up fashion.

Figure 8. Example of a mapping to a generic, layer-independent concept

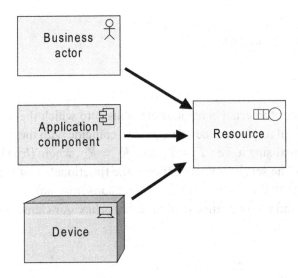

Figure 9. Example of a normalisation step

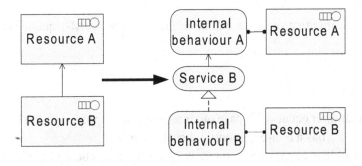

Step 1: Top-down workload calculation

For a normalised model, we can calculate the arrival rate for any node a with the following recursive expression:

$$\lambda_a = f_a + \sum_{i=1}^{d_a^+} n_{a,k_i} \lambda_{k_i},$$

(1)

where d_a^+ denotes the out-degree of node a and k_i is a child of a. In other words, the arrival rate for a node is determined by adding the requests from higher layers to the local arrival frequency f_a.

Step 2: Bottom-up performance calculation

Once the workloads on the various model components have been calculated, we can proceed with the bottom-up calculation of the performance measures. The approach is similar to the top-down approach.

We focus here on the bottom-up propagation of performance measures. The following recursive expressions apply:

- The utilisation of any resource r is

$$U_r = \frac{1}{C_r} \sum_{i=1}^{d_r} \lambda_{k_i} T_{k_i},$$

  where d_r is the number of internal behaviour elements k_i to which the resource is assigned.

- The processing time and response time of a service s coincide with these measures for the internal behaviour element b realising it, i.e.: $T_s = T_b$ and $R_s = R_b$, where (b, s) is the *realisation* relation with a as end point. (The service merely exposes the functionality of the internal behaviour element to the environment: there is no additional time consumption).

- The processing time and response time of an internal behaviour element a is computed using the following recursive formulas:

$$T_a = S_a + \sum_{i=1}^{d_a^-} n_{k_i,a} R_{k_i} \qquad R_a = F(a, r_a),$$

  where d_a denotes the in-degree of node a, k_i is a parent of a and r_a is the resource assigned to a; F is the response time expressed as a function of attributes of a and r_a.

For example, if we assume that the node can be modelled as an M/M/1 queue (Harrison and Patel, 1992), this function is

$$F(a, r_a) = \frac{T_a}{(1 - U_{r_a})}.$$

We can replace this by another equation in case other assumptions apply: e.g., the Pollaczek-Khinchine formula for an M/G/1 if T_a has a non-exponential distribution.

In most cases, this will lead to approximate results because the queueing networks are not separable (Harrison and Patel, 1992). At the architectural level, where we are generally interested in global performance estimates, we expect such approximations to be good enough. In case more precise results would be required, instead of simple queueing formulas, more detailed techniques such as simulation can be applied in combination with our approach.

Cost Analysis

In contrast to performance analysis, cost analysis only requires a bottom-up analysis phase, because costs do not depend on workloads (with our method, we calculate the cost for a single request).

Step 1: Bottom-up cost calculation

The following recursive expressions apply:

- The total cost K_a of an internal behaviour element a is

$$K_a = k_a + k_{r_a} + Sv_{r_a} \sum_{i=1}^{d_a^-} n_{s_i,a} K_{s_i} + \sum_{j=1}^{d_a^+} n_{a,o_j} k_{o_j}$$

where d_a^- denotes the number of incoming 'used by' relations of node a, s_i is a service used by a, d_a^+ denotes the number of outgoing 'access' relations of node a, o_j is an object accessed by a and r_a is the resource assigned to a.

- The cost of a service s coincides with the cost of the internal behaviour element b realising it, i.e.: $K_s = K_b$, where (b, s) is the *realisation* relation with a as end point.

Optionally, a variable cost V_a can be determined for each node a (i.e., the cost per time unit associated with that node), given that the workload λ_a has also been determined (as described in the previous section): $V_a = \lambda_a K_a$ for each internal behaviour element or service, and $V_a = \lambda_a k_a$ for each resource or object.

Example

In this section we give an example to illustrate the analysis approach. In the example, we restrict ourselves to performance analysis (but a cost analysis can be carried out in a similar way, as described in the previous section).

Consider an insurance company using a document management system for the storage of damage reports. We assume that the document management system is a centralised system, used by multiple offices throughout the country, which means that it is quite heavily used. We show how performance measures of this system can be derived using a model of the architecture of the system (see Figure 10). This model covers the whole stack from business processes and actors, through applications, to the technical infrastructure.

There are three applications offering services that are used directly by the business actors. The Administrator can *search* in the metadata database, resulting in short descriptions of the reports that meet the query and *view* reports that are returned by a search. The *report scanning application* is used to scan, digitise and store damage reports (e.g., in PDF-format).

In addition to the two applications that are used directly by the end-user, there are two supporting application components: a *database access* component, providing access to the metadata database, and a *document management* component, providing access to the document base. Finally, the model shows the physical devices of which the database access and document management components make use. They use file access services provided by these devices.

In the model we also specify the analysis inputs. On the 'used by' relations, we specify workloads, in terms of the average number of uses n of the corresponding service. For the business processes, an arrival frequency f is specified. Finally, for services we may specify a service time S. We now proceed to analyse this model, using the three steps described in the previous section.

Figure 10. Example model

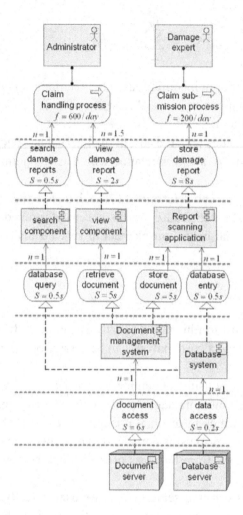

Model Normalisation

We first derive a normalised model using a model transformation as described in Section 5.1. Figure 11 shows the normalised version of the model in Figure 10. The input parameters for the workload on the 'used by' relations are the same as in the original model. The service times are now transferred also to the inserted internal behaviour elements.

Analysis step 1: Top-down workload analysis

Figure 12 shows the workload for the services s in the model, in terms of the arrival rates λ_s. The arrival rates depend on the frequencies of the customer input requests and the cardinalities n of the 'used by' relations. The table also shows the scaled arrival rates expressed in arrivals/second (assuming that systems are operational eight hours per day).

Figure 11. Normalised model

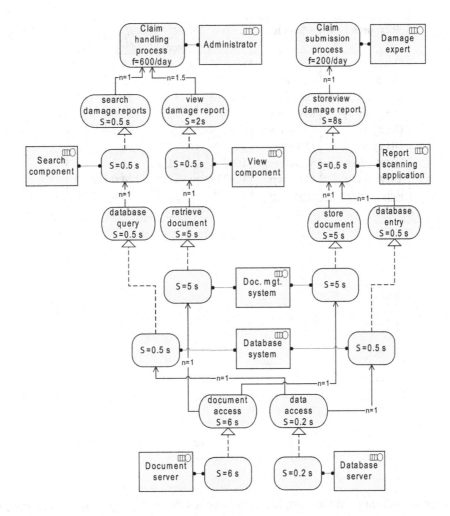

Analysis step 2: Bottom-up performance analysis

Figure 12 shows the performance results for the example, i.e., the processing and response times for the services and the utilisations for the resources at the application and infrastructure layer.

The results show that queueing times from the lower layers accumulate in the higher layers, resulting in response times that are orders of magnitude greater than the local service times. E.g., the 'view' component of the 'claim handling support' application has a utilisation of over 84%, which results in a response time of the 'view damage report' application service of almost 3 minutes.

Using our approach, it is easy to study the effect of input parameter changes on the performance. For example, the graph in Figure 12 shows how the response time of the View component depends on the arrival frequency associated with the Administrator (assuming a fixed arrival frequency for the Damage expert). The maximum arrival frequency, which results in an utilisation of the View component of

Figure 12. Workloads and performance results

Resource (r)	Service (s)	λ_s (sec^{-1})	T_s (sec)	R_s (sec)	U_a (%)
Doc. srv.	doc. acc.	0.0382	6.0	7.8	22.9
DB srv.	data acc.	0.0278	0.2	0.2	0.6
Doc.mgt. sys.	retr. doc.	0.0313	12.8	25.0	48.8
Doc.mgt. sys.	store doc.	0.0069	12.8	25.0	48.8
DB syst.	DB query	0.0278	0.7	0.7	1.9
DB syst.	DB entry	0.0069	0.7	0.7	1.9
Search comp.	search rep.	0.0278	1.2	1.2	2.5
View comp.	view rep.	0.0313	27.0	174.0	84.3
Rep.scanning	store rep.	0.0069	33.7	44.0	23.4

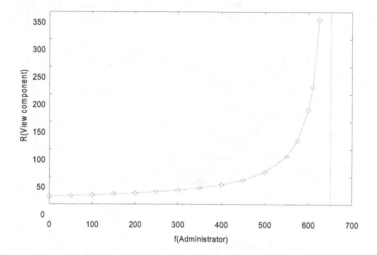

100%, is 651 arrivals per day. In the design stage these results may help us to decide, e.g., if an extra View component is needed.

CONCLUSION AND FUTURE WORK

Starting from the observation that current approaches to model-driven development of applications and services have a strong focus on functionality, we argue for the necessity of including non-functional aspects describing qualities of this functionality. This is not limited to detailed designs; non-functional aspects should be included as early as possible in the design process, starting from the architectural (computational independent) level and going through all MDA layers.

Orthogonal to the MDA layered view, we distinguished two modelling spaces, the design space and the analysis space. Model-to-model transformations play a central role in the integration of these spaces. These can be combined with vertical model-to-model transformations, both in the design space and in the analysis space, when moving towards the platform-specific models.

Most existing approaches to quantitative evaluation focus on detailed models within a specific domain. Many of these approaches may find their place in the framework that we presented, as we illustrated in (Jonkers *et al.*, 2005). In this paper we demonstrated the applicability of quantitative modelling and analysis techniques for the effective evaluation of design choices at the architectural level, by introducing a new approach for the propagation of workload and performance measures through a service-oriented architectural model. This can be used as an analysis framework where existing methods for detailed performance analysis, based on, e.g., queueing models, Petri nets or simulation, can be plugged in. The presented example illustrates the use of our top-down and bottom-up techniques to evaluate the performance of a document management system for the storage and retrieval of damage reports. Using a simple queueing formula for the response times, we showed that queueing times from the lower layers of the architecture accumulate in the higher layers, which results in response times that are orders of magnitude greater than the local service times. A prototype has been developed for further illustration and validation of the approach.

Several improvements and extensions to the approach are conceivable. E.g., in Iacob and Jonkers (2004) it is shown that our 'vertical' approach to propagate workloads and performance measures can be combined with 'horizontal' analysis techniques to evaluate completion times in business processes (Jonkers *et al.*, 1999). An obvious extension is the development of analysis algorithms for other quality attributes, besides performance and cost. Further study and case studies are required to assess the viability of really integrating the analysis results from multiple detailed design models. Finally, a tighter integration of the analysis techniques in the overall architectural design and analysis process is needed: e.g., as indicated in Section 4.4, the integration of our approach with the ATAM/CBAM methodology might be an interesting research direction to pursue.

ACKNOWLEDGMENT

This paper combines results from the ArchiMate (http://archimate.telin.nl) and Freeband A-MUSE (http://a-muse.freeband.nl) projects. The ArchiMate consortium consisted of ABN AMRO, Stichting Pensioenfonds ABP, the Dutch Tax and Customs Administration, Ordina, Telematica Instituut, Centrum voor Wiskunde en Informatica, Radboud Universiteit Nijmegen, and the Leiden Institute of Advanced Computer Science. Freeband (http://www.freeband.nl) is sponsored by the Dutch government under contract BSIK 03025.

We thank René van Buuren, Timber Haaker, Hugo ter Doest, Marc Lankhorst and Patrick Strating for their useful remarks that helped to improve this approach.

REFERENCES

Alsaadi, A. (2004, January). A performance analysis approach based on the UML class diagram. In *Proc 4th International Workshop on Software and Performance: ACM SIGSOFT Software Engineering Notes*, 29(1).

Andrews, T., Curbera, F., Dholakia, H., Goland, Y., Klein, J., Leymann, F., Liu, K., Roller, D., Smith, D., & Thatte, S. (ed.), Trickovic, I., Weerawarana, S. (2002). *Business Process Execution Language for Web Services version 1.1.*

Balsamo, S., Simeoni, M. (2001a). Deriving Performance Models from Software Architecture Specifications. *Proceedings of the 15th European Simulation Multiconference (ESM2001)*, SCS - Society for Computer Simulation.

Balsamo, S., Simeoni, M. (2001b). On Transforming UML models into performance models, Technical Report Saladin Project R-SAL-51, *WTUML: Workshop on Transformations in UML*, ETAPS 2001 Satellite Event Genova, Italy, April 7th.

Bernardi, S., Donatelli, S., & Merseguer, J. (2002). From UML sequence diagrams and statecharts to analysable Petri net models. In *Proc. 3rd International Workshop on Software and Performance*, Rome, Italy, 35 – 45.

BiZZdesign (2007). http://www.bizzdesign.nl.

Boehm, B. W., & Sullivan, K. J. (2000). Software economics: a roadmap. In *Proceedings Conference on the Future of Software Engineering*. Limerick, Ireland, June, pp. 319-343.

Boekhoudt, P., Jonkers, H., & Rougoor, M. (2000). Graph-based analysis of business process models. In N. Mastorakis (ed.), *Mathematics and Computers in Modern Science, Proc. of the WSES/MIUE/HNA International Conference*, Montego Bay, Jamaica, Dec., pp. 227-235.

Bosch, J., & Grahn, H. (1998). Characterising the performance of three architectural styles. In *Proceedings First International Workshop on Software and Performance*, Santa Fe, NM, Oct.

BPMI (2003), *Business Process Management Initiative: Business process modeling notation.* working draft (1.0), Aug.

Broens, T., Halteren, A. van Sinderen, M. Van, & Wac, K. (2005). Towards an application framework for context-aware m-health applications", in *Proc. 11th Open European Summer School (EUNICE 2005)*, Colmenarejo, Spain, July.

Bucher, T., Fischer, R., Kurpjuweit, S., & Winter, R. (2006). Enterprise architecture analysis and application – An exploratory stury. In *Proc. EDOC Workshop on Trends in Enterprise Architecture Research (TEAR 2006)*, Hong Kong.

Buuren, R. van, Jonkers, H., Iacob, M.-E., & Strating, P. (2004). Composition of relations in enterprise architcture models. In H. Ehrig, G. Engels, F. Parisi-Presicce, and G. Rozenberg, editors, *Graph Transformations – Proceedings of the Second International Conference* (LNCS 3256), pages 39–53, Rome, Italy, Sept.

Canevet, C., Gilmore, S., Hillston, J., Kloul, L., & Stevens, P. (2004, January). Analysing UML 2.0 activity diagrams in the software performance engineering process. In *Proc 4th International Workshop on Software and Performance: ACM SIGSOFT Software Engineering Notes*, 29(1).

Cortellessa, V., & Mirandola, R. (2000). Deriving a queueing network based performance model from UML diagrams. In *Proceedings 2nd International Workshop on Software and Performance*, Ottawa, Canada, Sept., pp. 58 – 70.

Di Marco, A., & Inverardi, P. (2004). Compositional generation of software architecture performance QN models. In J. Magee *et al.* (eds.), *Proc. 4th Working IEEE/IFIP Conference on Software Architecture* (WICSA2004), Oslo, Norway, June, pp 37–46.

Eck, P. van, Blanken, H., & Wieringa, R. (2004, September). Project GRAAL. Towards operational architecture alignment, *International Journal of Cooperative Information Systems,* 13(3), 235-255.

Eertink H., Janssen, W., Oude Luttighuis, P., Teeuw, W., & Vissers, C. (1999). A business process design language. In *Proc. 1st World Congress on Formal Methods*, Toulouse, France.

Gordijn, J., & Akkermans, H. (2001). Designing and evaluating E-Business models. *IEEE Intelligent Systems, 16*(4), 11-17.

Gu, G. P., & Petriu, D. C. (2002). XSLT transformation from UML models to LQN performance models. In *Proc. 3rd International Workshop on Software and Performance*, Rome, Italy, 2002, pp. 227–234.

Harrison, P., & Patel, N. (1992). *Performance Modelling of Communication Networks and Computer Architectures*. Addison-Wesley.

Herzog, U. (2001). Formal methods for performance evaluation, In *Lectures on Formal Methods and Performance Analysis: First EEF/Euro Summer School on Trends in Computer Science* (LNCS 2090), pages 1–37. Springer Verlag, 2001.

Huang, K. (2007). *Towards an information technology infrastructure cost model*. M.Sc. Thesis, Massachusetts Institute of Technology.

Iacob, M.-E., & Jonkers, H. (2004). *Quantitative Analysis of Enterprise Architectures*. Technical Report ArchiMate D3.5b, Telematica Instituut, Enschede, the Netherlands, Mar.

Iacob, M.-E., & Jonkers, H. (2005), Quantitative analysis of enterprise architectures. In *Proc. 1st International Conference on Interoperability of Enterprise Software and Applications* (INTEROP-ESA'05), Geneva, Switzerland, Feb. 2005.

IEEE (2000). *IEEE standard 1471-2000: Recommended practice for architectural description of software-intensive systems.*

Jonkers, H., Janssen, W., Verschut, A., & Wierstra, E. (1998). A unified framework for design and performance analysis of distributed systems. In *Proc. 3rd Annual IEEE International Computer Performance and Dependability Symposium* (IPDS'98), Durham, NC, USA, Sept., pp. 109-118.

Jonkers, H., Boekhoudt, P., Rougoor, M., & Wierstra, E. (1999). Completion time and critical path analysis for the optimisation of business process models. In Obaidat, M., Nisanci, A. and Sadoun, B. editors, *Proceedings of the 1999 Summer Computer Simulation Conference*, pages 222–229, Chicago, IL, July.

Jonkers, H., & Swelm, M. van (1999). Queueing analysis to support distributed system Design, in Obaidat, M.S. and Ajmone Marsan, M. (eds.), *Proceedings of the 1999 Symposium on Performance Evaluation of Computer and Telecommunication Systems*, pages 300–307, Chicago, IL, July 1999.

Jonkers, H., Lankhorst, M., Buuren, R. van, Hoppenbrouwers, S., Bonsangue, M., & Torre, L. van der (2004, September). Concepts for Modelling Enterprise Architectures, *International Journal of Cooperative Information Systems, 13*(3), 257-287.

Jonkers, H., Iacob, M.-E., Lankhorst, M., & Strating, P. (2005). Integration and Analysis of Functional and Non-Functional Aspects in Model-Driven E-Service Development. In *Proc. 9th International Enterprise Distributed Object Computing Conference* (EDOC 2005), Enschede, The Netherlands, Sept.

Karsai, G., & Agrawal, A. (2003). Graph transformations in OMG's Model-Driven Architecture, in J.L. Pfaltz, M. Nagl and B. Böhlen (eds.), *Proceedings 2nd International Workshop on Applications of Graph Transformations with Industrial Relevance* (AGTIVE 2003), Charlottesville, VA, USA, Sept. 2003, pp. 243-259.

Kazman, R., Bass, L., Abowd, G., & Webb, M. (1994). SAAM: A method for analyzing the properties of software architectures. In *Proceedings 16th International Conference on Software Engineering*, pages 81–90, Sorento, Italy.

Kazman, R., Klein, M., & Clements, P. (2000). ATAM:Method for Architecture Evaluation, Technical Report CMU/SEI-2000-TR-004 ESC-TR-2000-004, August.

Kazman, R., Asundi, J., & Klein, M. (2002). *Making Architecture Design Decisions: An Economic Approach,* Technical Report CMU/SEI-2002-TR-035 ESC-TR-2002-035, September.

Leeuwen, D. van, Doest, H. Ter, & Lankhorst, M. (2004). A tool integration workbench for enterprise architecture. In *Proc. 6th International Conference on Enterprise Information Systems* (ICEIS 2004), Porto, Portugal, April.

López-Grao, J. P., Merseguer J., & Campos, J. (2004, January). From UML activity diagrams to Stochastic Petri Nets: Application to software performance engineering. In *Proceedings 4th International Workshop on Software and Performance: ACM SIGSOFT Software Engineering Notes*, 29(1).

Lung, C.-H., Jalnapurkar, A., & El-Rayess, A. (1998). Performance-oriented software architecture analysis: An experience report. In *Proceedings First International Workshop on Software and Performance*, Santa Fe, NM, Oct.

Miller, J., & Mukerji, J. (eds.), (2003). *MDA Guide Version 1.0.1*, Object Management Group, June.

Misof, D. (2007). Process costing with ARIS Business Optimizer. ARIS Expert Paper, IDS Scheer, Jan.

OMG (2003), UML *Profile for Schedulability,Performance and Time Specification*, Version 1.0 (formal/03-09-01), Sept.

OMG (2004), UML *Profile for Modeling Quality of Service and Fault Tolerance Characteristics and Mechanisms* (ptc/2004-06-01), 2004.

Pooley, R., (1999). Using UML to Derive Stochastic Process Algebra Models, in N. Davies and J. Bradley, editors. UKPEW '99, *Proceedings of the Fifteenth UK Performance Engineering Workshop*, The University of Bristol, July 1999, pp23-33.

Scheer, A.-W. (1994). *Business Process Engineering: Reference Models for Industrial Enterprises*, Springer, Berlin, 2nd ed.

Schomig, A. and Rau, H. (1995). A petri net approach for the performance analysis of business processes. Technical Report 116, Lehrstuhl fur Informatik III, Universitat Wurzburg.

Scott, K. (2004). *Fast Track UML 2.0*. Apress.

Skene, J., & Emmerich, W. (2003a). Model driven performance analysis of enterprise information systems. In *Proc. International Workshop on Test and Analysis of Component Based Systems (ETAPS/TACoS)*, 82(6). Warsaw, Poland, April 2003. Electronic Notes in Theoretical Computer Science

Skene, J., & Emmerich, W. (2003b). A model driven architecture approach to non-functional analysis of software architectures. In *Proc. 18th IEEE Conference on Automated Software Engineering* (ASE'03), Toronto, Canada. Oct.

Smith, C. (1990). *Performance Engineering of Software Systems*. Addison-Wesley.

Smith, C. U., & Williams, L. G. (2000). Performance and scalability of disributed software architectures: An SPE approach. *Parallel and Distributed Computing Practices*, 3(4).

Soley, R., & the OMG Staff Strategy Group (2000). *Model Driven Architecture*. Object Management Group White Paper, Draft 3.2, Nov.

Sowa, J. F., & Zachman, J. A. (1992). Extending and formalizing the framework for information systems architectures. *IBM Systems Journal*, *31*(3), 590-616.

Spitznagel, B., & Garlan, D. (1998). Architecture-based performance analysis. In *Proceedings 1998 Conference on Software Engineering and Knowledge Engineering*, San Francisco Bay, June.

Steen, M. W. A., Akehurst, D. H., Doest, H. W. L. ter, & Lankhorst, M. M. (2004). Supporting viewpoint-oriented enterprise architecture. In *Proc. 8th International Enterprise Distributed Object Computing Conference* (EDOC 2004), Monterey, CA, USA, Sept., pp. 201-211.

ENDNOTE

[1]   See http://www.ids-scheer.com/en/Software/ARIS_Software/ARIS_ArchiMate_Modeler/21980.html

Chapter V
Significance of Analytical Hierarchy Process (AHP) and Nominal Group Technique (NGT) in ERP Implementation

S. Parthasarathy
Thiagarajar College of Engineering, India

ABSTRACT

Enterprise Resource Planning (ERP) system is an integrated software system reflecting the business processes of an enterprise. Enterprise Resource Planning (ERP) system is a generic term for integrated systems for corporate computing that supersedes concepts such as Materials Requirements Planning (MRP) of the 1970s and, later, Manufacturing Resource Planning (MRP II) of the 1980s. The objective of customization in ERP implementation is to achieve a fit between the ERP system and the business process that the system supports. Literature review reveals that the customization is the major annoyance in most of the ERP projects. A solution is proposed using a process framework that incorporates participatory learning and decision-making processes based on Nominal Group Technique (NGT) and the evaluation methodology adopting the Analytical Hierarchy Process (AHP). A case study is presented to illustrate its applicability in practice. The upshot of the study is the identification of various customization possibilities for ERP implementation. This study is meant to help managers think about the various feasible customization options available to them. Future research work that can be done in ERP software customization is also indicated.

INTRODUCTION

According to the AMR Research Report (www.amrresearch.com), the ERP market had a spectacular year, with total revenue growing by 14% and license revenue up an amazing 18% from 2005. While sales of traditional ERP applications were very healthy in 2006, many vendors also saw substantial revenue growth from the acquisition of other software companies. Large organizations continue to roll out SAP or Oracle, while many SMEs or smaller divisions of the large organizations are still in the ERP selection process, searching for the right point product or upgrading applications. As per the AMR Research report on ERP called "Enterprise Resource Planning Spending Report, 2006-2007," U.S. companies will increase their ERP budgets by 11.3% in 2007. It also states that the enterprise resource planning (ERP) applications market grew to $25.4B in 2005, reached $29B in 2006 and over the next five years, the market will grow at an average of 10%.

Growth in ERP spending is fueled by several factors. As midsize organizations fight for market share against increasingly diverse global competition, increased profitability, revenue growth, and customer satisfaction become priorities. In addition, with globalization, the pool of potential customers is ever growing, creating a need for streamlined processes to help meet demand. "We found that midsize companies, whether divisions of large enterprises or stand-alone small businesses, are prepared to make the necessary investments to support profitable growth in today's global economy," said Simon Jacobson, senior research analyst at AMR Research. In addition, by 2010, 43% of companies would like to employ a single, global financial and shared services ERP system.

The success of an ERP system is assured when there is a perfect fit between the ERP system and the organizational processes it supports (Holland & Light, 1999; Robey, Ross & Boudreau, 2002). The significance of ERP systems is that they are packaged software solutions rather than customized systems. The ERP systems come to the customers as a pack with all the required business processes. In traditional information systems development, the software is designed and developed to fit the organization.

A key issue in ERP implementation is finding a match between the organization's business processes and the ERP system by appropriately customizing both the system and the organization. One has to be very careful during the process of customization as over-customization will result in a system with reduced flavour of an integrated system and it fails miserably to reap the full benefits of a packaged software solution. ERP vendors deploy technical consultants and functional consultants for carrying out this hectic process. The objective of customization in ERP implementation is to achieve a fit between the ERP system and the process that the system supports.

In this paper, we use a framework proposed by Wenhong Luo & Strong (2004) for evaluating ERP implementation choices. This framework does not determine decisions for the management; rather it provides the possibilities for customization and indicates the level of technical and organizational change needed to implement each possible customization option. Hence, in this study, we enable the management to make decisions on ERP customization choices in two steps as follows:

- Step 1: Use the Nominal Group Technique (NGT) to define the criteria based on which the framework has to be viewed.
- Step 2: Apply the Analytical Hierarchy Process (AHP) to the framework for evaluating ERP implementation choices.

The outcome of the study is the identification of various customization possibilities for the business processes as well as ERP systems and it is expected to determine decisions available for managers. This study is meant to help managers think about the various feasible customization options available to them. The application of the NGT and the AHP to the framework is illustrated with the data collected from an organization preparing for ERP implementation.

LITERATURE REVIEW

Software that fails to meet the requirements of the customer can have devastating consequences. There is a history of poor matching between the customer's requirements and the enterprise resource planning software, which has had a negative impact on the actual and perceived performance of enterprise resource planning system. Among the research axes that are now active in ERP, it is noticed that there is a growing interest in the customization of ERP systems (Botta-Genoulaz et al., 2005). Enterprise Resource Planning (ERP) is a constantly changing and evolving concept (Klaus, Rosemann & Gable, 2000).

The rapid global deployment of electronic business (e-business) and information systems has required managers to make decisions that seek to balance technical factors with strategic business goals (Raisinghani et al., 2007). ERP systems have gradually been designed, developed and improved by ERP vendors in response to new technologies and emerging business requirements (Mabert, Soni & Venkataramanan, 2003). Ease of customization is judged to be an important criterion, while ease of implementation and vendor reputation was not found to be significant (Mark Keil & Amrit Tiwana, 2006). Functionality and reliability of packaged software depend solely on the degree of customization.

Information system success is dependent upon the effectiveness of requirements elicitation (Mitzi G. Pitts & Glenn J. Browne, 2007). Several studies have demonstrated that the implementation of ERP systems requires the examination of many business processes and it is vital for the company's processes to be accurately aligned with those of the ERP system if the full benefits are to be realized (Redouane et al., 2006). This clearly indicates the need for carefully carrying out the customization during ERP implementation.

Customization is believed to be the critical success factor for ERP implementation (Markus & Tanis, 2000; Holland & Light, 1999; Van Everdingen, Hilergersberg & Waarts, 2000; Hong & Kim, 2002). Hong and Kim (2002) assessed the impact of data, process and user fit between ERP system and organizational requirements on implementation success. They found a positive correlation between the initial organizational fit and the implementation success. However, for most organizations, such a fit can only be achieved through the mutual adaptation of the ERP systems and the organization processes (Lassila & Brancheau, 1999).

Carmel and Sawyer (1998) compared the packaged software with traditional information systems. Their analysis shows that vendors of packaged software have to satisfy many customers with varying needs and requirements in order to capture the necessary market share and profit to justify their investment. Hence customizing the ERP system and organization's business processes becomes essential to fine tune the performance of ERP implementation.

Today enterprises face many forces that compel them to take a larger view of their systems. These forces include globalization, regulatory changes, commerce, cost, multiple customer-access channels, product development cycles, changing business processes, etc. Companies ask for help from their own internal information systems (IS) organizations as well as from external services consultants, product developers, and packaged solutions vendors (Leishman, 1999).

From the viewpoint of system adaptation, Davenport (1998), Brehm (2001) and Glass (1998) say that ERP systems need to be changed to fit existing or reengineered business processes. From the viewpoint of organization adaptation, Boudreau (1999) and Robey (2002) say that organizations need to be changed to fit the ERP system. As user participation is limited during the development of ERP software, the gap between the ERP system and the organizational business processes is inevitable (Sawyer, 2000; Gefen, 2002). Clemons (1991) explained the divergences among organizations in the use of IT and in the benefits they have gained from the usage. This is one of the major reasons for the organizations to choose different ERP customization options during ERP implementation.

ERPs are information systems that manage the data for a company's main business processes, from customer orders to accountability. Their functions include data capture, processing and customized distribution to any end user (Nicolas Serrano & Jose Maria Sarriegi, 2006). Technical changes are costly and can lead to schedule slippage because they are complex and need significant testing. To avoid high maintenance costs or to deploy a standard corporate model in an international group, some corporations implement ERP systems without or with minimal customization (Ghost et al., 2002).

It is found during the literature review that the major research contribution for customization of ERP packages is the framework proposed by Wenhong Luo & Diane M. Strong (2004) for supporting management decision-making on customization choices. Of course, Ben Light (2005) has identified the various problems in customization of ERP packages, but no solution has been suggested to overcome those problems.

It is observed that the various factors affecting the software projects have to be examined again and the process of requirements analysis alone cannot be held responsible for failure of information system projects (Manish Agrawal & Kaushal Chari, 2007). The various risks in information system projects are financial risk, technical risk, functionality risk, project risk and political risk. Of all these risks, functionality risk is the worst affected due to increased customization in ERP projects. The risk factor may come into play if a significant amount of customization is required (Amrit Tiwana & Mark Keil, 2006).

We reviewed the ERP implementation issues and a summary is provided in Table 1. From this literature review, we find that the customizations that must be carried over from one version of enterprise software to the next are the biggest technology headache in ERP implementation. Hence, in this study we have exemplified the application of Nominal Group Technique (NGT) and the Analytical Hierarchy Process (AHP) to a framework to enable the top management and ERP consultants to find a suitable feasible customization option in ERP implementation, which will increase the success rate of the ERP software.

CUSTOMIZATION IN ERP IMPLEMENTATION

Deciding the degree of customization for an ERP system and the business process is a crucial decision which needs to be taken by the organization with the help of consultants as it is indispensable in ERP's success. The process of customization will not take place properly unless there is a strong working knowledge of ERP systems. Customization not only accounts for ERP's success but also for achieving

Table 1.

Review of literature	ERP implementation issues
Manish Agrawal and Kaushal Chari (2007)	There is a need to reexamine the various factors affecting the software project development.
Kai A. Olsen and Per Saetre (2007)	A major problem in ERP implementation is that the ERP system has an inherent business model that does not conform to the needs of the company.
Amrit Tiwana & Mark Keil (2006)	Risk factor may come into play if a significant amount of customization is required.
Redouane El Amrani & Frantz Rowe & Benedicte Geffroy-Maronnat (2006)	It is vital for the company's processes to be accurately aligned with those of the ERP system if the full benefits are to be realized
Mark Keil & Amrit Tiwana (2006)	Ease of customization is judged to be an important criterion in ERP implementation.
Robert C. Beatty & Craig D. Williams (2006)	Over-customizing the standard ERP software modules will make the organization unable to take any ERP upgrade initiative.
Nicolas Serrano & Jose Maria Sarriegi (2006)	ERP is an information system which needs customization to reap its full benefits
Ben Light (2005)	It is difficult for ERP vendors to keep pace with changing industry requirements and to nuance their products for use by a range of customers.
Botta-Genoulaz, Millet & Grabot (2005)	ERP systems must be flexible enough to support newly discovered customer trends.
Konstanflons Chertouras (2004)	Consultants play a crucial role in ERP customization. They tailor the system according to business processes.
Diane M. Strong (2004)	Adjusting the software to fit the organization should be the only form of ERP customization.
Boudreau & Robey (1999); Robey, Ross & Boudreau (2002)	Organizational needs to be changed to fit the ERP systems
Fiona Fui-Hoon Nah & Janet Lee-Shang Lau (2001)	Customization is one critical success factor for ERP implementation.
Sawyer (2000) & Gefen (2002)	User participation is limited during the development of ERP software
Jeanne W. Ross (1999)	Process change is inevitable with an ERP because we have to fit the organization around the software.

continued on following page

Table 1. continued

Bingi, Sharma & Godla (1999); Holland & Light (1999); Reel (1999); Sumner (2000)	BPR and minimum customization lead to successful ERP implementation.
Davenport (1998); Brehm, Heinzl & Markus (2001); Glass (1998)	ERP systems need to be changed to fit existing business processes

user-satisfaction. As ERP is basically packaged software and each organization's strategies, structures and systems are different, substantial customization is necessary.

Customization is an integral part of ERP implementation. The rate of customization is directly proportional to ERP success. Customization tends to pose a challenge to time and the funds allocated. The challenge of successful management lies in balancing them and making both ends meet. It is a difficult task but the success speaks for the process. The major issues that require attention in the process of customizing ERP are strong knowledge about the current system and the likelihood of innovations in ERP.

The prime goal of customization in ERP implementation is to ensure that the company's requirements match with the ERP solution. This can be achieved by either changing our existing business processes to those of the ERP system, as ERP provides the best practices in the industry, or, on the other hand, changing the system according to the business processes. The former process is called Process Customization and the latter process is called System Customization. The decision on the degree of customization and the method of doing it in ERP implementation is really a challenging task for the management and the ERP consultants.

Wenhong Luo & Diane M. Strong (2004) designed a framework (Refer Table 2) for supporting management decision making on ERP customization choices. From Table 2, we find that there are nine customization options available to the management and the ERP consultants. Companies have three types of technical customization options namely module selection, table configuration and code modification and three process customization options namely no change, incremental change and radical change in the business processes.

In general, the ERP vendors have the opinion that the higher the degree of customization, the lower the performance of the ERP software (Leishman, 1999). It is evident that the incremental change of business process customization will lead to Total Quality Management (TQM) (Hammer & Stanton, 1999). In Table 2, the cell "No customization" refers to the business process that fits the system process and in which no customization is necessary. Process adaptation deals with the system process that is ideal and business processes which are close to it. Process conversion refers to the business process that is far from system process. The cell "fit system to process" indicates that business process change is not necessary and it is better to fit the system process to the business process. The cell "mutual adaptation" is meant for making minor modifications to both the system process and the business process.

The cell "Fit process to system" means minor system process changes are necessary and this can be achieved by redesigning the business process to system process. System conversion refers to a situation where business process change is not desirable and customizing system process to business process is desired. System conversion and process adaptation suggest that minor business process changes are desirable and customizing system process to business process is therefore essential. The last cell in the framework, "System and Process Reengineering" is least preferred in ERP implementation as it involves total redesign of business and system processes.

NOMINAL GROUP TECHNIQUE (NGT)

The Nominal Group Technique (NGT) enables the ERP implementation team to define criteria based on which the ERP framework (Shown in Table 2) has to be viewed. Using these criteria, the inputs will be supplied to the AHP by the ERP team members to arrive at the various customization choices for the ERP implementation. NGT is a structured methodology that enables assimilation of ideas and judgments of knowledgeable individuals towards building a group of consensus over the desired outcome (Oslen, 1982). The outcome of the NGT is the list of criteria for the ERP team to adopt when they use the AHP to determine the various ERP customization choices available to them. The steps involved in the NGT are as follows:

i. Each one of the ERP team members write down the strategy and the criteria on which the ERP customization has to be done.
ii. Each member presents their views but does not discuss them. The ERP team leader records all the points presented by the team members.
iii. The ERP team leader throws each point to the team members for analysis and explanation.
iv. The ERP team leader asks each member to write down the points (strategy/criteria) that seem especially important. The leader then goes down the list and records the number of people who consider each item a priority.
v. Finally, members rate each item from no importance (0) to top priority (10). The leader then collects and calculates the ratings and records the cumulative rating for each item.

ANALYTICAL HIERARCHY PROCESS (AHP)

Thomas L. Saaty (Saaty, 1980) evolved the Analytical Hierarchy Process (AHP). It is a methodology for multi-criteria analysis and decision-making which can enable decision makers to represent the interac-

Table 2.

		Process Customization Options		
Technical Customization Options	**Parameter**	**No Change (NC)**	**Incremental Change (IC)**	**Radical Change (RC)**
	Module Customization (M)	No Customization (MNC)	Process Adaptation (MIC)	Process Conversion (MRC)
	Table Customization (T)	Fit System to Process (TNC)	Mutual Adaptation (TIC)	Fit Process to System (TRC)
	Code Customization (C)	System Conversion (CNC)	System Conversion and Process Adaptation (CIC)	System and Process Reengineering (CRC)

tion of multiple factors in complex situations. The process requires the decision makers to develop a hierarchical structure for the factors which are explicit in the given problem and to provide judgements about the relative importance of each of these factors to specify a preference for each decision alternative with respect to each factor. It provides a prioritized ranking order indicating the overall preference for each of the decision alternatives.

AHP uses a hierarchy to structure a decision problem, which deconstructs the problem into its component elements, groups the elements into homogeneous sets and arranges them hierarchically. Based on the hierarchical model, the AHP provides a method to assign numerical values to subjective judgements on the relative importance of each element and then to synthesize the judgements to determine which elements have the highest priority.

The general approach of AHP is to decompose the total problem into smaller sub-problems in such a way that each sub-problem can be analyzed and appropriately handled with practical perspectives in terms of data and information. The objective of decomposition of the total problem into several levels is to enable pairwise comparisons of all the elements on a given level with respect to the related elements in the level just above. The solution process consists of three stages:

i.   Determination of the relative importance of the attributes;
ii.   Determination of the relative importance of each of the alternatives with respect to each attribute; and
iii.   Overall priority weight determination of each of these alternatives.

With various objectives, a number of methods namely scoring, ranking, mathematical optimization and multi-criteria decision analysis have been applied in the past to ERP projects (Chun-chin Wei, 2005) and a summary is given in Table 3. We prefer the AHP as the methodology to evaluate the ERP implementation choices as the major advantage of AHP over the other multi-criteria decision making methods is that AHP is designed to incorporate tangible as well as intangible factors especially where the subjective judgements of different individuals constitute an important part of the decision process.

Table 3.

Methods in practice	Review of literature
Scoring method	This method according to Lucas & Moore (1976) is intuitive, but reflects opinions of decision makers.
Ranking approach	Buss (1983) proposed a ranking approach to compare computer projects and has found that this method has some limitations.
Non-Linear programming model	Santhanam & Kyparisis (1996) proposed a nonlinear programming model to optimize resource allocation allowing for the interaction of factors.
0-1 Goal programming model	Badri & Davis (2001) presented the 0-1 Goal Programming Model. This method could not get the required attributes from an ERP system and hence got weakened.
AHP Method	Saaty (1980) discovered the AHP method and was used by Schniederjans and Wilson (1991) in the ERP software selection process and was found useful.
Nominal group technique (NGT)	Teltumbde (2000) used NGT and AHP to select an ERP system and found AHP useful.

In this study, the Analytical Hierarchy Process (AHP) is used as the methodology to evaluate the ERP implementation choices using the framework shown in Table 2. The AHP provides nine customization options which are prioritized on the basis of the priority value obtained by this method for each cell in the framework. The AHP provides a method to assign numerical values to subjective judgements on the relative importance of each element and then to synthesize the judgements to determine which elements have the highest priority. AHP is a method that advocates the comparison of two requirements at one moment. Please refer to Saaty (1980) for detailed explanation on using the AHP method. It consists of the following steps.

- Step 1. Choose the requirements to be prioritized.
- Step 2. Set the requirements into the rows and columns of the n x n AHP matrix.
- Step 3. Perform a pair-wise comparison of the requirements in the matrix according to a set of criteria.
- Step 4. Sum the columns.
- Step 5. Normalize the sum of rows.
- Step 6. Calculate the row averages.

APPLICATION OF NGT AND AHP

The application of the NGT and the AHP to the framework shown in Table 2 was done for a public sector undertaking company (PSC) in India in order to evaluate the feasible customization options available during ERP implementation in that organization. A team of twelve people, five from the business and seven from the information system, participated in this process. They were supplied with the scale for pairwise comparison table (Refer Table 4) to give their degree of preference for the various attributes to give input to the 3 x 3 AHP matrices.

As a first step, the criteria based on which the inputs must be given to the AHP were defined using the NGT. The ERP team members followed the procedure discussed in the previous section for using the NGT and identified the following factors as the basis for evaluating ERP customization choices. They are: [1] Existing business processes in PSC [2] Capability of the ERP team to execute the customiza-

Table 4.

Degree of preference	Definition
1	Equally preferred
3	Moderately preferred
5	Strongly preferred
7	Very strongly preferred
9	Extremely preferred
2, 4, 6, 8	Intermediate preferences between the two adjacent judgements
Reciprocal of the above non-zero numbers	If criterion L is assigned one of the above non-zero numbers when it is compared with criterion J, J has the reciprocal value when it is compared with L

tion [3] Risk management [4] Hardware and software configurations requirements [5] Expected project duration [6] End user training and [7] Costs for carrying out the ERP customization. These factors play a key role in choosing the degree of preference for various attributes in the framework.

These people were asked to provide input to the 3 x 3 AHP matrices A, B, C and D given below. Matrix A represents the input values for the major attributes to compute relative priorities of the major attributes namely module customization (MC), table customization (TC) and code customization (CC). Matrix B, Matrix C and Matrix D represent the input values for the various sub-attributes to compute the inter-criterion priority weights. All these four matrices were used to compute the overall priority weights for each cell in the framework as shown in Table 5 and Table 6.

The application of AHP must be carried out during the initial stage of ERP implementation so that it provides us with the various customization options in terms of its importance. This will vary from one ERP project to another as the input from the ERP team varies. Finally, all the four 3 x 3 AHP matrices given above were evaluated using the six steps presented earlier to find the priority values of each attribute.

Three sets of results were obtained. They are: (A) Priority weights of each of the major attributes namely module customization, table customization and code customization; (B) Priority weights of the sub-attributes namely no change, incremental change and radical change attached to all the major attributes; (C) Overall priority weights for each cell in the framework using the results obtained in (A) and (B).

The AHP analysis showing the relative priorities of the major attributes, the inter-criterion priority weights and the overall priority weights for each cell in the framework are shown in Table 5 and Table

	MC	TC	CC
MC	1	3	4
TC	1/3	1	3
CC	1/4	1/3	1

3 x 3 AHP Matrix A

	MNC	MIC	MRC
MNC	1	3	4
MIC	1/3	1	3
MRC	1/4	1/3	1

3 x 3 AHP Matrix B

	TNC	TIC	TRC
TNC	1	3	4
TIC	1/3	1	4
TRC	1/4	1/4	1

3 x 3 AHP Matrix C

	CNC	CIC	CRC
CNC	1	3	5
CIC	1/3	1	4
CRC	1/4	1/4	1

3 x 3 AHP Matrix D

6. The outcome of the application of the AHP to the framework is the identification of nine feasible customization options available to the management and the ERP team.

It is observed that the cell with higher priority value is strongly recommended and the cell with low priority value is the least preferred. The intermediate values give the various other options available for customization. Table 5 gives the priority values for the major attributes, the sub-attributes and the over all composite score. It is also observed that the consistency ratio for all the matrices is less than 0.1 and hence the decision maker's pairwise comparison matrices are acceptable.

FINDINGS

The application of Nominal Group Technique (NGT) determines the base for giving the inputs to the AHP, thereby enabling all the ERP team members to apply the AHP to the framework under a common objective. Before deciding the type of customization required for the ERP implementation, it is very much essential to bring a consensus among the ERP team members about the criteria on which the decision to select a feasible customization option for their enterprise. Hence, in this research study, at first, the ERP team uses the NGT and then applies the AHP to the framework. The NGT has found that there are seven factors to consider while giving inputs to the AHP.

The application of the AHP to the framework (Shown in Table 2) provides us nine customization options. Choosing the right option is now made easier as a consensus among the ERP team members can be achieved using the NGT. The results obtained using the AHP are tabulated in Table 6 and Figure 1. The results depend on the factors determined by the ERP team members using the NGT. It is necessary

Table 5.

Major Attributes	Priority Value	Sub-Attributes	Priority Value	Customization Options	Overall Priority Value	Priority / Rank
Module (M)	0.607	No change (NC)	0.608	MNC	0.369	1
		Incremental change (IC)	0.271	MIC	0.164	2
		Radical change (RC)	0.119	MRC	0.072	6
Table (T)	0.271	No change (NC)	0.593	TNC	0.160	3
		Incremental change (IC)	0.295	TIC	0.079	4
		Radical change (RC)	0.109	TRC	0.029	8
Code (C)	0.119	No change (NC)	0.619	CNC	0.073	5
		Incremental change (IC)	0.283	CIC	0.033	7
		Radical change (RC)	0.096	CRC	0.011	9

to mention here that choosing the right customization option also depends on the technical and domain knowledge of the ERP consultants.

Table 6 and Figure 1 show the various customization options in ERP implementation in terms of their priority value obtained using the AHP. In Table 6, the value in the square bracket and the closed brackets in each cell represent the rank and priority value of the respective customization option. In figure 1, the X-axis represents the various customization options and the Y-axis represents the priority value obtained using the AHP. We find that nine options are available, out of which the first cell "MNC" is the most preferred and recommended. The least preferred cell is "CRC". We find that "MIC" and "TNC" carry equal weightage. Hence if the customization becomes essential, the vendor can choose module customization rather than touching upon the other functionality of the ERP system. ERP vendors must remember that the business processes have many touch-points, many of which will not have access to the ERP system.

From Table 5, we find that less customization is preferred to incremental changes and radical changes that can be done to the module, table and source code of an ERP software. The cell "CRC" carries the least value, which confirms the fact that completely reengineering the business processes of an enterprise and redesigning the ERP software accordingly would significantly affect future competitiveness and performance of a company. As we have already discussed, the priority values vary from one ERP implementation to another and hence the preference of the cells also varies depending on the data provided by the ERP team based on the business processes and the chosen ERP system.

Most organizations that implement ERP make some customizations to an ERP vendor's basic product offering, but many make the mistake of over-customizing their application modules. The responsibility of carrying out customization lies with the entire ERP team and the management. In particular, the functional consultants and the technical consultants involved in ERP implementation play a crucial role. This study strongly recommends module customization rather than table and source code customization. Identifying the suitable module for ERP implementation will solve many problems, which many companies fail to do.

From Figure 1, we find that unanimously the ERP team has given low priority value to source code customization, as it requires significant testing. Source code customization must ensure that the changes made to one segment of the code do not affect the other. In addition, a complete walkthrough has to be

Table 6.

		NC	IC	RC
M		**MNC** [1] (0.369)	**MIC** [2] (0.164)	**MRC** [6] (0.072)
T		**TNC** [3] (0.160)	**TIC** [4] (0.079)	**TRC** [8] (0.029)
C		**CNC** [5] (0.073)	**CIC** [7] (0.033)	**CRC** [9] (0.011)

Figure 1.

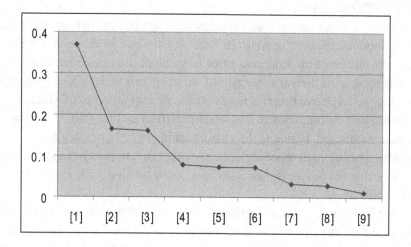

done for the ERP system. All these activities not only lengthen the project duration but also leave the ERP software incomplete at the end. Also, the cell "CRC" involves certain risk factors.

Thus, we learn that customization leads to increased project duration, schedule slippage, losing standards embedded in the ERP system and at last the objective of adopting the best practices in the industry through the ERP system fades away. Above all, success is in the bag if the system users understand how the ERP system should be integrated into the overall company operation (Umble et al., 2003).

CONCLUSION

ERP system is an effective tool to plan an enterprise's resources. ERP system helps us to achieve maximum utilization of available resources in an enterprise. With increasing competitive pressure in the market, ERP projects will continue to occupy dominant space in IT investments in the coming years. We have applied Nominal Group Technique (NGT) and the Analytical Hierarchy Process (AHP) to a framework found in the literature. Data were collected from the ERP team in an organization preparing for ERP implementation.

In this study, a list of factors to be considered for ERP software customization by the ERP team has been identified using the NGT. These factors will act as the basis for giving the inputs to the AHP. Nine customization options found in the framework were prioritized based on the priority values computed using the AHP. It helps the management and the ERP team to determine the decision on choosing a feasible customization option for successful ERP implementation. Especially, it accelerates the reaching of consensus among multiple decision makers involved in ERP implementation.

Contributions to Practice

The NGT is simple and user-friendly to the ERP team members. It quickly brings a consensus among the ERP team members to determine the criteria for the ERP software customization. The purpose of using the AHP to select a feasible customization option is to view ERP implementation as a portfolio of software projects. Different projects will require different customization options. Thus, they should be managed in their own ways. This study is meant to help the management and the ERP team to understand the process of customization and to evaluate it based on the way an organization does its business.

Contributions to Research

Most of the research work in Enterprise Resource Planning (ERP) addresses managerial issues and a few frameworks in the literature only suggest the possibility of adapting an ERP system to the business processes. Our research study goes beyond these in several ways. In this study, we have considered both technical customization and process customization. Furthermore, the frameworks already proposed in the literature do not determine decisions for managers in executing customization, which is fulfilled in our study.

Limitations

Data provided by the ERP team from an organization preparing for ERP implementation were used. The outcome of using this framework with the AHP has to be analyzed to validate the framework. Data from different ERP team members from different ERP projects should be used to improve this framework and apply the AHP accordingly. This framework with the AHP has to be accompanied by other existing tools for project management to meet issues like change management, project scheduling, etc.

Future Research

A future research study could compare the framework used in this study with other frameworks available in the literature. All these frameworks have to be validated and the AHP has to be applied to the finest framework. A new framework could be developed that will address the customization process as well as its impact on other factors like project cost, project scheduling, project team capabilities, change management, etc. The future research study could evolve a model for the ERP customization using the NGT and the AHP, which shall act like a channel for the ERP team to determine the best customization choice for their enterprise as well as the formula to execute it successfully.

REFERENCES

Amrit, T., & Keil, K. (2006, August). Functionality Risk in Information Systems Development: An Empirical Investigation. *IEEE Transactions on Engineering Management, 53*(3), 412-425.

Badri, M. A., & Davis, D. (2001). A comprehensive 0–1 goal programming model for project selection. *International Journal of Project Management, 19*, 243–252.

Beatty, R. C., & Williams, C. D. (2006, March). ERP II: Best practices for successfully implementing an ERP upgrade. *Communications of ACM, 49*(3), 105-109.

Ben light. (2005, May). Potential pitfalls in packaged software adoption. *Communications of ACM, 48*(5), 119-120.

Bingi, P., Sharma, M. K., & Godla, J. (1999). Critical issues affecting an ERP implementation. *Information Systems Management, 16*(3), 7-14.

Botta-Genoulaz, V., Millet, P. A., & Grabot, B. (2005). A survey on the recent research literature on ERP systems. *Computers in Industry, 56*, 510-522

Boudreau, M. C., & Robey, D. (1999, December). Organizational transition to enterprise resource planning systems: Theoretical choices for process research. *Proceedings of 20th International conference on Information Systems*, Charlotte, 291-299.

Brehm, L., Heinzl, A., & Markus, M. L. (2001). Tailoring ERP systems: A spectrum of choices and their implications. *Proceedings of 34th Annual Hawaii International Conference on System Sciences*, IEEE Press, Maui, Hawaii.

Buss, M. D. J. (1983). How to rank computer projects. *Harvard Business Review, 61*(1), 118–125.

Carmel, E., & Sawyer, S. (1998). Packaged software development teams: what makes them different? *Information Technology People, 11*(1), 7-19.

Chun-chin, W., Chen-fu, C. & Mao-jiun, J. W. (2005). An AHP based approach to ERP system selection. *International Journal on Production Economics, 96*, 47-62.

Clemon, E. K., & Row, M. C. (1991). Sustaining IT advantage: The role of structural differences. *MIS quarters*, 275-292.

Davenport, T. H. (1998, July/August). Putting the enterprise into the enterprise system. *Harvard Business Review, 76*(4), 121-131.

Diane, M. S., & Volkoff, O. (2004, June). A Roadmap for Enterprise System Implementation. *Computer*, 22-28.

Fiona, F.-H. N.& Lee-Shang L. J. (2001). Critical factors for successful implementation of enterprise systems. *Business Process Management Journal, 7*(3), 285-296.

Gefen, D. (2002). Nurturing clients' trust to encourage engagement success during the customization of ERP systems. *Omega, 30*(4).

Ghost, A. K., & Howell, C., & Whittaker, J. A. (2002). Building software securely from the ground up. *IEEE software, 19*(1), 14-16.

Glass, R. L. (1998). Enterprise Resource Planning—Breakthrough and/or term problems. *Database for Advances Information System, 29*(2), 14-16.

Hammer, M., & Stanton, S. (1999, November-December). How process enterprises really work. *Harvard Business Review*, 108-118.

Holland, C. P., & Light, B. (1999, May-June). A critical success factors model for ERP implementation. *IEEE Software, 16*(3), 30-36

Holland, P., & Light, B., & Gibson, N. (1999). A critical success factor model for enterprise resource planning implementation. *Proceedings of the 7th European conference on information systems, 1*, 273-297.

Hong, K., & Kim, Y. (2002). The Critical success factors for ERP implementation: An organizational fit perspective. *Information Management, 40*(1), 25-40.

Jeanne, W. R. (1999, July-August). Surprising facts about implementing ERP. *IT Pro*, 65-67

Kai, A. O., & Per, S. (2007). IT for niche companies: Is an ERP system the solution? *Information Systems Journal, 17*, 37-58.

Klaus, H., Rosemann, M., & Gable, G. G. (2000). What is ERP? *Information System Frontiers, 2*(2), 141-162.

Konstanflons, C. (2004, June). ERP systems deployment problems in the real world: From Blue prints to Go Live. *26ᵗʰ International conference on information technology interfaces*, ITI 2004, Cavtat, croatia, 71-76.

Lassila, K. S., & Brancheau. (1999). Adoption and utilization of commercial software packages: Exploring utilization equilibria, transitions, triggers and tracks. *Journal of Management Information System, 16*(2), 63-90.

Leishman, D. A. (1999). Solution customization. *IBM Systems Journal, 38*(1), 76-97.

Lucas, H. C., & Moore Jr., J. R. (1976). A Multiple-criterion scoring approach to information system project selection. *Info., 14*(1), 1–12.

Manish, A., & Kaushal, C. (March 2007). Software Effort, Quality and Cycle Time: A Study of CMM Level 5 Projects. *IEEE Transaction on Software Engineering, 33*, (3), 145-156.

Mark, K., & Amrit, T. (2006). Relative importance of evaluation criteria for enterprise systems: a conjoint study. *Information Systems Journal*, (16), 237-262.

Mabert, V. A., Soni, A., & Venkataramanan, M. A. (2003). The impact of organization size on ERP implementations in US manufacturing sector. *The International Journal of Management Science, 31*, 235-246.

Markus, M. L., & Tanis, C. (2000). The enterprise systems experience-From adoption to success. In *framing the Domains of IT Research: Glimpsing the Future through the Past*, R. W. Zmud, Ed. Cincinnati, OH: Pinnaflex Educational Resources Inc., pp. 173-207.

Mitzi, G. P., & Glenn, J. B. (2007). Improving requirements elicitation: An empirical investigation of procedural prompts. *Information Systems Journal, 17*, 89-110.

Nicolas, S., & Sarriegi, J. M. (2006, May/June). Open source software ERPs: A new alternative for an old need. *IEEE Software*, 94 -96

Olsen, S. A. (1982). *Group Planning and Problem Solving Methods in Engineering Management*. New York: Wiley.

Raisinghani, M. S., Meade, L., & Schkade, L. L. (2007). Strategic E-Business Decision Analysis Using The Analytic Network Process. *IEEE Transactions on Engineering Management, 54*(4), 673-686.

Reel., J. S. (1999). Critical success factors in software projects. *IEEE Software, 16*(3), 18-23.

Redouane, EI A., Rowe, F., & Benedicte G-M.(2006). The effects of enterprise resource planning implementation strategy on cross-functionality. *Information Systems Journal*, (16), 79-104.

Robey, D., Ross, J. W., & Boudreau, M. C. (2002). Learning to implement enterprise systems: An exploratory case study of the dialectics change. *Journal of Management Information Systems, 19*(1), 17-46.

Saaty, T. L. (1980). *The Analytic Hierarchy Process (AHP)*. New York: McGraw-Hill.

Santhanam, R., & Kyparisis, G. J. (1996). A decision model for interdependent information system project selection. *European Journal of Operational Research, 89*, 380–399.

Sawyer, S. (2000). Packaged software: Implications of the differences from custom approaches to software development. *European Journal of Information System, 9*, 47-58.

Schniederjans, M. J., & Wilson, R. L. (1991). Using the analytic hierarchy process and goal programming for information system project selection. *Information & Management, 20*, 333-342.

Sumner, M. (2000). Risk factors in Enterprise-Wide/ERP projects. *Journal of Information Technology, 15*(4), 317-327.

Teltumbde, A. (2000). A framework for evaluating ERP projects. *International Journal of Production Research, 38*(17), 4507–4520.

Umble, E. J., Halt, R. R., & Umble, M. M. (2003). Enterprise Resource Planning: Implementation procedures and critical success factors. *European Journal of Operational Research, 146*(2), 241-257.

Van Everdingen, Y., Hilsberg, J., & Waarts, E. (2000). ERP adoption by European midsize companies. *Communications of ACM, 43*(2), 27-31.

Wenhong, L., & Strong, D. M. (2004). A framework for evaluating ERP implementation choices. *IEEE transactions on Engineering Management, 51*(3), 322-332.

Chapter VI
Specifying Software Models with Organizational Styles

Manuel Kolp
Université Catholique de Louvain Place des Doyens, Belguim

Yves Wautelet
Université Catholique de Louvain Place des Doyens, Belguim

Stéphane Faulkner
University of Namur Rempart de la Vierge, Belgium

ABSTRACT

Organizational Modeling is concerned with analyzing and understanding the organizational context within which a software system will eventually function. This chapter proposes organizational patterns motivated by organizational theories intended to facilitate the construction of organizational models. These patterns are defined from real world organizational settings, modeled in i* and formalized using the Formal Tropos language. Additionally, the chapter evaluates the proposed patterns using desirable qualities such as coordinability and predictability. The research is conducted in the context of Tropos, a comprehensive software system development methodology.

INTRODUCTION

Analyzing the organizational and intentional context within which a software system will eventually operate has been recognized as an important element of the organizational modeling process also called early requirements engineering (see e.g., (Anton 1996, Dardenne, van Lamsweerde & Fickas 1993, Yu 1995)). Such models are founded on primitive concepts such as those of actor and goal. This paper focuses on the definition of a set of organizational patterns that can be used as building blocks for constructing such models. Our proposal is based on concepts adopted from organization theory and strategic alliances literature. Throughout the paper, we use i* (Yu 1995) as the modeling framework in terms of which the proposed patterns are presented and accounted for. The research reported in this paper is being conducted within the context of the Tropos project (Giorgini, Kolp, Mylopoulos & Pistore 2004, Giorgini, Kolp, Mylopoulos & Castro 2005), whose aim is to construct and validate a software development methodology for agent-based software systems. The methodology adopts ideas from multi-agent system technologies, mostly to define the implementation phase of our methodology. It also adopts ideas from Requirements Engineering, where actors and goals have been used heavily for early requirements analysis. The project is founded on that actors and goals are used as fundamental concepts for modeling and analysis during all phases of software development, not just early requirements, or implementation. More details about Tropos can be found in (Giorgini et al. 2005). The present work continues the research in progress about social abstractions for the Tropos methodology. In (Kolp, Giorgini & Mylopoulos 2002*a*), we have detailed a social ontology for Tropos to consider information systems as social structures all along the development life cycle. In (Giorgini, Kolp & Mylopoulos 2002, Kolp, Giorgini & Mylopoulos 2002*b*, Kolp, Giorgini & Mylopoulos 2006), we have described how to use this Tropos social ontology to design multi-agent systems architectures, notably for e-business applications (Kolp, Do & Faulkner 2004). As a matter of fact, multi-agent systems can be considered structured societies of coordinated autonomous agents. In the present paper, which is a extended and revised version of (Kolp, Giorgini & Mylopoulos 2003), we emphasize the use of organizational patterns based on organization theory an strategic alliances for early requirements analysis, with the concern of modeling the organizational setting for a system-to-be in terms of abstractions that could better match its operational environment (e.g., an enterprise, a corporate alliance, . . .)

The paper is organized as follows. Section 2 describes organizational and strategic alliance theories, focusing on the internal and external structure of an organization. Section 3 details two organizational patterns – the structure-in-5 and the joint venture – based on real world examples of organizations. These patterns are modeled in terms of social and intentional concepts using the i* framework and the Formal Tropos specification language. Section 4 identifies a set of desirable non-functional requirements for evaluating these patterns and presents a framework to select a pattern with respect to these identified requirements. Section 5 overviews the *Tropos* methodology. Finally, Section 6 summarizes the contributions of the paper and overviews related work.

STRUCTURING ORGANIZATIONS

Organizational structures are primarily studied by *Organization Theory* (e.g., (Mintzberg 1992, Scott 1998, Yoshino & Rangan 1995)), that describes the structure and design of an organization and *Strategic Alliances* (e.g., (Dussauge & Garrette 1999, Gomes-Casseres 1996, Morabito, Sack & Bhate 1999, Segil 1996)), that model the strategic collaborations of independent organizational stakeholders who have agreed to pursue a set of agreed upon business goals.

Both disciplines aim to identify and study organizational patterns that describe a system at a macroscopic level in terms of a manageable number of subsystems, components and modules inter-related through dependencies.

In this paper, we are interested to identify, formalize and apply, for organizational modeling, patterns that have been already well-understood and precisely defined in organizational theories. Our purpose is not to categorize them exhaustively nor to study them on a managerial point of view. The following sections will thus only insist on patterns that have been found, due to their nature, interesting candidates also considering the fact that they have been studied in great detail in the organizational literature and presented as fully formed patterns.

Organization Theory

"An organization is a consciously coordinated social entity, with a relatively identifiable boundary, that functions on a relatively continuous basis to achieve a common goal or a set of goals" (Morabito et al. 1999). Organization theory is the discipline that studies both structure and design in such social entities. Structure deals with the descriptive aspects while design refers to the prescriptive aspects of a social entity. Organization theory describes how practical organizations are actually structured, offers suggestions on how new ones can be constructed, and how old ones can change to improve effectiveness. To this end, since Adam Smith, schools of organization theory have proposed models and patterns to try to find and formalize recurring organizational structures and behaviors.

In the following, we briefly present organizational patterns identified in Organization Theory. The structure-in-5 will be studied in detail in Section 3.

The Structure-in-5. An organization can be considered an aggregate of five substructures, as proposed by Minztberg (Mintzberg 1992). At the base level sits the *Operational Core* which carries out the basic tasks and procedures directly linked to the production of products and services (acquisition of inputs, transformation of inputs into outputs, distribution of outputs). At the top lies the *Strategic Apex* which makes executive decisions ensuring that the organization fulfils its mission in an effective way and defines the overall strategy of the organization in its environment. The *Middle Line* establishes a hierarchy of authority between the Strategic Apex and the Operational Core. It consists of managers responsible for supervising and coordinating the activities of the Operational Core. The *Technostructure* and the *Support* are separated from the main line of authority and influence the operating core only indirectly. The Technostructure serves the organization by making the work of others more effective, typically by standardizing work processes, outputs, and skills. It is also in charge of applying analytical procedures to adapt the organization to its operational environment. The Support provides specialized services, at various levels of the hierarchy, outside the basic operating workflow (e.g., legal counsel, R&D, payroll, cafeteria). We describe and model examples of structures-in-5 in Section 3.

The pyramid pattern is the well-know hierarchical authority structure. Actors at lower levels depend on those at higher levels. The crucial mechanism is the direct supervision from the Apex. Managers and supervisors at intermediate levels only route strategic decisions and authority from the Apex to the operating (low) level. They can coordinate behaviors or take decisions by their own, but only at a local level.

The chain of values merges, backward or forward, several actors engaged in achieving or realizing related goals or tasks at different stages of a supply or production process. Participants who act as intermediaries, add value at each step of the chain. For instance, for the domain of goods distribution, providers are expected to supply quality products, wholesalers are responsible for ensuring their massive exposure, while retailers take care of the direct delivery to the consumers.

The matrix proposes a multiple command structure: vertical and horizontal channels of information and authority operate simultaneously. The principle of unity of command is set aside, and competing bases of authority are allowed to jointly govern the workflow. The vertical lines are typically those of functional departments that operate as "home bases" for all participants, the horizontal lines represents project groups or geographical arenas where managers combine and coordinate the services of the functional specialists around particular projects or areas.

The bidding pattern involves competitivity mechanisms, and actors behave as if they were taking part in an auction. An auctioneer actor runs the show, advertises the auction issued by the auction issuer, receives bids from bidder actors and ensures communication and feedback with the auction issuer who is responsible for issuing the bidding.

Strategic Alliances

A strategic alliance links specific facets of two or more organizations. At its core, this structure is a trading partnership that enhances the effectiveness of the competitive strategies of the participant organizations by providing for the mutually beneficial trade of technologies, skills, or products based upon them. An alliance can take a variety of forms, ranging from arm's-length contracts to joint ventures, from multinational corporations to university spin-offs, from franchises to equity arrangements. Varied interpretations of the term exist, but a strategic alliance can be defined as possessing simultaneously the following three necessary and sufficient characteristics:

- The two or more organizations that unite to pursue a set of agreed upon goals remain independent subsequent to the formation of the alliance.
- The partner organizations share the benefits of the alliances and control over the performance of assigned tasks.
- The partner organizations contribute on a continuing basis in one or more key strategic areas, e.g., technology, products, and so forth.

In the following, we briefly present organizational patterns identified in Strategic Alliances. The joint venture will be studied in details in Section 3.

The joint venture pattern involves agreement between two or more intra-industry partners to obtain the benefits of larger scale, partial investment and lower maintenance costs. A specific joint management actor coordinates tasks and manages the sharing of resources between partner actors. Each partner can manage and control itself on a local dimension and interact directly with other partners to exchange resources, such as data and knowledge. However, the strategic operation and coordination of such an organization, and its actors on a global dimension, are only ensured by the joint management actor in which the original actors possess equity participations. We describe and model examples of joint ventures in Section 3.

The arm's-length pattern implies agreements between independent and competitive, but partner actors. Partners keep their autonomy and independence but act and put their resources and knowledge together to accomplish precise common goals. No authority is lost, or delegated from one collaborator to another.

The hierarchical contracting pattern identifies coordinating mechanisms that combine arm's-length agreement features with aspects of pyramidal authority. Coordination mechanisms developed for arm's-length (independent) characteristics involve a variety of negotiators, mediators and observers at different levels handling conditional clauses to monitor and manage possible contingencies, negotiate and resolve conflicts and finally deliberate and take decisions. Hierarchical relationships, from the executive apex to the arm's-length contractors restrict autonomy and underlie a cooperative venture between the parties.

The co-optation pattern involves the incorporation of representatives of external systems into the decision-making or advisory structure and behavior of an initiating organization. By co-opting representatives of external systems, organizations are, in effect, trading confidentiality and authority for resource, knowledge assets and support. The initiating system has to come to terms with the contractors for what is being done on its behalf; and each co-optated actor has to reconcile and adjust its own views with the policy of the system it has to communicate.

MODELING ORGANIZATIONAL PATTERNS

We will define an organizational pattern as a metaclass of organizational structures offering a set of design parameters to coordinate the assignment of organizational objectives and processes, thereby affecting how the organization itself functions. Design parameters include, among others, goal and task assignments, standardization, supervision and control dependencies and strategy definitions.

This section describes two of the organizational patterns presented in Section 2: the structure-in-5 and the joint-venture.

Structure-in-5

To detail and specify the structure-in-5 as an organizational pattern, this section presents two case studies: LDV Bates (Bates 2006) and GMT (GMT 2006). They will serve to propose a model and a semi-formal specification of the structure-in-5.

LDV Bates. Agate Ltd is an advertising agency located in Belgium that employs about fifty staff, as detailed in Table 1.

The *Direction* – four directors responsible for the main aspects of LDV Bates's *Global Strategy* (advertising campaigns, creative activities, administration, and finances) – forms the *Strategic Apex*. The *Middle Line,* composed of the *Campaigns Management* staff, is in charge of finding and coordinating advertising campaigns (marketing, sales, edition, graphics, budget, . . .). It is supported in these tasks by the *Administration and Accounts* and *IT and Documentation* departments. The *Administration and Accounts* constitutes the *Technostructure* handling administrative tasks and policy, paperwork, purchases and budgets. The Support groups the IT and Documentation departments. It defines the *IT policy* of Agate, provides *technical means* required for the management of campaigns, and ensures services for *system support* as well as information retrieval (*documentation* resources). The *Operational Core* includes the *Graphics and Edition* staff in charge of the creative and artistic aspects of realizing *campaign* (texts, photographs, drawings, layout, design, logos).

Figure 1 models LDV Bates in structure-in-5 using the i* strategic dependency model. i* is a modeling framework for organizational modeling (Yu 1995), which offers goal-and actor-based notions such as *actor, agent, role, position, goal, softgoal, task, resource, belief* and different kinds of social dependency between actors. Its strategic dependency model describes the network of social *dependencies* among actors. It is a graph, where each node represents an acto*r* and each link between two actors indicates that one actor depends on the other for some goal to be attained. A dependency describes an "agreement" (called *dependum*) between two actors: the *depender* and the *dependee*. The depender is

Table 1. Organization of LDV Bates

Direction	Edition	
1 Campaigns Director	2 Editors	**IT**
1 Creative Director	4 Copy writers	1 IT manager
1 Administrative Director		1 Network administrator
1 Finance Director	**Documentation**	1 System administrator
	1 Media librarian	1 Analyst
Campaigns Management	1 Resource librarian	1 Computer technician
2 Campaign managers	1 Knowledge worker	
3 Campaign marketers		
1 Editor in Chief	**Administration**	**Accounts**
1 Creative Manager	3 Direction assistants	1 Accountant manager
	4 Manager Secretaries	1 Credit controller
Graphics	2 Receptionists	2 Accounts clerks
6 Graphic designers	2 Clerks/typists	2 Purchasing assistants
2 Photographers	1 Filing clerk	

the depending actor, and the dependee, the actor who is depended upon. The type of the dependency describes the nature of the agreement. *Goal* dependencies represent delegation of responsibility for fulfilling a goal; *softgoal* dependencies are similar to goal dependencies, but their fulfillment cannot be defined precisely (for instance, the appreciation is subjective or fulfillment is obtained only to a given extent); *task* dependencies are used in situations where the dependee is required to perform a given activity; and resourc*e* dependencies require the dependee to provide a resource to the depender. As shown in Figure 1, actors are represented as circles; dependums – goals, softgoals, tasks and resources – are represented as ovals, clouds, hexagons and rectangles; respectively, and dependencies have the form *depender → dependum → dependee.*

GMT is a company specialized in telecom services in Belgium. Its lines of products and services range from phones & fax, conferencing, line solutions, internet & e-business, mobile solutions, and voice & data management. As shown in Figure 2, the structure of the commercial organization follows the structure-in-5. An *Executive Committee* constitutes the *Strategic Apex*. It is responsible for defining the *general strategy* of the organization. Five chief managers (*finances, operations, divisions management, marketing,* and *R&D*) apply the specific aspects of the *general strategy* in the area of their competence: *Finances & Operations* is in charge of *Budget* and Sales *Planning & Control, Divisions Management* is responsible for *Implementing Sales Strategy,* and *Marketing* and *R&D* define *Sales Policy* and *Technological Policy.*

The *Divisions Management* groups managers that coordinate all managerial aspects of product and service sales. It relies on *Finance & Operations* for handling *Planning* and *Control* of products and services, it depends on *Marketing* for accurate *Market Studies* and on R&D for *Technological Awareness.*

The *Finances & Operations* departments constitute the *technostructure* in charge of management *control* (financial and quality audit) and sales *planning* including *scheduling* and *resource management.*

Figure 1. LDV Bates as a Structure-in-5

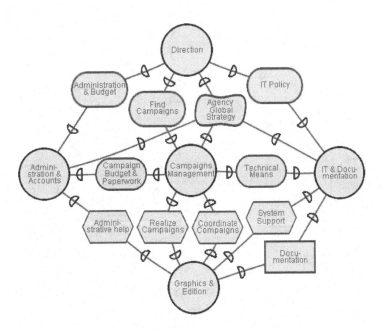

The *Support* involves the staff of *Marketing* and *R&D*. Both departments jointly define and support the *Sales* Policy. The Marketing department coordinates *Market Studies* (customer positionment and segmentation, pricing, sales incentive, . . .) and provides the *Operational Core* with *Documentation* and *Promotion* services. The *R&D* staff is responsible for defining the technological policy such as *technological awareness* services. It also assists *Sales people* and *Consultants* with *Expertise Support* and *Technology* Training.

Finally, the *Operational Core* groups *the Sales people* and *Line consultants* under the supervision and coordination of *Divisions Managers*. They are in charge of selling products and services to actual and potential customers.

Figure 3 abstracts the structures explored in the case studies of Figures 1 and 2 as a Structure-in-5 pattern composed of five actors. The case studies also suggested a number of constraints to supplement the basic pattern:

- The dependencies between the *Strategic Apex* as depender and the *Technostructure, Middle Line* and *Support* as dependees must be of type goal
- A softgoal dependency models the strategic dependence of the *Technostructure, Middle Line* and *Support* on the *Strategic Apex*
- The relationships between the *Middle Line* and *Technostructure* and *Support* must be of goal dependencies
- The *Operational Core* relies on the *Technostructure* and *Support* through task and resource dependencies
- Only task dependencies are permitted between the *Middle Line* (as depender or dependee) and the *Operational Core* (as dependee or depender).

Figure 2. GMT's sales organization as a Structure-in-5

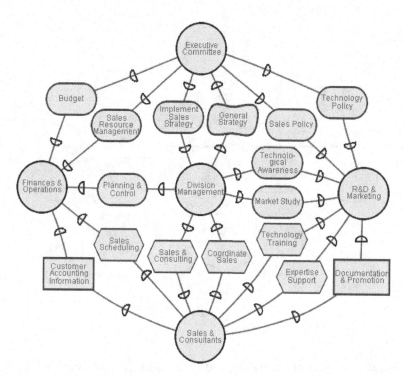

Figure 3. The structure-in-5 pattern

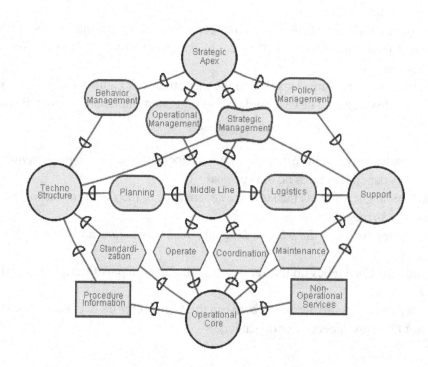

To specify the formal properties of the pattern, we use *Formal Tropos* (Fuxman, Liu, Mylopoulos, Roveri & Traverso 2004), which extends the primitives of *i** with a formal language comparable to that of KAOS (Dardenne et al. 1993). Constraints on *i** specifications are thus formalized in a first-order linear-time temporal logic. *Formal Tropos* provides three basic types of metaclasses: *actor, dependency, and entity* (Giorgini, Kolp & Mylopoulos 2002). The attributes of a *Formal Tropos* class denote relationships among different objects being modeled.

Metaclasses
Actor := **Actor** name[attributes] [creation-properties] [invar-properties][actor-goal]
With subclasses:
Agent(with attributes occupies: Position, play: Role)
Position(with attributes cover: Role)
Role
Dependency := **Dependency** name type mode **Depender** name **Dependee** name [attributes] [creation-properties] [invar-properties] [fulfill-properties]
Entity:=**Entity** name [attribute] [creation-properties][invar-properties]
Actor-Goal := (**Goal**|**Softgoal**) name mode **FulFillment**(actor-fulfill-property)

Classes: Classes are instances of Metaclasses.

In Formal Tropos, constraints on the lifetime of the (meta)class instances are given in a first-order linear-time temporal logic (see (Fuxman et al. 2004) for more details). Special predicates can appear in the temporal logic formulas: predicate *JustCreated*(x) holds in a state if element x exists in this state but not in the previous one; predicate *Fulfilled*(x) holds if x has been fulfilled; and predicate *JustFulfilled*(x) holds if *Fulfilled*(x) holds in this state, but not in the previous one.

In the following, we only present some specifications for the *Strategic Management* and *Operational Management* dependencies.

Actor StrategicApex
Actor MiddleLine
Actor Support
Actor Technostructure
Actor OperationalCore

Dependency StrategicManagement
Type SoftGoal
Depender te: Technostructure, ml: MiddleLine, su: Support
Dependee sa: StrategicApex
Invariant
$\forall dep : Dependency$ (*JustCreated*(dep) $\rightarrow$ *Consistent*(*self, dep*)) $\forall ag : Actor - Goal$ (*JustCreated*(ag) $\rightarrow$ *Consistent*(*self, ag*))
Fulfillment
$\forall dep : Dependency$ (*dep.type = goal* $\wedge$ *dep.depender = sa* $\wedge$
(*dep.dependee = te dep.dependee = ml dep.dependee = su*)) $\wedge$
Fulfilled(*self*) $\rightarrow$ ◆*Fulfilled*(*dep*)

[Invariant properties specify, respectively, that the strategic management softgoal must be consistent with any other dependency of the organization and with any other goal of the actors in the organization. The predicate Consistent depends on the particular organization we are considering and it is specified in terms of goals' properties to be satisfied. The fulfillment of the dependency necessarily implies that the goal dependencies between the Middle Line, the Technostructure, and the Support as dependees, and the Strategic Apex as depender have been achieved some time in the past]

Dependency OperationalManagement **Type** Goal
Mode achieve
Depender sa: StrategicApex
Dependee ml: MiddleLine
Invariant
Consistent(self, StrategicM anagement)
$\exists c : Coordination (c.type = task \land c.dependee = ml \land c.depender = OperationalCore \land ImplementedBy(self, c))$
Fulfillment
$\forall ts : Technostructure, dep : Dependency (dep.type = goal \land$
$dep.depender = ml \land dep.dependee = ts) \land Fulfilled(self)) \rightarrow \blacklozenge Fulfilled(dep)$

[The fulfillment of the Operational management goal implies that all goal dependencies between the Middle Line as depender and the Technostructure as dependee have been achieved some time in the past. Invariant properties specifies that Operational Management goal has to be consistent with Strategic Management softgoal and that there exists a coordination task (a task dependency between MiddleLine and Operational Core) that implement (ImplementedBy) the OperationalManagaemnt goal.]

In addition, the following structural (global) properties must be satisfied for the Structure-in-5 pattern:

* $\forall inst1, inst2 : StrategicApex \rightarrow inst1 = inst2$
    [There is a single instance of the Strategic Apex (the same constraint also holds for the Middle Line, the Technostructure, the Support and the Operational Core)]
* $\forall sa : StrategicApex, te : Technostructure, ml : MiddleLine,$
    $su : Support, dep : Dependency$
    $(dep.dependee = sa \land (dep.depender = te \lor dep.depender = ml$
    $\lor dep.depender = su) \rightarrow dep.type = softgoal)$
    [Only softgoal dependencies are permitted between the Strategic Apex as dependee and the Technostructure, the Middle Line, and the Support as dependers]
* $\forall sa : StrategicApex, te : T echnostructure, ml : M iddleLine,$
    $su : Support, dep : Dependency :$
    $(dep.depender = sa \land (dep.dependee = te \lor dep.dependee =$
    $ml \lor dep.dependee = su) \rightarrow dep.type = goal)$
    [Only goal dependencies are permitted between the Technostructure, the Middle Line, and the Support as dependee, and the Stategic Apex as depender]

- $\forall su : Support, ml : MiddleLine, dep : Dependency$

    $((dep.dependee = su \land dep.depender = ml) \rightarrow dep.type = goal)$

    [Only task dependencies are permitted between the Middle Agency and the Operational Core]

- $\forall te : Technostructure, oc : OperationalCore, dep : Dependency$

    $((dep.dependee = te \land dep.depender = oc) \rightarrow$

    $(dep.type = task \lor dep.type = resource))$

    [Only resource or task dependencies are permitted between the Technostructure and the Operational Core (the same constraint also holds for the Support)]

- $\forall a : Actor, ml : MiddleLine,$

    $(\exists dep : Dependency(dep.depender = a \land dep.dependee =$

    $ml) \lor (dep.dependee = a \land dep.depender = ml) \rightarrow$

    $((\exists sa : StrategicApex(a = sa)) \lor (\exists su : Support(a = su) \lor$

    $(\exists te : Technostructure(a = te)) \lor (\exists op : OperationalCore$

    $(a = op))$

    [No dependency is permitted between an external actor and the Middle Agency (the same constraint also holds for the Operational Core)]

This specification can be used to establish that a certain *i** model does constitute an instance of the Structure-in-5 pattern. For example, the *i** model of Figure 1 can be shown to be such an instance, in which the actors are instances of the Structure-in-5 actor classes (e.g., *Direction* and *IT&Documentation* are instances of the *Strategic Apex* and the *Support*, respectively), dependencies are instances of Structure-in-5 dependencies classes (e.g., *Agency Global Strategy* is an instance the *Strategic Management*), and all above global properties are enforced (e.g., since there are only two task dependencies between *Campaigns Management* and *Graphics&Edition*, the fourth property holds).

Joint Venture

We describe here two alliances – Airbus (Dussauge & Garrette 1999) and a more detailed one, Carsid (Wautelet, Kolp & Achbany 2006) – that will serve to model the joint venture structure as an organizational pattern and propose a semi-formal specification.

Airbus. The Airbus Industrie joint venture coordinates collaborative activities between European aeronautic manufacturers to built and market airbus aircrafts. The joint venture involves four partners: British Aerospace (UK), Aerospatiale (France), DASA (Daimler-Benz Aerospace, Germany) and CASA (Construcciones Aeronauticas SA, Spain). Research, development and production tasks have been distributed among the partners, avoiding any duplication. Aerospatiale is mainly responsible for developing and manufacturing the cockpit of the aircraft and for system integration. DASA develops and manufactures the fuselage, British Aerospace the wings and CASA the tail unit. Final assembly is carried out in Toulouse (France) by Aerospatiale. Unlike production, commercial and decisional activities have not been split between partners. All strategy, marketing, sales and after-sales operations are entrusted to the Airbus Industrie joint venture, which is the only interface with external stakeholders such as customers. To buy an Airbus, or to maintain their fleet, customer airlines could not approach one or other of the partner firms directly, but has to deal with Airbus Industrie. Airbus Industrie, which is a real manufacturing company, defines the alliance's product policy and elaborates the specifications of each new model of aircraft to be launched. Airbus defends the point of view and interests of the alliance as a whole, even against the partner companies themselves when the individual goals of the latter enter into conflict with the collective goals of the alliance.

Figure 4 models the organization of the Airbus Industrie joint venture using the *i** strategic dependency model. Airbus assumes two roles: Airbus Industrie and Airbus Joint Venture.

Airbus Industrie deals with demands from customers, *Customer* depends on it to receive airbus aircrafts or maintenance services. The *Airbus Joint Venture* role ensures the interface for the four partners (*CASA, Aerospatiale, British Aerospace* and *DASA*) with *Airbus Industrie* defining Airbus strategic policy, managing conflicts between the four Airbus partners, defending the interests of the whole alliance and defining new aircrafts specifications. *Airbus Joint Venture* coordinates the four partners ensuring that each of them assumes a specific task in the building of Airbus aircrafts: wings building for *British Aerospace*, tail unit building for *CASA*, cockpit building and aircraft assembling for *Aerospace* and fuselage building for *DASA*. Since Aerospatiale assumes two different tasks, it is modeled as two roles: *Aerospatiale Manufacturing* and *Aerospatiale Assembling*. *Aerospatiale Assembling* depends on each of the four partners to receive the different parts of the planes.

Carsid (Carolo-Sidérurgie) is a joint venture that has recently arisen from the global concentration movement in the steel industry. The alliance, physically located in the steel basin of Charleroi in Belgium, has been formed by the steel companies Duferco (Italy), Usinor (France) – that also partially owns Cockerill-Sambre (Belgium) through the Arcelor group – and Sogepa (Belgium), a public investment company, representing the Walloon Region Government. Usinor has also brought its subsidiary Carlam in the alliance.

Roughly speaking, the aim of a steel manufacturing company like CARSID is to extract iron from the ore and to turn it into semi-finished steel products. Several steps compose the transformation process, each step is generally assumed by a specific metallurgic plant:

Figure 4. The Airbus Industrie Joint Venture

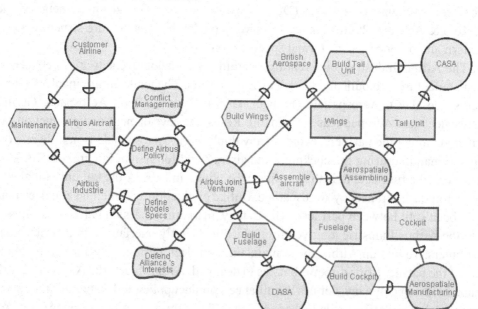

- *Sintering Plant.* Sintering is the preparation of the iron ore for the blast furnace. The minerals are crushed and calibrated to form a sinter charge.
- *Coking Plant.* Coal is distilled (i.e., heated in an air-impoverished environment in order to prevent combustion) to produce coke.
- *Blast Furnace.* Coke is used as a combustion agent and as a reducing agent to removes the oxygen from the sinter charge. The coke and sinter charge are loaded together into the blast furnace to produce cast iron.
- *Steel Making Plant.* Different steps (desulphuration, oxidation, steel adjustment, cooling, . . .) are necessary to turn cast iron into steel slabs and billets. First, elements other that iron are remove to give molten steel. Then supplementary elements (titanium, niobium, vanadium, . . .) are added to make a more robust alloy. Finally, the result – finished steel – is solidified to produce slabs and billets.
- *Rolling Mill.* The manufacture of semi-finished products involves a process known as hot rolling. Hot-rolled products are of two categories: flat (plates, coiled sheets, sheeting, strips, . . .) produced from steel slabs and long (wire, bars, rails, beams, girders, . . .) produced from steel billets.

Figure 5 models the organization of the Carsid joint venture in *i**. Carsid assumes two roles Carsid S.A. ("Société Anonyme" – the english equivalent is "Ltd") and Carsid Joint Venture.

Carsid S. A. is the legal and contractual interface of the joint venture. It handles the sales of *steel semi-finished products* (bars, plates, rails, sheets, etc. but also slabs, billets) and *co-products* (coke that does not meet blast furnace requirements, rich gases from the different plants, godroon, naphtalin, etc.) to external *industries* such as vehicle (automobile, train, boat, . . .) manufacturers, foundries, gas companies, building companies. It is also in charge of the *proper environment policy*, a strategic aspect for steelworks that are polluting plants. Most important, Carsid has been set up with the help of the

Figure 5. The Carsid Joint Venture

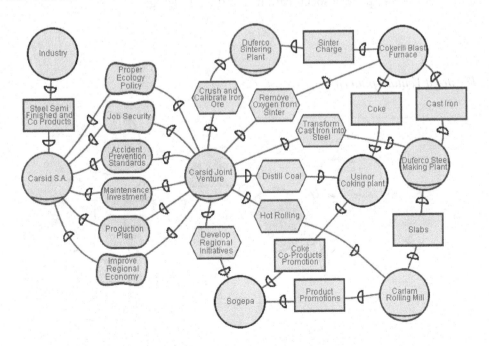

Walloon Region to guarantee *job security* for about 2000 workers in the basin of Charleroi. Indeed, the steel industry in general and the Walloon metallurgical basins in particular are sectors in difficulty with high unemployment rates. As a corrolar, the joint venture is committed to *improve regional economy* and maintain work in the region. Carsid has then been contractually obliged to plan *maintenance investment* (e.g., blast furnace refection, renovation of coke oven batteries, . . .) and develop *production plans* involving regional sub contractors and suppliers. Since steelmaking is a hard and dangerous work sector, Carsid, like any other steelworks, is legally committed to respect, develop and promote *accident prevention standards*.

The *Carsid joint venture* itself coordinates the steel manufacturing process. The sintering phase to *prepare iron ore* is the responsibility of *Duferco Sintering Plant* while *Usinor Coking Plant, distills coal* to turn it onto *coke*. The *sinter charge* and *coke* are used by Cokerill Blast Furnace to produce *cast iron* by *removing oxygen from sinter. Duferco Steel Making Plant transforms cast iron into steel* to produce slabs and billets for *Carlam Rolling Mill* in charge of the *hot rolling* tasks. Carlam (Carolo-Laminoir). *Sogepa*, the public partner, has the responsibility to *develop regional initiative* to promote Carsid activities, particularly in the Walloon Region and in Belgium.

Figure 6 abstracts the joint venture structures explored in the case studies of Figures 4 and 5. The case studies suggest a number of constraints to supplement the basic pattern:

- Partners depend on each other for providing and receiving resources.
- Operation coordination is ensured by the joint manager actor which depends on partners for the accomplishment of these assigned tasks.
- The joint manager actor must assume two roles: a private interface role to coordinate partners of the alliance and a public interface role to take strategic decisions, define policy for the private interface and represents the interests of the whole partnership with respect to external stakeholders.

Part of the Joint Venture pattern specification is in the following:

Figure 6. The Joint Venture pattern

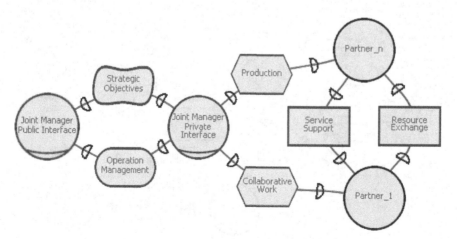

Role JointManagerPrivateInterface Goal
    CoordinatePatterns
Role JointManagerPublicInterface
    Goal TakeStrategicDecision
    SoftGoal RepresentPartnershipInterests
Actor Partner

and the following structural (global) properties must be satisfied:

- $\forall jmpri1, jmpri2 : JointManagerPrivateInterface$
  $(jmpri1 = jmpri2)$
  [Only one instance of the joint manager]

- $\forall p1, p2 : Partner, dep : Dependency (((dep.depender = p1 \land dep.dependee = p2) \lor (dep.depender =$
  $p2 \land dep.dependee = p1)) \rightarrow (dep.type = resource))$
  [Only resource dependencies between partners]

- $\forall jmpri : JointManagerPrivateInterface, p : Partner, dep : Dependency((dep.dependee = p \land dep.depender = jmpri)$
  $\rightarrow dep.type = task)$
  [Only task dependencies between partners and the joint manager, with the joint manager as depender]

- $\forall jmpri : JointManagerPrivateInterface, jmpui : JointManagerPublicInterface, dep : Dependency$
  $((dep.depender = jmpri \land dep.dependee = jmpui)$
  $\rightarrow (dep.type = goal \lor dep.type = softgoal))$
  [Only goal or softgoal dependencies between the joint manager roles]

- $\forall dep : Dependency, p1 : Partner ((dep.depender = p1 \lor dep.dependee = p1) \rightarrow$
  $((\exists p2 : Partner(p1 \neq p2 \land (dep.depender = p2 \lor dep.dependee = p2)) \lor (\exists jmpi : JointManagerPrivateInterface$
  $((dep.depender = jmpi \lor dep.dependee = jmpi))))$
  [Partners only have relationships with other partners or the joint manager private interface]

- $\forall dep : Dependency, jmpi : JointManagerPrivateInterface ((dep.depender = jpmi \lor dep.dependee = jpmi) \rightarrow$
  $((\exists p : Partner((dep.depender = p \lor dep.dependee = p))) \lor (\exists jmpui : JointManagerPublicInterface ((dep.depender = jmpui \lor dep.dependee = jmpui))))$
  [The joint manager private interface only has relationships with the joint manager public interface or partners]

EVALUATION

Patterns can be compared and evaluated with quality attributes (Shaw & Garlan 1996), also called non-functional requirements (Chung, Nixon, Yu & Mylopoulos 2000) For instance, the requirements seem particularly relevant for organizational structures (Do, Faulkner & Kolp 2003, Kolp et al. 2006):

    Predictability (Woods & Barbacci 1999). Actors can have a high degree of autonomy (Wooldridge & Jennings 1995) in the way that they undertake action and communication in their domains. It can be then difficult to predict individual characteristics as part of determining the behavior of the system at large. Generally, predictability is in contrast with the actors capabilities to be adaptive and responsive: actors must be predictable enough to anticipate and plan actions while being responsive and adaptive to unexpected situations.

Security. Actors are often able to identify their own data and knowledge sources and they may undertake additional actions based on these sources (Woods & Barbacci 1999). Strategies for verifying authenticity for these data sources by individual actors are an important concern in the evaluation of overall system quality since, in addition to possibly misleading information acquired by actors, there is the danger of hostile external entities spoofing the system to acquire information accorded to trusted domain actors.

Adaptability. Actors may be required to adapt to modifications in their environment. They may include changes to the component's communication protocol or possibly the dynamic introduction of a new kind of component previously unknown or the manipulations of existing actors.

Generally, adaptability depends on the capabilities of the single actors to learn and predict the changes of the environments in which they act (Weiss 1997), and also their capability to make diagnosis (Horling, Lesser, Vincent, Bazzan & Xuan 1999), that is being able to detect and determine the causes of a fault based on its symptoms. However, successful organization environments tend to balance the degree of reactivity and predictability of the single actors with their capabilities to be adaptive.

Coordinability. Actors are not particularly useful unless they are able to coordinate with other agents. Coordination is generally (Jennings 1996) used to distribute expertise, resources or information among the actors (actors may have different capabilities, specialized knowledge, different sources of information, resources, responsibilities, limitations, charges for services, etc.), solve interdependencies between actors' actions (interdependence occur when goal undertaken by individual actors are related), meet global constraints (when the solution being developed by a group of actors must satisfy certain conditions if is to be deemed successful), and to make the system efficient (even when individuals can function independently, thereby obviating the need for coordination, information discovered by one actor can be of sufficient use to another actor that both actors can solve the problem twice as fast).

Coordination can be realized in two ways:

- **Cooperativity**. Actors must be able to coordinate with other entities to achieve a common purpose or simply their local goals. Cooperation can either be communicative in that the actors communicate (the intentional sending and receiving of signals) with each other in order to cooperate or it can be non-communicative (Doran, Franklin, Jennings & Norman 1997). In the latter case, actors coordinate their cooperative activity by each observing and reacting to the behaviour of the other. In deliberative organizations, actors jointly plan their actions so as to cooperate with each other.
- **Competitivity**. Deliberative negotiating organization (Doran et al. 1997) are like deliberative one, except that they have an added dose of competition. The success of one actors implies the failure of others.

Availability. Actors that offer services to other actors must implicitly or explicitly guard against the interruption of offered services.

Fallibility-Tolerance. A failure of one actor does not necessarily imply a failure of the whole organization. The organization then needs to check the completeness and the accuracy of information and knowledge transactions and workflows. To prevent failure, different actors can have similar or replicated capabilities and refer to more than one actor for a specific behavior.

Modularity (Shehory 1998) increases efficiency of service execution, reduces interaction overhead and usually enables high flexibility. On the other hand, it implies constraints on inter-organization communication.

Aggregability. Some actors are parts of other actors. They surrender to the control of the composite entity. This control results in efficient workflow execution and low interaction overhead, however prevents the organization to benefit from flexibility.

As an illustration, we evaluate the patterns with respect to coordinativity, predictability, fallibility-tolerance and adaptability. The evaluation can be done in a similar way for the other non-functional requirements. Due to the lack of space, we refer the author to the bibliography for the other attributes.

- **The structure-in-5** improves coordinativity among actors by differentiating the data hierarchy -the support actor -from the control hierarchy -supported by the operational core, technostructure, middle agency and strategic apex. The existence of three different levels of abstraction (1 -Operational Core; 2 -Technostructure, Middle Line and Support; 3 -Strategic Apex) addresses the need for managing predictability. Besides, higher levels are more abstract than lower levels: lower levels only involve resources and task dependencies while higher ones propose intentional (goals and soft-goals) relationships. Checks and control mechanisms can be integrated at different levels of abstraction assuming redundancy from different perspectives and increase considerably fallibility-tolerance. Since the structure-in-5 separates data and control hierarchies, integrity of these two hierarchies can also be verified independently. The structure-in-5 separates independently the typical components of an organization, isolating them from each other and allowing then dynamic adaptability. But since it is restricted to no more than 5 major components, more refinement has to take place inside the components.

- The joint venture supports coordinativity in the sense that each partner actor interacts via the joint manager for strategic decisions. Partners indicate their interest, and the joint manager either returns them the strategic information immediately or mediates the request to some other partners. However, since partners are usually heterogeneous, it could be a drawback to define a common interaction background. The central position and role of the joint manager is a means for resolving conflicts and preventing unpredictability. Through its joint manager, the joint-venture proposes a central communication controller. It is less clear how the joint venture pattern addresses fallibility-tolerance, notably reliability. However, exceptions, supervision, and monitoring can improve its overall score with respect to these qualities. Manipulation of partners can be done easily to adapt the structure by registering new ones to the joint manager. However, since partners can also exchange resources directly with each other, existing dependencies should be updated as well. The joint manager cannot be removed due to its central position.

Table 2 summarizes the strengths and weaknesses of the reviewed patterns.

To cope with non-functional requirements and select the pattern for the organizational setting, we go through a means-ends analysis using the non functional requirements (NFRs) framework (Chung et al. 2000). We refine the identified requirements to sub-requirements that are more precise and evaluates alternative organizational patterns against them, as shown in Figure 7. The analysis is intended to make explicit the space of alternatives for fulfilling the top-level requirements. The patterns are represented as operationalized requirements (saying, roughly, "model the organizational setting of the system with the *pyramid, structure-in-5, joint venture, arm's-length* . . . pattern").

Table 2. Strengths and weaknesses of some patterns

	Structure-in-5	Joint-Venture
Coordinativity	++	+
Predictability	+	+
Fallibility-Tolerance	++	+
Adaptability	+	+

The evaluation results in contribution relationships from the patterns to the non-functional requirements, labeled "+", "++", "–", "– –". Design rationale is represented by claims drawn as dashed clouds. They make it possible for domain characteristics (such as priorities) to be considered and properly reflected into the decision making process, e.g., to provide reasons for selecting or rejecting possible solutions (+, –). Exclamation marks (! and !!) are used to mark priority requirements while a check-mark "√" indicates an accepted requirements and a cross " X " labels a denied requirement.

Relationships types (AND, OR, ++, +, –, and – –) between NFRs are formalized to offer a tractable proof procedure. AND/OR relationships corresponds to the classical AND/OR decomposition relationships: if requirement R0 is AND-decomposed (respectively, OR-decomposed) into $R1,R2,...,Rn$ then all (at least one) of the requirements must be satisfied for the requirement R0 to be satisfied. So for instance, in Figure 7, Coordinativity is AND decomposed into Distributivity, Participability, and Commonality. Relationships "+" and "– " model respectively a situation where a requirement contributes positively or negatively towards the satisfaction of another one. For instance, in Figure 7, Joint Venture contributes positively to the satisfaction of Distributivity and negatively to the Reliability. In addition, relationships "++" and "– –" model a situation where the satisfaction of a requirement implies the satisfaction or denial of another goal. In Figure 7, for instance, the satisfaction of Structure-in-5 implies the satisfaction of requirements Reliability and Redundancy.

The analysis for selecting an organizational setting that meets the requirements of the system to build is based on propagation algorithms presented in (Giorgini, Mylopoulos, Nicchiarelli & Sebastiani 2002). Basically, the idea is to assign a set of initial labels for some requirements of the graph, about their satisfiability and deniability, and see how this assignment leads to the labels propagation for other requirements. In particular, we adopt from (Giorgini, Mylopoulos, Nicchiarelli & Sebastiani 2002) both qualitative and a numerical axiomatization for goal (requirements) modeling primitives and label propagation algorithms that are shown to be sound and complete with respect to their respective axiomatization. In the following, a brief description of the qualitative algorithm.

To each requirement R, we associate two variables $Sat(R), Den(R)$ ranging in $\{F, P, N\}$ (full, partial, none) such that $F > P > N$, representing the current evidence of satisfiability and deniability of the requirement R. E.g., $Sat(R_i) >= P$ states there is at least a partial evidence that A_i is satisfiable. Starting from assigning an initial set of input values for $Sat(R_i), Den(R_i)$ to (a subset of) the requirements in the graph, we propagate the values through the propagation rules of Table 3. Propagation rules for AND (respectively OR) relationship are min-value function for satisfiability (max-value function) and max-value function (min-value function) for deniability. A dual table is given for deniability propagation.

The schema of the algorithm is described in Figure 8. *Initial, Current* and *Old* are arrays of pairs $Sat(R_i), Den(R_i)$, one for each R_i of the graph, representing respectively the initial, current and previous labeling status of the graph.

Figure 7. Partial evaluation for organizational patterns

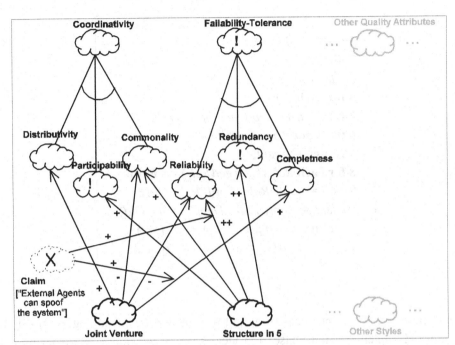

The array *Current* is first initialized to the initial values *Initial* given in input by the user. At each step, for every requirement R_i, $Sat(R_i)$, $Den(R_i)$ is updated by propagating the values of the previous step. This is done until a fixpoint is reached, that is, no updating is mode possible (*Current == Old*). The updating of $Sat(R_i)$, $Den(R_i)$ works as follows. For each relation Rel_i incoming in G_i, the satisfiability and deniability values sat_i and $deni_i$ derived from the old values of the source requirements are computed by applying the rules of Table 3. Then, it is returned the maximum value between those computed and the old values.

A REQUIREMENTS-DRIVEN METHODOLOGY

This research is conducted in the context of the *early requirements* phase of *Tropos* (Giorgini et al. 2004, Giorgini et al. 2005), a software development methodology for building multi-agent systems which is founded on the concepts of actor and goal.

Table 3. Propagation rules for satisfiability in the qualitative framework. A dual table is given for deniability propagation.

	+ $G2 \rightarrow G1$	- $G2 \rightarrow G1$	++ $G2 \rightarrow G1$	-- $G2 \rightarrow G1$
$Sat(G1)$ $Den(G1)$	$min\{ Sat(G2), P \}$ N	$min\{ Sat(G2), P \}$ N	$Sat(G2)$ N	N $Sat(G2)$

Figure 8. Schema of the label propagation algorithm

```
1 Current=Initial;
2 do
3 Old=Current;
4 for each Rᵢ do
5 Current[i] = Update label(i, Old);
6 until not (Current==Old);
7 return Current;
8 for each Relᵢ s.t. target(Relᵢ) == Ri do
9 satij = Apply Rules Sat(i, Relᵢ, Old);
10 denij = Apply Rules Den(Rᵢ, Relᵢ, Old);
11 return max(maxᵢ(satiᵢ), Old[i].sat),
12        max(maxᵢ(deniᵢ), Old[i].den);
```

The *Tropos* methodology adopts ideas from multi-agent systems technologies, mostly to define the detailed design and implementation phase, and ideas from requirements engineering and organizational modeling, where agents/actors and goals have been used heavily for early requirements analysis (Dardenne et al. 1993, Yu 1995). In particular, the *Tropos* project adopts Eric Yu's *i** model which offers actors (agents, roles, or positions), goals, and actor dependencies as primitive concepts for analyzing an application during organizational modeling. The key assumption which distinguishes *Tropos* from other methodologies is that actors and goals are used as fundamental concepts for analysis and design during *all phases of software development*, not just requirements analysis. That means that, in the light of this paper, *Tropos* describes in terms of the same concepts and patterns the organizational environment within which a system will eventually operate, as well as the system itself. *Tropos* spans four phases of software development:

1. Organizational modeling, concerned with the understanding of a problem by studying an organizational setting; the output is an organizational model which includes relevant actors, their goals and dependencies.
2. Requirements analysis, in which the system-to-be is described within its operational environment, along with relevant functions and qualities.
3. Architectural design, in which the system's global architecture is defined in terms of subsystems, interconnected through data, control and dependencies.
4. Detailed design, in which behaviour of each architectural component is defined in further detail.

CONCLUSION

Modelers need to rely on patterns, styles, and idioms, to build their models, whatever the purpose. We argue that, as with other phases of software development, organizational modeling can be facilitated by the adoption of organizational patterns. This paper focuses on two such patterns and studies them in detail, through examples, a formalization using Formal Tropos, and an evaluation with respect to desirable requirements. There have been many proposals for software patterns (e.g., (Kolp, Do & Faulkner 2005)) since the original work on design patterns (Gamma, Helm, Johnson & Vlissides 1995). Some of this work focuses on requirements patterns. For example, (Konrad & Cheng 2002) proposes a set of requirements patterns for embedded software systems. These patterns are represented in UML and cover both structural and behavioral aspects of a requirements specification. Along similar lines, (Fowler 1997) proposes some general patterns in UML. In both cases, the focus is on requirements analysis, and the modeling language used is UML. On a different path, (Gross & Yu 2002) proposes a systematic approach for evaluating design patterns with respect to non-functional requirements (e.g., security, performance, reliability). Our approach differs from this work primarily in the fact that our proposal is founded on ideas from Organization Theory and Strategic Alliances literature. We have already described organizational patterns but to be used for designing multi-agent system architectures (Kolp et al. 2006) and e-business systems (Kolp et al. 2004). Considering real world organizations as a metaphor, systems involving many software actors, such as multi-agent systems could benefit from the same organizational models. In the present paper, we have focused on patterns for modeling organizational settings, rather than software systems and emphasized the need for organizational abstractions to better match the operational environment of the system-to-be during organizational modeling.

REFERENCES

Anton, A. I. (1996). Goal-based requirements analysis. *In Proceedings of the 2nd Int. Conf. On Requirements Analysis, ICRE'96'*, Colorado Spring, USA, pp. 136–144.

Bates, LDV (2006), *Advertising Agency*. At http://www.ldv.be.

Chung, L. K., Nixon, B., Yu, E., & Mylopoulos, J. (2000), *Non-Functional Requirements in Software Engineering*. Kluwer Publishing.

Dardenne, A., van Lamsweerde, A., & Fickas, S. (1993). Goal-directed requirements acquisition. *Science of Computer Programming, 20*(1–2), 3–50.

Do, T. T., Faulkner, S., & Kolp, M. (2003). Organizational multi-agent architectures for information systems. *In Proc. of the 5th Int. Conf. on Enterprise Information Systems, ICEIS'03'*, Angers, France, pp. 89–96.

Doran, J. E., Franklin, S., Jennings N. R., & Norman, T. J. (1997). On cooperation in multi-agent systems. *Knowledge Engineering Review, 12*(3), 309–314.

Dussauge, P., & Garrette, B. (1999). *Cooperative Strategy: Competing Successfully Through Strategic Alliances*. Wiley and Sons.

Fowler, M. (1997), *Analysis Patterns: Reusable Object Models*. Addison-Wesley.

Fuxman, A., Liu, L., Mylopoulos, J., Roveri, M., & Traverso, P. (2004). Specifying and analyzing early requirements in tropos. *Requirements Engineering, 9*(2), 132–150.

Gamma, E., Helm, R., Johnson, J., & Vlissides, J. (1995). *Design Patterns: Elements of Reusable Object-Oriented Software*. Addison-Wesley.

Giorgini, P., Mylopoulos, J., Nicchiarelli, E., & Sebastiani, R. (2002). Reasoning with goal models. *In Proceedings of the 21st International Conference on Conceptual Modeling (ER 2002)*. Tampere, Finland, pp. 167–181.

Giorgini, P., Kolp, M., & Mylopoulos, J. (2002), Multi-agent and software architecture: A comparative case study. *In Proc. of the 3rd International Workshop on Agent Software Engineering, AOSE'02'*, Bologna, Italy, pp. 101–112.

Giorgini, P., Kolp, M., Mylopoulos, J., & Castro, J. (2005). A requirements-driven methodology for agent-oriented software. In B. Henderson-Sellers & P. Giorgini, (Eds.), *Agent Oriented Methodologies*. Idea Group Publishing, pp. 20–46.

Giorgini, P., Kolp, M., Mylopoulos, J., & Pistore ,M. (2004). The tropos methodology. *In* M.-P. G. F. Bergenti & F. Zambonelli, (eds.), *Methodologies and Software Engineering for Agent Systems*. Kluwer, pp. 89–105.

GMT (2006). Gmt consulting group. http://www.gmtgroup.com/.

Gomes-Casseres, B. (1996). *The alliance revolution: the new shape of business rivalry*. Harvard University Press.

Gross, D., & Yu, E. (2002). From non-functional requirements to design through patterns. *Requirements Engineering, 6*(1), 18–36.

Horling, B., Lesser, V., Vincent, R., Bazzan, A., & Xuan, P. (1999). *Diagnosis as an integral part of multi-agent adaptability*. Technical Report UM-CS-1999-003, University of Massachusetts.

Jennings, N. R. (1996). Coordination techniques for distributed artificial intelligence. In G. M. P. O'Hare & N. R. Jennings, (eds.), *Foundations of Distributed Artificial Intelligence*. Wiley, pp. 187–210.

Kolp, M., Giorgini, P., & Mylopoulos, J. (2002*a*). Information systems development through social structures. *In Proc. of the 14th Int. Conf. on Software Engineering and Knowledge Engineering, SEKE'02'*. Ishia, Italy, pp. 183–190.

Kolp, M., Giorgini, P., & Mylopoulos, J. (2002*b*), Organizational multi-agent architecture: A mobile robot example. *In Proc. of the 1st Int. Conf. on Autonomous Agent and Multi Agent Systems, AAMAS'02'*. Bologna, Italy, pp. 94–95.

Kolp, M., Giorgini, P., & Mylopoulos, J. (2003). Organizational patterns for early requirements analysis. *In Proc. of the 15th Int. Conf. on Advanced Information Systems, CAiSE'03'*. Velden, Austria, pp. 617–632.

Kolp, M., Giorgini, P., & Mylopoulos, J. (2006). Multi-agent architectures as organizational structures. *Autonomous Agents and Multi-Agent Systems, 13*(1), 3–25.

Kolp, M., Do, T., & Faulkner, S. (2004). A social-driven design of e-business system. *In Software Engineering for Multi-Agent Systems III, Research Issues and Practical Applications.* Edinburg, UK, pp. 70–84.

Kolp, M., Do, T., & Faulkner, S. (2005). Introspecting agent-oriented design patterns. *In*

S. K. Chang, (ed.), *Handbook of Software Engineering and Knowledge Engineering, 3,* Recent Advances', World Scientific, pp. 151–177.

Konrad, S. & Cheng, B. (2002). Requirements patterns for embedded systems. *In Proc. of the 10th IEEE Joint International Requirements Engineering Conference, RE'02'.* Essen, Germany, pp. 127–136.

Mintzberg, H. (1992). *Structure in fives: Designing effective organizations.* Prentice-Hall.

Morabito, J., Sack, I., & Bhate, A. (1999). *Organization modeling: Innovative architectures for the 21st century.* Prentice Hall.

Scott, W. R. (1998). *Organizations: Rational, natural, and open systems.* Prentice Hall.

Segil, L. (1996). *Intelligent business alliances: How to profit using today's most important strategic tool.* Times Business.

Shaw, M., & Garlan, D. (1996). *Software Architecture: Perspectives on an Emerging Discipline,* Prentice Hall.

Shehory, O. (1998). *Architectural properties of multi-agent systems.* Technical Report CMU-RI-TR-98-28, Carnegie Mellon University.

Wautelet, Y., Kolp, M., & Achbany, Y. (2006). *S-tropos: An iterative spem-centric software project management process.* Technical Report IAG Working paper 06/01, IAGISYS Information Systems Research Unit, Catholic University of Louvain, Belgium. http://www.iag.ucl.ac.be/wp/.

Weiss, G., (ed.) (1997). *Learning in DAI Systems.* Springer Verlag.

Woods, S. G., & Barbacci, M. (1999). *Architectural evaluation of collaborative agent-based systems.* Technical Report SEI-99-TR-025, SEI, Carnegie Mellon University, Pittsburgh, USA.

Wooldridge, M., & Jennings, N. R. (1995). Intelligent agents: Theory and practice. *Knowledge Engineering Review, 2*(10).

Yoshino, M. Y., & Srinivasa Rangan, U. (1995). *Strategic alliances: An entrepreneurial approach to globalization.* Harvard Business School Press.

Yu, E. (1995). Modelling Strategic Relationships for Process Reengineering. PhD thesis, University of Toronto, Department of Computer Science.

Chapter VII
Towards Identifying the Most Important Attributes of ERP Implementations

Piotr Soja
Cracow University of Economics, Poland

Dariusz Put
Cracow University of Economics, Poland

ABSTRACT

Enterprise resource planning (ERP) systems have been implemented in various and diverse organizations. The size of companies, their industry, the environment, and the number of implemented modules are examples of their heterogeneity. In consequence, a single procedure which leads to the success of implementation does not appear to exist. Therefore, there have been many implementations that have failed during, and also after, the implementation process. As a result, a considerable amount of research has been trying to identify issues influencing ultimate project success and also to recognize the best implementation projects. The aim of this work is to identify the most important characteristics of ERP implementation which affect project success. This study builds on data gathered using a questionnaire directed toward people playing leading roles in ERP implementations in a few dozen companies. Twelve attributes were identified and divided into three sets representing: effort, effect, and the synthetic measure of success calculated on the basis of the obtained data. Two agglomeration methods were employed to identify exemplar and anti-exemplar groups and objects. These elements were thoroughly analyzed, which led to identifying the most and the least desired attributes of an ERP implementation project. The findings are discussed and related with the results of prior research. Finally, implications for practitioners and concluding remarks summarise the chapter.

INTRODUCTION

The implementation of an ERP system is a great challenge for a company making the effort of introducing such a system into its organisation. The implementation project is usually connected with sizeable expenses for computer software and hardware, as well as for the implementation services provided by a system solution supplier (e.g., Sarkis & Gunasekaran, 2003). The implementation effects could be very diverse, beginning from the considerable enhancement of enterprise activity and increase of its profitability, to the rejection of the system introduced (e.g., Holland *et al.*, 1999; McNurlin & Sprague, 2002). The companies introducing ERP packages into their organisations differ quite significantly. The implementation endeavours called ERP projects comprise both simple installations of single modules of a system and complex solutions dealing with the installation of many system modules in numerous units of a company (Parr & Shanks, 2000).

Therefore, ERP implementation projects form a very diverse population and in order to compare particular implementations, one has to keep this diversity in mind so that such a comparison is reasonable (e.g., Stensrud & Myrtveit, 2003). Thus, it seems appropriate to group purposefully implementation projects into homogenous collections, where the comparison of projects is feasible and sensible. Only in this situation can we talk about a "model" implementation project and examine the project discovered in order to reveal the most needed characteristics.

Among the methods of projects grouping suggested by prior studies, there are those employing company size (e.g., Bernroider & Koch, 2001; Buonanno *et al.*, 2005; Everdingen *et al.*, 2000; Loh & Koh, 2004) and those relying on a criterion of the number of user licenses (Sedera *et al.*, 2003). While previous research indicates that company size is an important criterion influencing ERP project conditions, the results regarding the benefits achieved are mixed. Some research works suggest that benefits gained by large and small sized organisations seem to be similar (e.g., Shang & Seddon, 2000; Soja, 2005) and other studies advocate that benefits differ by company size (Mabert *et al.*, 2003).

Prior studies also suggest other criteria of ERP projects grouping that might influence implementations' conditions. These criteria include the extent of ERP package modification (Soh & Sia, 2005), implementation scope and duration time (Soja, 2005, 2006). The results imply that the implementations' conditions are diverse depending on project type defined by dividing criteria. Moreover, the project type can have an impact on the effects achieved by a company as a result of ERP implementation. In particular, the project duration seems to have an important influence on achieved results (Soja, 2005).

The multitude of potential factors influencing ERP projects is illustrated by the complex division presented by Parr and Shanks (2000). They suggest the following categories for the division of projects: implementation physical scope (single or multiple site), extent of organisational changes, level of system modification, module implementation strategy, and allocated resources in terms of time and budget. Taking into consideration the above-mentioned criteria of a division, there are a great many implementation types. Therefore, Parr and Shanks distinguish three main categories of ERP implementations: comprehensive, averagely complicated (middle-road) and simple (vanilla).

Overall, it seems that it is hard to find a generally accepted division of ERP projects into groups, which would constitute homogenous collections of similar implementations. Prior studies suggest various criteria of ERP projects grouping and these divisions take into consideration merely the variables defining the efforts made in order to implement a system, but they completely omit the issue of achieved effects. Meanwhile, incorporating the parameters describing implementation results could lead to interesting conclusions.

The goal of this paper is an attempt to discover the most desired attributes of a model ERP implementation project. The article is based on research conducted among a few dozen companies introducing an ERP system into their organisations in Poland. In order to achieve the paper's goal, the statistical methods of element grouping were employed, which allowed us to extract the groups of homogenous projects that were then ordered on the basis of the measure of achieved success. This procedure allowed us to distinguish the projects having the most desirable characteristics, as well as those with the least desirable attributes.

LITERATURE REVIEW

The idea of discovering issues determining the success of enterprise system (ES) implementation projects attracted the attention of a considerable number of researchers. There are a great many research approaches which investigate numerous issues and employ various understandings of project success. The works differ in various aspects, i.e. the employed methodologies and chosen variables. Some scholars examine the actual implementation process, others focus on the post-implementation phase, there are also those who treat ES adoption as a continuous endeavour without a clearly defined end point. The investigated issues vary from technological, through organisational to those connected with people, and from operational to strategic considerations. The following section summarises major findings achieved by prior research connected with the attributes and characteristics of successful ES adoption projects.

Among many issues analysed by researchers, knowledge seems to play a paramount role in enterprise system adoption. In particular, the researchers emphasize the need of adequate knowledge transfer from external consultants to clients in an adopting organisation (Ko *et al.*, 2005). This process should be dealt with by several parties participating in ES adoption: vendors, consultants and IS/IT managers. They should pay attention to improve not only the quality of ERP products, but also user's knowledge and involvement. They should also be aware of the importance of choosing suitable consultants and suppliers (Wu & Wang, 2007). Furthermore, emphasizing the role of knowledge transfer, McGinnis and Huang (2007) introduced the idea of constituting a knowledge-sharing community which may play the crucial role of a platform that can be used to provide a common frame of reference to all ERP activities. The authors also highlight the concept that the actual implementation does not finish the whole adoption endeavour, which should be still monitored and handled after the system rollout. The quality of the actual implementation process influences the course of the post-implementation phase. In particular, Nicolaou (2004) suggests five critical dimensions which affect the whole adoption project, including the post-implementation stage. These issues relate to the review of overall project scope and planning, the review of driving principles for project development, the effectiveness of misfit resolution strategies, the evaluation of attained benefits, and the evaluation of learning.

The enterprise system adoption projects differ greatly as regards the scope of the implementation. In general, the most complicated full-scope and highly-integrated enterprise system adoption projects are perceived as more likely to bring the best benefits for the company. This issue is illustrated by Ranganathan and Brown (2006), who conclude that a company's announcement of ERP adoption positively influences stock market returns. The authors suggest that the greater the project's scope (in terms of number of locations and the extent of introduced functionality) the stronger the influence.

Researchers highlight the need for identifying adequate characteristics of enterprise system in order to achieve its successful adoption. The enumerated features which appear to be the most important encompass system quality (Kositanurit *et al.*, 2006) together with other quality dimensions related to information and service (Chien & Tsaur, 2007), and perceived usefulness of the system (Amoako-Gyampah, 2007). In particular, on the basis of research conducted among 571 respondents and employing Technology Acceptance Model, Amoako-Gyampah (2007) suggests that users' intention to use an ERP might depend more on how useful they perceived the system than on their level of involvement or how easy it will be to use the system. Furthermore, the author advocates that perceived usefulness influences the users' involvement and beliefs concerning the necessity of changes. However, on the other hand, Amoako-Gyampah points out the role of legacy systems and related people's habits and expertise, which may negatively influence their attitudes towards ERP.

Identifying the desired features of the enterprise system is a necessary condition for successful adoption. However, equally important is the appropriate implementation process, during which one of the most crucial issues is to achieve an alignment between the system's capabilities and the company's needs. Sharma and Vyas (2007) emphasize this issue by talking about the synergy between technology and management, which is advocated as an important element influencing the success of ERP adoption.

Enterprise system adoption is inevitably connected with some extent of organisational changes which are carried out in the adopting company. The more radical approach to organisational changes is called business process reengineering (BPR), while the less radical method bears the name of business process improvement (BPI) (Law & Ngai, 2007). Schniederjans and Kim (2003), on the basis of a survey conducted among 115 US electronic manufacturing firms, advocate that business process change should precede the enterprise system implementation. Furthermore, Law and Ngai (2007), drawing for the experience of 96 companies, conclude that during enterprise system adoption firms should undertake business process improvement and ought to have dual focus: operational and strategic. The authors demonstrate that firms which had only operational focus achieved lower performance than those having dual or strategic focus. In short, the discussion above illustrates that enterprise system adoption should be first and foremost an organisational and business project. It should be treated as a business-led endeavour, in contrast to an IT related initiative (e.g., Law & Ngai, 2007; Nicolaou, 2004; Tinham, 2006).

The ES adoption project needs constant monitoring as regards employed resources, both internal and external. As far as internal resources are considered, Peslak (2006), on the basis of the opinions of over 200 top financial executives, advocates that cost and time were found to be major determinants of project success and should be carefully measured and monitored. Further, the author also points out that the use of external consultants for implementation should be carefully controlled since it was found to adversely impact cost performance.

The enterprise system adoption projects form a very diverse group differing in several aspects. This issue is discussed by Stensrud and Myrtveit (2003), who examined 30 ERP projects using Data Envelopment Analysis Variable Returns to Scale (DEA VRS) to measure the productivity of software projects and employed the method to identify outstanding projects of ERP systems that may serve as role models. As a result, they suggest that the average efficiency among investigated projects is approximately 50%. Furthermore, the authors notice that there were significant differences in productivity between projects in various industries. Therefore, one should exhibit caution when benchmarking and comparing projects across industries. The authors suggest that performance assessments should include both productivity and quality indicators, and it should also take into account other external factors such as schedule constraints.

As regards the difficulties with the comparison of different ES adoption projects, the impact of organisational size on ES project conditions was studied by several researchers. The majority of authors defined organisational size taking into consideration the number of employees; other studies understood the size of a company in terms of the level of revenues (Mabert *et al.*, 2003) or defined the size of an ES project as a number of installed licences of the system (Sedera *et al.*, 2003). While investigating ES projects, the scholars employed research approaches based on case studies, interviews and surveys. Their respondents were mainly adopters; however, some studies also enquired system supplier representatives (e.g., Mabert *et al.*, 2003).

The results of prior works illustrate that in the case of small firms, the most important issues comprise available human resources and system fit into company's organisation (Bernroider & Koch, 2001; Buonanno *et al.*, 2005; Mabert *et al.*, 2003; Muscatello *et al.*, 2003; Raymond & Uwizeyemungu, 2007), which result in a shorter implementation time, lower costs, and lack of the need for significant organisational changes (Adam & O'Doherty, 2000; Bernroider & Koch, 2001; Mabert *et al.*, 2003). The paramount significance of human resources in the case of small and medium-size companies is expressed by Sun *et al.* (2005), who claim that a great emphasis during ERP implementation should be placed on people.

It is worth noting that the issues connected with organisational changes are not perceived unambiguously by researchers: some point out the lack of willingness to perform organisational changes in the case of small firms, others claim that small companies are more likely to change their processes to fit the system (Mabert *et al.*, 2003). The cited research works also suggest that benefits realized by small and large companies differ: larger firms achieve greater benefits, with a special emphasis on a financial indicators improvement, while smaller companies accomplish first and foremost the improvement of manufacturing and logistics activities. The idea of limited benefits achieved by small and medium-size companies is reflected in the research of Sun *et al.* (2005), who conclude that as the implementation schedule increases, the cost increases accordingly, while the achievement increases to some point, beyond which there is no significant achievement benefit.

RESEARCH METHODOLOGY

This study is based on exploratory research conducted among enterprises introducing an ERP package into their organisations. A field study was adopted as a general research approach, and a questionnaire was employed as a data-gathering technique (e.g., Boudreau *et al.*, 2001). The research question posed in this study could be expressed as follows: *What are the most desired attributes of an ERP implementation project?*

The research questionnaire was comprised of questions with a mixture of scale, multiple choice and open questions. The purpose of these queries was to provide demographic data and details necessary to assess project conditions and implementation effects. The list of respondent enterprises was prepared on the basis of reports analysing the ERP market in Poland and databases containing companies' address data. The resulting list contains firms that introduced an ERP package into their organisations with a broad scope, estimated on the basis of available data.

The questionnaire was directed toward the people playing leading roles (the project leader, if possible) in the implementation. With the help of the questionnaire, data has been gathered regarding the conditions of implementation projects, efforts incurred, as well as results achieved. The collected data contain various pieces of information regarding both the implementation process and achieved results. Part of the data contains objective items, while the other (subjective) include respondents' individual evaluations. The achieved collection of projects is varied; hence, an attempt to identify the model object, having the most desired attributes which led to the completion of implementation goals, is not an easy task.

The group of objects was characterised by 12 attributes, which were divided into 3 distinct subsets. In the first subset, there were input indicators of an implementation process—let us call them "effort indicators". The second group was comprised of variables relating to the implementation results—called "effect indicators" (see Table 1). The third, one-element subset, contained the calculated variable being a synthetic measure of implementation success, which was calculated on the basis of data gathered from the enterprises (Soja, 2004). In the next stage of the research, this measure was used to establish the hierarchy of the groups.

The success synthetic measure, based on the understanding of success in the information systems domain (e.g., Lyytinen, 1988), employs 5 partial measures: (1) the actual scope of an implementation with respect to the planned implementation, (2) the actual duration with respect to the assumed duration, (3) financial budget with regard to the planned budget, (4) users' level of satisfaction from the system introduced, and (5) the existence and achievement of project goals (Soja, 2006).

In the research conducted, two agglomeration methods were employed: hierarchical Ward's method (e.g., El-Hamdouchi & Willett, 1986), which is the most commonly used agglomerative method employed for forming clusters (Everitt, 1993) and non-hierarchical k-Means method. The aim of Ward's method is to join objects together into ever increasing sizes of clusters using a measure of similarity of distance. K-means, on the other hand, is a simple non-parametric clustering method that minimises the within-cluster variability and maximises the between cluster variability. The k-means method requires that the number of clusters is specified beforehand (National Statistics 2001 area classification, 2001). One possibility for obtaining the number is to run Ward's method and use the outcome as initial configuration for k-means.

Since in the k-Means method a researcher has to arbitrarily provide the number of clusters, the two-phased approach is common in cluster analysis research. In the first stage, the hierarchical method is applied in order to determine a preliminary number of clusters (e.g., Ward's method), and in the second step the actual classification of objects using the k-Means method takes place (e.g., Everitt *et al.*, 2001). This approach was adopted during this research and is illustrated in Figure 1.

Table 1. Implementation effort and effect variables

Effort variables	Effect variables
• Company size measured by number of employees (*Size*)	• Actual duration time of an implementation (*AD*)
• Planned duration time of an implementation (*PD*)	• Measure of financial budget spending with regard to the planned budget (*Bud*)
• Zero-one variable bearing information whether the MRP Explosion module was implemented (*MRP*)	• Implemented scope (*Scope*)
• Number of implemented modules except MRP Explosion (*Mod*)	• User satisfaction indicator (*US*)
	• Level of achievement of project goals (*Goal*)
	• Subjective measure of positive effects of an implementation (*PE*)
	• Subjective measure of negative effects of an implementation (*NE*)

The procedure is aimed at the separation of object groups which are similar to each other but differing to a greater extent from the objects belonging to the remaining groups (e.g., Kaufman & Rousseeuw, 1990). Firstly, the standardization of variables was carried out, which allowed us to remove the excessive influence of variables having a wide range of values from the outcome of the research. In the next step, the Ward's hierarchical grouping method was applied. On the basis of a distance diagram obtained, two decisions were made:

1. Some objects were excluded from further processing. The objects most dissimilar to other items or those forming small, two-element groups, were treated as accidental measurement. Their exclusion allowed us, at the next stage, to receive more homogenous clusters, containing objects the most similar to each other and laying closer to the hypothetical centre of a cluster.
2. The k value was selected for the applied k-Means method. The greater the k, the more the clusters. These clusters tend to be smaller and contain more similar objects. A small k means, on the other hand, fewer groups and more diverse objects within each subset. In order to determine the k value, the distance diagram achieved with the use of Ward's method was employed. After excluding objects dissimilar to other items, the visual analysis of number clusters in the diagram was performed.

During the next stage, the k-Means method was applied. The calculations were performed three times: (1) for effort indicators only, (2) for effect indicators only, and (3) for all eleven indicators of effort and effect together. As a result, the separated groups of similar objects were extracted, together with the distance of each object from the hypothetical centre of a cluster. For each cluster, the average value of success measure was calculated using synthetic success measures evaluated for objects belonging to a particular group, and on the basis of this value, hierarchy of the group was determined. The cluster having the greatest average value of success measures was recognised as containing objects with the

Figure 1. Research model

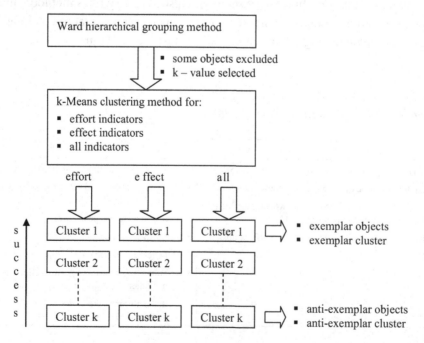

most desired characteristics. Simultaneously, the cluster with the least average value of success measures was recognised as having objects with the least desirable attributes.

Within each of these two extreme groups, one object having the smallest distance from the hypothetical centre of a cluster was distinguished. The object coming from "the best" group was regarded as exemplar (a model implementation), while the object extracted from the group having the least average value of success measure was perceived as anti-exemplar (an anti-model implementation). Since the calculation was performed three times, three exemplars and three anti-exemplars were extracted, characterising the most needed and, also, the least desirable attributes of variables describing efforts, effects as well as efforts and effects jointly (in some cases two objects were distinguished, since both were equidistant from the centre).

The detailed analysis of the attributes of exemplar and anti-exemplar objects, as well as basic statistics calculated for clusters distinguished as the best and the worst, allowed us to draw conclusions as regards to the most needed and the least desired parameters of an implementation project. Thus, the research question can be answered, i.e. the most desired attributed of an ERP project can be elicited. These conclusions could be a suggestion for people responsible for running ERP implementation projects, so that they pay attention to certain facts, which contribute to project success or failure.

RESEARCH DATA

During the research, 223 enterprises were contacted and 68 (30%) answers were obtained from enterprises representing the whole country and various industries. From among the questionnaires received, 64 were accepted for further analysis. All enterprises investigated in this study represent companies which introduced an ERP system into their organisations. The companies classified by industry type are described as shown in Table 2, where the number of companies belonging to particular industries was provided. As can be easily seen, the vast majority of companies comprise of manufacturing enterprises (75%).

For the purpose of analysis, this study adopted the criterion defining enterprise size as the number of employees. The understanding of "small" and "large" companies is derived from the European

Table 2. Companies by industry

Branch / Industry	n	%
Machinery Manufacturing	12	19%
Food Manufacturing	12	19%
Chemical Products Manufacturing	11	17%
Metal Products Manufacturing	8	13%
Trade	6	9%
Electrical Equipment Manufacturing	5	8%
Power Industry	5	8%
Construction	2	3%
Finance	2	3%
Other	1	2%

Table 3. Companies by number of workers

Number of workers	n	%
20 to 50	3	5%
51 to 100	3	5%
101 to 200	10	16%
201 to 300	10	16%
301 to 500	11	17%
501 to 1000	14	21%
over 1000	13	20%

Community's definition for small and medium-sized companies (e.g., The Commission of the European Community, 1996).

The investigated enterprises differ significantly in their size regarding the number of employees, which can be seen in Table 3. It contains, in subsequent rows, the number of companies (column *n*) employing a number of workers which falls within a specified range. The largest group is formed by companies employing from 501 to 1000 workers, and constitutes more than one fifth of the companies researched. The second largest group is made up by the biggest companies employing over 1000 workers, which represents 20% of enterprises evaluated. Certainly, the least numerous group is formed by small companies, employing not more than 100 workers.

The implementation projects researched make up quite a diverse group when project duration time is taken into consideration. Among the companies examined, there are projects lasting not more than a couple of months, as well as implementations with a duration time longer than 3 years. Table 4 illustrates the number of projects as regards planned and actual duration time.

The examined projects are also diverse as regards to the implementation scope defined by the number of installed modules of an ERP system. The following modules were taken into consideration: Finance, Purchasing, Inventory, Sales, Shop Floor Control and MRP Explosion. The last module is treated with special attention, because its implementation is exceptionally difficult and usually requires previous implementation and established use of several key modules of a system. Table 5 contains the number of companies implementing subsequent modules of a system, and Table 6 includes numbers of companies by the total number of modules introduced, with the exception of the module MRP Explosion.

Table 4. Projects by duration time

Duration time	Number of companies by project duration	
	planned	actual
up to 6 months	11	9
6 to 12 months	19	18
1 to 1,5 year	18	14
1,5 to 2 years	4	9
2 to 3 years	9	7
3 and more years	3	7

Table 5. Projects by implemented modules

Module	n	%
Finance	61	95%
Inventory	59	92%
Sales	55	86%
Purchasing	54	84%
Shop Floor Control	37	58%
MRP Explosion	29	45%

Table 6. Projects by number of implemented modules (without MRP Explosion)

Number of modules (without MRP Explosion)	n	%
1	4	6%
2	1	2%
3	6	9%
4	23	36%
5	30	47%

Finally, it seems interesting to present the range of implemented ERP packages, which is visible in Table 7. It contains ERP system names and the number of companies adopting a particular package (column #). As can be seen, the projects researched form a very varied collection, introducing 26 various packages. The world's leader, SAP R/3, is clearly the most popular solution and was introduced in 25% of the projects researched. Then came IFS Applications, then MicroMRP, and MFG/Pro. It is interesting to note that their usage is three times lower than SAP's. Also, it is interesting that the vast

Table 7. Number of ERP packages implemented

#	ERP Package
17	R/3
7	IFS Apps
6	MMRP (MicroMRP)
5	MFG/Pro
3	Baan IV, Exact, Scala
2	Adaptix*, Digitland Enterprise*, MAX (ICL), Movex, Tetra cs/3
1	ASW, Concorde, Fourth Shift, JDEdwards, Komadres*, Manager II*, Mapics, One World, Oracle Apps, Platinum ERA, Prodis, Promis S/4, System 21, Triton

* package developed in Poland

majority of researched companies introduced localised foreign solutions – only 6 firms implemented packages developed and known in Poland (9%).

RESULTS

Pictures 1–3 contain distance diagrams achieved by application of the Ward's method, consecutively using effort variables, effect variables, and all variables. On the basis of diagram analysis, the selected observations were excluded from further processing – they were different in each case. The longer the vertical line on the diagram (see Figure 2-4), the less the observation is similar to the others. Those which were represented by the longest lines or constituted small two-element groups where excluded. Table 8 contains the list of objects together with the ultimate cardinality of the object sets used in further research. This table also includes the k value determined on the basis of the analysis of object clusters classified for further processing.

The outcome of the division of object collection with the help of k-Means method is presented in Table 9. The clusters are ordered from the largest to the smallest average value of success measure. This means that the group having a smaller identifier contains objects with more desired properties from an implementation efficiency point of view. Along with each object identifier, the distance from the hypothetical centre of an appropriate cluster was placed. The table also contains an average success measure determined for each cluster.

Exemplar and Anti-Exemplar Objects' Characteristics

On the basis of the data obtained by employing k-Means method, the exemplar and anti-exemplar objects were chosen. The achieved results were put together in Table 10.

Figure 2. Distance diagram obtained with the use of Ward's method applied for 4 effort variables

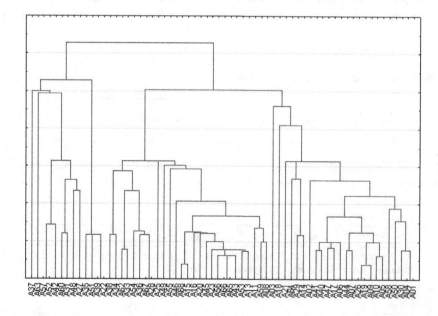

Figure 3. Distance diagram obtained with the use of Ward's method applied for 7 effect variables

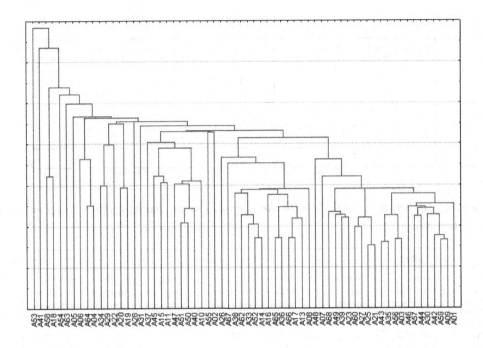

Figure 4. Distance diagram obtained with the use of Ward's method applied for all 11 variables

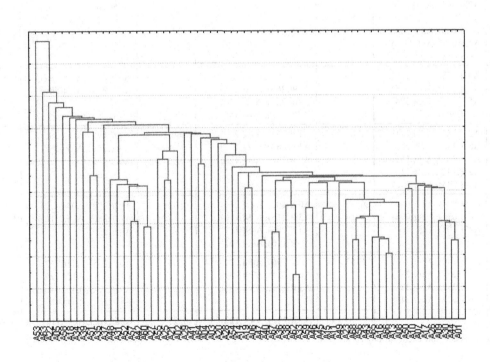

Table 8. List of objects excluded from further processing on the basis of Ward's distance diagram analysis (see Figures 2, 3, 4)

	Measurement for 4 effort variables	Measurement for 7 effect variables	Measurement for all 11 variables
Excluded objects	A37, A63, A25, A49, A03, A18, A21, A02	A53, A41, A58, A18, A54, A63, A05, A28, A31, A37, A55, A02, A26, A67, A48, A07	A53, A63, A22, A05, A58, A18, A34, A39, A51, A35, A37, A29, A41, A03, A20, A28, A54, A14
Number of objects selected for further analysis	56	48	46
Chosen *k* value	7	8	8

Table 9. Hierarchy of clusters obtained with the use of k-Means method, determined on the basis of average success measure

Group ID	For 4 effort variables		For 7 effect variables		For all 11 variables	
	Object identifiers (distance from cluster centre in parentheses)	Average success measure	Object identifiers (distance from cluster centre in parentheses)	Average success measure	Object identifiers (distance from cluster centre in parentheses)	Average success measure
1	A27(.328), **A31(.068)** A42(.395), A48(.542) A52(.277), A57(.277) A60(.082)	.8339	A01(.209), A03(.134) A35(.166), A43(.172) **A44(.122)**, A56(.200) A57(.217)	.8528	A27(.232), A31(.251) A42(.347), A48(.432) A52(.298), A57(.234) **A60(.179)**	.8339
2	A22(.000), A35(.117) A39(.000), A51(.117)	.8013	A08(.255), A14(.127) A33(.079), A38(.281) A52(.133), A62(.166)	.7979	A01(.191), A10(.261) A30(.166), A44(.232) A50(.233)	.8059
3	A08(.216), A11(.247) A13(.104), A15(.158) A16(.250), A20(.126) A23(.065), A43(.096) A45(.219), A53(.142) A56(.038), A59(.294) A65(.038), A66(.038) A68(.158)	.7553	A21(.215), A25(.131) A27(.156), A46(.248) A60(.038)	.7950	A08(.303), A13(.220) A16(.252), A23(.301) A43(.282), A49(.285) A56(.162), A65(.203) A66(.153), A68(.201)	.7983
4	A01(.188), A04(.188) A30(.154), A46(.383) A50(.195), A55(.394) A58(.238)	.7536	A10(.294), A11(.230) A19(.265), A20(.285) A40(.224), A47(.254) A50(.167), A51(.142)	.7853	A07(.243), A09(.187) A17(.219), A26(.206)	.7812
5	A05(.282), A07(.101) A09(.142), A10(.225) A14(.303), A19(.142) A26(.142), A29(.318) A44(.033), A64(.396)	.7402	A13(.161), A16(.255) A17(.086), A36(.174) A65(.168), A66(.123)	.7681	A33(.192), A38(.285) A46(.279), A59(.288) A62(.176)	.7679
6	A06(.094), A17(.059) A40(.071), A41(.093), A47(.108)	.6525	A09(.102), A23(.253) A30(.215), A39(.160) A42(.156), A49(.177) A59(.196), A68(.167)	.7671	A02(.272), A04(.432) A21(.286), A25(.310) A55(.228)	.6902
7	A28(.140), A33(.244) A34(.257), A36(.235) A38(.292), **A54(.133)** A62(.177), A67(.140)	.6363	A04(.396), **A06(.222)** A22(.331), A29(.249) A34(.310), A64(.286)	.6499	A06(.265), **A11(.263)** A15(.284), A19(.279) A40(.274), A45(.449) A47(.304), A64(.463)	.6746
8			**A15(.122), A45(.122)**	.6327	**A36(.112), A67(.112)**	.6023

Note: Exemplar and anti-exemplar objects are bold

The data in Table 10 allow us to draw certain conclusions regarding the characteristics of exemplar and anti-exemplar objects. In all three cases, exemplars are characterised by quite a long implementation time. The whole undertaking is well planned: actual implementation time is similar to the planned one (although in all cases slightly exceeded), and budget is only insignificantly exceeded. Correspondingly, the planned scope of an implementation was 100 percent completed. Predictably, the level of goals achievement is very high (equal to 3 to 5, where 5 is a maximum value), and the satisfaction level of users is estimated at the level of 4 (maximum 5) in all cases. Furthermore, the great advantage of subjective positive effects indicated by respondents over negative effects demonstrates user satisfaction, and, indirectly, project success.

The objects distinguished as anti-exemplars are characterised mainly by a short planned implementation time, together with a relatively large number of implemented modules. In decidedly most cases, the companies did not implement the MRP module; therefore, they could not be treated as the most extensive projects introducing a system in its full functionality. The budget was exceeded, which could suggest that the project was not properly planned. In these companies, the implementation scope was not entirely realised; therefore, the level of goal completion is estimated to be lower than in the case of positive implementations (below 3 except for 2 cases). The users perceive a somewhat small number of positive and negative effects from the implementation, and, what seems to be interesting, their number is similar, and in 3 cases there were more positive effects than negative ones.

It is worth noting that the R/3 package from SAP was implemented in the case of exemplar projects obtained on the basis of both effort variables and effects variables. However, on the other hand, an exemplar project which was distinguished on the basis of all variables introduced the IFS system. The interesting fact is that in the case of effect variables, both exemplar and anti-exemplar projects

Table 10. Exemplar and anti-exemplar objects of implementation process

	ID	Succ	Size	Industry	System	Mod	MRP	PD	AD	Bud	Scope	US	Goal	PE	NE
					Effort variables										
Exemplar	A31	.877	>1000	Transport	R/3	4	0	24	30	110	98	4	5	4	0
Anti-exemplar	A54	.363	>500	Food	Concorde	3	0	5	5	200	25	3	2	1	0
					Effect variables										
Exemplar	A44	.891	>300	Food	R/3	5	1	12	13	110	98	4	5	4	1
Anti-exemplar	A15	.676	>300	Food	R/3	4	0	6	6	110	90	2	2	2	2
	A45	.589	>200	Food	Exact	4	0	1	1	100	80	1	1	1	2
	A06*	.574	>100	Electrical Eq.	MMRP	5	1	8	18	150	90	3	3	2	3
					All variables										
Exemplar	A60	.822	>1000	Power	IFS	3	0	24	30	100	100	4	3	4	1
Anti-exemplar	A36	.635	>500	Chemical	Exact	4	0	3	5	130	80	4	2	3	0
	A67	.569	>500	Chemical	Scala	4	0	6	6	130	80	3	0	3	0
	A11*	.689	>100	Metal	Manager II	5	0	12	12	130	80	3	3	2	2

Symbols: ID – company identifier, Succ – average success measure, Other – as in Table 1

* – chosen from the next to last group, because anti-exemplars A15 and A45 as well as A36 and A67 belonged to two-element groups

implemented the R/3 package, and both were from the food industry. Practically all model objects introduced foreign packages, only one "all variables' anti-exemplar" object implemented Polish software (Manager II). The results show that there is no single ERP package connected with exceptional implementation performance.

Exemplar and Anti-Exemplar Clusters' Characteristics

In order to verify the observations achieved on the basis of exemplar and anti-exemplar object analysis, for all extreme clusters (containing the best and the worst objects), the basic statistics were estimated (average, minimum and maximum) on the basis of attribute values of objects belonging to particular clusters. The results are presented in Table 11, where the clusters having the objects with the most desired characteristics are depicted, and in Table 12 containing data regarding clusters with the worst objects. The first table comprises two parts (instead of three) because the analysis performed with the use of effort variables and all variables yielded the same exemplar groups containing the same objects.

The analysis of data put together in Tables 10 and 11 leads to certain general conclusions regarding the implementation process in those pattern companies. The objects included in exemplar clusters represent various industries, while the anti-exemplar groups mainly comprise companies from chemical (6 companies out of 12) and food (4 companies) industries. Planned duration time is longer in exemplar clusters than in anti-exemplar groups, while the number of implemented modules is similar or even bigger in anti-exemplar groups. This means that, in the case of anti-exemplar projects, the implementation duration time was estimated too optimistically. The implementation scope is near 100 percent among exemplars and is considerably lower among anti-exemplars. User satisfaction is definitely greater in the case of exemplar clusters; furthermore, the apparent advantage of subjective positive effects over negative results was observed. Nevertheless, in the case of anti-exemplar clusters, positive effects were more often recognised than negative outcomes; however, to a lesser extent than among exemplar projects.

Table 11. Average, minimum and maximum values of variables estimated for clusters containing objects with the best parameters

	Succ	Size	Industry	System	Mod	MRP*	PD	AD	Bud	Scope	US	Goal	PE	NE
				Effort variables and all variables. number of objects = 7										
Avg	.834	>1000	4 power	3 IFS	3.6		22.9	24.4	106	97	3.57	3.9	3.3	0.7
Min	.776	>1000	1 machinery 1 food	3 R/3	2	0%	14	14	100	90	3	3	2	0
Max	.877	>1000	1 transport	1 One World	5		36	36	110	100	4	5	4	1
				Effect variables. number of objects = 7										
Avg	.853	>500	2 food	2 MMRP	3.9		9.6	9.6	103	93	3.57	4.4	4	1
Min	.775	>50	1 chemical 1 machinery	2 R/3 1 Exact	1	57%	3	4	100	80	3	4	3	1
Max	.909	>1000	1 metal 1 power	1 IFS	5		18	18	110	100	4	5	5	1

* % of companies in group implementing MRP module

Table 12. Average, minimum and maximum values of variables estimated for clusters containing objects with the worst parameters

	Succ	Size	Industry	System	Mod	MRP*	PD	AD	Bud	Scope	US	Goal	PE	NE
Effort variables. number of objects = 8														
Avg	.636	>500	4 chemical 2 food 1 machinery 1 power	2 Adaptix 1 Concorde 1 Exact 1 IFS 1 Oracle 1 Scala 1 R/3	3.1	0%	8.4	11.4	124	82	3.38	1.8	2.8	0.8
Min	.363	>500			1		3	5	100	25	3	0	1	0
Max	.843	>500			4		14	18	200	100	4	4	4	4
Effect variables. number of objects = 2														
Avg	.633	>200	2 food	1 Exact 1 R/3	4	0%	3.5	3.5	105	85	1.5	1.5	1.5	2
Min	.589	>200			4		1	1	100	80	1	1	1	2
Max	.676	>300			4		6	6	110	90	2	2	2	2
All variables. number of objects = 2														
Avg	.602	>500	2 chemical	1 Exact 1 Scala	4	0%	4.5	5.5	130	80	3.5	1	3	0
Min	.569	>500			4		3	5	130	80	3	0	3	0
Max	.635	>500			4		6	6	130	80	4	2	3	0

* % of companies in group implementing MRP module

The exemplar group extracted on the basis of both effort and all variables consists of the largest companies employing more that 1000 people. This suggests that in the largest enterprises the ERP implementation brings about the best results. However, within this group, on average less that 4 system modules were introduced, and none of the projects installed an MRP Explosion module. Hence, these implementations can not be recognised as the most complicated. On the other hand, the most complicated full-scope implementations make up the majority of projects reaching the best effects, i.e. belonging to the exemplar group obtained on the basis of effect variables. Namely, 57 percent of the "best effects" exemplar implementations introduced an MRP Explosion module and the projects of this kind, on average, installed 4 other modules.

The exemplar groups contain projects implementing only foreign systems, mainly those most popular among implementations researched, i.e. R/3, IFS, and MMRP. Naturally, this can be partially explained by the frequency of their occurrence. However, the presence of well known foreign packages, which have mature software solutions and implementation methodologies rooted in long-term experience, suggests that the system solution reliability is the deciding factor. On the other hand, practically all exemplar packages were present among anti-exemplar projects or clusters. This suggests that the deciding factor is not only the system itself, but rather the way it is implemented into a particular organisation.

DISCUSSION OF FINDINGS

Lessons Learned

On the basis of the research results, the following observations can be made.

- The company type does not seem to be a factor deciding about ERP implementation success. Companies obtaining the best effects as a consequence of ERP implementation are mainly manufacturing enterprises, though it is difficult to indicate any specific industry that they belong to – they represent mainly food, but also metal, machinery, and other industries. However, on the other hand, almost all anti-exemplar companies were manufacturing enterprises.
- The lowest success level in implementing ERP system was reached by companies operating in food and chemical industries, as well as those belonging to the group of medium enterprises as regards to the number of employees. Therefore, the results suggest that company industry can be a significant factor for the project success.
- Implementations tended to be more successful in large enterprises of 1000 or more employees. On the other hand, implementations ended with failure, i.e. achieved a very low level of success measure, mainly among medium sized enterprises of 500 to 1000 employees.
- Exceptionally good effects were achieved by companies implementing an ERP system within its full functionality. Moreover, all anti-exemplar clusters include only partial projects. Thus, the integrating aspect of a system is seen when it embraces the company holistically.

The above-mentioned observations raise the issue of ERP system fit, i.e., whether a particular system solution fits a given company, and, also, whether a company really needs such a complicated system. A good illustration of this is the fact that chemical companies were present among the worst performers. However, none of them used the packages renown for their outstanding performance in chemical industry, like SAP R/3 (Stefanou, 2001).

Furthermore, the results suggest that a particular system solution is not a factor determining project success. It turned out that the particular package was present both among outstanding projects and worst performers. Instead, the way of introducing the system seems to play a vital role for project outcome.

Comparison with Prior Research

This study's findings, claiming that the company type does not seem to be a deciding factor in ERP implementation success, partially support the findings of Ettlie *et al.* (2005). Namely, the authors concluded that the strategic predictors of a successful enterprise system deployment do not depend on a company's industry, which is defined very broadly as the firm's core activity: manufacturing versus service. This definition of a company's industry seems equivalent to the understanding of company type employed by this study. Nonetheless, this research results imply that a company's actual industry plays a crucial role and that practitioners have to pay special attention while implementing ERP system in chemistry and food industries companies. These findings are consistent with the results of Stensrud and Myrtveit (2003), who concluded that there were significant differences in productivity between projects in different industries, and, also, that projects conducted in the process industry were the least efficient.

As regards the role of company size in enterprise system adoption, as was already mentioned, there are mixed results presented by various researchers. This study's findings also contribute to this debate and suggest that results achieved by large companies are greater than by small firms, which supports the findings of some prior research (e.g., Mabert *et al.*, 2003). In particular, they are consistent with the results of Sun *et al.* (2005) and their claims that small and medium sized companies' achievement increases to some point, beyond which there is no significant achievement benefit. Nonetheless, we must bear in mind that there are other research works suggesting that the benefits achieved by small and large companies are similar (e.g., Shang & Seddon, 2000). Also, there are research works suggesting that difficulties experienced during enterprise system adoption generally do not differ across company size (Soja & Paliwoda-Pękosz, 2007). However, on the other hand, Sun *et al.* (2005) emphasize that for small and medium sized companies people related issues are of paramount importance.

The results illustrating the vital need for an adequate amount of time planned for an implementation project are consistent with findings regarding difficulties during enterprise system implementation and impediments to its success. The prior studies recognize mainly organisational problems connected with time over-runs (Kremers & van Dissel, 2000; Soja, 2008; Themistocleous *et al.*, 2001) and the alignment of organisational structure with enterprise system (Kim *et al.*, 2005; Wright & Wright, 2002). This study's results confirm the findings of Peslak (2006) who perceive time and budget as the major determinants of project success. ES adopting companies should use time wisely and adequately plan education and training so that when the system goes live, users are comfortable with it and understand what they are supposed to be doing, how and why. This should also be ongoing long after the implementation is complete (Tinham, 2006).

The second impediment most often recognized by prior research, i.e. the alignment of organisational structure with enterprise system, is illustrated by the issue of system fit and implementation scope, raised by this study outcome. Prior research suggests that the issue of system fit especially concerns smaller companies, who tend to suffer more from the system misfit (e.g., Soja & Paliwoda-Pękosz, 2007). The idea of fit between the system characteristics and the company's needs is highlighted by Peslak (2006), who advocates that modification to enterprise systems should be minimized since they negatively affect both cost and time performance.

The fit between the system features and companies' needs is also connected with the scope of an implementation project perceived in terms of introduced functionality. This study's findings illustrate that better results were achieved by companies which implemented greater scope of ERP modules. These results are consistent with the findings of Ranganathan and Brown (2006) who discovered that the announcements of ERP adoptions created greater abnormal stock market returns for ERP adoptions with greater functional scope than for those with lesser functional scope.

Finally, the outcome of this study is consistent with the research works illustrating that enterprise system implementation should be treated as a business-led project, in contrast to an IT related initiative (Law & Ngai, 2007; Nicolaou, 2004; Tinham, 2006). In particular, this study's results reveal that the best projects demonstrated the greatest number of declared goals and the highest level of goals' achievement. This suggests that the best projects among the sample investigated were treated as business-driven endeavours.

Implications for Practitioners

Taking the research results into consideration, a series of suggestions for practitioners dealing with ERP projects could be formulated. Making use of these suggestions can have a positive influence on an implementation project course and its final outcome.

- The implementation endeavour has to be well planned – the best results were achieved by companies where actual duration time was similar to the planned time; also budget was as planned or only insignificantly exceeded. It is necessary to ensure adequate time for system implementation; haste can be a factor causing problems and having influence on a weak ultimate effect. In the research conducted, projects from the weakest group had an average time planned and usually exceeded this time.
- Special attention should be paid to partial scope implementations; according to the results obtained, such implementations too often end with failure. This could be connected with an underestimation of the importance of a project and the lack of care during execution.
- It is necessary to be careful in the case of implementation projects conducted in the food and chemical industry – the projects in companies representing those two branches most often ended with failure. This also suggests the need for further research on the influence of a company's industry on the project as a whole.
- The implementers should pay special attention to the choice of a particular system solution. They have to ensure the proper fit between a system and the adopting organisation.

CONCLUSION

The study examines the ERP implementations and, using the statistical methods of elements grouping, extracts the projects with best and worst parameters. The core contribution of this paper is that it illustrates the new method of estimating ERP implementation success factors by employing combined methods of clustering analysis. The study's results can be useful for practitioners as they suggest some recommendations towards ERP implementation improvement. These suggestions emphasise the need for the proper organisation of the project and the issue of system fit to the particular business environment. Furthermore, this study should benefit the academic community as it shows an innovative method of investigating the issues influencing ERP project outcome. Further research can enhance the process described by introducing more variables capturing project's effects and efforts, and, also can establish new categories of projects' estimation, such as implementation efficiency. The main limitation of this study is the sample of respondents. Though the number of research participants is quite substantial (64), further analysis should cover more companies and ensure better distribution of projects. Particularly, this suggestion applies to package type, since having comparable samples of adopters of various packages would allow us to better investigate the issues connected with a system fit and its performance. The results also suggest the need for further research on the projects' conditions depending on a company's industry.

REFERENCES

Adam F., & O'Doherty, P. (2000). Lessons from enterprise resource planning implementation in Ireland – towards smaller and shorter ERP projects. *Journal of Information Technology, 15,* 305-316.

Amoako-Gyampah, K. (2007). Perceived Usefulness, User Involvement and Behavioral Intention: an Empirical Study of ERP Implementation. *Computers in Human Behavior, 23,* 1232-1248.

Bernroider, E., & Koch, S. (2001). ERP selection process in midsize and large organizations. Business Process Management Journal, *7*(3), 251-257.

Boudreau, M., Gefen, D., & Straub, D. (2001). Validation in IS Research: A State-of-the-Art Assessment. *MIS Quarterly, 25*(1), 1-16.

Buonanno, G., Faverio, P., Pigni, F., Ravarini, A., Sciuto, D., & Tagliavini, M. (2005). Factors affecting ERP system adoption: A comparative analysis between SMEs and large companies. *Journal of Enterprise Information Management, 18*(4), 384-426.

Chien, S.-W., & Tsaur, S.-M. (2007). Investigating the Success of ERP Systems: Case Studies in Three Taiwanese High-Tech Industries. *Computers in Industry, 58*(8-9), 783-793.

El-Hamdouchi, A., & Willett, E. (1986). Hierarchic Document Classification Using Ward's Clustering Method. In *Proceedings of the 9th International ACM SIGIR Conference on Research and Development in Information Retrieval.* New York: ACM Press, pp. 149-156.

Ettlie, J. E., Perotti, V. J., & Joseph, D. A. (2005). Strategic predictors of successful enterprise system deployment. *International Journal of Operations & Production Management, 25*(10), 953-972.

Everdingen, Y., Hillegersberg, J., & Waarts, E. (2000). ERP adoption by European midsize companies. *Communications of the ACM, 43*(4), 27-31.

Everitt, B. S. (1993). *Cluster Analysis.* Edward Arnold, London.

Everitt, B. S., Landau, S., & Leese, M. (2001). *Cluster Analysis.* London: Edward Arnold

Holland, C., Light, B., & Gibson, N. (1999). A Critical Success Factors Model for Enterprise Resource Planning Implementation. In *Proceedings of the 7th European Conference on Information Systems ECIS,* Copenhagen Business School, Copenhagen, Denmark, 273-287.

Kaufman, L., & Rousseeuw, P. J. (1990). *Finding Groups in Data: An Introduction to Cluster Analysis.* New York: John Wiley & Sons,

Kim, Y., Lee, Z., & Gosain, S. (2005). Impediments to successful ERP implementation process. *Business Process Management Journal, 11*(2), 158-170.

Ko, D. G., Kisrch, L. J., & King, W. R. (2005). Antecedents of Knowledge Transfer from Consultant to Clients in Enterprise System Implementations. *MIS Quarterly,* 29(1), 59-85.

Kositanurit, B., Ngwenyama, O., & Osei-Bryson, K.-M. (2006). An Exploration of Factors that Impact Individual Performance in an ERP Environment: An Analysis Using Multiple Analytical Techniques. *European Journal of Information Systems, 15,* 556-568.

Kremers, M., & van Dissel, H. (2000). ERP System Migrations. *Communications of the ACM, 43*(4), 53-56.

Law, C. C. H., & Ngai, E. W. T. (2007). ERP Systems Adoption: An Exploratory Study of the Organizational Factors and Impacts of ERP Success. *Information & Management, 44*, 418-432.

Loh, T. C., & Koh, S. C. L. (2004). Critical elements for a successful enterprise resource planning implementation in small- and medium-sized enterprises. *International Journal of Production Research, 42*(17), 3433-3455.

Lyytinen, K. (1988). Expectation failure concept and systems analysts view of information systems failures: Results of an exploratory study. *Information and Management, 14*(1), 45-56.

Mabert, V. A., Soni, A., & Venkataramanan, M. A. (2003). The impact of organization size on enterprise resource planning (ERP) implementations in the US manufacturing sector. *International Journal of Management Science, 31*, 235-246.

McGinnis, T. C., & Huang, Z. (2007). Rethinking ERP Success: A New Perspective from Knowledge Management and Continuous Improvement. *Information and Management, 44*(7), 626-634.

McNurlin, B. C., & Sprague, R. H. Jr. (2002). *Information Systems Management in Practice*. 5th edition, Upper Saddle River.

Muscatello, J. R., Small, M. H., & Chen I. J. (2003). Implementing ERP in small and midsize manufacturing firms. *International Journal of Operations and Production Management, 23*, 850–871.

National Statistics 2001 area classification (2001). *Area classification for statistical wards*. http://www.statistics.gov.uk/about/methodology_by_theme/area_classification/wards/downloads/area_classification_for_statistical_wards_methods.pdf, retrieved 2006-01-20.

Nicolaou, A. I. (2004). ERP Systems Implementation: Drivers of Post-Implementation Success, *Decision Support in an Uncertain and Complex World, The IFIP TC8/WG8.3 International Conference*, 589-597.

Parr, A., & Shanks, G. (2000). A Taxonomy of ERP Implementation Approaches. In *Proceedings of the 33rd Hawaii International Conference on System Sciences HICSS*, Maui, Hawaii, USA, 2424-2433.

Peslak, A. R. (2006). Enterprise Resource Planning Success. An Exploratory Study of the Financial Executive Perspective. *Industrial Management & Data Systems, 106*(9), 1288-1303.

Ranganathan, C., Brown, C. V. (2006). ERP Investments and the Market Value of Firms. *Information Systems Research, 17*(2), 145-161.

Raymond, L., & Uwizeyemungu, S. (2007). A profile of ERP adoption in manufacturing SMEs. *Journal of Enterprise Information Management*, 20 (4), 487-502.

Sarkis, J., & Gunasekaran, A. (2003). Enterprise resource planning – modeling and analysis, *European Journal of Operational Research*, 146, 229-232.

Schniederjans, M. J., & Kim, G.C. (2003). Implementing Enterprise Resource Planning Systems with Total Quality Control and Business Process Reengineering, *International Journal of Operations & Production Management, 23*(4), 418-429.

Sedera, D., Gable, G., & Chan, T. (2003). ERP Success: Does Organization Size Matter? In *Proceedings of the Pacific Asia Conference on Information Systems (PACIS)*, 10–13 July, Adelaide, South Australia, 1075-1088.

Shang, S., & Seddon, P.B. (2000). A Comprehensive Framework for Classifying Benefits of ERP Systems. In *Proceedings of the 6th Americas Conference on Information Systems*, Long Beach, CA, USA, 1005-1014.

Sharma, A., & Vyas P. (2007). DSS (Decision Support Systems) in Indian Organised Retail Sector, *Indian Institute Of Management*.

Soh, C. & Sia, S.K. (2005). The challenges of implementing "vanilla" version of enterprise systems. *MIS Quarterly Executive, 4*(3), 373-384.

Soja, P. (2004). Success Factors in ERP Systems Implementations. Result of research on the Polish ERP market. In *Proceedings of the 10th Americas Conference on Information Systems AMCIS*, New York, USA, 3914-3922.

Soja, P. (2005). The Impact of ERP Implementation on the Enterprise – an Empirical Study. In *Proceedings of the 8th International Conference on Business Information Systems*, Poznan, Poland, 389-402.

Soja, P. (2006). Success factors in ERP systems implementations: lessons from practice. *Journal of Enterprise Information Management, 19*(4), 418-433.

Soja, P. (2008). Difficulties in Enterprise System Implementation in Emerging Economies: Insights from an Exploratory Field Study in Poland. *Information Technology for Development. Special Issue on Information Technology Investments in Emerging Economies, 14*(1), 31-51.

Soja, P., & Paliwoda-Pękosz, G. (2007). Towards the Causal Structure of Problems in Enterprise System Adoption. In *Proceedings of the 13th Americas Conference on Information Systems,* Keystone/Colorado, USA.

Stefanou, C. J. (2001). A framework for the ex-ante evaluation of ERP software. *European Journal of Information Systems, 10*(4), 204-215.

Stensrud, E., & Myrtveit, I. (2003). Identifying High Performance ERP Projects. *IEEE Transactions on Software Engineering, 29*(5), 398-416.

Sun, A. Y. T., Yazdani, A., & Overend, J. D. (2005). Achievement Assessment for Enterprise Resource Planning (ERP) System Implementations Based on Critical Success Factors (CSFs). *International Journal of Production Economics, 98*, 189-203.

The Commission of the European Community (1996). (96/280/EC) Commission recommendation of 3 April 1996 concerning the definition of small and medium-sized enterprises. In *Official Journal* No. L 107 30/04/1996, pp.4-9.

Themistocleous, M., Irani, Z., O'Keefe R. M., & Paul, R. (2001). ERP Problems and Application Integration Issues: An Empirical Survey. In *Proceedings of the 34th Hawaii International Conference on System Sciences*.

Tinham B. (2006). Your Guide to Choosing and Implementing ERP. *Manufacturing Computer Solutions*.

Wright, S., & Wright, A. M. (2002). Information System Assurance for Enterprise Resource Planning Systems: Unique Risk Considerations. *Journal of Information Systems, 16* Supplement, 99-113.

Wu, J.-H., & Wang, Y.-M. (2007). Measuring ERP Success: The Key-Users' Viewpoint of the ERP to Produce a Viable IS in the Organization. *Computers in Human Behavior, 23*, 1582-1596.

Chapter VIII
A Voice–Enabled Pervasive Web System with Self–Optimization Capability for Supporting Enterprise Applications

Shuchih Ernest Chang
National Chung Hsing University, Taiwan

ABSTRACT

Other than providing Web services through popular Web browser interfaces, pervasive computing may offer new ways of accessing Internet applications by utilizing various modes of interfaces to interact with their end-users, and its technology could involve new ways of interfacing with various types of gateways to back-end servers from any device, anytime, and anywhere. In this chapter, mobile phone was used as the pervasive device for accessing an Internet application prototype, a voice-enabled Web system (VWS), through voice user interface technology. Today's Web sites are intricate but not intelligent, so finding an efficient method to assist user searching is particularly important. One of these efficient methods is to construct an adaptive Web site. This chapter shows that multimodal user-interface pages can be generated by using XSLT stylesheet which transforms XML documents into various formats including XHTML, WML, and VoiceXML. It also describes how VWS was designed to provide an adaptive voice interface using an Apache Web server, a voice server, a Java servlet engine, and a genetic algorithm based voice Web restructuring mechanism.

INTRODUCTION

Mobile phone and Internet brought us to a new era by offering a new way for person to person communication and facilitating companies and their customers in conducting business through electronic commerce (Gulliver, Serif & Ghinea, 2004; Toye, Sharp, Madhavapeddy & Scott, 2005; Roussos, Marsh & Maglavera, 2005). Because of the pervasive nature of empowering people to use it anywhere and anytime, mobile phone is becoming one of the most pervasive devices in the world (Chang & Chen, 2005; Ballagas, Borchers, Rohs & Sheridan, 2006). With the rapid spread of mobile phone devices and the convergence of the phone and the personal digital assistant (PDA), there is an increasing demand for a multimodal platform that combines the modalities of various interface devices to reach a greater population of users. While there is a growing demand for technologies that will allow users to connect to the Internet from anywhere through devices that are not suitable for the use of traditional keyboard, mouse, and monitor (Zhai, Kristensson & Smith, 2005), the constraints of a typical mobile device, such as small screen size, slow speed, and inconvenient keyboard, make it cumbersome to access lengthy textual information (Anerousis & Panagos, 2002). In Taiwan, the penetration rate of mobile phone (104.6%)[1] is much higher than the penetration rates of other major telecom services, including local telephone: 58.2%, Internet: 71.3%, and broadband Internet: 68.7% (Institute for Information Industry, 2007). However, the same survey also shows that the utilization rate of accessing Internet from wireless devices is relatively low, with a penetration rate slightly lower than 50%, mainly because the text-based interaction between mobile devices and Web sites is very limited. However, voice interface does not have these limitations, because voice interaction could escape the physical limitations on keypads and displays as mobile devices become ever smaller and it is much easier to say a few words than it is to thumb them in on a keypad where multiple key presses may be needed for entering each letter or character (Rebman, Aiken & Cegielski, 2003). Using voice as a medium to operate mobile devices also enables user's hands to engage in some other activities without losing the ability to browse the Internet through voice commands (Feng, Sears & Karat, 2006).

According to a study from Telecom Trends International, the number of mobile commerce users worldwide will grow from 94.9 million in 2003 to 1.67 billion in 2008, and the global revenues generated from mobile commerce are expected to expand from $6.86 billion in 2003 to $554.37 billion in 2008 (de Grimaldo, 2004). A report from ZDNetAsia states that more than half of 3G traffic would be voice and voice is still the platform on which our business is run (Tan, 2005). A study reported by the Kelsey Group claims that expenditures for speech-related services worldwide are expected to reach $41 billion by 2005 (The Kelsey Group, 2001). This report also estimates a 60-65% average annual growth rate for voice services globally by 2005, with the U.S. market expected to be 20-25% of this total. A recent example to the continuation of this trend can be illustrated by an outstanding growth (350 percent increase in quarterly revenue) of speech self-service marketplace reported by Voxify, Inc. (Market Wire, 2006). It is believed that the demand for mobile commerce has created a market for voice-enabled applications accessible by mobile phone.

Traditionally, Interactive Voice Response (IVR) systems are based on proprietary hardware and software technology, with development and deployment tightly integrated on the same hardware platform (Turner, 2004). This has resulted in high development costs. Non-portable proprietary software cannot be deployed on different platforms and it is also inherently difficult to upgrade or modify (Dettmer, 2003). A multi-modal language is needed to support human-computer dialogs via spoken input and audio output. As an optimum solution, VoiceXML (Voice eXtensible Markup Language), a markup language for creating voice-user interfaces, bridges the gap between the Web and the speech world by utilizing speech and telephone touchtone recognition for input and prerecorded audio and text-to-speech synthesis (TTS) for output (Larson, 2003). It is based on the World Wide Web Consortium's (W3C's) eXtensible Markup Language (XML) and leverages the Web paradigm for application development and deployment. By having a common language, application developers, platform vendors, and tool providers can all benefit from code portability and reuse. Furthermore, to reduce the cost of building and delivery of new capabilities to telephone customers, providing voice access to Web-based applications is an attractive option. VoiceXML makes it possible for companies to write shared business logic once and focus their resources on developing only the specific user interface for each device they support.

Due to the above mentioned facts and analyses, a voice-enabled web system (VWS), utilizing the voice user interface technology, was designed and implemented through our project conducted in Taiwan. Voice mobile phone was chosen as the pervasive device for accessing our Internet application prototype, a VWS-based service, for two reasons. Firstly, as mentioned earlier the penetration rate of mobile phone is much higher than the rates of other major telecom services, and mobile phone is associated tightly with people's daily life. Secondly, the use of speech for input and output is inherent in the minds of mobile phone users. The system implemented in this research has several advantages over systems using other mobile devices such as Palm PDA, BlackBerry, and Pocket PC. For example, VWS users can obtain information through voice instead of looking at the monitor, and VWS eliminates the requirement of keyboard or mouse through the use of voice user interface.

Voice channels which differ from the Web have some limitations. For instance, the greatest limitation is that voice channels only support one type of access, acoustic, from a phone. Tomorrow's voice Web sites will serve up voice user interfaces (VUIs) alongside the graphical user interfaces (GUIs) they serve up today (Teo & Pok, 2003). The primary objective for VUIs must be creating a positive experience for the users. In addition, getting responses promptly is also an important concern for users. A voice Web site may have hundreds of pages. When users visit the pages by a phone, they only depend on the voice to navigate the site. Users must wait for the voice menus by sequences, so they spend relatively longer time using the voice channel than a Web browser in waiting for and/or selecting their desired choices. Unduly designed VUIs will be inefficient and fail to serve users' needs for promptness. It not only causes users' dissatisfaction, but also introduces unnecessary inefficiency and redundancy to the system (especially for the voice recognition and synthesis components). Thus, it is necessary to design a voice user interface optimization mechanism in the voice-enabled Web system (VWS) application. The proposed VWS system would apply genetic algorithms (GAs) to find a reasonably good arrangement of the site map in a voice Web site, so the restructured site map will make users' voice browsing experience more responsive. This GA-based VUI optimization mechanism was implemented as a software application so that it can be integrated with the VWS system.

The subsequent sections of this chapter are organized as follows. Section 2 provides the backgrounds on voice-enabled Web system, adaptive Web site, and genetic algorithm. Section 3 describes the architecture of the VWS system and how to generate multimodal user-interface pages by using XSLT stylesheet. To illustrate how the GA-based VUI optimization process works, the experiment method together with two simple examples was presented in Section 4. Section 5 covers more comprehensive experiment results, and Section 6 concludes this chapter after the discussions.

LITERATURE REVIEW

Voice-Enabled Web System

A voice-enabled Web system is a system which provides users a voice channel, such as telephone, to access Web applications. With voice-enabled Web systems, firms can provide desirable voice-based Internet services, such as online customer service, online transaction service, and self-served service, through both the conventional browser interface and the new voice interface. Our voice-enabled Web system combines XML based mark-up languages, automatic speech recognition (ASR), text to speech (TTS), and Web technologies. We use the emerging standard markup language, VoiceXML, which defines a common format to allow people to access Web content via any phone (Larson, 2003). The VoiceXML uses XML tags to represent call flows and dialogs. The development of the VoiceXML standard by AT&T, IBM, Lucent Technologies, and Motorola has led to a proliferation in recent years of voice-enabled Web systems. By using this standard Web-based language, data then can be easily exchanged in voice-enabled Web systems.

Voice-enabled Web technology is being deployed in a broad range of industries such as banking and retailing. With the launch of the first "voice portal", which provides telephone users with speech-enabled access (via the nature language interface) to Web-based information and applications, the voice-enabled Web technology caught people's attention. It is speculated that various industries will soon adopt it to develop suitable Web system to serve their own business purposes. Internet portal companies such as AOL and Yahoo and other companies like Tellme Networks, Hey Anita, and Internet Speech have been developing voice portals for providing several services. Generally speaking, a voice portal, like an Internet portal, is a single place where content from a number of sources is aggregated. For example, information services such as traffic reports, weather reports, stock quotes, bill inquiry/pay, restaurant/hotel recommendations, department store promotion information, cinema reviews, news, and e-mail can be accessed via voice portal. Recently, an emerging term called "v-commerce" has been used to describe the technology and its applications related to the users' activities of navigating voice portals with voice commands. V-commerce examples include the use of speech technology over the telephone in commercial applications such as buying cinema/airline tickets, banking, account transferring, stock trading, and purchasing from mail-order companies (Goose, Newman, Schmidt & Hue, 2000; Yamazaki, Iwamida & Watanabe, 2004).

Adaptive Web Site

Web users often get lost on the Internet due to its complicated structure and the information overload problem. One of the most important functions of a Web site is to assist users in searching information by using various Web intelligence methods (Li & Zhong, 2004). One of those efficient methods is to construct an adaptive Web site. Adaptive Web sites are sites that automatically improve their organization and presentation by learning from visitor access patterns (Kohrs & Merialdo, 2001).

Joachims, Freitag, and Mitchell (1997) initiated an adaptive Web project called WebWatcher, which is a "tour guide" agent for the World Wide Web, and its strategy for giving advice is learned from feedback from earlier tours. WebWatcher uses the paths of people who indicated success as examples of successful navigations. It groups people based on their stated interests rather than customizing to each individual. Perkowitz and Etzioni (2000) focused on the problem of index page synthesis. An index page is a page consisting of links to a set of pages that cover a particular topic at a site. Their goal is to transform the Web site into a better one – a new index page. They assume these groups of pages represent coherent topics in users' minds, and analyze the Website's access logs to find groups of pages that often occur together in user visits. Su, Yang, Zhang, Xu, Hu, and Ma (2002) designed an adaptive Web interface based on Web log analysis and Web page clustering. They also tried to improve users' performance by introducing index pages that minimize overall user browsing costs. Smith and Ng (2003) presented LOGSOM, a prototype system that organizes Web pages on a self-organizing map (SOM) according to user navigation patterns. They clustered the Web pages according to the users' navigation behaviors, rather than according to the Web content. Instead of organizing the Web pages according to the words contained in the Web pages, they kept track of the interest of the Web users, and organized the Web pages according to their interest. In this way, the SOM provided by LOGSOM can be updated regularly to reflect the current interest of the Web users. In addition, for the purpose of personalization or recommendation, many different kinds of adaptive Web sites have been explored recently. A simple but common example is that some Web sites allow users to personalize the sites for themselves such as customizing the lists of favorite links. Some other more complicated approaches may use various data mining, Web mining, content-based filtering, collaborate filtering, and other techniques to offer users personalized or adapted information and services (Chang, Changchien & Huang, 2006; Changchien, Lee & Hsu, 2004; Wang & Shao, 2004).

As mentioned in the previous subsection, a voice-enabled Web system provides landline and mobile telephone users a new channel for voice-based Web browsing, which allows users to navigate and traverse the structure of the Web site entirely by voice. In terms of voice browsing or navigating the VUI structure of voice-enabled Web sites, it would be more desirable to reduce users' navigation time, mainly because of the one dimensional nature of the voice channel which causes the users to spend much time in sequentially listening to various choices. In our research, a simple genetic algorithm (SGA) based voice user interface optimization mechanism, which will be described later in this chapter, was designed to realize an adaptive voice-enabled Web site by automatically adapting the site map (i.e., the Web site structure). The process of our voice user interface optimization is illustrated in Figure 1. According to the needs specified in a time-based or event-driven configuration file, VWS can extract its site map and invoke the VUI optimization mechanism to derive a restructured site map, which is used to substitute the original one for providing users a better browsing experience with a more efficient and more effective voice navigation paths.

Genetic Algorithm: Basic Concepts

Genetic algorithms (GAs), which use randomized search and optimization techniques, are designed to simulate processes in natural system necessary for evolution, that is, the solutions to a problem solved

Figure 1. The process of voice user interface optimization

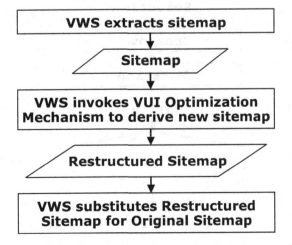

by GAs are derived through an evolutionary process, which is based on a mechanism of natural selection to search for an improved solution that optimizes a given fitness function. As shown in Figure 2, GA begins with a set of randomly created solutions called population. Pairs of solutions are taken and used to produce offspring of next generation, that is, a new population. This is motivated by a hope, that the new population will be better than the old one. In the selection stage, parent solutions (which are selected to produce offspring solutions) are selected according to their fitness – the more suitable they are the more chances they get to reproduce. Crossover operates on selected parent solutions to create new (offspring) solutions. The simplest way to do that is to choose randomly some crossover point and copy everything before this point from the first parent and then copy everything after the crossover point from the other parent. Specific crossover made for a specific problem can improve performance of the genetic algorithm. Mutation, which randomly modifies the genetic structures of some members of each new generation, is intended to prevent falling of all solutions in the population into a local optimum of the solved problem. Culling, which takes place each time before going to the next generation, is for updating the population. This iteration/revolution process is repeated until an acceptable or optimum solution is found or until some fixed time limit.

In contrast to the above described simple genetic algorithms (SGAs) that rely on the concept of biological evolution, the hybrid genetic algorithms (HGAs), which are based on ideas evolution (Misevicius, 2003; Moscato & Cotta, 2003), apply an improvement procedure to each offspring or mutated individual. Instead of random solutions, HGAs operate with the improved solutions. This leads to a more effective algorithm while comparing it with an SGA. HGAs may allow to escape from a local optimization and to find better solutions. SGA is currently used in our initial implementation of the VUI optimization mechanism, and for future research we plan to experiment on various HGA improving approaches,

Figure 2. The procedure of a genetic algorithm

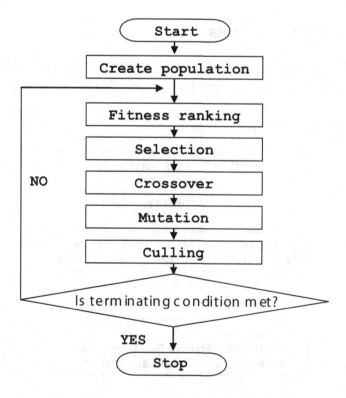

such as *ruin and recreate* (Misevicius, 2003), *tabu search* (Moscato & Cotta, 2003), *branch and bound* (Al-Khayyal & Sherali, 2000), and *simulated annealing* (Kirkpatrick, Gelatt & Vecchi, 1983).

SYSTEM ARCHITECTURE

Our VWS prototype was implemented using open technologies including eXtensible HyperText Markup Language (XHTML), XML, eXtensible Stylesheet Language for Transformations (XSLT), VoiceXML, MySQL database, Apache Web server, Apache Tomcat application server, and various Java APIs, such as: Java Servlet, Java Server Page (JSP), Java Database Connection (JDBC), Java Cryptography Extension (JCE), and others. Not only is Java suggested as the "write once, run everywhere" computer language in writing application for various smart phones (Chang & Chen, 2005), but Java's modular nature allows it to expand and develop solutions for new computational problems. It has been evolving from a popular client applet language to a cross platform GUI builder and an application server platform. This same modular nature now allows Java to drive wireless and multimodal applications. Java 2 Platform, Micro Edition (J2ME) is designed for nonbrowser-based devices and it is not exactly a subset of Java 2 Platform, Standard Edition (J2SE) (Sun Microsystems, 2004). J2ME keeps some of the J2SE core library application programming interfaces (APIs), but substitutes others with lightweight components through the javax.microedition package. As shown in Figure 3, a multimodal application architecture, which offers new ways of accessing web applications from any device at any location, was adopted in this study by utilizing various modes of interfaces to interact with end users (Chang and Minkin, 2006).

In addition to the conventional browser interface and the targeted voice interface, our multimodal web system approach also provides the ability to access web-based information and applications from multiple methods or channels such as a PDA, smart phone, Pocket PC, or BlackBerry. This multimodal

Figure 3. The multimodal approach for supporting voice-enabled web applications

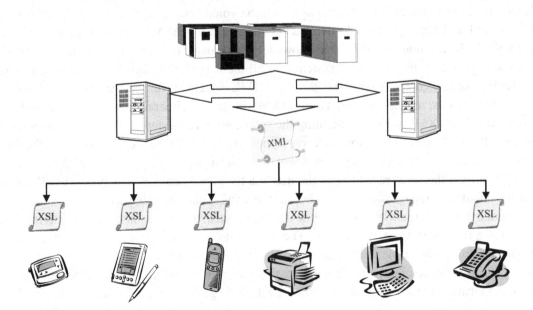

approach facilitates the sharing of the business logic and back-end processes in a multiple-tiered application environment, and thus freeing up the time and resources for concentrating on the design and implementation specifics of user interface for each device. Multimodal applications may use both wireless and voice devices. It is obvious from the name of the platform that J2ME supports wireless technologies such as PDA or smart phone. Many J2ME-enabled devices will support a voice channel, and as such may also be used to interact with VoiceXML-based services over the phone voice connection.

To build the VWS prototype, a voice server was used as the platform that enabled the creation of voice applications through industry standards, including XML, VoiceXML and Java (Burke, 2001; Rodriguez, Ho, Kempny, Pedreschi, & Richards, 2002). XML facilitates the concept of application integration and data sharing, and enables the exchange of self-describing information elements between computers. In addition to combining XML based mark-up languages, automatic speech recognition (ASR), text to speech (TTS), and Web technologies, our VWS also uses the emerging standard markup language, VoiceXML, which defines a common format to allow people to access Web content via any phone (Chang & Minkin, 2006). There were two options considered in our study for enabling telephony hardware to integrate with the voice server: Intel Dialogic-based voice server system and Cisco telephony platform. The voice server on the Dialogic platform utilizes a specialized telephony card manufactured by Dialogic, which is connected directly to the telephony interface. Calls are then managed by the Dialogic platform to pass incoming calls to the Voice Server application. The other one uses the Cisco telephony platform. The voice server facilitates the deployment of voice applications by interfacing with various voice standards (Rodriguez et al., 2002). The voice server for Cisco utilizes the Voice over IP (VoIP) protocol. Normally the voice server would be configured to work with a Cisco voice router that has a telephony interface connection. When a phone call is made, the voice router will convert the call to VoIP and then redirect the voice packets to the voice server. The system architecture is illustrated in Figure 4.

When Voice Server starts, VoiceXML browsers start up and wait for calls. Each VoiceXML browser works for one telephone call. When a user places a call to a designated phone number, a computer on the voice site (i.e. the voice server) answers the call and retrieves the initial VoiceXML script from a VoiceXML content server, which can be a Web server located anywhere on the Web. An interpreter on the voice site parses and executes the script by playing prompts, capturing responses, and passing the responses to a speech recognition engine on the voice system. Just as a Web browser renders HyperText Markup Language (HTML) documents visually, a VoiceXML interpreter on the voice site renders VoiceXML documents audibly and allows telephone users to access services that are typically available to Web users. Once the voice system gets all the necessary information from the caller, the interpreter translates them into a request to the VoiceXML content server, i.e. the web server. When the web server receives the request, it returns a VoiceXML page with either a canned response or dynamically generated VoiceXML scripts, containing the information requested by the caller. Responses are passed from the Web server to the voice site via HyperText Transfer Protocol (HTTP). Finally, the text to speech (TTS) engine, which is a key component of the voice server, converts VoiceXML scripts into speech and delivers the voice responses to the user via telephone channel. The process will continue, simulating a natural language conversation between the caller and the voice server.

We decided to use Java servlets to access the database, and used Java Database Connectivity (JDBC) to connect to a relational database, MySQL. The driver that we used was mysql-connector-java-3.1.1-alpha-bin.jar, which is available for free download at http://dev.mysql.com. Java servlets were used for validating login, constructing user request, processing the request from end user, and generating output results in the form of an XML document (Burke, 2001; Rodriguez et al., 2002). Afterwards, XSLT was

Figure 4. The architecture of the VWS system

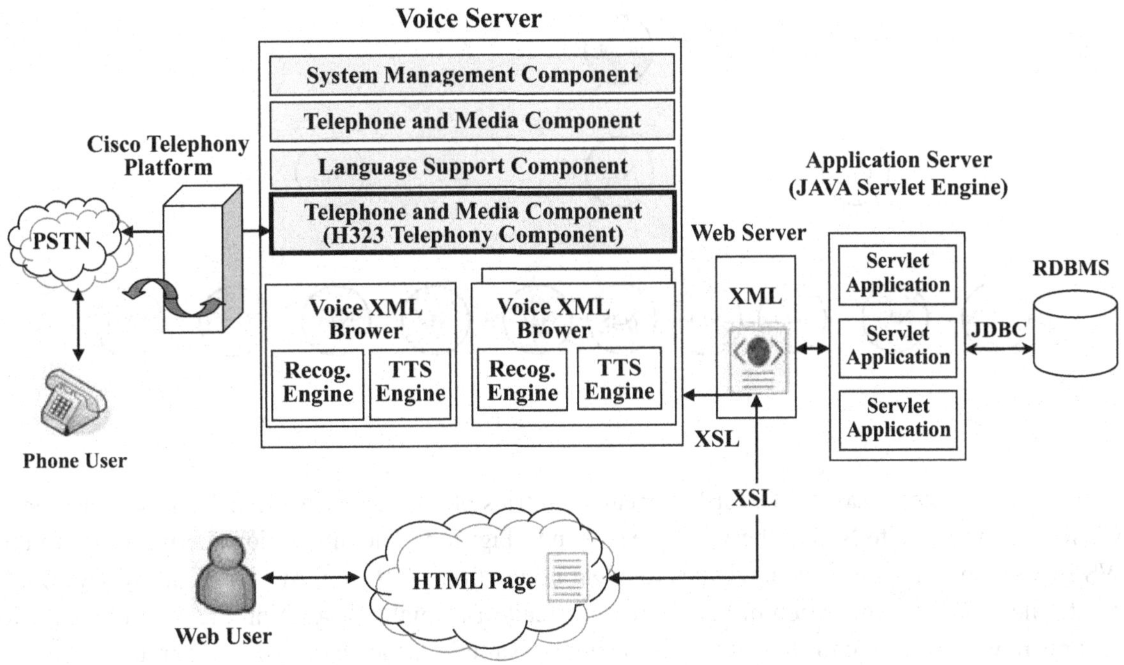

used to convert XML documents (generated by Java servlets) into XHTML documents, VoiceXML documents, and WML (Wireless Markup Language) decks to suit different devices. XSLT can be used to perform additional tasks within an application that uses XML as its main data representation model (Burke, 2001). The voice server, which contains the voice recognition and the synthesis engines used to automate the conversation between the site and the caller, is set up between the phone and the web server to interpret the VoiceXML documents and act as a middleware processor. Any web site can be a VoiceXML content server. Services provided by this VWS system can give subscribers access to contents offered by different sources of Internet applications and services through PSTN (Public Switched Telephone Network) telephones, wired or wireless.

EXPERIMENT METHOD FOR VUI OPTIMIZATION

One of our research objectives is to find a reasonably good arrangement of the site map in a voice Web site. To serve this need, a simulation approach was designed to experiment with various hierarchically structured site maps (i.e., VUI structures or VUI trees), which were modeled by a tree structure as illustrated in Figure 5. When a user, Joe, uses his mobile phone and makes a phone call to the VWS site, he will reach the root node of the VUI tree and hear a greeting message, which may look like "Welcome to XYZ online service portal. If you would like to get a stock quote please say ONE, for restaurant reservation please say TWO, for weather report please say THREE, ..." Joe may say THREE and traverse the VUI tree to N13, the node at the next level for weather report. For the moment, Joe will be answered with more choices such as: for domestic weather report please say ONE, for other

Figure 5. A VUI tree for modeling the hierarchically structured site map

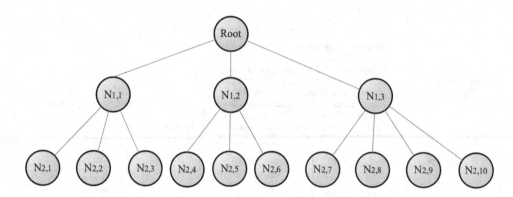

countries in Asia please say TWO, for European countries please say THREE, ...," and Joe may opt to say TWO and traverse to N28 of the VUI tree shown in Figure 5. The interactions between Joe and the VWS service continue until Joe navigates to a leaf node of the VUI tree. At this point, Joe can finally listen to the weather information of his interest. Instead of formally describing the VUI optimization mechanism, we would like to show it first by a simple example, which can easily illustrate not only the principle and the potential improvement of the VUI optimization process but also the model used in the optimization experiments.

An Example of VUI Optimization

In this simulation example, *root* node is at level 0, and $N_{i,j}$ is the *j*th node at level *i*. *Node access time* is the time length of audio heard by users during each visit to the node. *Node access count* is the frequency users navigate through and access to the node in a specific term. *Leaf node access time* is the total access time users navigate from *Root* to the leaf node. *Total time* is the summations of every *leaf node access time* multiply *leaf node access count*.

In a voice site, users' destination must end at leaf nodes; therefore, we focus on the leaf nodes in our model. It means only leaf nodes have the property of "access counts." The properties of the nodes used in this example are described in Table 1. In this case, the values of *node access time* are randomly created in the range between 3 and 8 seconds, the values of *node access count* are only applicable to leaf nodes and randomly generated between 40 and 100, and each value of *leaf node access time* is derived from the values of *node access time* of all nodes on the path from the *root* navigating to that particular leaf node. For example, the *leaf node access time* of $N_{2,1}$ is the summation of *node access time* values of the *root*, $N_{1,1}$, and $N_{2,1}$ (i.e., 5 + 6 + 5 = 16), and the *leaf node access time* of $N_{2,6}$ is the summation of *node access time* values of the *root*, $N_{1,1}$, $N_{1,2}$, $N_{2,4}$, $N_{2,5}$, and $N_{2,6}$ (i.e., 5 + 6 + 5 +8 + 5 + 4 = 33).

Using the VUI optimization mechanism, we can restructure the VUI tree and calculate the new total time. The new tree structure is shown in Figure 6, in which the nodes annotated with star marks [*] were restructured, and the properties of the nodes of the restructured tree are described in Table 2. Note that while the values of *node access time* and *node access count* on all nodes are unchanged, the values of *leaf node access time* on some leaf nodes are changed because the VUI tree is restructured.

Table 1. The properties of the nodes in the VUI tree shown in Figure 5.

Node	Root	$N_{1,1}$	$N_{1,2}$	$N_{1,3}$	$N_{2,1}$	$N_{2,2}$	$N_{2,3}$	$N_{2,4}$	$N_{2,5}$	$N_{2,6}$	$N_{2,7}$	$N_{2,8}$	$N_{2,9}$	$N_{2,10}$
Node access time	5	6	5	4	5	3	6	8	5	4	7	4	8	3
Leaf node access time	n/a	n/a	n/a	n/a	16	19	25	24	29	33	27	31	39	42
Node access count	n/a	n/a	n/a	n/a	70	100	40	40	60	100	70	100	50	60

In this case, the total time
= 16*70 + 19*100 + 25*40 + 24*40 + 29*60 + 33*100 + 27*70 + 31*100 + 39*50 + 42*60
= 1,120 + 1,900 + 1,000 + 960 + 1,740 + 3,300 + 1,890 + 3,100 + 1,950 + 2,520
= 19,480 (seconds) -------- (1)

Figure 6. A restructured VUI Tree [Nodes with star mark (*) were restructured.]

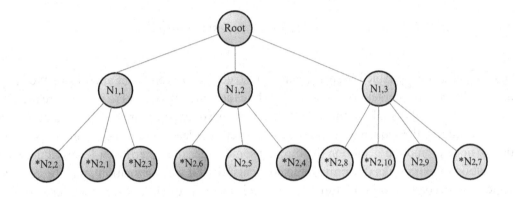

Table 2. The properties of the nodes in the restructured voice Web site tree

Node	Root	$N_{1,1}$	$N_{1,2}$	$N_{1,3}$	*$N_{2,2}$	*$N_{2,1}$	*$N_{2,3}$	*$N_{2,6}$	$N_{2,5}$	*$N_{2,4}$	*$N_{2,8}$	*$N_{2,10}$	$N_{2,9}$	*$N_{2,7}$
Node access time	5	6	5	4	3	5	6	4	5	8	4	3	8	7
Leaf node access time	n/a	n/a	n/a	n/a	14	19	25	20	25	33	24	27	35	42
Node access count	n/a	n/a	n/a	n/a	100	70	40	100	60	40	100	60	50	70

In the new condition, the total time
= 14*100 +19*70 + 25*40 + 20*100 + 25*60 + 33*40 + 24*100 + 27*60 + 35*50 + 42*70
= 1,400 + 1,330 + 1,000 + 2,000 + 1,500 + 1,320 + 2,400 + 1,620 + 1,750 + 2,940
= 17,260 (seconds) -------- (2)

In this sample case of using our optimization model, the improvement (time decreases) is about 11.40% ([(1) − (2)] / (1) ⬝ 0.1139), even though this is just a simple illustration. As voice pages increase numerically and calculations are adopted in computerized computations, it is expected that the improvements, achieved by GA-based optimization approaches for the proposed voice-enabled Web system, will be very attractive and better than the result of this illustration.

Genetic Algorithm for VUI Optimization

The VUI optimization process of restructuring a voice-enable Web site can be modeled by a tree structure (i.e., the VUI tree) as shown in Figure 5. For each VUI optimization experiment, our simulation program will create a VUI tree, with the values of *node access time* of all nodes and the values of *node access count* of all leaf nodes randomly generated. These values will remain unchanged throughout the entire GA evolution process. However, since each value of *leaf node access time* of a leaf node is derived from the values of *node access time* of all nodes on the path from the *root* navigating to that particular leaf node, it may change when the VUI structure changes. As illustrated in the previous example, each possible solution of this problem can be represented by a VUI tree, and the fitness function of this GA-based optimization is the *total time*, which is the summations of every *leaf node access time* multiply *leaf node access count*. Thus, the objective of our optimization process is to minimize the fitness function:

$$F(X) = \sum_{i=k}^{n} \left[LeafNodeAccessTime(i) \times LeafNodeAccessCount(i) \right]$$

The VUI tree of a voice-enabled Web site can be restructured to represent alternative Web site maps offering exactly the same contents and services. While there are many ways to restructure the VUI tree, in our initial design of the VUI optimization experiment we only consider the most straightforward approach of rearranging the sequence of choices under every nonleaf node. Other approaches, such as the operation of node promotion/demotion (by moving some nodes to higher/lower levels of the VUI tree), and the creation of extra links (for providing short-cuts to VUI tree navigation), may be considered in other experiments conducted in the future. Changing the order of child nodes for every nonleaf node can create many different restructured VUI trees, and every VUI tree represents a possible solution. Thus, for a VUI tree with hundreds of nodes, the potential number of restructured VUI trees can be very high. For example, let's consider a VUI tree with 200 nonleaf nodes and assume each nonleaf node has six child nodes (i.e. there are 6 choices available on each non-leaf node), then there could be potentially up to $(6!)^{200} = 2.9275 * 10^{571}$ restructured VUI trees, or possible solutions to be considered in our problem of VUI optimization. This permutation procedure is randomly applied to all non-leaf nodes of the initial VUI tree to generate nine more trees, and all these ten trees are put into the *population* for subsequent evolutions.

In our genetic algorithm, every nonleaf node is encoded by the sequence of choices available in that node. For a non-leaf node *N* randomly selected from tree *A*, its sequence of choices (or order of child nodes) can be represented as N(A) = 1 2 3 4 5 6 7 8 9, and at the same time, the same non-leaf node *N* in tree *B* may have a different sequence of choices represented as N(B) = 4 5 6 9 1 2 7 3 8. The representations of GA variables can also be called *chromosomes*. Assume that our algorithm randomly selects tree A and tree B from the population, identifies node N for the *crossover* operation, and then selects two positions, for example, the 3rd and the 5th positions, to define how to crossover *chromosomes* for producing new chromosomes, that is:

N(A) = 1 2 <u>3 4 5</u> 6 7 8 9   → crossover →   N(A) = 1 2 <u>6 9 1</u> 6 7 8 9
N(B) = 4 5 <u>6 9 1</u> 2 7 3 8   → crossover →   N(B) = 4 5 <u>3 4 5</u> 2 7 3 8

The mapping relationship of this crossover operation can be identified as:

$$3 \leftrightarrow 6 \quad 4 \leftrightarrow 9 \quad 5 \leftrightarrow 1$$

Then, the mapping relationships are applied to the unexchanged part of the chromosomes to create the following chromosomes for their offspring.

N′(A) = 5 2 6 9 1 3 7 8 4
N′(B) = 9 1 3 4 5 2 7 6 8

Mutation may also be applied randomly, at a pre-defined probability rate, to the chromosomes. For example, the chromosome of N′(B) = 9 1 3 4 5 2 7 6 8 can further be encoded into a binary string:

N′(B) = 1001 **0001** 0011 **0100** 0101 **0010** 0111 **0110** 1000

The algorithm can randomly modify some bits to simulate the mutation operation, such as:

N′(B) = 1001 **0001** 0111 **0100** 0100 **0010** 0111 **0110** 1000 = 9 1 7 4 4 2 7 6 8

The mapping relationship of this mutation operation can be identified as:

$$3 \leftrightarrow 7 \quad 5 \leftrightarrow 4$$

Again, the mapping relationships are applied to the unexchanged part of the chromosome to create the following new chromosome:

N″(B) = 9 1 7 5 4 2 3 6 8

From the above mentioned *population creation*, *selection*, *crossover*, and *mutation* operations, new chromosomes can be created and used to generate new VUI trees (solutions). Each newly generated VUI tree is evaluated by the fitness function to decide whether it is a better solution, and this evaluated value is used by the *culling* operation to decide whether the newly generated VUI tree should be placed into the *population* for replacing other less qualified VUI tree.

EXPERIMENT RESULT

Our system was implemented on a 1.73 GHz Pentium M 740 laptop PC with 1 GB RAM, and on another 2.8 GHz Pentium 4 desktop PC with 2 GB RAM. Both machines are running Microsoft Windows XP operating system. The simulation results obtained from 22 experiments are summarized in Table 3, and the simulation results derived from 15 additional experiments are summarized in Table 4. In these experiments, a total of 37 VUI trees were generated with different parameter settings (including the level of VUI tree, the number of children for each nonleaf node, the number of simulation cycles, access time, access count, and so on). Furthermore, the *initial total time* and the *optimized better total time* derived in each experiment were used to calculate the improvement by the following straightforward formula:

Improvement (%) = (Initial Total Time – Better Total Time) / Initial Total Time

Both Table 3 and Table 4 show the experiment results obtained from the aforementioned SGA simulations. As you can see, most cases in these two tables have improvements over 15%, and it is noted that the improvements of some cases even reach nearly 50%. Besides, we noticed that the results of large tree structures are not significant (shown as gray-highlighted items in Table 3 and Table 4), so we tried to increase searching iterations and recalculate them.

As shown in Table 5, when we changed searching iterations from 20,000 times to 500,000 times, we found the improvement got a dramatic increase. It means the more searching iterations we give, the more improvement we get. In other words, for large tree structures, we can eventually get satisfied improvements, only if we increase searching iterations.

Table 3. Results of SGA simulations (number of children = fixed; access time = 2 ~ 15; access counts = 1 ~10,000)

Level	Number of Children	Iterations	Initial Total Time (s)	Better Total Time (s)	Improvement (%)
2	3	20,000	1,886,608	960,008	49.1
2	4	20,000	5,008,968	2,705,967	46.0
2	5	20,000	9,297,450	5,156,684	44.5
2	6	20,000	14,627,224	9,079,845	37.9
3	3	20,000	7,160,233	3,804,627	46.9
3	4	20,000	25,905,538	16,690,080	35.6
3	5	20,000	65,340,923	45,643,277	30.1
3	6	20,000	155,856,635	109,391,621	29.8
4	3	20,000	33,264,675	23,520,746	29.3
4	4	20,000	139,935,642	107,410,143	23.2
4	5	20,000	431,157,562	331,317,272	23.2
4	6	20,000	1,132,148,584	879,033,227	22.4
5	3	20,000	124,114,791	92,712,893	25.3
5	4	20,000	652,978,855	535,596,066	18.0
5	5	20,000	2,700,049,188	2,450,119,893	9.3
5	6	20,000	8,416,055,793	7,975,813,132	5.2
6	3	20,000	419,713,448	339,456,804	19.1
6	4	20,000	3,194,265,541	2,680,976,660	16.1
6	5	20,000	16,141,177,101	15,988,455,697	1.0
6	6	20,000	60,592,359,070	60,590,742,389	0.0

Table 4. Results of SGA simulations (number of children = varied; access time = 2 ~ 15; access counts = 1 ~10,000)

Level	Number of Children	Iterations	Initial Total Time (s)	Better Total Time (s)	Improvement (%)
2	4 to 5	20,000	6,671,516	4,049,286	39.3
2	3 to 6	20,000	5,841,651	3,263,079	44.1
2	2 to 7	20,000	3,803,479	2,071,459	45.5
3	4 to 5	20,000	49,441,465	35,029,192	29.2
3	3 to 6	20,000	34,589,124	24,112,238	30.3
3	2 to 7	20,000	26,332,244	20,114,552	23.6
4	4 to 5	20,000	310,882,476	249067717	19.9
4	3 to 6	20,000	237,910,059	195,086,909	18.0
4	2 to 7	20,000	167,725,927	134,812,794	19.6
5	4 to 5	20,000	1,637,790,586	1,249,947,619	23.7
5	3 to 6	20,000	1,434,332,917	1,258,053,217	12.3
5	2 to 7	20,000	931,088,499	816,875,439	12.3
6	4 to 5	20,000	8,997,595,006	8,892,944,474	1.2
6	3 to 6	20,000	7,832,316,476	7,731,169,501	1.3
6	2 to 7	20,000	4,932,297,039	4,744,909,127	3.8

Table 5. Results of SGA simulations with more iterations (access time = 2 ~ 15; access counts = 1 ~10,000)

Level	Number of Children	Iterations	Initial Total Time (s)	Better Total Time (s)	Improvement (%)
5	6	500,000	8,416,055,793	7,087,376,995	15.8
6	6	500,000	60,592,359,070	53,334,886,394	12.0
6	4 to 5	500,000	8,997,595,006	7,338,143,520	18.4
6	3 to 6	500,000	7,832,316,476	6,768,258,648	13.6

DISCUSSION AND CONCLUSION

While pervasive computing continues to affect more and more people in the world, there will be inevitably plenty of opportunity and revolutionary benefits for everyone who participates. The most significant pervasive computing applications have been in the enterprise market rather than the consumer sector; however, the future of pervasive computing will be supplemented by applications used by a wider variety of professionals and by more horizontal applications. Eventually the access to the conventional desktop and Internet applications through pervasive devices will become very attractive and could lead to pervasive computing being used as much in the consumer sector as it is in the enterprise world. To support various types of pervasive devices in a conventional way, multiple applications have to be independently developed with each to satisfy one type of devices. This practice will exponentially increase the cost, complexity, and manageability of a system when new devices or changes are introduced. To resolve this issue, our project researched on both theoretical concepts of the technologies and practical applications of the concepts by adopting a new software application architecture (see Figure 3) that enables one single application simultaneously interfacing with various types of distributed devices such as PC's, handheld computers, PDA's, WAP-enabled wireless devices, phones, and others. This multimodal application architecture overcomes the difficulties by singularizing the business and application logic while expanding device interfaces. Since common business and application logic is centralized, the maintenance and enhancement become much easier. Our multimodal web system, VWS, was designed and implemented based on this architecture to serve as a "proof of concept" example of this new e-commerce application paradigm.

Nowadays, mobile and wireless technologies are becoming increasingly prevalent, and there is a growing demand for technology that will allow users to connect to the Internet from anywhere through devices that are not suitable for the use of traditional keyboard, mouse, and monitor. In the near future, human-computer voice interfaces will become important tools for solving the accessibility limitations of conventional human-computer interfaces. Based on the multimodal architecture, this chapter describes how a voice-enabled web system (VWS) prototype could be implemented to provide an interactive voice channel using an Apache web server, a voice server, and a Java servlet engine. We also showed through our project that multimodal user interface pages could be generated by using technologies including: eXtensible Markup Language (XML), eXtensible Stylesheet Language for Transformations (XSLT) (Burke, 2001), VoiceXML (Larson, 2003), and Java technology (Sun Microsystems, 2004). As a matter of fact, it is also reconfirmed from our project that voice interfaces may not only help solve the accessibility limitations of conventional human-computer interfaces, but enable mobile device users' hands to engage in some other activities without losing the ability to browse the Internet through voice commands.

In terms of enhancing users' experience and improving the overall system performance, a GA-based dynamic structure approach, which can restructure the site map according to users' demand or the overall performance needs of a system, was applied to our VWS system. Our experiment results showed that this optimization approach may be adopted by an adaptive VWS Systems for supporting large-scale enterprise applications. To ameliorate the rate of convergence of the optimization approach used by the adaptive VWS system, we plan to add some heuristic rules, such as ruin and recreate (Misevicius, 2003) and tabu search (Moscato & Cotta, 2003), to improve the simple genetic algorithm used in the VWS system, which will eventually have the ability of self-learning to optimize itself automatically, dynamically, and effectively.

In their influential paper on the challenges associated with nomadic or pervasive computing, Lyytinen and Yoo (2002) outline eight research themes and twenty research questions, covering a wide range of topics in the heart land of information systems research. If we are to choose a research question posed by them that comes nearest to what we do here, it is their research question 1.1, namely: "How do we design and integrate sets of personalized mobile services that support users' task execution in multiple social and physical contexts?" (Lyytinen & Yoo, 2002, p. 380). Our contribution lies in showing how VWS can be designed to provide an interactive voice channel using readily available information technology products, such as Apache web server, the voice server, and the servlet engine. Furthermore, we describe how multimodal user-interface pages for supporting various wireless devices have been implemented by using technologies including eXtensible Markup Language (XML), eXtensible Stylesheet Language for Transformations (XSLT), and Java technologies. The last but never the least, compared with the Web browser based interface the voice channel is slower, and therefore, there is a need to apply the optimization techniques, such as the GA-based algorithm described in this chapter, to enhance the responsiveness of the VWS based services and applications.

ACKNOWLEDGMENT

The editorial efforts and the invaluable comments from the editor are highly appreciated. The author would also like to thank the National Science Council, Taiwan, for financially supporting this work under contract number NSC-96-2221-E-005-088-MY2.

REFERENCES

Al-Khayyal, F. A., & Sherali, H. D. (2000). On finitely terminating branch-and-bound algorithms for some global optimization problems. *SIAM Journal on Optimization, 10*(4), 1049-1057.

Anerousis, N., & Panagos, E. (2002). Making voice knowledge pervasive. *IEEE Pervasive Computing, 1*(2), 42-48.

Ballagas, R., Borchers, J., Rohs, M., & Sheridan, J. G. (2006). The smart phone: A ubiquitous input device. *IEEE Pervasive Computing, 5*(1), 70-77.

Burke, E. (2001). *JAVA & XSLT.* California: O'Reilly.

Chang, S. E., Changchien, S. W., & Huang, R-H. (2006). Assessing users' product-specific knowledge for personalization in electronic commerce. *Expert Systems with Applications, 30*(4), 682-693.

Chang, S. E., Minkin, B. (2006). The implementation of a secure and pervasive multimodal Web system architecture. *Information and Software Technology, 48*(6), 424-432.

Chang, Y.-F., & Chen, C. S. (2005). Smart phone - the choice of client platform for mobile commerce. *Computer Standards and Interfaces, 27*(4), 329-336.

Changchien, S. W., Lee, C. F., & Hsu, Y. J. (2004). Online personalized sales promotion in electronic commerce. *Expert Systems with Applications, 27*(1), 35-52.

Dettmer, R. (2003). It's good to talk (speech technology for online services access). *IEE Review, 49,* 30-33.

Feng, J., Sears, A., Karat, C.-M. (2006). A longitudinal evaluation of hands-free speech-based navigation during dictation. *International Journal of Human-Computer Studies, 64*(6), 553-569.

Goose, S., Newman, M., Schmidt, C., & Hue, L. (2000). Enhancing Web accessibility via the Vox Portal and a Web-hosted dynamic HTML <-> VoxML converter. *Computer Networks, 33,* 583-592.

de Grimaldo, S.W., (2004). *Mobile Commerce Takes off.* Telecom Trends International, Inc., Virginia. Retrieved November 15, 2007, from http://www.telecomtrends.net/reports.htm

Gulliver, S. R., Serif, T., & Ghinea, G. (2004). Pervasive and standalone computing: the perceptual effects of variable multimedia quality. *International Journal of Human-Computer Studie*s, 60(5/6), 640-665.

Institute for Information Industry (2007). *Survey on the mobile Internet in Taiwan for Q3 2007.* ACI-FIND, focus on Internet news and data. Retrieved January 2, 2008, from http://www.find.org.tw/find/home.aspx?page=many&id=184

Joachims, T., Freitag, D., & Mitchell, T. (1997). WebWatcher: A tour guide for the World Wide Web. In *Proceedings of IJCAI-97, Fifteenth Joint Conference on Artificial Intelligence, Nagoya, Japan* (pp. 770-775).

The Kelsey Group (2001, March). *The global voice ecosystem* (Analyst Report), The Kelsey Group.

Kirkpatrick, S., Gelatt, C.D. Jr., & Vecchi, M.P. (1983). Optimization by simulated annealing. *Science, 220*(4598), 671-680.

Kohrs, A., & Merialdo, B. (2001). Creating user-adapted Web sites by the use of collaborative filtering. *Interacting with Computers, 13*, 695-716.

Larson, J.A. (2003) VoiceXML and the W3C speech interface framework. *IEEE Multimedia, 10*, 91-93.

Li, Y., & Zhong, N. (2004). Web mining model and its applications for information gathering. *Knowledge-Based Systems, 17*(3), 207-217.

Lyytinen, K., & Yoo, Y. (2002). The next wave of nomadic computing. *Information Systems Research, 13*(4), 377-388

Market Wire (2006). *Voxify Reports Outstanding Growth, Increased Momentum in the Speech Self-Service Marketplace.* Retrieved August 10, 2006, from http://www.findarticles.com/p/articles/mi_pwwi/is_200605/ai_n16136434

Misevicius, A. (2003). Genetic algorithm hybridized with ruin and recreate procedure: Application to the quadratic assignment problem. *Knowledge-Based Systems, 16*(5-6), 261-268.

Moscato, P., & Cotta, C. (2003). Gentle introduction to memetic algorithms. In F. Glover & G. Kochenberger (Eds.), *Handbook of metaheuristics* (pp. 105-144). Boston: Kluwer Academic Publishers.

Perkowitz, M., & Etzioni, O. (2000). Towards adaptive Web sites: Conceptual framework and case study. *Artificial Intelligence, 118*, 245-275.

Rebman Jr., C. M., Aiken, M. W., Cegielski, C.G.., 2003, Speech recognition in the human-computer interface. *Information & Management, 40*(6), 509-519.

Rodriguez, A., Ho, W.-K., Kempny, G., Pedreschi, M., & Richards, N. (2002). *IBM WebSphere Voice Server 2.0 Implementation Guide.* IBM Redbooks, IBM.

Roussos, G., Marsh, A. J., & Maglavera, S. (2005). Enabling pervasive computing with smart phones. *IEEE Pervasive Computing, 4*(2), 20-27.

Su, Z., Yang, Q., Zhang, H., Xu, X., Hu, Y-H., & Ma, S. (2002). Corellation-based Web document clustering for adaptive Web interface design. *Knowledge and Information Systems, 4*, 151-167.

Sun Microsystems (2004). Information on J2ME and J2SE. Retrieved June 2, 2007, from http://java.sun.com/j2me/ and http://java.sun.com/j2se/

Smith, K. A., & Ng, A. (2003) Web page clustering using a self-organizing map of user navigation patterns. *Decision Support Systems, 35*, 245-256.

Tan, A. (May 2005). Voice to dominate 3G traffic, says expert. *ZDFNetAsia*. Retrieved June 2, 2007, from http://www.zdnetasia.com/news/communications/0,39044192,39231956,00.htm

Teo, T., & Pok, S. (2003). Adoption of WAP-enabled mobile phones among Internet users. *Omega: The International Journal of Management Science, 31*, 483-498.

Toye, E., Sharp, R., Madhavapeddy, A., & Scott, D. (2005). Using smart phones to access site-specific services. *IEEE Pervasive Computing, 4*(2), 60-66.

Turner, K. (2004). Analysing interactive voice services. *Computer Networks, 45*(5), 665-685.

Wang, F. H., & Shao, H. M. (2004). Effective personalized recommendation based on time-framed navigation clustering and association mining. *Expert Systems with Applications, 27*(3), 365-377.

Yamazaki, Y., Iwamida, H., & Watanabe, K. (2004). Technologies for voice portal platform. *Fujitsu Scientific and Technical Journal, 40*(1), 179-186.

Zhai, S., Kristensson, P.-O., Smith, B. A., (2005). In search of effective text input interfaces for off the desktop computing. *Interacting with Computers, 17*(3), 229–250.

Chapter IX
The Impact of Culture on the Perception of Information System Success

Hafid Agourram
Bishop's University, Canada

ABSTRACT

Research has showed that social and socio-technical concepts are influenced by culture. The objective of this chapter is to explore how the socio-technical concept of information system success is defined and perceived by a group of French managers. The results show that culture does influence IS success perception. The study has many implications for both academic and practice communities. The results are especially important to multinational organizations that standardize IS in different cultures including France. The research case is a multibillion dollar Canadian multinational organization which decided to standardize an Enterprise Resource Planning (ERP) system in all its worldwide subsidiaries.

INTRODUCTION

One of the most enduring research topics in the field of information systems is that of information systems success (Markus, Axline, Petrie, and Tanis, 2000). DeLone and McLean (1992) argued that if information systems research is to make a contribution to the world of practice, a well-defined outcome measure is essential. On the other hand, cross-cultural researchers have largely suggested that it is not possible to take existing models and theories and apply them to different contexts or cultures (Hofstede, 1980; Laurent, 1983; Maurice, 1979; Tayeb, 1994; Trompenaars, 1993, Pauleen et al., 2006). This problem becomes apparent in large organizations or multinational organizations which conduct business activities in different cultures because "the meaning of information and effectiveness of an information system can vary substantially in different cultures" (Jordan, 1996. p.2). This problem becomes even more complex in cases where a multinational organization seeks to standardize IS in its subsidiaries that are located in different cultures. The multinational organization would face two challenges. First, the system needs to be implemented successfully. Second, the multinational organization in due time, needs to measure the success of the system. However, before we measure a concept, we need to define it (Adam et al. 2000; Brown et al. 2003; Makus et al. 2000 and Ford et al. 2003). In reviewing the literature, we couldn't find specific studies that deal with how people in different cultures define and operationalize IS success. The intent of this research is to focus on this issue by developing culturally sensitive models of IS success in France.

REVIEW OF LITERATURE

IS Success

The DeLone and McLean (1992, 2003) model is probably one of the most cited models in the IS community. Their 1992 model was successfully tested in many empirical studies (Rai, Lang and Welker, 2002; Ivari, 2005). IS success definition and measurement is still problematic for many factors (Seddon, Staples, Patnayakuni, and Bowetell, 1999). The first factor is the mixture of the technical and social aspects of an IS (Kanellis, Lycett, and Paul, 1998). Second, Alter (2000) argues that information technology and work practices are now so intertwined that it is difficult to identify their respective contributions to success. Other researchers link the difficulty of defining IS success to the methodological aspects involved in measuring IS success "Specifying a dependent variable is difficult because of the many theoretical and methodological issues involved in measuring IS success" (Garrity and Sanders; 1998, p. 14). Seddon et al. (1999) argue that IS success is still a fuzzy concept contingent upon different stakeholders and different types of IT. In the practice community, Markus and Tanis (2000) claimed that there is a fundamental gap in both practical and academic thinking between the lack of consensus and the clarity about the meaning of success, where information systems are concerned.

IS Success in the International Context

The problem of IS definition and measurement becomes more difficult and more complicated if we add the international dimension (Ishman,1998; Garrity and Sanders,1998). The international dimension includes cultural terms such as values and assumptions which may be at the heart of the differing perceptions and interpretations. Shing-Kao (1997) argues that «Research has shown that people notice, interpret and retain information based on their values, assumptions and expectations. Different assumptions and values lead to different ways of looking at the same thing» (p. 13).

This international differing perception of the meaning of a phenomenon is an important topic in International Management or Cross-cultural Management disciplines. Do theories and concepts born in a specific culture apply or have the same meaning in other cultures? Hofstede (1993), for example, after a large survey on work-related values in sixty countries, concluded that management theories and findings are not automatically transferable from one context to another. Shing-Kao (1997), Kedia and Bhagat (1988), and Robichaux and Cooper (1998) add that the majority of theories of management have a Western and, therefore, generally, an American perspective which is based on the embedded values that influence the ways in which Americans perceive and think about the world.

Rosenzweig (1994) argues that a central concern in scientific research is external validity. That is, the extent to which a theorized or observed relationship among variables can be generalized to other settings. Rosenzweig (1994) claims that the main question should not be, «Are scientific management theories that interest us valid elsewhere? But how can we best understand management, as it exists around the world? » (p.37); this is exactly the main goal of this research project where we seek to understand the meaning of IS success in France.

CULTURE

Culture is a term that was originally developed in the field of anthropology and has recently become a prevalent research area in organizational studies. Unfortunately, a consistent definition of this ambiguous concept is extremely difficult to isolate (Lammers and Hickson,1979). The complexity of the concept of culture derives then from the multiplicity of the perspectives that investigate it. One thing that all researchers agree upon it the fact that culture is related to people. In 1952, the anthropologists Kroeber and Kluckholn claimed that there were more than 150 definitions of the concept of culture. Baligh (1994) also argues that there are many ways to describe and define culture and that one may conceive of culture in terms of its parts and its components, and the two are related. Culture concerns a group of people who share a common understanding and meaning of things around them. It is a shared system of meaning (Trompenaars and Hampden-Turner, 1998) or, the collective programming of the human mind that distinguishes members of one group from another (Hofstede, 1993). Trompenaars and Hampden-Turner (1998) propose the following model to understand culture.

The above model indicates that the products of a culture (observable artefacts) are symbols of the norms and values of the people, which in turn are based on fundamental basic assumptions about human existence and life. National culture is a major type of culture.

National Culture

National culture is a concept that helps determine similarities and differences between the cultures of the countries.

Figure 1. Trompenaars and Hampden-Turner (1998) cultural model

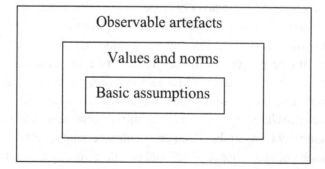

The literature provides some models which try to capture the concept of national culture. Hall (1976) uses a single dimension; high context versus low context to differentiate between national cultures. The context dimension draws upon the degree of communication between individuals in a particular national culture. Individuals from high context cultures use informal information and informal communication mediums to satisfy their information needs. Individuals from low context cultures use objective data and explicit information that may be stored in computer databases and in written reports to seek knowledge.

Hofstede (1980) proposes a multidimensional model and suggests that national culture and values, as they affect the work environment and its management, could be categorized on the basis of four dimensions, namely: power distance, uncertainty avoidance, individualism–collectivism, and masculinity-femininity.

The values of people in a particular culture are the most widely used concept or variable in cross-cultural studies (Glenn and Glenn, 1981; Hofstede, 1980; Triandis, 1982). The reason for the popularity of values as cross-cultural research variables is the deeper layer of culture; basic assumptions are preconscious (taken for granted) and are powerful because they are less debatable than espoused values (Lachman, Nedd, and Hinings, 1994). Trompenaars and Hampden-Turner (1998) suggest differentiating between norms and values in claiming that values direct our feelings of good and evil, and that norms are the basis by which a group of people judge something as right or wrong.

Based on his research on national culture, Hofstede (1993) developed many types of organizational models. Among the five dimensions that he developed, "power distance" and "uncertainty avoidance" are considered the most important in studying organizations in different national cultures. The combination of these dimensions yields a four-quadrant framework, which represents profiles of organizations in each organizational model: Machine, Market, Pyramid and Family. Each part of the organizational model includes all countries that share a common degree of national culture dimensions.

RESEARCH FRAMEWORK

Figure 2 shows our research framework which will guide the research questions, data collection and analysis procedures. The framework is made of two main components: national culture and the meaning of IS success at the system, the user and the organizational levels in France. The framework is not a model that needs to be tested by the present study. The arrow simply indicates the logic that national culture would impact the meaning of IS success and the aim of the study is to determine that meaning. The system, user and organizational classification was borrowed from DeLone and McLean (1992) model of IS success and our study develops IS success categories in each level.

The Research Question

The research questions follow from the research framework. The framework stipulate that national culture and in our case the French culture would influence the meaning of IS success at at least three levels. The following research questions are asked to construct that meaning:

- How is the concept of IS success defined and perceived by a group of French people at the system level?

Figure 2. Research framework

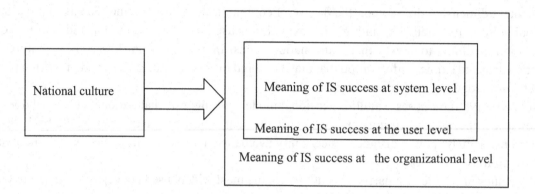

- How is the concept of IS success defined and perceived by a group of French people at the user level?
- How is the concept of IS success defined and perceived by a group of French people at the organizational level?

METHODOLOGY

An inductive process is followed in this study. That is, from data that is grounded in its own context, we construct IS success models. Since this research aims to explore and to find the meaning of IS success in France, a qualitative approach is employed. The emerging theory will be developed from words and their associated meanings as described by the researcher participants. A case study is used in this research as a strategy.

Grounded theory analysis which seeks to develop theory that is grounded in the data (Myers, 1997) is used in this study. Grounded theory is a method in which the researcher attempts to derive a theory by using multiple stages of data collection and refinement and interrelationships of categories of information (Strauss and Corbin, 1999). This is exactly the aim of the present study. Our models are to be grounded from the participants' data as they are collected and analyzed in the participants' context. The three basic elements of grounded theory are: concepts, categories and propositions. Concepts are the lowest level of abstraction of raw data as stressed by Corbin and Strauss (1990). Categories are higher theoretical abstraction than concepts. The difference between concepts and categories is the level of theoretical abstraction.

A two-stage process is conducted in this study. Stage one concerns the analysis of data by the researcher. In stage two, we asked two experts in information systems from a well known university to verify our findings. They were asked to verify that each concept belongs to its category and that the name of the category accurately represents its meaning. The following figure summarizes the steps of our research design.

Figure 3.

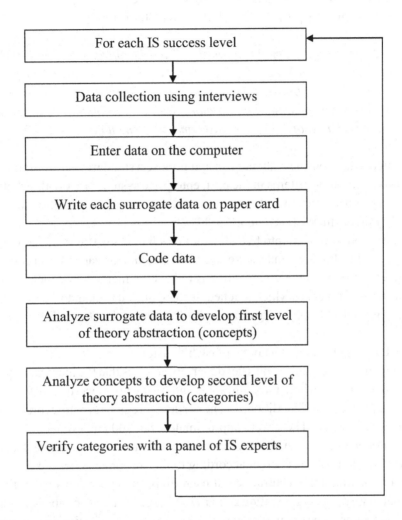

The Case

We first met with management at the headquarters' of the organization in Canada. Top management decided to implement a large scale project in which information system standardization constitutes only a subproject. The organization has decided to adopt a common strategy across its groups and business units. The objectives and expected benefits were: reduce software acquisition costs, reduce implementation costs, reduce operation costs, produce benefits in the business sectors, and minimize implementation and ongoing risks. Since the time the decision was made, no unit or division is allowed to purchase or select a software package that is not fully compatible with the future standard information system. Information systems' components acquisition and implementation across all units of the multinational organization becomes centralized. The mains objective of this strategy is to receive real time information about the business activities.

Our case has shifted to IS standardization to implement its strategy and achieve its objectives. It decided to implement an Enterprise Resource Planning system (ERP) in all the subsidiaries. A standard system is chosen and a multibillion-dollar contract was signed. A complete definition of Enterprise Resource Planning Systems was provided by Markus and Tanis (2000):

Enterprise systems are clearly a phenomenon in the IT marketplace. Their potential significance for computer-using organizations cannot be overstated. They represent a nearly complete rearchitecting of an organization's portfolio of transactions-processing applications systems to achieve integration of business processes, systems and information along with corresponding changes in the supporting computing platform: hardware, software, database, and telecommunication (p. 175).

ERP systems dictate how business should run and impose a standard and centralized organizational architecture. "Unlike computer systems in the past, enterprise systems are off-the-shelf solutions. They impose their own logic on a company's strategy, culture, and organizations, often forcing companies to change the way they do business" (Davenport, p. 121).

Our case organization is divided into five divisions. Each division offers different products and services, requires different technology and marketing strategies and is headed by a president and the chief operation officer. The mission of the organization is to lead the markets in which it operates.

About 92% of the total revenues which reached thirteen billion Canadian dollars in 2000 originated from foreign markets, and 44% of the organization's workforce is located in Europe and 52% in North America.

Table 1 shows the main business locations of each division.

Senior management at the organization's headquarters believes that the increasingly diverse nature of the organization's markets, from both the geographic and product perspectives, affords the organization a further measure of protection. If conditions in one particular region turn unfavorable, only a portion of the activities would be affected. There were approximately 80, 000 employees in the organization. All the divisions are autonomous. This autonomy is a vital requirement that allows each division to meet its planned objectives which must be coherent according to the corporate general policies and guidelines. Power and decision-making are decentralized at each division. This allows each division to act in a rapid and coordinated way. The organization encourages interdivisional collaboration, involvement and engagement of its personnel. The organization puts a great deal of emphasis on its management philosophy. It believes that even though it does not in any way aim to have all the subsidiaries look alike, they must share a common management philosophy. The organization strongly believes that each subsidiary needs to adapt its products to the market which it serves (local market responsiveness) and to adhere to the management philosophy of the corporate office (consistency with headquarters' policies). It is thus a

Table 1. Business locations of each division

Division	Locations
1	Canada, United States of America, Northern Ireland.
2	Canada, United States of America, Mexico, Germany, France, Austria, Belgium, Czech Republic, United Kingdom, Switzerland, China.
3	Canada, United States of America, Austria, Finland.
4	United States of America, Canada, Finland, France,.
5	China, Canada.

multinational organization which believes that the ideal objective is to reach an optimum balance between market responsiveness and consistency with headquarters. Some of the organization's core beliefs are: drive for profitable growth, foster an entrepreneurial spirit in all our businesses, constantly innovate in products, operating processes, and systems of management, set up autonomous business units within a tight strategic governance system, and combine speed with discipline when pursuing acquisitions.

Data Collection

Data collection took place in a real context, that is, in the research participants' working place. Data collection was mainly based on open interviews. The open interview question is the same as the research question. Data was collected from eight managers from different functional areas. The notes of the interviews were taken on paper and most of them were recorded. Four participants refused to be recorded even though they were assured that the information would be kept private and no one would have access to it. Apart from those rare occasions, recording the interview proved to be a beneficial technique. After each interview, the notes and tapes were reviewed so as to insure that no relevant information was missed. The notes of each interview were entered in a computer using a word processing package. They were then printed and each raw data was written on card. Each card has a code. The coding mechanism is structured as follows: two digit number to represent the participant number and a single character to designate the level of analysis. For example, 06O represents raw data of IS success meaning at the organizational level of participant number 6. The same process was repeated for all the notes of the participants in each level.

RESULTS

Table 3 shows the amount of raw data of IS success at each level: system, user and organizational levels. The "Other" cell includes all the data that was not used in the analysis because this data could not be considered as attributes of IS success. Raw data elements are statements that the research participant provides to the researcher in response to the research questions. A raw data element is also a statement that provides details or different ways of describing the same phenomenon. The following are examples of raw data: "reports are easy to read", "the presentation is intuitive", "rapid access to data", "impact on relationships with suppliers", and "impact on the work method".

A total of 256 raw data were obtained during the interviews, as indicated in Table 2. Of these 256, 188 raw data were used in our analysis.

Table 2. The amount of raw data per IS success level

Level	Amount of raw data
Systems level	100
Individual level	59
Organizational level	29
Other	68
Total	**256**

Results at the System Level

The emerging categories at the system level are:

1. **Data quality:** Expressed in terms of intrinsic data quality, contextual data quality, representational data quality, and accessibility. These categories were borrowed from Wang and Strong's (1996) model which is indicated in appendix A;
2. **User-system interaction quality:** Emphasizes the quality of the interaction between the user and the system;
3. **Data processing system quality:** Emphasizes the hardware, the networks, and the processing attributes of a successful information system.

The Table 3 summarizes the categories of IS success at the systems level.

Results at the User Level

The Table 4 provides the emerged categories of IS success at the user level

The "Impact on individual task" category refers to the extent to which information can influence and modify the tasks that are executed by the user. The system should provide relevant information to

Table 3. Categories of IS success at the systems level

Category
Intrinsic data quality
Contextual data quality
Representational data quality
Accessibility
User-System interaction quality
Data processing systems quality

Table 4. IS success categories at the user level

Category
Impact on individual task
Impact on the user's career
Impact on decision making
User satisfaction
User independence from IS professionals
User power over the system
Use
Impact on individual skills and knowledge

help the user perform his or her job. The system should handle the routine activities and let the user perform more intelligent tasks.

The "Impact on the user's career" category refers to the ability of the system to influence the position and the long term career of its users. This mainly concerns promotions and new responsibilities in the organization.

The "Impact on decision making" category refers to the extent to which an information system supports its users in their decision-making process. The system would then be the basis of more specific applications that support the decision making process, such as: decision support systems, group support systems, executive information systems, and expert systems.

The "User satisfaction" category refers to the overall satisfaction of the user.

The "User independence from IS professionals" category refers to the extent to which the user of a successful information systems can use the system without relying much on IS professionals.

The "User's power over the system" category refers to the extent to which the user must dominate the system and not vice versa. That is, the logic and the rules of work are provided by the user and not the system.

The "Use" category refers to the degree of using the system. The more the system is used, the more successful it is. However, DeLone and McLean (1992) argues that the "Use" category can be misleading because there are two situations in which an IS can be used. The first one is where the user can perform his or her job without using the system, but he is using it to get information. In this case, a high degree of systems usage is a good indicator of IS success. The second scenario is where the user must use the system to perform his or her job. The system is mandatory. In this case using the "Use" category would lead to a biased conclusion about IS success. "Use" in our case refers to the first scenario.

We also came upon the "Impact on user's skills and knowledge" category. The French participants consider that a successful IS is one that gives them the freedom to perform the types of queries they like. A system that gives them freedom and liberty. A system that opens their eyes and help them try things and learn. This is a logical category in that the participant will try to find alternatives in response to the close-mindedness of the managers. They no longer count on management and therefore they need to explore other means by which they can gain freedom and independence. This is also related to the category of "User independence from IS professional" in the sense that IS professionals exercise power on users, and dictate to users very specific procedures to follow to use the system.

Results at the Organizational Level

The Table 5 displays the list of the emerged categories of IS success at the organizational level.

The following paragraphs provide information about the meaning of the emerging categories at the organizational level.

The category "Financial impact" refers to the extent to which a successful information system enables the financial growth of the organization.

The category "Business process redesign" refers to the extent to which a successful information system can reengineer business processes. The reengineering is possible only by introducing information technology in the different phases of business processes.

The fit between the systems and the human logic of work is highly emphasized by the French: "Should not externalize our rules of work", "Be a logical system", "We are the owners of our ideas", and "Must have our hands on the system".

Table 5. IS success categories at the organizational level

Category
Financial impact
Business process redesign
Fit between systems and human model of work
User integration and communication in the group

The user integration and communication in the group is implied by the unwillingness of the user to rely on managers and IS professionals. French users would rather approach colleagues that hold the same status in terms of hierarchy. The fit between the systems and the human logic of work is highly emphasized by the French: "Should not externalize our rules of work", "Be a logical system", "We are the owners of our ideas", and "Must have our hands on the system".

DISCUSSION

The score of the "Power distance" in France is 68. This is considered a high score on this dimension. This means that the French tend to accept unequal distribution of power in their organizations. This indicates that the decisions made by managers are likely to be considered legitimate and should not be disputed. Power is then believed to be an important value in French society. The "User independence from IS professionals" and "User power over the system" justify and support the high score of "Power distance" dimension. This means that a successful IS should maintain the values held by the users of the system. Users want to maintain power over the system. They want to make decisions themselves and not by relying on the system. They want to have more power on IS professionals. As power is legitimated, the users of the system want the system to provide them with more power. They believe that a successful IS should enable individual skills knowledge development. This means that knowledge justifies the power they may have and they want to learn as much as they can in order to become more knowledgeable and therefore more powerful. The "User integration and communication in the group" means that the users want to enhance their technical knowledge about the system and learn fro each other which may explain the "User independence from IS professionals". IS success is also characterized by the "Fit between human and systems models of work". This again means that the systems should not impose a work model or a business philosophy. People are more powerful than the system and the latter should at least follow the users' model of work. IS is a tool and should remain so.

France scores very high on the uncertainty avoidance dimension, 86 out of 100. This means that the French do not like unstructured situations and ambiguity. They would prefer to lower the risk and reduce surprises. Therefore they would implement strategies and procedures in organizations that all employees would follow.

Our research supports Rosensweig's (1994) theory concerning the internationalization of management science. The author argued that the internationalization of management science research that concerns socio-technical and social systems is impossible mainly because the variables, the measurement of the variables, and the relationship between the variables are all affected by the values of people who use them. From this perspective, we found that IS success, a concept that concerns socio-technical systems, is indeed affected by national culture. Many popular authors such as Hofstede (1980), Laurent (1983), Maurice (1979), Tayeb (1994), Trompenaars (1993), suggested not to automatically apply existing models and theories without local adaptation. In the field of information systems, Shing-Kao (1997), Kedia and Bhagat (1988), and Robichaux and Coopers (1998) add that the majority of management theories have a western perspective that is based on the embedded values of Americans. The findings of our research also support Jordan (1996) who claimed that the meaning of information and effectiveness of information systems could vary substantially in different cultures. The implementation failure of the ERP system in one specific national culture in which our organization has a subsidiary lends support to Robey and Rodriguez-Diaz (1989). The authors claimed that MNC face difficulties in implementing IS in different subsidiaries because culture may impede implementation effort due to differences in the way IS are interpreted and given meaning. We also answer Rosensweig's (1994) major request in which he invited researchers not to question whether or not existing theories are valid elsewhere but to inquire into how people in different places perceive and define the research object in question.

Our findings at the systems level will help the implementation team of the ERP system to succeed the implementation phase of the project. By implementation, we mean the technical aspect of the system implementation and not the social aspect. If the above categories and concepts are implemented in the ERP system, the systems acceptance is very likely to occur because it would be based on how the systems future users perceive the conditions of an acceptable and good system. The implementation team should take each of the categories: "Intrinsic data quality", "Contextual data quality", "Representational data quality", "Accessibility", "User-system interaction quality", and "Data processing systems quality", along with its corresponding concepts and implement the system.

IMPLICATIONS

The results of this study will help the management in our case organization measure IS success (long term success) at the systems level, the user, and the organizational level by continually developing a questionnaire that includes our emerging categories as well as their corresponding concepts. On the other hand, our research can be considered as a starting point of a research program in the field of information systems. According to our literature review, our research is the first of its kind that searches for IS success in a specific cultures.

LIMITATIONS

There are also a number of limitations in our research. First, we don't claim generalisation of our results to all organizations in France. We do however, seek analytical generalisation. That is, if the same research is conducted in the same environment, the finding would be similar. Second, although numbers don't count much in qualitative research, the number of research respondents is not as high as we wished. Finally, the selection of our respondents was done by our sponsor in the multinational organization. We wished we could select them ourselves so that we can have perfect cocktails of different functional perspectives.

CONCLUSION

It has been argued that national culture affect social and socio-technical system. This cross-cultural research was conducted to understand the affect of national culture on the perception of the meaning of IS success. A multinational organization has decided to standardize information systems in all its subsidiaries around the world. This organization was selected because 1) it has subsidiaries of the same business activity in many cultures and 2) it was concerned about how its people would define the performance of Information systems before the implementation of a standard ERP package. We found that the French culture does influence the meaning of IS success at the system, the user and the organizational levels. The findings of this research are imperative for the multinational organization in which the research took place. Our research is the first of its kind to study IS success in a multicultural environment. We invite other researchers to replicate our study and therefore strengthen the categories buy adding more categories and enhancing existing ones. Future research is also demanded to discover IS success in other countries such as China, Arab counteies and South American countries as large organizations are turning to these countries for the business advantages they offer.

REFERENCES

Adam, F., & O'Doherty, P. (2000). Lessons from enterprise resource planning implementations in Ireland—Towards smaller and shorter ERP projects. *Journal of Information Technology, 15*, 305-316.

Alter, S. (2000). The Siamese Twin Problem: A Central Issue Ignored by Dimensions of Information Effectiveness. *Communication of AIS, 2*(20), 1-55.

Baligh, H. H. (1994). Components of Culture: Nature, Interconnections, and Relevance to the Decisions on the Organization Structure. *Management Science, 40*(1), 14-27.

Brown, C. V., & Vessey, I. (2003). Managing The Next Wave of Enterprise Systems: Leveraging Lessons from ERP. *MS Quarterly Executive, 2*(1), 65-77.

Corbin, J., & Strauss, A. (1990). Grounded theory research: Procedures, canons, and evaluative criteria. *Qualitative Sociology, 13*, 3-21.

Davenport, T. H (1998). Putting the enterprise into the enterprise system. *Harvard Business Review, 76*(4), 121-131.

DeLone, W. H., & McLean, E. R. (1992). Information Systems Success: The Quest for The Dependent Variable. *Information Systems Research, 3*(1), 60-95.

DeLone, W. H., & McLean, E. R. (2003). The Delone and McLean model of Information systems success: A ten-year update. *Journal of Information Systems Management, 19*(4), 9-26.

Ford, D., Connelly, C., & Meister, D. (2003). Information systems research and Hofstede's Culture's Consequences: An uneasy and incomplete partnership. *IEEE Transactions on Engineering Management, 50*(1), 8-25.

Garrity, E. J. & Sanders, G. L. (1998). Introduction to Information Systems Success Measurement. *In* E. J. Garrity and G. L, Sanders (dir.), *Information Systems Success Measurement,* 1-12. Idea Group Publishing.

Glenn, E. S., & Glenn, C. G. (1981). *Man and Mankind: Conflict and Communication between Cultures.* Northwood, NJ: Ablex.

Hall, E. T. (1976). *Beyond culture.* New York: Anchor Press.

Hofstede, G. (1993). *Cultures and organizations: software of the mind.* London: McGraw-Hill.

Hofstede, G. (1980). Motivation, Leadership and Organization: Do American theories apply abroad? *Organizational Dynamics, 75*(1), 42-63.

Ishman, M. (1998). Measuring Information Success at the individual level in cross-cultural Environments. *In* E.J. Garrity and G.L, Sanders (dir), *Information Systems Success Measurement.* Idea Group Publishing.

Ivari, J. (2005). An Empirical Test of the DeLone-McLean Model of Information System Success. *Database for Advances in Information Systems, 36*(2), 8-27.

Jordan, E. (1996). National Culture and Organizational Culture: Their use in information. http://www.is.cityu.edu.hk/ Research/WorkingPapers/paper/9408.pdf

Kanellis, P., Lycett, M., & Paul, R. (1999). Evaluating business information systems fit: From concept to practical application. *European Journal of Information Systems, 18*(1), 65-76.

Kedia, B. L., & Bhagat, R. S. (1988). Cultural Constraints on Transfer of Technology Across Nations: Implications for Research in International and Comparative Management. *Academy of Management Review, 13*(4), 559-571.

Kroeber, A., & Kluckholn, C. (1952). Culture: A critical review of concepts and definitions. Cambridge, MA.

Lachman, R., Nedd, A., & Hinings, B. (1994). Analyzing Cross-national Management and Organizations: A Theoretical Framework. *Management Science, 40*(1), 40-55.

Lammers, C. J., & Hickson, D. J. (1979). *Organizations* alike and unlike: Toward a comparative sociology of organizations. London: Routledge and Kegan Paul.

Laurent, A. (1983). The cultural diversity of western conceptions of Management. *International Studies of Management and Organizations, 23*(2), 75-96.

Laurent, A. (1983). The cultural diversity of western conceptions of Management. *International Studies of Management and Organizations, 23*(2), 75-96.

Markus, M L., & Tanis, C. (2000). The Enterprise System Experience – From Adoption to Success. In R. Zmud (dir.), *Framing the Domain of IT Management*, 173-207, Pinnaflex.

Markus, M. L., Axline, S., Petrie, D., & Tanis, C. (2000). Learning from Adopters' Experience with ERP: Problems Encountered and Success Achieved. *Journal of Information Technology, 15*, 245-265.

Maurice, M. (1979). For a study of the societal effect: the universality and specificity in organizational research. In C. J. Lammers and D. J. Hickson (dir.), *Organizations Alike and Unlike*. London: Routledge and Kegan Paul

Myers, M. D. (1997). *Qualitative Research in Information Systems*. Entered on May 20th 1997 from http://www.qual.auckland.ac.nz/

Pauleen, D., Evaristo, R., Davison, R., Ang, S., Alanis, M., & Klein (2006). Cultural Bias in Information Systems Research and Practice: Are You Coming from the same place I am? *Communications of the AIS, 17*, 354-372.

Rai A., Lang S. S., & Welker R. B. (2002). Assessing the Validity of IS Success Models: An Empirical Test and Theoretical Analysis. *Information Systems Research, 13*(1), 50-69.

Robey, D., & Boudreau M. C. (2000). Organizational Consequences of Information Technology: Dealing with Diversity in Empirical Research. In R. Zmud (dir.), *Framing the Domain of IT Management*, 51-61. Pinnaflex.

Robichaux, B. P., & Cooper, R. B. (1998). GSS Participation: A Cultural Examination. *Information and Management, 33*, 287-300.

Rosenzweig, P. M. (1994). When Can Management Science Research Be Generalized Internationally? *Management Science, 40*(1), 28-39.

Seddon, P. B., Staples, S., Patnayakuni, R., & Bowetell, M. (1999). Dimensions of Information Success. *Communication of the ACM, 2*(20), 1-40.

Shing-Kao, L. (1997). *A study of National Culture versus Corporate Culture in International Management*. Dissertation abstract international, Nova South-eastern University.

Strauss, A., & Corbin, J. (1999). *Basics of qualitative research: Grounded theory procedures and techniques*. Newbury Park, CA, Sage.

Tayeb, M. (1994). Organizations and national culture: methodology considered. *Organizations Studies, 15*(3), 429-446.

Triandis, H. C. (1982). Dimensions of Cultural Variation as Parameters of Organizational Theories. *International Studies of Management and Organizations, 12*, 139-169.

Trompenaars, F. T., & Hampden-Turner, C. H. (1998). *Riding The Waves of Culture—Understanding Diversity in Global Business*. McGraw-Hill.

Trompenaars, F. (1993). Riding the waves of culture: Understanding Cultural Diversity in Business. Economics Books, London.

APPENDIX

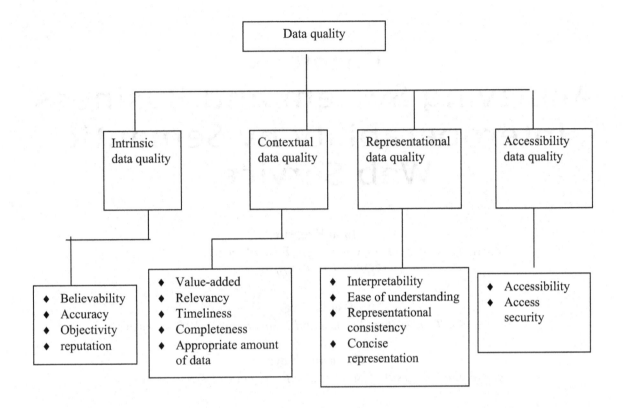

Chapter X
Achieving System and Business Interoperability by Semantic Web Services

John Krogstie
Norwegian University of Science and Technology (NTNU), Norway
SINTEF ICT, Norway

Csaba Veres
Norwegian University of Science and Technology (NTNU), Norway

Guttorm Sindre
Norwegian University of Science and Technology (NTNU), Norway

Øyvind Skytøen
Norwegian University of Science and Technology (NTNU), Norway

ABSTRACT

Much of the early focus in the area of Semantic Web has been on the development of representation languages for static conceptual information; while there has been less emphasis on how to make Semantic Web applications practically useful in the context of knowledge work. To achieve this, a better coupling is needed between ontology, service descriptions, and workflow modeling, including both traditional production workflow and interactive workflow techniques. This chapter reviews the basic technologies involved in this area to provide system and business interoperability, and outlines what can be achieved by merging them in the context of real-world workflow descriptions.

INTRODUCTION

Information systems interoperability has become a critical success factor for process and quality improvement both in private enterprises and the public sector (Linthicum, 2003), and recent technological advances to achieve this include web services and semantics encoded in ontologies. "The Semantic Web" (Berners-Lee, Hendler & Lassila, 2001) is seen as the next generation of web systems, providing better information retrieval, better services, and enhanced interoperability between different information systems. The Semantic Web initiative is currently overseen in the semantic web activity of the W3C, and includes a number of core technologies. Some core technologies that will be relevant to this overview are XML, RDF, RDF/S, OWL, and Web Services (SOAP, WSDL, UDDI). Also newer initiatives such as OWL-S and WSMO are relevant to our work, and will be described in more detail in the article. While these technologies are promising, it can still be argued that alone, they are not sufficient to achieve interoperability in the business domain, allowing for a smooth integration between different information systems within and between organizations. For this to be accomplished, it is not enough to describe ontological metadata about the information and services available – one also needs to know the work context in which the different types of information and services are requested. As observed in (Bubenko, 2007) this is often a challenge, as many ontologists focus on domain ontologies as such, more than their potential usage in applications, as well as having limited knowledge of advances in other areas of conceptual modeling during the last decades. Hence there is a need to integrate ontologies and service descriptions with models of workflows and business processes. Most of the work within these areas focuses on automating routine tasks. While computerization automates routine procedures, knowledge-based cooperation remains a challenge, where we see a role for interactive process models. To the extent that different enterprises use different modeling languages, the interoperability between various models would also emerge as a challenge in its own respect, in which case some unification effort might be needed (Opdahl & Sindre, 2007), one effort in this direction is the Unified Enterprise Modeling Language (UEML)[1], not to be confused with the UML.

The purpose of this paper is as follows:

a) To provide an overview of the relevant technologies (ontology, service models, workflow models, including those being based on interactive models).

b) To show how these technologies fit together, both in theory (presented as "The interoperability pyramid") and in practice.

The rest of this paper is structured as follows: The next three sections survey ontologies, service models, and workflow models, respectively. Then an integrated approach to enterprise and IS development is presented, where interoperability among the various systems (and enterprises) would be a major focus. Finally, the last section provides some concluding remarks.

BASE TECHNOLOGIES AND ONTOLOGY

We here briefly describe core technologies within the area, including XML, RDF, RDF Schema, and ontologies including an overview of OWL.

XML

XML will receive the least coverage in this review. It is the most general and widespread of the technologies we consider, and is therefore likely to be familiar to the majority of readers. Basically, XML defines a set of syntax rules that can be used to create semantically rich markup languages for particular domains. Once a markup language is defined and the semantics of the tags known, the document content can be annotated. The XML language thus defined can include specification of formatting, semantics, document meta-data (author, title, etc.), and so on. XML allows for the creation of *elements* which are XML containers consisting of a start tag, content, and an end tag.

Because of the flexibility of XML in defining domain specific, meaningful markups, it has been widely adapted as a standard for application independent data exchange. These properties combine to make XML the foundational technology for the semantic web, providing a common syntax for authoring web content. XML provides means for syntactic interoperability, as well as ways to ensure the validity of a document, and most importantly the necessary syntax to define the meaning of elements in a domain specific application. On the other hand providing the syntax for defining meaning is only a necessary, but not sufficient condition for the specification of semantics that allows interoperability

Building on the XML specification also becomes necessary because the hierarchical structure of XML documents makes them difficult to use for extensible, distributed data definitions. Much of the information about relationships in the data is implicit in the structure of the document, making it difficult to use and update this information in a flexible and application independent way. This is where RDF comes into the picture.

RDF

The first level at which a concrete data model is defined on XML is the Resource Description Framework (RDF). Actually, RDF as a data model is independent of XML, but we consider it as a layer extending the XML because of the widely practiced XML *serialization* of RDF in semantic web applications (RDF/XML[2]).

The basic structure of RDF is a triple consisting of two nodes and a connecting edge. These basic elements are all kinds of *RDF resources*, and can be variously described as <things> <properties> <values> (Manola & Miller, 2004), <object> <attribute> <value> (Broekstra, Kampman, & van Harmelen, 2003), or <subject> <predicate> <object> (Powers, 2003). There are alternative serializations of RDF, including N3[3], N-Triples[4], and Turtle[5]. Each of these professes some advantages, for example human readability, but RDF/XML is the normative syntax for writing RDF.

This relatively simple basic model has several features that make it a powerful data model for integrating data in dispersed locations (Butler 2002).

1. RDF is based on triples, in contrast to simple attribute-value pairs. The advantage of using triples is that this makes the subject of the attribute value pair explicit.
2. RDF distinguishes between resources and properties that are globally qualified, i.e., are associated with a URI, and those that are locally qualified. The advantage of a globally qualified resource or property is it can be distinguished from other resources or properties in different vocabularies that share the same fragment name, in a fashion that is analogous to XML namespaces.

3. As a result of the first two properties, RDF can be used to make statements about Web resources, by relating one URI to another.

4. It is easy to encode graphs using RDF as it is based on triples, whereas XML documents are trees so encoding graphs is more complicated and can be done in several different ways.

5. RDF has an explicit interpretation or model theory; there is an explicit formal, application independent interpretation of an RDF model (Hayes, 2004). XML documents also have interpretations but they are often implicit in the processor or parser associated with that particular type of XML document.

But in spite of the apparent usefulness of RDF, there is relatively slow adoption of RDF compared with XML (Batzarov, 2004).

There are many possible reasons for this slow adoption. (Daconta, Obrst, & Smith, 2003) take an optimistic position and attribute the long lead-in time to poor tutorials, minimal tool support, and poor demonstration applications, arguing that once the practical limitations have been overcome, adoption will grow rapidly. However, we must not ignore the presence of dissatisfaction with RDF in both practitioner and research communities. Some of the challenges for RDF in light of this dissatisfaction are as follows:

1. RDF / XML (or XHTML) integration needs improvement. The W3C RDF Working Group is working on solutions for successfully embedding RDF within XHTML (RDF/A[6]), and tools such as SMORE[7] purport to making HTML markup easier. But so far there are no high profile, compelling applications to showcase the advantages of RDF. For example microformats[8], which can be seen as a very simple version of RDF/A but are "designed for humans first and machines second", have enjoyed a rapid uptake. For example, both Yahoo! and Google can run specialized searches on microformats.

2. The RDF data model can be complex and confusing because it mixes metaphors and introduces new concepts that can be tricky to model. For instance the standard notion of RDF as composed of subject-predicate-object is linguistically derived, but its relationship to concepts in other representations is somewhat unclear, e.g., class-property-value (object-oriented), node-edge-node (graph theory), source-link-destination (web link), entity-relation-entity (database), and can cause confusion. One of the particularly tricky constructs is reification, which introduces an unproven modeling construct that is foreign to most data modeling communities. Reification can cause confusion because it can be used to arbitrarily nest statements, possibly negating the stated truth value of statements (Daconta, Obrst, & Smith, 2003).

3. The RDF/XML serialization is confusing and difficult to work with, especially in the absence of proper tool support. The striped syntax (Brickley, 2001) can make it difficult to understand the proper interpretation of statements. For instance it is often impossible to tell whether an XML element in the RDF serialization represents an edge, or a node. The complexity of the syntax is partially responsible for a relative support of the RSS1.0[9] specification. RSS1.0 is an RDF based variant of the popular RSS format, and is probably the most high profile use of RDF on the Internet. However, it is losing ground in terms of popularity to the non-RDF based, and syntactically much simpler RSS 2.0[10].

Clearly there is a great deal of work to be done in establishing RDF as a core technology that adds value to the widely adopted XML syntax alone. There are some fledgling ventures launched in 2007, backed by high profile investors, which attempt to bring the advantages of RDF to mainstream social networking applications[11]. Should they become successful, then RDF will become more prominent in the public eye.

But RDF is also important as a foundation layer for *Ontologies,* making it relatively simple to express higher level ontological constructs. Implementing ontologies in XML and XML Schema without RDF is tricky for several reasons. In describing a procedure for translating an ontology into an XML Schema, (Klein et al., 2003) note several important problems. First, superclass/subclass inheritance is problematic and has to be overcome with artificial workarounds in the XML specification, and defining multiple inheritance is not possible at all in XML/S. Second, the possibility of fully automating the translation process is questionable, limiting its use for large ontologies.

In order to use RDF as a means of representing knowledge it is necessary to enrich the language in ways that fixes the interpretation of parts of the language. As described thus far, RDF does not impose any interpretation on the kinds of resources involved in a statement beyond the roles of subject, predicate and object. It has no way of imposing some sort of agreed meaning on the roles, or the relationships between them. The RDF schema is a way of imposing a simple ontology on the RDF framework by introducing a system of simple types.

RDF Schema

We have seen that RDF provides a means to relate resources to one another in a graph based formalism connecting subjects to objects via predicates. The RDF schema, (RDF/S) provides modeling primitives that can be used to capture basic semantics in a domain neutral way. That is, RDF/S specifies metadata that is applicable to the entities and their properties in all domains. The metadata then serves as a standard model by which RDF tools can operate on specific domain models, since the RDF/S meta-model elements will have a fixed semantics in all domain models. The RDF/S elements are shown in Table 1 and 2.

RDF/S provides simple but powerful modeling primitives for structuring domain knowledge into classes and sub-classes, properties and sub- properties, and can impose restrictions on the domain and range of properties, and defines the semantics of containers.

Table 1. RDF/S classes

Class name	comment
rdfs:Resource	The class resource, everything.
rdfs:Literal	The class of literal values, e.g. textual strings and integers.
rdfs:Class	The class of classes.
rdfs:Datatype	The class of RDF datatypes.
rdfs:Container	The class of RDF containers.
rdfs:ContainerMembershipProperty	The class of container membership properties, rdf:_1, rdf:_2, ..., all of which are sub-properties of 'member'.

Table 2. RDF/S properties

Property name	comment	domain	range
rdfs:subClassOf	The subject is a subclass of a class.	rdfs:Class	rdfs:Class
rdfs:subProper-tyOf	The subject is a subproperty of a property.	rdf:Property	rdf:Property
rdfs:domain	A domain of the subject property.	rdf:Property	rdfs:Class
rdfs:range	A range of the subject property.	rdf:Property	rdfs:Class
rdfs:label	A human-readable name for the subject.	rdfs:Resource	rdfs:Literal
rdfs:comment	A description of the subject resource.	rdfs:Resource	rdfs:Literal
rdfs:member	A member of the subject container.	rdfs:Resource	rdfs:Resource
rdfs:seeAlso	Further information about the subject resource.	rdfs:Resource	rdfs:Resource
rdfs:isDefinedBy	The definition of the subject resource.	rdfs:Resource	rdfs:Resource

The simple meta-modeling elements can limit the expressiveness of RDF/S. Some of the main limiting deficiencies are identified in (Antoniou & van Harmelen, 2004):

- *Local scope of properties*: in RDF/S it is possible to define a range on properties, but not so they apply to some classes only. For instance the property eats can have a range restriction of food that applies to all classes in the domain of the property, but it is not possible to restrict the range to plants for some classes and meat for others.
- *Disjointness* of classes cannot be defined in RDF/S.
- *Boolean combinations of classes* are not possible. For example Person cannot be defined as the union of the classes Male and Female.
- *Cardinality restrictions* cannot be expressed.
- *Special characteristics of properties* like transitivity cannot be expressed.

Ontologies

A good starting point for understanding what *ontology* entails, is to consider Figure 1, adopted from (Daconta, Obrst, & Smith,2003), which places a number of knowledge models on a continuum. As you go from the lower left corner to the upper right, the richness of the expressible semantics increases. This is shown on the right side of the arrow with some typical expressions that have some sort of defined semantics for the particular model. The names for the knowledge models are given on the left of the arrow. It is important to note that all of the terms on the left hand side have been called "ontology" by at least some authors, which is part of the source for confusion about the word.

Models based on the various points along the ontology spectrum have different uses (McGuinness, 2003). In the simplest case, a group of users can agree to use a controlled vocabulary for their domain. This of course does not guarantee that they will use the terms in the same way all the time, but if all the users including database designers chose their terms from an accepted set, then the chances of mutual understanding are greatly enhanced.

Perhaps the most publicly visible use for simple ontologies is the taxonomies used for site organization on the World Wide Web. This allows designers to structure information and users to browse and

Figure 1. The ontology spectrum

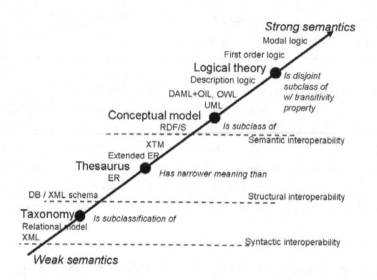

search. Taxonomies can also help with sense disambiguation since the context of a term is given by the more general terms in the taxonomy.

Structured ontologies provide more sophisticated usage scenarios. For instance, they can provide simple consistency and completeness checks. If all *products* must have a *price* then web sites can automatically be checked for missing or conflicting information. Such ontologies can also provide completion where partially specified information can be expanded automatically by reference to the terms in the ontology. This expanded information could also be used for refining search, for instance. Ontologies can also facilitate interoperability, by aligning different terms that might be used in different applications (McGuinness, 2003).

Now we are in a position to see why the ontologies on the most formal end of the spectrum are often taken as the default interpretation in the context of the semantic web, providing the conceptual underpinning for " ... making the semantics of metadata machine interpretable" (Staab & Stuber, 2004). But for the semantics of a domain model to be machine interpretable in any interesting way, it must be in a format that allows automated reasoning in a flexible manner. Obviously, taxonomies can specify little in this sense. Database schemas are more powerful, but limit the interpretation to a single model in terms of reasoning over the knowledge base and the only automated reasoning that can be performed is what is allowed by the relational model, i.e., retrieval of tuples actually represented in the database. Formal logic based reasoning about ontologies can consider multiple possible models (Bordiga & Brachman, 2003). They are at the same time more formally constrained and more semantically flexible than database schemas. Ontologies based on different logics can support different kinds of inference, but a minimal set of services should include reasoning about class membership, class equivalence, consistency, and classification (Antoniou & van Harmelen, 2004).

The ontology representation language adopted by the Web Ontology Working Group of the W3C[12] is the Web Ontology Language (OWL). OWL is a response to a number of requirements (Smith, Welty, & McGuinness, 2004) including the need for a language with formal semantics that enables automated reasoning, and to address the inherent limitations of RDF/S as described above.

OWL

According to the original design goal, OWL was to be a straightforward extension of RDF/S, guaranteeing downward compatibility such that an OWL aware processor could also understand RDF/S documents without modification. Unfortunately this did not succeed because the generality of some RDF/S elements (e.g. the semantics of *class* as *"the class of all classes"*) does not make RDF/S expressions tractable in the general case. In order to maintain computational tractability, OWL processors include restrictions that prevent the interpretation of some RDF/S expressions. The OWL specification defines three sublanguages: OWL Full, OWL DL, and OWL Lite: OWL Full is upward and downward compatible with RDF but OWL DL and OWL Lite are not.

The names of the three sub languages of OWL describe their expressiveness, keeping in mind a fundamental tradeoff between expressiveness, efficiency of reasoning, and support for human understanding. OWL Full has constructs that make the language undecidable. Developers should therefore only use OWL Full if the other two sub languages are inadequate for modeling the relevant domain, or if they wish to maintain full compatibility with RDF. Similarly, OWL DL should be used if OWL Lite is not sufficient. Details of the syntax and semantics can easily be obtained from the technical documentation web site of the W3C.

WEB SERVICES

There is a great deal of interest about web services (Alonso et al., 2004) and service oriented architectures in general. A useful definition can be found in (Daconta, Obrst, & Smith, 2003): "Web services are software applications that can be *discovered, described,* and *accessed* based on XML and standard Web protocols over intranets, extranets, and the Internet." This definition exposes the main technical aspects of web services, to do with discovery and description, as well as the role of WWW (e.g. XML) technologies for data exchange and communication. Also the definition is abstract enough to exclude low level protocols like RPC as web services. These core concepts along with the associated technologies are shown in Figure 2 below.

It is important to situate the role of Web services in the real world. (Daconta, Obrst, & Smith, 2003) argue that the most important factor for determining the future of a new technology is not "... how well it works or how "cool" it is ..." but on business adoption. Along this line they see a bright future for Web

Figure 2. The basic layers of Web services

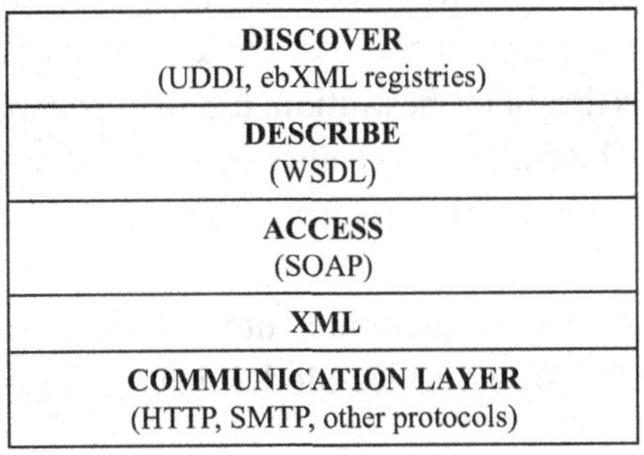

DISCOVER
(UDDI, ebXML registries)
DESCRIBE (WSDL)
ACCESS (SOAP)
XML
COMMUNICATION LAYER (HTTP, SMTP, other protocols)

services which is being promoted by Microsoft, IBM, Sun, as well as the open source community. But why such widespread support? One reason is the promise of interoperable systems. Once businesses adopt standardized web service descriptions, the possibility of exchanging data and sharing the cost of services increases. In addition, the open standards prevent monopolization of applications, preventing the dreaded "vendor lock-in" associated with proprietary solutions. Finally, a widespread adoption of Web service protocols means that existing applications can be leveraged by turning them into Web services. As an example, it is possible for .NET clients and servers to talk to J2EE servers using SOAP.

The point of all this is that Web services enable interoperability at the level of business processes without having to worry about interoperating between different applications, data formats, communication protocols, and so on. We will see later in the article that this influences the way workflows and knowledge based work processes are modeled and instantiated in particular work environments.

As describe above web services must be discovered, described, and appropriately connected in an implementation independent way. (Berardi et al., 2005) outline 3 different approaches for web service discovery, on a trade-off between ease of provision and accuracy: 1) natural language keyword matching, 2) ontology based keyword matching (increasing precision through a controlled vocabulary), and 3) semantic matchmaking, based on precise semantic descriptions of services and service needs. Currently, service descriptions in UDDI, for example, are primarily text descriptions with no semantic markup, requiring a lot of manual input, and not facilitating the more advanced approaches to discovery.

Service Composition

As for service composition (Berardi et al., 2005) distinguishes between *synthesis*, building the specification of the composite service from its sub-services, and *orchestration*, which is the run-time management of the composite service (scheduling, invoking sub-services, etc.). Synthesis can be done either manually or automatically, the latter requiring that services have been specified formally. The orchestration problem for web services has a lot in common with similar issues in workflow management, which will be discussed in the next section. (Dijkman & Dumas, 2004) identify four different viewpoints from which the control-flow aspects of web services can be described, distinguishing between *choreography*, which is a collaboration between service providers and user to achieve a certain goal, and *orchestration,* which is what a service provider performs internally to realize a service it provides. (The other two viewpoints are *behavior interface* and *provider interface*).

There are two ongoing standardization efforts related to service composition (Barros, Dumas & Oaks, 2005), the Web Service Business Process Execution Language (WS-BPEL), formerly known as BPEL4WS, and the Web Service Choreography Description Language (WS-CDL). WS-BPEL (Arkin et al., 2005) is meant to specify both abstract and executable business processes, and the language contains one section of core concepts (needed for both kinds of specifications) as well as sections with extensions for executable processes and abstract processes (a.k.a. business protocols), respectively. The main viewpoint taken in WS-BPEL is that of orchestration, requiring centralized control of the business process. WS-CDL (Cavantzas et al., 2005), takes the alternative viewpoint of choreography, meaning that this language is better suited for describing interplay between several independent parties in a shared control domain.

There are several proposed frameworks to facilitate automatic support for describing, finding and composing web services: METEOR-S[13], Web Service Modeling Ontology (WSMO)[14], Internet Reasoning Service (IRS)[15], and OWL-S[16].

METEOR-S

The METEOR-S project is run at the LSDIS Lab at the University of Georgia, as a successor of the METEOR project, whose focus was on workflow management in a more traditional transaction-oriented perspective. METEOR-S take a more semantic and dynamic perspective on workflow management. The METEOR-S architecture consists of three main components: the process designer, the configuration module, and the execution environment. The process designer module supports the design of abstract work processes represented inWS-BPEL. The Jena toolkit is used for building and processing ontologies. The process configuration module is responsible for dynamically finding and binding services for the defined processes. The METEOR-S Web Service Annotation Framework (MWSAF)[17] tool is used for semi-automatically annotating web services with semantics using the WSDL-S[18] language. The execution environment consists of a logical layer over a web process execution engine. The execution engine uses proxies for each virtual partner of the process. To support run-time and deployment-time binding the configuration module can change the service bound to the proxies.

At the time of writing (December 2007) the METEOR-S framework is in version 0.8, with a couple of finished tools. Currently, the MWSAF tool seems to be the only one publicly available for download.

WSMO

The Web Service Modeling Ontology (WSMO) is a prject undertaken by the WSMO Working group under the SDK[19] project cluster (EU). WSMO consists of three main components: a modeling framework of core elements for semantic web services, a formal description language (Web Service Modeling Language - WSML) and an execution environment (WSMX). The WSMO core elements are

1. Ontologies – provide the formally specified terminology of the information used by all other components
2. Goals – objectives that a client wants to achieve by using Web Services
3. Web Services – semantic description of web services including functional capability and usage interface
4. Mediators – connectors between components with mediation facilities for handling heterogeneities

Each of these elements is further described by non-functional properties including the Dublin Core Metadata Set, versioning information, quality of service information, and other relevant annotations.

Together these components are able to define the terminology of the domain and how it relates to applications, and to describe the service in terms of its pre-conditions, post-conditions, effects, and mediators required during the discovery and execution of the service.

Several tools related to WSMO are publicly available, the most important ones being the Web Service Execution Environment (WSMX), the Web Service Modeling Toolkit (WSMT), and the WSML Validator.

Internet Reasoning Service

The Internet Reasoning Service (IRS) is an ongoing project at the Knowledge Media Institute at the Open University. IRS has many similarities with WSMO, as it actually uses the WSMO's ontology as a basis, but then providing several extensions. In particular, the concepts of goal and web service have been extended in IRS relative to the original WSMO definition. The latest implementation is IRS-III, supporting the following activities for building semantic web services (Cabral et al., 2006):

- Use of domain ontologies
- Description of client requests as goals
- Semantic description of deployed web services
- Resolution of conceptual mismatches
- Publication and invocation of the described web services

The support for these activities is achieved by the IRS-III server, having the following components:

- The SWS library, where the semantic descriptions of web services are stored.
- Interpreters for choreography and orchestration, respectively
- The Mediation Handler, supporting brokering in the process of selecting, composing and invoking web services.
- The Invoker, which communicates with the service publishing platform, sends input from the client to the invoked services, and returns the results back to the client.

The IRS server is written in LISP and is available as an executable file. The publishing platforms for web services are available as Java web applications. Also available is the WebOnto[20] tool for visualizing and editing IRS-III ontologies defined in the language OCML (Operational Conceptual Modeling Language)[21].

OWL-S

OWL-S is a W3C initiative to provide an ontology and language to describe web services. It is less revolutionary than WSMO or IRS, as is evidenced by its closer ties to current standards like WSDL and UDDI. Its primary role is to assist discovery, which it fulfils by specifying three key components of a service as parts of its Upper Ontology of Services:

- *What does the service provide for prospective clients?* The answer to this question is given in the Service Profile which is used to advertise the service.
- *How is it used?* The answer to this question is given in the "process model." This perspective is captured by the ServiceModel class.
- *How does one interact with it?* The answer to this question is given in the "grounding." A grounding provides the needed details about transport protocols.

Thus each service presents a Service Profile (what it does), is described by a Service Model (how it works), and supports a Service Grounding (how to access it).

Available implementations for OWL-S include OWL files for the Upper Ontology of Services and other relevant ontologies used by this Upper Ontology. Moreover, a set of relevant tools have been released, mostly by third parties, for instance:

- The OWL-S Protégé-based editor[22]
- Another OWL-S Editor[23] developed at the University of Malta
- ASSAM Web Service Annotator (Hess et al., 2004)
- Semantic Web Service Composer[24]
- OWL-S matcher[25], to assess the degree of correspondence between different service descriptions

Comparison of the Frameworks

While OWL-S is a less comprehensive approach, there are certain similarities between this and the WSMO-based approaches.

- OWL-S Service Profile ≈ WSMO capability + goal + non-functional properties. WSMO separates provider (capabilities) and requester points of view (goals) while OWL-S Profiles combine existing capabilities (advertisements) and desired capabilities (requests)
- OWL-S process model ≈ WSMO Service Interfaces. The process model in the OWL-S ServiceModel roughly corresponds to the interfaces in the WSMO Web Services descriptions of WSMO.
- OWL-S Grounding ≈ WSMO Grounding. Both provide a mapping to WSDL.

Nevertheless, clear differences exist in the overall architecture as well as the reliance of WSMO on explicitly defined mediators. A key objective of the WSMO is to define a taxonomy of mediators to translate between message produced by one Web service and those expected by another. In the OWL-S vision this is a step which can detract from the primary purpose of discovery. To be sure the translation problems still need to be solved, but OWL-S assumes this will be possible through some form of

Table 1. Comparison of the four frameworks

SWS Activity	METEOR-S	WSMO	IRS-III	OWL-S
Publishing	Process Designer	WSMO Editor / Service Repository	Publishing Client / Handler	Not detailed
Discovery	Config. Module	Matchmaker	Mediation Handler	Matcher
Composition	Config. Module	Matchmaker	Mediation Handler	Not detailed
Selection	Config. Module	Selector	Mediation Handler	Matcher
Invocation	Execution Engine	Communication Manager	Invocation Handler / Publishing Platf.	Not detailed
Deployment	MWSAF	Matchmaker	Publishing Platf.	Not detailed
Ontology management	MWSAF	WSMO Editor	Mediation Handler	OWL-S Editors

composition (Ankolekar et al., 2004). But this has some implications for the use of each system in a specific context, such as the system described in subsequent sections.

The comparison of the four discussed frameworks is summed up in Table 3, concerning the available support for various activities related to the development and running of applications based on semantic web services.

As can be seen from this comparison, OWL-S is the framework which is most different from the others, in the sense that it specifies less of the surrounding architecture for service and application development. While the other three include some kind of supporting tools for all the 7 tasks indicated in the left column of the table, OWL-S has not provided any specific support for publishing, composition, invocation and deployment.

WORKFLOW AND ENTERPRISE PROCESS MODELING

The unprecedented flexibility of web services provides a particular challenge for how to integrate their use in enterprise work practices. On the one hand, demand based service provision promises to be a blessing for facilitating problem solving; on the other hand, the instance based variability provided through the relatively free range of solutions offered in service composition could result in a serious challenge to established workflow modeling paradigms.

Process modeling implicates a family of techniques used to document and explicate a set of business and work processes in a way that allows their analysis at various levels, and for various purposes. Our specific interest here is to use workflow modeling to analyze the work contexts that are likely to be involved in the day to day activities of an enterprise, with the aim of improving the timely delivery of appropriate information related resources and services. The purpose is to integrate workflow modeling with the potential of web services, to capture the likely usage scenarios under which the services will need to operate and to model this integrated use. The aim is that the model of work practices will allow better specification of actual information needs, which will in turn allow for richer requirements for the service descriptions expected from a web service, which will facilitate service composition and interoperability. The research problems therefore complement one another: workflow modeling helps web service design, but the availability of these services in turn improves workflow modeling techniques.

The challenge for us is to construct modeling approaches that maintain sufficient expressive power for the required points of view as well as to allow flexibility for changing situations. (Jørgensen, 2004; Krogstie & Jørgensen, 2004) argue that static workflow models cannot handle the changing demands of real world situations, and that adaptive models, while providing greater flexibility, still cannot adequately handle the instance based user driven modifications needed in many situations. They argue for interactive models that can be dynamically configured by users.

Workflow and Process Modeling Languages

Workflow modeling has been used to learn about, guide and support practice in a number of different areas including software process improvement (Bandinelli et al., 1995; Derniame, Kaba & Wastell, 1998), enterprise modeling (Fox & Grüninger, 2000), process centric software engineering (Ambriola, Conradi & Fuggetta 1997), and workflow systems (Fischer, 2001). The process modeling languages employed in these areas have been usefully categorized into one of the following types: transformational, conversational, role-oriented, constraint-based, and systemic (Carlsen, 1997). A summary of each type is given in (Jørgensen, 2004) where they are considered for their suitability as interactive modeling paradigms.

Transformational languages represent the majority of process modeling languages in use, adopting an input-process-output approach. Some well known languages adopting this approach are Data Flow Diagrams (DFD), IDEF-0, Activity diagrams, BPMN, Event-driven Process Chains (EPC), and Petri nets. While there are clear differences between the formalisms, it is possible to generalize in terms of their basic expressive commitments and therefore suitability for modeling dynamic, flexible workflows (Conradi & Jaccheri, 1998; Curtis, Kellner & Over, 1992; Green & Rosemann, 2000; Lei & Singh, 1997). The standards defined by the Workflow Management Coalition (Fischer, 2001), the Internet Engineering Task Force (IETF) (Bolcer & Kaiser, 1999), and the Object Management Group (OMG, 2000) are all predicated on a common perspective. We consider a few languages from this perspective.

The WfMC standards for process definition interchange between systems (WfMC, 1999) include a large portion of the primitives involved in transformational languages. Processes are modeled with hierarchical decomposition, control flow structures for sequences, iteration, AND and XOR branching. Activities can be associated with organizational roles and actors, tools and applications. The core terminology of the WfMC is found in (Fischer, 2001). Importantly, there is a distinction between process definition (idealized process) and instance (actual work).

From past experience with developing flexible groupware and workflow systems (Carlsen, 1998; Jørgensen, 2001, 2003; Jørgensen & Carlsen, 1999; Natvig & Ohren, 1999), we have defined an interactive models approach to flexible information systems (Jørgensen, 2004). Models are normally defined as explicit representations of some portions of reality as perceived by some actor (Wegner & Goldin, 1999). A model is active if it directly influences the reality it reflects. Model activation involves actors interpreting the model and adjusting their behavior accordingly. This process can be

- Automated, where a software component interprets the model,
- Manual, where the model guides the actions of human actors, or
- Interactive, where prescribed aspects of the model are automatically interpreted and ambiguous parts are left to the users to resolve.

We define a model to be interactive if it is interactively activated. By updating such a model, users can adapt the system to fit their local plans, preferences and terminology.

The Business Process Modeling Language (BPML) (Arkin, 2002) defines a *web service* interface description language, which presents obvious promise concerning the present requirements. BPML emphasizes low-level execution and contains several control flow primitives for loops (foreach, while, until), branching (manual choice or rule based switch, join), decomposition (all, sequential, choice), instantiation (call, spawn), properties (assign), tools (action), exceptions (fault), and transactions (compensate). The ability to define manual as well as rule based branching is promising for use in flexible systems. Unfortunately the promise is only partially realized since different primitives are used for the two cases, implying that the automation boundary must be defined during process design. Additionally, BPML has weak support for local change and unforeseen exceptions. A visual notation, for BPML, BPMN has been developed and is getting increasing support both among researchers and in industrial practice (BPMI. org and OMG, 2006). The further standardization of BPMN is taken over by OMG, which have also standardized The Business Process Definition Metamodel (BPDM) which applies MDA principles to provide a consistent end-to-end approach for business process modeling. The development of

BPMN was based on the revision of other notations, including UML, IDEF, ebXML, RosettaNet, LOVeM and EPCs, and stemmed from the demand for a graphical language that complements the BPEL standard for executable business processes. Although this gives BPMN a technical focus, it has been the intention of the BPMN designers to develop a modeling language that can be applied for typical business modeling activities as well. The complete BPMN specification defines thirty-eight distinct language constructs plus attributes, grouped into four basic categories of elements, viz., Flow Objects, Connecting Objects, Swimlanes and Artefacts. Flow Objects, such as events, activities and gateways, are the most basic elements used to create Business Process Diagrams (BPDs). Connecting Objects are used to interconnect Flow Objects through different types of arrows. Swimlanes are used to group activities into separate categories for different functional capabilities or responsibilities (e.g., different roles or organizational departments). Finally, Artefacts may be added to a diagram where deemed appropriate in order to display further related information such as processed data or other comments.

BPDM on its side acknowledges that business process definitions are frequently used for purposes that do not required automation (for example, simulation and optimization of manual processes). In cases where a business process is to be (partially) automated, the BPDM enables sufficient detail to be added to a process definition to completely specify the process to the level of detail that is required to generate executable runtime artifacts (e.g. by providing a mapping from BPMN to BPEL).

There is some recognition for the need to separate design components from run-time components for increased flexibility. This is realized in the WfMC's XML Process Definition Language (WfMC, 2002). But even here, the separation is focused mainly for facilitating the reuse of design components across different workflow engines and design tools. There is little support for user driven interaction at run-time.

It appears that current approaches are not designed with the flexibility required to accommodate the adaptive workflows that are enabled by Web Services technologies. One approach that be recon is worth pursuing is the use of interactive models, which we will look on in more detail below.

INTEGRATING ENTERPRISE AND IS DEVELOPMENT AND INTEROPERABILITY

Different approaches to model-driven development are appropriate for supporting different types of processes, from very static, to very dynamic, even emergent processes. The different process types decide the extent to which the underlying technology can be based on hard-coded, predefined, evolving or implicit process models. This gives a number of development approaches as illustrated in Figure 3: on one extreme; systems are manually coded on top of a traditional runtime environment, and on the other enterprise models are used directly to generate process-support solutions. In between these, we have the approaches typically described in OMGs Model-Driven Architecture approach (MDA), namely the development of Platform Independent Models (PIMs) for code-generation (e.g. on top of a UML Virtual Machine, denoted PIM EE in the figure), or for Platform Specific Models (PSMs) for more traditional code-generation or manual implementation.

In Figure 4, we outline the different types of interoperability-possibilities between these types of development. Whereas traditional systems use special APIs and approaches such as EDI for interchange

Figure 3. Overview of different execution environment for different process models

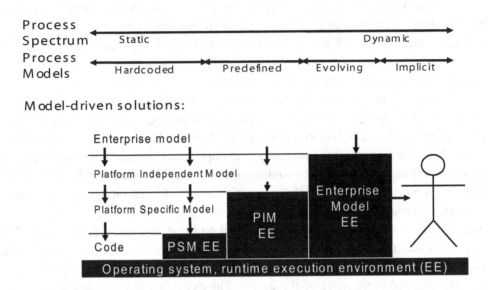

Figure 4. Interoperability between different platforms

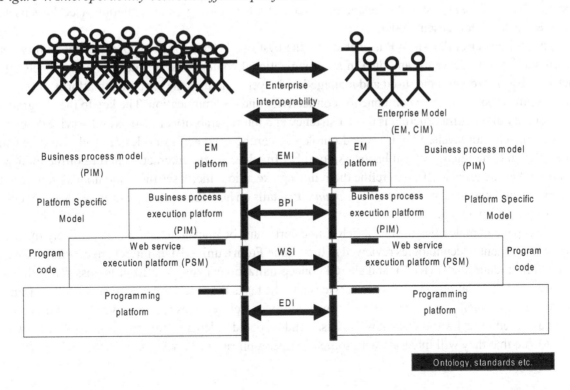

of data, on the next level (PSM), we can identify the standard Web Services Interfaces (WSI). Above this level, there is a lot of work being performed on specific business process execution platform, with a possibility to exchange directly using a BPI (Business Process Interface).

Finally, projects such as EXTERNAL[26], MAPPER[27] and ATHENA[28] have provided solutions for how to interoperate on the enterprise model level, potentially supporting interoperability across models developed using different modeling languages and different tools (Krogstie, 2007).

The EXTERNAL project developed an infrastructure to support networked organizations, defined in three basic layers: the *information and communication technology* (ICT) layer (1); the *knowledge representation* layer (2); the *work performance and management* layer (3). The "business end" of the infrastructure is layer 3 with support for modeling and implementing customer solutions, and generating work environments as personalized and context-sensitive user interfaces available through portals. The task performers may access desktop tools, organizational information systems, web services, or automated processes through this user environment.

User environments are generated dynamically based on the definition of tasks using EEML (Extended Enterprise Modeling Language, (Krogstie, 2008). Forms and components for interacting with different model objects are selected and composed based on generic user interface policies and on the personal and role-oriented preferences of the users. The dynamically generated work management interface includes services for work performance, but also for process modeling and meta-modeling. The model-generated workplace (MGWP) is the main component in this interface. In addition to the services for performing and managing the task, it contains links to all knowledge in the process models that is relevant for the task. Since the MGWP is dynamically generated, subject to personal preferences, the skill levels of task performers can be taken into account. Similarly, customized MGWPs for project management can support the project management team. The contents may include an overview of the project, adopted management principles, applicable methodologies, project work-break-down structure, results, plans and tasks, technologies and resources, status reporting and calculations (see Jørgensen, 2004; Krogstie & Jørgensen, 2004).

The full power of the MGWP is enabled by the first two layers, which enable interoperability between applications, services, and data in an organizational context. Layer 2 defines how models and meta-models are represented, used and managed and layer 1 defines the execution platform, software architectures, tools, software components, connectivity and communication. The key to the integrated functionality of the infrastructure is the consistency and interoperability of models and service descriptions at all relevant levels. Standards and ontologies can be used across all levels, and also between levels to make the interoperation happen smoothly. In addition, the interactive nature of the models, meaning that the users are free to refine them during execution, increases their potential as sources of experience and knowledge. As such they *document* details on how the work was actually done, not only how it was once planned.

Clearly the complexities of such a rich framework must be managed, and this is precisely the role for the fundamental technologies reviewed in this paper. From a unified data interchange format (XML) to a common data model (RDF), and shared conceptualizations (using OWL), it is possible to define services, and the relationships between services and the tasks they are supposed to support, in a transparent and reproducible way. Moreover, the availability of web services can be driven by requirements as documented in real world workflow models. Vendors could independently implement solutions with a guarantee that they will integrate with some existing application framework.

CONCLUSION AND FURTHER WORK

This paper has provided a survey of relevant technologies for achieving semantic interoperability in the context of enterprise information systems, namely ontologies, service descriptions, and tool support frameworks for developing and executing service-oriented applications, as well as workflow models including both automated and interactive tasks. The overview of interoperability between different platforms, together with the example explanations of this, illustrates how the combination of these technologies can provide more advanced interoperability than with current systems.

We suggest that "interoperability" in the abstract may be an untenable goal, at least in the immediate future. But interoperability in the context of dynamic and interactive workflows, as the next best thing, is very much within our reach. Important future work on our approach is as indicated above related to integrating the results from the current work on semantic web services, in addition to operationalizing the semantic annotation approach.

ACKNOWLEDGMENT

Csaba Veres was funded by the Norwegian Research Council through the WISEMOD project while much of the work behind this paper was carried out. John Krogstie has in addition been funded by the projects ATHENA (http://www.athena-ip.org) and the Norwegian Research Council-project MONESA. The ideas of this paper were pursued in the context of the EU NoE project INTEROP and its continuation INTEROP-VLab, and we thank other partners of INTEROP for valuable inspiration. The paper does not represent the view of the funding organizations or project consortia and the authors are solely responsible for the paper's content.

REFERENCES

Alonso, G., Casati, F., Kuno, H., & Machiraju, V. (2004). *Web Services: Concepts, Architecture and Applications*. Berlin: Springer.

Ambriola, V., Conradi, R., & Fuggetta, A. (1997). Assessing Process-Centered Software Engineering Environments. *ACM Transactions on Software Engineering and Methodology, 6*(3), 283-328.

Ankolekar, A., Martin, D., McGuinness, D., McIlraith, S., Paolucci, M., & Parsia, B. (2004). *OWL-S' Relationship to Selected Other Technologies*, Technical report, W3C Member Submission 22 November 2004. Retrieved 1 Feb, 2006, from http://www.w3.org/Submission/OWL-S-related/

Antoniou, G., & van Harmelen, F. (2004). Web Ontology Language: OWL. In S. Staab & R. Studer (Eds.), *Handbook on Ontologies* (pp. 67-92). Berlin: Springer.

Arkin, A. (2002). *Business Process Modelling Language*. Retrieved 23 Aug, 2003, from http://www.bpmi.org/bpmi-downloads/BPML-SPEC-1.0.zip

Arkin, A., Askary, S., Bloch, B., Curbera, F., Goland, Y., Kartha, N., et al. (Eds.) (2005) Web *Services Business Process Execution Language Version 2.0*, Technical report, OASIS Open, Inc., Committee

Draft, 21 Dec, 2005. Retrieved 15 Feb 2006 from http://www.oasis-open.org/committees/download. php/16024/wsbpel-specification-draft-Dec-22-2005.htm

Bandinelli, S., Fuggetta, A., Lavazza, L., Loi, M., & Picco, G. (1995). Modelling and Improving an Industrial Software Process. *IEEE Transactions on Software Engineering, 21*(5), 440-454.

Barros, A., Dumas, M., & Oaks, P. (2005). *A Critical Overview of the Web Services Choreography Description Language*. BPTrends (www.bptrends.com), March 2005, pp 1-24.

Batzarov, Z. (2004). *Orbis Latinus: Linguistic Terms*. Retrieved 3 Apr, 2005, from http://www.orbilat. com/General_References/Linguistic_Terms.html

Berardi, D., Cabral, L., Cimpian, E., Domingue, J., Mecella, M, Stollberg, M., & Sycara, K. (2005). *ESWC Semantic Web Services Tutorial*. Retrieved 15 Feb, 2006, from http://stadium.open.ac.uk/dip/

Berners-Lee, T., Hendler, J., & Lassila, O. (2001). *The Semantic Web*. Scientific American, 284(5), 34-43.

Bolcer, G. A., & Kaiser, G. (1999). SWAP: Leveraging the Web To Manage Workflow. *IEEE Internet Computing, 3*(1), 85-88.

Borgida, A., & Brachman, R. (2003). Conceptual Modeling with Description Logics. In F. Baader, D. Calvanese, D. McGuinness, D. Nardi, & P. Patel-Schneider (Eds.) *The Description Logic Handbook: Theory*, Implementation and Applications. Cambridge University Press.

BPMI.org and OMG. (2006). *Business Process Modeling Notation Specification. Final Adopted Specification*. Object Management Group, http://www.bpmn.org (February 20, 2006).

Brickley, D. (2001). *RDF: Understanding the Striped RDF/XML Syntax*. Retrieved 25 Sep, 2002, from http://www.w3.org/2001/10/stripes/.

Broekstra, J., Kampman, A., & van Harmelen, F. (2003). Sesame: An Architecture for Storin gand Querying RDF Data and Schema Information. In D. Fensel, J. A. Hendler, H. Lieberman & W. Wahlster (Eds.), *Spinning the Semantic Web: Bringing the World Wide Web to Its Full Potential* [outcome of a Dagstuhl seminar] (pp. 197-222). Cambridge, MA: MIT Press.

Bubenko Jr., J. (2007). From Information Algebra to Enterprise Modelling and Ontologies – A Historical Perspective on Modelling for Information Systems. In J. Krogstie, A. L. Opdahl & S. Brinkkemper (Eds.): *Conceptual Modelling in Information Systems Engineering*. Berlin: Springer, pp. 1-18.

Butler, H. (2002). *Barriers to real world adoption of Semantic Web technologies*. Hewlett-Packard.

Cabral, L., Domingue, J., Galizia, S., Gugliotta, A., Tanasescu, V., Pedrinaci, C., & Norton, B. (2006). IRS-III: A broker for semantic web services based applications. In I. Cruz et al. (Eds.). *Proc. ISWC'06, LNCS 4273,*.201-214.

Carlsen, S. (1997). *Conceptual Modelling and Composition of Flexible Workflow Models*. PhD thesis, Dept of Computer and Inforamtion Science, Norwegian University of Science and Technology, Trondheim, Norway.

Carlsen, S. (1998). Action Port Model: A Mixed Paradigm Conceptual Workflow Modeling Language. *Proceedings of the 3rd IFCIS International Conference on Cooperative Information Systems (CoopIS'98),* pp. 300-308. Los Alamitos, CA: IEEE CS Press.

Cavantzas, N., Burdett, D., Ritzinger, G., Fletcher, T., Lafon, Y., & Barreto, C. (Eds.) (2005). *Web Services Choreography Description Language Version 1.0.* Technical report, W3C Candidate Recommendation, 9 Nov, 2005. Retrieved 10 Feb, 2006, from http://www.w3.org/TR/2005/CR-ws-cdl-10-20051109/

Conradi, R., & Jaccheri, L. (1998). Process Modelling Languages. In J.-C. Derniame, B. A. Kaba & D. G. Wastell (Eds.), *Software Process: Principles, Methodology, and Techniques* (pp. 27-52). Berlin: Springer LNCS 1500.

Curtis, B., Kellner, M., & Over, J. (1992). Process Modeling. *Communications of the ACM, 35*(9), 75-90.

Daconta, M., Orbst, L., & Smith, K. (2003). The Semantic Web: A guide to the future of XML, Web Services and Knowledge Management. London: Wiley.

Derniame, J.-C., Kaba, B. A., & Wastell, D. G. (Eds.). (1998). Software Process: Principles, Methodology, Technology. Berlin: Springer (LNCS 1500).

Dijkman, R. & Dumas, M. (2004). Service-Oriented Design. A Multi-Viewpoint Approach. *International Journal of Cooperative Information Systems, 13*(4), 337-368.

Fischer, L. (Ed.). (2001). The Workflow Handbook 2001. Lighthouse Point, FL: Workflow Management Coalition (WfMC).

Fox, M., & Grüninger, M. (1998). Enterprise Modeling. *AI Magazine, 19*(3), 109-121.

Green, P., & Rosemann, M. (2000). Integrated Process Modelling: An Ontological Evaluation. *Information Systems, 25*(2), 73-87.

Haake, J. M., & Wang, W. (1997). Flexible support for business processes: extending cooperative hypermedia with process support. *In Proceedings of GROUP'97, International Conference on Supporting Group Work.* The Integration Challenge.

Hayes, P. (2004). *RDF Semantics.* Technical report, W3C, 10 Feb 2004. Retrieved Mar 3, 2005, from http://www.w3.org/TR/rdf-mt/

Hess, A., Johnston, E., & Kushmerick, N. (2004). ASSAM: A Tool for Semi-automatically Annotating Semantic Web Services. In S.A. McIlraith et al. (Eds.). *Proc. ISWC'04, Springer LNCS 3298,* 320-334.

Jørgensen, H. D. (2001). Interaction as a Framework for Flexible Workflow Modelling. In: C. Ellis & I. Zigurs (Eds.), *Proceedings of the International ACM SIGGROUP Conference on Supporting Group Work 2001.* September 30 - October 3, 2001, Boulder, Colorado, USA. p.32-41.

Jørgensen, H. D. (2003). Model-Driven Work Management Services. In R. Jardim-Goncalves, H. Cha, A. Steiger-Garcao (Eds.), *Proceedings of the 10th International Conference on Concurrent Engineering (CE 2003),* July 2003, Madeira, Portugal. A.A. Balkema Publishers.

Jørgensen, H. D. (2004). *Interactive Process Models*. PhD thesis, Department of Computer and Information Science, Norwegian University of Science and Technology, Trondheim, Norway.

Jørgensen, H. D., & Carlsen, S. (1999) Emergent Workflow: Integrated Planning and Performance of Process Instances. In J. Becker, M. zur Mühlen, M. Rosemann (Eds.) *Proceedings of the 1999 Workflow Management Conference: Workflow-based Applications*, 9 Nov, Univ., Münster, Germany, pp 98-116.

Klein, M., Broekstra, J., Fensel, F., van Harmelen, F., & Horrocks, I. (2003). Ontologies and Schema Languages on the Web. In D. Fensel, J. A. Hendler, H. Lieberman & W. Wahlster (Eds.), *Spinning the Semantic Web: Bringing the World Wide Web to Its Full Potential* [outcome of a Dagstuhl seminar] (pp. 95-139). Cambridge, MA: MIT Press.

Krogstie, J. (2004). Integrating Enterprise and IS Development Using a Model-Driven Approach. In O. Vasilecas, A. Caplinskas, G. Wojtkowski, W. Wojtkowski, J. Zupancic (Eds.) *Information Systems Development Advances in Theory, Practice, and Education*. (Proc. ISD'04). Boston, MA: Kluwer.

Krogstie, J., & Jørgensen, H. (2004). Interactive Models for Supporting Networked Organizations. In A. Persson & J. Stirna (Eds.), *Advanced Information Systems Engineering, 16th International Conference (CAiSE'04)*, Berlin: Springer (LNCS 3084).

Krogstie, J. (2007). Modelling of the People, by the People, for the People. In J. Krogstie, A. L. Opdahl & S. Brinkkemper (Eds.), *Conceptual Modelling in Information Systems Engineering*. Berlin: Springer, pp. 305-318.

Krogstie, J. (2008). Integrated Goal, Data and Process modeling: From TEMPORA to Model-Generated Work-Places. In, Johannesson and Søderstrøm, (eds.), *Information Systems Engineering*. IGI Publishing 2008.

Kuntz, J., Christiansen, T., Cohen, G., Jin, Y. & Levitt, R. (1998). The virtual design team: A Computational simulation model of project organizations. *Communications of the ACM, 41*(11), 84-92.

Lei, Y., & Singh, M. (1997). A Comparison of Workflow Metamodels. *Paper presented at the ER'97 Workshop on Behavioral Models and Design Transformations: Issues and Opportunities in Conceptual Modeling*, Los Angeles, CA.

Lillehagen, F. (1999). Visual extended enterprise engineering embedding knowledge management systems engineering and work execution. *IFIP International Enterprise Modeling Conference (IEMC'99)*, Verdal, Norway.

Linthicum, D. (2003). *Next Generation Application Integration: From Simple Information to Web Services*. Boston: Addison-Wesley.

Loos, P., & Allweyer, T. (1998). *Process Orientation and Object Orientation - An Approach for Integrating UML* (Technical Report). Saarbrücken, Germany: Institut für Wirtschaftsinformatik, University of Saarland.

Manola, F., & Miller, E. (2004, 10 Feb). RDF Primer. Retrieved 15 Aug, 2005, from http://www.w3.org/TR/rdf-primer/

McGuinness, D. L. (2003). Ontologies Come of Age. In D. Fensel, J. A. Hendler, H. Lieberman & W. Wahlster (Eds.), *Spinning the Semantic Web: Bringing the World Wide Web to Its Full Potential* [outcome of a Dagstuhl seminar] (pp. 171-195). Cambridge, MA: MIT Press.

Miles, A. (2006, February). *RDFMolecules:Evaluating Semantic Web Technology in a Scientific Application*. Available at http://www.w3c.rl.ac.uk/SWAD/ papers/RDFMolecules_final.doc (Feb 20, 2006)

Natvig, M. K., & Ohren, O. (1999). Modeling shared information spaces (SIS). *In GROUP '99: Proceedings of the international ACM SIGGROUP conference on Supporting group work*, Phoenix, AZ, Nov 14-17, pp. 99-108. New York: ACM Press.

OMG (2000). Workflow Management Facility Specification, v.1.2. Needham, MA: Object Management Group.

Opdahl, A. L., & Sindre, G. (2007). Interoperable Management of Conceptual Models, In J. Krogstie, A. L. Opdahl & S. Brinkkemper (Eds.), *Conceptual Modelling in Information Systems Engineering*. Berlin: Springer, pp. 75-90.

OWL-S Coalition (2004). OWL-S 1.1 Release. Retrieved 9 Aug, 2005, from http://www.daml.org/services/owl-s/

Powers, S. (2003). Practical RDF. Sebastopol, CA: O'Reilly.

Scheer, A.-W., & Nuttgens, M. (2000). ARIS Architecture and Reference Models for Business Process Management. In W. M. P. van der Aalst, J. Desel & A. Oberweis (Eds.), *Business Process Management* (pp. 376-390). Berlin, Germany: Springer (LNCS 1806).

Smith, M., Welty, C., & McGuinness, D. L. (Eds.) (2004, 10 Feb). *OWL Web Ontology Language Guide*. Retrieved 25 Feb, 2005, from http://www.w3.org/TR/owl-guide/

Staab, S., & Studer, R. (Eds.). (2004). Handbook on Ontologies. Berlin, Germany: Springer.

van der Aalst, W. M. P. (1999). Formalization and Verification of Event-driven Process Chains. *Information and Software Technology, 41*(10), 639-650.

Wegner, P., & Goldin, D. (1999). Interaction as a Framework for Modeling. In P. P. Chen, J. Akoka, H. Kangassalo, & B. Thalheim (Eds.), *Conceptual Modeling*. Berlin: Springer (LNCS 1565), pp. 100-114

WfMC (1999). *Workflow Management Coalition Interface 1: Process Definition Interchange Process Model* (Technical report No. WfMC TC-1016-P). Lighthouse Point, FL: Workflow Management Coalition.[gsl]

WfMC (2002). *Workflow Process Definition Interface - XML Process Definition Language* (Technical report No. WFMC-TC-1025). Lighthouse Point, FL: Workflow Management Coalition.

WSMO Working Group (2005). *The Web Service Modeling Language WSML*. Retrieved Aug 20, 2005, from http://www.wsmo.org/wsml/wsml-syntax

ENDNOTES

[1]   http://is.uib.no/wiki/UEML/UEML

[2]   http://www.w3.org/TR/rdf-syntax-grammar/

[3]   http://www.w3.org/DesignIssues/Notation3

[4]   http://www.w3.org/TR/2004/REC-rdf-testcases-20040210/#ntriples

[5]   http://www.dajobe.org/2004/01/turtle/

[6]   http://www.w3.org/2001/sw/BestPractices/HTML/2006-01-24-rdfa-primer

[7]   http://www.mindswap.org/2005/SMORE/

[8]   http://microformats.org/

[9]   http://web.resource.org/rss/1.0/spec

[10]   http://www.rssboard.org/rss-specification

[11]   http://www.radarnetworks.com/

[12]   http://www.w3.org/2001/sw/WebOnt/

[13]   http://lsdis.cs.uga.edu/projects/meteor-s/

[14]   http://www.wsmo.org/

[15]   http://kmi.open.ac.uk/projects/irs/

[16]   http://www.daml.org/services/owl-s/

[17]   http://lsdis.cs.uga.edu/projects/meteor-s/downloads/mwsaf/

[18]   http://www.w3.org/Submission/WSDL-S/

[19]   http://sdk.semanticweb.org/index.html

[20]   http://kmi.open.ac.uk/projects/webonto/

[21]   http://kmi.open.ac.uk/projects/ocml/

[22]   http://www.daml.org/services/owl-s/tools.html, http://owlseditor.semwebcentral.org/

[23]   http://staff.um.edu.mt/cabe2/supervising/undergraduate/owlseditFYP/OwlSEdit.html

[24]   http://alphaworks.ibm.com/tech/ettk

[25]   http://owlsm.projects.semwebcentral.org/

[26]   http://research.dnv.com/external/default.htm

[27]   http://193.71.42.92/websolution/UI/Troux/07/Default.asp?WebID=260&PageID=1

[28]   http://www.athenaip.org

Chapter XI
Integrated Research and Training in Enterprise Information Systems

Chen-Yang Cheng
Penn State University, USA

Vamsi Salaka
Penn State University, USA

Vittal Prabhu
Penn State University, USA

ABSTRACT

The success of implementing Enterprise Information System (EIS) depends on exploring and improving the EIS software, and EIS software training. However, the synthesis of the EIS implementation approach has not been investigated. In this chapter, the authors propose an integrated research and training approach for students and employees about enterprise information systems (EIS) that are encountered in an organization. Our integrated approach follows the different stages of a typical EIS project from inception to completion. These stages, as identified, are modeling, planning, simulation, transaction, integration, and control. This ensures that an employee who is trained by this plan has an acquaintance with the typical information systems in an organization. Further, for training and research purposes the authors developed prototype information systems that emulate the ones usually found in organizations. This ensures the EIS software logic is consistent with the business logic. This chapter also discuss some of the case studies conducted with the prototype systems.

INTRODUCTION

Enterprise Information Systems (EIS) constitute the spectrum of information technology solutions used by an organization and influence nearly all aspects of operations of an organization. Typical EIS systems such as Enterprise Resource Planning (ERP), Customer and Supplier Relationship Management (CRM and SRM), and Manufacturing Execution Systems (MES). It is widely accepted that EIS deliver great rewards, but the risks these systems carry are equally important. If an organization rolls out an EIS without analyzing the business implications, the logic of the system may conflict with the logic of the business (Subramanian & Hoffer, 2005). This may result in failure of implementation, wasting vast sums of money, and weakening important sources of organization's competitive advantage.

Prior research has investigated and identified the critical factors that influence the successful implementation of EIS. Education and training of employees on EIS is one of the most widely recognized factors (Umble & Haft, 2003) (H. Hutchins, 1998; Ptak & Schragenheim, 2000) (Laughlin, 1999). EIS implementation requires the knowledge of the employees to smoothly carry on the business process and further solve problems that arise from the new system. Even with good technical assistance, the complete potential of EIS cannot be realized without employees having an appreciation of the capabilities and limitations of the system (Somers & Nelson, 2001). To make the employee training successful, it is agreed that it should start early, preferably well before the rollout of EIS begins. The upper management in large manufacturing enterprises often underestimate the level of education and training necessary to implement EIS and as well as its associated costs. It has been suggested that reserving 10–15% of the total EIS implementation budget is a good practice to ensure the employees receive enough training (McCaskey & D. Okrent, 1999) (Umble & Haft, 2003). With the estimated budgets for implementing EIS in billions of dollars the cost of training the employees on these systems is a very sizeable portion (Hong & Kim, 2002). These costs can be brought down if the employees have a prior education and training on EIS. Hence, at the Center for Manufacturing and Enterprise Integration (CMEI) at the Penn State University focuses on training students and working professional in EIS and related enterprise integration issues. Further, as part of research at CMEI, projects are undertaken to study the information system infrastructure for planning in Small Manufacturing Enterprise (SME). These projects were aimed at improving the operations management for SMEs with the help of Information Technology (IT). We found many avenues for improvement both in operations management and information systems, but there were barriers in implementing such projects. These barriers vary from capital and complexity of the systems to human inertia to change. But the key barrier we noticed among SMEs is the lack of tools or expertise for handling the EIS software. Most of the EIS software available requires extensive training for its use and maintenance. SMEs cannot afford this training as it involves hiring specialized engineers and consultants. Based on our experience with SMEs and to reduce training costs for EIS deployment in large manufacturing enterprises, we developed a rollout plan which encompasses the different settings in an organization that employees use EIS. The important stages that we identified are the Modeling, Planning, Simulation, Integration, Execution and Control. We developed prototype software for each stage that emulates the functionalities of typical organizational software. In the following sections, we present an overall view of our rollout plan and then elaborate on the individual stages. In this work, our focus has been mostly centered on information systems that are typical in manufacturing organizations, but it can be readily extend to other industry segments.

ROLLOUT PLAN FOR TRAINING IN ENTERPRISE INFORMATION SYSTEMS

The rollout plan developed for training in EIS was modeled to follow the different stages that a new project undergoes from inception to completion as shown in Figure 1. Following this procedure it is envisioned that training employees or students would introduce them to the spectrum of EIS software that are used in an organization. We have developed prototype software that would emulate the working of industry standard EIS software. It is important to note that the purpose of developing prototype software for different stages in the rollout plan is to reduce the complexity while maintaining the fundamental concepts found in industrial strength software. The different stages that are part of our rollout plan are as follows:

- In the modeling phase the requirements and objectives of a project are established. In general the requirements are captured by enterprise models using modeling techniques such as data flow diagrams (DFD), and unified modeling language (UML). The typical software used in industry for developing enterprise models are Microsoft Visio® and Rational Rose®. For training purposes we developed a tool customizing Microsoft Visio® to provide user friendly interfaces supporting a wide variety of modeling techniques (Mathew, 2003).

- The planning phase is where organizations evaluate alternatives, do what-if analysis for designing and to come up with a plan of execution. In general the planning phase is strongly tied with the simulation phase where the feasibility and the success of the proposed plans are evaluated by the developed simulation models. For training purposes, we developed Sensors to Suppliers (S2S) planning and simulation tool (Mehta, 2003).

- The integration phase is where we focus our discussion on the need and advantages of seamless integration of various information systems within the organization. To train and demonstrate how data level integration works, we have developed Schema Lens software, which extracts the schema from a source database and has the capabilities to map it with transformations to a destination.

- The transaction phase is where organizations execute the business process to create customer value. In general, the transaction system in an enterprise constitutes the Customer Relationship Management (CRM), and Enterprise Resource Planning (ERP) system. CRM provide a single view of all customer interactions, and campaign management for personalized services. ERP systems execute a fixed sequence of defined functions such as purchasing or selling. They lack the flexibility to implement varying business process. Hence, we developed the automated workflow system which integrates the ERP system with web services.

- The control phase in manufacturing systems is where the data collected from the shop floor is fed back to business systems to make informed decisions. Here we discuss the Radio Frequency Identification (RFID) data collection techniques with distributed computing to solve computational problems in manufacturing. For training purposes, we implemented the RFID-based Manufacturing Execution System (MES) for updating the cutting tool information in real-time and built a library for distributed computing (Cheng & Prabhu, 2007a, , 2007b, , 2007c).

Figure 1. Rollout plan for training in EIS

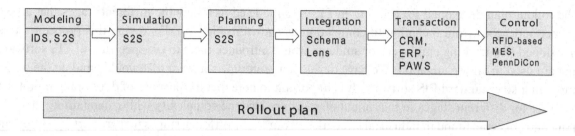

ENTERPRISE MODELING

There is a general lack of documentation and standardization of business processes in organizations. This lack of documentation leads to inconsistent formats and data. The flow of documents is often not clear, leading to gaps in these processes. For implementation of information systems, it is very important that an organization has standardized business processes. Enterprise modeling facilitates the understanding of business processes and relations that exist within and across the various departments of an organization (Kamath, Dalal, Chaugule, Sivaraman, & Kolarik, 2003). It is important to train the users of an EIS system in enterprise modeling to familiarize them with the organization's business process and provide an understanding of how EIS software drives the business process. For the purpose of training and conducting related research we developed an Integrated Decision Support (IDS) framework by enriching the interfaces in Microsoft Visio® for more specific data collection and modeling requirements. The customized environment is shown in Figure 2.

There exists a number of enterprise modeling techniques employed in the industry and are discussed by (Kamath, Dalal, Chaugule, Sivaraman, & Kolarik, 2003). We support a wide range of them in IDS for the following reasons: A particular modeling tool can be better suitable for expressing a part of the problem; and different users can have their own preference and comfort with a particular modeling tool. In one of the case studies we conducted with this tool, we were able to work with a defense and aerospace organization to capture their business process and IT infrastructure to identify the requirements for enterprise integration. Further, we were able to evaluate various available integration choices collaboratively based on the estimates of cost and complexity. The detailed functioning of IDS along with the case study is presented in a related work (Salaka & Prabhu, 2006).

PLANNING AND SIMULATION

One of the most common information system deployments in manufacturing is for identifying planning requirements. These systems maintain order status and explode it into material and operational requirements based on bill of materials. Further, these systems act as a bookkeeping tool and are linked to accounting. Simulation allows the quantitative analysis of the operation policies made in the planning phase. As computing power becomes inexpensive, using software simulation for analysis is becoming much widely acceptable. In general the planning phase is strongly tied with simulation where the feasibility and the success of the proposed plans are evaluated by the developed simulation models. We

Figure 2. Enterprise modeling environment customized in Microsoft Visio®

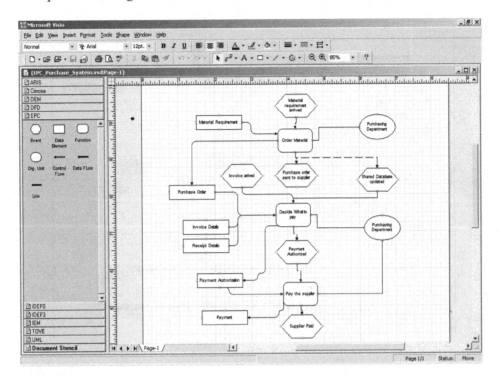

developed a Sensors to Supplier (S2S) tool that enables both planning and simulation in manufacturing systems with their complex structure and behavior. A brief description of the S2S tool is presented in the following section.

Sensor to Supplier Planning and Simulation Tool

The S2S simulation tool contains a rich library of components that can be configured to represent a particular business. The components support different policies and, the user controls decision-making rules and the quantitative variables. Apart from that, the tool provides an interactive and intuitive user interface for model development and performance analysis. The elements of the modeling tool and their function are shown in Figure 3. The objective of the tool is to capture the business model as quickly as possible and in as much detail as desired by the user. Once the business model is captured, it can be simulated and desired metrics can be analyzed. The user can then iteratively change planning policies and quantitative variables of the model, add and remove components to gain insights under different scenarios. S2S is implemented in object oriented programming language on the Microsoft .Net platform. The simulation is executed by having objects, representing business components interacting with each other. Using the development interface, business models can be created, modified, saved and merged.

S2S is currently being used in an academic setting to educate and train students in simulation for evaluating various planning policies in manufacturing systems. Further, it has been an attractive tool for SMEs who lack the capital, experience, and expertise in using other commercial simulation tools. We

Figure 3. S2S Modeling tool

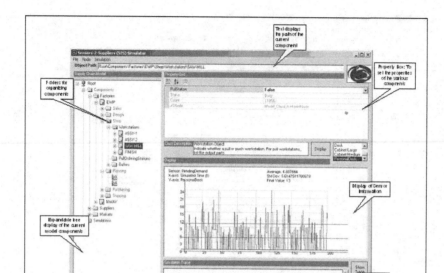

demonstrated the use of S2S in SMEs by a case study performed in a wood manufacturing enterprise. The details of the case study are presented in a related work (Salaka, Mehta, & Prabhu, June 2005).

ENTERPRISE INTEGRATION

Enterprise integration (EI) is creating new business solutions by effectively utilizing the capabilities of existing software applications by allowing rapid movement of information between them. EI is strategically important for improved business process management. The market for EI was valued at $8.3 Billion for the year 2004-2005 and was expected to grow 20% during the year 2005-2006 (Salaka & Prabhu, 2006), which indicates the emphasis on integration in the industry. The knowledge of enterprise integration is an essential part of training on EIS software for students and organizational employees to make them realize the potential of integrated enterprises. As part of our rollout plan, we train students on the contemporary standards and techniques in EI. The training plan on integration includes familiarizing the undergraduate students with typical XML features that are supported currently by most of the industry software for data integration. For this, we demonstrate the XML features that are in Microsoft Office® software and how these features can be used in migrating data between software applications. Figure 4 shows one of the demonstrations to the students as part of the training. For research purposes and acquaint students industry standard integration software, we developed Schema Lens data level integration software, which is described next.

Figure 4. Demonstration of XML features in Microsoft Office®

Figure 5. Framework of Schema Lens

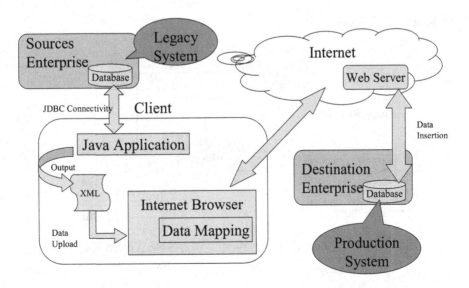

Schema Lens

Figure 5 shows the framework of the software. Schema Lens transfers the data from a legacy system to a production system extracting schema and data as an XML file from the source database using a Java® application. The front end for the application is a web browser. The browser connects to a web application residing in a web server. Further the web server contacts the destination database and enables the mapping XML data from the source to the tables and columns of the destination database. Currently, Schema Lens is being used as a test bed for a PhD student's work.

CONTROL OF MANUFACTURING SYSTEMS

The general idea of control is to use feedback mechanism from sensor to adjust a system to obtain desired results. In a manufacturing system, the feedback from shop floor can improve business decisions. We developed RFID-based Manufacturing Execution System for the purpose of training and related research in latest advances of manufacturing control with the advent of RFID technology. The current system is modeled to address the tool management issues in machining. Further, to demonstrate the importance of having faster solution frameworks that can take advantage of large data generated from RFID technology in manufacturing control, we built PennDiCon, a library for distributed computing. In the following sections, we detail the functioning of the above system.

RFID-Based Manufacturing Execution System

Figure 6 illustrates the RFID-based Manufacturing Execution System framework for tool management. Each Computer Numerical Control (CNC) tool is attached with a RFID tag that records the tool's usage time, preset data (projection, edge radius, and effective diameter), and operation data (speeds, feeds and depth of cut). When the tool is attached to the spindle, the RFID reader on the CNC machine is

Figure 6. RFID-base MES System

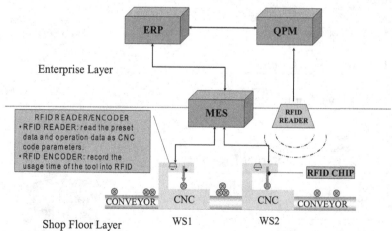

configured to read the data from the RFID tags. The purpose of this avoids all sources of potential data entry error, tool offsetting errors and possible tool crashes. After the completion of each operation, the RFID encoder on the CNC machine is programmed to write the usage time of the tool onto the RFID tag and further update the Quality Performance Management (QPM) system. Based on the demand for tool replacement as scheduled by QPM, a purchase order can be created from ERP in advance to avoid stock shortages and reduce downtime.

Distributed Computing -PennDiConn

PennDiCon is a distributed computing library that provides several communication functionalities such as peer-to-peer, multicast and broadcast, which can be called from C/C++ programs. In distributed computing environment, any entity can communicate with another entity or a group of entities using PennDiCon, allowing it to dynamically discover resources in the system. The detailed architecture of PennDiConn along with the case study is presented in a related work (Sharma & Prabhu, 2005).

TRANSACTION IN ENTERPRISE INFORMATION SYSTEM

A business transaction is a process that has two or more partners communicating to synchronize the related activity states in all information systems for the purpose of creating customer value. The transaction system of the outbound business comprises CRM system. CRM enables business to track and manage all of their customers' interactions over the lifetime, from first contact through to purchase and post-sales. On the other hand, the transaction system in an enterprise constitutes ERP system. ERP systems execute a fixed sequence of defined functions such as purchasing or selling. However, existing CRM or ERP systems fail to adapt to frequent requests for changing business processes. Therefore, we developed a workflow system, Process Automation with Web Services (PAWS), which support modification of business logics at runtime. A brief description of the training and research in transaction system is presented in the following section.

Outbound Transaction System

Outbound transaction covers the types of retailing, channels, tools for data collection, and transaction standard. The adopting of Information technologies in the outbound transaction system includes CRM, point of sale systems, barcode, RFID/EPC, global data synchronization, EDI, XML, and web services. Students learn the hands-on experimentation/demonstrations such as Microsoft CRM, PC-based POS terminals, scanners, RFID tags and readers, and integrated software for store and home office using Microsoft Retail Management System (RMS). Training course includes a group project in which students will design and construct an IT application focused on retail. A single view of all customer interactions, and campaign management for personalized services using MSCRM software is adopted in training. It helps student to learn how to target new customers, and manage marketing campaigns, enabling closer relationships with customers.

Inbound Transaction System- ERP

ERP constitutes the typical transaction system within an organization. This system provides information systems support for planning, production, marketing, and finance. Hence, it is important to educate students and employees about this software. To learn the prevalent ERP software, we currently have the training on Production Planning module of SAP® part of a senior undergraduate class on manufacturing systems. Typically, this training incorporates a day or two of lectures on how business processes need to work in tandem to make a business successful and how an ERP software such as SAP® are used in the industry to accomplish the same. For a small to medium size company, ERP software could be in-house development software such as TEAM (Total Enterprise Application Manger). TEAM was developed in Microsoft Access® by Georgia Technology Economic Development Institute, shown in Figure 7. By using Visual Basic Application, (VBA), students can learn to develop or extend the ERP software, and also get exposure to the software through hands-on exercises.

Process Automation with Web Services (PAWS)

PAWS is an automatic workflow system for tool quotation process within and between the supply chains. It extends the RFID-based MES discussed in the previous section. Figure 8 illustrates the framework of PAWS. In PAWS, ERP broadcasts the tool requirements to the web services of certificated suppliers registered with the Universal Description Discovery and Integration (UDDI) server. The web services in each supplier's server verify the inventory and price in its own database and respond to the quotation based on its current status. The business logic of the Request for Quotation (RFQ) process in PAWS decides the candidate supplier and starts another RFQ process for logistic provider. This automation workflow system not only integrates the inner-business process including QPM, ERP, and mailing system, but also combines the business-to-business (B2B) process in the supply chain. Figure 9 shows the

Figure 7. Mastering Scheduling in the TEAM ERP

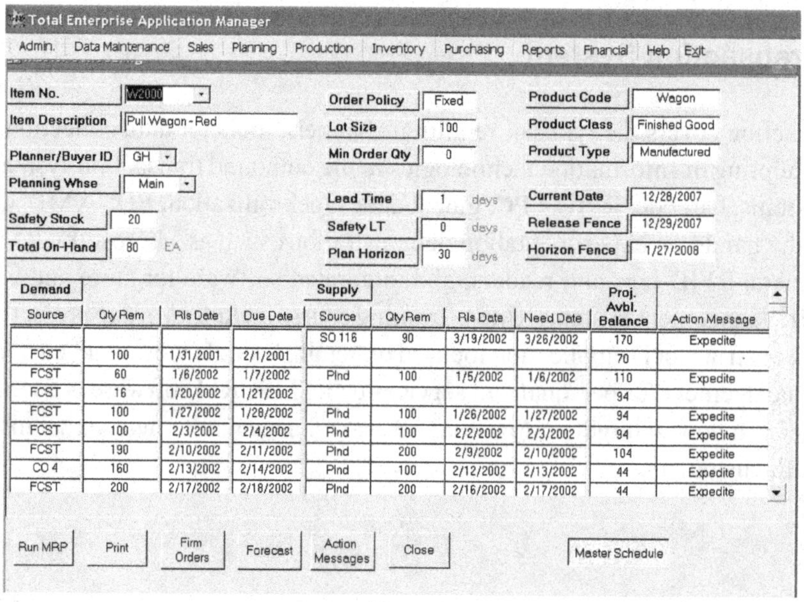

Figure 8. The framework of PAWS execution

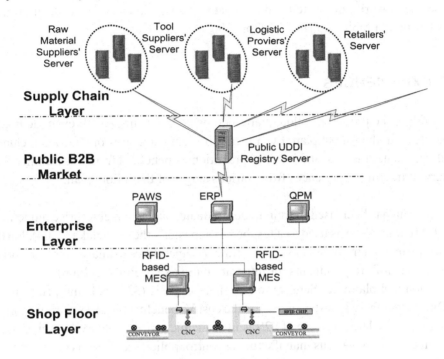

Figure 9. Quotation process

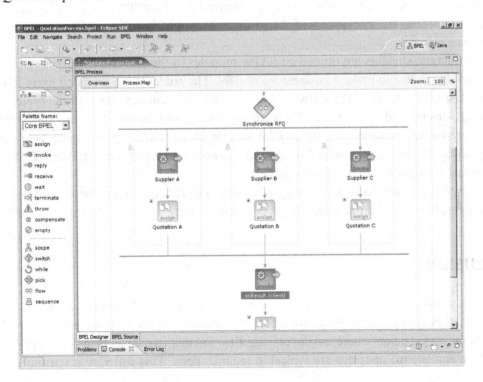

quotation process which broadcasts the RFQ synchronous to each supplier. Thus PAWS demonstrates to students the use of work flow systems to automate a transaction process to shrink time consuming RFQ process(Cheng & Prabhu, 2007a, , 2007b, , 2007c).

STUDENT EXPERIENCES

Given the breadth of the proposed rollout plan, there is no one course or an example that can be used to train the students in the rollout plan. Even then, different categories of students including graduate students, undergraduate students, and industry practitioners benefited from this training. The following is the summary of training experiences from various stages of the rollout plan:

- Microsoft Visio has been used to train undergraduate students in enterprise modeling techniques such as UML and IDS was used as a test bed in a master's thesis (Salaka, 2004). Further, IDS has been used in an industry project to demonstrate its capabilities to analyze an enterprise's business process and identify requirements for integration (Salaka & Prabhu, 2006).
- In simulation and planning, Sensors to Suppliers Chassis (S2S) is being primarily used in two ways. One way to show industry managers the cost Vs benefit analysis of various policies in manufacturing systems. The other use of S2S is in academic settings where it is being used to educate students in evaluating various manufacturing control policies and as an example to train students in object-oriented software. Also S2S is being used in an undergraduate honors thesis to study the advantages of the tie-in between a simulation environment and an ERP system.
- In the integration part of the rollout plan, undergraduate students are trained on XML features in software applications useful in integrating software applications. Further, they are familiarized with web services and the impact of service oriented architectures on an enterprise's business process. Further, the software tool Schema Lens developed is being used as a test bed for a PhD student's research.
- In transaction, students are trained on SAP® modules to illustrate how business processes need to work in tandem to make a business successful. The students are provided login to the SAP® systems to learn some of the software functions and get familiarized with the typical data flow among various modules of the SAP® systems that support various business functionalities encountered in an organization. Further, PAWS, the workflow software developed, helps to illustrate to graduate students how a workflow system can work in tandem with ERP and MES systems to automate an organization's business process.
- The control software developed is being used as a test bed in a graduate course to study various control algorithms for manufacturing systems. It is also being used by a PhD student for research.

CONCLUSION

In this work, we identified the need for a rollout map for education and training in implementing enterprise information systems (EIS). In accordance, we proposed a rollout map that encompassed different settings in an organization where employees use EIS. Further, we developed prototype information systems that emulate the ones that are typical in organizations. This software is currently being used in academic settings to educate and train students in using EIS. The current authors are working to incorporate the rollout plan part of the courses taught in graduate and undergraduate curriculum. The student response so far to the training has been very positive. The important takeaway for other researchers and academicians is that following this rollout plan the students can be familiarized with the broad spectrum of EIS systems in a systematic way. In the future, we plan to extend this training to small manufacturing enterprises that lack the experience in using EIS.

REFERENCES

Cheng, C. Y., & Prabhu, V. (2007a). Applying RFID for Cutting Tool Supply Chain Management. *Proceedings of the 2007 Industrial Engineering Research Conference*, 637-642:

Cheng, C. Y., & Prabhu, V. (2007b). Complexity Metrics for Business Process Enabled by RFID and Web Services. *Proceedings of 17th International Conference on Flexible Automation and Intelligent Manufacturing (FAIM 2007)*, 812-819:

Cheng, C. Y., & Prabhu, V. (2007c). Performance Modeling of Business Processes Enabled by RFID and Web Services. *Proceedings of 6th IEEE/ACIS International Conference on Computer and Information Science (ICIS 2007)*, 718-723:

N/A (1998). 7 key elements of a successful implementation, and 8 mistakes you will make anyway. *APICS 1998 International Conference Proceedings*. Falls Church, VA, 356–358:

Hong, K. K., & Kim, Y. G. (2002). The critical success factors for ERP implementation: an organizational fit perspective. *Information & Management, 40*, 25–40.

Hutchins, H. (1998). *APICS 1998 International Conference Proceedings*, Falls Church, VA, 1998, pp. 356–358.

Kamath, M., Dalal, N., Chaugule, A., Sivaraman, E., & Kolarik, W. (2003). A review of enterprise process modeling techniques. In V. V. Prabhu, S. Kumara & M. Kamath (Eds.), *In Scalable Enterprise Systems: An Introduction to Recent Advances* (pp. 1–32). Boston, MA: Kluwer Academic Publishers.

Laughlin, S. (1999). An ERP game plan. *Journal of Business Strategy, 20*(1), 32-37.

Mathew, S. (2003). *Quantitative Models for Total Cost of Ownership of Integrated Enterprise Systems*. Pennsylvania State University, University Park.

McCaskey, & Okrent, M. D. (1999). Catching the ERP second wave. *APICS—The Performance Advantage, 34*–38:

Mehta, R. (2003). *Software Modeling Tool for Analysis of Manufacturing and Supply Networks*. Pennsylvania State University, University Park.

Ptak, C., & Schragenheim, E. (2000). *ERP: Tools, Techniques, and Applications for Integrating the Supply Chain*. Boca Raton, FL: St. Lucie Press.

Salaka, V., Mehta, R., & Prabhu, V. V. (June 2005). Sensors-to-Suppliers Simulation Modeling of Manufacturing Supply Chains. *Proceedings of the 15th International Conference on Flexible Automation and Intelligent Manufacturing (FAIM 2005)*, Bilbao, Spain,

Salaka, V., & Prabhu, V. V. (2006). Project Management for Enterprise Integration. *The tenth IEEE conference on enterprise computing (EDOC 2006)*, Hong Kong,

Sharma, A., & Prabhu, V. V. (2005). Computing and Communication Quality of Service for Distributed Time-scaled Simulation in Heterarchical Manufacturing Control. *International Journal of Modelling and Simulation.*

Somers, T. M., & Nelson, K. (2001). The impact of critical success factors across the stages of enterprise resource planning implementations. *Proceedings of the 34th Hawaii International Conference on System Sciences*, Hawaii, USA, 1–10:

Umble, E. J., & Haft, R. R. (2003). Enterprise resource planning: implementation procedures and critical success factors. *European Journal of Operational Research, 146*(2), 241-257.

Chapter XII
Service–Oriented Middleware for Managing Inter–Enterprise Collaborations

Lea Kutvonen
University of Helsinki, Finland

Toni Ruokolainen
University of Helsinki, Finland

Sini Ruohomaa
University of Helsinki, Finland

Janne Metso
University of Helsinki, Finland

ABSTRACT

Participation in electronic business networks has become necessary for the success of enterprises. The strategic business needs for participating in multiple networks simultaneously and for managing changes in these networks are reflected as new requirements for the supporting computing facilities. The Pilarcos architecture addresses the needs of managed collaboration and interoperability of autonomous business services in an inter-organisational context. The Pilarcos B2B middleware is designed for lowering the cost and effort of collaboration establishment and to facilitate the management and maintenance of electronic business networks. The approach is a federated one: All business services are developed independently, and the provided B2B middleware services are used to ensure that technical, semantic, and pragmatic interoperability is maintained in the business network. In the architecture and middleware functionality design, attention has been given to the dynamic aspects and evolution of the network. This chapter discusses the concepts provided for application and business network creators, and the supporting middleware-level knowledge repositories for interoperability support.

INTRODUCTION

The globalization of business and commerce makes enterprises increasingly dependent on their partners. Competition takes place between supply chains and networks of enterprises. In this competition, the flexibility of enterprise information systems becomes critical. The IT systems and development teams should be able to respond in a timely manner to the requirements arising from the changing co-operation networks and their communications needs.

Traditionally, inter-enterprise collaboration has been supported by business process driven solutions that focus on the business functionality needs and the technology-homogenizing needs of the collaboration. This leads to situations where a change in the business processes induces large re-development projects. Furthermore, technology changes may cause domino effects cascading on the computing systems of dependent collaborators.

The present goal, instead, is to narrow the gap between business management concepts and the computing solutions. This introduces a new category of dynamic management aspects to the computing facilities, which isolates business processes from the technology, and thus improves the agility of enterprises when it comes to participating in new business networks. In addition, the wave of service-oriented computing facilities creates new possibilities for enhancing the automation of services as building blocks of many different types of business networks simultaneously.

In this work, the major challenge is to develop a middleware that takes the burden of managing these loosely-coupled collaborations and maintains the correct interoperation between business services in a way that supports business management concepts more directly. In comparison to traditional integration solutions, the global solution must lean on federating B2B middleware services that support the management of contract-governed collaborations, as will be discussed below.

We present an overview of the middleware solutions suggested by the Pilarcos project for inter-enterprise collaboration management. Section 2 first outlines the model of global networked business and the B2B middleware role in supporting it, addressing the new computing challenges that are arising. The activities addressed include negotiating and describing new business networks, developing new business services for the open service markets, contracting with partners about a collaboration and forming a new business network, acting as a partner providing agreed-upon business services, and monitoring potential risks and breaches during the activities. As the partners are autonomous and only contractually bound to a common goal, there is no technical guarantee of correct behavior in the business or technical sense. Therefore, a feedback loop for creating a "social pressure" effect is needed: the architecture includes a reputation-based trust management system.

Section 3 in turn outlines the Pilarcos middleware architecture. Since interoperability knowledge is a key issue to address in the architecture, Section 4 gives additional details on the essential knowledge types and roles of the repositories globally available. This interoperability knowledge has several important roles in the architecture: the pieces of information play a role a) in the service and collaboration creation processes, b) in the verification and observation of interoperability at operational time, and c) as elements in the contract structures needed for defining the business goals of the collaborations, which thus enables the validation or breach detection in the business operation across the inter-enterprise collaboration. Section 5 gives further insight into the realization methods of some management activities.

Finally, the discussion is turned to the relationship of the Pilarcos architecture to other current research and development directions, and concludes with usability issues, impacts and future work.

MODEL OF BUSINESS NETWORKS AND THEIR MANAGEMENT

The world of business is going through a revolution that emphasises open markets and agility, and extends the concept of autonomous actors from enterprises to governmental organisations, user communities and individuals.

In order to provide the right set of concepts and processes to support inter-enterprise collaborations, i.e. business networks, in this context, we need to choose the global enterprise architecture; the selection of business management activities is dependent on that.

Our model for the global business environment of the future is based on open service markets.

The enterprises and other autonomous entities can provide services freely in the network, and those willing to use the services are provided with facilities on finding and selecting the services, and contracting on their use. The support should cover not only the establishment of the business network, but the operational and termination phases too. Furthermore, the environment should provide support for gathering information about the trustworthiness of potential partners, and enforce regulatory rules on the business networks.

It is commonly expected that the old traditional business domain silos (such as metal industry, forestry, medical services, media) will lose their standing and be forced to compete with the more flexible service industry, where software-based services provide a major growth potential. Traditional examples of business networks include supply chains and subcontractor networks. Collaboration rules have become defined by best practices in the field, traditions, standards, or through the enforcing power of the leading role operator on the domain. Services have been developed slowly and with high investments; inter-enterprise processes for collaborations have caused problems in terms of re-engineering, and re-investments. The computing systems expected to support information exchange between parties are monolithic and thus difficult to adapt to new circumstances; they have different assumptions on the basic business processes, and fail in sharing understanding of the exchanged information.

Another strong trend is the emphasis on the role of clients in regulating and reforming services, even innovatively co-creating services, in addition to just using them according to a prescribed interaction pattern. Both trends bring up the need for viewing business scenarios as multiparty constellations, where each partner has a distinct role and a related interaction pattern to follow. Moreover, both trends bring up the need to take into consideration the autonomous nature of each partner in the scenario. With autonomy we mean the ability to make independent decisions on participation in business scenarios, technological choices, policies that govern security and privacy needs, and decisions on providing information or services to other parties, just to mention a few aspects. This is in contrast to the traditional collaborations between autonomous enterprises, for example in the form of supply chains or subcontractor networks.

In this inter-enterprise architecture, the essential concepts are business service interoperability and contract-governed collaboration between business services. We understand interoperability, or the capability to collaborate, as the effective capability to mutually communicate information in order to exchange proposals, requests, results, and commitments (i.e., to exchange speech acts common in business). The term covers technical, semantic and pragmatic interoperability. Technical interoperability is concerned with connectivity between the computational services, allowing messages to be transported from one application to another. Semantic interoperability means that the message content becomes understood in the same way by the senders and the receivers. This concerns both information representation and messaging sequences. Pragmatic interoperability captures the willingness of partners to perform the actions needed for the collaboration. This willingness to participate refers both to the capability of performing a requested action, and to policies dictating whether it is preferable for the enterprise.

We call all types of the inter-enterprise collaborations *business networks*. This is because the business management activities appearing in different types of business scenarios (e.g., supply chains, virtual enterprises, and subcontractor networks; even digital business ecosystems) largely repeat the same pattern. Looking at the common business scenarios from the supporting technology point of view, we can separate external business processes that express what interactions the players in the business network must take, and the service processing software at the location of each player. The nature of the supply chain or virtual enterprise becomes expressed and defined by the business processes, while the supporting technical environment can be identical for all types. From the technical point of view, we can consider that the primary goal of each independent organisation in these scenarios is to provide added-value services by combining existing services provided by different enterprises. However, because of different responsibility models, which are important for the business management perspective, we need to preserve the following separation:

- Orchestration, where the coordinator of the composed service takes on the obligations of providing the service; and
- Collaboration, where a mutual contract is formed and the members of the collaboration are equal and have their contracted obligations; the coordination of the collaboration is maintained by the supporting infrastructure.

Therefore, each business network is viewed as a collaboration between autonomously administered business services. A business network is established dynamically to serve a certain business scenario or opportunity that is made commonly known by publishing a business network model (BNM). The business network model captures all external business processes that are relevant for the business scenario. The business network model also gives structure to the eContract, which is in the technical core of governing the collaboration at runtime; the eContract captures most of the social behaviour requirements in the collaboration. A business service is realised by a business application implementation, running under the administration of a single authority. The wide potential of activities of the business application is restricted and controlled by enterprise policies to the degree that the enterprise is prepared to make available for its clients. The business services can fill in roles in multiple business networks simultaneously, based on their ability to fulfil the behavioural and non-functional requirements of the role and the eContract.

The methodology for building the business networks is semi-automated: based on a selected business network model and service offers published by service providing enterprises, the B2B middleware is able to suggest eContracts that are ensured to represent interoperable collaborations. The expected way of business services to fit into the collaboration and into each other is defined in terms of interoperability and collaboration contract requirements and breaches. These aspects are to be continuously monitored during the collaboration lifecycle, at times triggering management actions.

The set of tools supporting this methodology addresses the repeating business management activities for the different types of business networks:

1. *Designing the collaboration strategy and goals* involves business process design and reengineering activities. In (Ruokolainen & Kutvonen, 2007; Kutvonen, 1998), we have proposed a service-

oriented software engineering (SOSE) tool chain for producing business network models and service types with related property frameworks, and publishing service offers. This information is made available in globally accessible interoperability knowledge repositories within the B2B middleware. In (Kutvonen, 2002; Kutvonen, Ruokolainen, & Metso, 2007), we have explained how these meta-information elements carry the functional aspects of a collaboration, and where placeholders for non-functional aspects are located. This management activity is supported by a global network of business network model repositories, as discussed in Sections 4 and 5.

2. *Development and provision of new services* by an enterprise involves definition of service interfaces, and the policies governing the behaviour of the service in collaborations. This activity is supported by a network of service type repositories that make existing service descriptions available and mappable to similar services for interoperability support.

3. *Involvement in eContract negotiation and contract establishment* comprises finding potential new partners and selecting from them, determining the services agreed on, the expected level of service quality, payments and costs, definition of breaches and resolution methods for breaches. In (Kutvonen, Ruokolainen, & Metso, 2007) we have proposed a B2B middleware layer represented by an enterprise-based agent to provide protocols for refining contract negotiation, state management, breach notifications, and interfaces for requesting services for suggesting a business network and joining or leaving a community. Furthermore, the enterprise's negotiation support services facilitate control of enterprise policies and memberships in the collaborations, for example. This management activity is supported by a global network of service offer repositories; the semantic interoperability of service offer repositories is maintained by service type definitions (see Sections 4 and 5).

4. *Management of each business service by the service provider enterprise* is addressed by local service management and policy management facilities. This includes provision of the services and provisioning of the interactions with other services. Further, it specifically must take into account the contract-driven government of services within the collaboration. As the services are independently administered, monitoring must be used for detecting potential deviations from the contract. In connection to this,

5. *Monitoring of the operation according to functional and non-functional criteria* is supported by the B2B middleware facilities embedded in communication channels. In (Kutvonen, Metso, & Ruokolainen, 2005), we have addressed how the functional meta-information and monitoring are related. Both the management of business services and communication between them and monitors has been addressed earlier by the group (Kutvonen, Ruokolainen, & Metso, 2007; Kutvonen & Metso, 2005; Nurmela & Kutvonen, 2007; Ruokolainen, Metso, & Kutvonen, 2007). These management activities are further discussed in Section 5, which also shows how service type and eContract information is utilized.

6. *Termination of the collaboration either as the collaboration goals have been reached or due to breaches* is supported by the monitoring facilities and process descriptions embedded into eContracts for these purposes. In collaboration termination, it is possible to collect valuable information about the successfulness or failures of the collaboration, thus providing further guidance for business-strategic decisions later, for example in the form of reputation information. Because the enterprises are autonomous, there are no technical means to enforce policies and behavior on them; the social peer pressure supported by reputation and future potential for collaborations has a fundamental controlling role in the architecture. The mechanisms and effects on the collabora-

tion establishment phase (Kutvonen, Metso, & Ruohomaa, 2006) and operational time (Kutvonen, Metso, & Ruohomaa, 2007) has been discussed in earlier work.

THE PILARCOS MIDDLEWARE SERVICES AND ELEMENTS

The Pilarcos architecture proposes a model of inter-enterprise collaborations as eCommunities, consisting of independently developed business services. A business service denotes a set of functionalities provided by an enterprise to its clientele and partners. It is governed by the enterprise's own business rules and policies, as well as by business contracts and regulatory systems controlling the business area. Furthermore, as the business service is realised by software, the service is also defined by the computing, information representation, and communication facilities used and required.

The functionalities supported by the B2B middleware include

- A set of B2B middleware services for establishing, modifying, monitoring, and terminating eCommunities, or looking from the business service point of view, operations for joining and leaving an eCommunity either voluntarily or by community decision and leaving a trace in the global business world about the success of the collaboration; and
- A set of repositories for storage of meta-models for communities, ontologies of service types, and services, to support interoperability validation.

The business service providers are responsible for providing supporting meta-information to the B2B middleware repositories, but are otherwise freed from implementing any of the eCommunity life-cycle management. Instead, they are expected to use local middleware services for it.

The eCommunity life-cycle is mainly controlled in an eCommunity contract, or eContract. The eContract comprises the business network model, BNM (to define the network structure), information about the member services at each role, information about the expected nonfunctional properties of the services and their mutual communication (such as non-repudiation, security, privacy preservation), some overview state information about the progress of the external business processes, and methods for changing the contract itself.

In the eCommunity establishment process (and operational time management), the eContract is used to gather together all relevant information about both the business and the technical level details for the eCommunities. Figure 1 illustrates how contractual information derived from different sources becomes part of the eCommunity contract, and is used to govern a computational service in order to bring it up to represent the intended business service. In the following, these steps are discussed in more detail.

The strategical requirements of a business network are expressed as a meta-level model that defines a set of external business processes (upper right corner of Figure 1). We call this the business network model. The structure is defined in terms of roles and interactions between the roles. For each role, assignment rules define additional requirements for the service offer that can be accepted to fulfill it, and conformance rules determine limits for acceptable behavior during the eCommunity operation. The explicit use of such a model allows comparison and matching of strategic and pragmatic goals of members in the network by giving a working structure for comparable and negotiable service offers. The business network models should take into consideration all relevant legal and regulatory systems in the application area.

An enterprise that is able to run a computational service, i.e., an application constellation of software components providing interfaces for functionalities of a business service, can make it available for other parties by publishing its interface and property information (upper left corner of Figure 1). In addition, we expect the service offer to be considered as a commitment to provide the service with the identified properties, terms, and conditions. The information elements required in the service offer are determined by two aspects: first, by the requirements of the B2B middleware concepts, and second, by the mandatory properties defined for the service type in question, which will finally match the business network role requirements. Essential for the offer structure is that the contract terms relevant for the business area become represented in a way that allows them to be compared.

The contracting process between the business services is governed by the selected business network model. The basic properties of the business service become defined by the service offer, although the mechanism does not technically enforce the offer to be truthful or the service implementation to conform to the offer. However, in business terms, the enterprise loses credibility by false offers, and increased certainty levels can be acquired by external conformance testing and certifications. The process of enforcing enterprises to provide accurate service offers is mainly an organizational issue, not fully addressable by technical solutions. Computationally, it is possible to control that exporters of service offers are authorized by their organizations for making external commitments, and that there are technical facilities to follow the thread of delegations and negotiations for determining the party responsible for each commitment.

The resulting contract object contains both business network regulations and the agreed constraints for joint behavior. This context information is configured, in suitable phases, to the monitor object governing all service requests passing in or out through the computational services interface. Thus the business rules and terms are passed to the monitor for controlling that the actual business service behavior is not violated by the computational service, which is capable of more varied behaviors.

Figure 1. Source of business-level and technical-level information to control software behavior to fulfill the business service commitments and restrictions

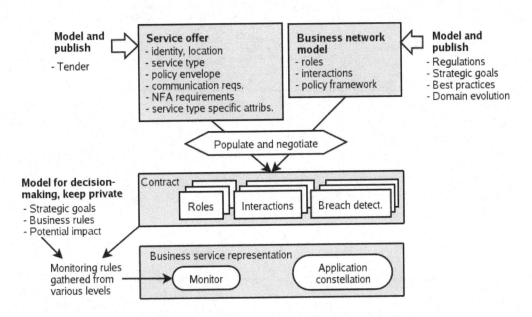

Because the business services are provided by autonomous service providers, there is no inherent guarantee that they would form an interoperable eCommunity. Therefore, special functionality for interoperability checking takes place when establishing a community, or entering a new service into an existing community. The applications themselves need only to concentrate on the local business logic, implemented on their local computing platform. For the eCommunity management functionality, it is necessary that the underlying B2B middleware is able to evaluate the interoperability of business services based on their service offers and to monitor the interoperability during the operational time.

The main functional elements needed for establishing and controlling eCommunities can be seen in Figure 2. The following will explain the main functionality of each module.

The upper part represents the breeding environment services, including the populator, service offer repository, business network model repository and type repository. These services can be placed in the public domain to be used by any enterprise. Breeding environment services like populators and type repositories are not required from all sites, but can be provided as infrastructure services as a business in its own right.

For the support of the populator, the business network model (BNM) design process involves the introduction and verification of new models to be stored into the repositories. The implementation of new services or the introduction of legacy applications involves interaction with the type repository. New business services are published for use by exporting service offers to the corresponding repositories. Deployment processes are naturally augmented with service offer exports. These processes feed in meta-level knowledge of potential participants in communities to be formed. The feeding processes are independent of each other, and even withdrawing or deprecating information may take place.

Figure 2. Service agents of the operational environment; arrows represent communication relationships boxes are active agents, and cylinders data stores

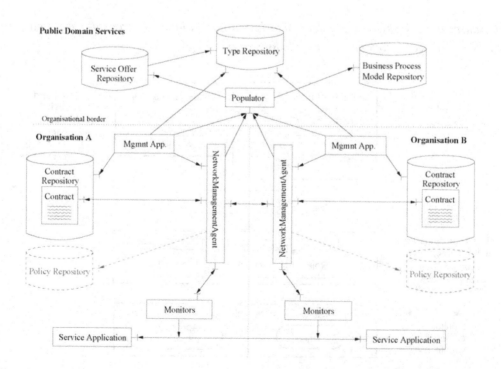

The two lower parts of Figure 2 represent two autonomous enterprises. By autonomy we mean the potential for control over the private computing systems, and moreover on strategic business processes and policies. Each site or administrative domain, representing an autonomous ICT system, is expected to run a business process management agent. The lower part of the figure also shows the network management agents (NMAs) and eContracts as the major players of the operational environment. As discussed in the previous section, the eCommunity contract captures shared meta-information about the collaboration. At operational time, reflective methods are used to keep the real system at each involved computing site in correspondence with this meta-information. At each administrative computing domain, there is a local agent for management of knowledge about locally deployed services. The local management interfaces are homogenized by a protocol for requesting the system to prepare for running a service (resourcing), querying about communication points, releasing the service, etc. Likewise, all relevant changes in the real system are notified and thus change the meta-information accordingly. The eCommunity contract is an active object itself, and includes logic that may react to changes in the meta-information and request local sites for further negotiations or changes in the system state.

The *Populator* uses a given BNM for ensuring the pragmatic interoperability of partners to an eCommunity; it also uses a set of compulsory aspects in service offers to determine service types, communication channel requirements, and nonfunctional aspects to be agreed upon for the eCommunity. The populator represents a breeding process where services are selected for eCommunity roles. The population process is a constraint satisfaction challenge between candidates' attribute value spaces and constraints given for roles in the business network model. The service type definitions dictate the attributes and attribute value sets necessary to describe the service, and the actual values for each published service is found in the service offer repository. As there are dependencies between selected offers in interacting roles (on channels and NFA), the process is complex. The populator provides its clients with a set of interoperable communities from which to choose during negotiations. Replacement of partners in an existing community, or one partner changing to a significantly different service implementation are also situations where interoperability preconditions need to be checked.

The eCommunity management is performed in cooperation with *Network Management Agent* (NMA) and the *Contract* object. The NMAs are responsible for managing the inter-organizational coordination and management protocols, while the contract object is responsible for making decisions regarding the eCommunity it represents. The NMAs are located so that there is an agent acting as a representative between the eCommunity and the local service-providing system at each administrative domain. The contract object is made available across all involved domains; redundancy is required for availability to be ensured also in most common failure situations. The NMAs provide three interfaces. For the local administrator, there is an eCommunity management interface for triggering renegotiations on conditions and memberships. Between each other, the agents have a protocol for notifications of task completions and contract breaches, and another interface for negotiation and commitment protocols for joint contract changes. For communication with the local monitors, the NMAs provide an interface for receiving notifications of contract breaches and task completion and another for feeding monitoring instructions to the monitor. The protocols are described in detail in (Metso & Kutvonen, 2005). It is essential for the NMA role that it acts on behalf of the administrative domain it represents, and is able to access relevant policy information, which is private for the enterprise. Based on local policies and guidelines, the NMA is able to enforce decisions, for example, on the significance of the breach notifications received from the monitors, and subsequently decide on which protocol to trigger between the NMAs.

The eCommunity contract is itself a key element in the architecture, because it makes aspects from different levels/viewpoints of the business network available at operational time. The community contract describes technical, semantic, (external business) process-related, and pragmatic aspects. Technical information includes service types and related behavior descriptions, binding types between services, implementation-specific messages or function parameters, and policies used in the eCommunity. The structuring element of the contract is the business network model (BNM) used for the eCommunity: each role is supplemented with information from the participant's service offer, each binding with connector parameterization information. Semantic aspects cover information representation formats in messages exchanged. The pragmatic aspects covered include functional description of business processes, policies constraining roles, and nonfunctional aspects. The non-functional aspects govern features like trust, security and QoS, which are traditionally considered to require additional platform-level service solutions. In addition, non-functional aspects related to business process models capture more business-oriented features, like business rules (captured as policies and monitoring rules here). These main elements of the eContract are presented in Figure 3.

The structure of the contract is directly determined by the business network model in use. Most of the contract structure is a copy of the associated business network model. The business network model lacks identification of the business services as members, and only gives acceptable ranges for some negotiable policies. The business network model is also independent of the bindings (interaction support) the business services need to deploy among themselves. The model can, in addition, set requirements for the services beyond those set by the service type, such as support for transactions.

Monitors are part of the communication channel between participating services. A monitor has a generic sensor element that can be configured to filter traffic by classifying it to expected and unexpected event sequences (task started / completed, unacceptable traffic or lack of expected traffic). The network management agents provide each monitor with a behavior automaton to follow based on the service choreographies described for the corresponding role. The monitors can be used both to monitor the behavior of the roles provided by their own organization and the roles of the other organizations. Monitoring reports can be acted on in various ways, scaling from post-operational auditing to proactive

Figure 3. Information contents of the eContract

- Reference to the business network model;
- information about the epoch (operational phase) in which the network is;
- process for changing epoch

For each role,
- assignment rules that specify the requirements on:
  - service type;
  - nonfunctional aspects;
  - restrictions on identity, participation in other business networks, etc.
- conformance rules that are used for determining conformance to the role which the assigned component is in the role; similar as above.

For each interaction relationship between roles,
- channel requirements;
- locations of the channel endpoints;
- QoS agreement; security agreement;
- information presentation formats

For each policy that governs the choices between alternative behaviour patterns in the business network model,
- acceptable values or value ranges;

- references to alternative breach recovery processes;
- objective of the business network as business rules

prevention of unwanted events. In Pilarcos, the intent is to allow major breaches on agreed behavior or policies to be acted on during the eCommunity operation, and allowing automatic recovery processes to be started. In this respect, the Pilarcos approach differs from related projects (like (Neal et al., 2003)) that otherwise use similar techniques. Because the definition of "severe breach" and the appropriate methods of potentially replacing misbehaving partners are specific to each application domain, those rules and process definitions are compulsory parts of BNMs.

The monitors have two very important tasks in the architecture, both involved with business aspects and (mis)trust in the global markets.

First, the monitors provide a method for enforcing the business-level policies and enterprise wide operational policies onto the computational service constellations. In the operational environment, the monitor and the computational service constellation together form a representation of the business service.

Second, the monitors report suspicious events to NMAs, thus triggering announcements on misbehavior or contract breaches, and providing a data source for reputation information.

INTEROPERABILITY KNOWLEDGE AND ITS MANAGEMENT

The three meta-information repositories in the B2B middleware – business network model repository, service type repository, and service offer repository – have a central role in establishing a knowledge base that allows interoperability tests on to be made. Essential target concepts are service types, service offers, and business network models. Each repository is distributed for scalability and improved accessibility. Due to different types of load, the good distribution styles differ (Kutvonen, 1998).

Service types and business network models (BNM) have separate life-cycles. This provides isolation layers that keep local changes from involving the whole eCommunity, and minimizes the effects of BNM enhancements to local services. Furthermore, the creation of each model requires only a reasonably narrow expertise. In addition to direct relationships between models, the repositories store transformation rules and components for improved transformer/interceptor reusability (Kutvonen, 1998). We will return to transformers and interceptors later in this section.

In addition to these three repositories, reputation information networks feed information about the experience gathered in eCommunities about the behaviour of business services.

The service elements of the Pilarcos breeding environment address the need of joining four important processes:

- Introduction of BNMs to the model repository, and introduction of supporting service types to the type repository;
- Software engineering processes to provide implementations that correspond to the known service types and thus are applicable for the known BNMs;
- Deployment of services and export of corresponding service offers to traders, effectively making a commitment to keep the service consistent with the service offer; and
- An eCommunity establishment process using the provided information.

These processes are only loosely interleaved. Business network models and the actual business services can be developed independently from each other; indeed, their development forms quite separate professions. In the platform, these concepts have to meet at the service description level.

Type and Service Offer Repositories

The *type repository* provides a structured storage for type information related to services and their access interfaces. Operations are provided for publishing new types, comparing types, and creating relationships between types.

Service types are abstract descriptions of business service functionality. Service descriptions are used to ensure technical connectivity, semantic interoperation and behavioral compatibility in possibly heterogeneous environments. Service descriptions do not expose internal properties of business services, as this decreases the possibilities of reuse and evolution of services. Implementation-specific information, such as binding of a service into a specific communication protocol or address, is not covered by service type. Service type is like a contract, which an actual service must implement.

Service types are XML-based descriptions which define interface signatures, service attributes and an interface protocol. Interface signature in Pilarcos is described using a WSDL description without technical binding information (see (WSDL, 2001)). Each service supports only one kind of behavior; different behavior implies different service types. We refer to the definition of service behavior as interface protocol, which is a behavioral description defining externally visible behavior at one endpoint of a bilateral communication. Interface protocols in Pilarcos are based on session types (see (Takeuchi, Honda, & Kubo, 1994; Gay & Hole, 1999)). For behavioral descriptions, we have a simple XML-based process description language. Semantic interoperability of services is supported by binding ontological concepts to the exchanged documents. XML based ontology description languages, such as general-purpose description languages RDF(S) and OWL (RDF-S, 2004; OWL, 2004) or more specialized XML-based ontologies such as RosettaNet, can be used (RosettaNet Consortium, 2004). The rules of the type system are based on behavioral session types, structural matching of syntactic information and semantic relations based on description logic (Takeuchi et al., 1994; Jha, Palsberg, & Zhao, 2002; Nardi & Brachman, 2002). Sub typing-like relationships that support service evolution are also important (Di Cosmo, Pottier, & Rémy, 2005; Gay & Hole, 1999; Nardi & Brachman, 2002).

The type discipline in the Pilarcos platform is strictly managed. Every type definition must be contained by a type repository. Each type name, i.e. URI, must also identify the type repository responsible for managing the corresponding namespace and its type definitions. Without strict management of typing information, it would be impossible to ensure that types are unambiguously named, persistently stored, verified to be correct, and relationships between types verified and intact (Kutvonen, 1998). Type repositories can also be organized into a hierarchy for partitioning of namespaces.

Service types are published by institutions responsible for a business domain or by enterprises willing to promote use of new kinds of services. Standardization of a new service type is not necessary, however, because the applicability and adoption of the service type is determined by peer acceptance.

The relationships of interest for the type repository users are: no match, similar types (equality of text or reference, sub typing), and interoperable with interception. The comparison and judgment is not fully automated and cannot be made (due to performance issues) at the time of query. Instead, the service type publication process involves verification of the type, comparison to other named types, and verification of the type relationships. The process of creating interceptors (i.e., transformers that change the inputs and outputs of one interface type so that they become suitable for another) is external to the type repository. The service types can thus be matched with each other in a more relaxed way, only limited with an interoperability requirement. As an enhancement, the cost of connection can be added to direct users to choose "native" types instead of transformed connections.

The initial Pilarcos type repository was designed and developed during the work on the ODP type repository function standard (IS14746, 1999), and OMG MOF specification (MOF, 2002). Although there are certain differences, most interfaces are similar. Thus the type repository offers operations (Kutvonen, 1998) for

- Publishing realisations of abstract types,
- Checking whether two type realisations are conformant and interchangeable,
- Retrieving subtypes or supertypes of a type realisation,
- Retrieving templates for a given abstract type,
- Translating one type realisation to another, and
- Retrieving names for abstract types and type realisations in other type domains.

The service offer repository refers to services (like UDDI (Belwood & et al., 2004) and the ODP trading service (IS13235, 1995)) for locating services that are published using a structured meta-information description of the service. We consider these descriptions commitments to provide the service. When a new service offer is published, type repository functionality is used to validate the conformance between the offer and the corresponding service type.

Given a service type and a service offer, the conformance validation algorithm verifies if the service offer corresponds to the behavioral and structural properties of the corresponding service type. Concerning behavior, each communication action described in the service offer has to be matched with the communication behavior defined in the service type. Both substitutability and compatibility relationships can be used as a behavioral matching criterion. For structural properties, similarity between the document structures used in the service offer and document types declared in the service type must be matched.

Functional properties of the type checking algorithm are characterized by the service-typing rules which are based on the session typing discipline (Takeuchi et al., 1994; Gay & Hole, 1999).

The session typing discipline provides formal characterizations for service substitutability and compatibility which are based on the notions of session sub typing and duality (Vallecillo, Vasconcelos, & Ravara, 2003). The algorithm for validating session sub typing is syntax-driven and is expected to be efficient in practice (Vallecillo et al., 2003); however, no formal validation of this claim has yet been given.

If the conformance validation is successful, the service offer is published into a service offer repository with the claimed service type. The service offer publishing process requires predefined service types. In the Pilarcos architecture, we expect service types to mandate properties for expressing issues affecting technical, semantic, and pragmatic interoperability. This is reflected by the structure required by service offers, as illustrated in Figure 4.

Business Network Model Repository

The business network model (BNM) repository provides interfaces for publishing models, verifying their properties, and comparing and querying models for population or software engineering processes.

The structure (topology) and properties of a business network are defined by its BNM, which explicates the roles of partners and the interactions between roles that are needed for reaching the objective of the eCommunity. A BNM comprises a collection of roles, a set of connectors and a set of architecture-

Figure 4. Structure of service offers in Pilarcos

```
- Interface syntax and protocol; either IDL or WSDL specification for the service interface, and
  partial ordering rules of operations;
- schema for information elements;
- list of nonfunctional aspects, such as QoS offers (acceptable range for QoS),
  trust requirements, or name for security mechanism to be used;
- requirements for platform;
- requirements for communication channel service level
```

specific nonfunctional properties. The approach combines ideas from the ODP enterprise viewpoint language (IS15414, 2003) and those of separating functional units and their interconnection into distinct concepts of components and connectors (Allen & Garlan, 1994).

A role represents a logical business service or entity in an administrative domain. The role definition expresses the functional and nonfunctional properties required. Role functionality is described as a composition of service types and role-specific synchronization patterns. Synchronization patterns express causal relationships between actions in distinct services of a role (by setting preconditions for interactions using the terms before, after etc).

Interaction relationships between roles are described by bilateral connectors between service interfaces. Connectors may define other communication-related properties, such as control or data adaption, eCommunity coordination and nonfunctional properties of communication.

Nonfunctional properties are managed as named values that are used for selecting the right technical configurations from the underlying platform. Some properties are used for dynamic branching of behavior at operational time. These decisions stem from the business level, but the negotiation and commitment protocols needed are preferably transparent to the business services.

The elements of the business network model descriptions required are presented in Figure 5.

Reputation Information

The overall architecture assumes that terminating eCommunities provide information to the global network of their satisfaction to the past collaboration. This information gives a basis for predicting the likely behavior of a partner in an eCommunity, and thus facilities for deciding on whether an action is worth the related risk of partner failure.

The required information must be associated to the business service in question, not only to the enterprise providing it, or the technical environment supporting it. Naturally, changing any of these aspects will change the reputed target as well. On the other hand, persistent enough identification of the responsible service providers is essential.

The reputation information is accumulated on two forums; it is the current, private view of a trustor's trustworthiness formed from local experience and shared third party experience. The reputation views building on these two very different sources are stored separately up until the moment of a trust decision.

Both external and local reputation views follow the same format. They count the outcomes of each type (experiences) for each asset, and tag the information with credibility information.

Figure 5. The contents of a business network model

```
- A set of named business process models, each presented in terms of named roles with
  - role assignment rules for guiding the populator to retrieve suitable service offers from the
    offer repository;
  - role conformance rules for guiding the monitors to notify its BNA about all deviations from
    these rules;
  - interaction pattern expected at each communicatino channel; may be simple invocation,
    announcement or full session specification;
  - name for the breach recovery process to be used;
- role association requirements expressing how a business service is required to
  simultaneously act in named roles of named business process models; this allows functional
  slicing of the model for reuse and design purposes;
- policy rules overarching the business network model; these policies provide invariants that
  need to be fulfilled;
- breach recovery process name and type (type for example "dissolving", "restarting", or
  "continuable with sanctions")
```

The assets selected so far are named monetary, reputation, control and fulfilment. The monetary asset can denote only concrete costs and gains, while the reputation asset encompasses both the enterprises reputation rating in any reputation systems, as well as the more abstract notion of its public relations, appearance in the media, and the attitudes of its associates, partners and customers towards it. The control asset represents the general need for an enterprise to protect itself from outside influences: to maintain control over its security, privacy and other aspects of its autonomy. The fulfillment asset is the one most tightly connected with a trustee. It encompasses whether the trustee does its part of what was agreed, leaves something relevant undone or does something it was not strictly expected to. Where the base for the monetary asset is the wealth of the organization, the base for fulfillment is the general trend of respected agreements, which reflects on the success of the organization.

The outcomes of actions are represented through their effect on assets: major negative effect, minor negative effect, no effect, minor positive effect, major positive effect, and unknown effect, if the outcome could not be determined for a particular asset (Ruohomaa & Kutvonen, 2008).

Relationships of Metadata

The meta-information repositories' contents are interdependent. A verified business network model acts as a template for the eCommunity. The model to be used as a contract template is first negotiated between the potential partners, involving comparison and matching of strategic, pragmatic goals of members in the network. As the matching of multiple network models is too hard a problem to solve by an automated process in general cases for a heterogeneous modeling environment, we require a single shared model to be agreed on at the eCommunity establishment. Checking that all parties expect the same business network model is one of the pragmatic interoperability aspects.

Within the business network models, service types are used as means to define requirements for role players. Again, the matching problem is too hard in a general theoretical sense, and therefore we have focused on practical goals: grouping of similar models, and identifying suitable transformers or adapters available when similar models need to be mapped together.

The service type repository is used for holding such a relationship between models and the associated transformation information. The actual adapters are produced in a separate process starting from the service type descriptions (Kutvonen, 2004b) for configuring a communication channel between peers so that the information exchange is understood correctly and there is no known deadlock in the sequence of message exchanges. The adapters can address modifications at multiple levels of interoperability, such as data representation modifications, and changing the communication pattern (for example, splitting a request of a task to a set of requests for subtasks from the peer).

The service publication functionality is similar to the UDDI (Belwood & et al., 2004) or the ODP trading mechanisms (IS13235, 1995); the type management system resembles the ODP type repository function (IS14746, 1999) and enforces a typing discipline to follow over service offer repositories.

In the service publication process, service providers send service offers to the service offer repository, to state claims about the type and properties of the services. A service offer describes functional and nonfunctional properties of the service to be published: the actual service interface signature, service behavior, requirements for technical bindings (e.g. transport protocol), and attributes such as service quality and trust-related commitments. The service offer repository then initiates a conformance validation process. For this purpose, a service type corresponding to the claimed service type is retrieved from the type repository. The service type defines syntactical structures for service interface signature and messages, externally visible service behavior and semantics for exchanged messages (Kutvonen, Ruokolainen, & Metso, 2007). Conformance validation is executed by the service type repository holding the corresponding service type. Only after a successful validation, the service offer is published; otherwise a service typing mismatch is reported between the service offer and its claimed type.

The BNM repository is a shared storage of business collaboration information that enables enterprises to share business transaction models, similar to the ebXML-repository (Kotok & Webber, 2001), although with a more automated and repeatable breeding process. The notations used are not discussed here, but they resemble the ODP enterprise language and use XML-style notations (see (Kutvonen, 2004a) and (Kutvonen, Ruokolainen, & Metso, 2007)).

For each eCommunity establishment process initiated by a willing partner, the corresponding business network model is first fetched from the BNM repository. The population process provides a set of interoperable eCommunity proposals where the roles of the BNM are filled with potential partners. For this purpose, the type repository is consulted for providing service types matching the requirements of the business network model, after which the service offer repository can be used to provide the corresponding service providers. After population, and the subsequent negotiation, the eCommunity contract is received and distributed to every participant.

The service interoperability and correct operation of the community assumes that the metalevel information on BNMs, service types, and service offers is correct. Therefore, we find it necessary to collect the meta-information into repositories, where the trustworthiness of the information source can be controlled, and the quality of the information can be validated by the repository management actions. These aspects must be weaved into the tasks involved with eCommunity establishment, such as service publication or discovery (Ruohomaa, Viljanen, & Kutvonen, 2006; Kutvonen, 1998).

ECOMMUNITY MANAGEMENT ASPECTS

This section presents some key management activities or aspects. First, development of business network models for the breeding environment is discussed. Then two aspects of the eCommunity lifecycle are detailed: semi-automated decision-making support for enterprise systems for participating business network activities, and verification and observation of interoperability.

Designing the Collaboration Strategy and Goals

Traditionally, the establishment of business networks starts by negotiation of the joint objectives and goals, and collaborative definition of the joint processes, and definition of the methods of connecting individual computing elements to a coherent whole. This phase is supported by breeding environments where selection of partners, learning about their capabilities, and designing the joint business network model takes place. In this process the set of functionality is determined, as well as a set of business policies that must be adopted.

Although all this is necessary for the business network establishment, it is not necessary to perform the whole process independently for each business network. Neither is it necessary to repeat the whole process when partners have wishes to make changes to the collaboration goals, processes, or supporting applications or computing platforms.

We have separated the business network design phase from the network establishment phase. On one hand, the business network models can be collaboratively designed, verified and validated for their suitability. On the other hand, these models provide a common vocabulary for enterprises to use at the business network establishment negotiations: When a collaboration is being established, the pragmatic interoperability (including processes and policies) is tested between partners. This means that the business services forming a collaboration do not necessarily have a joint history in the breeding environment that would enforce interoperability, but can simply be introduced to each other in a refining negotiation of the eContract.

As a consequence, the architecture

- Uses policies for refining the process models;
- Must include operational-time facilities for ensuring interoperability and breach detection between the partners;
- Uses policies for constraining the acceptability of a business service in a role of the business network; and
- Is able to support dynamic changes on the policies during the operational time.

In the business network model designs, it is beneficial to create rather abstract behavior groups within which actual business networks can vary, in order to support a wide potential for collaboration and evolution. Within each model, more precise alternative behavior can be chosen by setting the guiding policy value at the eContract.

The ability to perform dynamic policy management is a strong tool: selecting policy languages and targets suitably, most business management needs related to strategies and business rules can be modeled and transformed into rules that can be monitored at runtime. Effectively, the introduction of different types of policies allows mapping business domain guidelines directly to B2B middleware facilities.

The design of business network models is by nature a distributed activity: the resulting model should be acceptable for the business domain, represent the best practices, and even follow the regulations on that business domain or domains addressed. Therefore a common vocabulary is needed on-line for the designers to use, and strong guidance towards reuse of existing business process models is necessary.

Considering the present business process definition languages (e.g., BPMN, WS-BPEL, XPDL, WS-CDL; survey (W. van der Aalst, ter Hofstede, & Weske, 2003)) the main concepts are roles and interaction relationships between them. Then, the assignment criteria for roles, and interaction patterns are determined. We do not deviate from this general direction, but emphasize some special features that are relevant for service orientation, nonfunctional aspect management, and evolution support on the service markets.

First, the created models are published in an abstract (black box (Norta, 2007)) form, only revealing the obligated interactions between roles. This view is then to be refined by other design and configuration phases. The business network models are constructed by connecting together business processes that each have a single starting point, single termination point and one functional goal (which is essential for verification purposes as well (W. M. P. van der Aalst, Verbeek, & Kumar, 2001)). Connecting the processes together takes place by explicating which roles at each process model must collocate at a combined role. The new role inherits the service requirements from all these collocated roles. The business process models are annotated by criteria for assignment of business services and operational time criteria for not causing a breach. When the combined roles are created, annotations are added for restricting collocations, for example, to avoid legally invalid combinations where something expected to be externally supervised performs the supervision role itself.

Second, the business rules for the collaboration are explicitly defined, and thus changeable. The rules determining breaches are explicit, as is the agreement on what recovery process to use. For this purpose, a) multiple recovery business processes should be defined and consistently viewed as a set of best practices definitions, and b) all business network models should be analyzed to determine their recoverability style. Some networks are not able to recover from breaches but need to be terminated, while others may recover from the loss of some members, and further some require a set of compensation actions to take place before either continuing operation or terminating.

Third, all business network models should be analysed and verified for properties like liveliness, fairness, privacy-preservation (data flow sufficiency and minimality), termination of processes, and recoverability.

We have found it natural for the process designers to work process-wise; however, due to the autonomy of the domains providing the actual services, the models must be at least transformed to a role-based model. The basic structure of the business network model comes from the roles and functional interactions, while nonfunctional aspects are added on to collaboration, role and interaction levels. Each non-functional aspect may have its own domain-specific aspect language in use: the expressive requirements fall to the categories already present in current rule languages (e.g., RuleML (Grosof & Poon, 2003)), policy languages (e.g., Ponder (Damianou, Dulay, Lupu, & Sloman, 2001)), service level agreement languages (e.g., WSLA, WS-Policy; survey (Nurmela & Kutvonen, 2007)), or eContract languages (e.g., BCA (Milosevic, Jøsang, Patton, & Dimitrakos, 2002), (Goodchild, Herring, & Milosevic, 2000)).

Decision-Making Support

As the negotiation of the business network structure and goals have been factored to a separate step that results to an explicit, published model, the eContract negotiation between enterprises becomes more restricted in its scope. Effectively, the negotiation must result into a situation where it is ensured by static validation that interoperability at all levels exists between all parties, and that all parties are willing to participate in the collaboration. Furthermore, the refining negotiation must select the policy values to be used for this particular collaboration and stored into the eContract.

The supporting facilities to be used here are as follows (Kutvonen, Ruokolainen, & Metso, 2007; Kutvonen et al., 2006). First, the B2B middleware provides population of the business network followed by a generic negotiation protocol between the enterprise agents. The population process ensures that according to the claims in service offers the business services becoming members of the business network can be interoperable at all levels. Then, the proposed eContract draft is set to each enterprise to gather commitments of participation, or further refinements on the policies suggested. In the service offers, ranges of policy values are announced, so there is sufficient potential of finding shared values from the shared domain of potentially acceptable values.

The negotiation cycle ensures privacy of decision-making for each participant. In routine cases, it is possible for the agent that represents an enterprise to provide an automated response to the collaboration proposals. However, it is important that there is an explicit metapolicy guiding the agent to decide what cases can be considered as routine rejections or commitments. The cases can be detected, for example, by uncertainty of the trustworthiness of the peers, uncertainty of the strategic benefit of the collaboration, or uncertainty of the acceptability of negative reputation effects caused by a refusal.

Both for the automated decision-making and for the support of human intervention, we propose to use an expert system to gather the relevant knowledge and to feed governing policies to the enterprise system, i.e., the relevant non-functional aspects of the collaboration and its contributing services.

The decisions to join collaboration balance between the risk of failure or loss of assets as a consequence of participation, and the potential benefits of participation. That is, the expert system should compute a three-value outcome (agree, disagree, call for human intervention) on whether a service or a collaboration is dependable and beneficial for the enterprise in a given context and situation (Metso, 2007; Ruohomaa, 2007). By dependability we mean that the service fulfils its business purpose and the use of the service does not involve intolerable risk of monetary loss or reputation loss, for example caused by delivery failures or unacceptable delivery delays. Semantically, the decision to join the collaboration means two things. From the service provider's viewpoint, an outsourcing relationship to the rest of the collaboration community becomes effective. From the collaboration point of view, an insourcing relationship takes effect. We consider insourcing and outsourcing to have technically identical "clauses": three levels of interoperability and commitment to behavior according to the eContract.

Computationally, the system computes values for risk and risk tolerance, both of which are vectors over a set of assets, such as monetary assets, reputation, fulfillment of purpose, and control of autonomy (Ruohomaa et al., 2006). For the risk values, the essential input comes from reputation information, i.e., first-hand experiences and positive and negative recommendations by members of earlier collaborations. For the risk tolerance, the essential input is from the perceived importance of the tasks or business network. The starting values for the importance and loss scenarios should be created by an extensive risk analysis and strategic business analysis.

When the risk vector is compared to the tolerance vector, a simple and safe decision is made as follows:

- Agree, when no tolerance thresholds for acceptability are violated;
- Disagree, when no tolerance vector values for disagreeability are violated; and
- Propagate to human decision-making, when any tolerance vector value gets classified differently from the other vector values, all vector values fall between acceptability and disagreeability thresholds, or the metapolicy classifies the case as non-automatable.

When the request is forwarded to human consideration with all the relevant information; the formulations and scope are yet to be detailed. The information should support the understanding the proposed collaboration, its business values and risks, trust on potential partners, privacy preservation and so on. For the automated cases, the similar decision is based on a set of interoperability levels and nonfunctional aspects.

Besides the business network establishment phase, the same kind of decision-making takes place when entering significant tasks or business transactions within the collaboration.

Furthermore, during the operation of the business network, the monitors governing the business services can proactively or passively scan the messaging, reporting to enterprise level agents if the eContract is breached. The breaches can mean failing to fulfill an obligation, or failing to provide the agreed quality level of the service; more formally, failing to provide the level of dependability expected. At such situations, decisions are needed on whether the event is serious enough for terminating or leaving the business network. The same type of knowledge about the operational environment can be used, and again the expert system can make automated decisions or redirect the request for human intervention.

The concept of dependability, in terms of fulfilling the contracted aspects, can be concretized on two fields. There are general properties that can be set as service level expectations for any service, such as availability, timeliness, and privacy-preservation, or interaction relationship, such as non-repudiation and immutability. In addition, there are properties that are relevant for individual service types, each requiring a definition of value domain and metrics for defining the service levels relevant for the property. For example, reputation information (recommendations) can have a credibility property associated to it, determining how completely a recommendation from that source is assumed truthful. Another example is the traditional QoS levels with different metrics for data bandwidth and jitter in transfer.

The service level management lifecycle from property and metrics definition, to agreement establishment and control (Nurmela & Kutvonen, 2007) is present in the tool cycle illustrated earlier in Figure 1. The type definitions must include property frameworks; the property framework definitions form a common vocabulary for the domain and should represent standard definitions. Likewise, the type and business network model definitions can utilize policy framework definitions when expressing which part of the behavior can be changed at operational time. The property and policy frameworks form a common vocabulary and thus create a strong tool on expressing the market needs and also in directing the markets. In addition, the set of property frameworks and policy frameworks is evolvable, because the definitions are stored in common B2B middleware repositories and thus made available to all enterprises.

In relation to other work (e.g., survey (Medjahed, Benatallah, Bouguettaya, Ngu, & Elmagarming, 2003), eNegotiation (Chiu, Cheung, Hung, Chiu, & Chung, 2004), OMNI (Vaquez-Salceda, Dignum, & Dignum, 2005), (Neisse, Pereira, Granville, Almeida, & Tarouco, 2004)) and outsourcing management systems, we emphasize a) use of predefined contract templates that capture not only business level or technical level issues, but both; b) running a multi-partner negotiation instead of bilateral negotiations; c) support of contract template evolution through the facilities for creating new business network models and policy variations; d) agility of business networks gained by operational time negotiations and renegotiations that is based on ontologies and abstract enough behavior models created at design time; e) privacy of decision-making and using interoperability knowledge effectively for it; and f) potential to use multiple negotiation protocols for different types of collaborations (auctioning systems, simple commitment protocols).

Verification and Observation of Interoperability

The Pilarcos middleware aims for maintaining correct collaborative behavior in eCommunities, involving several aspects of interoperability requirements. The requirements cover technical, semantic, and pragmatic aspects, i.e., awareness of collaborative behavior and policies. Traditional verification and static analysis methods are complemented by dynamic observation of behavior conformance against the contracted BNM and policies.

The research and prototype building in the Pilarcos project focuses on interoperability and eCommunity management problems at the business service level, i.e. at the level of eCommunity, its participants, behavior and life-cycle. As we presume that services are implemented or wrapped using Web Services technology, technical interoperability at the lower protocol levels is well provided by a service-oriented technical middleware layer.

Interoperability problems in software systems stem mainly from components' implicit and incorrect assumptions about behavior of their surrounding environment (Garlan, Allen, & Ockerbloom, 1995). Every aspect of service and eCommunity functionality must be made explicit using unambiguous notations. Concepts of compatibility and substitutability are key issues in integration of autonomous services into communities; descriptions of services and communities must be founded on a formal basis.

When an eCommunity is established, we ensure sufficient conditions for interoperability of services during service discovery and population. Conditions for an interoperable eCommunity are fulfilled by three solutions. First, by the use of a verified BNM as a basic structuring rule for the eCommunity. The various business process models intertwined into the network model can be verified to be for example deadlock-free and complete by traditional protocol-verification tools. Second, by the use of constraint matching for accepting service offers to fulfill roles in the BNM. Previously verified compatibility and substitutability relationships between service types, provided by the type repositories, and validated conformance claims between service offers and corresponding services types are utilized in this process. Third, by augmentation of the constraint matching process by the interference of further constraints arising from the selected offers for neighbor roles.

Behavioral interoperability is considered in the extent of verifying that service offers and role requirements for service behavior match. By and large, this is accomplished by utilizing the already verified correspondences between service offers and services types. However, roles may also impose additional constraints for the behavioral patterns of the contained services, such as obligations to perform specific transactions. Other relevant issues in role-related constraints cover interface syntax with behavior descriptions, syntax of documents to be exchanged, semantic aspects of control and information flows, and nonfunctional aspects like trust and business policies that further restrict the behavior. The role specific constraints are validated during the design of the BNM (verifying that the constraints imposed by the role do not conflict with the properties of the corresponding service types), and during the operation of the community (verifying that the service implementations actually conform to these constraints). These validation procedures can be implemented using model checking techniques.

To promote the evolution and flexible use of syntactic structures utilized by the services, we will adopt principles of by-structure matching instead of by-name matching for service interface comparisons (Ruokolainen, 2004). Using structural typing constructors for WSDL and XML-Schema definitions we can decide if two WSDL interface descriptions are structurally equal. This interface matching is done using an approach similar to (Palsberg & Zhao, 2001; Jha et al., 2002). Service selection and matching based on semantic concepts is not addressed in the present version of the Pilarcos platform but it will be implemented in future versions. Matching of semantic concepts shall be implemented using standard theories and tools, similarly to (Peer, 2002; Srihare & Senivongse, 2003).

We do not even seek to completely prove that an eCommunity behaves correctly, as this would need verification of behaviors between every possible participant in an eCommunity during its establishment process. Even in theory, a complete pre-operational verification of an eCommunity behavior would be impossible due to dynamic changes in the system, such as evolving business policies. Instead, service types are considered as contracts, and the sub typing of session types as proof of conformance. Inevitable behavior and policy conflicts are observed and acted on during operational time by the monitoring system.

During runtime, however, participants of an eCommunity may behave incorrectly due to outdated service descriptions, changed business policies or technical problems. To overcome, or at least identify, interoperability problems during operation of communities, we have adopted an approach based on runtime monitoring of eCommunity contracts.

The monitoring system can be given a fairly free set of rules to monitor passing message traffic, and different informational and behavioural aspects are fairly straightforward to monitor (Kutvonen et al., 2005). The monitoring system reports detected situations (task started, completed, unacceptable traffic or lack of expected traffic). In monitoring, the challenges lie in the performance of the communication system, the design of monitoring rules, and decision engine.

Some breaches that can be detected by monitoring include a) messages from parties that are not partners in the eCommunity; b) transactions that are not acceptable in the current state of the eCommunity life-cycle or not fulfilling precedence requirements; c) information contents are not allowed to be exchanged (e.g., private documents, unknown structure); d) the expected flow of information is broken; and e) obligatory transactions are not performed.

Each administrative domain can have their own decision method on how critical a breach is considered. The eCommunity contract provides methods for network management agents (NMA) to invoke in case of breaches, either for information only, or for the removal of the partner in fault. The eCommunity contract carries these rules for deciding which recovery or sanction processes to use.

RELATED WORK

The Pilarcos architecture and services address the infrastructure requirements and solutions for bridging the gap between enterprise-level business considerations and the corresponding service management at the computing platforms. The global infrastructure services, transparently used by B2B middleware services at each enterprise, comprise partner service selection support, eContract management facilities, eCommunity life-cycle management, breach detection by business-rule aware monitors, and interoperability support facilities for technical, semantic, process-aware, and pragmatic aspects.

Traditionally, inter-enterprise collaboration has required integration of enterprise computing systems or applications. The topical integration techniques vary from new generation ERP systems and process-orientation to distributed workflow management systems. A significant amount of research is currently focusing on virtual-enterprise approaches. Virtual enterprises are joint ventures of independent enterprises joining a shared collaboration process. In many projects (like PRODNET (Afsamanesh, Garita, Hertzberger, & Santos Silva, 1997), MASSYVE (Rabelo, Camarinha-Matos, & Vallejos, 2000), FETISH-ETF (Camarinha-Matos & Afsarmanesh, 2001) and WISE (Lazcano, Alonso, Schuldt, & Schuler,

2000; Alonso, 1999)) the support environment consists of a breeding environment and operational environment. The breeding environment provides facilities for negotiating and modeling the collaboration processes; the operational environment controls the enactment of the processes. Many of the virtual enterprise support environments use a unified architecture approach: there is a shared abstract model to which all enterprises have to adapt their local services.

In contrast to this, the approach in the Pilarcos architecture is federated: enterprises seek out partners that have services with which they are able to interoperate (within the strategically acceptable limits). A collaboration model (business network model, BNM) is used for explicitly expressing what kind of collaboration is wanted and comparison of BNMs is used as a semantic interoperability verification tool. Enactment of services and local business processes, either by applications or a local workflow management system are required features of the service management facilities of each local computing system. This design choice has been made in order to make the evolution of BNMs and business networks themselves more flexible. Changes in the model to follow require that the model is explicitly available at the operational time, and that there is a synchronization and negotiation mechanism for partners to reach a safe point where new rules can be adopted.

Related to other toolsets for inter-enterprise collaboration management, the goal is rather different.

For example, ATHENA (Berre et al., 2007) appears to provide a knowledge base for finding out good solution examples for repeating problems. An other example is ECOLEAD (Camarinha-Matos & Afsarmanesh, 2006; Rabelo, Gusmeroli, Arana, & Nagellen, 2006) where the breeding environment of virtual enterprises is mainly aiming at providing strategic network facilities for automating the distributed business scenario, business process design and eContracting. The Pilarcos approach is not the only federated approach, however: (Montagut & Molva, 2005) and (Davidsson et al., 2006) present a rather similar management approach of a separate abstract business network that is populated with independent servers.

The fundamental difference between approaches is due to the changing goals of interoperability and with the changing maturity of B2B collaboration support. Each evolution phase has its characteristic challenges and solution architectures, as illustrated in Figure 6. The issues of interest focus on the second and third wave, while the first wave completes the picture by showing the traditional integration of application silos; typical solutions included data integration, presentation of joint portals, application integration, distributed workflow management and use of middleware (Linthicum, 2001).

The second wave introduces generated solutions that are based on shared models. The emergence of service-oriented architectures (SOA) (Papazoglou & Georgakopoulos, 2003) to a wide audience has secured the use of the concepts of services, e-contracts, and metainformation for describing services. On this basis, the model-driven engineering approach (MDE) (Schmidt, 2006) provides tools for creating a unifying model for collaboration and generation of services and workflows that ensure interoperation between services provided by collaborating enterprises. Interoperability is ensured by joint design efforts and interoperation of design tools used at each collaborators system. The interoperability challenges focus on the production tools, their ability to exchange models and to generate logically similar implementation skeletons onto technically differing platforms.

The third wave illustrates the future enterprise computing systems that contain common, generic facilities for federated management of inter-enterprise collaborations. This type of solution well matches to the EU FP7 work program (European Commission, 2007), and challenges raised by the enterprise interoperability cluster (Li, Crave, Gilo, & van den Berg, 2007). Likewise, solutions suggested for digi-

Figure 6. From manual integration to middleware supported interoperability

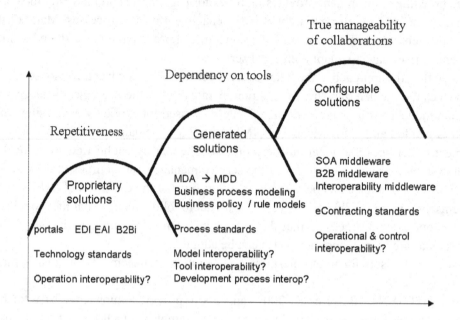

tal business ecosystems have similar goals (Nachira, Dini, A.Nicolai, Louarn, & Léon, 2007). We call them B2B middleware (Kutvonen et al., 2006). The goal of this middleware layer is to provide a breeding environment for the establishment of new collaborations, and an operational time environment for controlling them. The automation of processes in these environments requires, however, a well-formed set of knowledge about the interoperability features of services involved. Further, as the services and business processes of enterprises change, the interoperability knowledge must be dynamically increased. Thus, the interoperability knowledge is considered to be dynamically evolving, strictly typed and regulated by an evolving type discipline, heterogeneous in representation, and commonly available. Towards this goal, there is still lack of shared ontologies for eContracts, protocols for automated management of inter-enterprise collaborations, and control of the non-functional aspects of these collaborations.

Using the knowledge gathered into these repositories the B2B middleware agents can collect suggestions for new collaborations, and furthermore, check and negotiate for a multi-party contracts so that all partners a) share the intent of using the same business network model; b) conform to the role requirements given to them; c) share NFA models and communication channel types with those partners they have direct communication with; and d) conform to the generic policies (business rules for example) defined for the collaboration.

The Pilarcos architecture has been developed in interaction with RM-ODP (reference model of open distributed processing (IS10746, 1996)) and is founded on many of the principles also visible in current SOA (service oriented architecture (Papazoglou & Georgakopoulos, 2003)) trend. Shared foundations include the strong encapsulation of business services into autonomous units, introduction of meta-information services for service discovery and selection, and loose coupling of services for composites or collaborations.

The Pilarcos concept of eContracts ties together ICT-related viewpoints of ODP (Open Distributed Processing reference model (IS10746, 1996)), also ranging to some features of business aspects. The RM-ODP introduces information, computational, engineering and technical viewpoints. Each of these present interrelated but somewhat independent aspects of the collaboration features and their composition using more basic computing services. The Pilarcos contract structure captures these aspects in its BNMs, binding requirements, and behavioral and nonfunctional monitoring rules (Kutvonen, 2004a). The initial Pilarcos type repository was developed during the work on the ODP type repository function standard (IS14746, 1999), and OMG MOF specification (MOF, 2002). In other projects, like BCA (Milosevic, Linington, Gibson, Kulkarni, & Cole, 2004), contracts have legal and business level focus and detect contract breaches post-operatively (Quirchmayr, Milosevic, Tagg, Cole, & Kulkarni, 2002). Pilarcos aims for more real-time intervention.

The B2B middleware developed in the Pilarcos project series provides support for autonomously administered peer services that collaborate in a loosely coupled eCommunity. The eCommunity management by design excludes the need for distributed enactment services, but in contrast provides facilities for ensuring interoperability at the semantic and pragmatic level. In this respect the federated approach has a different focus from those in most other P2P community management systems, such as ADEPT (Reichert&Dadam, 1998) or METEOR (Aggarwal, Verma, Miller,&Milnor, 2004), and contract-driven integration approaches, such as ebXML (Kotok & Webber, 2001). Even most virtual enterprise support environments, such as CrossFlow (Grefen, Aberer, Hoffner, & Ludwig, 2000) and WISE (workflow-based Internet services) (Lazcano et al., 2000), rely on models for distributed business process enactment. However, the Pilarcos approach leaves enactment as a local business processing task, concentrating on interoperability monitoring.

In the Pilarcos middleware, the eCommunity life-cycle is built to be collaboration-process-aware. The architecture model acts on two abstraction layers, the upper layer involved with the abstract, external business process describing the collaboration requirements; the lower layer comprising actual services bound to the eCommunity dynamically. In this kind of environment, static verification of models and interoperability cannot be complete. In the B2B middleware provided by the Pilarcos project, we find it necessary to develop control environments for monitoring and reflectively restructuring the operational eCommunities, besides a breeding environment. The goals are similar to other projects, but the solution methods differ. While ADEPT supports direct modification of the workflow control structures, Pilarcos uses negotiated policy-values to choose between predefined behavioral alternatives. The Pilarcos solution even requires that well-formed contracts include suitable recovery processes that involve whole communities. In contrast to METEOR-S, the Pilarcos platform has no central tool for making the whole of an interoperability analysis, but partial static verification is done at the meta-data repositories, and monitoring is used to detect further problems.

The B2B middleware is in some extent comparable to agent-based approaches, such as MASSYVE (Rabelo et al., 2000). The main difference seems to be the separation of business services and B2B middleware services from each other. The Pilarcos middleware agents do not provide workflow execution, but expect local application management to play that part. In contrast to (Daskalopulu, Dimitrakos, & Maibaum, 2002), the middleware agents are responsible for semantic verification and failure resolution, and use separate monitors to help and report.

CONCLUSION

The Pilarcos architecture provides a B2B middleware layer that supports management of business networks. The management facilities are based on a shared vision of meta-information captured into an eContract. Changes in the contract are locally reflected to the enterprise computing system; and correspondingly, relevant progress and breach reports are delivered to partners through the eContract.

The architecture follows a federated approach: participating services are independent and pre-existing, and the collaborative behavior model is used only for watching conformance. Enforcement of the contract is reached through the independent monitoring facilities at each participant. The monitors basically react to events that should not take place at that service or resource interface. These self-protective reactions are then used as triggers for corrective actions for the benefit of the whole business network.

The Pilarcos approach supports autonomous services to form federated communities. A federated approach means that there is no overarching shared collaboration model from which the services would be derived. Instead, the services stand on their own and interoperability from the collaboration process, semantic and technical view must be maintained explicitly by B2B middleware. From the BNM, it would be possible to use the popular model-driven approach and generate applications, but those are not resistant to evolution needs. This is further discussed in (Kutvonen, 2004b, 2004a).

In this kind of environment, several strategical, process-related and technological needs can be attended by the business network management:

- Formation of new business networks that provide added value services for clients.
- Joining multiple networks at the same time without unnecessary restrictions on technologies or operational policies.
- Taking up new business processes and services with relatively low cost.
- Moving existing business networks to new phases of life-cycle so that new collaboration forms can be used.
- Monitoring the progress and correctness of the collaborative processes.
- Automating some collaboration establishment and correction events.
- Protecting local services and computing solutions from the changes and failures of the collaboration partner services and solutions.

The provision of the Pilarcos architecture requires further development of business process modeling techniques. The collaboration of business processes or workflows should be modeled without unnecessary revealing of local processing steps. Instead, only the collaborative part (external view) should be agreed on and monitored. Work has already been started by the component driven approach on splitting workflows into Web Services. The structural needs of business process models are also widened by the requirements of incorporating reusable sanctioning, recovery, and compensation processes into eCommunity contracts. Furthermore, shared ontologies and repositories for business process models should be made available. Such facilities would improve the potential for reaching interoperability in an environment where service components are truly developed independently from each other. More fundamentally, ontologies and repositories would create a facility for checking semantic similarity of a business process model as part of the interoperability tests during eCommunity establishment.

The federated approach has been criticized for the lack of advice for service elements to be developed. However, making existing business network models globally available and thus exposing repeating patterns of roles — i.e., expected local business processes — gives the required guidance. Such publishing has already taken place with RosettaNet etc; our solution is to provide a repository for external process descriptions that can be augmented on demand, and that will provide an element of evolution support. These model definitions can be added to the repositories at will, without interfering with already operational communities. Existing models can be frozen so that new communities are no more formed using them, but are not actually removed automatically. The verification and matching hierarchies within the repositories may depend on them, and of course, operational communities may do references.

Another criticism frequently arising is the performance penalty of the eCommunity interoperability checking. From our earlier prototype on the populator process, we can judge that the cost of the process and its scalability are acceptable (Kutvonen & Metso, 2005). The scalability of the open-ended search for potential partners from service offer repositories indicates a large search space; the matching process is further complicated by the interdependencies between selected partners in terms of available communication solutions and policies. The populator algorithms address the potentially exponential growth of the search space by limiting the resources used for the search, at the cost of the completeness of the results.

Specific features of the Pilarcos breeding environment include the level of automation expected, the relaxed matching of service types aimed for, and the use of explicit business network model repositories. The level of automation in eContracting has to be considered carefully. Enterprises are generally not ready to allow automated agents to take business-level decisions. Therefore, the automatically acceptable commitments have to be guarded by enterprise policies, and to be directed towards routine decisions. The main impact on the Pilarcos facilities is in providing control over technological and evolution-involved problems, not in the aggressive enhancement to new business partners. The major development on the architecture, however, is trust management, on which we have started a separate development project (Ruohomaa et al., 2006).

The federated type repository service is an essential element of a B2B middleware that supports the establishment of new business networks, or in a more simple case, connection between independently administered clients and servers. The role of the type repository is to provide a trustworthy source of service type information, and furthermore, provide transformation services for communication between almost similar interfaces. The service types can thus be matched with each other in a more relaxed way, only limited with the interoperability requirement. As an enhancement, the cost of connection can be added to direct users to choose "native" types instead of transformed connections. The service type matching approach supports evolution of services in a heterogeneous environment, where independent actors create new items, and where market forces has an effect on the usability of items, in addition to the verifiable correctness properties. Furthermore, the approach gives a natural tool for managing one type of transformation components needed in the current component-based, model-driven networking environment.

The use of explicit business network model repository is an ontology-defining tool that allows dynamic development and quick publication of new collaboration models. This is one of the key elements in the trial of developing evolution support for dynamic, inter-enterprise networks.

ACKNOWLEDGMENT

This article is based on work performed in the Pilarcos and web-Pilarcos projects at the Department of Computer Science at the University of Helsinki. The Pilarcos project was funded by the National Technology Agency TEKES in Finland, Nokia, SysOpen and Tellabs. In web-Pilarcos, active partners have been VTT, Elisa and SysOpen. The work integrates to a large degree with RM-ODP standards work, and has found an interesting context in the INTEROP-NoE collaboration.

REFERENCES

Afsamanesh, H., Garita, C., Hertzberger, B., & Santos Silva, V. (1997). Management of distributed information in virtual enterprises - the PRODNET approach. In *ICE'97 - International Conference on Concurrent Enterprising*.

Aggarwal, R., Verma, K., Miller, J., & Milnor, W. (2004, September). Constraint Driven Web Service Composition in METEOR-S. In *IEEE International Conference on Services Computing (SCC'04)* (pp. 23–30). Los Alamitos, CA, USA: IEEE Society Press.

Allen, R., & Garlan, D. (1994). Formalizing architectural connection. In *ICSE '94: Proceedings of the 16th international conference on Software engineering* (pp. 71–80). Los Alamitos, CA, USA: IEEE Computer Society Press.

Alonso, G. (1999). WISE: Business to Business e-Commerce. *In 9th workshop on research issues on data engineering (RIDE-VE'99)*. Sydney.

Belwood, T., & et al. (2004). *UDDI version 3.0.* (Retrieved September 1st, 2005, from http://uddi.org/pubs/uddi_v3.htm)

Berre, A.-J., Elvesaeter, B., Fgay, N., Guglielmina, C., Johnsen, S., Karlse, D., et al. (2007, March 28–30). The ATHENA Interoperability Framework. In *Enterprise Interoperability II*. Funchal, Portugal: Springer.

Camarinha-Matos, L. M., & Afsarmanesh, H.(2001, November). Service federation in virtual organisations. In *Prolamat'01*. Budabest, Hungary.

Camarinha-Matos, L. M., & Afsarmanesh, H. (2006, September). Modeling framework for collaborative networked organizations. In *Network-Centric Collaboration and Supporting Frameworks. Seventh IFIP Working Conference on Virtual Enterprises* (pp. 3–14). Springer.

Chiu, D. K. W., Cheung, S. C., Hung, P. C. K., Chiu, S. Y. Y., & Chung, A. K. K. (2004). Developing e-Negotiation support with a meta-modeling approach in a web services environment. *Decision Support Systems, 40*, 51–69. (ISSN:0167-9236, Special issue: Web services and process management)

Christensen, E., Curbera, F., Meredith, G., & Weerawarana, S. (2001, March). *Web Services Description Language (WSDL) 1.1.* (Retrieved September 1st, 2005, from http://www.w3c.org/TR/wsdl)

Damianou, N., Dulay, N., Lupu, E., & Sloman, M.(2001, January). The Ponder policy specification language. *In Workshop on policies for distributed systems and networks (Policy2001)* (Vol. 1995). HP Labs Bristol: Springer-Verlag.

Daskalopulu, A., Dimitrakos, T., & Maibaum, T. (2002). Evidence-Based Electronic Contract Performance Monitoring. *The INFORMS Journal of Group Decision and Negotiation.* (Special Issue on Formal Modelling in E-Commerce.)

Davidsson, P., Hederstierna, A., Jacobsson, A., Persson, J. A., Carlsson, B., Johansson, S. J., et al. (2006). The concept and technology of plug and play business. In *ICEIS 2006 - proceedings of the eighth international conference on enterprise information systems: Databases and information systems integration* (p. 213-217). Paphos, Cyprus.

Di Cosmo, R., Pottier, F., & Rémy, D. (2005, April). Subtyping Recursive Types modulo Associative Commutative Products. In P. Urzyczyn (Ed.), *7th International Conference on Typed Lambda Calculi and Applications (TLCA 2005) 3461*, 179–193. Berlin, Heidelberg, Germany: Springer-Verlag.

European Commission. (2007, June). *EC FP7 ICT Work Programme* (Tech. Rep.). EC.

Garlan, D., Allen, R., & Ockerbloom, J. (1995). Architectural mismatch or why it's hard to build systems out of existing parts. In *ICSE '95: Proceedings of the 17th international conference on Software engineering* (pp. 179–185). New York, NY, USA: ACM Press.

Gay, S. J., & Hole, M. (1999). Types and Subtypes for Client-Server Interactions. In ESOP *'99: Proceedings of the 8th European Symposium on Programming Languages and Systems, 1576*, 74–90. London, UK: Springer-Verlag.

Goodchild, A., Herring, C., & Milosevic, Z. (2000, June). Business contracts for B2B. In *Proceedings of the CAISE'00 Workshop on Infrastructure for Dynamic Business-to-Business Service Outsourcing ISDO'00.* Stockholm, Sweden: CEUR-WS.org.

Grefen, P., Aberer, K., Hoffner, Y., & Ludwig, H. (2000). CrossFlow: Cross-Organizational Workflow Management in Dynamic Virtual Enterprises. *International Journal of Computer Systems Sciences and Engineering, 15*(5), 277-290.

Grosof, B. N., & Poon, T. (2003). SweetDeal: Representing agent contracts with exceptions using XML rules, ontologies and process descriptions. In *Proceedings of the 12th international conference on the World Wide Web (WWW 2003).* Budapest, Hungary: ACM.

Information Technology – Open Distributed Processing – Reference Model – Enterprise Language. (2003). (IS15414)

Information Technology – Open Systems Interconnection, Data Management and Open Distributed Processing. ODP Trading Function. (1995). (IS13235)

Information Technology – Open Systems Interconnection, Data Management and Open Distributed Processing. Reference Model of Open Distributed Processing. (1996). (IS10746)

Information Technology – Open Systems Interconnection, Data Management and Open Distributed Processing. Reference Model of Open Distributed Processing. ODP Type repository function. (1999). (IS14746)

Jha, S., Palsberg, J., & Zhao, T. (2002). Efficient type matching. In *FoSSaCS '02: Proceedings of the 5th International Conference on Foundations of Software Science and Computation Structures* (pp. 187– 204). London, UK: Springer-Verlag.

Kotok, A., & Webber, D. R. R. (2001). *ebXML: The New Global Standard for Doing Business Over the Internet.* Boston, USA: New Riders.

Kutvonen, L. (1998). *Trading services in open distributed environments.* Department of Computer Science, University of Helsinki. (PhD thesis. A-1998-2)

Kutvonen, L. (2002). Automated management of inter-organisational applications. In *Proceedings of the Sixth International Enterprise Distributed Object Computing Conference (EDOC 2002)* (p. 27-38). Lausanne, Switzerland: IEEE.

Kutvonen, L. (2004a). Challenges for ODP-based infrastructure for managing dynamic B2B networks. In A. Vallecillo, P. Linington, & B. Wood (Eds.), *Workshop on ODP for Enterprise Computing (WODPEC 2004)* (pp. 57–64). Monterey, California.

Kutvonen, L. (2004b, September). Relating MDA and inter-enterprise collaboration management. In *Second European Workshop on Model Driven Architecture (MDA), EWMDA-2* (pp. 84–88). (Published as technical report No. 17-04 in University of Kent.)

Kutvonen, L., & Metso, J. (2005, September). Services, contracts, policies and eCommunities – Relationship to ODP framework. In P. Linington, A. Tanaka, S. Tyndale-Biscoe, & A. Vallecillo (Eds.), *Workshop on ODP for Enterprise Computing (WODPEC 2005)* (pp. 62–69). Enschede, The Netherlands.

Kutvonen, L., Metso, J., & Ruohomaa, S. (2006, October). From trading to eCommunity population: Responding to social and contractual challenges. In *Proceedings of the 10th IEEE international EDOC conference (EDOC 2006)* (pp. 199–210). Hong Kong: IEEE.

Kutvonen, L., Metso, J., & Ruohomaa, S. (2007, July). From trading to eCommunity management: Responding to social and contractual challenges. *Information Systems Frontiers (ISF) - Special Issue on Enterprise Services Computing: Evolution and Challenges,* 9(2–3), 181–194.

Kutvonen, L., Metso, J., & Ruokolainen, T. (2005, November). Inter-enterprise collaboration management in dynamic business networks. In *On the Move to Meaningful Internet Systems 2005: CoopIS, DOA, and ODBASE: OTM Confederated International Conferences, CoopIS, DOA, and ODBASE* (Vol. 3760). Agia Napa, Cyprus: Springer-Verlag.

Kutvonen, L., Ruokolainen, T., & Metso, J. (2007, January). Interoperability middleware for federated business services in Web-Pilarcos. *International Journal of Enterprise Information Systems, Special issue on Interoperability of Enterprise Systems and Applications,* 3(1), 1–21.

Lazcano, A., Alonso, G., Schuldt, H., & Schuler, C. (2000). The WISE approach to Electronic Commerce. *Computer Systems Science and Engineering,* 15(5), 345–357.

Li, M.-S., Crave, S., Gilo, A., & van den Berg, R. (2007). *Value propositon for enterprise interoperability.* EC.

Linthicum, D. S. (2001). *B2B Application Integration - eBusiness-Enable Your Enterprise.* Addison-Wesley.

Medjahed, B., Benatallah, B., Bouguettaya, A., Ngu, A. H. H., & Elmagarming, A. K. (2003). Business-to-business interactions: issues and enabling technologies. *The VLDB Journal* (12), 59-85.

Meta Object Facility (MOF) Specification — Version 1.4. (2002, April). (Retrieved September 1st, 2005, from http://www.omg.org/docs/formal/02-04-03.pdf)

Metso, J. (2007, April 26–27). Pragmatic aspects in computer-supported negotiations of virtual enterprise contracts. In *Web proceedings of the I-ESA '07 Doctoral symposium*. Funchal, Portugal. (To appear.)

Metso, J., & Kutvonen, L. (2005, September). Managing Virtual Organizations with Contracts. In *Workshop on Contract Architectures and Languages (CoALa2005)*. Enschede, The Netherlands.

Milosevic, Z., Jøsang, A., Patton, M., & Dimitrakos, T. (2002). Discretionary enforcement of electronic contracts. In *6th Enterprise Distributed Object Computing conference (EDOC 2002)*. Entschede, The Netherlands: IEEE Computer Society.

Milosevic, Z., Linington, P. F., Gibson, S., Kulkarni, S., & Cole, J. B. (2004). Inter-Organisational Collaborations Supported by E-Contracts. In W. Lamersdorf, V. Tschammer, & S. Amarger (Eds*.), Building The E-Service Society: E-Commerce, E-Business, and E-Government -IFIP 18th World Computer Congress TC6/TC8/TC11 4th International Conference on E-Commerce, E-Business, E-Government (I3E 2004)* (p. 413-429). Kluwer.

Montagut, F., & Molva, R. (2005). Enabling pervasive execution of workflows. In *International conference on collaborative computing: Networking, applications and worksharing*. San Jose, CA, USA: IEEE.

Nachira, F., Dini, P., A.Nicolai, Louarn, M., & Léon, L. (2007). *Digital business ecosystems*. European Commission.

Nardi, D., & Brachman, R. (2002). *The description logic handbook*. In F. Baader, D. Calvanese, D. L. McGuinnes, D. Nardi, & P. Pate-Schneider (Eds.), (pp. 5–44). Cambridge CB2 2RU, UK: Cambridge University Press.

Neal, S., Cole, J. B., Linington, P. F., Milosevic, Z., Gibson, S., & Kulkarni, S. (2003). Identifying requirements for Business Contract Language: a Monitoring Perspective. In *7th International Enterprise Distributed Object Computing Conference (EDOC 2003)* (pp. 50–61). Los Alamitos, CA, USA: IEEE.

Neisse, R., Pereira, E. D. V., Granville, L. Z., Almeida, M. J. B., & Tarouco, L. M. R. (2004). A hierarchical policy-based architecture for integrated management of grids and networks. In *Fifth IEEE International Workshop on Policies for Distributed Systems and Networks (POLICY'04)* (p. 103-106). New York, USA.

Norta, A. (2007). *Exploring dynamic inter-organisational business process collaboration*. Technicshe Universiteit Eindhoven, Department of Technology Management.

Nurmela, T., & Kutvonen, L. (2007, June). Service level agreement management in federated virtual organizations. In *Distributed applications and interoperable systems (DAIS2007)*. Paphos, Cyprus: Springer-Verlag.

OWL Web Ontology Language Guide. (2004, February). (W3C Recommendation 10 February 2004, Retrieved September 1st, 2005, from http://www.w3.org/TR/owl-guide/)

Palsberg, J., & Zhao, T. (2001). Efficient and flexible matching of recursive types. *Information and Computation, 171*(2), 364–387.

Papazoglou, M. P., & Georgakopoulos, D. (2003, October). *Service oriented computing. Communications of the ACM, 46*(10).

Peer, J. (2002). Bringing Together Semantic Web and Web Services. In *ISWC '02: Proceedings of the First International Semantic Web Conference on The Semantic Web* (pp. 279–291). London, UK: Springer-Verlag.

Quirchmayr, G., Milosevic, Z., Tagg, R., Cole, J., & Kulkarni, S. (2002). Establishment of Virtual Enterprise Contracts. In *Database and Expert Systems Applications : 13th International Conference* (Vol. 2453, pp. 236–248). London, UK: Springer-Verlag.

Rabelo, R. J., Camarinha-Matos, L. M., & Vallejos, R. V. (2000). Agent-based brokerage for virtual enterprise creation in the moulds industry. In *Proceedings of the IFIP TC5/WG5.3 Second IFIP Working Conference on Infrastructures for Virtual Organizations: Managing Cooperation in Virtual Organizations and Electronic Business towards Smart Organizations* (pp. 281–290). Deventer, The Netherlands: Kluwer, B.V.

Rabelo, R. J., Gusmeroli, S., Arana, C., & Nagellen, T. (2006). The ECOLEAD ICT infrastructure for collaborative networked organizations. In *Network-centric collaboration and supporting frameworks* (Vol. 224, p. 451-460). Springer-Verlag.

RDF Vocabulary Description Language 1.0: RDF Schema. (2004, February). (W3C Recommendation 10 February 2004. Retrieved September 1st, 2005, from http://www.w3.org/TR/rdf-schema/)

Reichert, M., & Dadam, P. (1998). ADEPTflex – Supporting Dynamic Changes of Workflow Without Losing Control. *Journal of Intelligent Information Systems - Special Issue on Workflow Management, 10*(2), 93-129.

RosettaNet Consortium.(2004). *RosettaNet Implementation Framework: Core Specification V02.00.00.* (Retrieved September 1st, 2005, from http://www.rosettanet.org/)

Ruohomaa, S.(2007, April 26–27). Trust management for inter-enterprise collaborations. In *Web proceedings of the I-ESA '07 Doctoral symposium.* Funchal, Portugal. (To appear.)

Ruohomaa, S., & Kutvonen, L. (2008, March). Making multi-dimensional trust decisions on inter-enterprise collaborations. In *Proceedings of the Third international conference on availability, reliability and security (ARES 2008).* Barcelona, Spain: IEEE.

Ruohomaa, S., Viljanen, L., & Kutvonen, L. (2006, March). Guarding enterprise collaborations with trust decisions—the TuBE approach. In *Interoperability for Enterprise Software and Applications. Proceedings of the Workshops and the Doctoral Symposium of the Second IFAC/IFIP I-ESA International Conference: EI2N, WSI, IS-TSPQ 2006* (pp. 237–248). Bordeaux, France: ISTE Ltd.

Ruokolainen, T. (2004). *Component interoperability.* University of Helsinki, Department of Computer Science. (MSc thesis C-2004-42. In Finnish.)

Ruokolainen, T., & Kutvonen, L.(2007, April). Service Typing in Collaborative Systems. In G. Doumeingts, J. Müller, G. Morel, & B. Vallespir (Eds.), *Enterprise Interoperability: New Challenges and Approaches* (pp. 343–354). Springer.

Ruokolainen, T., Metso, J., & Kutvonen, L. (2007, March). Ontology for federated management of business networks. In L. Kutvonen, P. Linington, J.-H. Morin, & S. Ruohomaa (Eds.), *Pre-proceedings of ISTSPQ 2007 — The 2nd international workshop on Interoperability solutions to Trust, Security, Policies and QoS for Enhanced Enterprise Systems* (pp. 41–54). University of Helsinki, Department of Computer Science Publications Series B, Report B-2007-3.

Schmidt, D. (2006, February). Model-driven engineering. *IEEE Computer, 39*(2), 25–31.

Sriharee, N., & Senivongse, T. (2003, November). Discovering Web Services Using Behavioural Constraints and Ontology. In J.-B. Stefani, I. Demeure, & D. Hagimont (Eds.), *Distributed Applications and Interoperable Systems: 4th IFIP WG6.1 International Conference (DAIS 2003)* (pp. 248–259). Springer-Verlag.

Takeuchi, K., Honda, K., & Kubo, M. (1994). An Interaction-based Language and its Typing System. In *PARLE '94: Proceedings of the 6th International PARLE Conference on Parallel Architectures and Languages Europe* (pp. 398–413). London, UK: Springer-Verlag.

Vallecillo, A., Vasconcelos, V. T., & Ravara, A.(2003). Typing the behavior of objects and components using session types. *Electronic Notes in Theoretical Computer Science, 68*(3). (Presented at FOCLASA'02)

van der Aalst, W., ter Hofstede, A., & Weske, M. (2003). Business process management: A survey. In *Proceedings of the First International Conference on Business Process Management*. Eindhoven, The Netherlands: Springer-Verlag.

van der Aalst,W. M. P., Verbeek, H. M.W., & Kumar, A.(2001). XRL/Woflan: Verification of an XML/Petri-net based language for inter-organisational workflows. In *Proceedings of the 6th Informs Conference on Information Systems and Technology (CIST-2001)* (p. 30-45).

Vaquez-Salceda, J., Dignum, V., & Dignum, F. (2005). Organizing multiagent systems. *Autonomous Agents and Multi-Agent Systems, 11*, 307–360.

Chapter XIII
Training and User Acceptance in a University ERP Implementation:
Applying the Technology Acceptance Model

Joseph Bradley
University of Idaho, USA

C. Christopher Lee
Pacific Lutheran University, USA

ABSTRACT

Training is still a neglected part of most ERP implementation projects. This case study investigates the relation between training satisfaction and the perceptions of ease of use, the perception of usefulness, effectiveness and efficiency in implementing an ERP system at a mid-sized organization. We view training satisfaction as a necessary condition for technology acceptance. Our surrogates for training satisfaction are (1) training level prior to implementation, (2) training level when measured after implementation, (3) understanding of features and functions, and (4) perceived need for more training because these factors contribute to perceived ease of use and usefulness. A survey of 143 employees involved in the implementation of ERP in a mid-sized university was conducted. ANOVA and t-tests were used to explore differences in training satisfaction among groups of users by gender, job type, and education level. We found that training satisfaction differed based on job type and gender but not education level. Multiple regression analysis suggests that (1) post implementation training satisfaction is related to ease of use and (2) current training satisfaction and user participation are related to our variables for usefulness, which are perceived efficiency and effectiveness of the ERP systems in doing respondents' jobs

INTRODUCTION

Enterprise Resource Planning (ERP) systems are complex, integrated, off-the-shelf IT solutions that promise to meet the information needs of an organization. ERP systems frequently replace aging and difficult-to-maintain legacy systems. Despite ERP's promise, these systems are difficult, time consuming and expensive to implement. Many failed implementation projects have been widely cited in the business and academic press (Davenport, 1998; Steadman, 1999; Steadman, 1999a; Wah, 2000; Nelson, 2007).

In response to today's constantly changing business conditions, many organizations are implementing ERP systems. Large sums are still being spent on ERP installations. A Forrester survey found that ERP and enterprise applications in general remain the top IT spending priority for 2005 (Hamerman & Wang, 2006). A survey of Society for Information Management members conducted in the summer of 2005 concluded that ERP is among the top six application concerns of its members (Luftman, Kempaiah, and Nash, 2006).

ERP systems allow organizations to put separate business processes together into one compact software system using what the vendors consider "best practices." Integration of different business processes using off-the-shelf ERP solutions is predicted to reap benefits that will outweigh the costs involved with the implementation; however, practice has shown that ERP implementation is not an easy task. Davenport (1998) identified unsuccessful implementation efforts at Fox-Meyer Drug, Mobile Europe, Dell and Applied Materials. Stedman (1999) found that after spending $112 million on an ERP project, Hershey Foods was unable to fill Halloween candy orders in 1999, resulting in a 19% drop in quarterly profits. Wah (2000) observes that "ERP projects have snarled internal processes in big companies like Whirlpool, Hershey's, Waste Management, Inc. and W. L. Gore & Associates." Nike's ERP implementation is included in a listing of "infamous failures in IT project management" because of a major inventory problem which resulted in a profit drop of $100 million in the 3rd quarter of 2000 (Nelson, 2007).

The case we report in this paper deals with a mid-sized university. Universities face many of the same problems as for profit organizations in installing ERP such as "the problems of coordinating resources, controlling costs, of stimulating and facilitating enterprise among the staff, and so on " (Pollock and Cornford, 2004, p. 32). In face of cut-backs in funding, many universities turned to ERP systems to improve efficiency and to become more responsive to student needs. Higher education institutions are not exempt from implementation difficulties. Universities often suffer lost revenue, wasted time, cost overruns and delays during ERP systems implementations. For example, the state of Ohio sued PeopleSoft for $510 million for fraud and breach of contract (Songini, 2004). The University of Massachusetts – Amherst experienced a "nightmare" at registration (Bray, 2004) and Indiana University experienced difficulties in financial aid payments (Songini, 2004a).

We know from the Technology Acceptance Model (Davis, 1989) that successful implementation requires user acceptance. Since ERP systems are potentially a disruptive technology change, organizations undertake training as a way to gain technology acceptance. Only a small number of existing studies examined the effectiveness of training and education in ERP system implementation at higher-education institutions. This lack of exploration of an important factor in successful ERP implementations is what led us to this study. The purpose of this paper is to explore the relationship of training and education to ERP project success. We use:

- User perceptions of ease of use,
- User perceptions of usefulness,
- Efficiency and
- Effectiveness

as predictors of use, an important element of ERP project success.

The data collected is from a medium sized public university in the northwestern region of the United States. The university experienced significant delays and unexpected costs during its ERP system implementation. We use multiple regression analysis to determine the effect of training satisfaction on use and usefulness. We use ANOVA on survey data to look for differences in perception of training satisfaction by gender, job type, education level, department, and longevity in current position.

RESEARCH PROBLEM

This research examines the relation between the users' perceptions of whether training is adequate before implementation and after implementation in terms of the users' perception of ease of use and usefulness in doing their job after the implementation. We sought to find out:

- How does training impact the technology acceptance model?
- Do different groups perceive training adequacy differently?
- What factors are related to the perceived ease of use, effectiveness and efficiency of the ERP system?

LITERATURE REVIEW AND HYPOTHESES

IS Success. Measuring the success in information systems is difficult. User acceptance and use are key factors in the success of any new technology in information systems. An example can be found in the DeLone-McLean IS success model. DeLone and McLean (1992 and 2003) reviewed 180 articles published between 1981 and 1987 and developed a taxonomy and model based on six dimensions of I/S success – systems quality, information quality, use, user satisfaction, individual impact and organizational impact. The constructs of the model which interest us in this paper are use and user satisfaction. Use is important in this model since "the amount of USE can affect the degree of user satisfaction -positively or negatively- as well as the reverse being true (DeLone, 1992, p. 83)." The DeLone-McLean model has proven very popular among IS researchers. In the period 1993 through mid-2002 285 refereed papers in journals and proceedings referenced the model. DeLone and McLean (2003) cite two studies, Seddon and Kiew (1994) and Rai, et al. (2002), which empirically test and validate the model. Many others have implicitly tested the model.

Another success model presented by Seddon (1997) respecifies and extends the DeLone-McLean model. In the area of IS use Seddon argues that IS success results from IS use. IS use "must precede impacts and benefits, but it does not cause them" (Rai, Lang & Welker, 2002, p. 56). Perceived usefulness and user satisfaction are both important constructs in the Seddon model.

Figure 1. DeLone-McLean success model (reprinted by permission)

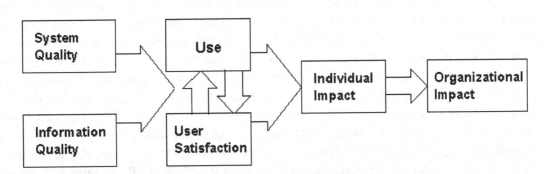

Technology Acceptance Model. Davis et al. (1989) develop the Technology Acceptance Model (TAM) based on the Theory of Reasoned Action. The TAM uses two variables, perceived usefulness and perceived ease of use, as determinants of use. The perceived usefulness is based on the observation that "people tend to use or not use the application to the extent they believe it will help them perform their job better (Davis, 1989, p. 320)." Even if an application is perceived as useful, it will only be used if it is perceived as easy to use, that is benefits of usage outweigh the effort of using the system. These two determinants result in the user's attitude toward using the software system, which in turn leads to the user's behavioral intention to use. The result is use of the system, a construct in the DeLone-McLean success model.

Lee et al. (2003) summarize research studies of the TAM, including studies of 21 external variables affecting the model. Neither training nor training satisfaction is included among these variables.

Our study examines the impact of training on the TAM model. We also the examine impact of personal characteristics on perceived ERP training satisfaction and perceived usefulness of the ERP systems. The proposed model is shown in Figure 2.

Training and ERP. Buchner (1999) argues that whatever your choice of software, ERP should allow you to integrate your existing business applications and data libraries to make migration for users easy, avoid downtime due to training, and reduce the costs associated with migrating data. Schaaf (1999) found that ERP systems create important implications for training. PeopleSoft (now a division of Oracle) launched a satellite-based system to deliver live training to hundreds or even thousands of workers at companies that buy its ERP applications (Stedman, 1999; Spacenet, 2006), emphasizing the importance of training.

Training plays a major role in ERP implementation and use, because ERP generally requires massive reengineering of the organization. Lassila and Brancheau (1999) investigated the implementation of new software packages and found that the initial user experience was important. This study also finds that firms tend to cut training cost in adopting commercial packages, resulting in "negative user attitudes and a low-integration equilibrium" (p. 84). Lassila and Brancheau (1999) also found that training should involve "both the packaged systems features and related work processes" (p. 85). Wheatly (2000) finds that ERP training is frequently compressed if implementation projects are running out of time and money. Wheatly also finds that ERP users would prefer allowing more time for training and obtain training around their own business processes.

Ferrando (2001) argues that when organizations change their business processes by the adoption of new technology, they must prepare their employees with comprehensive training. Employees reported that training classes helped them feel more comfortable using the system and helped reduce mistakes.

Brown (2001) expresses that budgeting for an ERP system should also include training and implementation time, not just the cost of purchasing the software and hardware. A Gartner Group study concluded that 25% of the ERP budget should be allocated to training users. (Coetzer, 2000) Because ERP systems take a considerable time and money to implement, they can disrupt a company's culture, create excessive training requirements, and even lead to productivity dips and mishandled customers orders (Stein, 1999). Grossman and Walsh (2004) refer to training as a "stepchild of most software implementations...that cannot be overlooked or underemphasized" (p. 40). Training contributes to reducing operational and cultural issues encountered during an implementation project (Grossman and Walsh 2004). Duplaga and Astani (2003) found in interviews conducted at 30 manufacturing firms of varying size that the implementation problem rated the highest is "lack of ERP training and education for affected employees" (p. 71).

Training and TAM. Amoako-Gyampah and Salam (2004) study the impact of a "belief construct" (described as "shared beliefs in the benefits of a technology") and training and communication on perceived usefulness and perceived ease of use during an ERP implementation in a large global organization using SAP R/3. They find that training influenced both shared beliefs and perceived ease of use, demonstrating the importance of training in technology acceptance. Therefore, we propose:

- $H_0 1$: Training satisfaction is not related to perceived usefulness of an ERP system.
- $H_0 2$: Training satisfaction is not related to perceived ease of use.

Personal and Job Characteristics

Okpara (2004) finds personal characteristics gender, age, education, income, and experience predict job satisfaction among Nigerian IT managers. We are interested in determining if such characteristics influence training satisfaction. The personal characteristics used in our study include gender, and education level. Job characteristics include job type and longevity in position.

Gender Differences. Venkatesh and Morris (2000) found gender differences in the individual adoption and sustained usage of technology in the workplace. Trauth (2004) identifies three theories to explain the under-representation of women in the IT profession. "The essentialist perspective dichotomizes gender based upon the presumption of significant inherent differences between men and women...The social construction perspective focuses on the social construction of IT as a male domain" (p. 114). Trauth advances a third theory based on "individual differences among women as they relate to the needs and characteristics of IT work and the IT workplace" (p. 115).

Harrison, Rainer and Hochwarter (1997) examine gender differences in computer related activities in a large university setting. They find that men have significantly more computer experience, less computer anxiety, and significantly higher computer self-efficacy and more positive anticipation of computer use than women. "Men reported more successful computer-related outcomes than women in all organizational occupations except clerical" (Smith, 2005, p. 15). These findings are consistent with the social construction of computer-related differences. On the other hand, Busch (1995) found no gender differences in computer attitudes or perceived self-efficacy regarding the completion of word processing and spreadsheet programs.

Ray, Sormunen, and Harris (1999) find women 1.) "possessed a more positive attitude toward the value of computers to productivity ," 2.) "were more positive about the impact of computers on people and their work environment," and 3.) "displayed a greater level of comfort with technology than men" (Smith, 2005, p. 15).

Pijpers and van Montfort (2006) investigated senior executives' acceptance of technology using the TAM and found that gender has no effect on perceived usefulness or perceived ease of use, but also found that gender affects positively actual usage frequency.

Men and women may learn differently and have different perceptions of the adequacy of ERP training provided. The differences in the literature led us to question the role of gender in perceived training satisfaction. In this study we use the following null hypotheses about gender differences:

- H_03: The quality of training prior to implementation is perceived equally by both genders.
- H_04: The quality of training following implementation is perceived equally by both genders.
- H_05: The quality of training in understanding features, functions, and abilities of ERP is perceived equally by both genders.
- H_06. The need for more training after implementation is perceived equally by both genders.

Attitudes and perceptions. Peppard and Ward (2005) observe that four factors influence individual attitudes and perception of enterprise systems (1) implementation-roles and responsibilities, (2) information asymmetry, (3) professional background, and (4) personal interests. We use job classification and educational level as proxies for these differing perceptions of the effectiveness of training.

Amoako-Gyampah (2004), in a single case study, found significant differences existed between the perceptions of user-managers (managers in this study) and end-users (clerical and technical support in this study). "End users felt less confident about their ability to use the system after going through the program than user-managers did" (p. 179). Amoako-Gyampah believes the different perceptions between user-managers and end-users are "the allegiance that end-users have toward the legacy systems that ERP systems are meant to replace." Because of the detailed familiarity of these end-users with the legacy systems, it may take more effort to convince them of the superiority of the ERP system. User-managers are closer to the decision-making process and may have more "buy-in" to the new technology.

The foregoing findings in the literature led to the following hypotheses on attitudes and perceptions:

- H_07: Clerical, technical and managerial personnel perceive equally the quality of training prior to implementation.
- H_08: Clerical, technical and managerial personnel perceive equally the current quality of training[1].
- H_09: Clerical, technical and managerial personnel perceive equally the quality of training in understanding features, functions, and abilities of ERP.
- H_010: Clerical, technical, and managerial personnel perceive equally the need for more training after implementation.

Education level. The educational level of the employee may affect their perception of the adequacy of training. Okpara (2004) found education to be a factor in job satisfaction. Bilgic (1998) found that there were fewer complaints about job related issue among employees with higher education level. Pijpers and van Montfort (2006) found education level influenced both perceived usefulness and perceived ease of use among senior executives. We wanted to see if education level was a factor in training satisfaction.

Therefore, we propose the following hypotheses.

- H_011: Employees of all educational levels perceive equally the quality of training prior to implementation.
- H_012: Employees of all educational levels perceive equally the quality of current training.
- H_013: Employees of all educational levels perceive equally the quality of training in understanding features, functions, and abilities of ERP.
- H_014: Employees of all educational levels perceive equally the need for more training after implementation.

Proposed Model

Based on the above examination of literature, we propose an extension of the technology acceptance model for ERP projects incorporating satisfaction with training as a factor in perceived usefulness of ERP systems and perceived ease of use of ERP systems. Additionally, we propose that personal and job characteristics influence training satisfaction. Our proposed model is shown in Figure 2.

Importance of Topic. Organizations implementing ERP systems face considerable challenges based on the cost and complexity of implementing ERP systems. The knowledge that training favorably impacts intention to use the system and user attitude toward using the system may convince management to allocate more resources to training to enhance the probability of ERP implementation success.

THE ERP IMPLEMENTATION PROJECT

The university studied implemented PeopleSoft for all its information needs. The first modules implemented involve human resource management. This project began in 2000. Two HR executives were sent to PeopleSoft training and then trained the staff that would be using the system. The second phase of the implementation targeted the university's accounting requirements. Training on this phase was conducted in a similar manner with the university's Information Technology Services conducting the training. Data was collected for this study in this time period. The university subsequently implemented the PeopleSoft academic records modules.

Figure 2. Proposed model

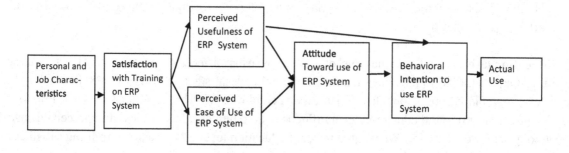

METHODS

Questionnaire. The instrument used in our survey is shown in Appendix I. The PeopleSoft Implementation Survey asks 26 questions.

- The first six questions are demographic. They asked the respondents job type, gender, department, education level, years in current position and level of involvement in ERP.
- Questions 7 through 23 are seven point Likert scale questions about aspects of the ERP implementation. Respondents were asked to indicate their agreement (on a 1 = Strongly disagree to 7 = strongly agree scale) with statements about the PeopleSoft implementation project.
- Questions 24-26 are open-ended questions soliciting the respondents' views about what was done well and what could have been done better in the implementation.

We were interested specifically in the following questions because they relate to our hypotheses:

1. Questions 11, 12, 14 and 20 relate to perceived training satisfaction.
2. Question 15 represents perceived ease of use. A similar question is used by Davis (1989) to develop a valid measurement scale for predicting user acceptance.
3. Questions 21 and 22 relate to the perceived usefulness of the ERP system. Similar questions were used by Davis (1989) to develop a valid measurement scale for predicting user acceptance although Davis used the terms "increased productivity" and "accomplish more work" rather than efficiency.

Table 1 lists the questions that were used in this study and the means and standard deviations of responses to non-demographic questions.

To test the relationship between user perceptions of ease of use and user perception of usefulness we performed multiple regressions for each of the dependent variables-ease of use, efficiency and effectiveness- with the independent variables to examine the relationship among these variables.

Hypothesis testing was used to determine whether there are statistically significant differences in the perspectives of ERP systems implementation among members of different genders, job types, and levels of education. If statistical significance is found on any hypothesis, it leads to a conclusion that its independent variables significantly impacted the perspectives of the ERP systems implementation and, hence, training should be different for that group. Our data was taken from the PeopleSoft Implementation Survey (shown in Appendix I), which was administered by coauthor Lee. Questionnaires were completed by 143 respondents, 30 of whom indicated they were not involved the implementation, leaving 113 usable questionnaires.

We performed t-tests or one-way ANOVA tests on each five independent vaiables with the four dependent variables used to measure training satisfaction, which are shown in Table 2. The reliability of the four variables used to measure training satisfaction was examined resulting in a Cronbach's alphas of 0.838 which exceeds the customary lower limit of 0.70 of reliability.

Statistical Results

Our first tests examine the relationship of training satisfaction to one variable representing perceived ease of use and two variables representing perceived usefulness-efficiency and effectiveness. In addi-

Table 1. Questions used in this study

Q1	Which of the following categories best describes your primary occupation? Technical Support Staff, clerical, Middle Manager, Top Management, Other		
Q2	What is your gender? Female, Male		
Q4	Please indicate the highest level of education completed. High School, Vocational/Technical School, Some College, College Graduate, Master's Degree, Doctoral Degree, Professional Certification, other		
Q5	How many years have you held your current position?		
Q6	What is your level of involvement in PeopleSoft implementation? Not exposed, planning, training, testing, or using the system at work.		
All scores below based on a scale range from 1=strongly disagree to 7=strongly agree, don't know or not applicable		Mean	S.D.
Q7	Do you feel you were a full participant in the design and building of the PeopleSoft system?	4.38	3.22
Q10	There are enough people in your workplace who are technically knowledgeable of computer programming.	3.84	2.64
Q11	Your level of training for the use of PeopleSoft was appropriate prior to the implementation.	2.84	2.03
Q12	Currently, your level of training for the use of PeopleSoft is appropriate.	3.24	2.08
Q14	You have gained a complete understanding of the features, functions, and abilities of PeopleSoft.	2.79	1.95
Q15	PeopleSoft is easy to use.	3.33	2.19
Q20	More training of PeopleSoft would help the implementation process.	6.42	.91
Q21	PeopleSoft has helped or will help you perform your job more effectively (achieve desired results).	4.12	2.19
Q22	PeopleSoft has helped or will help you perform your job more efficiently (faster).	3.98	2.14

Table 2. Dependent and independent variables –training satisfaction

Dependent Variables-Training Satisfaction		Independent Variables-Personal Characteristics
Q11. Training prior to implementation	Cronbach's Alpha =.838	Q1. Job Type
Q12. Current level of training		Q2. Gender
Q14. Understanding of features, etc.		Q3. Department
Q20. Need for more training		Q4. Education Level
		Q5. Longevity at current position

tion to the training success variables, we included in the regression analysis other variables collected in our survey, including personal and job characteristics.

Regression Analysis. To test $H_0 1$, perceived usefulness we included as variables the job and personal characteristics and other variables we had collected in our survey to determine if these variables related directly to usefulness without the training satisfaction variable, Standard multiple regression was conducted to determine the accuracy of the independent variables (training prior to implementation, current level of training, need for more training, technically knowledgeable people in workplace, participation in design and building of system, years in current position, education background, and gender) predicting the two variables related to perceived usefulness, efficiency and effectiveness. For efficiency, regression results indicate that the overall model significantly predicts efficiency in performing the respondent's job. The model accounts for 54% of the variance in efficiency. Only two (current level of training satisfaction and user participation in design and building of system) of the eight variables significantly contributed to the model. For effectiveness, standard regression results indicate that the overall model significantly predicts effectiveness in doing the respondents' respective jobs with People-Soft. The model accounts for 50.8% of the variance in efficiency. Only two (current level of training satisfaction and user participation in design and building of system) of the eight variables significantly contributed to the model. For usefulness, regression results indicate the overall model significantly predicts the usefulness of PeopleSoft. We had not anticipated in our model that participation in the design and building of the system would directly influence usefulness.

To test $H_0 2$, ease of use, standard multiple regression was conducted to determine the accuracy of the independent variables (training prior to implementation, current level of training, need for more training, technically knowledgeable people in workplace, participation in design and building of system, years at work, education background, and gender) predicting ease of use. The model accounts for 78.1% of the variance in ease of use. Only one (current level of training satisfaction) of the eight variables significantly contributed to the model. For ease of use, regression results indicate that the overall model significantly predicts the perceived ease of use of PeopleSoft.

Table 3 presents the model summary statistics for these regression analyses.

We now examine the influence of personal and job characteristic on training satisfaction by comparing the mean of each characteristic with the appropriate demographic variables.

Gender. Questions 11, 12, 14, and 20 in the survey are used to test hypotheses H3 through H6 concerning gender. The data were analyzed by gender with the results shown in Table 4. The findings are based on t-tests.

- A significant difference was found for satisfaction with the level of training[1] prior to implementation (Hypothesis $H_0 3$). Male response mean was 3.77, while female response mean was 2.66). Female respondents were less satisfied with training than male respondents.
- Female respondents were significantly less satisfied with the current level of training (Hypothesis $H_0 4$). Male response mean was 4.17, while female response mean was 3.07.
- No significant gender differences were found for understanding features, functions, and abilities of the software (Hypothesis $H_0 5$).

Table 3. Results of regression for ease of use, efficiency, and effectiveness

Dependent Variable(s)	Perceived Ease of Use	Perceived Usefulness	
		Efficiency	Effectiveness
	Current training	Current training, user participation	Current training, user participation
R^2	.784	.550	.518
R^2_{adj}	.781	.540	.508
F	F(1,93)=336.743	(F1,90)=8.212	F(1,90)=9.486
P	<.001	<.005	<.005
% variance accounted for	78.4%	55.0%	51.8%

Table 4. Results for gender differences

Gender	Male			Female					
t-test	n	mean	S.D	n	mean	S.D.	t	df	Prob.
Q11. Training prior to implementation	17	3.77	2.05	87	2.66	1.99	-2.09	102	.039*
Q12. Current level of training	18	4.17	1.82	97	3.07	2.09	-2.08	113	.040*
Q14. Understanding of features, etc.	18	3.00	1.68	96	2.75	2.01	-.50	112	.620
Q20. Need for more training	16	5.94	1.48	96	6.50	.75	2.34	110	.021*

All scores based on a scale range from 1=strongly disagree to 7=strongly agree
$* p<.05$ $** p<.001$

- Female respondents significantly wished for more training (Hypothesis $H_0 6$). Male response mean was 5.94, while female response mean was 6.50.

Job Type. Table 5 shows the results for job type. Questions 11, 12, 14, and 20 were used in an ANOVA analysis. The data were disaggregated into technical support, clerical, and management. Significant differences were found among the three groups for training prior to implementation (Q11), current level of training (Q12), and understanding of features (Q14). Respondents classified as management exhibited a much more favorable view of the level of training than technical support personnel or clerical per-

Table 5. Mean scores on training variables by job type

Job Type	Technical Support			Clerical			Management				
ANOVA	n	mean	S.D	n	mean	S.D.	n	mean	S.D	F Ratio	Prob.
Q11. Training prior to implementation	22	2.41	1.59	48	2.10	1.60	31	4.36	2.21	15.5	.000**
Q12. Current level of training	23	2.83	1.95	54	2.48	1.81	35	4.77	1.85	17.1	.000**
Q14. Understanding of features, etc.	22	2.36	1.59	54	1.96	1.27	35	4.43	2.12	25.0	.000**
Q20. Need for more training	22	6.59	.96	56	6.39	.82	32	6.34	1.04	.52	.597

All scores based on a scale range from 1=strongly disagree to 7=strongly agree
$* p<.05$ $** p<.001$

sonnel. This finding is consistent with the case study described by Amoako-Gyampah (2004) where user-managers were consistently more satisfied for critical issues in ERP implementation.

Other independent variables.
Education level. Education levels ranged from high school through post-graduate university degrees in our sample. No statistically significant differences were found in training level prior to or after implementation ("current"), the understanding of features, etc. or the need for more training based on education level. Hypotheses H11 through H14 are sustained.

Department and longevity in current position. Preliminary screening of the data found that these variables presented no significant differences, as expected.

DISCUSSION

In analyzing the literature we found agreement that training is important when implementing a new ERP system in a university or a large-scale organization. Yet practice does not follow this finding. Training budgets are frequently cut as implementation projects experience over-runs in cost and time.

Our examination of the relationship between training satisfaction and use supports the importance of training satisfaction to ERP system use which is an important factor in IS success models. The regression analyses for the dependent variables of perceived ease of use, perceived efficiency of the ERP system and perceived effectiveness of the ERP system showed these variables to be influenced by training satisfaction. Specifically:

- Satisfaction with the current level of training explained 78.4% of the variance in ease of use of the ERP system.
- Satisfaction with current training and user participation together explained 55.0% of the variance in ease of use in doing the respondents job with ERP.
- Satisfaction with current level of training and user participation accounted for 51.8% of the variance in effectiveness of doing the respondent's job with the ERP system.

In our regression models we included personal and job type characteristics as variables. None of these variables was included in the resulting models. This result shows that the characteristics do not directly influence ease of use or usefulness, further confirming our model.

The unanticipated result from our regression was the inclusion of participation in the design and building of the ERP system in the model for usefulness (efficiency and effectiveness). Our review of the literature did not lead us to anticipate this result. Participation has been studied as a critical success factor in ERP implementations with mixed results, but has not been related to usefulness or use. The literature has focused more on participation to reduce user resistance to change.

Our examination of the personal and job characteristic which influence training satisfaction found that gender and job classification influence this construct. Education level, department, and longevity in current position did not show any difference in the perception of training quality prior to implementation, current training quality, understanding of the system and need for more training.

Gender. Female respondents reported significantly lower levels of satisfaction with training prior to implementation, current level of training and higher agreement with the need for more training than male respondents. Since both male and female employees experienced the same training, this finding raises the question of whether different training methods might be appropriate for male and female employees. Another explanation may be that female workers are heavier users of the ERP systems and might need more training than the university provided. Our survey did not capture how extensively respondents used the PeopleSoft system.

Job type. Management level employees expressed higher satisfaction with training levels both prior to and after implementation and higher levels of understanding of the features, functions and abilities of PeopleSoft. Managers may not be as heavily involved in the use of the PeopleSoft system as clerical employees, especially in the data entry and file maintenance functions. Technical support employees also exhibited slightly higher levels of satisfaction than clerical personnel on these three variables. No difference by job type was shown for the need for more ERP training. All job types expressed the need for more training.

Responses to open ended questions at the end of the survey supported the importance of training. Responses to the question "how do you think the implementation process can be improved" included:

- Training and updating employees to the status of (implementation) process
- More training in all departments
- More training, more info to end users earlier in the process
- More training and more testing before putting this system on line.
- Training would be nice
- Don't implement a system unless you fell (sic) you will be able to ease the workload of those who are actual end users.
- Training…Instruction Manual…Something to help me learn this would be nice.
- More testing, training, and time before implementation.

These comments further confirm the importance of training to employees involved in the implementation process.

SUMMARY AND CONCLUSION

This analysis of factors affecting training and the attitudes toward acceptance of technology confirms the value of training when implementing an ERP system in a university or other large organization. The data analysis provides evidence that the perspectives of gender and job types affect the perception of the adequacy and completeness of training. This finding indicates the need for proper training when implementing an ERP system in a university.

The regression analysis shows that training satisfaction is a factor leading to usefulness, which we define as employee perceptions of the efficiency and effectiveness, and ease of use of the ERP system in doing their job. The results confirm that practitioners should allocate ample budgets for training and measure training satisfaction as a predictor of employee attitudes toward the ERP system during and after implementation.

LIMITATIONS AND FUTURE RESEARCH

Limitations of the present study include:

- The results may not be generalizable because only one organization was studied. ERP training at additional organizations should be studied.
- Self-reporting of perceptions creates inherent limitations. However, these limitations are quite difficult to overcome.
- Our sample size was not large enough to study joint effects such as gender and job type. Studies of larger implementations could be of help in addressing these issues.
- The questionnaire design limited our ability to use additional analytical tools.

Further research is needed to explore why different groups perceive training differently and how training satisfaction can be improved among all groups. The extension of the TAM model to include the effect of training satisfaction should be studied in other ERP projects and in other large IS systems.

REFERENCES

Amoako-Gyampah, K., (2004). ERP Implementation Factors: A comparison of managerial and end-user perspectives. *Business Process Management Journal*, 10(2), 171-183.

Amoako-Gyampah, K., & Salam, A. F (2004). An extension of the technology acceptance model in an ERP implementation environment. *Information & Management*, 41, 731-745.

Bray, H. (2004). Computer woes cause registration 'nightmare' at University of Massachusetts. *Knight Ridder Business News*, Washington, Sep 14, 2004, p. 1.

Brown, J. (2001, February). ERP Doomed By Poor Planning. *Computing Canada, 11.*

Buchner, M. (1999, August). ERP Application Integration. *Midrange Systems, 12.*

Busch, T. (1995). Gender differences in self-efficacy and attitudes toward computers. *Journal of Educational Computing Research*, 12(2), 147-158.

Coetzer, J. (2000, September 18). Survey-Enterprise Resource Planning-Analyse Before Implementing. *Business Day, 20.*

Davenport, T. H. (1998). Putting the Enterprise into the Enterprise System. *Harvard Business Review,* 76(4, July-August), 121-131.

Davis, F.D. (1989). Perceived Usefulness, Perceived Ease of Use, and User Acceptance of Information Technology, *MIS Quarterly, 13*(3), 319-340.

Davis, F. D., Bagozzi, R. P., & Warshaw, P. R. (1989). User Acceptance of Computer Technology: A Comparison of Two Theoretical Models. *Management Science, 35,* 8, 982-1003.

DeLone, W. H., & McLean, E. R., (1992). Information Systems Success: The Quest for the Dependent Variable. *Information Systems Research, 3*(1), 60-95.

DeLone, W.H. & McLean, E. R., (2003). The DeLone and McLean model of information systems success: A ten-year update. *Journal of Management Information Systems, 19*(4), 9-30.

Duplaga, E. A. & Astni, M. (2003). Implementing ERP in Manufacturing. *Information Systems Management, 20*(3), 68-75.

Ferrando, T. (2001). Training Employees to Use ERP Systems. *The American City & County..* September 2001, 12.

Grossman, T., & Walsh, J. (2004). Avoiding the Pitfalls of ERP System Implementations. *Information Systems Management, 21(2), 38-42.*

Hamerman, P., & Wang, R. (2006). ERP: Still a Challenge after All These Years. *Enterprise Applications.* Jan 29, 2006, p.1-2. Downloaded on Sept. 25, 2006 from http://www.networkcomputing.com/gswelcome/showArticle.jhtml?articleID=177104905

Harris, P. (2000). PeopleSoft hopes to recover fumble with Big Ten universities. *The Business Journal,* 17(38), 3. San Jose, Jan 07, 2000.

Harrison, A. W., Rainer, R. K., & Hochwarter, W.A. (1997) Gender differences in computing activities. *Journal of Social Behavior & Personality, 12*(4), 849-869.

Lassila, K. S., & Brancheau, J. C. (1999). Adoption and Utilization of Commercial Software Packages: Exploring Utilization Equilibria, Transitions, Triggers, and Tracks. *Journal of Management Information Systems, 12*(2), 63-90.

Lee, C.C, & Lee, H. (2001). Factors Affecting Enterprise Resource Planning Systems Implementation in a Higher Education Institution. *Issues in Information Systems, 2,* 207-212.

Lee, Y., Kozar, K., & Larsen, K.R.T. (2003). The Technology Acceptance Model: Past, Present and Future. *Communications of the Association for Information Systems, 12*(50), 752-780.

Luftman, J., Kempaiah, R., & Nash, E. (2006). Key Issues for IT Executives 2005. *MIS Quarterly Executive, 5*(2), 81-99.

Nelson, R. R. (2007). IT Project Management: Infamous failures, classic Mistakes, and Best Practices. MIS Quarterly Executive, 6(2), 67-78.

Okpara, J.O. (2004). Personal Characteristics as predictors of job satisfaction: An exploratory study of IT managers in a developing country. *Information Technology & People, 17*(3), 327-337.

Peppard, J., & Ward, J. (2005). Unlocking Sustained Business Value from IT Investments. *California Management Review, 48*(1), 52-70.

Pijpers, G. G. M., & van Montfort, K. (2006). An Investigation of Factors that Influence Senior Executives to Accept Innovations in Information Technology, *International Journal of Management, 23*(1), 11-23.

Pollock, N., & Cornford, J. (2004). ERP systems and the university as a "unique" organization. *Information, Technology & People, 17,* 1, 31-52.

Rai, A., Lang, S. S., & Welker, R. B. (2002). Assessing the Validity of IS Success Models: An Empirical Test and Theoretical Analysis. *Information Systems Research, 13*(1), March 2002, 50-69.

Ray, C.M., Sormunen, C., & Harris, T. M. (1999). Men's and women's attitudes toward computer technology: A comparison. *Office Systems Research Journal, 17*(1) Retrieved Oct. 14, 2006 from http://www.osra.org/itlpj/vol17no1.html

Schaaf, D. (1999, May). What Trainers Need to Know About ERP. *Training.* ET4- ET12.

Seddon, P. B. (1997). A respecification and extension of the DeLone and McLean model of IS success. *Information Systems Research.* 8(September) 240-253.

Seddon, P. B., & Kiew, M.-Y (1994). A partial test and development of the DeLone and McLean model of IS success. In J.I. De Gross, S. L. Huff, and M. C. Munro (eds.), *Proceedings of the International Conference on Information Systems,* Atlanta, GA: Association for Information Systems, 1994, 99-110.

Slater, D. (1998, January28). ERP Projects Cost More Than Their Immediate Payback. *CIO Enterprise,* 26.

Smith, S. M. (2005). The Digital Divide: Gender and Racial Differences in Information Technology Education. *Information Technology, Learning, and Performance Journal, 23,* 1.13-23.

Songini, M. (2004). University Pins $510M Lawsuit on PeopleSoft. *Computerworld.* March 29, 2004. p. 6.

Songini, M. (2004a). ERP System Doesn't Make the Grade in Indiana. *Computerworld.* Sep 13, 2004, p. 1.

Spacenet Inc. (2006). Corporate Communications & Distance Learning. Downloaded from http://www.vsat.cc/images/ehc_idl.pdf

Stedman, C. (1999). Failed ERP Gamble Haunts Hershey: Candy maker bites off more than it can chew and 'Kisses' big Halloween sales goodbye. *Computerworld, 1.*

Stedman, C. (1999a). ERP Problems Plague College. *Computerworld, 4.*

Stedman, C. (1999b). Oracle, PeopleSoft Offer New Approaches to Live Training. *Computerworld, 8.*

Stein, T. (1999, May). ROI: Making ERP Add Up. *InformationWeek, 59-68.*

Trauth, E. M., Quesenberry, J. L., & Morgan, A. J. (2004). Understanding the Under Representation of Women in IT: Toward a Theory of Individual Differences, SIGMIS '04, April 22-24, 2004, Tucson, Arizona, 114-119.

Venkatesh, V., & Morris, M.G. (2000). Why Don't Men Ever Stop To Ask for Directions? Gender, Social Influence and Their Role in Technology Acceptance and Usage Behavior. *MIS Quarterly, 24*(1), 115-139.

Wah, L. (2000, March). Give ERP a Chance. *Management Review,* 20-24.

Wheatly, M. (2000). ERP Training Stinks. *CIO Magazine, 13*(June 1), 86-96.

Woodie, A. (2006, January 25). AMR Sees 'Huge Surge' in ERP Spending, Most Likely at Microsoft. The Windows Observer. Retrieved on Feb. 9, 2006 from http:// www.itjungle.com/two/two012506

ENDNOTE

[1] All means are based on a seven-point Likert scale

APPENDIX 1

PeopleSoft Implementation Survey

INSTRUCTIONS: This is an anonymous survey. Please identify your answer to each question by circling the appropriate letter or number corresponding with your choice. Please answer every question to the best of your ability.

1. Which of the following categories best describes your primary occupation?
A) Technical Support Staff
B) Clerical
C) Middle Manager (Analyze data and report to superiors)
D) Top Management (Administrators, decision-makers)
E) Other_____

2. What is your gender?
A) Female
B) Male

3. What department do you work in?

A)	Human Resources	F)	Student Employment
B)	Accounting	G)	Payroll
C)	Student Services	H)	Registrar
D)	Financial Aid	I)	CTS
E)	Admissions	J)	Other_____

4. Please indicate the highest level of education completed?

A)	High School	E)	Master's Degree
B)	Vocational/Technical School	F)	Doctoral Degree
C)	Some College	G)	Professional Certification
D)	College Graduate	H)	Other_____

5. How many years have you held your current position? _____

6. What is your level of involvement in PeopleSoft implementation?

A) Not exposed
B) Planning
C) Training
D) Testing
E) Using the system at work

For questions 7-22 please use this scale:
1 = Strongly Disagree; 2 = Disagree; 3 = Somewhat disagree; 4 = neutral; 5 = somewhat agree; 6 = agree; 7 = strongly agree; [DK] = Don't know; [NA] = Not Applicable

7. You feel you were a full participant in the design and building of the PeopleSoft system.
1   2   3   4   5   6   7   [DK]   [NA]

8. Enough time was allocated to the planning (vendor research, other end-users, etc.) of the implementation.
1   2   3   4   5   6   7   [DK]   [NA]

9. Enough funding was allocated to the implementation of PeopleSoft.
1   2   3   4   5   6   7   [DK]   [NA]

10. There are enough people in your workplace who are technically knowledgeable of computer programming.
1   2   3   4   5   6   7   [DK]   [NA]

11. Your level of training for the use of PeopleSoft was appropriate prior to the implementation.
1   2   3   4   5   6   7   [DK]   [NA]

12. Currently, your level of training for the use of PeopleSoft is appropriate.
1   2   3   4   5   6   7   [DK]   [NA]

1 = Strongly Disagree; 2 = Disagree; 3 = Somewhat disagree; 4 = neutral; 5 = somewhat agree; 6 = agree; 7 = strongly agree; [DK] = Don't know; [NA] = Not Applicable

13. Sufficient research was conducted on PeopleSoft/ERP systems prior to implementation.
1   2   3   4   5   6   7   [DK]   [NA]

14. You have gained a complete understanding of the features, functions, and abilities of PeopleSoft.
1   2   3   4   5   6   7   [DK]   [NA]

15. PeopleSoft is easy for you to use.

1   2   3   4   5   6   7   [DK]   [NA]

16. There is satisfactory internal (CWU personnel) technical support to handle problems experienced with PeopleSoft.

1   2   3   4   5   6   7   [DK]   [NA]

17. Adequate service has been provided by outside consultants who are independent from PeopleSoft.

1   2   3   4   5   6   7   [DK]   [NA]

18. You have received adequate service from PeopleSoft Inc.'s own consultants.

1   2   3   4   5   6   7   [DK]   [NA]

19. The redesigning of business processes was completed effectively prior to the implementation.

1   2   3   4   5   6   7   [DK]   [NA]

20. More training of PeopleSoft would help the implementation process.

1   2   3   4   5   6   7   [DK]   [NA]

21. PeopleSoft has helped or will help you perform your job more effectively (achieve desired results).

1   2   3   4   5   6   7   [DK]   [NA]

22. PeopleSoft has helped or will help you perform your job more efficiently (faster).

1   2   3   4   5   6   7   [DK]   [NA]

23. You have been informed of the goals and progress of the PeopleSoft implementation.

1   2   3   4   5   6   7   [DK]   [NA]

Written Comments:

24. What do you feel has been done well in the implementation process?

25. How do you think the implementation process can be improved?

26. Additional Comments:

Chapter XIV
Measuring and Diffusing Data Quality in a Peer-to-Peer Architecture

Diego Milano
Università degli Studi di Roma, Italy

Monica Scannapieco
Università degli Studi di Roma, Italy

Tiziana Catarci
Università degli Studi di Roma, Italy

INTRODUCTION

Data quality is a complex concept defined by various dimensions such as accuracy, currency, completeness, and consistency (Wang & Strong, 1996). Recent research has highlighted the importance of data quality issues in various contexts. In particular, in some specific environments characterized by extensive data replication high quality of data is a strict requirement. Among such environments, this article focuses on Cooperative Information Systems.

Cooperative information systems (CISs) are all distributed and heterogeneous information systems that cooperate by sharing information, constraints, and goals (Mylopoulos & Papazoglou, 1997). Quality of data is a necessary requirement for a CIS. Indeed, a system in the CIS will not easily exchange data with another system without knowledge of the quality of data provided by the other system, thus resulting in a reduced cooperation. Also, when the quality of exchanged data is poor, there is a progressive deterioration of the overall data quality in the CIS. On the other hand, the high degree of data replication that characterizes a CIS can be exploited for improving data quality, as different copies of the same data may be compared in order to detect quality problems and possibly solve them.

In Scannapieco, Virgillito, Marchetti, Mecella, and Baldoni (2004) and Mecella et al. (2003), the DaQuinCIS architecture is described as an architecture managing data quality in cooperative contexts, in order to avoid the spread of low-quality data and to exploit data replication for the improvement of the overall quality of cooperative data.

In this article we will describe the design of a component of our system named as, quality factory. The quality factory has the purpose of evaluating quality of XML data sources of the cooperative system. While the need for such a component had been previously identified, this article first presents the design of the quality factory and proposes an overall methodology to evaluate the quality of XML data sources.

Quality values measured by the quality factory are used by the data quality broker. The data quality broker has two main functionalities: 1) quality brokering that allows users to select data in the CIS according to their quality; 2) quality improvement that diffuses best quality copies of data in the CIS.

As a further research contribution, this article will focus on the design and implementation features of the data quality broker as a Peer-to-Peer (P2P) system. More specifically, the data quality broker is implemented as a peer-to-peer distributed service: each organization hosts a copy of the data quality broker that interacts with other copies. While the functional specification of the data quality broker is not a contribution of this article, and has been presented in (Scannapieco et al., 2004; Mecella et al., 2003), its detailed design and implementation features as a P2P system are a novel contribution of this article. Moreover, we will present some results from tests made to prove the effectiveness and efficiency of our system. The data quality broker is implemented by a peer-to-peer architecture in order to be as less invasive as possible in introducing quality controls in a cooperative system. Indeed, cooperating organizations need to save their independency and autonomy requirements. Such requirements are well-guaranteed by the P2P paradigm which is able to support the cooperation without necessarily involving consistent re-engineering actions; in the section on Related Work, we will better detail this point, comparing our choice with a system that instead does not adopt a P2P architecture.

The rest of this article is organized as follows. The second section describes the main features of the quality factory and of the data quality broker. The third section presents the overall methodology and the fourth section details the architectural design of the quality factory, by focusing on the case of XML data sources. The fifth section describes the detailed design and implementation of the data quality broker as a peer-to-peer system, and each module of its component architecture. The set of performed experiments is described in the sixth section. Finally, related work and conclusions are presented in the seventh and eighth section respectively.

THE DATA QUALITY BROKER AND QUALITY FACTORY: GENERALITIES

In this section, we provide an overview of the main functionality of the data quality broker and we detail the interaction of such module with the quality factory, the design of which is provided in the third and fourth sections. The component architecture and implementation details of the data quality broker are instead described in the fifth section.

The Data Quality Broker Functionality

In the DaQuinCIS architecture, all cooperating organizations export their application data and quality data (i.e., data quality dimension values evaluated for the application data) according to a specific data model. The model for exporting data and quality data is referred to as Data and Data Quality (D^2Q)

model (Mecella et al., 2003). The data quality broker allows users to access data in the CIS according to their quality. Specifically, the data quality broker performs two tasks, namely *query processing* and *quality improvement.*

The data quality broker performs query processing according to a global-as-view (GAV) approach by unfolding queries posed over a global schema, that is, replacing each atom of the original query with the corresponding view on local data sources (Ullman, 1997; Lenzerini, 2002). Both the global schema and local schemas exported by cooperating organizations are expressed according to the D²Q model. The specific way in which the mapping is defined stems from the idea of performing a quality improvement function during the query processing step. Global schema concepts are defined by means of queries over the local sources that retrieve all data present in the system that can populate such concepts. When retrieving results, data coming from different sources can be compared and a best quality copy can be constructed. Specifically, in our setting, data sources have distinct copies of the same data with different quality levels, that is, there are instance-level conflicts. We resolve these conflicts at query execution time by relying on quality values associated to data: when a set of different copies of the same data are returned, we look at the associated quality values, and we select the copy to return as a result on the basis of such values. More details on the algorithm implemented for processing queries can be found in (Scannapieco et al., 2004). The best quality copy is also diffused to other organizations in the CIS as a quality improvement feedback.

Interaction Between the Data Quality Broker and the Quality Factory

The quality factory has the purpose of evaluating the quality of data stored by the cooperating sources. Such values will be used to populate the D²Q model with the quality values associated to the integrated data. Therefore, the principal role of the quality factory is to measure such quality values in order to make them accessible by the data quality broker. More specifically, at query time the data quality broker accesses quality values in order to solve instance level conflicts, and thus returning an answer to the user query. At query time, a further interaction may occur, as the data quality broker can send better data and associated quality values to specific organizations in the CIS, while performing the improvement functionality. In Figure 1, the interactions between the data quality broker and the quality factory are shown. Notice also the P2P deployment of the data quality broker that will be discussed in the fifth section.

The Data Quality Factory

The quality factory has the task of measuring the quality of the data that each organization makes available to the others. In this section we introduce the data quality evaluation methodology which is implemented by the quality factory. We then make some considerations about the architectural design of a quality factory module.

The definition of a data quality evaluation methodology is dependent on the data models used by organizations for their application data. As an example, the types of integrity constraints that are defined for the relational data model are of course different from the ones defined for a semi-structured data model, like the XML data model.

We focus on the case of data sources adopting the XML data model, showing how appropriate data quality measures can be devised in this case. We first start from a generic methodology, then we specify

Figure 1. Interaction between the data quality broker and the quality factory

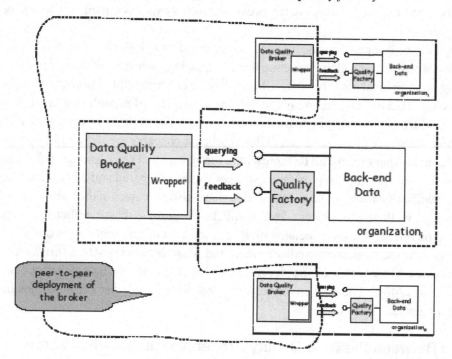

the methodology for XML data sources and we describe an example of definition of suitable metrics for quality evaluation.

A Data Quality Evaluation Methodology

The quality evaluation methodology is shown in Figure 2. The main idea is to measure data quality not by relying on the original schema of data sources, but through a comparison with a more constraining schema.

Indeed, many data quality problems are caused by the fact that data models and data management systems are often too weak at expressing several constraints that nonetheless exist in reality. On one hand, data management systems have the possibility to avoid some quality errors, such as the ones that can be introduced during data entry processes, or depend on applications behavior. As an example, relational DBMSs can perform various checks at data entry or when certain operations are performed; XML documents can be validated against a DTD or other kind of schema, and so forth. On the other hand, database management systems are currently not able to enforce all the constraints that must hold on the data in order for them to be error-free and consistent; both relational DBMSs and XML data storage systems are examples of the missing enforcement of such a wide range of constraints.

This may be due to failure of data management systems to support enforcement of some constraints, or in limitations of the expressivity of the data models used, to actually represent data that fail to support some of the constraints holding on the domain even if they are known. Good design approaches exist for relational databases. Such approaches usually start with a requirement analysis. The result of this phase of the design is a conceptual model that tries to capture all the details concerning the domain

Figure 2. Methodology for quality evaluation

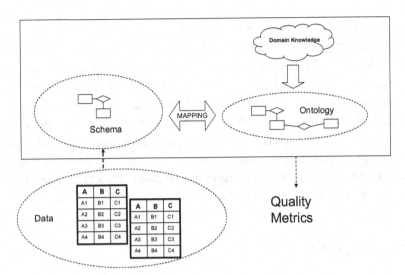

involved, including any possible constraint that should be enforced in order to guarantee the consistency of the database during the lifetime of the application. All the domain and application specific knowledge that is necessary to run the application is usually formalized through a high level, expressive language like the Entity Relationship model. However, the final relational schema cannot enforce some of the constraints identified during this process.

Furthermore, missing constraints can also be due to poor schema design. Conceptual XML design, for instance, is still an open problem that only recently has received attention from the research community (Conrad, Scheffner, & Freytag, 2000).

The methodology we propose aims at identifying data quality problems that can be imputed to inconsistency with "constraints" that should hold but are not actively enforced on data. In order to evaluate data quality a comprehensive schema is first created. Such a schema is built by complementing the knowledge contained in the original data schema with knowledge representing the specific application domain, gathered through a domain analysis activity (e.g., performed by a domain expert).

The language used should be expressive enough to allow representation of more complex constraints than those already holding on the data to be analyzed. Besides being expressive, the modelling language used to represent such knowledge should be formal and have a machine processable format, in order to be used in an automated quality evaluation process, that is, by the quality factory module. We call the resulting representation *reference ontology*. In the fourth section we will give details about the modelling language used for the reference ontology.

In order to allow evaluation of data based on this "rich" representation, it must be related to the schema describing the data. The correspondence between the original data schema and the ontology is established by a mapping, as detailed in the fourth section.

The main advantage of this approach is that referring to this high-level, formalized representation of the reality of interest provides a homogeneous and effective way to define metrics for quality evaluation.

Reference Ontology and Mapping

The reference ontology used in the above described methodology must be expressed in a language rich enough to model complex application domains and represent a wide range of constraints. Conceptual data models (Hull & King, 1987) like the Entity-Relationship model have been initially introduced to help the schema designer, and are capable of expressing rich constraints on the modelled reality. Lately, it has been shown that such models can be formalized through appropriate expressive description logics (Baader, Calvanese, McGuinness, Nardi, & Patel-Schneider, 2003), thus making available for them the basic logical reasoning services characterizing such description languages. A detailed formal description of a full-fledged ontology language to be used for this task is outside the scope of this article. Therefore, we introduce a simplified language, whose features are indeed sufficient to describe our methodology and to show an example of its application (see the fourth section).

REFERENCE ONTOLOGY

In the following, we will denote a reference ontology with Σ.

Syntactically, Σ is a tuple $< C, Prop, R >$ where:

- C is a set of *Concepts*.
- For each $c \in C$, *Prop(c)* denotes a set of named properties. We assume that on properties it is possible to express cardinality constraints that must be satisfied by instances of the concept. In particular, properties may be defined as optional or mandatory.
- R is a set of binary relationships of the form $< c, c' >$ where c and c' are concepts in C.

For the relationships in R, we require that some constraints can be expressed. In particular, given a relationship $r = < c, c' >$ in the ontology, we assume the ontology formalism allows:

- To specify cardinality constraints on both concepts c and c'.
- To specify a direction for the relationship. A relationship $r = < c, c' >$ on which a direction is defined is said to be a parent-child relationship. The concept c is said to have the role of parent and the concept c' is said to have the role of child.
- To specify a constraint over two properties p and p', belonging respectively to *Prop(c)* and *Prop(c')*, such that related instances of c and c' will have the same value for p and p'. A relationship on which this constraint holds is named as *join relationship*. If $r = < c, c' >$ is a join relationship with an equality constraint over the properties p of c and p' of c', we will also write $r = < c : p, c' : p' >$.

Though we have introduced only binary relationships, a generalization to higher arity relationships is straightforward. Besides creating the reference ontology, it is also necessary to establish a mapping between the original data schema and the ontology itself. This mapping links the original data to the ontology, thus allowing evaluating constraints holding on the ontology over the data populating the original schema. Starting from the ontology and the mapping, appropriate quality metrics can be defined. The language used to describe the reference ontology can be the same for each organization; instead, the mapping can be defined in several ways and is dependent on the particular data model and schema language used by each organization. Different mapping formalisms must be devised for example for the relational model, the various XML schema languages and so on.

In the following sections, we first illustrate a general architecture for the quality factory module based on the proposed methodology. Then, we show how the general architecture of the quality factory can be tailored for a specific data model, namely the XML data model. We also introduce a specific mapping formalism to map from the DTD schema language to our ontology language, and we show how quality metrics appropriate for such data model can be defined. In particular, we provide an example of the definition of metrics related to the *completeness* quality dimension.

The possibility of defining these metrics is of particular interest, since quality metrics for XML data have not yet been devised. The main motivations for choosing XML are: 1) DTD, which a widely diffused XML schema formalism, is particularly weak at expressing some constraints that are essential to ensure the quality of XML data; 2) while longtime established good design methodologies exist for the relational case, the problem of defining guidelines for XML schema design has been only recently addressed (Arenas & Libkin, 2004) and is far to be solved.

The approach described so far shares some ideas with (Milano, Scannapieco, & Catarci, 2005), where the purpose was a different one, namely cleaning XML data. Instead, here we focus on the evaluation of XML data quality in the context of a comprehensive system for data quality management.

Generic Architecture of the Quality Factory

The following considerations justify the architecture in order for a quality factory module described in this section. First, the organizations participating to a CIS might employ heterogeneous data models to store their data. Thus, appropriate quality metrics and quality evaluation strategies must be devised, that take into account such different models. Second, a quality factory not only has the duty to evaluate quality values, but also to manage such values and maintain a connection between such values and the data from which they were derived. After performing an evaluation of the quality of a data source, the quality factory stores the resulting quality values, making them available to a wrapper module which is responsible for presenting both data and quality trough the D²Q data model. At this stage, however, quality values are not related to data by a D²Q representation, as such representation is only built by the wrapper at query time. It is thus necessary to solve the problem of how to maintain a connection between the original data values and the evaluated quality values. We describe a possible solution to this problem for the XML case in the fourth section.

An alternative solution allows the quality factory to interact directly with data already represented through the (data part of the) D²Q model. This choice would indeed simplify the architecture of the system, as the quality factory would interact with a single data model and thus, being independent on data and schema heterogeneity, it could be used without changes within different organizations. Unfortunately, this option has some serious drawbacks. First, as previously explained, organizations export their data in the D²Q model simply by implementing a wrapper that allows access to the data in that format. This works coherently with the spirit of CISs, in which organizations cooperate preserving their independence, and can maintain their own data models. Data is never actually stored in the D²Q model, but it is only translated to this model at query time. If the quality factory interacted directly with the model, it should query the data trough the wrapper and then store the computed quality values, while preserving the links to original data values. This strategy imposes too strict constraints on the implementation of the wrapper. The choice of having the quality factory interact directly with the D²Q model has a second important drawback, namely quality evaluation would be performed independently from the original data model used by organizations to store their own data. Instead, we believe that structural properties of the underlying data models should be taken into proper account when evaluating quality. If all data are translated to a single model *before* quality evaluation, much information on the data structures and on the constraints would be lost.

A generic logical architecture for a quality factory module is presented in Figure 3. The figure shows the main logical components of the quality factory module, namely a quality storage, a quality evaluator, and a set of quality metrics. The figure also shows how the quality factory interacts with the data stored at the source. The interaction is driven by a reference ontology and mapping. The reference ontology and the mapping are built by a domain expert and they are organization specific. The quality storage is (logically) linked to the data stored inside the organizations. The details of such connection depend on the specific way the data storage itself is designed. When accessing a source, the wrapper module also accesses the quality storage and exploits this logical connection to retrieve the relevant quality values. The principal features of each module are briefly described in the following

Quality Storage

The quality storage is a logical component inside the quality factory that has the role of storing quality values evaluated by the quality evaluator component. The most important aspect in the design of a quality storage for a particular data model is how to maintain the connection between the data values and the quality values. In this article, we show a possible solution to this problem for an XML data source. A notable difference between the XML model and the relational one is that pieces of data must not only be identified with regard to their values, but also with regard to their position in the XML tree, as we describe in the fourth section.

Figure 3. The logical architecture of the quality factory

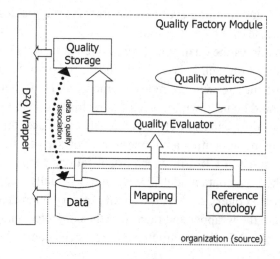

Quality Evaluator

The quality evaluator component has the role of actually accessing the data stored in the organization and assessing their quality. This is done on the base of the quality metrics defined for the particular data model used within the source. Besides considering the specific metrics to be evaluated, the quality evaluator must also implement efficient algorithms to "visit" the data at the source. Furthermore it must be able to manage changes in the data due to updates. Whenever possible, incremental evaluation strategies should be devised, in order to avoid the need for a new assessment each time the underlying source changes.

Quality Metrics

As already remarked, quality metrics depend on the particular data model considered. The quality metrics are identified as input to the quality evaluator because it is highly desirable that such component is parametric with respect to the metrics.

The Quality Factory for XML Data Sources

This section gives the architectural details of a quality factory module designed for an organization that stores its data as XML documents. As shown in Figure 3, the quality factory consists of various logical components. Such components can be better specified when referred to a specific data model, and we specify them for the XML data model. Later, we also describe an appropriate way of defining a mapping from the schema available for the original XML data to the reference ontology. Finally, an example of definition of metrics for the completeness data quality dimension is provided.

Quality Storage for XML Data

In order for the quality factory to store quality values, it is necessary to decide how quality values are linked to the related data values.

Our solution considers XML data that satisfy some general requirements. First, if the document is not explicitly modified, then the order of its nodes does not change between two subsequent accesses to it. Second, the quality factory and the D²Q wrapper can access the XML documents stored in a source directly, and not through a query language like XPath or XQuery. For example, the document-tree could be made accessible through a DOM interface. Finally, without loss of generality, we assume that the data at the sources is stored as a single logical XML document.

As we suppose that the XML documents are directly accessible, we can easily assign a unique identifier to each piece of data. This can be done, for instance, by associating each node in the XML tree to a label representing its number in a pre-order depth-first visit of the ordered XML tree. Another way is to describe the position of a node in the tree by means of node addresses, as proposed in (Buneman, Davidson, Fan, Hara, & Tan, 2001). Edges in an XML tree going from an element node to another element node or a text node can be labelled with the index of this sub node among the children of its parent. Thus, starting from the root, an element or text node can be uniquely identified from the concatenation of such indexes (e.g., 1#2#1#4) in the path that leads to that node. The XML model is a partially ordered tree, in that an order is not imposed among the attribute children of an element. However, attribute names are unique, and thus a unique attribute node address can be obtained by concatenating the node address of its parent and the name of the attribute itself (e.g., 1#2#2@name).

In order to store quality values, we use the following approach. Each node in the XML tree can be assigned a set of quality values, corresponding to values of quality dimensions; the considered quality dimensions are accuracy, completeness, consistency, and currency. These values are stored in an XML tree, called quality-tree; we call data-tree the XML tree storing application data. The quality-tree conforms to the following rules:

- For each element node e of the data-tree, the quality tree contains an element node q_e named after e and with the same address as e.
- For each text node t in the data-tree, the quality tree contains an element node q_t having the same address as t, and named "text".
- An element node in the quality tree contains four quality attributes that are used to store quality values related to the data-tree element or text node it represents. These attributes are named after the quality dimensions used in the system, that is, *accuracy, completeness, consistency* and *currency*.
- For each attribute node a in the data-tree, the element node of the quality-tree which corresponds to the parent of a will contain four additional attributes whose names are obtained by concatenating the name of a, with the names of the quality dimensions.

As an example, let us suppose that the data-tree contains the node:

```
<Xelem Xatt="...">...<Xelem/>
```

Then, the quality-tree will contain a node:

```
<Xelem
    accuracy=v₁
    completeness=v₂
    consistency=v₃
    currency=v₄
    XattAccuracy=v₅
    XattCompleteness=v₆ XattConsistency=v₇
    XattCurrency=v₈>
    ...
<Xelem/>
```

Where $v_1, \ldots, v_8$ are appropriate quality values.

Given the unique address of a node, this data structure allows to retrieve its associated quality values. The choice of representing this data structure with an XML document is motivated by two reasons. First, as the structure is a tree, XML is particularly well suited to represent it. Second, as the wrapper used to transform source data from its original model into the D²Q model must already manipulate XML data (those at the source itself), representing also the quality data in XML format simplifies the wrapper, allowing for the reuse of any XML manipulation facility already present in it. Notice that the names of the element used to construct this tree are not significant, only their order is. Also notice that we are not making any assumptions here on the fact that a certain node is actually assigned a quality value. This depends on how quality metrics are defined, on the reference ontology and on the defined mapping.

Quality Evaluator for XML Data Sources

In order to evaluate the quality of an XML source, given the storage model described above, the quality evaluator module can perform a pre-order, left-to-right, depth-first visit of the data-tree, evaluate the quality at each node, and construct a corresponding node in the quality-tree, with the following steps:

- Given the root of the data-tree r, construct the root q_r of the quality-tree as an element node having the same name as r. Then, for each quality dimension measured on r, add to q_r an attribute named after the quality dimension and having a value equal to the measured value. The addresses of these attribute nodes will be @accuracy, @completeness, @consistency, @currency.
- Given an element or text node d, let $addr(d) = addr(p)\#n$ be its address, where p is the parent of the node. This means that d is the n-th child of p. Furthermore, let q_p be the node corresponding to p in the quality-tree. Construct an element node q_d corresponding to d as n-th child of q_p, that is with address $addr(q_d) = addr(q_p)\#n$. If d is an element node, then q_d will be named after d. Otherwise, the name of q_d will be text. Then, for each quality dimension measured on d, add to q_d an attribute named after that quality dimension and having value equal to the measured value. The addresses of such attribute nodes will be $addr(q_p)\#n@$accuracy, $addr(q_p)\#n@$completeness, $addr(q_p)\#n@$consistency, $addr(q_p)\#n@$currency.
- Given an attribute node a let $addr(a) = addr(p)@name$ be its address, where p is the element node containing a and name is the name of a. Let q_p be the node corresponding to p in the quality-tree. For each quality dimension measured on a, add to q_p an attribute whose name is constructed by concatenating the name of the quality dimension and the name of a, as described before. The value of these attributes will be set to the measured values. The addresses of the attributes nodes added will be:

  *addr(qp)#n@name*Accuracy,
  *addr(qp)#n@name*Completeness,
  *addr(qp)#n@name*Consistency,
  *addr(qp)#n@name*Currency;

In this way, a new tree is constructed which has the same structure of the data-tree and contains the quality values measured for it. Figure 4 shows an example of how a (portion of) a quality tree is built starting from a data-tree. Figure 4(a) shows a simple data-tree. Attribute nodes have their names prefixed by a '@' symbol. Text nodes are depicted as nodes labelled with strings in double quotes. Figure 4(b) shows a first step in the construction of the quality-tree. An element with the same name of the data-tree root is built, and quality attributes are added. We show only two of such attributes to avoid visual cluttering. The values v_1, v_2 and so on are just placeholders for real quality values. In Figure 4(c), a bigger portion of the quality-tree has been built. Particularly, the tree contains attribute nodes corresponding to the "year" attribute in the data-tree, and nodes corresponding to the title node of the data-tree. A child of node "title" named "text" will be the next node to be created. The dashed line indicates that

Figure 4. An example of construction of quality-tree nodes

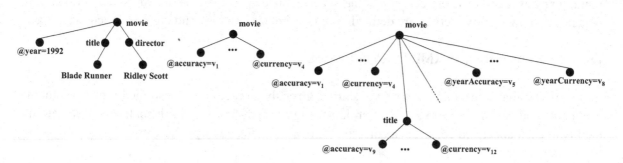

the quality node corresponding to node "director" will be created as second child of the node "movie" in the quality-tree, as it is the second child of the node "movie" in the data-tree.

This approach has the problem of maintaining the quality storage updated with regard to changes in the related XML data. We assume here that this task is performed by triggering a new quality evaluation each time the data is modified. Two issues must be considered. First, whenever a node is inserted, deleted or moved, the structural correspondence between the quality-tree and the data-tree might be partially or completely lost. Maintaining the alignment of the two trees only requires adding or deleting a node in the quality-tree to reflect the changes in the data-tree. Second, when a node is inserted, deleted or moved and when text and attributes values are updated, this change might have consequences also on the quality values of nodes that don't take part to this transformation, depending on how the quality metrics are defined and also on the given reference ontology and the mapping. We plan to address these problems in our future work.

Reference Ontology and Mapping for XML Data Sources

Before quality metrics can be introduced for the XML model, it is necessary to detail how a schema for this data model, such as a DTD, can be mapped to a reference ontology. When trying to establish a mapping between a DTD and a conceptual model, there is generally no adopted way to put in correspondence elements of an XML document with conceptual level constructs. Conceptual relationships might be represented in various ways, from simple nesting of elements to attribute-value based joins. XML elements can be used with different intended meaning, including to identify an object-type, a named relationship, or to represent a role name in a n-ary relationship.

In the following, we make some assumptions to capture the case of a reasonable representation in which: 1) elements are put in correspondence with types; 2) relationships are only established by means of nesting elements, namely *parent-child relationship*, and through value-based joins, considering both attribute values and text node values, namely *join relationships*. Let us note that the DTD formalism is expressive enough to capture some constraints over parent-child relationships, but cannot express almost any constraint over join-relationships.

The following definition of restricted DTD considers some structural limitations over the full generality of what a DTD can express. It is worthwhile to recall that DTD were originally conceived to represent (textual) document structure and not data, thus some limitations, similar to those proposed here, occur very often when considering XML as a data model.

Restricted DTD

A restricted DTD is a tuple $D = <T_v, T_c, t_r, A, def, attlist, req>$ where:

- T_v is a finite set of value-types
- T_c is a finite set of complex-types
- t_r is a separate type called the root type
- A is a finite set of attribute types
- For each $t \in Tc \cup \{t_r\}$, $def(t)$ is a regular expression called the element type definition of t. The language of the regular expressions used for element type definitions is described by the following grammar:

$$a ::= t_v \mid t_c \mid a|a \mid a,a \mid a* \mid \varepsilon$$

Where ε denotes the empty content, $t_v \in T_v$, $t_c \in T_c$ and the symbols "|", "," and "*" denote union, concatenation and Kleene closure.

- For each $t \in Tc \cup \{t_r\}$, $attlist(t) \subseteq A$ is a set of attribute types.

Notice that in this simplified model we explicitly disallow mixed content, that is, elements having both element and text children. Also, value-typed elements, that are elements containing only one text child, cannot have attributes. With these assumptions, it is quite straightforward to interpret elements containing a text child as representing "named values", as it is for attributes.

Based on this simplified version of DTD, and on the ontology language previously introduced, we can introduce the following way of establishing mappings between schemas and reference ontologies.

Mapping

Let $D = <T_v, T_c, t_r, A, def, attlist, req>$ be a restricted DTD and $\Sigma = <D,C,Prop,R>$ an ontology. We define a mapping M between D and Σ as a set of correspondences between types of D and elements of Σ such that:

- $\forall t \in Tc \cup \{t_r\}$, $M(t) = c \in C$
- $\forall t \in Tc, \forall t' \in Tv$ such that t' appears in $def(t)$, if $M(t) = c$ then $M(t, t')$ is a property $p \in Prop(c)$
- $\forall t \in Tc, \forall t' \in A$ such that $t' \in attlist(t)$, if $M(t) = c$ then $M(t, t')$ is a property $p \in Prop(c)$

Notice that, given an ontology and a restricted DTD, multiple mappings could be established between them.

DEFINING QUALITY METRICS: THE CASE OF COMPLETENESS

The quality factory evaluates the quality of the data inside the XML document following some quality metrics definitions. These metrics must only be defined once. They are specifically tailored for the XML data model, but they do not directly depend on the specific domain to which the data belongs (neither, of course, on the specific ontology which is used to describe such domain). The methodology we propose can be extended to take into account ad-hoc, domain-specific quality dimensions, and metrics. This only requires that the quality factory module allows for the addition of other metrics defined over generic reference ontology apart from those common to all the quality factories for XML documents.

Previously, we have formalized the concept of restricted DTD and XML document valid with respect to a restricted DTD. Furthermore, we have defined how to establish a mapping between a restricted DTD and a given ontology. We have shown how to define quality metrics for XML documents based on reference ontology and mapping. Specifically, we describe an example of quality metrics' definition focusing on a specific quality dimension, namely *completeness*. Completeness is generically defined as "the extent to which data are of sufficient breadth, depth, and scope for the task at hand." (Wang & Strong, 1996). We characterize completeness of XML data in a specific way by introducing a set of metrics that capture various forms of incompleteness of XML data. In the following definitions we consider a node n of type $t \in Tc$ and we consider $M(t) = c$ as the corresponding concept in the ontology Σ.

Value-Completeness

Let l be a leaf node of type $t' \in Tv$ such that $l \in subel(t)$ and $M(t, t') = p \in Prop(c)$. If p is a mandatory property, the leaf l is said to be value-complete if $value(l) \neq \varepsilon$. Notice that leaves corresponding to non mandatory properties are always considered to be value-complete.

Leaf-Completeness

Let p be a mandatory property of c. The node n is said to be leaf-complete w.r.t. p if it has at least one leaf child l such that $M(t, type(l)) = p$. Let $P = \{p_1, \ldots, p_n\} \subseteq Prop(c)$ be all the mandatory properties of c. The degree of leaf-completeness of n, written dl(n) is defined as the number of properties w.r.t. which n is leaf-complete divided by the cardinality of P.

Parent-Child Completeness

Let $r = <c,c'>$ be a directed (parent-child) relationship to which c participates with cardinality 1. . .* with the role of parent. We say that n is parent-child complete with respect to r if $\exists$ at least one child n' of n, such that $M(type(n')) = c'$. Let now $R_{pc} = \{r_1, \ldots, r_k\}$ be all the parent-child relationships to which c participates with cardinality $1...*$. Let $C_{pc} = \{cr_1, \ldots, cr_k\}$ be the concepts having role of child in the relationships of R_{pc}. The *degree of parent child completeness* of n, written $d_{pc}(n)$, is defined as the number of relationships in R_{pc} with respect to which n is parent-child complete, divided by the cardinality of R_{pc}. More formally, let us suppose that $R_{pc} = \{r_1 = <c,cr_1>, \ldots, r_s = <c,cr_s>\} \subseteq R_{pc}$ is the set of relationships such that $\forall r_i \in R_{pc} \exists n_{ri} \in subel(n)$ such that $M(type(n_{ri})) = c_i$. Then:

$$d_{pc}(n) = |R_{pc}| / |R_{pc}|$$

Join Completeness

Let n be a node of type t and $M(t) = c$ the corresponding concept in Σ. Let $r = < c: p, c': p' >$ be a join relationship to which c participates with cardinality $1. . .*$. We say that n is join-complete with respect to r if the following conditions hold:

- the node n has a leaf child l such *that $M(t, type(l)) = p$ and l is leaf-complete, that is value(l) $\neq \varepsilon$*
- there exist at least one node $n' \in N$ of type t' such that $M(t') = c'$ and n' has a leaf child l' such that $M(t', type(l')) = p'$ and l is leaf complete, that is *value(l) $\neq \varepsilon$*
- *value(l) = value(l').*

Let now $R_j = \{r_1 = <c : p_1, cr_1 : pr_1 >, . . . , r_k <c : p_k, cr_k : p_{rk} >\}$ be all the join relationships to which c participates with cardinality $1. . .*$. The *degree of join completeness* of n, written $d_j(n)$ is defined as the number of relationships in R_j with respect to which n is join complete, divided by the cardinality of R_j. More formally, let us suppose that $R_j = \{r_1, . . . , r_s\} \subseteq Rj$ is the set of relationships such that $\forall r_i \in R_j$ n is join complete w.r.t. r_i. Then:

$$d_j(n) = | R_j |/| R_j |$$

R-Completeness

Given a node n, let R_{pc} and R_j be respectively the set of parent-child and join relationships to which n participates with minimum cardinality one, and $R_{pc} \subseteq R_{pc}$, $R_j \subseteq R_j$ the above defined sets of relations with respect to which n is parent-child complete and join-complete. Then the *degree of parent-child completeness* of n, written $d_r(n)$, is defined as:

$$d_r(n) = | R_j \cup R_{pc} |/| R_{pc} R_j |$$

All the definitions provided have the purpose of showing that quality metrics can be defined on the basis of the reference ontology and the mapping with the original schema (a restricted DTD in our case) according to the quality evaluation methodology described in the third section.

The Data Quality Broker

In the second section, we described the main functionality of the data quality broker that allows query processing and quality improvement in cooperative systems. In this section we provide the detailed design and implementation of this component.

The data quality broker is implemented as a peer-to-peer distributed service: each organization hosts a copy of the data quality broker that interacts with other copies (see Figure 5, left side). Each copy of the data quality broker is internally composed by four interacting modules (see Figure 5, right side). The modules query processor and transport engine are general and can be installed without modifications in each organization. We have implemented both the query processor and the transport engine; details on their implementation will be provided in the next sections.

Figure 5. The data quality broker as a P2P system and its internal architecture

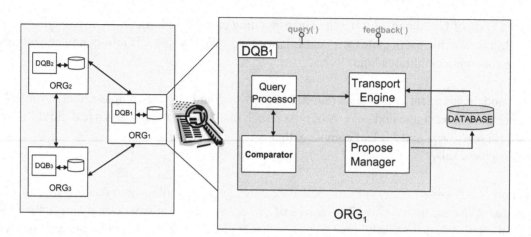

The wrapper has to be customized for the specific data management system and translates the query from the language used by the broker to that of the specific data source; it is a read-only module that accesses data and associated quality stored inside organizations without modifying them.

The Propose Manager receives feedbacks sent to organizations in order to improve their data. This module can be customized by each organization according to the policy internally chosen for quality improvement. As an example, if an organization chooses to trust quality improvement feedbacks, an automatic update of databases can be performed on the basis of the better data provided by improvement notifications.

The query processor is responsible for query execution. The copy of the query processor local to the user query receives the query and splits it into queries local to the sources, on the basis of the defined GAV mapping. Then, the local query processor also interacts with the local transport engine in order to send local queries to other copies of the query processor and receive the answers.

The transport engine provides general connectivity among all data quality broker instances in the CIS. Copies of the transport engine interact with each other in two different scenarios:

- **Query execution:** the requesting transport engine sends a query to the local transport engine of the target data source by executing the invoke() operation (see 5, right side) and asynchronously collects the answers.
- **Quality feedback:** when a requesting transport engine has selected the best quality result of a query, it contacts the local transport engines to enact quality feedback propagation. The propose() operation (see Figure 5, right side) is executed as a callback on each organization, with the best quality selected data as a parameter. The propose() can be differently implemented by each organization: a remote transport engine simply invokes this operation.

Another function performed by the transport engine is the evaluation of the availability of data sources that are going to be queried for data. This feature is encapsulated into the transport engine as it can be easily implemented exploiting transport engine's communication capabilities.

The data quality broker has been implemented by web services technologies. To implement web services, we have chosen the J2EE 1.4 Java Platform, specifically the Java API for XML-based Remote Procedure Call (JAX-RPC) (JSR-101-Expert-Group, 2003). In JAX-RPC, request/response of remote methods is performed through the exchange of SOAP messages over an HTTP connection. The implementation of the query processor and of the transport engine is better detailed in the next sections.

QUERY PROCESSOR: DESIGN AND IMPLEMENTATION ISSUES

The query processor module of the data quality broker implements the mediation function of data integration architecture (Wiederhold, 1992). It performs query processing according to a GAV approach, by unfolding queries posed over a global schema. Both the global schema and local schemas exported by cooperating organizations are expressed according to the D²Q model. The D²Q model is a semi structured model that enhances the semantics of the XML data model (Fernandez, Malhotra, Marsh, Nagy, & Walshand, 2002) in order to represent quality data. The schemas and instances of the D²Q model are almost directly translated respectively into XML Schemas and XML documents. Such XML-based representations are then easily and intuitively queried with the XQuery language (Boag et al., 2003). The unfolding of an XQuery query issued on the global schema can be performed on the basis of well-defined mappings with local sources. The exact definition of the mapping is described in (Milano, Scannapieco, & Catarci, 2004).

Query Processing Steps

Query processing is performed according to the sequence of steps described in Figure 6. The entire process may be logically divided into two phases: an *unfolding* phase, which involves a global query and

Figure 6. Sequence of steps followed in the query processing phase

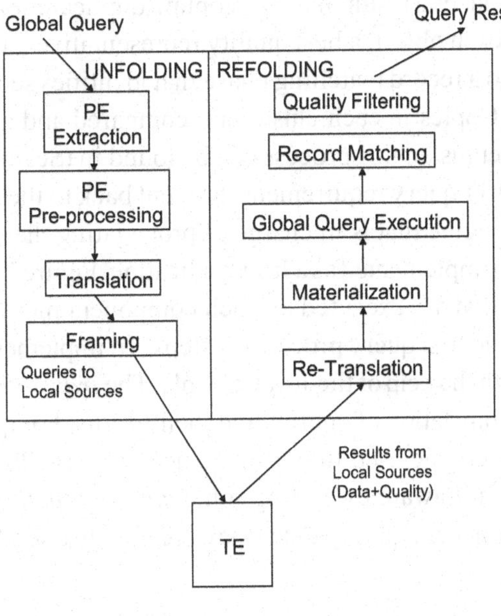

produces a set of sub-queries to be sent to local organizations, and a *refolding* phase, which collects the results of local sub-queries execution, rewrites the global query and finally executes the global query. In the following, we briefly revise the steps of these two phases.

The unfolding phase starts by receiving a global query and analyzing it in order to extract those path expressions that access data from the integrated view. Only these parts of the query are actually translated and sent to wrappers for evaluation. During the path expression extraction phase, the query processor looks for path expressions. The extraction is straightforward most of the times[1]. The result of the path expression extraction phase is a number of identified path expressions that need to be translated. Before the translation phase, they are submitted to a preprocessing step.

The preprocessing step decomposes each path expression into a set of path expressions whose concatenation produces a result equivalent to that of the original expression. The elements of this set are still expressed over the global schema alphabet, and are therefore translated into local organizations alphabets, according to the mapping specification.

After translation, sub-queries are ready to be executed at local sources. A further preliminary step is needed to make possible to re-translate their results. Usually, results of a query contain nodes and their descendants. Any information regarding their ancestors is lost. We adopt a framing mechanism in order to keep trace of ancestors and thus simplifying the retranslation phase. After retranslation, framing elements may be discarded and result fragments may be safely concatenated to form a single document.

After all the steps of the Unfolding phase have been completed, sub-queries may be passed to a transport engine module, which is in charge of redirecting them to local sources for execution and to subsequently collect results.

The Refolding phase starts with a step in which the received results are re-translated according to the global schema specification. Results coming from different organizations answering the same global path expression are then concatenated into a single temporary file. Each occurrence of a path expression previously extracted from the global query is replaced with a special path expression that accesses one of the temporary files built during the previous step. In this way, the global query is changed into a query that only uses local files, and can then be executed.

The execution of a query produces a result that may contain duplicate copies of the same objects coming from different sources. For each object, a best quality representative must be chosen or constructed. For this purpose, results undergo a record matching phase that identifies semantically equivalent objects and groups them into clusters. Copies in each cluster are compared and a best quality object is either selected or constructed; more details on this process can be found in (Scannapieco et al., 2004). Finally, the results best fitting with the user query requirements are sent back to the user. Moreover quality feedbacks are sent to the transport engine that is in charge of propagating them throughout the system.

The query processor has been implemented as a Java application. Figure 7 shows the main components; the phases of query processing that are executed by each component module are also represented.

The *query parser* performs the first query processing steps. To implement it, a parser for the XQuery language has been generated with the help of the JavaCC tools. The *translation/retranslator* module is in charge of the translation and retranslation of queries and their results. For query execution a third-party query engine may be used. The engine used in our implementation is IPSI-XQ (IPSI-XQ, n.d.). Let us note that we made IPSI-XQ quality-aware by adding some *quality functions* to it. These functions are written in XQuery, and allow to access quality data; they are simply added to the query prolog of each query submitted to the engine.

Figure 7. Internal modules of the query processor

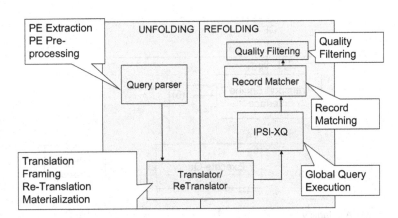

TRANSPORT ENGINE: DESIGN AND IMPLEMENTATION ISSUES

The transport engine component of the data quality broker provides the connectivity and communication infrastructure of the DaQuinCIS system. In Figure 8 the internal components of the transport engine are shown; the sequence of interactions among such modules is also depicted. The *availability tester* module works in background continuously executing connectivity tests with servers from other organizations. It executes a ping function on the servers in the cooperative system opening HTTP connections on them. The *transport engine interface* is the module that interfaces the query processor and the transport engine. Specifically, it uses a data structure to store queries and query results, once the latter have been gathered from each organization. The data structure is organized as an array: each element is representative of a single query execution plan and is composed by a list of queries that are specific of such a plan. Such queries are passed by the query processor (step 1). Then, the *transport engine interface* activates the *execute-query* module with plans as input parameters (step 2). The execute-query interacts with the *availability tester* module that performs an availability check of the sources involved in the query execution (step 3). Then, the *execute-query* activates the *Web service invoker* module that carries out the calls to the involved organizations (step 4). The call is performed in an asynchronous way by means of suitable proxy SOAP client. Before invoking data management web services, an availability check is performed by the Availability Tester module. When the result of the different plans are sent back, the *execute-qQuery* module stores them in a specific data structure and gives it to the *transport engine interface* (step 5) that, in turn, gives it back to the query processor (step 6). The data structure is very similar to the input one; the main difference is the substitution of the query field with a special record containing data and associated quality provided as query answers.

Notice that the same interaction among modules shown in Figure 8 occurs when quality feedbacks need to be propagated. The query processor selects the best quality copies among the ones provided as query answers and then sends the result back to the *transport engine Interface* that activates the *execute-query* module with the best quality copies and the organizations to be notified about them as input parameters. The best quality copies are then sent by the *Web service invoker*. On the receiver organization side, the *execute-query* module notifies the *propose manager* modules of involved organizations about the better quality data available in the system, thus implementing the quality feedback functionality that the data

Figure 8. Internal modules of the transport engine of organization i

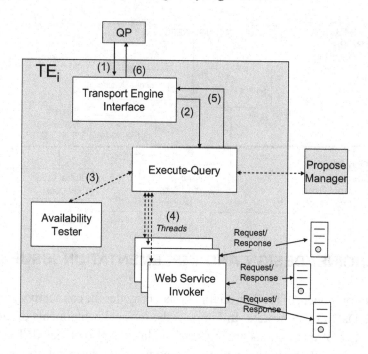

quality broker provides at query processing time. Also notice that the *execute-query* module, on the sender organization side interacts with the *availability tester* modules; this makes quality notification to not be performed in a one-step process. Instead, a transaction starts that commits only when the set of sources that has to be notified, is exhausted.

EXPERIMENTS

In this section, we first show the experimental methodology, and then we show quality improvement experiments and performance experiments.

Experimental Methodology

We perform a set of experiments in order to test the quality improvement functionality of the data quality broker and its performance features. We used two real data sets, each owned by an Italian public administration agency, namely: 1) the first data set is owned by the Italian Social Security Agency, referred to as INPS (in Italian, Istituto Nazionale Previdenza Sociale). The size of the database is approximately 1.5 million records; 2) the second data set is owned by the Chambers of Commerce, referred to as CoC (in Italian, Camere di Commercio). The size of the database is approximately 8 million records.

Some data are agency-specific information about businesses (e.g., employees social insurance taxes, tax reports, and balance sheets), whereas others are common to both agencies. Common items include one or more identifiers, headquarter and branches addresses, legal form, main economic activity, number of employees and contractors, and information about the owners or partners.

As far as quality improvement experiments, we have associated quality values to the INPS and CoC databases. Specifically, we have associated completeness and currency quality values to each field value. Completeness refers to the presence of a value for a mandatory field. As far as currency values, timestamps were already associated to data values in the two databases; such timestamps refer to the last date when data were reported as current. We have calculated the degree of overlapping of the two databases that is equal to about 970,000 records.

As far as performance experiments, a P2P environment has been simulated. Each data source has been wrapped by a web service; such web services have been deployed on different computers connected by a LAN at 100 Mbps and interacting with each other using the SOAP protocol.

Quality Improvement Experiments

The experimental setting consists of the two described real data bases plus a third source that has the purpose of querying the first two sources and cooperates with them. We have considered how this CIS behaves with regards to the quality of its data, in two specific cases. In the first case, a "standard" system is analyzed; this system does not perform any quality based check or improvement action. In the second case, the CIS uses the data quality broker functionality of query answering and quality improving. Values for the frequency of queries and updates on the data bases and average query result size are derived from real use cases. We have estimated the frequency of changes in tuples stored in the two databases to be around 5000 tuples per week. Average query frequency and query result size are, respectively, of 3000 queries per week and 5000 tuples per query. In a real setting, updates are distributed over a week. Anyway, to simplify our experimental setting, we have chosen to limit updates to the beginning of each week.

We consider how the quality of the entire CIS changes throughout a period of five weeks. Note that such variations are due to both updates on the databases and exchanges of data between them. In the standard system, these exchanges are only due to queries. With the data quality broker, each time a query is performed, an improvement feedback may be propagated. For both the data quality broker and the standard system, we calculate the overall Quality of the system, as the percentage of the high quality tuples in the system. We adopt simplified quality metrics by considering that a tuple has high quality if it is complete and current on all its fields. Conversely, a tuple has low quality if it is not complete and/or current on some fields.

To clarify how the two systems react to updates, we have considered an update set composed by both high quality and bad quality tuples equally distributed. In Figure 9, the behaviors of the data quality broker and the standard system with respect to quality improvement are shown. In the standard system (Figure 9.a), the overall quality is roughly constant, due to the same number of high quality and low quality tuples spread in the system. Instead, with the data quality broker (Figure 9.b), the improvement of quality in each period is enhanced by data quality feedbacks performed by the system and low quality data are prevented to spread. This causes a growing trend of the data quality broker curve, in spite of low quality inserted tuples. The actual improvement is about 0.12%; given that the size of the two databases is about 9.500.000 tuples, the improvement consists of about 11.500 tuples.

Performance Experiments

For the performance set of experiments, we have considered the data quality broker and the standard system behavior with fictitious sources, in order to vary some parameters influencing performance experiments.

The first performance experiment shows the time overhead of the data quality broker system with respect to the standard system. In such experiment we draw a normalized transaction time defined by the fraction:

$$\frac{DQBrokerElaborationTime - StandardElaboration\,Time}{StandardElaborationTime}$$

The elaboration time is the time required by the system for processing a query. The normalized transaction time is drawn when varying the degree of overlapping of data sources. The overlapping degree significantly influences the data quality broker. Indeed, the data quality broker accomplishes its functionalities in contexts where data sources overlap and such an overlapping can be exploited to

Figure 9. Data quality improvement in the standard system and with the data quality broker

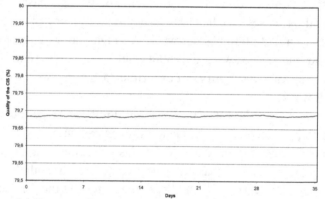

(a) Data quality improvement in the standard system

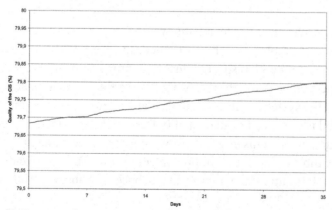

b) Data quality improvement with the data quality broker

Figure 10. Normalized transaction time wrt percentage of overlapping data sources (top) and normalized transaction time wrt query sizes (bottom)

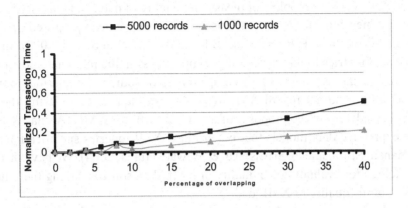

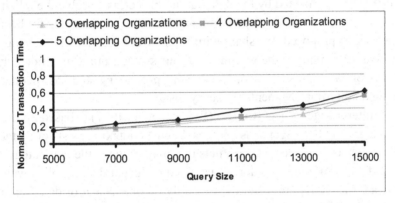

improve the quality of data. The Figure 10 (top) shows how the normalized transaction time varies in dependence on the percentage of data sources overlapping with two fixed query result sizes, namely q1=1000 tuples, q2= 5000 tuples. The number of overlapping sources is fixed to 3. This means that once a query is posed over the system, three sources have data that can be provided as answer to the query, though the system can have a larger number of sources. Figure 10 shows the actual time overhead of the data quality broker systems with respect to a standard system. The data quality broker system has an acceptable time overhead. The worst depicted case is for the query result size q2=5000 and a percentage of overlapping equal to 40%; in such a case, there is a 50% time overhead with respect to the standard system. The second performance experiment shows the normalized transaction time with query size varying (see Figure 10 bottom). For a fixed degree of overlapping equals to 15%, we draw the normalized transaction time for three different numbers of overlapping organizations, namely n1=3, n2=4 and n3=5. This experiment shows the behavior of the data quality broker when increasing the number of organizations and the size of queries. Specifically, the normalized transaction time increases slowly, with an almost linear trend. The positive result shown in Figure 10 is that when the number of overlapping data sources increases, the trend does not substantially change.

RELATED WORK

The quality factory deals with the problem of measuring quality of data. Data quality is typically characterized by a set of dimensions, for which various definitions have been proposed, including (Wang, 1998), (M. Bovee and Srivastava, R.P. and Mak, B.R., 2001) and (Liu & Chi, 2002). In (Scannapieco & Batini, 2004), a set of metrics for characterizing completeness in the relational model are described, while in (Naumann, Freytag, & Leser, 2004) completeness of sources in data integration settings is evaluated. Such definitions do not regard XML data. The problem of considering the quality of an XML document is considered by the proposal of a normal form for XML (Arenas & Libkin, 2004), and by new more expressive data models that better allow XML queries specification and execution (Jagadish, Lakshmanan, Scannapieco, Srivastava, & Wiwatwattana, 2004). We have instead described an original methodology for evaluating the quality of XML data sources, laying the foundations for a full characterization of the quality of XML data.

Quality-aware querying, performed by the data quality broker, is a problem explicitly addressed in a few works. In (Naumann, Leser, & Freytag, 1999), an algorithm for querying for best quality data in a LAV integration system is proposed. We share with such a work the idea of querying for best quality data; however, the main difference is the semantics of our system: our aim is not only querying, but also improving quality of data. To such a scope, the query processing step has specific semantics that allows for performing quality improvements on query results.

The MIT Context Interchange project (COIN) (Bressan et al., 1997) is based on the idea of modeling a "context" for integrating heterogeneous sources. Such a context consists of metadata that allows for solving problems, such as instance level conflicts that may occur in the data integration phase. The data quality broker differs mainly for considering a much more general and explicit way of representing quality of data. Instead, the COIN approach focuses only on one aspect of data quality, namely data interpretability.

In (Mihaila, Raschid, & Vidal, 2000), the basic idea is querying web data sources by selecting them on the basis of quality values on provided data. Specifically, the authors suggest publishing metadata, characterizing the quality of data at the sources. Such metadata are used for ranking sources and a language to select sources is also proposed. In the data quality broker system, we associate quality to data (at different granularity levels) rather than to a source as a whole. This makes things more difficult, but allows posing more specific queries.

As an e-government initiative, the Italian Public Administration in 1999 started a project, called "Services to Businesses", which involved extensive data reconciliation and cleaning (Bertoletti, Missier, Scannapieco, Aimetti, & Batini, 2005). The approach followed in this project consisted of three different steps: 1) linking once the databases of three major Italian public administrations, by performing a record matching process; 2) correcting matching pairs, and 3) maintaining such status of aligned records in the three databases by centralizing record updates and insertions only on one of the three databases. This required a substantial re-engineering of administrative processes, with high costs and many internal changes for each single administration. Differently from the approach adopted in the "Services to Businesses" project, the data quality broker is implemented in a completely distributed way through P2P architecture, thus avoiding bottlenecks on a single cooperating organization. Even more important, no kind of re-engineering actions need to be engaged when choosing to use the data quality broker, as query answering and quality improvement can be performed with a very low impact in terms of changes on cooperating organizations.

CONCLUDING REMARKS

We provided two major contributions. First, we described the issues related to the implementation of a quality factory in cooperative information systems, where a quality factory has the purpose of evaluating the quality provided by each cooperating organization. A general methodology for designing a quality factory is proposed and the design of a specific quality factory for XML data is described. Second, we provided the implementation details of the data quality broker module, responsible for data and quality exchanges in CIS.

The data quality broker has been implemented as a peer-to-peer system. Specifically, we have described the detailed design and implementation of two modules composing the data quality broker, namely the query processor and the transport engine. We have also described some experiments that validate our approach with respect to quality improvement effectiveness. Such experiments show that the data quality broker succeeds in controlling and improving quality of data in a CIS. Moreover, when compared to a standard system, that is, a system with no quality management features, the data quality broker exhibits limited performance degradation. Such performance degradation is not a serious problem in specific scenarios, such as e-government, in which the quality of data is the main enabling issue for service provisioning. Indeed, we remark that such scenarios are the reference ones for our system. Future works will address two main lines: 1) the quality factory will be extended with further metrics for quality measuring of XML data: besides completeness, we aim to investigate also metrics for accuracy and consistency; 2) the data quality broker will be more extensively validated, in particular by pushing the adoption of the proposed P2P system in some Italian e-government pilot initiatives.

REFERENCES

Arenas, M., & Libkin, L. (2004). A Normal Form for XML Documents. ACM Trans. Database Syst., 29.

Baader, F., Calvanese, D., McGuinness, D.L., Nardi, D., & Patel-Schneider, P.F. (2003). *The description logic handbook: Theory, implementation, and applications.* Cambridge University Press.

Bertoletti, M., Missier, P., Scannapieco, M., Aimetti, P., & Batini, C. (2005). *Improving government-to-business relationships through data reconciliation and process re-engineering.* In R. Wang (Ed.), Advances in Management Information Systems, Information Quality Monograph (AMIS-IQ) . Sharpe, M.E.

Boag, S., Chamberlin, D., Fernandez, M., Florescu, D., Robie, J., & Simeon, J. (2003, November). XQuery 1.0: An XML Query Language. W3C Working Draft. Available from http:///www.w3.org/TR/xquery.

Bouzeghoub, M., & Lenzerini, M. (2001). *Special Issue on Data Extraction, Cleaning, and Reconciliation. Information Systems*, 26(8).

Bressan, S., Goh, C., Fynn, K., Jakobisiak, M., Hussein, K., Kon, K., et al. (1997). The COntext INterchange Mediator Prototype. In *Proceedings ACM SIGMOD International Conference on Management of Data (SIGMOD 1997).*

Buneman, P., Davidson, S., Fan, W., Hara, C., & Tan, W. (2001). Keys for XML. In *Proceedings of WWW 2001.*

Conrad, R., Scheffner, D., & Freytag, J. (2000). Xml Conceptual Modeling Using UML. In *19th International Conference on Conceptual Modeling.*

Fernandez, M., Malhotra, A., Marsh, J., Nagy, M., & Walshand, N. (2002, November). *XQuery 1.0 and XPath 2.0 Data Model. W3C Working Draft.* Available from http:///www.w3.org/TR/query-datamodel.

Hull, R., & King, R. (1987). *Semantic database modeling: Survey, applications, and research issues. ACM Comput. Surv., 19*(3), 201-260. IPSI-XQ. (n.d.). Available from http://ipsi.fhg.de/oasys/projects/ipsi-xq/index e.html.

Jagadish, H., Lakshmanan, L., Scannapieco, M., Srivastava, D., & Wiwatwattana, N. (2004,). Colorful XML: One Hierarchy Isn't Enough. In *Proceedings of the 2004 ACM SIGMOD Conference (SIGMOD 2004).* JSR-101-Expert-Group. (2003, October). Java(tm) API for XML based Remote Procedure Call (jax-rpc) Specification Version 1.1. Sun Microsystems, Inc.

Lenzerini, M. (2002). Data Integration: A Theoretical Perspective. In *Proceedings of the 21st ACM Symposium On Principles Of Database Systems* (PODS 2002).

Liu, L., & Chi, L. (2002). Evolutionary Data Quality. In *7th International Conference on Information Quality.*

M. Bovee and Srivastava, R.P. and Mak, B.R. (2001). A conceptual framework and belief-function approach to assessing overall information quality. In *Proceedings of the 6th International Conference on Information Quality.*

Mecella, M., Scannapieco, M., Virgillito, A., Baldoni, R., Catarci, T., & Batini, C. (2003). The DaQuinCIS broker: Querying data and their quality in cooperative information systems. *Journal of Data Semantics, 1(1. Shorter version also appeared in CoopIS 2002.).*

Mihaila, G., Raschid, L., & Vidal, M. (2000). Using quality of data metadata for source selection and ranking. In *Proceedings of the 3rd International Workshop on the Web and Databases (WebDb'00).*

Milano, D., Scannapieco, M., & Catarci, T. (2004). Quality-driven query processing of xquery queries. In *Proceedings of the International Workshop on Data and Information Quality (DIQ 2004).*

Milano, D., Scannapieco, M., & Catarci, T. (2005). Using ontologies for xml data cleaning. In *Second INTEROP dissemination workshop.*

Mylopoulos, J., & Papazoglou, M. (1997). Cooperative information systems (Special Issue). *IEEE Expert Intelligent Systems & Their Applications, 12*(5).

Naumann, F., Freytag, J., & Leser, U. (2004). Completeness of integrated information sources. *Information Systems, 29*(7).

Naumann, F., Leser, U., & Freytag, J. (1999). Quality-driven integration of heterogenous information systems. In *Proceedings of 25th International Conference on Very Large Data Bases (VLDB'99).*

Scannapieco, M., & Batini, C. (2004). Completeness in the relational model: A comprehensive framework. In *9th International Conference on Information Quality*.

Scannapieco, M., Virgillito, A., Marchetti, M., Mecella, M., & Baldoni, R. (2004). The DaQuinCIS architecture: A platform for exchanging and improving data quality in cooperative information systems. *Information Systems, 29*(7).

Ullman, J. (1997). Information integration using logical views. In *Proceedings of the 6th International Conference on Database Theory (ICDT '97)*.

Wang, R. (1998). A product perspective on total data quality management. *Communications of the ACM, 41*(2).

Wang, R., & Strong, D. (1996). Beyond accuracy: What data quality means to data consumers. *Journal of Management Information Systems, 12*(4).

Wiederhold, G. (1992). Mediators in the architecture of future information systems. *IEEE Computer, 25*(3).

ENDNOTE

[1]   In some cases, a nested expression may contain direct or indirect references to data in the global view. Such cases must be handled in a slightly different way. Our current approach is to split any path expression containing a problematic step and to treat the two parts separately. Specifically, when reverse steps are involved, they must be taken into account to perform the splitting properly.

This work was previously published in International Journal of Enterprise Information Systems, Vol. 3, Issue 1, edited by A. Gunasekaran, pp. 61-84, copyright 2007 by IGI Publishing, formerly known as Idea Group Publishing (an imprint of IGI Global).

Chapter XV
Modeling Buyer–Supplier Relationships in Dynamic Supply Chains

Vipul Jain
Indian Institute of Technology Delhi, India

S. Wadhwa
Indian Institute of Technology Delhi, India

S. G. Deshmukh
Indian Institute of Technology Delhi, India

ABSTRACT

The key part of dynamic supply chain management is negotiating with suppliers and with buyers. Designing efficient business processes throughout the supply chain, and controlling their speed, timing, and interaction with one another, is decisive factors in a competitive and dynamic environment. Coordination is essential for successful supply chain management. Therefore, in this chapter, a novel Negotiation-to-Coordinate (N2C) mechanism is proposed to explore the interactive nature of the buyer-supplier relationships for dynamic environments. The proposed N2C mechanism uses prioritized fuzzy constraints to represent trade-offs among the different probable values associated with the negotiation issues and to signify how agents should make concessions. Supervisor agent in the N2C mechanism takes into account the conflicts of interest of buyer's agent and supplier's agent and the proposal and plan generated by supervisor agents helps in resolving the true and potential conflicts of interests for buyer's agent and supplier's agent. The proposed computational framework based on fuzzy constraints is suited for capturing the dynamics by modeling trade-offs between different attributes of a product leading to a fair and equitable deal for both suppliers and buyers. The proposed approach models the intricacies in the face of the imprecise, uncertain and conflicting nature of objectives. The efficacy of the proposed approach is demonstrated through an illustrative example.

INTRODUCTION

Traditionally, marketing, distribution, planning, manufacturing, and the purchasing of organizations along the supply chain operate independently. These organizations have their own objectives and they are often conflicting. Marketing's objectives of high customer service and maximum sales dollars conflict with the manufacturing and distribution goals. Many manufacturing operations are designed to maximize throughput and lower costs with little consideration for the impact on inventory levels and distribution capabilities. Purchasing contracts are often negotiated with very little information beyond historical buying patterns. The result of these factors is that there is not a single, integrated plan for the organization. *Clearly, there is a need for a mechanism through which these different functions can be integrated together.* Supply chain management is a strategy through which such an integration can be achieved. Supply chain management is typically viewed to lie between fully vertically integrated firms, where the entire material flow is owned by a single firm, and where each channel member operates independently. Therefore, coordination between the various players to the chain is key in its effective management (Jain *et al.* 2007).

Supply chains are complex operations and their analysis requires a carefully defined approach. Most of previous studies have neglected significant impacts of integration issues because of the modeling complexity required. Therefore, past models may be confined in their capability and applicability to analyze real supply chain process. An integrated quantitative model, addressing the above-mentioned issues becomes an imperative (Jain 2006). Moreover, with the increase in technological complexity, supply chains have become more dynamic and complex to solve. Consequently, it is easy to get lost in details and spend a large amount of effort for analyzing the supply chain. *There is growing interest from industry and academic disciplines regarding coordination in supply chains, particularly addressing the potential coordination mechanisms available to eliminate sub-optimization within supply chains* (Fung and Chen 2005, Jain 2006). Coordination, the process by which an agent reasons about its local actions and the actions of others to try to ensure the community acts in a coherent manner (Toledo and Jennings 2002), is an important issue in multi-agent systems. There are three main reasons why it is necessary for agents to coordinate. First, there are dependencies between agents' tasks or goals; second, there is a need to meet global constraints such as cost and time limits; and third, no individual agent has sufficient competence, resources, or information to solve the entire problem (Toledo and Jennings 2002).

Member enterprises in the chain need to cooperate with their business partners in order to meet customers' needs and to maximize their profit. *Managing multi-party collaboration in a supply chain, however, is a very difficult task because there are so many parties involved in the supply chain operation, each with its own resources and objectives.* There is no single authority over all the chain members. Cooperation is through negotiation rather than central management and control. The interdependence of multistage processes also requires real-time cooperation in operation and decision-making across different tasks, functional areas, and organizational boundaries in order to deal with problems and uncertainties. *The strategic shift of focus for mass customization, quick response, and high quality service cannot be achieved without more sophisticated cooperation and dynamic formation of supply chains (Chan et al. 2004).* One solution to this problem is to have intelligent interacting entities, which can provide domain-specific information to validate the decision-making system. Therefore, Multi-agent system (MAS) based approaches for supply chain modeling are proposed (Swaminathan *et al.* 1998, Ertogral and Wu 2000, Julka *et al.* 2002, Jain *et al.* 2007 etc).

Agents based modeling can be assumed to be a reasonable methodology for the examination of supply chains because in a supply chain a number of individual companies interact with each other using specific internal decision structures (Choi *et al.* 2001). Each of the players in the supply chain is modeled as an agent who negotiates with its immediate neighbour in pushing/pulling the part or product through the chain. The agents operate in multiagent systems and situations often arise in which their plans conflict with the plans of other agents. *For achieving effective multi agent coordination, conflict resolution is crucial. Negotiation is a predominant tool for resolving conflict of interests (Jain et al. 2007). However, with recent technological advances, the mechanisms available to carry out such activities have become increasingly sophisticated, and the environment in which these activities take place has become highly dynamic. A higher-level coordination mechanism with respect to distributed modeling of supply chains is generally not specified in the reported literature (Chan and Chan 2004).*

In this chapter, we explore the interactive nature of the buyer-supplier relationship in the dynamic supply chain environment. First, a prioritized fuzzy constraint based model is developed for bilateral multi issue negotiation in dynamic supply chain environments. A novel Negotiation to Coordinate (N2C) approach is proposed, which utilizes prioritized fuzzy constraints to represent trade-offs between the different possible values of the negotiation issues with a corresponding coordination mechanisms dedicated to dynamic supply chain networks.

The proposed Negotiation to Coordinate (N2C) approach has the following benefits:

- It enables the negotiation to be carried out over fuzzy constraints of multiple issues of a product. That is more efficient than negotiation that is carried out over single point solutions. The proposed model uses prioritized fuzzy constraints to represent trade-offs among the different probable values of the negotiation issues and to signify how agents should make concessions.
- The supervisor agent in the proposed mechanism takes into account the conflicts of interest of buyer's agent and supplier's agent and the proposal/plan generated by supervisor agents helps in resolving the true and potential conflicts of interests for buyer's agent and supplier's agent. The supervisor agent maintains dynamic updates of resource requirements.
- It is generic and can be used for a wide range of domains such as negotiation of supply contracts for flexible production networks. The model ensures a high degree of flexibility; it avoids deadlocks and enhances chances of willingness to a compromise. It guarantees that the outcome of the negotiation is Pareto optimal for both parties (if such a solution exists), yet the participating agents reveal minimal information about their preferences and constraints.

The chapter is organized as follows: Section 2 discusses supply chain and fuzzy system modeling. Section 3 addresses the prioritized fuzzy constraint satisfaction problem for supply chain networks. Section 4 discusses supplier buyer relationships in detail. Section 5 provides the details of the proposed N2C mechanism along with a numerical example. Finally, Section 6 presents the concluding remarks and the scope for future work.

SUPPLY CHAIN SYSTEMS AND FUZZY SYSTEMS MODELING

Petrovic *et al.* (1999) highlighted the uncertainties in supply chain system as follows: "A real supply chain operates in an uncertain environment. Different sources and types of uncertainty exist along the supply chain. They are random events uncertainty in judgment, lack of evidence, lack of certainty in judgment, lack of evidence, lack of certainty of evidence that appear in customer demand, production and supply. Each facility in the supply chain must deal with uncertainty demand imposed by succeeding facilities and uncertain delivery of the preceding facilities in the supply chain". Generally, supply chain networks include several subsystems with unlimited interfaces and relations. Every subsystem usually contains uncertainties. Obviously, uncertainties associated with each subsystem or components make the whole system vague. Also, the nature of interfaces in dynamic supply chains causes supply chains to function in completely imprecise and uncertain environment. These interfaces are rooted in the information flows, material flows and supplier-buyer relations Goyal and Gopalakrishnan (1996). Moreover, relations among entities of dynamic supply chains critically depend on human activities. This fact forms the main reason why emergent dynamic supply chains necessitates fuzzy system modeling.

Zadeh (1973) also states: "As the complexity of a system increases, our ability to make precise and yet significant statements about its behavior diminishes until a threshold is reached beyond which precision and significance (or relevance) become almost mutually exclusive characteristics. It is in this sense that precise quantitative analyses of the behavior of humanistic systems are not likely to have much relevance to the real-world societal, political, economic, and other types of problems which involve humans either as individuals or in groups". Turksen and Zarandi (1999) discussed many advantages of fuzzy system approach in real world applications and that motivate the authors to apply fuzzy modeling in dynamic supply chains.

1.   Fuzzy system models are flexible, and with any given system like dynamic supply chains, it is easy to handle it with fuzzy system models.

2.   Nearly all nonlinear functions of arbitrary complexity can be captured by fuzzy system models. Also fuzzy models are conceptually simple to understand.

3.   Superior communication between experts and managers is provided by Fuzzy system models. Moreover, these are based on natural languages and are tolerant of imprecise and vague data.

4.   Fuzzy system models can be constructed on the top of the experience of experts and can be mingled with conventional control techniques.

Dynamic supply chain network problems are characterized by their complexity and inherent decentralization. The application of fuzzy logic and multiagent systems techniques to this problem seems appropriate. Therefore, in this chapter, we have tap the properties of fuzzy logic and propose a N2C mechanism to capture dynamic negotiation between the sellers and the buyers.

PRIORITIZED FUZZY CONSTRAINT (PF_zC_{SP}) MODEL FOR DYNAMIC ENVIRONMENT

Several real world problems (e.g. Planning (Raghunathan, 1992), automated negotiation (Faratin *et al.*, 2002), etc) can be modeled as constraint satisfaction problems (CSP's). In the conventional framework for CSP's, constraints can never be violated i.e. solving a CSP involves finding an assignment of values to variables such that all its constraint hold. This is however, sometimes inflexible. For dealing with problems in which the satisfaction level of a constraint is not a simple zero-one matter, the formulation of CSP is too rigid. Thus, several efforts are made for combining conventional CSP with soft constraints, which can partially be violated. The extended framework includes fuzzy CSP's (Dubois and Prade 1999), probabilistic CSP's (Luo *et al.,* 2003) and more general valued CSP's (Dago and Verfaillie, 1996). We choose the PF_zC_{SP} as the basis of our proposed N2C in for the following reasons:

- Consider the trade-off involved in an agent deciding whether it prefers to acquire exactly the preferred value of an attribute that is very important or several sets of less good values for attributes that are less important to it. Such a trade-off can be modeled by fuzzy constraints. One of the primary things in negotiation is to represent trade-offs between the different possible values for parameters. A buyer's preferences on trade-offs between different attributes of the desired product can easily be modeled by fuzzy constraints.
- For a single characteristic of the preferred product, a buyer might prefer certain values over others. Such a preference can be expressed as a fuzzy constraint over a single attribute, and the preference level at a certain value of the attribute is the constraint's satisfaction degree for that value. Likewise, for multiple product attributes, a buyer might favor certain combinations of values over others. Such preferences can be expressed as fuzzy constraint over multiple attributes, and the preference level at a certain combination value of these attributes is the constraint's satisfaction degree for the combination value.
- In several cases, buyers do not know the precise details of the products they want to buy, and so their requirements are often expressed by constraints over multiple issues.
- A buyer's constraints are not for all time equally important. In order to deal with different levels of importance of different fuzzy constraints, researchers have introduced the concept of priority into fuzzy CSP's to form PF_zC_{SP}.
- When buyer's and sellers negotiate, it is hardly ever the case that an offer is totally acceptable or totally inconsistent with their respective constraints. Relatively, an offer usually satisfies the buyer's constraints more or less. The PF_zC_{SP} is suited for capturing constraints of this kind because fuzzy constraints can be partially satisfied or violated.

We define fuzzy constraint satisfaction problem as follows:

Definition 1: a fuzzy constraint satisfaction problem (F_zC_{SP}) is defined as a 3-tuple $(V_{AR}, D_{MN}, \Re^f)$.

1) $V_{AR} = \{V_{ARp} / p = 1,...m\}$ is a finite set of variables.
2) $D_{MN} = \{D_{MN}p / p = 1,...n\}$ is the set of domains. Each domain $D_{MN\,p}$ is a finite set containing the possible values for the corresponding variable V_{ARp} in V_{AR}
3) $\Re^f$ is a set of fuzzy constraints. That is

$$\Re^f = \{F_P{}^C / \mu_{F_P{}^C} : (\prod_{V_{ARe} \in V_{AR}(F_P{}^C)} D_{MNe}) \to [0,1], p = 1,...m\} \qquad (1)$$

where $V_{AR}(F_P{}^C)$ denotes the set of variables of fuzzy constraint $F_P{}^C$. The membership degree of a fuzzy constraint just indicates the local degree to which the constraint is locally satisfied with a compound label, and so the degree is also called the local satisfaction degree of the constraint for a compound label.

Definition 2: A prioritized fuzzy constraint satisfaction problem (PF_zC_{SP}) is a 4-tuple $(V_{AR}, D_{MN}, \Re^f, P^R)$, where $(V_{AR}, D_{MN}, \Re^f)$ is an F_zC_{SP}, and P^R: $\Re^f \to [0, \infty)$ is a priority function.

Definition 3: In a PF_ZC_{SP} $(V_{AR}, D_{MN}, \mathfrak{R}^f, P^R)$, given a compound label $V_{AR}*$ of all variables in V_{AR},

$$\alpha_p{}^R(VAR^*) = \oplus_{P^R}\{h(P^R(F^C), \mu_{F^C}(VAR(F^C))) \ /F^C \in \mathfrak{R}^f\} \tag{2}$$

where $\oplus_{P^R}: [0,1]^m \rightarrow [0,1]$ and $h:[0, +\infty] \times [0, 1] \rightarrow [0, 1]$, is said to be the global satisfaction degree, if the following properties are satisfied:

Property 1: If for the fuzzy constraint $F_{max}{}^C$, $P_{max}{}^R = P^R(F_{max}{}^C) = \max\{P^R(F^C) \ /F^C \in \mathfrak{R}^f\}$ then

$$\mu F_{max}{}^C(VAR(F_{max}{}^C)) = 0 \Rightarrow \alpha P^R(VAR^*) = 0 \tag{3}$$

Equation 3 means that in a PF_ZC_{SP}, although fuzzy constraints can be partially violated by a variable assignment, it is absolutely impossible for a variable assignment to be accepted as a solution, if one of the most important fuzzy constraints is completely violated by the variable assignment. This mirrors the situation that can occur reasonably often in the real-world supply chain networks.

Property 2: If $\exists P^R{}_o \in [0,1]$, $\forall F^C \in \mathfrak{R}^f$, $P^R(F^C) = P^R{}_o$, then

$$\alpha P^R(VAR^*) = \Delta\{\mu F^C(VAR(F^C)) \ /F^C \in \mathfrak{R}^f\} \tag{4}$$

Equation 4 reveals that since priorities are relative, their effect should disappear when they are the same.

Property 3: For $F_p{}^C$, $F_e{}^C \in \mathfrak{R}^f$, suppose $P^R(F_e{}^C) \geq P^R(F_e{}^C)$, and there are two different compound labels $V_{AR}*$ and $V_{AR}**$ such that $\forall F^C \in \mathfrak{R}^f$

a) When $F^C \neq F_p{}^C$ and $F^C \neq F_p{}^C$, $\mu F^C(VAR(F^C)) = \mu F^C(VAR(F^C))$

b) When $F^C \neq F_p{}^C$, $\mu F^C VAR(F^C) = \mu F^C(VAR^{**}(F^C)) + \beta_0$ (5)

c) When $F^C = F_p{}^C$, $\mu F^C(VAR^{**}(F^C)) = \mu F^C VAR(F^C) = \mu F^C(VAR(F^C)) + \beta_0$

If $h(P^R(F_p{}^C), \mu F_p{}^C(VAR(F_p{}^C)) \leq h(P^R(F_e{}^C), \mu F_e{}^C(VAR(F_e{}^C)))$ then

$$\alpha P^R(VAR^*) \geq \alpha P^R(VAR^{**})$$

The above equations capture the essential meaning of priorities. If one wants to raise the global satisfaction degree of all prioritized constraints, a constraint with a relatively high priority must be sufficiently satisfied prior to a constraint with a relatively low priority. The above equation 5 measures the relative importance among things in a group to determine only their relative precedence and signifies that the higher the priority of one thing, the earlier the thing should be handled or the more preferred is the thing. Consequently, the higher the priority of a constraint, the more preference satisfying the constraint should be given when finding a solution. That is precisely the reason why this kind of framework is called Prioritized.

Property 4: For two different compound labels $V_{AR}*$ and $V_{AR}**$, if $\forall F^C \in \Re^f$
$$\mu_{Fc}(V_{AR(F^C)}) \geq \mu_{Fc}(V_{AR}*_{(F^C)}) \text{ then}$$

$$\alpha_P^R(V_{AR}*) \geq \alpha_P^R(V_{AR}**) \tag{6}$$

Equation 6 captures the monotonicity of the aggregation operation: the global satisfaction degree of all prioritized fuzzy constraints in a PF_ZC_{SP} should increase when the local satisfaction degree of all the corresponding non-prioritized constraints increases.

Property 5: If there exists a compound labels $V_{AR}*$ such that $\forall F^C \in \Re^f$, $\mu_{Fc}(V_{AR(F^C)}) = 1$ then

$$\alpha_p^R(V_{AR}*) = 1 \tag{7}$$

The above equation means that when each corresponding non-prioritized constraint is locally satisfied completely with a compound label, there is no reason why the global satisfaction degree of all constraints in a PF_ZC_{SP} should not be 1. In addition, the generic PF_ZC_{SP} global satisfaction degree formula equation 1 implies that the result of an aggregation should not be affected by the aggregation ordering.

Definition 4: We exploit fuzzy truth prepositional logic in calculating the buyer's acceptability for a product. Fuzzy truth propositions are employed to represent the facts in the buyers profile model because these facts are often partial true (i.e. they have truth-values between "completely true" and "completely false". A fuzzy truth preposition system is a 5 tuple $(\rho, \ell, \wedge, \vee, \neg)$ where

1) $\rho = \{\rho_k \ / \ k=1, ...m\}$ is the set of primitive propositions.
2) $\ell : \rho \rightarrow [0,1]$ is a truth function, which associates each proposition ρ with a truth $\ell(\rho) \in [0,1]$ and
3) $\wedge, \vee$ and $\neg$ are logical operators.

A composite preposition CP of primitive propositions $\rho_1, \rho_2, ... \rho_n$ called a Boolean expression of $\rho_1, ... \rho_k$ is constructed from $\rho_1, ... \rho_n$ through the logical operators $\wedge, \vee$ and $\neg$. The truth $\rho(CP)$, of composite proposition CP is calculated recursively by:

$$\ell(\neg CPo) = 1 - \ell(CPo)$$

$$\ell(CP_1 \wedge CP_2) = min\{\ell(CP_1), \ell(CP_2)\}$$

$$\ell(CP_1 \vee CP_2) = min\{\ell(CP_1), \ell(CP_2)\}$$

where CP_0, CP_1 and CP_2 are primitive propositions or composite propositions. The truth $\ell(CP)$ of composite proposition CP is also denoted as $CP'\{\ell(\rho_1)... \ell(\rho_n)\}$.

In the next section, we present the buyer supplier relationships in detail.

THE BUYER SUPPLIER RELATIONSHIPS

One the most prevalent issues, among several which followed the introduction of E-Commerce systems, is the ability to establish a dynamic and flexible structures for buyer-supplier relationships which deterministically drive both parties toward strategic partnerships and coordination (Robert and Mckay, 1998). Before moving to a marketplace, most buyers and suppliers will have existing relationships that must be reflected in the marketplace. Suppliers can configure the system to reflect pre-negotiated discounts for certain buyers, which will automatically be applied when those buyers access the market place. This many-to-many marketplace combines the advantages of both sell-side and buy-side models, but since it is hosted, avoids setup and maintenance costs for the participants. Significantly, this can allow access to smaller organizations that would not otherwise have had the resources for B2B trade online. Both buyers and suppliers gain the advantage of a much broader trading community (Christopher *et al.*, 1991).

The study of buyer-supplier relationships is commissioned in some well-established frameworks such as transaction cost theory, political economy theory, social exchange theory and resource dependence theory (Robicheaux and Colman, 1994). The development of electronic interconnection has greatly reduced the time and cost of information exchange, effectively and tightly linking the process from supplier to buyer, helping them search, filter, and match parties relative to each transaction. These are the electronic interconnection effects identified by (Malone *et al.*, 1987): the electronic communication effect, the electronic brokerage effect, and the electronic integration effect. Another point of view, which is proposed by (Bakos, 1991) and is based on the idea of the relationship between suppliers and customers in a vertical market, is a distinguished vertical market inter-organizational system with information links and an electronic marketplace. Buyers and suppliers may mutually benefit from each other when more market opportunities are available for buyers to make purchasing choices, and suppliers can additionally charge for the market information they provide. The effects brought to market by the electronic market system, will prompt an evolution in the market from a biased environment to an unbiased, personalized market. Business practice exhorts customer and supplier firms to seek close, collaborative relationships with each other. This change in focus from value exchanges to value-creation relationships have led companies to develop a more integrative approach in marketing, one in which other firms are not always competitors and rivals but, are considered partners in providing value to the consumer. This has resulted in the growth of many partnering relationships such as business alliances and cooperative marketing ventures. Close, cooperative and interdependent relationships are seen to be of greater value than purely transactions based relationship (Kalwani and Narayandas, 1995).

Analysis of Relationship and Relationship Drivers

The growth of relationship orientation of marketing in post-industrial era is the rebirth of direct marketing between producers and consumers. Several environmental and organizational development factors are responsible for direct relationships between producers and consumers. At least five macro-environmental forces can be identified:

* Rapid technological advancements, especially in information technology;
* The adoption of total quality programs by companies;
* The growth of the service economy;

- Organizational development processes leading to empowerment of individuals and teams; and
- Increase in competitive intensity leading to concern for customer retention.

These forces are reducing the reliance of producers, as well as consumers, on middlemen for affecting the consummation and facilitation processes. An increasingly complex world has forced businesses to develop new ways of interacting with their customers or suppliers. Three interconnected forces are pushing firms to rethink the basic buying process.

- First, the need to maintain core capabilities while still building product becomes more difficult as the complexity within products increases, the push for lower and lower costs.
- Second, the drive for lower and lower costs is pushing firms to new relationship models and
- Third, rapidly changing technology challenges firms to focus on what core capabilities they will keep in house and what capabilities they will acquire through partnerships or relationships.

The buyer-supplier relationships are often characterized by reference to two major types: adversarial and collaborative (Wilson, 1995). The adversarial model, also referred to as the antagonistic model, has characteristics of tough negotiation, focus on price, short-term contracts and multiple sourcing (Matthyssens, 1994). Under the collaborative model, the buyers consideration of a preferred supplier is not simply only based on price or cost, but also on the factors that contribute more to the suppliers' competence in production, distribution and post purchase service. But the current trend of relationships is evolving towards a more collaborative form based on cooperation, mutual benefit and trust and relational exchange. It is also beneficial for suppliers to be able to get access to the business skill and expertise of their buyer partners. Both the buyer and seller extend the relationship to a new level of interdependence and cooperation in achieving mutual goals. It is important to understand what happens to the marketing and sales function as these relationships evolve in deeper relationships.

The buyer and the seller may have four alternative interaction strategies: collaboration, competition, dominance and compliance. However, real-life business relationships are usually combinations of these extreme strategies. Under each strategy the number of alternative partners, the use of power as well as the rules and expectations of the relationship differ (Alajoutsijarvi *et al.* 1999). Other factors, which influence the way buyers, choose their suppliers include the responsiveness of a supplier, the staying power and growing potential of a supplier, a long track record, and whether they will lose the ability to acquire or to fully use complementary products in the future. Trust is widely recognized as an essential dimension of relationship quality (Garbarino and Johnson, 1999). Trust is also defined as the most frequently used dimension in buyer supplier relationship built on the performance parameters (Wilson and Moller, 1991). This is because the presence of trust can reduce the specification and monitoring of contracts, provide material incentives for co-operation, and reduce uncertainty. The buyers are always seeking suppliers who can provide the highest level of customer service. The level of customer service often positively correlates with market response, such as market share, customer preference and satisfaction, total sale or profit.

For the buyers, the search for products or services with the lowest buying cost and highest level of quality in customer service is the most essential. The supplier's cost occur over the entire production process, from raw material to finished product and at every stage of procurement, production, manufacturing, distribution, and post-transaction. For the buyer, the costs include searching, identifying, and selecting or rejecting a supplier as well as he price paid for the execution of the transaction. The direct buyer-supplier link, which has advantages of cost reduction, faster delivery, quick response and better service, is the consequence of this new era. For those who may be buyers or suppliers participating in the execution of transactions, their own objectives will possibly differ with, or even conflict with the objectives of their transactional partners. The transaction is executed through the exchange of information and the delivery of products or services. Better understanding of the status and nature of the relationship between transactional partners is a means to improve the performance of supply chain management. Negotiation and compromise occur frequently, which characterizes the process of transaction although it is viewed rather as an art than a technique.

In this chapter, we propose a novel N2C mechanism with supervisor agent with negotiations to be carried out over fuzzy constraints of multiple issues of a product. The computational framework of fuzzy constraints is suited for capturing the dynamics by modeling trade-offs between different issues of a product leading to a fair and equitable deal for both suppliers and buyers. Sellers use B2B e-commerce to lower costs and access new customers. Buyers can use B2B marketplaces to reduce direct and indirect supply chain costs by leveraging their global scale, focusing their spending on preferred suppliers, and taking advantage of dynamic models such as auctions and bid-quote for efficient sourcing and spot buying. Beyond leveraging spend, new tools for logistics, payment and tax create new opportunities to build transparency in the supply chain, decreases logistics costs, increase inventory turns, and improve the overall performance of the manufacturing and procurement processes. The proposed N2C offer buyers and sellers uniquely powerful forums to reduce transaction costs, enhance sales and distribution processes, deliver and consume value-added services, and streamline customer management.

NEGOTIATION TO COORDINATE (N2C) MECHANISM

This section describes in detail the trade-offs between seller's agent, buyer's agent and supervisor agent for reaching a fair deal for both buyer and seller. The proposed N2C mechanism is show in Figure 1.

Seller Agent

A seller agent is a 6-tuple-knowledge system $(\nabla, \psi, \theta, \beta, \lambda, \eta)$ where:

1) $\nabla =$, called the product module, is the domain knowledge of the agent. It consists of the following attributes:
    $\nabla = \varphi\tau/\varphi\tau = (\partial_\tau, \delta_\tau, \hbar_\tau, \varepsilon_\tau), \varepsilon_\tau = (\alpha_{\tau 1}, ...\alpha_{\tau j}), 0 \leq \tau \leq \varpi$. Each attribute is defined as follows:
    ∂_τ: It is the constriction attached with the product ϕ_τ, which a buyer agent must satisfy in order to obtain the product. The restriction is expressed as a Boolean expression, which is given in definition 4.
    δ_τ: It is the award associated with product ϕ_τ, which the seller agent may use to persuade a buyer agent to purchase the product. The award is also expressed as Boolean expression given in definition 4.
    $\hbar_\tau$: It is the profit that the seller agent gets if product ϕ_τ is sold at a particular price.
    ε_τ: is called the product- characteristics, is the value vector of negotiable attributes (e.g. price, quality, model, volume, delivery date, expiry date, after-sale service and warranty) of product ϕ_τ.

Figure 1. The proposed N2C mechanism for electronic marketplace

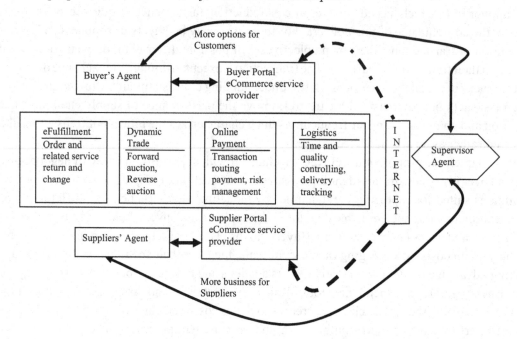

Finally, ϖ is the total number of products the seller agent possesses to sell.

2) $\psi = \{\vartheta_1, \vartheta_2, \vartheta_3, \vartheta_4, \vartheta_5, \vartheta_6, \vartheta_7\}$ is the set of primitive actions that seller agent can take during negotiations. These actions are described in Table 1.

3) θ is the behavior protocol that specifies the rules that the seller agent must obey during the course of the negotiation

4) $\beta = (\xi_s, \xi_\beta)$ is the communication port of the seller agent, where ξ_s, ξ_β are seller's offer and buyers offer respectively.

5) λ = (CS, SN, LS and PS) is the working memory of the seller agent where CS stores the constraints that a buyer agent has so far submitted to the seller agent. The SN stores the current solution that the seller agent finds according to the CS in the current round if negotiation. The LS stores the solution that the seller agent found in the last round of negotiation. The PS stores all the solutions that the seller agent found, before the current round, according to the same CS that the buyer had submitted.

6) η represents the dynamic update from the supervisor agent. This enables the buyer's agent and supplier's agent decision to be made on the basis of up-to-date information.

Buyer Agent

Similarly a Buyer agent is a 6-tuple-knowledge system denoted as $(\Pi, \psi, \theta, \beta, \lambda, \eta)$ where

1) $\Pi = (Ц, \gamma, \mu)$ is the domain knowledge of the buyer agent.
   $Ц = (\chi, \zeta, \pi, v, u)$ is the buyer's requirement model.
   (χ, ζ, π, v) is a $P_F C_{SP}$, where
   χ is the set of attributes of the product. Every domain $\zeta_i \in \zeta$ is a set of fuzzy constraints that

Table 1. Primitive actions taken by seller's agent during N2C negotiation

Symbols for actions	Primitive actions taken by seller's agent during N2C negotiation
ϑ_1	Puts forward a solution, from its product set, to satisfy the constraint set that a buyer has submitted. In order to guarantee the maximum profit for the seller agent, a solution with the highest profit is chosen; in case more than one solution satisfies the constraint set.
ϑ_2	Modifies (adds or deletes) constraints in a constraint set. The effect of deleting a constraint is to remove it from the set and then add its negation into the set.
ϑ_3	Proposes the constriction attached to a product.
ϑ_4	Proposes the award associated with a product.
ϑ_5	Receives an offer to a buyer agent.
ϑ_6	Sends an offer to a buyer agent.
ϑ_7	Presents information to the supervisor agent.

express the buyer's requirements on the attributes of the desired product. Each constraint $C_i^f \in \pi$ is associated with a priority $v(C_i^f) \in [0,+\infty]$ as well as a relaxing threshold $u(C_i^f) \in [0,1]$. However, a fuzzy constraint can be relaxed if the cut level, by which the fuzzy constraint induces a crisp constraint, is not less than the relaxing threshold.

$\gamma : \gamma = (\rho, \ell)$ is a fuzzy truth proposition system, representing the buyer's profile model. This is the background information it uses to evaluate the seller's offer.

$\rho = \{\rho_k \mid k = 1, \ldots j\}$ is a set of fuzzy propositions and $\ell : \rho \to [0,1]$ is a truth function.

$\mu \in [0,1]$ is the acceptability threshold which the seller's offer must surpass to be acceptable for the buyer agent.

2) $\psi = \{\Gamma_1, \Gamma_2, \Gamma_3, \Gamma_4, \Gamma_5, \Gamma_6, \Gamma_7, \Gamma_8\}$ is the set of primitive actions the buyer agent can take during negotiations. These actions are described in Table 2.

3) θ is the behavior protocol that specifies the rules that the seller agent must obey during the course of the negotiation.

4) $\beta = (x_s, x_b)$ is the communication port of the seller agent, where ξ_s, ξ_β are seller's offer and buyer's offer respectively.

5) $\lambda = (SC, CL)$ is the working memory of the buyer agent. The SC stores the constraints that the buyer agent has so far sent to the seller. The CL stores the current degree to which the fuzzy constraints are relaxed.

6) η represents the dynamic update from the supervisor agent. This can help buyer's agent and seller's agent to review their future development.

Inter-Agent Communication

We present performatives through which the seller agent can ask the buyer agent

- To check the product against its requirement and profile models.
- To relax the constraints associated with the products.

Table 2. Primitive actions taken by buyer's agent during N2C negotiation

Symbols for actions	Primitive actions taken by buyer's agent during N2C negotiation
Γ_1	Generates a crisp constraint induced from the fuzzy constraint with the highest priority in the buyer's constraint set. It does this by using cut-set technique at cut level 1. If there is more than one constraint with the highest priority, choose randomly between them.
Γ_2	Checks the attribute values of a seller offered product against the crisp constraints induced. It does this by using the cut-set technique at a given cut level, from the buyer's constraint set. If the test is passed, return "Correct" otherwise, return "Wrong".
Γ_3	Calculates the overall satisfaction degree of all the fuzzy constraints, whose induced crisp constraints have been submitted to the seller agent at the current point of the negotiation process.
Γ_4	Evaluates a seller's offer to find whether it is acceptable. This offer consists of the attribute values of the product plus its attached restriction condition (if any) and associated reward (if any).
Γ_5	Utilizes the cut set technique to induce a crisp constraint from the fuzzy constraint with the highest priority among those whose induced crisp constraints are violated by the seller's offer.
Γ_6	Relaxes the fuzzy constraint that has the lowest priority among the constraints that have already been submitted to the seller agent.
Γ_7	Receives an offer from a seller agent.
Γ_8	Sends an offer to a seller agent.

- The seller agent can also talk about the concessions and the flexibility associated with the products

Similarly the buyer agent can ask the seller agent to

- Find or refind a product compatible with the submitted constraints
- End the negotiation

A seller's agent offers message as:

$$\xi_S = (\Theta_1, \Theta_2, \Theta_3, \Theta_4)\ \text{where}$$

1) The item $\Theta_1 = (b_1, \ldots b_n)$ is a value vector of characteristics of the product that the seller agent considers satisfies the constraints submitted by the buyer agent.
2) The item Θ_2 denotes the restriction attached to the product. It is a Boolean expression given in definition 4.
3) The item Θ_3 denotes the reward associated with the product. It is also a Boolean expression and is given in definition 4.
4) The item Θ_4 denotes the performative i.e. the action that the seller agent wants the buyer agent to take after receiving the message. This include the following:

Confirm: The seller agent is asking the buyer agent to confirm whether the product is acceptable. That is, to confirm whether the product plus any accompanying information can convince its whole constraint set because some of the buyer's constraints may not yet have been revealed to the seller and whether the buyer's minimum interest (its acceptability threshold) can be guaranteed.

Unwind: The seller agent is asking the buyer agent to unwind one of the constraints it has submitted. This is sent while the seller agent cannot locate a product that satisfies the constraints submitted to the buyer agent.

Concessions: When the buyer cannot accept the seller's offer, the seller always tries to find a trade-off offer with the same profit to it as the previous offer. Only when the seller cannot do this, it makes some concessions i.e. provides another offer with less profit for it.

Flexi: The seller agent provides the information pertaining to the flexibilities associated with the product to find a trade-off.

The selection of the aforementioned performatives is based on the following assumptions:

Since negotiation involves shared agreement by both parties, if the seller locates a product that it believes satisfies the buyer's requirements (as extreme as specified) then what it would like to execute is ask the buyer to *confirm* whether the product does definitely meet all the constraints.

Sellers always prefer to make a profitable sale. So even if sellers cannot find products that satisfy the constraints submitted by buyers, they are unlikely to say, "Unsuccessful". Rather they prefer to ask the buyers to *unwind* their submitted constraints, will talk about *concessions* and *flexibility* to see if a compatible product can be found.

A buyer offers a message as follows:

$\xi_b = (CT, PF)$

1) The item CT contains the constraints that the buyer agent uses to specify the product it wants to buy. In particular, if the buyer agent wants to unwind a constraint C that it has already submitted it is represented as C'$\downarrow$ where C' is the unwinded constraint. If the buyer agent wants to add a new constraint C, the constraint is represented as C$\uparrow$.

2) The item PF represents the action that the buyer agent wants the seller agent to take after receiving the message. These include:

   - *Locate*: The buyer agent is asking the seller agent to find an alternative product for it. This is sent when the buyer cannot accept the product that it has just been offered.
   - *Relocate*: The buyer agent is asking the seller agent to locate an alternative product for it. This is sent when the buyer cannot accept the product that it has just been offered.
   - *Agreement*: The buyer agent is asking the seller agent to end their negotiation. It is sent when a successful deal has been made.
   - *Unsuccessful*: The buyer agent is asking the seller agent to end their negotiation. It is sent when the seller agent cannot offer a product compatible with the buyer's submitted constraints and the buyer cannot relax any constraints further.

The selections of the aforementioned performatives were based on the following intuitions:

- When a buyer submits a constraint to a seller, the buyer's intention is to ask the seller to *locate* a product satisfying the present constraint and any previously submitted ones.
- When a buyer reviews a seller's offer which does not violate any of its constraints at the current cut level, but does not reach its acceptability threshold, the buyer does not want to give up on the chance of reaching a deal. Thus, it asks the seller to *relocate* an alternative.

Figure 2. The value stream in the proposed N2C mechanism

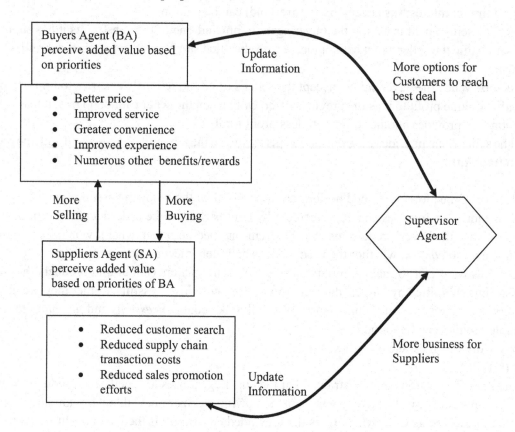

- The buyer needs a mean of signifying the end of a negotiation (whether a deal is made or not).

When the seller agent cannot offer a product compatible with the buyer's submitted constraints and the buyer cannot relax any constraints further, the buyer agent can ask the seller agent to end their negotiation. In such situations, when the plans of one agent conflict with the plans of other agents, conflict resolution is crucial for achieving effective coordination through negotiation. The value streams associated with the proposed negotiation mechanism is shown in Figure 2.

The proposed N2C model utilizes a supervisor agent, which maintains dynamic updates of resource requirements.

Behavior of Seller's agent in N2C model
Start negotiation
LS: = NIL; CS: = ϕ;
REPEAT
   Receive (ξ_β)
  IF ξ_β . PF= "Locate" OR "Relocate" THEN
    IF ξ_β . PF= "Locate" THEN
      CS: ϑ_2 (CS, ξ_β.CT)
      SN: = ϑ_1 (CS); PS: = ϕ;

ELSE

 SN: $= \vartheta_2(\text{CS} \cup \{ SN \notin PS \})$;

END IF;

IF SN $\neq$ NIL THEN

 $\xi_s.\Theta_1 := \text{SN}; \, \mathbf{x}_s \, \Theta_3 = \text{NIL}$;

 $\xi_s.\Theta_2 := \vartheta_3(\text{SN}.\Theta_1)$;

 $\xi_s.\Theta_4 := \text{Confirm}$

ELSE IF LS = NIL THEN

 $\xi_s.\Theta_4 = \text{Unwind}$

ELSE IF $\vartheta_4(\text{LS}.\Theta_1) \neq \text{NIL}$

  AND LS.$\Theta_3 = \text{NIL}$ THEN

 $\xi_s.\Theta_3 = \vartheta_4(\text{LS}.\Theta_1)$;

 $\xi_s.\Theta_1 = \text{LS}.\Theta_1$

 $\xi_s.\Theta_2 = \text{LS}.\Theta_2$

 $\xi_s.\Theta_4 = \text{Confirm}$

ELSE $\xi_s.\Theta_4 = \text{Unwind}$

END IF;

END IF;

END IF;

END IF;

IF $\xi_\beta.$ PF = "Agreement" THEN decision $= \xi_s$ END IF

IF $\xi_\beta.$ PF = "Unsuccessful" THEN decision $= \eta$ (dynamic update from supervisor agent) Present (ξ_s); LS $= \xi_s$

 PS = PS $\cup$ {LS};

UNTIL $\xi_\beta.$ PF = "Unsuccessful" OR "Agreement" END REPEAT;

Decision $= \eta$

RETURN Decision

End negotiation

The flowchart for the Coordination and structure generation in the proposed N2C mechanism is shown in Figure 3 and Figure 4 respectively.

Supervisor Agent

Supervisor agents are autonomous computational processes with internal structures (mental states) composed of beliefs (facts about the environment and the buyer's and supplier's agent), goals (world states to be achieved), plan templates (procedures for achieving specific world states), and supervision intentions (commitments to achieve world states or to perform actions). Supervisor agents try to execute their plans in an effective and competent way. They are not antagonistic and do not intentionally try to deceive or thwart the plans of buyer and sellers agent. Therefore, situations often arise in which the plans of buyer's agent conflict with the plans of seller's agent. A conflict of interests is defined as a social concept involving two or more agents that have plans requiring mutually exclusive world states to exist. These plans are called incompatible and cannot be executed together.

Figure 3. Flowchart for the coordination in the proposed N2C mechanism (from supplier's perspective)

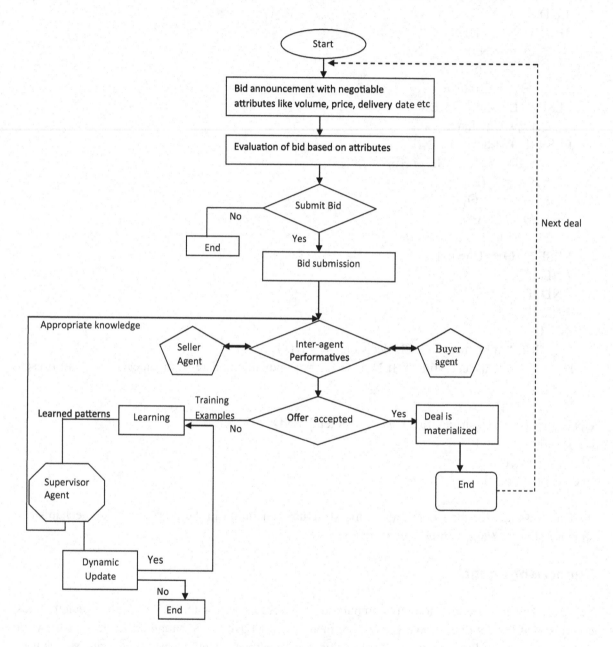

The mental state (MS) of supervisor agent is a 5 tuple given by:

$$MS = \{B_{LF}, G_L, P_{LN}, I_{NS}, E_{ED}\} \text{ where}$$

- B_{LF}: Signifies the set of beliefs representing facts about the world and the agent himself. We assume that beliefs persist by default over time and are continuously updated to reflect changes in the world.

Figure 4. Structure generation for N2C mechanism

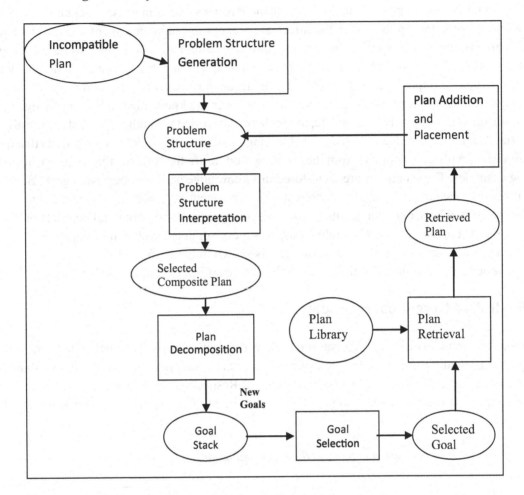

- G_L: Signifies the set of goals representing world states to be achieved. Each goal has associated a number of factors, including a priority or importance and a degree of urgency.
- P_{LN}: The supervisor agent has a library of plan templates representing known procedures for achieving specific goals. A plan template for supervisor agent is a 7 tuple denoted by
  $\{PT_1, PT_2, PT_3, PT_4, PT_5, PT_6 \text{ and } PT_7\}$ where
- PT_1: is a plan identifier, PT_2: is a plan name, PT_3: is a list of arguments, PT_4: is the type of plan template, PT_5 is the procedure for achieving the goal specified by PT_2 and PT_3.
- PT_6: is list of constraint (such as price, quality, model, volume, delivery date, expiry date, after-sale service and warranty) imposing a temporal order on the members of the body, on the types of arguments, on the relation between arguments, PT_7: is the list of conditions that must hold before processing the plan's body.
- I_{NS}: Consist of a list of supervision threads. Each supervision threads contain the plan adopted for achieving the goal. The supervisor agent commits to the plans he adopts and undertakes to reconsider them to monitor and resolve the existing conflicts between the buyer's agent and supplier's agent.

The supervisor agent monitors the trade-off between supplier's agent and buyer's agent by taking into account the potentials plan of supplier's agent and buyer's agent. Supervisor agent has a data structure called external description where the information about the supplier's agent and buyer's agent is stored. This information is obtained by explicit communication and corresponds to the belief, goals, and intentions (plans) of supplier's agent and buyer's agent. The supervisor agent maintains dynamic updates of resource requirements. This enables the decision of buyer's agent and supplier's agent to be made on the basis of up-to-date information. Whenever the knowledge in the knowledge base of Supervisor agent is found to be incomplete, the problem is rectified through incremental learning using appropriate additional training examples. The learning module is used to learn the patterns that exist in the training examples. The outputs from the learning module are the patterns that were extracted from training examples. These patterns are then stored in a knowledge base of supervisor agent. Supervisor agent takes into account the conflicts of interest of buyer's agent and supplier's agent and the proposal and plan generated by supervisor agents helps in resolving the true and potential conflicts of interests for buyer's and supplier's agent. The architecture of supervisor agent is shown in Figure 5.

The proposal generation is for supervisor agent is shown in Figure 6.

We demonstrate the efficacy of the proposed N2C mechanism by a numerical example.

An Illustrative Numerical Example

To exhibit the operation of our mechanism and to show its practicality, we have generated a hypothetical example for evaluating suppliers. In this example, there are 2 suppliers S_1 and S_2 with attributes Cost ($/item), Lead Time (days), Quantity (items), Reward, Restrictions and Profit associated with them. Such a scenario is typical of semi-competitive environment. That is, both supplier agent and buyer

Figure 5. Supervisor agent architecture for the proposed model

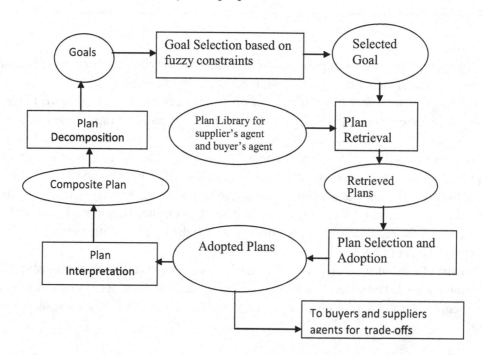

Figure 6. Proposal generation for supervisor agent

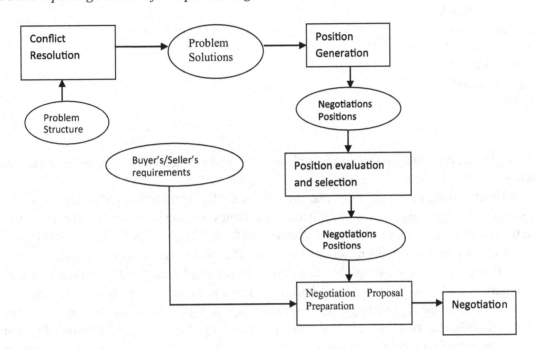

agent attempt to acquire the best deal they can since they both are self-interested. Towards this end, they should minimize the revelation of their private information since it could prevent them from getting good deals. However, as the seller desires to build or preserve his reputation (this should associate with more money in long term) and the buyer needs to settle down as soon as possible, it is also essential for them to cooperate to a certain extent in the negotiation. Table 3 shows the seller product model (i.e. the information about the available suppliers prepared by the seller agent).

We assume the following ranges for attributes:

Table 3. Product information held by supplier's agent

Supplier	Cost ($)	Lead time (days)	Quantity (items)	Award	Restriction
S_1	10-65	1-6	1-25	No	No
	10-63	7-12	1-80	No	No
	10-60	13-18	1-125	5 Units Free	Cash payment
S_2	10-65	1-4	1-10	No	No
	10-62	5-10	1-60	2 Units Free	No
	10-61	11-18	1-125	No	No

Cost (in $):
MIN= OPT= 10; MAX=65.
Lead Time (in days):
OPT= 2, 3, 4, 5, 6, 7, 8
MIN= 1; MAX= 18.
Quantity (in items):
MAX: OPT= 125
MIN: 1.

By varying the attributes and balancing with cost, we randomly generate 10 combinations as shown in Table 4.

For different configuration of suppliers, the proposed N2C mechanism will represent trade-offs among the different probable values of the negotiation issues. For the numerical example, we have assumed the priorities for Cost, Lead-time and Quantity as 0.40, 0.32 and 0.28 respectively. The proposed Pritorized fuzzy constraint problem formulations for B2B markets capture the essential meaning of priorities. If one wants to raise the global satisfaction degree of all prioritized constraints, a constraint with a relatively high priority must be sufficiently satisfied prior to a constraint with a relatively low priority. It measures the relative importance among things in a group to determine only their relative precedence and signifies that the higher the priority of one thing, the earlier the thing should be handled or the more preferred is the thing. Consequently, the higher the priority of a constraint, the more preference satisfying the constraint should be given when finding a solution. That is precisely the reason why this kind of framework is called Prioritized. Thus the sensitivity of these priorities can be checked that is how sensitive the choices are to the changes in criteria weights. This is useful in situations such as where uncertainties exist in the definition of the importance of different factors. Table 5, 6 and 7 shows the fuzzy constraint for cost, lead-time and quantity with priorities 0.40, 0.32 and 0.28 respectively.

The negotiation rounds for the proposed N2C mechanism is described as follows:

Table 4. Different combinations of supplier's agent

Configuration of Supplier	Cost ($/ item)	Lead time (days)	Quantity (Items)	Reward	Restrictions	Profit ($)
A (S_1)	10	2	75	No	No	75
B (S_1)	15	8	60	No	No	70
C (S_1)	10	6	125	No	No	76
D (S_1)	10	3	120	No	Cash payment	40
E (S_1)	20	6	90	No	No	60
F (S_2)	10	11	120	No	Cash Payment	35
G (S_2)	64	5	108	No	No	30
H (S_2)	58	6	90	2 Units Free	No	35
I (S_2)	65	15	125	No	No	45
J (S_2)	10	2	120	5 Units free	Cash payment	78

Table 5. Fuzzy constraints for cost with priority 0.40

Cost ($/item)	Satisfaction degree
$1 \leq \text{Cost} \leq 10$	100%
$11 \leq \text{Cost} \leq 20$	80%
$21 \leq \text{Cost} \leq 30$	60%
$31 \leq \text{Cost} \leq 40$	40%
$41 \leq \text{Cost} \leq 50$	20%
$51 \leq \text{Cost} \leq 65$	0%

Table 6. Fuzzy constraints for Lead Time with priority 0.32

Lead time range (days)	Satisfaction degree
$1 \leq \text{Lead time} \leq 3$	100%
$4 \leq \text{Lead time} \leq 6$	80%
$7 \leq \text{Lead time} \leq 9$	60%
$10 \leq \text{Lead time} \leq 12$	40%
$13 \leq \text{Lead time} \leq 15$	20%
$16 \leq \text{Lead time} \leq 18$	0%

Table 7. Fuzzy constraints for quantity with priority 0.28

Quantity (items)	Satisfaction degree
$1 \leq \text{Quantity} \leq 15$	0%
$16 \leq \text{Quantity} \leq 30$	15%
$31 \leq \text{Quantity} \leq 46$	30%
$47 \leq \text{Quantity} \leq 60$	45%
$61 \leq \text{Quantity} \leq 75$	60%
$76 \leq \text{Quantity} \leq 90$	75%
$91 \leq \text{Quantity} \leq 105$	90%
$106 \leq \text{Quantity} \leq 125$	100%

Round 1:

Buyer: Select the constraint with highest priority as follows:

$$\text{Cost} \leq 10 \tag{8}$$

Then Γ_8 present the seller agent with a message to ask it to *locate* supplier, which satisfy this constraint.

Seller: Receive the buyers offer message ξ_β x_b and accordingly action ϑ_2 modifies its current constraints set (empty at the moment i.e. LS = NIL; CS=ϕ) with constraint in equation (8). Thus its current constraint set becomes:

$$\{\text{Cost} \leq 10\} \tag{9}$$

Then action ϑ_2 put forwards a solution (C for S_1) to CSP (9). Further, action ϑ_3 try to propose the attached constriction for the solution. Here, there is no constriction. Finally, action ϑ_6 present the buyer agent with a message to ask it to *confirm* whether supplier C is acceptable according to the information (Unit Cost =10; 5 $\leq$ Leadtime $\leq$11; 1$\leq$Quantity $\leq$125). Notice that D and F also satisfy the constraint, but the profit $\hbar_\tau$ is highest for C.

Round 2:

Buyer: Receive the seller's offer message, and accordingly action Γ_2 verify C against its current constraints in order of their priorities. This shows that the constraint (1$\leq$ Lead time $\leq$3) is violated.

Thus, action Γ_8 present the seller agent with a message to ask it to *locate* a supplier which can satisfy the constraint (1$\leq$ Lead time $\leq$3) as well. Thus, the current constraint set becomes:

$$CS= \{\text{Cost} \leq 10, 1 \leq \text{Lead time} \leq 3\} \tag{10}$$

Then action ϑ_2 put forwards a solution, A to the CSP (a). Here, restriction is again none. Finally, action ϑ_6 present the buyer agent with a message to ask it to *Confirm* whether A is acceptable according to the constraints $\{\text{Cost} \leq 10, 1 \leq \text{Lead time} \leq 3\}$. Notice that A is chosen as profit $\hbar_\tau$ for A is highest.

Round 3:

Buyer: Receive the seller's offer message and action Γ_2 verify A against its current constraint set in order of their priorities. This shows that constraint (106 $\leq$Quantity $\leq$125) is violated.

Thus, action Γ_8 present the seller agent with a message to ask it to *locate* a supplier which can satisfy the constraint (106$\leq$ Quantity$\leq$ 125) as well. Thus, the current constraint set becomes:

$$CS= \{\text{Cost} \leq 10, 1\leq \text{Lead time} \leq 3, 106 \leq \text{Quantity} \leq 125\} \tag{11}$$

Then action ϑ_2 put forwards a solution, D to the CSP (a). Here, constriction is cash payment. Finally, action ϑ_6 present the buyer agent with a message to ask it to *Confirm* whether D is acceptable according to the constraints $\{\text{Cost} \leq 60, 1\leq \text{Lead time} \leq 3, 1\leq \text{Quantity} \leq 125\}$.

Round 4:

Buyer: Receive the seller's offer message and action Γ_2 verify D against its current constraint set. No violations are found. Second evaluate the Buyer's agent acceptability for D. According to the buyer's requirement model, D completely satisfies all its constraints.

$$\alpha = min\left\{\{\mu_{cost}-1\}\frac{P^R(Cost)}{P^R_{max}}+1,\{\mu_{Leadtime}-1\}\frac{P^R(Leadtime)}{P^R_{max}}+1,\{\mu_{Quantity}-1\}\frac{P^R(Quantity)}{P^R_{max}}+1\right\}$$

$= min\{(1-1)x\ 0.40/0.40+1,\ (1-1)x\ 0.32/0.40+1,\ (1-1)x\ 0.28/0.40+1\}$

$= 1$

According to the buyers profile model, D's constriction obedience $\beta = 0.43$. Since there is no award associated with D, award value υ is 0 for product δ_τ.

Acceptability (D) $= min\{\alpha, \beta\}\oplus_p ((1-\tau)\upsilon+\mu))$

$= min\ (1, 0.43)\ \oplus_p ((1-0.72)\ x\ 0+0.72)$

$= 0.43\ \oplus\ 0.72$

$=\{(1-0.72)\ x0.43x0.72\}/(1-0.72)\ x0.43x0.72+0.73x(1-0.42)(1-0.73)$

$= 0.46$

This value is less than the buyer's acceptability threshold of 0.65 and so D is not acceptable. Thus, action Γ_8 present the seller agent with a message to ask it to *Relocate* a supplier which can satisfy the constraint the buyer has submitted so far.

Seller: Receive the buyer's offer message, and action ϑ_2 put forwards an alternative solution, supplier J, which has the same profit as supplier D (i.e. J is a trade off solution of D). Further, purpose the attached restriction for the solution "Cash Payment". Thus, present the Buyer's agent with a message to ask it to *Confirm* whether J is acceptable with following constraints.

{Cost =10; 1≤Lead time≤5; 1≤Quantity≤120}, with constriction as "Cash Payment".

Round 5:

Buyer: Receive the seller's offer message, and through action Γ_2 verify J against its constraints. In this case, constraint {106≤ Quantity≤ 125} is violated. Then, present the buyer agent with a message to ask it to *locate* a supplier, which can also satisfy constraint {106 ≤Quantity≤ 125}

Seller: Receive the buyer's offer message, and accordingly action J_2 modifies its current constrained {Cost≤ 10, 1≤ Leadtime ≤5, 1 ≤Quantity≤120} with constraint {106 ≤Quantity ≤ 125}. Thus, its current constraint set becomes:

{Cost =10, 1 ≤Lead time ≤5, 106 ≤Quantity ≤125}   (12)

Then, try to generate a solution to the CSP but fail. Thus, propose the *award* for the last solution J; the seller agent can provide the buyer with "5 Units Free". Then, present the buyer agent with a message to ask it to *Confirm* again whether J is acceptable according to the revealed information plus the *award* "5 Units Free" and the constriction of cash payment.

Round 6:

Buyer: Receive the seller's offer message and *confirm* whether the acceptability for J is increased sufficiently by the *award*. According to the buyer requirement model, J's requirement satisfaction is:

$$\alpha = min \left\{ \{\mu_{cos\,t} - 1\} \frac{P^R(Cost)}{P^R_{max}} + 1, \{\mu_{Leadtime} - 1\} \frac{P^R(Leadtime)}{P^R_{max}} + 1, \{\mu_{Quantity} - 1\} \frac{P^R(Quantity)}{P^R_{max}} + 1 \right\}$$

$= min \{(1-1) \times 0.40/0.40+1, (1-1) \times 0.32/0.40+1, (1-1) \times 0.28/0.40+1\}$
$= 1$

According to the buyers profile model, J's constriction obedience $\beta = 0.6$. Since there is an award "5 Units Free" is associated with J, award value is 0.4 for product d_t .

Acceptability (J) $= min\{\alpha, \beta\} \oplus_p ((1-\tau)\upsilon + \mu))$
$= min (1, 0.6) \oplus_p ((1-0.72) \times 0+0.72)$
$= 0.72$

This value is greater than the buyer's acceptability threshold of 0.65. Thus, present the seller agent with a message to tell it that a deal has been made and that it can end its negotiation process.

Seller: Receive the buyer's offer message x_b and end the negotiation process.

The supervisor agent monitors the trade-off between supplier's agent and buyer's agent by taking into account the potentials plan of supplier's agent and buyer's agent. The negotiation rounds are summarized in Table 8.

Observations

From the above negotiation procedure, we know that suppliers configurations such as A, B, C, D, E, F, G, H, I are not acceptable to the buyer agent, but configuration J is acceptable. Also, the profit for seller agent is maximum for J. Therefore, from both the seller's and buyer's perspective J is the best solution. Our agents are autonomous in that they negotiate with each other on behalf of both sellers and buyers. Thus, they actually make the contract decision themselves. In this mechanism, the user's requirements on attributes of a product/service that fuzzy constraints can easily capture are represented.

The problem can be extended to *m* suppliers with *n* attributes and N2C mechanism can be carried out over fuzzy constraints of multiple issues of products, which is more efficient than doing it over single solutions. In many cases it is difficult for sellers and buyers to trust a mediator to act fairly on their behalf. Also, the privacy issue makes it almost impossible for sellers and buyers to expose their individual sensitive data to a third party. Since human negotiators are unwilling to disclose private information, decentralized methods for searching Pareto-optimal solutions in negotiation problems are necessary. The proposed N2C mechanism guarantees that the outcome of the negotiation is Pareto-optimal.

CONCLUDING REMARKS

From the point of view of electronic commerce, it is essential to recognize some of the elements of buyer-seller relationships that particularly seem to affect the development of electronic systems. Interdependency between companies, their bargaining power and product at hand are these kinds of important elements relevant.

Table 8. The negotiations round for the numerical example

Stages during negotiations	Offer received (from combination of suppliers)	Constraints offered during negotiation	Constraints Violated during negotiation	Interagent Performatives during N2C mechanisms — Buyer	Seller	Constrictions associated with suppliers	Awards associated with suppliers	Acceptability Index
Round 1		Cost ≤ 10		Locate	Confirm			
Round 2	C	Cost =10; 5 ≤ Lead time ≤11; 1≤Quantity ≤125	1 ≤ Lead time ≤ 3	Locate	Confirm			
Round 3	A	Cost =10; 1 ≤ Lead time ≤3; 1≤Quantity ≤95	106 ≤ Quantity ≤ 125	Locate	Confirm			
Round 4	D	Cost =10; 1 ≤ Lead time ≤3; 106≤Quantity ≤125		Relocate	Confirm	Cash Payment		0.46
Round 5	J	Cost =10; 1 ≤ Lead time ≤3; 1≤Quantity ≤120	106 ≤ Quantity ≤ 125	Locate	Confirm			
Round 6	J	Cost =10; 1 ≤ Lead time ≤3; 1≤Quantity ≤120		DEAL materialized		Cash Payment	5 Units Free	0.72

In this chapter, we develop a prioritized fuzzy constraint based model to explore the interactive nature of the buyer-supplier relationships in dynamic supply chain environments. One of the essential features of the approach is that there is frequently more than one alternative that can satisfy the interests of both buyers and suppliers. Thus, if the opponent cannot accept an offer then the proponent must endeavor to locate an alternative, which is uniformly acceptable to it, but more acceptable to the opponent. The proposed model uses prioritized fuzzy constraints to represent trade-offs among the different probable values of the negotiation issues and to signify how agents should make concessions. This chapter explores the role of the buyer- seller relationship when choosing a negotiation model for dynamic supply chains. The proposed Negotiation to Coordinate (N2C) mechanism enables the negotiation to be carried out over fuzzy constraints of multiple issues of a product that is more efficient than negotiation that is carried out over single point solutions. Supervisor agent takes into account the conflicts of interest of buyer's agent and supplier's agent and the proposal and plan generated by supervisor agents helps in resolving the true and potential conflicts of interests for buyer's agent and supplier's agent. The supervisor agent maintains dynamic updates of resource requirements. The proposed N2C mechanism is generic and can be used for wide range of domains especially in negotiations pertaining to supply contracts for flexible production networks. The model ensures a high degree of flexibility; it avoids deadlocks and encourages the parties willingness to a compromise. The proposed model exploits the notion of pritorized fuzzy constraint satisfaction problems as the basic representation scheme. It guarantees that the outcome of the negotiation is Pareto optimal, yet the participating agents reveal minimal information about their preferences and constraints. Efficacy and intricacy of the proposed model is demonstrated with the help of numerical examples. In future, the concept of Game theory can be employed to deal with the insight of agent behavior for effective portrayal of the characteristics of the agents, especially in the emerging dynamic B2B E-Commerce environment.

REFERENCES

Alajoutsijarvi, K., Moller, K., & Rosenbroijer, C-J. (1999) Relevance of Focal Nets in Understanding the Dynamics of Business relationships. *Journal of Business-to-Business Marketing*, 6(3), 3-35.

Bakos, J. Y. (1991) A Strategic analysis of electronics marketplaces. *MIS Quarterly*, 15(3), 295-310.

Chan, F. T. S., & Chan, H. K. (2004). A new model for manufacturing supply chain networks: a multiagent approach. *Journal of Engineering Manufacture*, 218, Part B, 443-454.

Chan, F. T. S., Chung, S. H., & Wadhwa, S. (2004). A heuristic Methodology for Order Distribution in a Demanddriven Collaborative Supply Chain. *International Journal of Production Research*, 42(1), 1-19.

Choi, T. Y., Dooley, K. J., & Rungtusanatham, M. (2001) Supply networks and complex adaptive systems: control versus emergence. *Journal of Operations Management*, 19(3), 351-366.

Dago, P., & Verfaillie, G., (1996). No good recordings for valued constraint satisfaction problems. *Proceedings of 8th IEEE International Conference on Tools with Artificial Intelligence*, Toulouse, 132–139, France.

Dubois, D., & Prade H. (1999). Qualitative possibility theory and its applications to constraint satisfaction and decision under uncertainty. *International Journal of Intelligent Systems, 14*, 45-61.

Ertogral, K., & Wu, S. D. (2000) Auction-Theoretic coordination of production planning in the supply chain. *IIE Transactions, 32*(10), 931-940.

Faratin, P., Sierra, C. & Jennings, N. R., (2002) Using Similarity criteria to make issue tradeoffs in automated negotiations. *Artificial Intelligence, 142*(2), 205-237.

Ford, D., Gadde, L. E., Hakansson, H., Lundgren, A., Snehota, I., Turnbull, P., & Wilson, D. (1988). *Managing Business Relationships*. John Wiley & Sons Ltd., Chichester.

Fung, R. Y. K., & Chen, T. (2005). A multiagent supply chain planning and coordination architecture. International Journal of Advanced Manufacturing Technology, 25, 811–819.

Garbarino, E., & Johnson, M. S. (1999). The Different Roles of Satisfaction, Trust and Commitment in Customer Relationships. *Journal of Marketing, 63*, 70-87

Goyal, S. K., & Gopalkrishnan, M. (1996). Production lot-sizing model with insufficient production capacity. *Production Planning and Control, 7*(4), 222-224.

Jain, V. (2006). Hybrid approaches to model supplier related issues in a dynamic supply chain. Unpublished Ph D Thesis, Mechanical Engineering Department, Indian Institute of Technology Delhi, India.

Jain, V., Wadhwa, S., & Deshmukh, S. G. (2007). A Negotiation-to-Coordinate (N2C) mechanism for Modeling Buyer-Supplier relationship in Dynamic Environment. *International Journal of Enterprise Information Systems, 3*(2),1

Julka, N., Srinivasan, R., & Karimi, I. (2002) Agent-based Supply Chain Management a Framework. *Computers & Industrial Engineering, 26*(12), 1755-1769.

Luo, X., Leung, H. F., Lee, J. H. M., & Jennings, N. R. (2003). Prioritized fuzzy constraint satisfaction problems: Axioms, instantiation and validation. *Fuzzy sets and Systems, 136*(2), 151-188.

Malone, T. W., Yates, J., & Benjamin, R. I. (1987). Electronic markets and electronics hierarchies. *Communications of the ACM, 30*(6), 484-497.

Matthyssens, P., & Van den Butle, C. (1994). Getting closer and nicer: Partnerships in the supply chain. *Long Range Planning, 27*(1), 72-83.

Petrovic D., Roy, R., & Petrovic R., (1999) Supply chain modeling using fuzzy sets. *International Journal of Production Economics, 59*(3), 443-453.

Raughunathan, S. (1992). A planning aid: an intelligent modeling system for planning problems based on constraint satisfaction. *IEEE Transactions on Knowledge Data Engineering, 4*(4), 317–335.

Roberts, B., & Mackay, M. (1998). IT supporting supplier relationship: The role of electronic commerce. *European Journal of Purchasing and Supply Management, 4*(2/3), 175-184.

Robicheaux, R. A., & Colman J. E. (1994). The Structure of Marketing Channel Relationships. *Journal of Academy of Marketing Science, 22*(1), 38-51.

Swaminathan, M. J., Smith, S. F., & Sadeh, N. M. (1998). Modelling Supply Chain Dynamics: A Multiagent Approach. *Decision Sciences*, *29*(3), 607-632.

Tang, J. E., Shee, D. Y., & Tang, T-I. (2001). A Conceptual model for interactive buyer-supplier relationship in Electronic Commerce. *International Journal of Information Management*, *21*, 49-68.

Toledo, C., Excelente, B., & Jennings, N. R. (2002). Learning to Select a Coordination Mechanism. In *Proc. AAMAS'02*, Bologna, Italy, July 15-19, 1106-1113.

Turksen, I. B., Zarandi, M. H. (1999). *Production planning and scheduling: Fuzzy and Crisp approaches*. Boston, Kluwer Academic publishers, pp. 479-529.

Wadhwa, S., & Rao, K. S. (2004) A Unified Framework for Manufacturing and Supply Chain Flexibility. *Global Journal of Flexible Systems Management*, *5*(1), 15-22.

Wadhwa, S., & Rao, K. S. (2003). Enterprise Modeling of Supply Chains Involving Multiple entity Flows: Role of Flexibility in Enhancing Lead Time Performance. *SIC Journal*, *12*(1), 5-20.

Wilson, D. T. (1995). An Integrated Model of Buyer-Seller Relationships. *Journal of the Academy of Marketing Science*, *23*(4), 335-345.

Zadeh, L. A. (1973). Outline of a new approach to the analysis of complex systems and decision processes. *IEEE Transactions on Systems, Man and Cybernetics*, *3*(1), 28-44.

Chapter XIV
Enterprise Systems, Control and Drift

Ioannis Ignatiadis
University of Bath, UK

Joe Nandhakumar
University of Warwick, UK

ABSTRACT

Enterprise Systems are widespread in current organizations and seen as integrating organizational procedures across functional divisions. An Enterprise System, once installed, seems to enable or constrain certain actions by users, which have an impact on organizational operations. Those actions may result in increased organizational control, or may lead to organizational drift. The processes that give rise to such outcomes are investigated in this chapter, which is based on a field study of five companies. By drawing on the theoretical concepts of human and machine agencies, as well as the embedding and disembedding of information in the system, this chapter argues that control and drift arising from the use of an Enterprise System are outcomes of the processes of embedding and disembedding human actions, which are afforded (enabled or constrained) by the Enterprise System.

INTRODUCTION

Implementation of an Enterprise System (also known as Enterprise Resource Planning-ERP System) in an organization may have profound impact on organizational processes (Boudreau & Robey, 1999; Koch, 2001; Martin & Cheung, 2000; Schrnederjans & Kim, 2003; Siriginidi, 2000), as well as on information flow and transparency (Bernroider & Koch, 1999; Besson & Rowe, 2001; Gattiker & Goodhue, 2004; Legare, 2002; Markus & Tanis, 2000; Newell et al., 2003; Shang & Seddon, 2000). Much of the research in Enterprise Systems however, is concerned with the implementation process and providing insights into success factors of Enterprise Systems implementation (e.g. Akkermans & van Helden, 2002; Al-Mashari & Al-Mudimigh, 2003; Bingi et al., 1999; Holland & Light, 1999; Hong & Kim, 2002; Nah et al., 2001; Shanks et al., 2000; Somers & Nelson, 2001). Only a few studies investigate issues relating to the post implementation of ES (e.g. Elmes et al., 2005). Hence we have limited understanding of issues affecting the use of Enterprise Systems in organizations and their potential for organizational impact.

This chapter therefore concentrates on the actual use of an Enterprise System, post-implementation. It examines the impact of actions performed by humans (users), or a machine (the Enterprise System), on control and drift within an organization. We propose a theoretical conceptualisation to describe the impact of those actions by drawing on a field study of five companies that have an Enterprise Resource Planning System installed. The significance of this research is twofold. First, our conceptualisation developed in this chapter enhances the understanding of the processes that result in organizational control (or drift) through the use of an Enterprise System. Second, our results also pinpoint issues of practical interest to companies that are using (or thinking of installing) an Enterprise System.

Although ERP systems were originally designed to be used within an organization, in the last years they have evolved considerably to include or link with external functionalities such as Customer Relationship Management (CRM), Supply Chain Management (SCM) and e-business (B2B and B2C). The current trend is also to repackage ERP systems as a collection of interoperable modules with standards-based interfaces, in accordance with the mandates of Service-Oriented Architectures. The examination of ERP systems in this chapter however only looked at internal operations, and the use of such systems referred only to internal actors, without examining external linkages, which was beyond the purposes of this research.

The rest of the chapter is structured as follows: in the following section, we review the relevant literature on Information Systems, control and drift, as well as human agency, which are topics central to our research. We then present our theoretical foundations, in which we frame our analysis and discussion. Our research approach is then outlined, followed by a description of the companies that participated in this research. We follow this with an analysis of the data gathered from the companies, across the dimensions of control and drift. We then discuss our findings and present our conceptualisation of Enterprise System use, and conclude with some theoretical and practical implications of our research.

LITERATURE REVIEW

Enterprise Systems, Control and Drift

The link of Information Systems with organizational control has been investigated by a variety of scholars in the field (e.g. Coombs et al., 1992; Duane & Finnegan, 2003; Malone, 1997; Tang et al., 2000). Many point to the paradox that while Information Systems can empower employees with increased decision-making capabilities, at the same time they can serve to increase control within the organization (e.g. Bloomfield & Coombs, 1992; Bloomfield et al., 1994; Orlikowski, 1991).

Although control in a general information systems setting has been examined to a large extent, the number of studies in an Enterprise Systems setting in particular is still quite limited. What distinguishes Enterprise Systems from other Information Systems is their scale, complexity, and potential for organizational impact. Because of this, they deserve special attention with regards to the issue of control. From the limited number of studies in this area, the characteristic ones are those by Hanseth et al. (2001), Sia et al. (2002), and Elmes et al. (2005). The main findings of these three studies are outlined below.

Hanseth et al. (2001) claim that Enterprise Systems (such as ERP systems), with their emphasis on standardization, streamlining, and integrating business processes, are an ideal control technology. However, they point to a surprising result: That implementing an ERP system over a global organization in order to enhance control may as well have the opposite effect, i.e. reduce control. This can be explained with the ubiquitous nature of side effects. In that sense, the more integrated the system is, the faster and farther side effects have an impact, and the bigger their consequences.

Sia et al. (2002) have examined the issues of empowerment and panoptic control of ERP systems. They summarize the panoptic control aspect of ERPs in three dimensions: comprehensive system tracking capability, enhanced visibility to management, and enhanced visibility to peers (through workflow dependency and data interdependency). The findings by Sia et al. (2002) indicate that although an ERP implementation has the potential for both employee empowerment and managerial control, managerial power seems to be perpetuated through an ERP implementation.

Elmes et al. (2005) have identified two seemingly contradictory theoretical concepts in an Enterprise System: reflective conformity and panoptic empowerment. Reflective conformity refers to the way that the integrated nature of the Enterprise System leads to greater employee discipline, while at the same time requiring them to be reflective in order to achieve organizational benefits from the system. Panoptic empowerment describes the greater visibility of information, which is provided by the shared database of the Enterprise System. This empowers employees to do their work more effectively and efficiently, but at the same time makes their work in the system more visible to others, who can then more easily exercise control over them.

Regarding the issue of drift, Ciborra (2002) defines drift as the processes of matching between situated human interventions of use and open technology. Technology drifting can be the result of passive resistance, learning-by-doing, sabotage, radical shifts in conditions, or plain serendipity In addition, Ciborra (2000) mentions the case when control has to decrease, when it is associated with the power to bring to life sophisticated and evolving infrastructures. Although Ciborra concentrates mainly on technology drift, this chapter is concerned with drift at the organizational level, which is implied by decrease of organizational control.

In particular regarding the issue of drift, van Fenema and van Baalen (2005) have looked into strategies for dealing with drift during the implementation of ERP systems. They distinguish between three such strategies, from which they argue the third strategy (drift containment) is the most realistic in ERP implementation projects:

- Control strategy aims at eliminating drifting and risk.
- Incremental strategy considers drifting to be a normal part of technology implementations. In this case "bricolage" is used to adapt technology to its context.
- Drift containment recognizes the inevitable drifting in technology implementations and the fact that drifting may even contribute to the stabilisation of technology. The question is then how to balance control and drift and use drift as a source of stabilisation of technology projects.

Although the above studies looked (amongst others) at either the issue of control or drift (but not both at the same time), Nandhakumar et al. (2005) have looked into the contextual forces of an ERP implementation, and how those influence control and drift during the implementation process. These contextual forces were interrelated, and referred to the affordance of the technology, as well as the social structure, practices and norms, either within the organization or external. The analysis by Nandhakumar et al. (2005) was based on examining managers' intentions, the power and cultural context within the organization, as well as the affordances of the technology.

Control was seen by Nandhakumar et al. to be an outcome of managerial intentions regarding the trajectory of implementation of the ERP system. This depended on both system affordances and social structure. (Technological) drift was then seen by Nandhakumar et al. (2005) to occur from the "organizational members' planned and unplanned actions in response to both previous technology and organizational properties they have enacted in the past" (p. 239). Unintended consequences of the implementation would then mean that the technology would drift from the planned implementation outcomes. Control and drift during the implementation of the ERP system in this case were interrelated, and would be operating in continuous cycles, in response to contextual forces shaping the actual implementation of the ERP system.

Although Nandhakumar et al. directly acknowledge the influence of users in accepting or rejecting the ERP system, their study mainly examined managerial as opposed to user intentions, and in the implementation, as opposed to the use stage of an ERP system. This chapter therefore complements the viewpoint by Nandhakumar et al. by arguing that the way users use the system according to the affordances of the technology also has a large part to play on impacting control and drift within an organization.

Enterprise System Use and Human Agency

One important strand of Enterprise System research which is also relevant to the current chapter is the linkage of Enterprise System (e.g. ERP) use with the agency of humans. Kallinikos (2004) for example argues that ERP systems help shape human agency and institute patterns of action and communication in organizations. They accomplish this by delineating the paths along which human agency should take place. This is afforded by the dissection of organizational activities in discreet terms, and the provision of the procedural sequences for the execution of particular tasks. In this sense, ERP systems are mostly concerned with streamlining, control and standardisation of organizational operations. In so doing, ERP systems enable the construction of accountable and governable patterns of behaviour in organizations.

Similarly, Boudreau & Robey (2005) have pointed to the fact that when looking at organizational change arising from the use of IT, an agency perspective may mean limited possibilities for radical IT-induced change. An agency perspective of IT in this case takes the position that IT is socially constructed and open to a variety of social meanings and potential uses. Boudreau & Robey argue that certain technologies allow for a greater degree of human agency and others to a lesser degree. Their views agree with those of Orlikowski (2000), who acknowledges that while users can and do use technologies as they were designed, they also can and do circumvent the intended uses of technologies, either by ignoring certain properties, working around them, or inventing new ones.

The research by Boudreau & Robey looked at ERP systems, which are seen as inflexible software packages constraining user-inspired action (human agency). Their results, however, indicate that although ERP systems are seen as rigid control mechanisms, there is still scope for human agency to take place within such systems, contradicting Kallinikos (2004). The research by Boudreau & Robey indicated that technical system constraints on human agency can be overcome through a process of initial inertia (rejection of the system), improvised learning as a result of pressure to use the system, and finally reinvention of usages of the system, to match their own previous experiences and background.

THEORETICAL FOUNDATIONS

This section presents our theoretical foundations for the development of our conceptualisation in the chapter. These theoretical foundations are the concepts of embedding-disembedding and agencies (human and machine). These concepts were chosen as they were deemed important in explaining the processes that lead to organizational control and drift. The theoretical foundations presented below together with the concepts of control and drift that were described in the previous section, will inform our analysis and discussion.

Embedding-Disembedding

Giddens (1990) defines disembedding as "the lifting out of social relations from local contexts of interaction and their restructuring across indefinite spans of time-space" (p. 21). Conversely, embedding (or reembedding) is according to Giddens, "the reappropriation or recasting of disembedded social relations so as to pin them down (however partially or transitorily) to local conditions of time and place" (pp. 79-80).

For Giddens (1990) there are two types of disembedding mechanisms: symbolic tokens and expert systems (not expert systems in an information systems sense). Although Giddens concentrates mainly on money, symbolic tokens in general are media of exchange that can be circulated without regard to specific characteristics of the people or groups that handle them. Expert systems are then organizations of technical accomplishment or professional expertise that make a significant contribution to the material and social environment in which we live.

In the current context of an Enterprise System, it can be argued that the expert system as defined by Giddens consists of the rules and procedures that are inscribed in the Enterprise System. The symbolic token is then the information that is held and represented within the Enterprise System. The social relations that are being disembedded and reembedded derive from the actions of users in the system. These actions are disembedded from the local context where they are carried out, to time-space stretches of the company's operations. Those actions are consequently reembedded, by impacting on, and being appropriated by, other users of the system.

Human and Machine Agency

Giddens (1984) defines agency is the "capability to make a difference, that is to exercise some sort of power" (p. 139). In other words, agency is synonymous to the carrying out (or intentionally not carrying out) of an action. With regards to actions in an Information Systems setting, Rose et al. (2003) have questioned the relationship between the social and technical aspects of IS, in other words, how do social systems act upon technology, and vice versa. Rose & Jones (2004) have drawn on both Actor-Network Theory and Structuration Theory, as well as Pickering (1995), to develop a model called the "Double Dance of Agency". In this model, the distinction is made between human agency and machine agency, but the two are interwoven and affect each other.

Rose & Truex (2000) have proposed to give an understanding of machine agency as perceived autonomy. Machine agency is then the emergent property of the development process and becomes embedded in the completed machine. However, Nandhakumar et al. (2005) in their study of an ERP implementation, draw from Gibson (1979) and Norman (1988) to view machine agency as affordance. They also draw from Giddens (1984), who attributes intentionality to human agency. In the context of this chapter, we will similarly assume that machine agency is characterised by affordance, whereas human agency is characterised by intentionality. The next section presents the research approach employed in our research.

RESEARCH APPROACH

Our research approach is interpretive case study (Walsham, 1993). In interpretivism, the reality is socially constructed by human agents (Walsham, 1995). Interpretive studies reject the notion of an objective or factual account of events and situations, seeking instead a relativistic, albeit shared, understanding of phenomena (Orlikowski & Baroudi, 1991).

In the current research, five companies (NGlobe, TechniCom, SecSys, FCom and TransCom – all pseudonyms) have been examined with regards to the use of their Enterprise System. The research took place between October 2004 and August 2005, and involved formal semi-structured (face-to-face mostly with a few telephone) interviews with company staff (office employees and managers). It also involved informal conversations with them, as well as observing user interactions with the system. Interviews were mostly with one person, although a couple of them involved two persons, and lasted anything between 40 minutes and 2 hours, with an average of 1 hour per interview. All of the interviews (with the exception of one due to personal sensitivities) were recorded and transcribed verbatim. The table below shows the interviews with members of the 5 companies researched.

Analysis was carried out using a qualitative data analysis approach proposed by Miles & Huberman (1994). They distinguish between three types of codes: *Descriptive* codes entail little interpretation, but attribute a class of the phenomena to a segment of text (such as interview transcript). The same segment could also be coded with an *interpretive* code, where the researcher uses some of his or her knowledge about the background of the phenomenon in order to interpret the segment of text. Thirdly, *pattern* codes are even more inferential and explanatory.

In the current research, coding was done with the aid of the qualitative analysis software NVivo. Within NVivo, descriptive coding was done through a first pass analysis of the interview transcripts, where the relevant text was examined, and portions of it (sentences, paragraphs, or sections) were assigned a code according to the phenomenon that they were describing. Some pattern coding also occurred at this stage, as codes were grouped into categories at various levels that linked those codes together. This coding was more akin to a grounded theory approach (Glaser & Strauss, 1967), where codes evolved directly from the data. Memos were also kept in NVivo about issues of interest that emerged, and reflections from the part of the researcher on the data examined. This prompted a second pass of coding, where the coding was more theory-driven, according to identified themes in the first pass, and literature that could support the concepts from the first pass of coding (e.g. relevant literature on control, drift, human action, machine action, intentionality, affordance, embedding, disembedding). The second pass of coding was more interpretive, in that segments of text were interpreted according to the chosen literature. However, data were not forced into predefined categories, as codes emerged

Table 1. Illustration of the interviews carried out

Area	Positions Interviewed	No. of Interviews
Company: NGlobe		
IS Department	- Business Centre IS Manager - General IS Manager	2
Finance Department	- Accounts Payable Employee - Cash Management and Treasury Process Director - Record to Report Process Director	3
Company: TechniCom		
Procurement	- Supply Chain Manager 1 - Supply Chain Manager 2	2
Company: SecSys		
Procurement	- Purchasing Manager	2
Company: FCom		
IT Department	- IT Manager	2
Company: TransCom		
Sales	- Sales Facilitator - Commercial Assistant	3
Finance	- Billing Clerk - Accounting Reports Manager - Accounts Payable Clerk - Assistant Accountant - Assistant Finance Manager	6
Service Management	- Maintenance Policy Leader - Head of Production - SAP Facilitator - Production Planner - Shift Planning Coordinator - Flow Repairable Controller - Reliability Group Leader - Abnormal Work Manager	12
Warehouse and Distribution	- Business Improvement Coordinator - Logistics Director - Inventory Planner	5
Materials Management	- Materials Controller 1 - Materials Controller 2 - Materials Planner	5
Purchasing	- Purchasing Manager	1
IT Management	- IT Manager - Global Information Systems Director	4
Total Interviews		**47**

not only from the literature, but also as a result of the first pass coding, which was grounded on the interview data. In addition, pattern coding also occurred at this stage, as several codes were grouped into higher-order patterns.

The analysis below is structured in terms of the two concepts of control and drift, also taking into account human and machine actions, and the respective intentionalities and affordances. Indicative quotes are also presented. Discussion of the results then incorporates the concepts of embedding and disembedding. The next section briefly describes the background of the companies participating in the research, followed by the analysis and discussion of our results.

COMPANY DESCRIPTIONS

The companies that participated in the research are described below (with pseudonyms). All of the companies have had an Enterprise System (ERP) installed for a minimum of 2 years. This was a criterion when selecting those companies, in order to be able to observe the impacts of the Enterprise System after it had been used for a number of years, and not during or immediately after implementation. The companies come from different sectors, have different customer markets, and use different ERP systems, which adds to the generalizability of the results.

TransCom

TransCom operates in the transport sector, and has 5 billion Euros in annual sales worldwide. TransCom is using the SAP R/3 ERP system, currently on version 4.5 in most places where it is installed, although there are some later versions (4.6) or earlier versions (e.g. 3.1, or even R/2) in some countries. The system was fully installed in January 2002 in the UK. In addition to the UK, SAP is currently fully installed in Spain, France, Sweden, Romania, Chile, and the USA. The modules of SAP used are Materials Management, Service Management, Finance, Sales & Distribution.

NGlobe

NGlobe has a presence in almost 200 countries, and generates most of its revenue by selling financial information. NGlobe has the Oracle 11i ERP system installed, used for the modules of Finance (accounts receivable, payable, general ledger, fixed assets, and purchasing) and HR. In addition, the Oracle's learning module is also installed. The design of the ERP system took place between 2000-2001, and NGlobe first went live in 2001, with the whole implementation finishing by the end of 2003. NGlobe was one of the first implementations of one global instance of Oracle. This was enabled by the fact that NGlobe is a very homogenous company.

TechniCom

TechniCom is a company in the technological sector. It has recently been restructured, and over a 4-year period TechniCom has bought 32 companies, all with different bespoke systems. TechniCom is using Oracle version 11 for the financials part, mainly for accounts payable and accounts receivable. For their HR function TechniCom is using the PeopleSoft ERP system. For billing they have had a bespoke system built for them, which harmonizes all the different billing systems from all the companies that TechniCom bought.

FCom

FCom is a vertical retail manufacturer, which means that the bulk of the products that they sell in the stores, they also manufacture themselves. It operates more like a family-run business, rather than a large corporate public company. FCom is a £55 million turnover company operating in the UK, currently having 61 stores and employing around 500 people. FCom has the SAP R/3 system installed. The modules used are Payroll, Finance, Manufacturing, and Sales and Distribution.

SecSys

SecSys is owned by an American company, and operates in the UK under the service support sector. There are around 25 offices of SecSys in the UK. SecSys has the SAP (R/3, version 3.1h) ERP system, which was installed in November 1998 in order to overcome the millennium issue. The modules of SAP that are currently used are Finance, Logistics, Materials Management, Inventory Management, Purchasing, Sales and Distribution. The company's intention within the next 2 years is to update their ERP system.

CASE EVIDENCE AND ANALYSIS

The field study data from the companies were analyzed based on the categories of control and drift, which are central to our research. The analysis also drew on the notions of the intentionality of human agency (users), and the affordances of the machine agency of the Enterprise System. Human agency in the analysis below is implied by words such as "intention" and "intentionality". Machine agency is implied by words such as "afford", "enable", "constrain". Only data from the companies that are relevant to the main theme of this research are presented here.

Before examining the actual use of the Enterprise System, our research data indicated that there are also factors which influence its use, and which are discussed next. The examination of these factors comes mostly from TransCom, due to the larger number of interviews carried out in that company.

Factors Impacting Enterprise System Use

Cultural and Organizational Context

In TransCom there was a global group responsible for the implementation and maintenance of the ERP system worldwide, named ERPGlobal. They interfaced with the UK via a local country group named ITUK. Within the sites examined in this research, there were some negative views about the ITUK team, as well as about ERPGlobal. As ERPGlobal wanted to keep the configuration and use of the ERP system as standard worldwide, it was very hesitant in carrying out updates to it, unless those would affect the majority of countries where the system was installed. Even in cases where updates were agreed by ERPGlobal however, those took a very long time to implement according to the users, and this was viewed negatively.

However, as most users in the UK interfaced with the ITUK team directly, and not with ERPGlobal, most of the negative criticisms were directed towards the ITUK team. This tended to put the ITUK team in an awkward position, as they needed sanctioning from ERPGlobal to carry out user requests, but ERPGlobal was reluctant to give its consent in many matters in order to avoid deviation from standards regarding the configuration and use of SAP. As a result, many users who did not have interaction with ERPGlobal blamed the ITUK team for being unresponsive to their needs, slow and inefficient. Some times there were tensions between users and the ITUK team, as well as between the ITUK team and ERPGlobal.

In addition, the ITUK team claimed that they were also understaffed, with the result that they could not respond very quickly to user requests. This impacted training as well, and one common complaint from most users of the system was that they had not received enough training, and that either they did not understand how the system worked, or could not use it to its full potential. As a result, the ITUK team who was responsible for training was seen as quite irresponsible and unresponsive with regards to the training needs of the users.

There were also cultural reasons which could influence the use of the system. For example, the implementation of SAP gave TransCom the opportunity to record and control time, and how long it actually took to do a job on a train. Nevertheless, the employees at the Manchester depot refused to do this when SAP was initially implemented at their site. On closer examination however, it was revealed that they would refuse to do this anyway, whether there was the SAP system or not. The intention of not recording time was a strong cultural aspect, but it was also local to the specific area. This refusal to record working times at the Manchester depot was in fact mentioned to be tied to contracts of employment and the influence of trade unions.

Resistance

In addition, when the SAP system was installed in TransCom, there was resistance to the system at various levels. Part of middle managers and users did not use the system fully. In order to overcome this, initial training regarding the system was carried out, in order for the employees to understand what the system could offer. However, there was still resistance from middle managers to fully use SAP as a management tool. SAP was seen by many managers in TransCom as a financial overhead, and consequently there was not a lot of enthusiasm in supporting it.

This also had on impact on the users of the system. Resistance was evident there, also because users were used to the old systems installed in TransCom, some of which were still operational. In that sense, there was resistance of SAP, also fuelled by the fact that many of the users were considered as technophobes, and were not used to computing systems. The main complaints about the system were then that the system was difficult to use, was not user friendly, and users did not understand what all the fields and text in SAP were used for. To this lack of knowledge and apprehension of the system also contributed the general lack of proper training. However, this type of resistance was considered normal, and seen to be overcome once the users felt more confident with the system:

That's just the normal resistance to a new system, because a lot of the people had other systems, which they knew and they were confident, and they knew what they could get out of them. And so it's just this transition to another system that they've got to learn and understand. But I'm sure once they can understand it, once they can use it, they'll be quite happy with it. (Reliability Group Leader, TransCom)

Implementation History

The implementation of SAP was also the impetus for creating a new business unit within TransCom, whose aim was to stock and supply the depots in the UK (and especially the West Coast area) with spare parts for trains. This was important, as TransCom did not have a proper parts business to deal with spare parts for trains, and therefore it also did not have the systems to manage the spare parts.

As a result, the business processes were written around the system, in order to make the system work. The system was conceived and implemented by a consultancy company, who looked at what the business strategy was, and the processes that TransCom required. They then tailored SAP to suit the business needs of the company at the time SAP was implemented, in terms of for example the order processes, purchasing, inventory, warehouse, and logistics.

As a parts business did not exist before, people within TransCom did not know in detail how the business should be supported by the ERP system. The consultancy company therefore implemented their own ideas to a large degree, resulting in a system that was according to the views of many interviewees very inadequate. The consultancy company was thought to be responsible for this, having implemented the system:

They [the consultancy company] thought they knew how to implement a spare parts management system in SAP, we did not have the expertise here in-house, which meant that they were always able to convince the people they were dealing with what the right answers were. And it was a very poor implementation. (Logistics Director, TransCom)

Power Differentials

During the implementation of SAP some employees of TransCom were released in order to participate in the implementation and contribute their business experience towards the development of the system. Many of these people did not have any proper training at all in SAP, but got to know it from working together with the consultants. Although those TransCom employees were released back to the business when the implementation of SAP finished, their experience of the system gained during its implementation made them become perceived as SAP experts by other users of the system:

And whilst the consultants were here for 3 months helping other people load their data, I sat with the consultants, learning the system, saying, right, if I do this, how does that happen, how do I do this, and things like that. And just general questions, saying, right, there's more information to get. One thing led to another, and I became one of the, sort of, SAP experts within the business. (Business Improvement Coordinator, TransCom)

As a result of gaining SAP technical knowledge, the perceived SAP experts at TransCom became the first point of contact when users had problems with the system, as opposed to logging their problems with the ITUK team, and the ITUK team then trying to identify what the solution would be. The help of the perceived SAP experts was asked as they could go to the users' desk quite quickly to see what the problem was, and explain to them what they were doing wrong. However, the business rules indicated that in case of problems users should be contacting the ITUK team in the first place. By bypassing those rules and seeking the help of the perceived SAP experts instead, the power of the latter was increased in the company, as they could influence the way that the ERP system was used by other users. This meant that the perceived SAP experts could direct the agency of other users in terms of the way they were using the system. If the directions given to the users were right, then the intended control from using the system would be re-enacted, if the directions given to them were flawed, then it would be possible that drift would be propagated, by the end users using the system incorrectly.

Having described some factors that could influence the use of the ERP system, the next section discusses the various ways that organizational control from the use of the Enterprise System could be enacted. Results from all the companies examined are presented, although TransCom provided the biggest case study of this research.

Organizational Control from Enterprise System Use

The case analyses indicated that amongst the managerial intentions for installing an Enterprise System, and the purpose of its configuration, was to increase control of the company's operations. Control was implemented with a variety of mechanisms in the Enterprise System. Those were the setting of access controls, the monitoring capabilities of the Enterprise System, the rules and procedures (process flow) that were embedded in the Enterprise System, and various checks carried out by the system.

Control from Access Profiles

With regards to the access profiles that specified which types of users had access to different types of information in the system, it could happen that those controls were either too strict, or too lax. In this sense, there were two ways by which those access controls could be changed: The first was to redefine what a particular access level allowed a person to do, and the second was that an individual could be given a less or more open type of user access. In general however, the system controls implemented through access profiles were seen to be quite strict at NGlobe, making it difficult to bypass them:

In terms of bypassing controls, the only ways to bypass a control are either to be given somebody else's password, or to do it in cahoots with somebody else. (Cash Management and Treasury Process Director, NGlobe)

At the time of the interviews there were many complaints from the users with regards to the setting of those profiles. Most of those complaints had to do with the limited access to screens and transactions in the system, when access was required, but was not given due to the incorrect setting of access levels. As one interviewee mentioned:

That's quite annoying for me, because I have the information that I need to put into SAP, I've got the information of how to do it, but I'm not given the access to it, because someone has made the decision that only one person in the company is allowed to do it. (Shift Planner, TransCom)

On the other hand, users also pointed out that although needed access was unnecessarily limited in many cases, there were also many other cases where users were allowed to carry out tasks in the system, which they did not necessarily need to. This increased access to the system was mainly due to the inattention that was paid to the correct setting of the access profiles. The result was that the intended controls in the system were seen to be very lax in some cases, because people had authorizations to do many things outside their immediate area.

In some cases users "abused" their increased access, because it was easier for them to do a transaction in the system themselves that they should not be doing, rather than asking the person that should be carrying out that transaction. As one interviewee mentioned:

For example, if there is something to be posted in the material master, because they [users outside the Materials Management area] have got authorisation and they've got some knowledge of the material master, they think, right, OK, I'll do it myself, rather than going to somebody who's got better knowledge, and say, right, OK, can you add this so I can carry on with my processing. (Business Improvement Coordinator, TransCom)

Control from Monitoring Capabilities of the Enterprise System

Our interviews indicated that the managerial intention of increased control through the use of an Enterprise System was also afforded by the monitoring capabilities of the Enterprise System. In this case the system tagged user actions in the system with information about who carried out a transaction. This could be examined if the need arose, and that was deemed beneficial by some of the interviewees:

You can see who's carried out the transaction, and you can take corrective action to understand why it happened. So, the system allows that visibility, to see where things have gone wrong, who's made what transactions, who's done what purchasing. (Purchasing Manager, SecSys)

The monitoring capabilities of the Enterprise System also resulted in power differentials, as people who were allowed to see the actions of other users in the system, had authority over the latter. In some cases, this could lead to uncertainties about how the information obtained by monitoring user actions in the system was used. As some users of the system mentioned:

I think people can use [monitoring] to their own advantage. Sometimes there's too much information there, if you make a mistake or whatever, it can be used to the wrong advantage, which I am not too happy about... It's there; it can be done. That's the worrying thing (Shift Planning Coordinator, TransCom).

The thing with SAP though, it's the traceability. If we were trying to bypass the system, it's all traceable. You can look into who did that, what changes you've made, they will come and hit you if you do try and bypass anything, because that's one thing with SAP, it doesn't lie, does it? It's got to put your name against everything, every time. (Inventory Planner 1, TransCom)

This apprehension with regards to monitoring of user actions in the system led some users to believe that anyone with the right access could go and monitor what other users were doing in the system, and this could be used to highlight areas of inefficiencies with respect to the work carried out by them. This was seen quite negatively by those users, who considered the system to be the means of giving people the opportunity to spy on other people's work, and then used for blaming them if something went wrong.

This apprehension of the system was also confirmed in the case of recording hours for a particular job done on a train in TransCom. Although this required the inputting of individual hours for each user that worked on a train, the company was only interested in the total amount of time it took to do a job, rather than how much each individual spent in doing that job. However, users seemed hesitant to follow the recommended procedure of inputting hours worked in the system, as they could not see the business benefit of it, and were worried about how their data would be used:

You have to record the individual's clock number. And that in itself is problematic, because you are identifying a particular individual, and they may think, oh well, you know, that's a bit too Big Brother, you're watching my every movement. But at the end of the day, we're not, as a business interested that it takes one man 20 minutes, but it takes another man 30 minutes to do a job. So, as a business we need to know that it took X man-hours for a particular job altogether. (SAP Facilitator 2, TransCom)

Control from Enterprise System's Process Flow

Our interviews also indicated that another way control was exercised through an Enterprise System was by the rules and procedures afforded by such a system. This meant that certain workflows were carried out in a certain order, and the output of one stage in the workflow was used as the input in the next stage. Therefore, the Enterprise System forced users in one department to complete their work before users in another department could start with their own work. This mechanism of forcing users to work in a certain way was mentioned by many managers, characteristically:

ERPs force you to undertake business in a certain way. And when I say force you, I mean the fact that you have to put a workflow in, to determine that these are the activities that need to be placed... Now you have a workflow, you put a control in. (Supply Chain Manager 2, TechniCom)

This mechanism [of ERP process flow] enables us to ensure that nothing goes on to the lorries to be delivered, unless it's also been flagged as having been physically finished within the factory. (IT Manager, FCom)

Control from System Checks

SAP in TransCom was configured to carry out various checks that would ensure the quality and integrity of data in the system. For example, users were constrained from inputting an invoice twice. This could occur for example when users tried to create an invoice as a copy of the original one. In this case the system would check whether an invoice for the particular work and customer already existed, and come up with a warning about this. This would stop the user from entering a duplicate invoice, and was seen as a good control mechanism in SAP, in terms of minimizing duplication of data.

Another example of checks carried out by the system was if VAT on invoices was entered (manually) incorrectly, which would result in an incorrect total balance in the end. This could happen more at month ends, when users at finance would be busy trying to input everything in the system. In this case mistakes would be more possible than other periods, and so the relative financial journals would not balance in SAP. The checking of the balance across various ledgers was done automatically by the clicking of a button, and if there were any mistakes SAP would come up with a warning saying that the changes could not be posted in the system because the relative journals would not balance. Other smaller-scale examples of checks carried out by the system also included the format of the fields entered (e.g. for numbers, dates, etc), the range of the values the field could accept, etc.

Although the system provided those checks to ensure a level of quality of the data that was input into the system, in other cases the system was not capable of carrying out some checks that users deemed necessary. For example, when an item needed to be returned as broken to the supplier, it needed to be recorded into the system as such. However, there were no checks that the item was not accidentally booked into the good stock, although it was declared as broken in the system. The users in the workshops in this case deemed it necessary to have a warning message coming up that would inform them that they were trying to book broken parts into good stock. However, the system as it was did not carry out those checks, and would let the users carry on. This was actually an example of drift that could occur instead of control due to required checks not being supported by the enterprise system.

In general however the four mechanisms described above (access profiles, monitoring capabilities, process flow, and system checks) aided the managerial intention to enhance control over the company's operations. The control mechanisms then applied on the users of the system and the way they carried out their work. However, while users worked on the system, it was possible that some degree of drift could occur. Our analysis indicated that this might be due to the configuration of the system, which could allow the omission of important information, as well as possibly allowing the bypassing or work-around of controls by users; the use of systems outside the Enterprise System was also identified as conducive to drift. Each of these factors will be examined in turn below, with relevant evidence from the companies quoted.

Organizational Drift from Enterprise System Use

System Configuration

Based on our analysis, it was evident that the actual configuration of the system was quite important in ensuring that the required controls were properly implemented. If the controls described in the previous section were not correctly configured, this could result in users taking actions in the system that they shouldn't, and this could have a "ripple" effect to other departments. For example, as one interviewee mentioned, lax system controls allowed individuals to carry out transactions in the system that they were not allowed to, and this had an impact on various departments of the company:

Somebody from the other sites went and built some transaction on my site the other day, which messed up my stock basically ... [The impact of this transaction would be] financial, because the figures wouldn't have matched. (Materials Controller 1, TransCom)

However, the system could be intentionally configured to allow more lax controls, in order to cater for business necessities, for example:

There are benefits to being able to do it, like for example, if say, the person who places the order in another site is off sick, and there's only say, somebody here who can place the order, then that means that he can carry out the transaction. (Materials Controller 1, TransCom)

In other cases, the affordance of the system could force to choose a configuration of the system (e.g. setting of access profiles) amongst a range of limited possibilities, which did not accurately reflect the needs of the company. In this case, drift could occur if the intention to use the system in other than the prescribed ways was there. As one interviewee mentioned:

Say for instance with the guys out the back who change bin locations, that means they've got access to the material master. So they can change it if they want to. But unfortunately you can't separately set it so that they can only view it. They've got access to it or not. So if they wanted to, not that they would, but they have access to change anything. (Materials Controller 2, TransCom)

The way that the system was configured, according to the business necessities and what was afforded by it, could result in users using it in other than the prescribed ways, by working around intended controls, or not inputting important information in the system. Those two reasons for drift are now presented below.

Bypassing or Workaround of Controls

Our analysis indicated that organizational drift could arise from users bypassing the system controls, or working around them. The degree to which they could do this was enabled or constrained by the properties of the Enterprise System. It also depended on how the access profiles in the system were configured. For example, as one interviewee mentioned, although access to information on one screen was not allowed, the same information could be obtained by accessing an alternative screen:

Now, if I go into Oracle inquiry for Accounts Receivable for example, I can see invoice information, but I can't see credits in there... If I go into Business Objects with my inquiry access, it runs invoices and credits and it does so pretty happily. So I can get them that way. (Cash Management and Treasury Process Director, NGlobe)

Although there might not have been intention in doing so, controls could still be bypassed unconsciously, because it was easier to bypass them than follow the prescribed ways of working with the system. For example, although access controls could be imposed with the use of usernames and passwords, if those were shared by the employees then the intended controls lost their meaning:

Everybody has their own login. But if say there were 4 or 5 of us on duty today, somebody wouldn't come to it and log on, we'd use whatever was in, just for speed. I suppose really, if I walk away from it, I should log off, and the next person who comes would log in. But it just takes time to keep logging off and logging in when you're busy. (Materials Planner, TransCom)

Using one log-in for everybody in the workshop essentially meant that the intended controls in the system were bypassed by the users. If a generic logon approach was followed, then it would be difficult to tell who was or was not using the system. It would also be impossible if the need arose to identify in the system which user actually carried out a transaction.

In addition, in the implementation of SAP at TransCom there existed a "source list", which contained the suppliers from which the company could buy items required for the maintenance and repairing of trains. The source list existing in the system was created and maintained by the system administrators at ITUK, and a block was put in the system to disallow other users from amending it, so that only authorised suppliers identified in the source list could be used to buy materials from. However, users identified a way to bypass this, by creating a new source list in the system, rather than using the one created for them by the ITUK team. This meant that they could effectively include any supplier in their own source list, and buy from any of them, without reference to the approved suppliers in the ITUK-maintained source list.

Missing Information

From the interviews carried out we realised that users could choose not to enter important information in the system. This might be due to lack of this information, or users resisting the system by not inputting this information. It could also be because users didn't understand the workings of the system, and the impact that their inaction of inputting that information had on other departments and the company as a whole. If important information was missing in the system, negative organizational consequences were certain to occur. In this case, money might be lost, as one interviewee indicated:

There are vehicles coming to our depot, and we don't know who's sending them. There's no contract set up for them, so the commercial department can't allocate working hours... We did quite a lot of work for these customers, but we don't have any idea who to bill, or how to get the money back, or how much. (Production Planner, TransCom)

One way to overcome the effects of missing information in the system was by introducing mandatory fields, or using the affordances of the system to carry out checks that this information was there. However, although appealing this approach might seem, there were practical considerations that would make it unworkable:

If it was for me, I would say, make all the fields mandatory, and you have to fill them all in. In the real world, you could never do that. There are time constraints for one, availability of information, two. So you would have the end user who wouldn't use the system. (SAP Facilitator, TransCom)

The quality of information that was input into the system was generally recognised as very important for the correct functioning of the system:

I think the big problem we've got with SAP at the moment is the quality of data being entered. I think there is a perception that nobody is using SAP, for once the information is entered, it's forgotten, it's never used again. And therefore a lot of the information that gets put in is completely rubbish. And that can only be changed by the people using it, there's nothing SAP could do to make that any better, that's entirely human. (Reliability Group Leader, TransCom)

In addition to the issue of the quality of information that was input into the system, the timing of inputting that information was also important. For example, due to the vast number of jobs done on trains in TransCom and the associated number of service orders, work on a train could start before the relevant service order was created in SAP. If this mistake was realised later on the same day or the next day, this could be too late, as the train would be repaired by then, and left the depot. This would then mean that it would be difficult to identify without any records what work was done on a train. Even worst, if this mistake was not found at all and the service order was not created, then the train would have been repaired for free, without charging the customer for it.

Use of External Systems

In all of the companies examined, most of their reporting requirements were carried out by extracting data from the system and inputting them for manipulation into Excel. In SecSys for example, a key process within the supply chain was customer order satisfaction, examining where the company was able to satisfy customer orders within the delivery time that the customer wanted. The relevant data was extracted from SAP into Excel in this case, in order to produce a management report that was presented on a monthly basis to senior management. Similarly in TransCom, some of the reports that were running included for example the number of open and closed service orders in a given period, the number of purchase invoices processed per site, number of materials issued, received or transferred in a certain period, etc.

Although some of the reports taken directly out of the system would give all the information that was needed, the layout would generally be not right for showing those reports to management; therefore the need to manipulate these data in Excel. Excel in this case was considered more advanced, in terms of being able to summarize and carry out calculations on the data, produce graphs, manage the layout, etc. However, by taking data out of the ERP system and manipulating them in another piece of software (Excel) that did not impose access restrictions, data could be (intentionally or unintentionally) falsified, producing erroneous results. If this occurred, then control over the accuracy and truthfulness of those data would be lost, and drift would occur:

You have that functionality, it's very good, you can export it [data from the system]. The problem is, that you can then manipulate the data [in Excel] into any way you want, you know, anyhow you want. And for me, that's potential loss of control, because, OK, if you imagine, 2 groups of people are producing the same data in theory, manipulating it slightly differently, and potentially you turn up with 2 individuals at the same meeting, with 2 different sets of data. (SAP Facilitator 2, TransCom)

The use of Excel was also not always a panacea for the production of reports. Users had to know Excel quite well, in order to be able to manipulate the data coming out of the Enterprise System. In the Materials Management area in TransCom for example, the output from more than one areas of SAP had to be extracted at a time, and each of those outputs had to be entered into an Excel spreadsheet and then combined using specialist functions such as vlookup. This was seen to be too complicated and time-consuming to do, distracting the users from the main job that they should be doing, rather than having to learn complex functions in Excel to manipulate the data that were taken out of the system.

DISCUSSION AND THEORY DEVELOPMENT

In this section we draw on the analysis presented above on the ways control and drift can occur, as well as our theoretical concepts of disembedding / reembedding and human and machine agencies, in order to develop our theoretical conceptualisation that explains the processes that lead to control and drift within the context of an Enterprise System.

Human and Machine Agencies

The actual use of the system in the analysis of the five companies can be conceptualised by the interplay between human and machine agencies. A human agency position in the use of the Enterprise System in this case assumes that humans (Enterprise System users in this case) could choose to use the system minimally, invoke it according to needs, or improvise in ways that could produce unanticipated consequences (Boudreau & Robey, 2005; Orlikowski, 2000). On the other hand, machine agency is assumed to embody rules guiding human action, limiting choice alternatives and monitoring human action (Boudreau & Robey, 2005; Winner, 1977; Zuboff, 1988). Although machines themselves are products of human agency (when the development stage is considered), when they are installed and left to operate they then become constraints or enablers of human agency (Boudreau & Robey, 2005; Nandhakumar et al., 2005; Rose et al., 2003).

In other words, the assumption in the handling of agency in this chapter is that human (user) agency is characterised by intentionality to perform certain actions in the system, while machine (system) agency is characterised by affording (enabling or constraining) the intended human actions in the system. This position follows amongst others the works of Jones (1999), Rose and Jones (2004) and Rose et al. (2003), who argue that by defining agency as the "capacity to make a difference" (Giddens, 1984), both machines and humans can be viewed as possessing agency. However, humans have intentionality and self and social awareness, which result in capabilities for interpretation of particular situations and actions. Machines however lack those capabilities (at least to a large degree relative to humans and based on current technologies).

Embedding-Disembedding of Human Agency

In this chapter we argue that human agency can also be further elaborated into the disembedding and reembedding of user actions in the system. This refers to the ways that actions of one user are disembedded to other users, and these actions then being reembedded by them as input for their own work in the system. The disembedding of actions in this case can be linked to data input by users in the system, and the reembedding of actions can be linked to data use by users of the system. Disembedded actions refer to users in one department using the system to carry out a transaction (such as finance giving authorisation to do the stock count). This action then gets disembedded for example from the finance area to other departments or users concerned (for example the Materials Management area). This disembedded action then gets reembedded locally (in this case by the Materials Management users) in terms of being able to use it as input for their own work (in this case carrying out the stock count).

The disembedding and reembedding of human actions in the system can be seen to be facilitated by the workflow that is inscribed in the Enterprise System, and the single database that enables monitoring of user actions. Authorisations for the disembedding and reembedding of information are then made possible with the use of access profiles that specify which users could disembed and reembed various pieces of information in the system. Because of the workflow inscribed in the ERP system, the disembedding and reembedding of information could be seen to operate in cycles, i.e. the output of one phase of the workflow being used as the input in the next phase of the workflow. This would also mean that an action of a user in the system would impact other users of the system, in a cause and effect, or action/consequence manner.

However, we argue that the employment of the disembedding/reembedding concepts goes a step further from simply describing cause and effect. Due to the global and integrative nature of the Enterprise System, the action of a user in the system is not simply the cause for another action by another user, but also entails visibility across geographical, functional and time dimensions. This means that the disembedded action in the system is recorded, and could be examined by authorised users in other locations of the company, in other functional areas, or in the future if need arose. This action therefore then ceases to be local, but is "disembedded" across time and space.

As discussed, the disembedding and reembedding of human actions in the system can be seen to be facilitated by the machine agency of the Enterprise System. For example, the fact that the system consists of a single global database enables the user actions to be disembedded in terms of being visible to other users. The single database also enables other users to view disembedded actions in the system and reembed them, in terms of using them as the input for their own work. The disembedding and reembedding of human actions can also be seen to be facilitated by the workflow and access controls in the ERP system, which specify which actions users could take in the system in order for them to be disembedded, and to which other users those actions would impact upon, in terms of those actions being reembedded by them.

When the user actions in the system are disembedded however, any errors, omissions or inconsistencies by the user are disembedded as well. This could have a "ripple" effect to the company's operations as a whole, and therefore drift might occur. As has been discussed in the analysis section, this drift might occur because of the system configuration, which could allow for missing information in the system, the bypassing of controls by users, or the use of external systems such as Excel.

Conceptualisation of Enterprise System Use and Organizational Consequences (Control and Drift)

The figure below presents our conceptualisation of the organizational impact (classified as control or drift) of the use of Enterprise Systems, according to the data we gathered from the case study companies and the theoretical frameworks that we employed.

Although the factors from Enterprise System use in Figure 1 are shown to lead to organizational control and/or drift, this result is in essence the interpretation of the researcher according to the unique context where these factors are identified. It can be argued for example however, that the same factors could be interpreted in another way in a different context.

For example, while missing information was interpreted as resulting in organizational drift, it could be argued that such missing information was the outcome of users not inputting the required information in order to signal problems with the system or data incompatibilities, and this could be viewed as a control factor (e.g. Kavanagh, 2004; Marakas & Hornik, 1996; Markus, 1983). Similarly, with the case of the monitoring of user actions afforded by the Enterprise System which was interpreted to lead to organizational control, in other contexts it could potentially lead to users resisting the system. In this sense, some users in TransCom have expressed their perception of the visibility offered by the ERP system as a kind of "Big Brother". Although these users were subsequently educated and trained to use the system, the visibility functionality of the ERP system could otherwise potentially result in user resistance which would be detrimental to the company (Kossek et al., 1994; Martinko et al., 1996), and which would therefore cause organizational drift as far as the use of the system is concerned. As such, the interpreted nature of the factors from ERP use leading to either organizational control or drift must be mentioned, which depends on the context where these factors are encountered.

The importance of this conceptualisation then does not lies in enumerating the various factors affecting ERP use, as well as the factors from ERP use leading to either control or drift. The importance of the conceptualisation lies more in sensitizing the reader with regards to the need to examine the context where an Enterprise System is used, as well as the actual use of the system and its outcome in terms of organizational control and drift. This means that when examining the use of an ERP system, the factors impacting its use must be examined, as well as the affordances of the system, the actions of users in the system, and the interdependencies between actions of different users (through the disembedding and reembedding of those actions).

CONCLUSION AND IMPLICATIONS

The aim of this chapter has been to present and theorize the impact of actions related to an Enterprise System on organizational control and drift. We have taken an agency perspective, where humans (users) and machine (the Enterprise System) both possess and exhibit agency. We have based our conceptualisation on the assumption that the Enterprise System acts by affording (enabling or constraining) states of control and drift. We have also based our conceptualisation on the assumption that human actions are characterised by intentionality, and have shown that those actions can be embedded and disembedded, consequently having an impact on organizational control and drift.

Our findings draw upon and complement the findings by Hanseth et al. (2001), where side effects can lead to loss of control (drift) due to the integrative nature of an ERP, through which these side effects are "rippled". We have enhanced this understanding by arguing that drift can occur through the disembedding and reembedding of user actions in the system (see Figure 1). Our results also refine Boudreau & Robey (2005), who argue that although ERPs can constrain human agency, this can still take place within such systems. We argue that this exercise of human agency from the part of users can lead to drift, as shown in Figure 1. Finally, we argue that the concept of panoptic empowerment as identified by Elmes et al. (2005), occurs through the disembedding and consequent reembedding of user actions in the system.

For practitioners, our findings indicate that attention needs to be paid to the setting of access profiles, according to what is afforded by the system. Attention should also be paid to the actual configuration of the system, to minimize the bypassing of controls and the unwanted or unauthorised use of the system, which can lead to drift. The importance of inputting required information in the system should also be emphasized to employees, although the system may not force users to enter it. This also links to user training in order to increase the understanding of the system. If users don't understand how the system works and how their actions in the system impact other users, then errors, omissions or inconsistencies will keep occurring and the effects of those will be "rippled" across the company, resulting in drift.

On the other hand, too tight controls in the system can reduce the resiliency of the company to respond to future challenges and adapt to new realities (Ignatiadis & Nandhakumar, 2005). In that sense, some degree of calculated drift may be beneficial, as long as it is not caused by inadvertent or uninformed user

Figure 1. The impact of enterprise systems on control and drift: A human and machine agency perspective through the embedding and disembedding of human actions

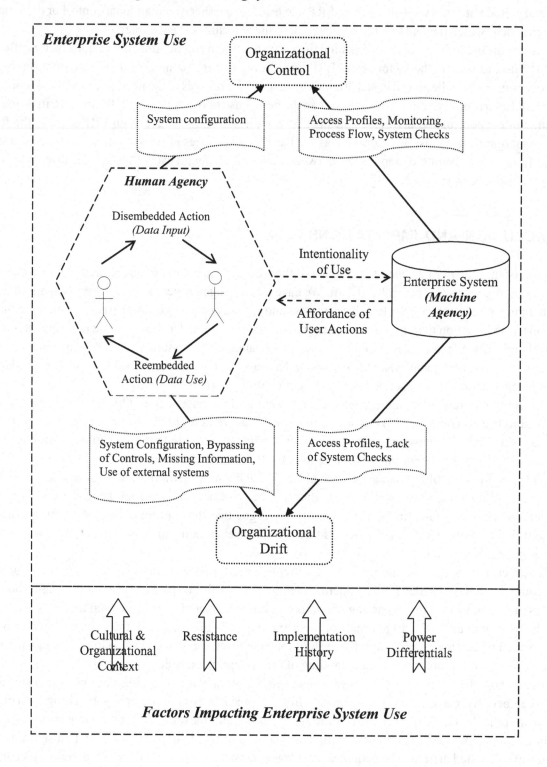

actions. The thin line between control and drift is different for each company, and depends on factors internal and external to it. Our model presents an understanding of the processes that lead to control and drift, so that managers can tailor these processes according to the idiosyncrasies of their companies.

REFERENCES

Akkermans, H., & van Helden, K. (2002). Vicious and virtuous cycles in ERP implementation: a case study of interrelations between critical success factors. *European Journal of Information Systems, 11*(1), 35-46.

Al-Mashari, M., & Al-Mudimigh, A. (2003). Enterprise Resource Planning: A taxonomy of critical factors. *European Journal of Operational Research, 146*(2), 352-364.

Bernroider, E., & Koch, S. (1999). *Decision making for ERP investments from the perspective of organizational impact - Preliminary results from an empirical study.* Paper presented at the 5th Americas conference on information systems, Milwaukee, WI, USA.

Besson, P., & Rowe, F. (2001). ERP project dynamics and enacted dialogue: perceived understanding, perceived leeway, and the nature of task-related conflicts. *The DataBase for Advances in Information Systems, 32*(4), 47-65.

Bingi, P., Sharma, M. K., & Godla, J. (1999). Critical Issues Affecting an ERP Implementation. *Information Systems Management, 16*(3), 7-14.

Bloomfield, B. P., & Coombs, R. (1992). Information Technology, Control and Power: The Centralization and Decentralization Debate Revisited. *Journal of Management Studies, 29*(4), 459-484.

Bloomfield, B. P., Coombs, R., & Owen, J. (1994). The social construction of information systems - the implications for management control. In R. Mansell (Ed.), *Management of Information and Communication Technologies - Emerging Patterns of Control* (pp. 143-157). London: Aslib.

Boudreau, M.-C., & Robey, D. (1999). *Organizational transition to enterprise resource planning systems: theoretical choices for process research.* Paper presented at the 20th International Conference on Information Systems, Charlotte, North Carolina, United States.

Boudreau, M.-C., & Robey, D. (2005). Enacting Integrated Information Technology: A Human Agency Perspective. *Organization Science, 16*(1), 3-18.

Ciborra, C. U. (2000). A Critical Review of the Literature on the Management of Corporate Information Infrastructure. In C. U. Ciborra, K. Braa, A. Cordella, B. Dahlbom, A. Failla, O. Hanseth, V. Hepso, J. Ljungberg, E. Monteiro & K. A. Simon (Eds.), *From Control to Drift - The Dynamics of Corporate Information Infrastructures* (pp. 15-40). Oxford: Oxford University Press.

Ciborra, C. U. (2002). *The Labyrinths of Information: Challenging the Wisdom of Systems.* Oxford: Oxford University Press.

Coombs, R., Knights, D., & Willmott, H. C. (1992). Culture, Control and Competition; Towards a Conceptual Framework for the Study of Information Technology in Organizations. *Organization Studies, 13*(1), 51-72.

Duane, A., & Finnegan, P. (2003). Managing empowerment and control in an intranet environment. *Information Systems Journal, 13*(2), 133-158.

Elmes, M. B., Strong, D. M., & Volkoff, O. (2005). Panoptic empowerment and reflective conformity in enterprise systems-enabled organizations. *Information and Organization, 15*(1), 1-37.

Gattiker, T. F., & Goodhue, D. L. (2004). Understanding the local-level costs and benefits of ERP through organizational information processing theory. *Information & management, 41*(4), 431-443.

Gibson, J. J. (1979). *The ecological approach to visual perception.* Boston: Houghton Mifflin.

Giddens, A. (1984). *The Constitution of Society: Outline of the Theory of Structuration.* Cambridge: Polity Press.

Giddens, A. (1990). *The Consequences of Modernity.* Cambridge: Polity Press.

Glaser, B. G., & Strauss, A. (1967). *The discovery of grounded theory: Strategies for qualitative research.* New York: Aldine.

Hanseth, O., Ciborra, C. U., & Braa, K. (2001). The Control Devolution: ERP and the Side Effects of Globalization. *The DataBase for Advances in Information Systems, 32*(4), 34-46.

Holland, C. P., & Light, B. (1999). A critical success factors model for ERP implementation. *IEEE Software 1999*, 30-36.

Hong, K. K., & Kim, Y. G. (2002). The critical success factors for ERP implementation: an organizational fit perspective. *Information & management, 40*, 25-40.

Ignatiadis, I., Nandhakumar, J. (2007). The impact of Enterprise Systems on organizational resilience. *Journal of Information Technology, 22*(1), 36-43.

Jones, M. R. (1999). Information Systems and the Double Mangle: Steering a Course between the Scylla of Embedded Structure and the Charybdis of Strong Symmetry. In T. J. Larsen, L. Levine, J. I. DeGross (Eds.), *Information Systems: Current Issues and Future Changes* (pp. 287-302). New York: OmniPress.

Kallinikos, J. (2004). Deconstructing information packages: Organizational and behavioural implications of ERP systems. *Information Technology & People, 17*(1), 8-30.

Kavanagh, J. F. (2004). Resistance as Motivation for Innovation: Open Source Software. *Communications of the Association for Information Systems, 13*, 615-628.

Koch, C. (2001). BPR and ERP: Realising a vision of process with IT. *Business Process Management Journal, 7*(3), 258-265.

Kossek, E. E., Young, W., Gash, D., & Nichol, V. (1994). Waiting for Innovation in the Human Resources Department: Godot Implements a Human Resource Information System. *Human Resource Management, 33*(1), 135-160.

Legare, T. L. (2002). The role of organizational factors in realizing ERP benefits. *Information Systems Management, 19*(4), 21.

Malone, T. W. (1997). Is Empowerment Just a Fad? Control, Decision Making, and IT. *Sloan Management Review, 38*(2), 23-35.

Marakas, G. M., & Hornik, S. (1996). Passive Resistance Misuse: Overt Support and Covert Recalcitrance in IS Implementation. *European Journal of Information Systems, 5*(3), 208-220.

Markus, M. L. (1983). Power, Politics, and MIS Implementation. *Communications of the ACM, 26*(6), 430-444.

Markus, M. L., & Tanis, C. (2000). The Enterprise Systems experience - From adoption to success. In R. W. Zmud (Ed.), *Framing the domains of IT management: Projecting the future through the past.* Cincinnati, OH: Pinnaflex Educational Resources, Inc.

Martin, I., & Cheung, Y. (2000). SAP and Business Process Reengineering. *Business Process Management, 6*(2), 131-121.

Martinko, M. J., Henry, J. W., & Zmud, R. W. (1996). An attributional explanation of individual resistance to the introduction of information technologies in the workplace. *Behaviour & Information Technology, 15*(5), 313-330.

Miles, M. B., & Huberman, A. M. (1994). *Qualitative Data Analysis* (2nd ed.). Thousand Oaks, California: Sage Publications.

Nah, F. F., Lau, J. L., & Kuang, J. (2001). Critical factors for successful implementation of enterprise systems. *Business Process Management Journal, 7*(3), 285-296.

Nandhakumar, J., Rossi, M., & Talvinen, J. (2005). The dynamics of contextual forces of ERP implementation. *Journal of Strategic Information Systems, 14*(2), 221-242.

Newell, S., Huang, J. C., Galliers, R. D., & Pan, S. L. (2003). Implementing Enterprise Resource Planning and knowledge management systems in tandem: fostering efficiency and innovation complementarity. *Information and Organization, 13*(1), 25-52.

Norman, D. A. (1988). *The Psychology of Everyday Things.* New York: Basic Books.

Orlikowski, W. J. (2000). Using Technology and Constituting Structures: A Practice Lens for Studying Technology in Organizations. *Organization Science, 11*(4), 404-428.

Orlikowski, W. J. (1991). Integrated Information Environment or Matrix of Control? The Contradictory Implications of Information Technology. *Accounting, Management and Information Technologies, 1*(1), 9-42.

Orlikowski, W. J., & Baroudi, J. J. (1991). Studying Information Technology in Organizations: Research Approaches and Assumptions. *Information Systems Research, 2*(1), 1-28.

Pickering, A. (1995). *The Mangle of Practice: Time, Agency and Science.* Chicago: University of Chicago Press.

Rose, J., & Jones, M. R. (2004). *The Double Dance of Agency: a socio-theoretic account of how machines and humans interact.* Paper presented at the ALOIS Workshop: Action in Language, Organizations and Information Systems, Linkoping, Sweden.

Rose, J., Jones, M. R., & Truex, D. (2003). The problem of agency: How humans act, how machines act. *Paper presented at the ALOIS Workshop: Action in Language, Organizations and Information Systems,* Linkoping University, Linkoping, Sweden.

Rose, J., & Truex, D. (2000). Machine agency as perceived autonomy; an action perspective. In R. L. Baskerville, J. Stage & J. I. DeGross (Eds.), *Organizational and Social Perspectives on Information Technology* (pp. 371–390). Aalborg, Denmark: Kluwer.

Schrnederjans, M. J., & Kim, G. C. (2003). Implementing enterprise resource planning systems with total quality control and business process reengineering survey results. *International Journal of Operations and Production Management, 23*(3/4), 418-429.

Shang, S. S. C., & Seddon, P. B. (2000). *A comprehensive framework for classifying the benefits of ERP systems.* Paper presented at the Americas Conference on Information Systems, Long Beach, California.

Shanks, G., Parr, A., Hu, B., Corbitt, B., Thanasankit, T., & Seddon, P. B. (2000). Differences in critical success factors in ERP systems implementation in Australia and China: a cultural analysis. *Paper presented at the European Conference on Information Systems,* Vienna, Austria.

Sia, S. K., Tang, M., Soh, C., & Boh, W. F. (2002). Enterprise Resource Planning (ERP) Systems as a Technology of Power: Empowerment or Panoptic Control? *The DataBase for Advances in Information Systems, 33*(1), 23-37.

Siriginidi, S. R. (2000). Enterprise Resource Planning in Reengineering Business. *Business Process Management Journal, 6*(5), 376 - 391.

Somers, T., & Nelson, K. (2001). *The Impact of Critical Success Factors across the Stages of Enterprise Resource Planning Implementations.* Paper presented at the Hawaii International Conference on Systems Sciences.

Tang, M., Sia, S. K., Soh, C., & Boh, W. F. (2000). A Contingency Analysis of Post-bureaucratic Controls in IT-related Change. *Paper presented at the 21st International Conference on Information Systems,* Brisbane, Queensland, Australia.

van Fenema, P. C., & van Baalen, P. J. (2005). *Strategies for Dealing with Drift during Implementation of ERP Systems.* Rotterdam: Erasmus Research Institute of Management.

Walsham, G. (1993). *Interpreting Information Systems in Organizations.* Chichester: John Wiley & Sons.

Walsham, G. (1995). The Emergence of Interpretivism in IS Research. *Information Systems Research, 6*(4), 376-394.

Winner, L. (1977). *Autonomous Technology. Technics-out-of-Control as a Theme in Political Thought.* London: MIT Press.

Zuboff, S. (1988). *In the Age of the Smart Machine: The Future of Work and Power*. Oxford, UK: Heinemann Professional Publishing.

Compilation of References

Abboud, L., & Vara, V. (2007, January 23). SAP Trails Nimble Start-Ups As Software Market Matures. *Wall Street Journal*, C1.

ACW Team (2004, August 23). SSA Global releases converged ERP with manufacturing capabilities. *Asia Computer Weekly*, 1.

Adam F., & O'Doherty, P. (2000). Lessons from enterprise resource planning implementation in Ireland – towards smaller and shorter ERP projects. *Journal of Information Technology*, 15, 305-316.

Adam, F., & O'Doherty, P. (2000). Lessons from enterprise resource planning implementations in Ireland—Towards smaller and shorter ERP projects. *Journal of Information Technology*, 15, 305-316.

Afsamanesh, H., Garita, C., Hertzberger, B., & Santos Silva, V. (1997). Management of distributed information in virtual enterprises - the PRODNET approach. In *ICE'97 - International Conference on Concurrent Enterprising*.

Aggarwal, R., Verma, K., Miller, J., & Milnor, W. (2004, September). Constraint Driven Web Service Composition in METEOR-S. In *IEEE International Conference on Services Computing (SCC'04)* (pp. 23–30). Los Alamitos, CA, USA: IEEE Society Press.

Aiken, P. (2002). *Enterprise resource planning (ERP) considerations*. VA, Richmond: VCU/Institute for Data Research.

Akkermans, H., & van Helden, K. (2002). Vicious and virtuous cycles in ERP implementation: a case study of interrelations between critical success factors. *European Journal of Information Systems*, 11(1), 35-46.

Aladwani, A. M. (2002). IT project uncertainty, planning and success: An empirical investigation from Kuwait. *Information Technology & People*, 15(3), 210-226.

Alajoutsijarvi, K., Moller, K., & Rosenbroijer, C-J. (1999) Relevance of Focal Nets in Understanding the Dynamics

of Business relationships. *Journal of Business-to-Business Marketing*, 6(3), 3-35.

Al-Khayyal, F. A., & Sherali, H. D. (2000). On finitely terminating branch-and-bound algorithms for some global optimization problems. *SIAM Journal on Optimization*, 10(4), 1049-1057.

Allen, R., & Garlan, D. (1994). Formalizing architectural connection. In *ICSE '94: Proceedings of the 16th international conference on Software engineering* (pp. 71–80). Los Alamitos, CA, USA: IEEE Computer Society Press.

Al-Mashari, M. (2002). Enterprise resource planning (ERP) systems: A research agenda. *Industrial Management and Data Systems*, 102(3), 165-170.

Al-Mashari, M., & Al-Mudimigh, A. (2003). Enterprise Resource Planning: A taxonomy of critical factors. *European Journal of Operational Research*, 146(2), 352-364.

Al-Mashari, M., & Al-Mudimigh, A. (2003). ERP Implementation: lessons from a case study. *Information Technology & People*, 16(1), 21-33.

Alonso, G. (1999). WISE: Business to Business e-Commerce. *In 9th workshop on research issues on data engineering (RIDE-VE'99)*. Sydney.

Alonso, G., Casati, F., Kuno, H., & Machiraju, V. (2004). *Web Services: Concepts, Architecture and Applications*. Berlin: Springer.

Alsaadi, A. (2004, January). A performance analysis approach based on the UML class diagram. In *Proc 4th International Workshop on Software and Performance: ACM SIGSOFT Software Engineering Notes*, 29(1).

Alter, S. (2000). The Siamese Twin Problem: A Central Issue Ignored by Dimensions of Information Effectiveness. *Communication of AIS*, 2(20), 1-55.

Ambriola, V., Conradi, R., & Fuggetta, A. (1997). Assessing Process-Centered Software Engineering Environments. *ACM Transactions on Software Engineering and Methodology, 6*(3), 283-328.

Amoako-Gyampah, K. (2007). Perceived Usefulness, User Involvement and Behavioral Intention: an Empirical Study of ERP Implementation. *Computers in Human Behavior, 23*, 1232-1248.

Amoako-Gyampah, K., & Salam, A. F (2004). An extension of the technology acceptance model in an ERP implementation environment. *Information & Management, 41*, 731-745.

Amoako-Gyampah, K., (2004). ERP Implementation Factors: A comparison of managerial and end-user perspectives. *Business Process Management Journal,* 10(2), 171-183.

Amoako-Gympah, K. (2005). Perceived usefulness, user involvement and behavioral intention: An empirical study of ERP implementation. *Computers in Human Behavior,* Available online January 11, 20005: http://www.sciencedirect.com/science/journal/07475632.

Amoako-Gympah, K., & Salam, A. M. (2004). An extension of the technology acceptance model in an ERP implementation environment. *Information & Management, 41*(6), 731-745.

Amrit, T., & Keil, K. (2006, August). Functionality Risk in Information Systems Development: An Empirical Investigation. *IEEE Transactions on Engineering Management, 53*(3), 412-425.

Andrews, T., Curbera, F., Dholakia, H., Goland, Y., Klein, J., Leymann, F., Liu, K., Roller, D., Smith, D., & Thatte, S. (ed.), Trickovic, I., Weerawarana, S. (2002). *Business Process Execution Language for Web Services version 1.1.*

Anerousis, N., & Panagos, E. (2002). Making voice knowledge pervasive. *IEEE Pervasive Computing, 1*(2), 42-48.

Ankolekar, A., Martin, D., McGuinness, D., McIlraith, S., Paolucci, M., & Parsia, B. (2004). *OWL-S' Relationship to Selected Other Technologies*, Technical report, W3C Member Submission 22 November 2004. Retrieved 1 Feb, 2006, from http://www.w3.org/Submission/OWL-S-related/

Anton, A. I. (1996). Goal-based requirements analysis. *In Proceedings of the 2nd Int. Conf. On Requirements Analysis, ICRE'96',* Colorado Spring, USA, pp. 136–144.

Antoniou, G., & van Harmelen, F. (2004). Web Ontology Language: OWL. In S. Staab & R. Studer (Eds.), *Handbook on Ontologies* (pp. 67-92). Berlin: Springer.

Arenas, M., & Libkin, L. (2004). A Normal Form for XML Documents. ACM Trans. Database Syst., 29.

Arinze, B., & Anandarajan, M. (2003). A framework for using OO mapping methods to rapidly configure ERP systems. Association for Computing Machinery. *Communications of the ACM, 46*(2), 61.

Arkin, A. (2002). *Business Process Modelling Language.* Retrieved 23 Aug, 2003, from http://www.bpmi.org/bpmi-downloads/BPML-SPEC-1.0.zip

Arkin, A., Askary, S., Bloch, B., Curbera, F., Goland, Y., Kartha, N., et al. (Eds.) (2005) Web *Services Business Process Execution Language Version 2.0*, Technical report, OASIS Open, Inc., Committee Draft, 21 Dec, 2005. Retrieved 15 Feb 2006 from http://www.oasis-open.org/committees/download.php/16024/wsbpel-specification-draft-Dec-22-2005.htm

Baader, F., Calvanese, D., McGuinness, D.L., Nardi, D., & Patel-Schneider, P.F. (2003). *The description logic handbook: Theory, implementation, and applications.* Cambridge University Press.

Badri, M. A., & Davis, D. (2001). A comprehensive 0–1 goal programming model for project selection. *International Journal of Project Management, 19*, 243–252.

Bair, J., & Gereffi, G. (2001). Local Clusters in Global Chains: The Causes and Consequences of Export Dynamism in Torreon's Blue Jeans Industry. *World Development, 29*(11), 1185-1903.

Bakos, J. Y. (1991) A Strategic analysis of electronics marketplaces. *MIS Quarterly, 15*(3), 295-310.

Bakos, Y. (1998). The Emerging Role of Electronic Marketplaces on the Internet. *Communications of the ACM, 41*(8), 35-42.

Baligh, H. H. (1994). Components of Culture: Nature, Interconnections, and Relevance to the Decisions on the Organization Structure. *Management Science, 40*(1), 14-27.

Ballagas, R., Borchers, J., Rohs, M., & Sheridan, J. G. (2006). The smart phone: A ubiquitous input device. *IEEE Pervasive Computing, 5*(1), 70-77.

Balsamo, S., Simeoni, M. (2001a). Deriving Performance Models from Software Architecture Specifications. *Proceedings of the 15th European Simulation Multiconference (ESM2001),* SCS - Society for Computer Simulation.

Balsamo, S., Simeoni, M. (2001b). On Transforming UML models into performance models, Technical Report Saladin Project R-SAL-51, *WTUML: Workshop on Transformations in UML*, ETAPS 2001 Satellite Event Genova, Italy, April 7th.

Bandinelli, S., Fuggetta, A., Lavazza, L., Loi, M., & Picco, G. (1995). Modelling and Improving an Industrial Software Process. *IEEE Transactions on Software Engineering, 21*(5), 440-454.

Barney, J. (1991). Firm Resources and Sustained Competitive Advantage. *Journal of Management, 17*(1), 99-120.

Barros, A., Dumas, M., & Oaks, P. (2005). *A Critical Overview of the Web Services Choreography Description Language*. BPTrends (www.bptrends.com), March 2005, pp 1-24.

Bates, LDV (2006), *Advertising Agency*. At http://www.ldv.be.

Batzarov, Z. (2004). *Orbis Latinus: Linguistic Terms*. Retrieved 3 Apr, 2005, from http://www.orbilat.com/General_References/Linguistic_Terms.html

Beatty, R. C., & Williams, C. D. (2006, March). ERP II: Best practices for successfully implementing an ERP upgrade. *Communications of ACM, 49*(3), 105-109.

Beheshti, H. M. (2006). What managers should know about ERP/ERP II. *Management Research News, 29*(4), 184-193.

Belwood, T., & et al. (2004). *UDDI version 3.0*. (Retrieved September 1st, 2005, from http://uddi.org/pubs/uddi_v3.htm)

Ben light. (2005, May). Potential pitfalls in packaged software adoption. *Communications of ACM, 48*(5), 119-120.

Berardi, D., Cabral, L., Cimpian, E., Domingue, J., Mecella, M, Stollberg, M., & Sycara, K. (2005). *ESWC Semantic Web Services Tutorial*. Retrieved 15 Feb, 2006, from http://stadium.open.ac.uk/dip/

Bernardi, S., Donatelli, S., & Merseguer, J. (2002). From UML sequence diagrams and statecharts to analysable Petri net models. In *Proc. 3rd International Workshop on Software and Performance*, Rome, Italy, 35 – 45.

Berners-Lee, T., Hendler, J., & Lassila, O. (2001). *The Semantic Web*. Scientific American, 284(5), 34-43.

Bernroider, E., & Koch, S. (1999). *Decision making for ERP investments from the perspective of organizational*

impact - *Preliminary results from an empirical study*. Paper presented at the 5th Americas conference on information systems, Milwaukee, WI, USA.

Bernroider, E., & Koch, S. (2001). ERP selection process in midsize and large organizations. Business Process Management Journal, *7*(3), 251-257.

Berre, A.-J., Elvesaeter, B., Fgay, N., Guglielmina, C., Johnsen, S., Karlse, D., et al. (2007, March 28–30). The ATHENA Interoperability Framework. In *Enterprise Interoperability II*. Funchal, Portugal: Springer.

Bertoletti, M., Missier, P., Scannapieco, M., Aimetti, P., & Batini, C. (2005). *Improving government-to-business relationships through data reconciliation and process reengineering*. In R. Wang (Ed.), Advances in Management Information Systems, Information Quality Monograph (AMIS-IQ) . Sharpe, M.E.

Besson, P., & Rowe, F. (2001). ERP project dynamics and enacted dialogue: perceived understanding, perceived leeway, and the nature of task-related conflicts. *The DataBase for Advances in Information Systems, 32*(4), 47-65.

Bhattacharjee, D., Greenbaum, J., Johnson, R., Martin, M., Reddy, R., Ryan, H. L., White, C., & McKie, S. (2002). *Intelligent Enterprise, 5*(6), 28-33.

Bingi, P., Sharma, M. K., & Godla, J. (1999). Critical issues affecting an ERP implementation. *Information Systems Management, 16*(3), 7-14.

Bingi, P., Sharma, M. K., & Godla, J. (1999). Critical Issues Affecting an ERP Implementation. *Information Systems Management, 16*(3), 7-14.

Bingi, P., Sharma, M., & Golda, J. (1999). Critical issues affecting an ERP implementation. *Information Systems Management, 16*(3), 7-14.

BiZZdesign (2007). http://www.bizzdesign.nl.

Bloomfield, B. P., & Coombs, R. (1992). Information Technology, Control and Power: The Centralization and Decentralization Debate Revisited. *Journal of Management Studies, 29*(4), 459-484.

Bloomfield, B. P., Coombs, R., & Owen, J. (1994). The social construction of information systems - the implications for management control. In R. Mansell (Ed.), *Management of Information and Communication Technologies - Emerging Patterns of Control* (pp. 143-157). London: Aslib.

Boag, S., Chamberlin, D., Fernandez, M., Florescu, D., Robie, J., & Simeon, J. (2003, November). XQuery 1.0:

An XML Query Language. W3C Working Draft. Available from http:///www.w3.org/TR/xquery.

Boehm, B. W., & Sullivan, K. J. (2000). Software economics: a roadmap. In *Proceedings Conference on the Future of Software Engineering*. Limerick, Ireland, June, pp. 319-343.

Boekhoudt, P., Jonkers, H., & Rougoor, M. (2000). Graph-based analysis of business process models. In N. Mastorakis (ed.), *Mathematics and Computers in Modern Science, Proc. of the WSES/MIUE/HNA International Conference*, Montego Bay, Jamaica, Dec., pp. 227-235.

Bolcer, G. A., & Kaiser, G. (1999). SWAP: Leveraging the Web To Manage Workflow. *IEEE Internet Computing, 3*(1), 85-88.

Borgida, A., & Brachman, R. (2003). Conceptual Modeling with Description Logics. In F. Baader, D. Calvanese, D. McGuinness, D. Nardi, & P. Patel-Schneider (Eds.) *The Description Logic Handbook: Theory*, Implementation and Applications. Cambridge University Press.

Bosch, J., & Grahn, H. (1998). Characterising the performance of three architectural styles. In *Proceedings First International Workshop on Software and Performance*, Santa Fe, NM, Oct.

Botta-Genoulaz, V., Millet, P. A., & Grabot, B. (2005). A survey on the recent research literature on ERP systems. *Computers in Industry, 56*, 510-522

Boudreau, M. C., & Robey, D. (1999, December). Organizational transition to enterprise resource planning systems: Theoretical choices for process research. *Proceedings of 20th International conference on Information Systems*, Charlotte, 291-299.

Boudreau, M., Gefen, D., & Straub, D. (2001). Validation in IS Research: A State-of-the-Art Assessment. *MIS Quarterly, 25*(1), 1-16.

Boudreau, M.-C., & Robey, D. (2005). Enacting Integrated Information Technology: A Human Agency Perspective. *Organization Science, 16*(1), 3-18.

Bouzeghoub, M., & Lenzerini, M. (2001). *Special Issue on Data Extraction, Cleaning, and Reconciliation. Information Systems, 26*(8).

Boynton, A. C., Zmud, R. W., & Jacobs, G. C. (1994). The influence of IT management practice on IT use in large organizations. *MIS Quarterly*, September, 299-318.

BPMI (2003), *Business Process Management Initiative: Business process modeling notation.* working draft (1.0), Aug.

BPMI.org and OMG. (2006). *Business Process Modeling Notation Specification. Final Adopted Specification.* Object Management Group, http://www.bpmn.org (February 20, 2006).

Bradford, M., & Florin, J. (2003). Examining the role of innovation diffusion factors on the implementation success of enterprise resource planning systems. *International Journal of Accounting Information Systems, 4*(3), 205-225.

Brannon, J., James, D., & Lucker, W. (1994). Generating and Sustaining Backward Linkages between Maquiladoras and Local Suppliers in Northern Mexico. *World Development, 22*(12), 1933-1945.

Bray, H. (2004). Computer woes cause registration 'nightmare' at University of Massachusetts. *Knight Ridder Business News*, Washington, Sep 14, 2004, p. 1.

Brehm, L., Heinzl, A., & Markus, M. L. (2001). Tailoring ERP systems: A spectrum of choices and their implications. *Proceedings of 34th Annual Hawaii International Conference on System Sciences*, IEEE Press, Maui, Hawaii.

Bressan, S., Goh, C., Fynn, K., Jakobisiak, M., Hussein, K., Kon, K., et al. (1997). The COntext INterchange Mediator Prototype. In *Proceedings ACM SIGMOD International Conference on Management of Data (SIGMOD 1997)*.

Brickley, D. (2001). *RDF: Understanding the Striped RDF/XML Syntax*. Retrieved 25 Sep, 2002, from http://www.w3.org/2001/10/stripes/.

Broekstra, J., Kampman, A., & van Harmelen, F. (2003). Sesame: An Architecture for Storin gand Querying RDF Data and Schema Information. In D. Fensel, J. A. Hendler, H. Lieberman & W. Wahlster (Eds.), *Spinning the Semantic Web: Bringing the World Wide Web to Its Full Potential* [outcome of a Dagstuhl seminar] (pp. 197-222). Cambridge, MA: MIT Press.

Broens, T., Halteren, A. van Sinderen, M. Van, & Wac, K. (2005). Towards an application framework for context-aware m-health applications", in *Proc. 11th Open European Summer School (EUNICE 2005)*, Colmenarejo, Spain, July.

Brown, C. V., & Vessey, I. (2003). Managing The Next Wave of Enterprise Systems: Leveraging Lessons from ERP. *MS Quarterly Executive, 2*(1), 65-77.

Brown, J. (2001, February). ERP Doomed By Poor Planning. *Computing Canada, 11.*

Bubenko Jr., J. (2007). From Information Algebra to Enterprise Modelling and Ontologies – A Historical

Perspective on Modelling for Information Systems. In J. Krogstie, A. L. Opdahl & S. Brinkkemper (Eds.): *Conceptual Modelling in Information Systems Engineering.* Berlin: Springer, pp. 1-18.

Bucher, T., Fischer, R., Kurpjuweit, S., & Winter, R. (2006). Enterprise architecture analysis and application – An exploratory stury. In *Proc. EDOC Workshop on Trends in Enterprise Architecture Research* (TEAR 2006), Hong Kong.

Buchner, M. (1999, August). ERP Application Integration. *Midrange Systems, 12.*

Buckhout, S., Frey, E., & Nemec, J. (1999). Making ERP succeeds: Turning fear into promise. *Strategy + Business magazine, 4*(2), 60-72.

Buneman, P., Davidson, S., Fan, W., Hara, C., & Tan, W. (2001). Keys for XML. In *Proceedings of WWW 2001.*

Buonanno, G., Faverio, P., Pigni, F., Ravarini, A., Sciuto, D., & Tagliavini, M. (2005). Factors affecting ERP system adoption: A comparative analysis between SMEs and large companies. *Journal of Enterprise Information Management, 18*(4), 384-426.

Burke, E. (2001). *JAVA & XSLT.* California: O'Reilly.

Burns, M. (2007, September). Work in process: Enterprise software survey 2007. *CA Magazine,* 18-20.

Busch, T. (1995). Gender differences in self-efficacy and attitudes toward computers. *Journal of Educational Computing Research, 12*(2), 147-158.

Buss, M. D. J. (1983). How to rank computer projects. *Harvard Business Review, 61*(1), 118–125.

Butler, H. (2002). *Barriers to real world adoption of Semantic Web technologies.* Hewlett-Packard.

Buuren, R. van, Jonkers, H., Iacob, M.-E., & Strating, P. (2004). Composition of relations in enterprise architcture models. In H. Ehrig, G. Engels, F. Parisi-Presicce, and G. Rozenberg, editors, *Graph Transformations – Proceedings of the Second International Conference* (LNCS 3256), pages 39–53, Rome, Italy, Sept.

Cabral, L., Domingue, J., Galizia, S., Gugliotta, A., Tanasescu, V., Pedrinaci, C., & Norton, B. (2006). IRS-III: A broker for semantic web services based applications. In I. Cruz et al. (Eds.). *Proc. ISWC'06, LNCS 4273,*.201-214.

Calisir. F., & Calisir, F. (2004). The relation of interface usability characteristics, perceived usefulness, and perceived ease of use to end-user satisfaction with enterprise resource planning (ERP) systems. *Computers in Human Behavior, 20*(3), 505-515.

Camarinha-Matos, L. M., & Afsarmanesh, H. (2006, September). Modeling framework for collaborative networked organizations. In *Network-Centric Collaboration and Supporting Frameworks. Seventh IFIP Working Conference on Virtual Enterprises* (pp. 3–14). Springer.

Camarinha-Matos, L. M., & Afsarmanesh, H.(2001, November). Service federation in virtual organisations. In *Prolamat'01.* Budabest, Hungary.

Canevet, C., Gilmore, S., Hillston, J., Kloul, L., & Stevens, P. (2004, January). Analysing UML 2.0 activity diagrams in the software performance engineering process. In *Proc 4th International Workshop on Software and Performance: ACM SIGSOFT Software Engineering Notes, 29*(1).

Carlsen, S. (1997). *Conceptual Modelling and Composition of Flexible Workflow Models.* PhD thesis, Dept of Computer and Inforamtion Science, Norwegian University of Science and Technology, Trondheim, Norway.

Carlsen, S. (1998). Action Port Model: A Mixed Paradigm Conceptual Workflow Modeling Language. *Proceedings of the 3rd IFCIS International Conference on Cooperative Information Systems (CoopIS'98),* pp. 300-308. Los Alamitos, CA: IEEE CS Press.

Carmel, E., & Sawyer, S. (1998). Packaged software development teams: what makes them different? *Information Technology People, 11*(1), 7-19.

Cavantzas, N., Burdett, D., Ritzinger, G., Fletcher, T., Lafon, Y., & Barreto, C. (Eds.) (2005). *Web Services Choreography Description Language Version 1.0.* Technical report, W3C Candidate Recommendation, 9 Nov, 2005. Retrieved 10 Feb, 2006, from http://www.w3.org/TR/2005/CR-ws-cdl-10-20051109/

Chan, F. T. S., & Chan, H. K. (2004). A new model for manufacturing supply chain networks: a multiagent approach. *Journal of Engineering Manufacture, 218,* Part B, 443-454.

Chan, F. T. S., Chung, S. H., & Wadhwa, S. (2004). A heuristic Methodology for Order Distribution in a Demanddriven Collaborative Supply Chain. *International Journal of Production Research, 42*(1), 1-19.

Chang, S. E., Changchien, S. W., & Huang, R-H. (2006). Assessing users' product-specific knowledge for personalization in electronic commerce. *Expert Systems with Applications, 30*(4), 682-693.

Chang, S. E., Minkin, B. (2006). The implementation of a secure and pervasive multimodal Web system architecture. *Information and Software Technology, 48*(6), 424-432.

Chang, Y.-F., & Chen, C. S. (2005). Smart phone - the choice of client platform for mobile commerce. *Computer Standards and Interfaces, 27*(4), 329-336.

Changchien, S. W., Lee, C. F., & Hsu, Y. J. (2004). Online personalized sales promotion in electronic commerce. *Expert Systems with Applications, 27*(1), 35-52.

Cheng, C. Y., & Prabhu, V. (2007). Applying RFID for Cutting Tool Supply Chain Management. *Proceedings of the 2007 Industrial Engineering Research Conference*, 637-642:

Cheng, C. Y., & Prabhu, V. (2007). Complexity Metrics for Business Process Enabled by RFID and Web Services. *Proceedings of 17th International Conference on Flexible Automation and Intelligent Manufacturing (FAIM 2007)*, 812-819:

Cheng, C. Y., & Prabhu, V. (2007). Performance Modeling of Business Processes Enabled by RFID and Web Services. *Proceedings of 6th IEEE/ACIS International Conference on Computer and Information Science (ICIS 2007)*, 718-723:

Chien, S.-W., & Tsaur, S.-M. (2007). Investigating the Success of ERP Systems: Case Studies in Three Taiwanese High-Tech Industries. *Computers in Industry, 58*(8-9), 783-793.

Chiu, D. K. W., Cheung, S. C., Hung, P. C. K., Chiu, S. Y. Y., & Chung, A. K. K. (2004). Developing e-Negotiation support with a meta-modeling approach in a web services environment. *Decision Support Systems, 40*, 51–69. (ISSN:0167-9236, Special issue: Web services and process management)

Choi, T. Y., Dooley, K. J., & Rungtusanatham, M. (2001) Supply networks and complex adaptive systems: control versus emergence. *Journal of Operations Management, 19*(3), 351-366.

Christensen, E., Curbera, F., Meredith, G., & Weerawarana, S. (2001, March). *Web Services Description Language (WSDL) 1.1.* (Retrieved September 1st, 2005, from http://www.w3c.org/TR/wsdl)

Chun-chin, W., Chen-fu, C. & Mao-jiun, J. W. (2005). An AHP based approach to ERP system selection. *International Journal on Production Economics, 96*, 47-62.

Chung, L. K., Nixon, B., Yu, E., & Mylopoulos, J. (2000), *Non-Functional Requirements in Software Engineering.* Kluwer Publishing.

Chung, S., & Sherman, M. (2002). Emerging Marketing. *McKinsey Quarterly, 2*, 62-71.

Chung, S., & Snyder, C. (2000). ERP adoption: A technological evolution approach. *International Journal of Agile Management Systems, 2*(1), 24-32.

Ciborra, C. U. (2000). A Critical Review of the Literature on the Management of Corporate Information Infrastructure. In C. U. Ciborra, K. Braa, A. Cordella, B. Dahlbom, A. Failla, O. Hanseth, V. Hepso, J. Ljungberg, E. Monteiro & K. A. Simon (Eds.), *From Control to Drift - The Dynamics of Corporate Information Infrastructures* (pp. 15-40). Oxford: Oxford University Press.

Ciborra, C. U. (2002). *The Labyrinths of Information: Challenging the Wisdom of Systems.* Oxford: Oxford University Press.

Clemon, E. K., & Row, M. C. (1991). Sustaining IT advantage: The role of structural differences. *MIS quarters*, 275-292.

Coetzer, J. (2000, September 18). Survey-Enterprise Resource Planning-Analyse Before Implementing. *Business Day, 20.*

Cohen, J., & Cohen, P. (1983). *Applied Multiple Regression/Correlation Analysis for the Behavioral Sciences.* NJ: Lawrence Erlbuam Associates Hillsdale.

Connolly, S. (1999, March 1). ERP: Corporate cleanup. *Computerworld*, 23-26

Conrad, R., Scheffner, D., & Freytag, J. (2000). Xml Conceptual Modeling Using UML. In *19th International Conference on Conceptual Modeling.*

Conradi, R., & Jaccheri, L. (1998). Process Modelling Languages. In J.-C. Derniame, B. A. Kaba & D. G. Wastell (Eds.), *Software Process: Principles, Methodology, and Techniques* (pp. 27-52). Berlin: Springer LNCS 1500.

Conway, C. (2001). Top 20 Visionaries. *Comments of Craig Conway, 1724*, 35. *VARbusiness*: Manhassett.

Coombs, R., Knights, D., & Willmott, H. C. (1992). Culture, Control and Competition; Towards a Conceptual Framework for the Study of Information Technology in Organizations. *Organization Studies, 13*(1), 51-72.

Cooper, R., & Zmud, R. (1990). Information technology implementation research: a technological diffusion approach. *Management Science, 36*(2), 123-139.

Corbin, J., & Strauss, A. (1990). Grounded theory research: Procedures, canons, and evaluative criteria. *Qualitative Sociology, 13*, 3-21.

Cortellessa, V., & Mirandola, R. (2000). Deriving a queueing network based performance model from UML diagrams. In *Proceedings 2nd International Workshop on Software and Performance*, Ottawa, Canada, Sept., pp. 58 – 70.

Cravey, A. (1997). The Politics of Reproduction: Households in the Mexican Industrial Transition. *Economic Geography, 73*(2), 166-186.

Curtis, B., Kellner, M., & Over, J. (1992). Process Modeling. *Communications of the ACM, 35*(9), 75-90.

Daconta, M., Orbst, L., & Smith, K. (2003). The Semantic Web: A guide to the future of XML, Web Services and Knowledge Management. London: Wiley.

Dago, P., & Verfaillie, G., (1996). No good recordings for valued constraint satisfaction problems. *Proceedings of 8th IEEE International Conference on Tools with Artificial Intelligence*, Toulouse, 132–139, France.

Dahlen, C., & Elfsson, J. (1999). An analysis of the current and future ERP market. Master's Thesis, Industrial Economics and Management. The Royal Institute of Technology, Stockholm, Sweden.

Dalal, N. P., Kamath, M., Kolarik, W. J., & Sivaraman, E. (2004). Toward an Integrated Framework for Modeling Enterprise Resources. *Communications of the ACM, 47*(3), 83-87.

Damianou, N., Dulay, N., Lupu, E., & Sloman, M.(2001, January). The Ponder policy specification language. *In Workshop on policies for distributed systems and networks (Policy2001)* (Vol. 1995). HP Labs Bristol: Springer-Verlag.

Dardenne, A., van Lamsweerde, A., & Fickas, S. (1993). Goal-directed requirements acquisition. *Science of Computer Programming, 20*(1–2), 3–50.

Daskalopulu, A., Dimitrakos, T., & Maibaum, T. (2002). Evidence-Based Electronic Contract Performance Monitoring. *The INFORMS Journal of Group Decision and Negotiation.* (Special Issue on Formal Modelling in E-Commerce.)

Davenport, T. (2000). *Mission Critical: Realizing the Promise of Enterprise Systems.* MA, Cambridge: Harvard Business School Press.

Davenport, T. H (1998). Putting the enterprise into the enterprise system. *Harvard Business Review, 76*(4), 121-131.

Davenport, T. H. (1998). Putting the Enterprise into the Enterprise System. *Harvard Business Review, 76*(4, July-August), 121-131.

Davenport, T. H. (1998, July/August). Putting the enterprise into the enterprise system. *Harvard Business Review, 76*(4), 121-131.

Davidsson, P., Hederstierna, A., Jacobsson, A., Persson, J. A., Carlsson, B., Johansson, S. J., et al. (2006). The concept and technology of plug and play business. In *ICEIS 2006 - proceedings of the eighth international conference on enterprise information systems: Databases and information systems integration* (p. 213-217). Paphos, Cyprus.

Davis, F. D., Bagozzi, R. P., & Warshaw, P. R. (1989). User Acceptance of Computer Technology: A Comparison of Two Theoretical Models. *Management Science, 35*, 8, 982-1003.

Davis, F.. Bagozzi, R., & Warshaw, P. (1989). User acceptance of computer technology: A comparison of two theoretical models. *Management Science, 35*(8), 982-1003.

Davis, F.D. (1989). Perceived Usefulness, Perceived Ease of Use, and User Acceptance of Information Technology, *MIS Quarterly, 13*(3), 319-340.

Davison, R. (2002). Cultural complications of ERP. Association for Computing Machinery. *Communications of the ACM, 45*(7), 109.

de Grimaldo, S.W., (2004). *Mobile Commerce Takes off.* Telecom Trends International, Inc., Virginia. Retrieved November 15, 2007, from http://www.telecomtrends.net/reports.htm

DeLone, W. H., & McLean, E. R. (1992). Information Systems Success: The Quest for The Dependent Variable. *Information Systems Research, 3*(1), 60-95.

DeLone, W. H., & McLean, E. R. (2003). The Delone and McLean model of Information systems success: A ten-year update. *Journal of Information Systems Management, 19*(4), 9-26.

DeLone, W. H., & McLean, E. R., (1992). Information Systems Success: The Quest for the Dependent Variable. *Information Systems Research, 3*(1), 60-95.

Delone, W., & McLean, E. (1992). Information systems success: the quest for the dependent variable. *Information Systems Research, 3*(1), 60-95.

DeLone, W.H. & McLean, E. R., (2003). The DeLone and McLean model of information systems success: A ten-year update. *Journal of Management Information Systems, 19*(4), 9-30.

Derniame, J.-C., Kaba, B. A., & Wastell, D. G. (Eds.). (1998). Software Process: Principles, Methodology, Technology. Berlin: Springer (LNCS 1500).

Dettmer, R. (2003). It's good to talk (speech technology for online services access). *IEE Review, 49*, 30-33.

Di Cosmo, R., Pottier, F., & Rémy, D. (2005, April). Subtyping Recursive Types modulo Associative Commutative Products. In P. Urzyczyn (Ed.), *7th International Conference on Typed Lambda Calculi and Applications (TLCA 2005) 3461*, 179–193. Berlin, Heidelberg, Germany: Springer-Verlag.

Di Marco, A., & Inverardi, P. (2004). Compositional generation of software architecture performance QN models. In J. Magee *et al.* (eds.), *Proc. 4th Working IEEE/IFIP Conference on Software Architecture* (WICSA 2004), Oslo, Norway, June, pp 37–46.

Diane, M. S., & Volkoff, O. (2004, June). A Roadmap for Enterprise System Implementation. *Computer*, 22-28.

Dijkman, R. & Dumas, M. (2004). Service-Oriented Design. A Multi-Viewpoint Approach. *International Journal of Cooperative Information Systems, 13*(4), 337-368.

Do, T. T., Faulkner, S., & Kolp, M. (2003). Organizational multi-agent architectures for information systems. *In Proc. of the 5th Int. Conf. on Enterprise Information Systems, ICEIS'03'*, Angers, France, pp. 89–96.

Doran, J. E., Franklin, S., Jennings N. R., & Norman, T. J. (1997). On cooperation in multi-agent systems. *Knowledge Engineering Review, 12*(3), 309–314.

Duane, A., & Finnegan, P. (2003). Managing empowerment and control in an intranet environment. *Information Systems Journal, 13*(2), 133-158.

Dubois, D., & Prade H. (1999). Qualitative possibility theory and its applications to constraint satisfaction and decision under uncertainty. *International Journal of Intelligent Systems, 14*, 45-61.

Duplaga, E. A. & Astni, M. (2003). Implementing ERP in Manufacturing. *Information Systems Management, 20*(3), 68-75.

Dussauge, P., & Garrette, B. (1999). *Cooperative Strategy: Competing Successfully Through Strategic Alliances*. Wiley and Sons.

Dutta, S., Lanvin, B., & Paua, F. (2003). *The Global Information Technology Report 2002-2003: Readiness for the Networked World*, Oxford University Press.

Eck, P. van, Blanken, H., & Wieringa, R. (2004, September). Project GRAAL. Towards operational architecture alignment, *International Journal of Cooperative Information Systems, 13*(3), 235-255.

Eertink H., Janssen, W., Oude Luttighuis, P., Teeuw, W., & Vissers, C. (1999). A business process design language. In *Proc. 1st World Congress on Formal Methods*, Toulouse, France.

Ehie, I. C., & Madsen, M. (2005). Identifying critical issues in enterprise resource planning (ERP) implementation. *Computers in Industry, 56*(6), 545-557.

El-Hamdouchi, A., & Willett, E. (1986). Hierarchic Document Classification Using Ward's Clustering Method. In *Proceedings of the 9th International ACM SIGIR Conference on Research and Development in Information Retrieval*. New York: ACM Press, pp. 149-156.

Elmes, M. B., Strong, D. M., & Volkoff, O. (2005). Panoptic empowerment and reflective conformity in enterprise systems-enabled organizations. *Information and Organization, 15*(1), 1-37.

Enterprise Information Systems. A definition from Wikipedia.com http://en.wikipedia.org/wiki/Enterprise_information_systems, accessed 20 November 2007.

Ertogral, K., & Wu, S. D. (2000) Auction-Theoretic coordination of production planning in the supply chain. *IIE Transactions, 32*(10), 931-940.

Ettlie, J. E., Perotti, V. J., & Joseph, D. A. (2005). Strategic predictors of successful enterprise system deployment. *International Journal of Operations & Production Management, 25*(10), 953-972.

European Commission. (2007, June). *EC FP7 ICT Work Programme* (Tech. Rep.). EC.

Everdingen, Y., Hillegersberg, J., & Waarts, E. (2000). ERP adoption by European midsize companies. *Communications of the ACM, 43*(4), 27-31.

Everitt, B. S. (1993). *Cluster Analysis*. Edward Arnold, London.

Everitt, B. S., Landau, S., & Leese, M. (2001). *Cluster Analysis*. London: Edward Arnold

Faratin, P., Sierra, C. & Jennings, N. R., (2002) Using Similarity criteria to make issue tradeoffs in automated negotiations. *Artificial Intelligence, 142*(2), 205-237.

Feng, J., Sears, A., Karat, C.-M. (2006). A longitudinal evaluation of hands-free speech-based navigation during dictation. *International Journal of Human-Computer Studies, 64*(6), 553-569.

Fernandez, M., Malhotra, A., Marsh, J., Nagy, M., & Walshand, N. (2002, November). *XQuery 1.0 and XPath 2.0 Data Model. W3C Working Draft*. Available from http:///www.w3.org/TR/query-datamodel.

Ferrando, T. (2001). Training Employees to Use ERP Systems. *The American City & County..* September 2001, 12.

Field, A. (2000). *Discovering Statistics: using SPSS for Windows.* London: SAGE Publications.

Filippi, F. (2005). Aspectos Teoricos de las Maquiladoras y la Migración. *Boletin Chiapas al Dia, 485,* 1-5.

Fiona, F.-H. N.& Lee-Shang L. J. (2001). Critical factors for successful implementation of enterprise systems. *Business Process Management Journal, 7*(3), 285-296.

Fischer, L. (Ed.). (2001). The Workflow Handbook 2001. Lighthouse Point, FL: Workflow Management Coalition (WfMC).

Ford, D., Connelly, C., & Meister, D. (2003). Information systems research and Hofstede's Culture's Consequences: An uneasy and incomplete partnership. *IEEE Transactions on Engineering Management, 50*(1), 8-25.

Ford, D., Gadde, L. E., Hakansson, H., Lundgren, A., Snehota, I., Turnbull, P., & Wilson, D. (1988). *Managing Business Relationships.* John Wiley & Sons Ltd., Chichester.

Fowler, M. (1997), *Analysis Patterns: Reusable Object Models.* Addison-Wesley.

Fox, M., & Grüninger, M. (1998). Enterprise Modeling. *AI Magazine, 19*(3), 109-121.

Fullerton, T., Barraza de A., & Martha P. (2003). Maquiladoras Prospect in a Global Environment. *Texas Business Review,* October, 1-5.

Fung, R. Y. K., & Chen, T. (2005). A multiagent supply chain planning and coordination architecture. International Journal of Advanced Manufacturing Technology, 25, 811–819.

Fuxman, A., Liu, L., Mylopoulos, J., Roveri, M., & Traverso, P. (2004). Specifying and analyzing early requirements in tropos. *Requirements Engineering, 9*(2), 132–150.

Gable, G. (1998). Large package software: A neglected technology. *Journal of Global Information Management, 6*(3), 3-4.

Gamma, E., Helm, R., Johnson, J., & Vlissides, J. (1995). *Design Patterns: Elements of Reusable Object-Oriented Software.* Addison-Wesley.

Garbarino, E., & Johnson, M. S. (1999). The Different Roles of Satisfaction, Trust and Commitment in Customer Relationships. *Journal of Marketing, 63,* 70-87

Garbellotto, G. (2007, October). The Data Warehousing Disconnect. *Strategic Finance,* 59-61.

Garlan, D., Allen, R., & Ockerbloom, J. (1995). Architectural mismatch or why it's hard to build systems out of existing parts. In *ICSE '95: Proceedings of the 17th international conference on Software engineering* (pp. 179–185). New York, NY, USA: ACM Press.

Garrity, E. J. & Sanders, G. L. (1998). Introduction to Information Systems Success Measurement. *In* E. J. Garrity and G. L, Sanders (dir.), *Information Systems Success Measurement,* 1-12. Idea Group Publishing.

Gattiker, T. F., & Goodhue, D. L. (2004). Understanding the local-level costs and benefits of ERP through organizational information processing theory. *Information & management, 41*(4), 431-443.

Gay, S. J., & Hole, M. (1999). Types and Subtypes for Client-Server Interactions. In ESOP '99: *Proceedings of the 8th European Symposium on Programming Languages and Systems, 1576,* 74–90. London, UK: Springer-Verlag.

Gefen, D. (2002). Nurturing clients' trust to encourage engagement success during the customization of ERP systems. *Omega, 30*(4).

Genovese, Y., Bond, B.A., Zrimsek, B., & Frey, N. (2001). The Transition to ERP II: Meeting the Challenges. http://www.gartner.com/DisplayDocument?doc_dc=101237, accessed on 7 July 2005.

Ghost, A. K., & Howell, C., & Whittaker, J. A. (2002). Building software securely from the ground up. *IEEE software, 19*(1), 14-16.

Gibbs, J., Kreamer, K. L., & Dedrick, J. (2003). Environment and Policy Factors Shaping Global E-Commerce Diffusion: A Cross-Country Comparison. *The Information Society, 19,* 5-18.

Gibson, J. J. (1979). *The ecological approach to visual perception.* Boston: Houghton Mifflin.

Giddens, A. (1984). *The Constitution of Society: Outline of the Theory of Structuration.* Cambridge: Polity Press.

Giddens, A. (1990). *The Consequences of Modernity.* Cambridge: Polity Press.

Giorgini, P., Kolp, M., & Mylopoulos, J. (2002), Multi-agent and software architecture: A comparative case study. *In Proc. of the 3rd International Workshop on Agent Software Engineering, AOSE'02',* Bologna, Italy, pp. 101–112.

Giorgini, P., Kolp, M., Mylopoulos, J., & Castro, J. (2005). A requirements-driven methodology for agent-oriented software. In B. Henderson-Sellers & P. Giorgini, (Eds.), *Agent Oriented Methodologies*. Idea Group Publishing, pp. 20–46.

Giorgini, P., Kolp, M., Mylopoulos, J., & Pistore ,M. (2004). The tropos methodology. *In* M.-P. G. F. Bergenti & F. Zambonelli, (eds.), *Methodologies and Software Engineering for Agent Systems*. Kluwer, pp. 89–105.

Giorgini, P., Mylopoulos, J., Nicchiarelli, E., & Sebastiani, R. (2002). Reasoning with goal models. *In Proceedings of the 21st International Conference on Conceptual Modeling (ER 2002)*. Tampere, Finland, pp. 167–181.

Glaser, B. G., & Strauss, A. (1967). *The discovery of grounded theory: Strategies for qualitative research.* New York: Aldine.

Glass, R. L. (1998). Enterprise Resource Planning—Breakthrough and/or term problems. *Database for Advances Information System, 29*(2), 14-16.

Glenn, E. S., & Glenn, C. G. (1981). *Man and Mankind: Conflict and Communication between Cultures.* Northwood, NJ: Ablex.

GMT (2006). Gmt consulting group. http://www.gmt-group.com/.

Gomes-Casseres, B. (1996). *The alliance revolution: the new shape of business rivalry.* Harvard University Press.

Goodchild, A., Herring, C., & Milosevic, Z. (2000, June). Business contracts for B2B. In *Proceedings of the CAISE'00 Workshop on Infrastructure for Dynamic Business-to-Business Service Outsourcing ISDO'00.* Stockholm, Sweden: CEUR-WS.org.

Goose, S., Newman, M., Schmidt, C., & Hue, L. (2000). Enhancing Web accessibility via the Vox Portal and a Web-hosted dynamic HTML <-> VoxML converter. *Computer Networks, 33*, 583-592.

Gordijn, J., & Akkermans, H. (2001). Designing and evaluating E-Business models. *IEEE Intelligent Systems, 16*(4), 11-17.

Goyal, S. K., & Gopalkrishnan, M. (1996). Production lot-sizing model with insufficient production capacity. *Production Planning and Control, 7*(4), 222-224.

Green, J. (2003). Responding to the challenge. *Canadian Transportation Logistics, 106*(8), 20-21.

Green, P., & Rosemann, M. (2000). Integrated Process Modelling: An Ontological Evaluation. *Information Systems, 25*(2), 73-87.

Grefen, P., Aberer, K., Hoffner, Y., & Ludwig, H. (2000). CrossFlow: Cross-Organizational Workflow Management in Dynamic Virtual Enterprises. *International Journal of Computer Systems Sciences and Engineering, 15*(5), 277-290.

Grosof, B. N., & Poon, T. (2003). SweetDeal: Representing agent contracts with exceptions using XML rules, ontologies and process descriptions. In *Proceedings of the 12th international conference on the World Wide Web (WWW 2003)*. Budapest, Hungary: ACM.

Gross, D., & Yu, E. (2002). From non-functional requirements to design through patterns. *Requirements Engineering, 6*(1), 18–36.

Grossman, T., & Walsh, J. (2004). Avoiding the Pitfalls of ERP System Implementations. *Information Systems Management, 21(2)*, 38-42.

Gruben, W., & Kiser, S. (2001). *NAFTA and Maquiladoras: Is the Growth Connected?* Federal Reserve Bank of Dallas. Retrieved from http://www.dallasfed.org/research/border/tbe_gruben.html

Gu, G. P., & Petriu, D. C. (2002). XSLT transformation from UML models to LQN performance models. In *Proc. 3rd International Workshop on Software and Performance*, Rome, Italy, 2002, pp. 227– 234.

Gulliver, S. R., Serif, T., & Ghinea, G. (2004). Pervasive and standalone computing: the perceptual effects of variable multimedia quality. *International Journal of Human-Computer Studies, 60*(5/6), 640-665.

Haake, J. M., & Wang, W. (1997). Flexible support for business processes: extending cooperative hypermedia with process support. *In Proceedings of GROUP'97, International Conference on Supporting Group Work.* The Integration Challenge.

Hair, J., Anderson, R., Tatham, R., & Black, W. (1995). *Multivariate data analysis with readings*. NJ: Prentice-Hall.

Hair, J., Anderson, R., Tatham, T., & Black, W. (1998). *Multivariate Data Analysis*. Fifth Edition, Prentice Hall, New Jersey.

Hall, E. T. (1976). *Beyond culture*. New York: Anchor Press.

Hamerman, P., & Wang, R. (2006). ERP: Still a Challenge after All These Years. *Enterprise Applications*. Jan 29, 2006, p.1-2. Downloaded on Sept. 25, 2006 from http://

www.networkcomputing.com/gswelcome/showArticle.jhtml?articleID=177104905

Hammer, M., & Stanton, S. (1999, November-December). How process enterprises really work. *Harvard Business Review*, 108-118.

Hanseth, O., Ciborra, C. U., & Braa, K. (2001). The Control Devolution: ERP and the Side Effects of Globalization. *The DataBase for Advances in Information Systems, 32*(4), 34-46.

Harris, P. (2000). PeopleSoft hopes to recover fumble with Big Ten universities. *The Business Journal,* 17(38), 3. San Jose, Jan 07, 2000.

Harrison, A. W., Rainer, R. K., & Hochwarter, W. A. (1997) Gender differences in computing activities. *Journal of Social Behavior & Personality, 12*(4), 849-869.

Harrison, P., & Patel, N. (1992). *Performance Modelling of Communication Networks and Computer Architectures.* Addison-Wesley.

Hayes, P. (2004). *RDF Semantics.* Technical report, W3C, 10 Feb 2004. Retrieved Mar 3, 2005, from http://www.w3.org/TR/rdf-mt/

Herzog, U. (2001). Formal methods for performance evaluation, In *Lectures on Formal Methods and Performance Analysis: First EEF/Euro Summer School on Trends in Computer Science* (LNCS 2090), pages 1–37. Springer Verlag, 2001.

Hess, A., Johnston, E., & Kushmerick, N. (2004). ASSAM: A Tool for Semi-automatically Annotating Semantic Web Services. In S.A. McIlraith et al. (Eds.). *Proc. ISWC'04, Springer LNCS 3298*, 320-334.

Higgins, K. (2005, May 23). ERP Goes On The Road. *Information Week, 1040*, 52-53.

Hofstede, G. (1980). Motivation, Leadership and Organization: Do American theories apply abroad? *Organizational Dynamics, 75*(1), 42-63.

Hofstede, G. (1993). *Cultures and organizations: software of the mind.* London: McGraw-Hill.

Holland, C. P., & Light, B. (1999). A critical success factors model for ERP implementation. *IEEE Software 1999*, 30-36.

Holland, C. P., & Light, B. (1999, May-June). A critical success factors model for ERP implementation. *IEEE Software, 16*(3), 30-36

Holland, C., Light, B., & Gibson, N. (1999). A Critical Success Factors Model for Enterprise Resource Planning Implementation. In *Proceedings of the 7th European Conference on Information Systems ECIS,* Copenhagen Business School, Copenhagen, Denmark, 273-287.

Holland, P., Light, B., & Gibson, N. (1999, June 23-25). *A critical success factors model for enterprise resource planning implementation.* Seventh European Conference on Information Systems, Copenhagen.

Holsapple, C., & Sena, M. (2005). ERP plans and decision support benefits. *Decision Support Systems, 38*(4), 575-590.

Hong, K., & Kim, Y. (2002). The Critical success factors for ERP implementation: An organizational fit perspective. *Information Management, 40*(1), 25-40.

Horling, B., Lesser, V., Vincent, R., Bazzan, A., & Xuan, P. (1999). *Diagnosis as an integral part of multi-agent adaptability.* Technical Report UM-CS-1999-003, University of Massachusetts.

Huang, K. (2007). *Towards an information technology infrastructure cost model.* M.Sc. Thesis, Massachusetts Institute of Technology.

Hull, R., & King, R. (1987). *Semantic database modeling: Survey, applications, and research issues. ACM Comput. Surv., 19*(3), 201-260. IPSI-XQ. (n.d.). Available from http://ipsi.fhg.de/oasys/projects/ ipsi-xq/index e.html.

Hutchins, H. (1998). *APICS 1998 International Conference Proceedings*, Falls Church, VA, 1998, pp. 356–358.

Iacob, M.-E., & Jonkers, H. (2004). *Quantitative Analysis of Enterprise Architectures.* Technical Report ArchiMate D3.5b, Telematica Instituut, Enschede, the Netherlands, Mar.

Iacob, M.-E., & Jonkers, H. (2005), Quantitative analysis of enterprise architectures. In *Proc. 1st International Conference on Interoperability of Enterprise Software and Applications* (INTEROP-ESA'05), Geneva, Switzerland, Feb. 2005.

IEEE (2000). *IEEE standard 1471-2000: Recommended practice for architectural description of software-intensive systems.*

Ignatiadis, I., Nandhakumar, J. (2007). The impact of Enterprise Systems on organizational resilience. *Journal of Information Technology, 22*(1), 36-43.

INEGI (Instituto Nacional de Estadistica, Geografia, e Informatica). Retrieved November 2007 from www.inegi.gob.mx.

Information Technology – Open Distributed Processing – Reference Model – Enterprise Language. (2003). (IS15414)

Information Technology – Open Systems Interconnection, Data Management and Open Distributed Processing. ODP Trading Function. (1995). (IS13235)

Information Technology – Open Systems Interconnection, Data Management and Open Distributed Processing. Reference Model of Open Distributed Processing. (1996). (IS10746)

Information Technology – Open Systems Interconnection, Data Management and Open Distributed Processing. Reference Model of Open Distributed Processing. ODP Type repository function. (1999). (IS14746)

Institute for Information Industry (2007). *Survey on the mobile Internet in Taiwan for Q3 2007.* ACI-FIND, focus on Internet news and data. Retrieved January 2, 2008, from http://www.find.org.tw/find/home.aspx?page=many&id=184

Ishman, M. (1998). Measuring Information Success at the individual level in cross-cultural Environments. *In* E.J. Garrity and G.L, Sanders (dir), *Information Systems Success Measurement.* Idea Group Publishing.

IT toolbox ERP Implementation Survey (2004). Retrieved July 7, 2005, from http://supplychain.ittoolbox.com/research/survey.asp?survey=corioerp_survey&p=2

Ivari, J. (2005). An Empirical Test of the DeLone-McLean Model of Information System Success. *Database for Advances in Information Systems, 36*(2), 8-27.

Jagadish, H., Lakshmanan, L., Scannapieco, M., Srivastava, D., & Wiwatwattana, N. (2004,). Colorful XML: One Hierarchy Isn't Enough. In *Proceedings of the 2004 ACM SIGMOD Conference (SIGMOD 2004).* JSR-101-Expert-Group. (2003, October). Java(tm) API for XML based Remote Procedure Call (jax-rpc) Specification Version 1.1. Sun Microsystems, Inc.

Jain, V. (2006). Hybrid approaches to model supplier related issues in a dynamic supply chain. Unpublished Ph D Thesis, Mechanical Engineering Department, Indian Institute of Technology Delhi, India.

Jain, V., Wadhwa, S., & Deshmukh, S. G. (2007). A Negotiation-to-Coordinate (N2C) mechanism for Modeling Buyer-Supplier relationship in Dynamic Environment. *International Journal of Enterprise Information Systems, 3*(2),1

Jeanne, W. R. (1999, July-August). Surprising facts about implementing ERP. *IT Pro,* 65-67

Jennings, N. R. (1996). Coordination techniques for distributed artificial intelligence. In G. M. P. O'Hare & N. R. Jennings, (eds.), *Foundations of Distributed Artificial Intelligence.* Wiley, pp. 187–210.

Jha, S., Palsberg, J., & Zhao, T. (2002). Efficient type matching. In *FoSSaCS '02: Proceedings of the 5th International Conference on Foundations of Software Science and Computation Structures* (pp. 187– 204). London, UK: Springer-Verlag.

Joachims, T., Freitag, D., & Mitchell, T. (1997). WebWatcher: A tour guide for the World Wide Web. In *Proceedings of IJCAI-97, Fifteenth Joint Conference on Artificial Intelligence, Nagoya, Japan* (pp. 770-775).

Jones, K. L., & Tullous, R. (2001). E-Commerce Attitudes and Involvement in the U.S. and Mexico, *Proceedings of the Academy of Business & Administrative Science Conference,* July 2001, Quebec, Canada.

Jones, M. R. (1999). Information Systems and the Double Mangle: Steering a Course between the Scylla of Embedded Structure and the Charybdis of Strong Symmetry. In T. J. Larsen, L. Levine, J. I. DeGross (Eds.), *Information Systems: Current Issues and Future Changes* (pp. 287-302). New York: OmniPress.

Jonkers, H., & Swelm, M. van (1999). Queueing analysis to support distributed system Design, in Obaidat, M.S. and Ajmone Marsan, M. (eds.), *Proceedings of the 1999 Symposium on Performance Evaluation of Computer and Telecommunication Systems,* pages 300–307, Chicago, IL, July 1999.

Jonkers, H., Boekhoudt, P., Rougoor, M., & Wierstra, E. (1999). Completion time and critical path analysis for the optimisation of business process models. In Obaidat, M., Nisanci, A. and Sadoun, B. editors, *Proceedings of the 1999 Summer Computer Simulation Conference,* pages 222–229, Chicago, IL, July.

Jonkers, H., Iacob, M.-E., Lankhorst, M., & Strating, P. (2005). Integration and Analysis of Functional and Non-Functional Aspects in Model-Driven E-Service Development. In *Proc. 9th International Enterprise Distributed Object Computing Conference* (EDOC 2005), Enschede, The Netherlands, Sept.

Jonkers, H., Janssen, W., Verschut, A., & Wierstra, E. (1998). A unified framework for design and performance analysis of distributed systems. In *Proc. 3rd Annual IEEE International Computer Performance and Dependability Symposium* (IPDS'98), Durham, NC, USA, Sept., pp. 109-118.

Jonkers, H., Lankhorst, M., Buuren, R. van, Hoppenbrouwers, S., Bonsangue, M., & Torre, L. van der (2004, September). Concepts for Modelling Enterprise Architectures, *International Journal of Cooperative Information Systems, 13*(3), 257-287.

Jordan, E. (1996). National Culture and Organizational Culture: Their use in information. http://www.is.cityu.edu.hk/ Research/WorkingPapers/paper/9408.pdf

Jørgensen, H. D. (2001). Interaction as a Framework for Flexible Workflow Modelling. In: C. Ellis & I. Zigurs (Eds.), *Proceedings of the International ACM SIG-GROUP Conference on Supporting Group Work 2001.* September 30 - October 3, 2001, Boulder, Colorado, USA. p.32-41.

Jørgensen, H. D. (2003). Model-Driven Work Management Services. In R. Jardim-Goncalves, H. Cha, A. Steiger-Garcao (Eds.), *Proceedings of the 10th International Conference on Concurrent Engineering (CE 2003),* July 2003, Madeira, Portugal. A.A. Balkema Publishers.

Jørgensen, H. D. (2004). *Interactive Process Models.* PhD thesis, Department of Computer and Information Science, Norwegian University of Science and Technology, Trondheim, Norway.

Jørgensen, H. D., & Carlsen, S. (1999) Emergent Workflow: Integrated Planning and Performance of Process Instances. In J. Becker, M. zur Mühlen, M. Rosemann (Eds.) *Proceedings of the 1999 Workflow Management Conference: Workflow-based Applications,* 9 Nov, Univ., Münster, Germany, pp 98-116.

Julka, N., Srinivasan, R., & Karimi, I. (2002) Agent-based Supply Chain Management a Framework. *Computers & Industrial Engineering, 26*(12), 1755-1769.

Kai, A. O., & Per, S. (2007). IT for niche companies: Is an ERP system the solution? *Information Systems Journal, 17,* 37-58.

Kallinikos, J. (2004). Deconstructing information packages: Organizational and behavioural implications of ERP systems. *Information Technology & People, 17*(1), 8-30.

Kamath, M., Dalal, N., Chaugule, A., Sivaraman, E., & Kolarik, W. (2003). A review of enterprise process modeling techniques. In V. V. Prabhu, S. Kumara & M. Kamath (Eds.), *In Scalable Enterprise Systems: An Introduction to Recent Advances* (pp. 1–32). Boston, MA: Kluwer Academic Publishers.

Kanellis, P., Lycett, M., & Paul, R. (1999). Evaluating business information systems fit: From concept to practical application. *European Journal of Information Systems, 18*(1), 65-76.

Karahanna, E., Evaristo, J., Srite, M. (2005). Levels of Culture and Individual Behavior: An Integrative Perspective. *Journal of Global Information Management, 13*(2), 1-20.

Karsai, G., & Agrawal, A. (2003). Graph transformations in OMG's Model-Driven Architecture, in J.L. Pfaltz, M. Nagl and B. Böhlen (eds.), *Proceedings 2nd International Workshop on Applications of Graph Transformations with Industrial Relevance* (AGTIVE 2003), Charlottesville, VA, USA, Sept. 2003, pp. 243-259.

Kaufman, L., & Rousseeuw, P. J. (1990). *Finding Groups in Data: An Introduction to Cluster Analysis.* New York: John Wiley & Sons,

Kavanagh, J. F. (2004). Resistance as Motivation for Innovation: Open Source Software. *Communications of the Association for Information Systems, 13,* 615-628.

Kazman, R., Asundi, J., & Klein, M. (2002). *Making Architecture Design Decisions: An Economic Approach,* Technical Report CMU/SEI-2002-TR-035 ESC-TR-2002-035, September.

Kazman, R., Bass, L., Abowd, G., & Webb, M. (1994). SAAM: A method for analyzing the properties of software architectures. In *Proceedings 16th International Conference on Software Engineering,* pages 81–90, Sorento, Italy.

Kazman, R., Klein, M., & Clements, P. (2000). ATAM: Method for Architecture Evaluation, Technical Report CMU/SEI-2000-TR-004 ESC-TR-2000-004, August.

Kedia, B. L., & Bhagat, R. S. (1988). Cultural Constraints on Transfer of Technology Across Nations: Implications for Research in International and Comparative Management. *Academy of Management Review, 13*(4), 559-571.

Khalil, O. E. M., & Mady, T. (2005). IT Adoption and Industry Type: Some Evidence from Kuwaiti Manufacturing Companies. *International Journal of Enterprise Information Systems, 1*(4), 39-55.

Kim, Y., Lee, Z., & Gosain, S. (2005). Impediments to successful ERP implementation process. *Business Process Management Journal, 11*(2), 158-170.

Kirkpatrick, S., Gelatt, C.D. Jr., & Vecchi, M.P. (1983). Optimization by simulated annealing. *Science, 220*(4598), 671-680.

Klaus, H., Rosemann, M., & Gable, G. G. (2000). What is ERP? *Information System Frontiers, 2*(2), 141-162.

Klein, M., Broekstra, J., Fensel, F., van Harmelen, F., & Horrocks, I. (2003). Ontologies and Schema Languages on the Web. In D. Fensel, J. A. Hendler, H. Lieberman & W. Wahlster (Eds.), *Spinning the Semantic Web: Bringing the World Wide Web to Its Full Potential* [outcome of a Dagstuhl seminar] (pp. 95-139). Cambridge, MA: MIT Press.

Knapen, J. (2007, May 14). SAP Sees Growth Ahead. *The Wall Street Journal Online*, http://online.wsj.article_print/SB1179166926818022214.html accessed 11 November 2007.

Ko, D. G., Kisrch, L. J., & King, W. R. (2005). Antecedents of Knowledge Transfer from Consultant to Clients in Enterprise System Implementations. *MIS Quarterly*, 29(1), 59-85.

Koch, C. (2001). BPR and ERP: Realising a vision of process with IT. *Business Process Management Journal*, 7(3), 258-265.

Koch, C. (2004). *Koch's IT Strategy: The ERP Pickle*. Retrieved June 16, 2005, from http://www.cio.com/blog_view.html?CID=935

Kohrs, A., & Merialdo, B. (2001). Creating user-adapted Web sites by the use of collaborative filtering. *Interacting with Computers, 13*, 695-716.

Kolp, M., Do, T., & Faulkner, S. (2004). A social-driven design of e-business system. *In Software Engineering for Multi-Agent Systems III, Research Issues and Practical Applications*. Edinburg, UK, pp. 70–84.

Kolp, M., Do, T., & Faulkner, S. (2005). Introspecting agent-oriented design patterns. *In*

Kolp, M., Giorgini, P., & Mylopoulos, J. (2002). Information systems development through social structures. *In Proc. of the 14th Int. Conf. on Software Engineering and Knowledge Engineering, SEKE'02'*. Ishia, Italy, pp. 183–190.

Kolp, M., Giorgini, P., & Mylopoulos, J. (2002), Organizational multi-agent architecture: A mobile robot example. *In Proc. of the 1st Int. Conf. on Autonomous Agent and Multi Agent Systems, AAMAS'02'*. Bologna, Italy, pp. 94–95.

Kolp, M., Giorgini, P., & Mylopoulos, J. (2003). Organizational patterns for early requirements analysis. *In Proc. of the 15th Int. Conf. on Advanced Information Systems, CAiSE'03'*. Velden, Austria, pp. 617–632.

Kolp, M., Giorgini, P., & Mylopoulos, J. (2006). Multi-agent architectures as organizational structures. *Autonomous Agents and Multi-Agent Systems, 13*(1), 3–25.

Konrad, S. & Cheng, B. (2002). Requirements patterns for embedded systems. *In Proc. of the 10th IEEE Joint International Requirements Engineering Conference, RE'02'*. Essen, Germany, pp. 127–136.

Konstanflons, C. (2004, June). ERP systems deployment problems in the real world: From Blue prints to Go Live.

26th *International conference on information technology interfaces*, ITI 2004, Cavtat, croatia, 71-76.

Kopinak, B. (2005). The Relationship Between Employment in Maquiladora Industries in Mexico and Labor Migration to the United Status. *The Center for Comparative Immigration Studies, 1-18*. University of California, San Diego.

Kositanurit, B., Ngwenyama, O., & Osei-Bryson, K.-M. (2006). An Exploration of Factors that Impact Individual Performance in an ERP Environment: An Analysis Using Multiple Analytical Techniques. *European Journal of Information Systems, 15*, 556-568.

Kossek, E. E., Young, W., Gash, D., & Nichol, V. (1994). Waiting for Innovation in the Human Resources Department: Godot Implements a Human Resource Information System. *Human Resource Management, 33*(1), 135-160.

Kotok, A., & Webber, D. R. R. (2001). *ebXML: The New Global Standard for Doing Business Over the Internet*. Boston, USA: New Riders.

Kremers, M., & Dissel, H. V. (2000). ERP system migrations. Association for Computing Machinery. *Communications of the ACM, 43*(4), 52-56.

Kremers, M., & van Dissel, H. (2000). ERP System Migrations. *Communications of the ACM, 43*(4), 53-56.

Kroeber, A., & Kluckholn, C. (1952). Culture: A critical review of concepts and definitions. Cambridge, MA.

Krogstie, J. (2004). Integrating Enterprise and IS Development Using a Model-Driven Approach. In O. Vasilecas, A. Caplinskas, G. Wojtkowski, W. Wojtkowski, J. Zupancic (Eds.) *Information Systems Development Advances in Theory, Practice, and Education*. (Proc. ISD'04). Boston, MA: Kluwer.

Krogstie, J. (2007). Modelling of the People, by the People, for the People. In J. Krogstie, A. L. Opdahl & S. Brinkkemper (Eds.), *Conceptual Modelling in Information Systems Engineering*. Berlin: Springer, pp. 305-318.

Krogstie, J. (2008). Integrated Goal, Data and Process modeling: From TEMPORA to Model-Generated Work-Places. In, Johannesson and Søderstrøm, (eds.), *Information Systems Engineering*. IGI Publishing 2008.

Krogstie, J., & Jørgensen, H. (2004). Interactive Models for Supporting Networked Organizations. In A. Persson & J. Stirna (Eds.), *Advanced Information Systems Engineering, 16th International Conference (CAiSE'04)*, Berlin: Springer (LNCS 3084).

Kumar, K., & Hillegersberg, J. V. (2000). ERP experiences and evolution. Association for Computing Machinery. *Communications of the ACM, 43*(4), 22-26.

Kuntz, J., Christiansen, T., Cohen, G., Jin, Y. & Levitt, R. (1998). The virtual design team: A Computational simulation model of project organizations. *Communications of the ACM, 41*(11), 84-92.

Kutvonen, L. (1998). *Trading services in open distributed environments*. Department of Computer Science, University of Helsinki. (PhD thesis. A-1998-2)

Kutvonen, L. (2002). Automated management of inter-organisational applications. In *Proceedings of the Sixth International Enterprise Distributed Object Computing Conference (EDOC 2002)* (p. 27-38). Lausanne, Switzerland: IEEE.

Kutvonen, L. (2004a). Challenges for ODP-based infrastructure for managing dynamic B2B networks. In A. Vallecillo, P. Linington, & B. Wood (Eds.), *Workshop on ODP for Enterprise Computing (WODPEC 2004)* (pp. 57–64). Monterey, California.

Kutvonen, L. (2004b, September). Relating MDA and inter-enterprise collaboration management. In *Second European Workshop on Model Driven Architecture (MDA), EWMDA-2* (pp. 84–88). (Published as technical report No. 17-04 in University of Kent.)

Kutvonen, L., & Metso, J. (2005, September). Services, contracts, policies and eCommunities – Relationship to ODP framework. In P. Linington, A. Tanaka, S. Tyndale-Biscoe, & A. Vallecillo (Eds.), *Workshop on ODP for Enterprise Computing (WODPEC 2005)* (pp. 62–69). Enschede, The Netherlands.

Kutvonen, L., Metso, J., & Ruohomaa, S. (2006, October). From trading to eCommunity population: Responding to social and contractual challenges. In *Proceedings of the 10th IEEE international EDOC conference (EDOC 2006)* (pp. 199–210). Hong Kong: IEEE.

Kutvonen, L., Metso, J., & Ruohomaa, S. (2007, July). From trading to eCommunity management: Responding to social and contractual challenges. *Information Systems Frontiers (ISF) - Special Issue on Enterprise Services Computing: Evolution and Challenges, 9*(2–3), 181–194.

Kutvonen, L., Metso, J., & Ruokolainen, T. (2005, November). Inter-enterprise collaboration management in dynamic business networks. In *On the Move to Meaningful Internet Systems 2005: CoopIS, DOA, and ODBASE: OTM Confederated International Conferences, CoopIS, DOA, and ODBASE* (Vol. 3760). Agia Napa, Cyprus: Springer-Verlag.

Kutvonen, L., Ruokolainen, T., & Metso, J. (2007, January). Interoperability middleware for federated business services in Web-Pilarcos. *International Journal of Enterprise Information Systems, Special issue on Interoperability of Enterprise Systems and Applications, 3*(1), 1–21.

Lachman, R., Nedd, A., & Hinings, B. (1994). Analyzing Cross-national Management and Organizations: A Theoretical Framework. *Management Science, 40*(1), 40-55.

Lammers, C. J., & Hickson, D. J. (1979). *Organizations alike and unlike: Toward a comparative sociology of organizations*. London: Routledge and Kegan Paul.

Landau S. (2005). Globalization, Maquilas, NAFTA and the State. *Journal of Developing Societies, 21*(3/4), 9.

Larson, J.A. (2003) VoiceXML and the W3C speech interface framework. *IEEE Multimedia, 10*, 91-93.

Lassila, K. S., & Brancheau, J. C. (1999). Adoption and Utilization of Commercial Software Packages: Exploring Utilization Equilibria, Transitions, Triggers, and Tracks. *Journal of Management Information Systems, 12*(2), 63-90.

Lassila, K. S., & Brancheau. (1999). Adoption and utilization of commercial software packages: Exploring utilization equilibria, transitions, triggers and tracks. *Journal of Management Information System, 16*(2), 63-90.

Latour, M. S., Hanna, J. B., Miller, M. D. & Pitts, R. E. (2002). Consumer Involvement with Personal Computer Technology: A Multi-Sample Analysis. *American Business Review*, June, 1-11.

Laughlin, S. (1999). An ERP game plan. *Journal of Business Strategy, 20*(1), 32-37.

Laurent, A. (1983). The cultural diversity of western conceptions of Management. *International Studies of Management and Organizations, 23*(2), 75-96.

Laurent, A. (1983). The cultural diversity of western conceptions of Management. *International Studies of Management and Organizations, 23*(2), 75-96.

Law, C. C. H., & Ngai, E. W. T. (2007). ERP Systems Adoption: An Exploratory Study of the Organizational Factors and Impacts of ERP Success. *Information & Management, 44*, 418-432.

Lazcano, A., Alonso, G., Schuldt, H., & Schuler, C. (2000). The WISE approach to Electronic Commerce. *Computer Systems Science and Engineering, 15*(5), 345–357.

Lee, C.C, & Lee, H. (2001). Factors Affecting Enterprise Resource Planning Systems Implementation in a Higher

Education Institution. *Issues in Information Systems, 2*, 207-212.

Lee, J., Siau, K., & Hong, S. (2003). Enterprise integration with ERP and EAI. Association for Computing Machinery. *Communications of the ACM, 46*(2), 54.

Lee, Y., Kozar, K., & Larsen, K.R.T. (2003). The Technology Acceptance Model: Past, Present and Future. *Communications of the Association for Information Systems, 12*(50), 752-780.

Leeuwen, D. van, Doest, H. Ter, & Lankhorst, M. (2004). A tool integration workbench for enterprise architecture. In *Proc. 6th International Conference on Enterprise Information Systems* (ICEIS 2004), Porto, Portugal, April.

Legare, T. L. (2002). The role of organizational factors in realizing ERP benefits. *Information Systems Management, 19*(4), 21.

Lei, Y., & Singh, M. (1997). A Comparison of Workflow Metamodels. *Paper presented at the ER'97 Workshop on Behavioral Models and Design Transformations: Issues and Opportunities in Conceptual Modeling*, Los Angeles, CA.

Leishman, D. A. (1999). Solution customization. *IBM Systems Journal, 38*(1), 76-97.

Lenzerini, M. (2002). Data Integration: A Theoretical Perspective. In *Proceedings of the 21st ACM Symposium On Principles Of Database Systems* (PODS 2002).

Letzing, J. (2007, April 25). Big Rivals Move In on Salesforce.com's Turf. *The Wall Street Journal*, B3G.

Levy, M., & Powell, P. (2003). Exploring SME Internet Adoption: Towards a Contingent Model. *Electronic Markets, 13*(2), 173-181.

Li, M.-S., Crave, S., Gilo, A., & van den Berg, R. (2007). *Value propositon for enterprise interoperability*. EC.

Li, Y., & Zhong, N. (2004). Web mining model and its applications for information gathering. *Knowledge-Based Systems, 17*(3), 207-217.

Lillehagen, F. (1999). Visual extended enterprise engineering embedding knowledge management systems engineering and work execution. *IFIP International Enterprise Modeling Conference (IEMC'99)*, Verdal, Norway.

Linthicum, D. (2003). *Next Generation Application Integration: From Simple Information to Web Services.* Boston: Addison-Wesley.

Linthicum, D. S. (2001). *B2B Application Integration - eBusiness-Enable Your Enterprise*. Addison-Wesley.

Liu, L., & Chi, L. (2002). Evolutionary Data Quality. In *7th International Conference on Information Quality*.

Loh, T. C., & Koh, S. C. L. (2004). Critical elements for a successful enterprise resource planning implementation in small- and medium-sized enterprises. *International Journal of Production Research, 42*(17), 3433-3455.

Loos, P., & Allweyer, T. (1998). *Process Orientation and Object Orientation - An Approach for Integrating UML* (Technical Report). Saarbrücken, Germany: Institut für Wirtschaftsinformatik, University of Saarland.

Lope, P. F. (1992). CIMII: the integrated manufacturing enterprise. *Industrial Engineering, 24*, 43-45.

López-Grao, J. P., Merseguer J., & Campos, J. (2004, January). From UML activity diagrams to Stochastic Petri Nets: Application to software performance engineering. In *Proceedings 4th International Workshop on Software and Performance: ACM SIGSOFT Software Engineering Notes, 29*(1).

Lucas, H. C., & Moore Jr., J. R. (1976). A Multiple-criterion scoring approach to information system project selection. *Info., 14*(1), 1–12.

Luftman, J., Kempaiah, R., & Nash, E. (2006). Key Issues for IT Executives 2005. *MIS Quarterly Executive, 5*(2), 81-99.

Lung, C.-H., Jalnapurkar, A., & El-Rayess, A. (1998). Performance-oriented software architecture analysis: An experience report. In *Proceedings First International Workshop on Software and Performance*, Santa Fe, NM, Oct.

Luo, X., Leung, H. F., Lee, J. H. M., & Jennings, N. R. (2003). Prioritized fuzzy constraint satisfaction problems: Axioms, instantiation and validation. *Fuzzy sets and Systems, 136*(2), 151-188.

Lyytinen, K. (1988). Expectation failure concept and systems analysts view of information systems failures: Results of an exploratory study. *Information and Management, 14*(1), 45-56.

Lyytinen, K., & Yoo, Y. (2002). The next wave of nomadic computing. *Information Systems Research, 13*(4), 377-388

M. Bovee, Srivastava, R.P., & Mak, B.R. (2001). A conceptual framework and belief-function approach to assessing overall information quality. In *Proceedings of the 6th International Conference on Information Quality*.

Mabert, V. A., Soni, A., & Venkataramanan, M. A. (2003). The impact of organization size on enterprise resource planning (ERP) implementations in the US manufacturing sector. *International Journal of Management Science, 31*, 235-246.

Mabert, V. A., Soni, A., & Venkataramanan, M. A. (2003). The impact of organization size on ERP implementations in US manufacturing sector. *The International Journal of Management Science, 31*, 235-246.

Malone, T. W. (1997). Is Empowerment Just a Fad? Control, Decision Making, and IT. *Sloan Management Review, 38*(2), 23-35.

Malone, T. W., Yates, J., & Benjamin, R. I. (1987). Electronic markets and electronics hierarchies. *Communications of the ACM, 30*(6), 484-497.

Mandal, P. (2006). Behavioral Factors and Information Technology Infrastructure Considerations in Strategic Alliance Development. *International Journal of Enterprise Information Systems, 2*(4), 77-88.

Manish, A., & Kaushal, C. (March 2007). Software Effort, Quality and Cycle Time: A Study of CMM Level 5 Projects. *IEEE Transaction on Software Engineering, 33*, (3), 145-156.

Manola, F., & Miller, E. (2004, 10 Feb). RDF Primer. Retrieved 15 Aug, 2005, from http://www.w3.org/TR/rdf-primer/

Marakas, G. M., & Hornik, S. (1996). Passive Resistance Misuse: Overt Support and Covert Recalcitrance in IS Implementation. *European Journal of Information Systems, 5*(3), 208-220.

Mark, K., & Amrit, T. (2006). Relative importance of evaluation criteria for enterprise systems: a conjoint study. *Information Systems Journal*, (16), 237-262.

Market Wire (2006). *Voxify Reports Outstanding Growth, Increased Momentum in the Speech Self-Service Marketplace*. Retrieved August 10, 2006, from http://www.findarticles.com/p/articles/mi_pwwi/is_200605/ai_n16136434

Markus M, L., Tanis, C., & Van Fenema, P. C. (2000). Multisite ERP implementations. *Communications of the ACM, 43*(4), 42-46.

Markus, M L., & Tanis, C. (2000). The Enterprise System Experience – From Adoption to Success. In R. Zmud (dir.), *Framing the Domain of IT Management*, 173-207, Pinnaflex.

Markus, M. L. (1983). Power, Politics, and MIS Implementation. *Communications of the ACM, 26*(6), 430-444.

Markus, M. L., & Tanis, C. (2000). The enterprise systems experience-From adoption to success. In *framing the Domains of IT Research: Glimpsing the Future through the Past*, R. W. Zmud, Ed. Cincinnati, OH: Pinnaflex Educational Resources Inc., pp. 173-207.

Markus, M. L., & Tanis, C. (2000). The Enterprise Systems experience - From adoption to success. In R. W. Zmud (Ed.), *Framing the domains of IT management: Projecting the future through the past*. Cincinnati, OH: Pinnaflex Educational Resources, Inc.

Markus, M. L., Axline, S., Petrie, D., & Tanis, C. (2000). Learning from Adopters' Experience with ERP: Problems Encountered and Success Achieved. *Journal of Information Technology, 15*, 245-265.

Markus, M. L., Tanis, C., & van Fenema, P. C. (2000). Multisite ERP implementations. Association for Computing Machinery. *Communications of the ACM, 43*(4), 42-46.

Martin, I., & Cheung, Y. (2000). SAP and Business Process Reengineering. *Business Process Management, 6*(2), 131-121.

Martinko, M. J., Henry, J. W., & Zmud, R. W. (1996). An attributional explanation of individual resistance to the introduction of information technologies in the workplace. *Behaviour & Information Technology, 15*(5), 313-330.

Mathew, S. (2003). *Quantitative Models for Total Cost of Ownership of Integrated Enterprise Systems*. Pennsylvania State University, University Park.

Matthyssens, P., & Van den Butle, C. (1994). Getting closer and nicer: Partnerships in the supply chain. *Long Range Planning, 27*(1), 72-83.

Maurice, M. (1979). For a study of the societal effect: the universality and specificity in organizational research. In C. J. Lammers and D. J. Hickson (dir.), *Organizations Alike and Unlike*. London: Routledge and Kegan Paul

McCaskey, & Okrent, M. D. (1999). Catching the ERP second wave. *APICS—The Performance Advantage, 34–38:*

McGinnis, T. C., & Huang, Z. (2007). Rethinking ERP Success: A New Perspective from Knowledge Management and Continuous Improvement. *Information and Management, 44*(7), 626-634.

McGuinness, D. L. (2003). Ontologies Come of Age. In D. Fensel, J. A. Hendler, H. Lieberman & W. Wahlster (Eds.), *Spinning the Semantic Web: Bringing the World Wide Web to Its Full Potential* [outcome of a Dagstuhl seminar] (pp. 171-195). Cambridge, MA: MIT Press.

McNurlin, B. C., & Sprague, R. H. Jr. (2002). *Information Systems Management in Practice*. 5th edition, Upper Saddle River.

Mecella, M., Scannapieco, M., Virgillito, A., Baldoni, R., Catarci, T., & Batini, C. (2003). The DaQuinCIS broker: Querying data and their quality in cooperative information systems. *Journal of Data Semantics, 1(1. Shorter version also appeared in CoopIS 2002.)*.

Medjahed, B., Benatallah, B., Bouguettaya, A., Ngu, A. H. H., & Elmagarming, A. K. (2003). Business-to-business interactions: issues and enabling technologies. *The VLDB Journal* (12), 59-85.

Mehta, R. (2003). *Software Modeling Tool for Analysis of Manufacturing and Supply Networks*. Pennsylvania State University, University Park.

Mercado, A. (2001). El Comercio Mediante la Red Electronica en Mexico y su Industria Maquiladora, Red de Economia Fronteriza, 1-18. Available at: http://www.nobe-ref.org/Conferences/2001/PANELII_AMERCADO.pdf.

Meta Object Facility (MOF) Specification — Version 1.4. (2002, April). (Retrieved September 1st, 2005, from http://www.omg.org/docs/formal/02-04-03.pdf)

Metso, J. (2007, April 26–27). Pragmatic aspects in computer-supported negotiations of virtual enterprise contracts. In *Web proceedings of the I-ESA '07 Doctoral symposium*. Funchal, Portugal. (To appear.)

Metso, J., & Kutvonen, L. (2005, September). Managing Virtual Organizations with Contracts. In *Workshop on Contract Architectures and Languages (CoALa2005)*. Enschede, The Netherlands.

Mihaila, G., Raschid, L., & Vidal, M. (2000). Using quality of data metadata for source selection and ranking. In *Proceedings of the 3rd International Workshop on the Web and Databases (WebDb'00)*.

Milano, D., Scannapieco, M., & Catarci, T. (2004). Quality-driven query processing of xquery queries. In *Proceedings of the International Workshop on Data and Information Quality (DIQ 2004)*.

Milano, D., Scannapieco, M., & Catarci, T. (2005). Using ontologies for xml data cleaning. In *Second INTEROP dissemination workshop*.

Miles, A. (2006, February). *RDFMolecules:Evaluating Semantic Web Technology in a Scientific Application*. Available at http://www.w3c.rl.ac.uk/SWAD/ papers/RDFMolecules_final.doc (Feb 20, 2006)

Miles, M. B., & Huberman, A. M. (1994). *Qualitative Data Analysis* (2nd ed.). Thousand Oaks, California: Sage Publications.

Miller, J., & Mukerji, J. (eds.), (2003). *MDA Guide Version 1.0.1*, Object Management Group, June.

Milosevic, Z., Jøsang, A., Patton, M., & Dimitrakos, T. (2002). Discretionary enforcement of electronic contracts. In *6th Enterprise Distributed Object Computing conference (EDOC 2002)*. Entschede, The Netherlands: IEEE Computer Society.

Milosevic, Z., Linington, P. F., Gibson, S., Kulkarni, S., & Cole, J. B. (2004). Inter-Organisational Collaborations Supported by E-Contracts. In W. Lamersdorf, V. Tschammer, & S. Amarger (Eds.*), Building The E-Service Society: E-Commerce, E-Business, and E-Government -IFIP 18th World Computer Congress TC6/TC8/TC11 4th International Conference on E-Commerce, E-Business, E-Government (I3E 2004)* (p. 413-429). Kluwer.

Mintzberg, H. (1992). *Structure in fives: Designing effective organizations*. Prentice-Hall.

Misevicius, A. (2003). Genetic algorithm hybridized with ruin and recreate procedure: Application to the quadratic assignment problem. *Knowledge-Based Systems, 16*(5-6), 261-268.

Misof, D. (2007). Process costing with ARIS Business Optimizer. ARIS Expert Paper, IDS Scheer, Jan.

Mitzi, G. P., & Glenn, J. B. (2007). Improving requirements elicitation: An empirical investigation of procedural prompts. *Information Systems Journal, 17*, 89-110.

Montagut, F., & Molva, R. (2005). Enabling pervasive execution of workflows. In *International conference on collaborative computing: Networking, applications and worksharing*. San Jose, CA, USA: IEEE.

Morabito, J., Sack, I., & Bhate, A. (1999). *Organization modeling: Innovative architectures for the 21st century*. Prentice Hall.

Moscato, P., & Cotta, C. (2003). Gentle introduction to memetic algorithms. In F. Glover & G. Kochenberger (Eds.), *Handbook of metaheuristics* (pp. 105-144). Boston: Kluwer Academic Publishers.

Muscatello, J. R., Small, M. H., & Chen I. J. (2003). Implementing ERP in small and midsize manufacturing firms. *International Journal of Operations and Production Management, 23*, 850–871.

Muscatello, J., Small, M., & Chen, I. (2003). Implementing enterprise resource planning (ERP) systems in small and midsize manufacturing firms. *International Journal of Operations & Production Management, 23*(8), 850-871.

Myers, M. D. (1997). *Qualitative Research in Information Systems*. Entered on May 20ᵗʰ 1997 from http://www.qual.auckland.ac.nz/

Mylopoulos, J., & Papazoglou, M. (1997). Cooperative information systems (Special Issue). *IEEE Expert Intelligent Systems & Their Applications, 12*(5).

N/A (1998). 7 key elements of a successful implementation, and 8 mistakes you will make anyway. *APICS 1998 International Conference Proceedings*. Falls Church, VA, 356–358:

Nachira, F., Dini, P., A.Nicolai, Louarn, M., & Léon, L. (2007). *Digital business ecosystems*. European Commission.

Nah, F. F., Lau, J. L., & Kuang, J. (2001). Critical factors for successful implementation of enterprise systems. *Business Process Management Journal, 7*(3), 285-296.

Nandhakumar, J., Rossi, M., & Talvinen, J. (2005). The dynamics of contextual forces of ERP implementation. *Journal of Strategic Information Systems, 14*(2), 221–242.

Nardi, D., & Brachman, R. (2002). *The description logic handbook*. In F. Baader, D. Calvanese, D. L. McGuinnes, D. Nardi, & P. Pate-Schneider (Eds.), (pp. 5–44). Cambridge CB2 2RU, UK: Cambridge University Press.

National Statistics 2001 area classification (2001). *Area classification for statistical wards*. Retrieved from http://www.statistics.gov.uk/about/methodology_by_theme/area_classification/wards/downloads/area_classification_for_statistical_wards_methods.pdf, retrieved 2006-01-20.

Nattkemper, J. (2000). An ERP evolution. *HP Professional, 14*(8), 12-15.

Natvig, M. K., & Ohren, O. (1999). Modeling shared information spaces (SIS). *In GROUP '99: Proceedings of the international ACM SIGGROUP conference on Supporting group work*, Phoenix, AZ, Nov 14-17, pp. 99-108. New York: ACM Press.

Naumann, F., Freytag, J., & Leser, U. (2004). Completeness of integrated information sources. *Information Systems, 29*(7).

Naumann, F., Leser, U., & Freytag, J. (1999). Quality-driven integration of heterogenous information systems. In *Proceedings of 25th International Conference on Very Large Data Bases (VLDB'99)*.

Neal, S., Cole, J. B., Linington, P. F., Milosevic, Z., Gibson, S., & Kulkarni, S. (2003). Identifying requirements for Business Contract Language: a Monitoring Perspective. In *7th International Enterprise Distributed Object Computing Conference (EDOC 2003)* (pp. 50–61). Los Alamitos, CA, USA: IEEE.

Neisse, R., Pereira, E. D. V., Granville, L. Z., Almeida, M. J. B., & Tarouco, L. M. R. (2004). A hierarchical policy-based architecture for integrated management of grids and networks. In *Fifth IEEE International Workshop on Policies for Distributed Systems and Networks (POLICY'04)* (p. 103-106). New York, USA.

Nelson, R. R. (2007). IT Project Management: Infamous failures, classic Mistakes, and Best Practices. MIS Quarterly Executive, *6*(2), 67-78.

Newell, S., Huang, J. C., Galliers, R. D., & Pan, S. L. (2003). Implementing Enterprise Resource Planning and knowledge management systems in tandem: fostering efficiency and innovation complementarity. *Information and Organization, 13*(1), 25-52.

Nicolaou, A. I. (2004). ERP Systems Implementation: Drivers of Post-Implementation Success, *Decision Support in an Uncertain and Complex World, The IFIP TC8/WG8.3 International Conference*, 589-597.

Nicolas, S., & Sarriegi, J. M. (2006, May/June). Open source software ERPs: A new alternative for an old need. *IEEE Software*, 94 -96

Nikolopoulos, K., Metaxiotis, K., Lekatis, N., & Assimakopoulos, V. (2003). Integrating industrial maintenance strategy into ERP. *Industrial Management & Data Systems, 103*, 3/4, 184-192.

Norman, D. A. (1988). *The Psychology of Everyday Things*. New York: Basic Books.

Norta, A. (2007). *Exploring dynamic inter-organisational business process collaboration*. Technicshe Universiteit Eindhoven, Department of Technology Management.

Nunnally, J.C. (1978). *Psychometric Theory*. New York: McGraw-Hill.

Nurmela, T., & Kutvonen, L. (2007, June). Service level agreement management in federated virtual organizations. In *Distributed applications and interoperable systems (DAIS2007)*. Paphos, Cyprus: Springer-Verlag.

O'Brien, J. M. (2002). J.D. Edwards follows 5 with ERP upgrade. *Computer Dealer News, 18*(12), 11.

Okpara, J.O. (2004). Personal Characteristics as predictors of job satisfaction: An exploratory study of IT managers in a developing country. *Information Technology & People*, *17*(3), 327-337.

Olsen, S. A. (1982). *Group Planning and Problem Solving Methods in Engineering Management*. New York: Wiley.

OMG (2000). Workflow Management Facility Specification, v.1.2. Needham, MA: Object Management Group.

OMG (2003), UML *Profile for Schedulability,Perform ance and Time Specification*, Version 1.0 (formal/03-09-01), Sept.

OMG (2004), UML *Profile for Modeling Quality of Service and Fault Tolerance Characteristics and Mechanisms* (ptc/2004-06-01), 2004.

Opdahl, A. L., & Sindre, G. (2007). Interoperable Management of Conceptual Models, In J. Krogstie, A. L. Opdahl & S. Brinkkemper (Eds.), *Conceptual Modelling in Information Systems Engineering*. Berlin: Springer, pp. 75-90.

Orlikowski, W. J. (1991). Integrated Information Environment or Matrix of Control? The Contradictory Implications of Information Technology. *Accounting, Management and Information Technologies, 1*(1), 9-42.

Orlikowski, W. J. (2000). Using Technology and Constituting Structures: A Practice Lens for Studying Technology in Organizations. *Organization Science, 11*(4), 404-428.

Orlikowski, W. J., & Baroudi, J. J. (1991). Studying Information Technology in Organizations: Research Approaches and Assumptions. *Information Systems Research, 2*(1), 1-28.

OWL Web Ontology Language Guide. (2004, February). (W3C Recommendation 10 February 2004, Retrieved September 1st, 2005, from http://www.w3.org/TR/owl-guide/)

OWL-S Coalition (2004). OWL-S 1.1 Release. Retrieved 9 Aug, 2005, from http://www.daml.org/services/owl-s/

Palsberg, J., & Zhao, T. (2001). Efficient and flexible matching of recursive types. *Information and Computation, 171*(2), 364–387.

Papazoglou, M. P., & Georgakopoulos, D. (2003, October). *Service oriented computing. Communications of the ACM, 46*(10).

Parr, A., & Shanks, G. (2000). A Taxonomy of ERP Implementation Approaches. In *Proceedings of the 33rd*

Hawaii International Conference on System Sciences HICSS, Maui, Hawaii, USA, 2424-2433.

Pauleen, D., Evaristo, R., Davison, R., Ang, S., Alanis, M., & Klein (2006). Cultural Bias in Information Systems Research and Practice: Are You Coming from the same place I am? *Communications of the AIS, 17*, 354-372.

Peer, J. (2002). Bringing Together Semantic Web and Web Services. In *ISWC '02: Proceedings of the First International Semantic Web Conference on The Semantic Web* (pp. 279–291). London, UK: Springer-Verlag.

Peppard, J., & Ward, J. (2005). Unlocking Sustained Business Value from IT Investments. *California Management Review, 48*(1), 52-70.

Perkowitz, M., & Etzioni, O. (2000). Towards adaptive Web sites: Conceptual framework and case study. *Artificial Intelligence, 118*, 245-275.

Peslak, A. R. (2006). Enterprise Resource Planning Success. An Exploratory Study of the Financial Executive Perspective. *Industrial Management & Data Systems, 106*(9), 1288-1303.

Petrovic D., Roy, R., & Petrovic R., (1999) Supply chain modeling using fuzzy sets. *International Journal of Production Economics, 59*(3), 443-453.

Pickering, A. (1995). *The Mangle of Practice: Time, Agency and Science*. Chicago: University of Chicago Press.

Pijpers, G. G. M., & van Montfort, K. (2006). An Investigation of Factors that Influence Senior Executives to Accept Innovations in Information Technology, *International Journal of Management, 23*(1), 11-23.

Pollock, N., & Cornford, J. (2004). ERP systems and the university as a "unique" organization. *Information, Technology & People, 17*, 1, 31-52.

Pooley, R., (1999). Using UML to Derive Stochastic Process Algebra Models, in N. Davies and J. Bradley, editors. UKPEW '99, *Proceedings of the Fifteenth UK Performance Engineering Workshop*, The University of Bristol, July 1999, pp23-33.

Poon, S., & Swatman, P (1999). An Exploratory Study of Small Business Internet Commerce Issues. *Information and Management, 35*, 9-18.

Poston, R., & Grabski, S. (2001). Financial impacts of enterprise resource planning implementations. *International Journal of Accounting Information Systems, 2*(4), 271-294.

Powers, S. (2003). Practical RDF. Sebastopol, CA: O'Reilly.

Ptak, C., & Schragenheim, E. (2000). *ERP: Tools, Techniques, and Applications for Integrating the Supply Chain*. Boca Raton, FL: St. Lucie Press.

Quinteros C. (2005). Corporate responsibility and the US–Central America Free Trade Agreement (CAFTA): Are they compatible? *Development in Practice, 15*(3/4), 572-583.

Quirchmayr, G., Milosevic, Z., Tagg, R., Cole, J., & Kulkarni, S. (2002). Establishment of Virtual Enterprise Contracts. In *Database and Expert Systems Applications : 13th International Conference* (Vol. 2453, pp. 236–248). London, UK: Springer-Verlag.

Rabelo, R. J., Camarinha-Matos, L. M., & Vallejos, R. V. (2000). Agent-based brokerage for virtual enterprise creation in the moulds industry. In *Proceedings of the IFIP TC5/WG5.3 Second IFIP Working Conference on Infrastructures for Virtual Organizations: Managing Cooperation in Virtual Organizations and Electronic Business towards Smart Organizations* (pp. 281–290). Deventer, The Netherlands: Kluwer, B.V.

Rabelo, R. J., Gusmeroli, S., Arana, C., & Nagellen, T. (2006). The ECOLEAD ICT infrastructure for collaborative networked organizations. In *Network-centric collaboration and supporting frameworks* (Vol. 224, p. 451-460). Springer-Verlag.

Rai A., Lang S. S., & Welker R. B. (2002). Assessing the Validity of IS Success Models: An Empirical Test and Theoretical Analysis. *Information Systems Research, 13*(1), 50-69.

Rai, A., Lang, S. S., & Welker, R. B. (2002). Assessing the Validity of IS Success Models: An Empirical Test and Theoretical Analysis. *Information Systems Research, 13*(1), March 2002, 50-69.

Raisinghani, M. S., Meade, L., & Schkade, L. L. (2007). Strategic E-Business Decision Analysis Using The Analytic Network Process. *IEEE Transactions on Engineering Management, 54*(4), 673-686.

Rajagopal, P. (2002). An innovation-diffusion view of implementation of enterprise resource planning (ERP) systems and development of research model. *Information & Management, 40*(2), 87-114.

Ramaseshan, B., Bejou, D., Jain, S., Mason, C., & Pancras, J. (2006). Issues and Perspectives in Global Customer Relationship Management. *Journal of Service Research, 9*(2), 195-207.

Ranganathan, C., Brown, C. V. (2006). ERP Investments and the Market Value of Firms. *Information Systems Research, 17*(2), 145-161.

Raughunathan, S. (1992). A planning aid: an intelligent modeling system for planning problems based on constraint satisfaction. *IEEE Transactions on Knowledge Data Engineering, 4*(4), 317–335.

Ray, C.M., Sormunen, C., & Harris, T. M. (1999). Men's and women's attitudes toward computer technology: A comparison. *Office Systems Research Journal, 17*(1) Retrieved Oct. 14, 2006 from http://www.osra.org/itlpj/vol17no1.html

Raymond, L., & Uwizeyemungu, S. (2007). A profile of ERP adoption in manufacturing SMEs. *Journal of Enterprise Information Management, 20* (4), 487-502.

RDF Vocabulary Description Language 1.0: RDF Schema. (2004, February). (W3C Recommendation 10 February 2004. Retrieved September 1st, 2005, from http://www.w3.org/TR/rdf-schema/)

Rebman Jr., C. M., Aiken, M. W., Cegielski, C.G.., 2003, Speech recognition in the human-computer interface. *Information & Management, 40*(6), 509-519.

Redouane, EI A., Rowe, F., & Benedicte G-M.(2006). The effects of enterprise resource planning implementation strategy on cross-functionality. *Information Systems Journal*, (16), 79-104.

Reel., J. S. (1999). Critical success factors in software projects. *IEEE Software, 16*(3), 18-23.

Reichert, M., & Dadam, P. (1998). ADEPTflex – Supporting Dynamic Changes of Workflow Without Losing Control. *Journal of Intelligent Information Systems - Special Issue on Workflow Management, 10*(2), 93-129.

Roberts, B., & Mackay, M. (1998). IT supporting supplier relationship: The role of electronic commerce. *European Journal of Purchasing and Supply Management, 4*(2/3), 175-184.

Robey, D., & Boudreau M. C. (2000). Organizational Consequences of Information Technology: Dealing with Diversity in Empirical Research. In R. Zmud (dir.), *Framing the Domain of IT Management*, 51-61. Pinnaflex.

Robey, D., Ross, J. W., & Boudreau, M. C. (2002). Learning to implement enterprise systems: An exploratory case study of the dialectics change. *Journal of Management Information Systems, 19*(1), 17-46.

Robey, D., Smith, L., & Vijayasarathy, L. (1993). Perceptions of conflict and success in information systems development projects'. *Journal of Management Information Systems, 10*(1), 123-39.

Robichaux, B. P., & Cooper, R. B. (1998). GSS Participation: A Cultural Examination. *Information and Management, 33*, 287-300.

Robicheaux, R. A., & Colman J. E. (1994). The Structure of Marketing Channel Relationships. *Journal of Academy of Marketing Science, 22*(1), 38-51.

Rodriguez, A., Ho, W.-K., Kempny, G., Pedreschi, M., & Richards, N. (2002). *IBM WebSphere Voice Server 2.0 Implementation Guide.* IBM Redbooks, IBM.

Rose, J., & Jones, M. R. (2004). *The Double Dance of Agency: a socio-theoretic account of how machines and humans interact.* Paper presented at the ALOIS Workshop: Action in Language, Organizations and Information Systems, Linkoping, Sweden.

Rose, J., & Truex, D. (2000). Machine agency as perceived autonomy; an action perspective. In R. L. Baskerville, J. Stage & J. I. DeGross (Eds.), *Organizational and Social Perspectives on Information Technology* (pp. 371–390). Aalborg, Denmark: Kluwer.

Rose, J., Jones, M. R., & Truex, D. (2003). The problem of agency: How humans act, how machines act. *Paper presented at the ALOIS Workshop: Action in Language, Organizations and Information Systems*, Linkoping University, Linkoping, Sweden.

Rosenzweig, P. M. (1994). When Can Management Science Research Be Generalized Internationally? *Management Science, 40*(1), 28-39.

RosettaNet Consortium.(2004). *RosettaNet Implementation Framework: Core Specification V02.00.00.* (Retrieved September 1st, 2005, from http://www.rosettanet.org/)

Roussos, G., Marsh, A. J., & Maglavera, S. (2005). Enabling pervasive computing with smart phones. *IEEE Pervasive Computing, 4*(2), 20-27.

Ruohomaa, S.(2007, April 26–27). Trust management for inter-enterprise collaborations. In *Web proceedings of the I-ESA '07 Doctoral symposium.* Funchal, Portugal. (To appear.)

Ruohomaa, S., & Kutvonen, L. (2008, March). Making multi-dimensional trust decisions on inter-enterprise collaborations. In *Proceedings of the Third international conference on availability, reliability and security (ARES 2008).* Barcelona, Spain: IEEE.

Ruohomaa, S., Viljanen, L., & Kutvonen, L. (2006, March). Guarding enterprise collaborations with trust decisions—the TuBE approach. In *Interoperability for Enterprise Software and Applications. Proceedings of the Workshops and the Doctoral Symposium of the Second IFAC/IFIP I-ESA International Conference: EI2N, WSI, IS-TSPQ 2006* (pp. 237–248). Bordeaux, France: ISTE Ltd.

Ruokolainen, T. (2004). *Component interoperability.* University of Helsinki, Department of Computer Science. (MSc thesis C-2004-42. In Finnish.)

Ruokolainen, T., & Kutvonen, L.(2007, April). Service Typing in Collaborative Systems. In G. Doumeingts, J. Müller, G. Morel, & B. Vallespir (Eds.), *Enterprise Interoperability: New Challenges and Approaches* (pp. 343–354). Springer.

Ruokolainen, T., Metso, J., & Kutvonen, L. (2007, March). Ontology for federated management of business networks. In L. Kutvonen, P. Linington, J.-H. Morin, & S. Ruohomaa (Eds.), *Pre-proceedings of ISTSPQ 2007 — The 2nd international workshop on Interoperability solutions to Trust, Security, Policies and QoS for Enhanced Enterprise Systems* (pp. 41–54). University of Helsinki, Department of Computer Science Publications Series B, Report B-2007-3.

S. K. Chang, (ed.), *Handbook of Software Engineering and Knowledge Engineering, 3,* Recent Advances', World Scientific, pp. 151–177.

Saaty, T. L. (1980). *The Analytic Hierarchy Process (AHP).* New York: McGraw-Hill.

Salaka, V., & Prabhu, V. V. (2006). Project Management for Enterprise Integration. *The tenth IEEE conference on enterprise computing (EDOC 2006),* Hong Kong,

Salaka, V., Mehta, R., & Prabhu, V. V. (June 2005). Sensors-to-Suppliers Simulation Modeling of Manufacturing Supply Chains. *Proceedings of the 15th International Conference on Flexible Automation and Intelligent Manufacturing (FAIM 2005),* Bilbao, Spain,

Sandoe, K., Corbitt, G., & Boykin, R. (2001). *Enterprise Integration.* NY: Wiley.

Sane, V. (2005). *Enterprise Resource Planning Overview.* Ezine articles. Retrieved July 2, 2005, from http://ezinearticles.com/?Enterprise-Resource-Planning-Overview&id=37656

Santhanam, R., & Kyparisis, G. J. (1996). A decision model for interdependent information system project selection. *European Journal of Operational Research, 89,* 380–399.

Sargent, J., & Matthews, L. (2003). Boom or Bust: Is it the end of the Maquiladoras? *Business Horizons,* March-April, 57-64.

Sargent, J., & Matthews, L. (2004). *What Happens When Relative Costs Increase in Export Processing Zones? Technology, Regional Production Networks, and Mexico's Maquiladoras*", Working Paper #2002-19, Center of Border Economic Studies, The University of Texas – Pan American.

Sarkis, J., & Gunasekaran, A. (2003). Enterprise resource planning – modeling and analysis, *European Journal of Operational Research*, 146, 229-232.

Sawyer, S. (2000). Packaged software: Implications of the differences from custom approaches to software development. *European Journal of Information System*, 9, 47-58.

Scannapieco, M., & Batini, C. (2004). Completeness in the relational model: A comprehensive framework. In *9th International Conference on Information Quality*.

Scannapieco, M., Virgillito, A., Marchetti, M., Mecella, M., & Baldoni, R. (2004). The DaQuinCIS architecture: A platform for exchanging and improving data quality in cooperative information systems. *Information Systems, 29*(7).

Schaaf, D. (1999, May). What Trainers Need to Know About ERP. *Training.* ET4- ET12.

Scheer, A.-W. (1994). *Business Process Engineering: Reference Models for Industrial Enterprises*, Springer, Berlin, 2nd ed.

Scheer, A.-W., & Habermann, F. (2000). Making ERP a Success. Association for Computing Machinery. *Communications of the ACM, 43*(4), 57-61.

Scheer, A.-W., & Nuttgens, M. (2000). ARIS Architecture and Reference Models for Business Process Management. In W. M. P. van der Aalst, J. Desel & A. Oberweis (Eds.), *Business Process Management* (pp. 376-390). Berlin, Germany: Springer (LNCS 1806).

Schmidt, D. (2006, February). Model-driven engineering. *IEEE Computer, 39*(2), 25–31.

Schniederjans, M. J., & Kim, G.C. (2003). Implementing Enterprise Resource Planning Systems with Total Quality Control and Business Process Reengineering, *International Journal of Operations & Production Management, 23*(4), 418-429.

Schniederjans, M. J., & Wilson, R. L. (1991). Using the analytic hierarchy process and goal programming for information system project selection. *Information & Management, 20*, 333-342.

Schomig, A. and Rau, H. (1995). A petri net approach for the performance analysis of business processes. Technical Report 116, Lehrstuhl fur Informatik III, Universitat Wurzburg.

Schrnederjans, M. J., & Kim, G. C. (2003). Implementing enterprise resource planning systems with total quality control and business process reengineering survey results. *International Journal of Operations and Production Management, 23*(3/4), 418-429.

Scott, K. (2004). *Fast Track UML 2.0*. Apress.

Scott, W. R. (1998). *Organizations: Rational, natural, and open systems*. Prentice Hall.

Seddon, P. B. (1997). A respecification and extension of the DeLone and McLean model of IS success. *Information Systems Research*. 8(September) 240-253.

Seddon, P. B., & Kiew, M.-Y (1994). A partial test and development of the DeLone and McLean model of IS success. In J.I. De Gross, S. L. Huff, and M. C. Munro (eds.), *Proceedings of the International Conference on Information Systems*, Atlanta, GA: Association for Information Systems, 1994, 99-110.

Seddon, P. B., Staples, S., Patnayakuni, R., & Bowetell, M. (1999). Dimensions of Information Success. *Communication of the ACM, 2*(20), 1-40.

Sedera, D., Gable, G., & Chan, T. (2003). ERP Success: Does Organization Size Matter? In *Proceedings of the Pacific Asia Conference on Information Systems (PACIS)*, 10–13 July, Adelaide, South Australia, 1075-1088.

Segil, L. (1996). *Intelligent business alliances: How to profit using today's most important strategic tool*. Times Business.

Shang, S. S. C., & Seddon, P. B. (2000). *A comprehensive framework for classifying the benefits of ERP systems*. Paper presented at the Americas Conference on Information Systems, Long Beach, California.

Shang, S., & Seddon, P.B. (2000). A Comprehensive Framework for Classifying Benefits of ERP Systems. In *Proceedings of the 6th Americas Conference on Information Systems*, Long Beach, CA, USA, 1005-1014.

Shanks, G., Parr, A., Hu, B., Corbitt, B., Thanasankit, T., & Seddon, P. B. (2000). Differences in critical success factors in ERP systems implementation in Australia and China: a cultural analysis. *Paper presented at the European Conference on Information Systems*, Vienna, Austria.

Sharma, A., & Prabhu, V. V. (2005). Computing and Communication Quality of Service for Distributed Time-scaled Simulation in Heterarchical Manufacturing Control. *International Journal of Modelling and Simulation.*

Sharma, A., & Vyas P. (2007). DSS (Decision Support Systems) in Indian Organised Retail Sector, *Indian Institute Of Management.*

Shaw, M., & Garlan, D. (1996). *Software Architecture: Perspectives on an Emerging Discipline*, Prentice Hall.

Shehory, O. (1998). *Architectural properties of multi-agent systems.* Technical Report CMU-RI-TR-98-28, Carnegie Mellon University.

Shing-Kao, L. (1997). *A study of National Culture versus Corporate Culture in International Management.* Dissertation abstract international, Nova South-eastern University.

Sia, S. K., Tang, M., Soh, C., & Boh, W. F. (2002). Enterprise Resource Planning (ERP) Systems as a Technology of Power: Empowerment or Panoptic Control? *The DataBase for Advances in Information Systems, 33*(1), 23-37.

Siriginidi, S. R. (2000). Enterprise Resource Planning in Reengineering Business. *Business Process Management Journal, 6*(5), 376 - 391.

Skene, J., & Emmerich, W. (2003a). Model driven performance analysis of enterprise information systems. In *Proc. International Workshop on Test and Analysis of Component Based Systems (ETAPS/TACoS),* 82(6). Warsaw, Poland, April 2003. Electronic Notes in Theoretical Computer Science

Skene, J., & Emmerich, W. (2003b). A model driven architecture approach to non-functional analysis of software architectures. In *Proc. 18th IEEE Conference on Automated Software Engineering* (ASE'03), Toronto, Canada. Oct.

Slater, D. (1998, January28). ERP Projects Cost More Than Their Immediate Payback. *CIO Enterprise,* 26.

Slevin, D., & Pinto, J. (1986). The project implementation profile: new tool for project managers. *Project Management Journal, 17*(4), 57-70.

Smith G. (2004). Made In The Maquilas -- Again. *Business Week, 3896,* 45.

Smith, C. (1990). *Performance Engineering of Software Systems.* Addison-Wesley.

Smith, C. U., & Williams, L. G. (2000). Performance and scalability of disributed software architectures: An SPE approach. *Parallel and Distributed Computing Practices, 3*(4).

Smith, K. A., & Ng, A. (2003) Web page clustering using a self-organizing map of user navigation patterns. *Decision Support Systems, 35,* 245-256.

Smith, M., Welty, C., & McGuinness, D. L. (Eds.) (2004, 10 Feb). *OWL Web Ontology Language Guide.* Retrieved 25 Feb, 2005, from http://www.w3.org/TR/owl-guide/

Smith, S. M. (2005). The Digital Divide: Gender and Racial Differences in Information Technology Education. *Information Technology, Learning, and Performance Journal, 23,* 1.13-23.

Soh, C. & Sia, S.K. (2005). The challenges of implementing "vanilla" version of enterprise systems. *MIS Quarterly Executive, 4*(3), 373-384.

Soh, C., Kien, S. S., & Yap, J. T. (2000). Cultural fits and misfits: Is ERP a universal solution. Association for Computing Machinery. *Communications of the ACM,* 43(4), 47-51.

Sohal, A. S., Moss, S., & Ng, L. (2000). Using information technology productivity: practices and factors that enhance the success of IT. *International Journal of Technology Management, 20*(3/4), 340-353.

Soja, P. (2004). Success Factors in ERP Systems Implementations. Result of research on the Polish ERP market. In *Proceedings of the 10th Americas Conference on Information Systems AMCIS,* New York, USA, 3914-3922.

Soja, P. (2005). The Impact of ERP Implementation on the Enterprise – an Empirical Study. In *Proceedings of the 8th International Conference on Business Information Systems,* Poznan, Poland, 389-402.

Soja, P. (2006). Success factors in ERP systems implementations: lessons from practice. *Journal of Enterprise Information Management, 19*(4), 418-433.

Soja, P. (2008). Difficulties in Enterprise System Implementation in Emerging Economies: Insights from an Exploratory Field Study in Poland. *Information Technology for Development. Special Issue on Information Technology Investments in Emerging Economies, 14*(1), 31-51.

Soja, P., & Paliwoda-Pękosz, G. (2007). Towards the Causal Structure of Problems in Enterprise System Adoption. In *Proceedings of the 13th Americas Conference on Information Systems,* Keystone/Colorado, USA.

Soley, R., & the OMG Staff Strategy Group (2000). *Model Driven Architecture*. Object Management Group White Paper, Draft 3.2, Nov.

Somers, T. M., & Nelson, K. (2001). The impact of critical success factors across the stages of enterprise resource planning implementations. *Proceedings of the 34th Hawaii International Conference on System Sciences*, Hawaii, USA, 1–10:

Somers, T., & Nelson, K. (2001). *The Impact of Critical Success Factors across the Stages of Enterprise Resource Planning Implementations*. Paper presented at the Hawaii International Conference on Systems Sciences.

Somers, T., & Nelson, K. (2004). A taxonomy of players and activities across the ERP project life cycle. *Information & Management, 41*(3), 257-278.

Songini, M. (2004). University Pins $510M Lawsuit on PeopleSoft. *Computerworld*. March 29, 2004. p. 6.

Songini, M. (2004). ERP System Doesn't Make the Grade in Indiana. *Computerworld*. Sep 13, 2004, p. 1.

Sowa, J. F., & Zachman, J. A. (1992). Extending and formalizing the framework for information systems architectures. *IBM Systems Journal, 31*(3), 590-616.

Spacenet Inc. (2006). Corporate Communications & Distance Learning. Downloaded from http://www.vsat.cc/images/ehc_idl.pdf

Spitznagel, B., & Garlan, D. (1998). Architecture-based performance analysis. In *Proceedings 1998 Conference on Software Engineering and Knowledge Engineering*, San Francisco Bay, June.

Sriharee, N., & Senivongse, T. (2003, November). Discovering Web Services Using Behavioural Constraints and Ontology. In J.-B. Stefani, I. Demeure, & D. Hagimont (Eds.), *Distributed Applications and Interoperable Systems: 4th IFIP WG6.1 International Conference (DAIS 2003)* (pp. 248–259). Springer-Verlag.

Staab, S., & Studer, R. (Eds.). (2004). Handbook on Ontologies. Berlin, Germany: Springer.

Stedman, C. (1999). Failed ERP Gamble Haunts Hershey: Candy maker bites off more than it can chew and 'Kisses' big Halloween sales goodbye. *Computerworld, 1*.

Stedman, C. (1999a). ERP Problems Plague College. *Computerworld, 4*.

Stedman, C. (1999b). Oracle, PeopleSoft Offer New Approaches to Live Training. *Computerworld, 8*.

Steen, M. W. A., Akehurst, D. H., Doest, H. W. L. ter, & Lankhorst, M. M. (2004). Supporting viewpoint-oriented enterprise architecture. In *Proc. 8th International Enterprise Distributed Object Computing Conference* (EDOC 2004), Monterey, CA, USA, Sept., pp. 201-211.

Stefanou, C. J. (2001). A framework for the ex-ante evaluation of ERP software. *European Journal of Information Systems, 10*(4), 204-215.

Stein, T. (1999, May). ROI: Making ERP Add Up. *InformationWeek,* 59-68.

Stensrud, E., & Myrtveit, I. (2003). Identifying High Performance ERP Projects. *IEEE Transactions on Software Engineering, 29*(5), 398-416.

Straub, D. (1989). Validating instruments in MIS research. *MIS Quarterly, 13*(2), 147-169.

Strauss, A., & Corbin, J. (1999). *Basics of qualitative research: Grounded theory procedures and techniques.* Newbury Park, CA, Sage.

Su, Z., Yang, Q., Zhang, H., Xu, X., Hu, Y-H., & Ma, S. (2002). Corellation-based Web document clustering for adaptive Web interface design. *Knowledge and Information Systems, 4*, 151-167.

Subramanian, G. H., & Hoffer, C. S. (2005) An Exploratory Case Study of Enterprise Resource Planning Implementation. *International Journal of Enterprise Information Systems, 1*(1), 23-38.

Sumner, M. (2000). Risk factors in Enterprise-Wide/ERP projects. *Journal of Information Technology, 15*(4), 317-327.

Sun Microsystems (2004). Information on J2ME and J2SE. Retrieved June 2, 2007, from http://java.sun.com/j2me/ and http://java.sun.com/j2se/

Sun, A. Y. T., Yazdani, A., & Overend, J. D. (2005). Achievement Assessment for Enterprise Resource Planning (ERP) System Implementations Based on Critical Success Factors (CSFs). *International Journal of Production Economics, 98*, 189-203.

Swaminathan, M. J., Smith, S. F., & Sadeh, N. M. (1998). Modelling Supply Chain Dynamics: A Multiagent Approach. *Decision Sciences, 29*(3), 607-632.

Takeuchi, K., Honda, K., & Kubo, M. (1994). An Interaction-based Language and its Typing System. In *PARLE '94: Proceedings of the 6th International PARLE Conference on Parallel Architectures and Languages Europe* (pp. 398–413). London, UK: Springer-Verlag.

Tan, A. (May 2005). Voice to dominate 3G traffic, says expert. *ZDFNetAsia*. Retrieved June 2, 2007, from http://www.zdnetasia.com/news/communications/0,39044192,39231956,00.htm

Tang, J. E., Shee, D. Y., & Tang, T-I. (2001). A Conceptual model for interactive buyer-supplier relationship in Electronic Commerce. *International Journal of Information Management, 21*, 49-68.

Tang, M., Sia, S. K., Soh, C., & Boh, W. F. (2000). A Contingency Analysis of Post-bureaucratic Controls in IT-related Change. *Paper presented at the 21st International Conference on Information Systems*, Brisbane, Queensland, Australia.

Tayeb, M. (1994). Organizations and national culture: methodology considered. *Organizations Studies, 15*(3), 429-446.

Teltumbde, A. (2000). A framework for evaluating ERP projects. *International Journal of Production Research, 38*(17), 4507–4520.

Teo, T., & Pok, S. (2003). Adoption of WAP-enabled mobile phones among Internet users. *Omega: The International Journal of Management Science, 31*, 483-498.

The Commission of the European Community (1996). (96/280/EC) Commission recommendation of 3 April 1996 concerning the definition of small and medium-sized enterprises. In *Official Journal* No. L 107 30/04/1996, pp.4-9.

The Kelsey Group (2001, March). *The global voice ecosystem* (Analyst Report), The Kelsey Group.

Themistocleous, M., Irani, Z., O'Keefe R. M., & Paul, R. (2001). ERP Problems and Application Integration Issues: An Empirical Survey. In *Proceedings of the 34th Hawaii International Conference on System Sciences.*

Tinham B. (2006). Your Guide to Choosing and Implementing ERP. *Manufacturing Computer Solutions.*

Toledo, C., Excelente, B., & Jennings, N. R. (2002). Learning to Select a Coordination Mechanism. In *Proc. AAMAS'02*, Bologna, Italy, July 15-19, 1106-1113.

Toye, E., Sharp, R., Madhavapeddy, A., & Scott, D. (2005). Using smart phones to access site-specific services. *IEEE Pervasive Computing, 4*(2), 60-66.

Trauth, E. M., Quesenberry, J. L., & Morgan, A. J. (2004). Understanding the Under Representation of Women in IT: Toward a Theory of Individual Differences, SIGMIS '04, April 22-24, 2004, Tucson, Arizona, 114-119.

Triandis, H. C. (1982). Dimensions of Cultural Variation as Parameters of Organizational Theories. *International Studies of Management and Organizations, 12*, 139-169.

Trompenaars, F. (1993). Riding the waves of culture: Understanding Cultural Diversity in Business. Economics Books, London.

Trompenaars, F. T., & Hampden-Turner, C. H. (1998). *Riding The Waves of Culture—Understanding Diversity in Global Business.* McGraw-Hill.

Turban, E., Aronson, J.& Liang, T. (2005). *Decision Support Systems & Intelligent Systems.* NJ: Prentice Hall.

Turksen, I. B., Zarandi, M. H. (1999). *Production planning and scheduling: Fuzzy and Crisp approaches.* Boston, Kluwer Academic publishers, pp. 479-529.

Turner, K. (2004). Analysing interactive voice services. *Computer Networks, 45*(5), 665-685.

Ullman, J. (1997). Information integration using logical views. In *Proceedings of the 6th International Conference on Database Theory (ICDT '97).*

Umble, E. J., & Haft, R. R. (2003). Enterprise resource planning: implementation procedures and critical success factors. *European Journal of Operational Research, 146*(2), 241-257.

Umble, E. J., Halt, R. R., & Umble, M. M. (2003). Enterprise Resource Planning: Implementation procedures and critical success factors. *European Journal of Operational Research, 146*(2), 241-257.

Vallecillo, A., Vasconcelos, V. T., & Ravara, A.(2003). Typing the behavior of objects and components using session types. *Electronic Notes in Theoretical Computer Science, 68*(3). (Presented at FOCLASA'02)

van der Aalst, W. M. P. (1999). Formalization and Verification of Event-driven Process Chains. *Information and Software Technology, 41*(10), 639-650.

van der Aalst, W., ter Hofstede, A., & Weske, M. (2003). Business process management: A survey. In *Proceedings of the First International Conference on Business Process Management*. Eindhoven, The Netherlands: Springer-Verlag.

van der Aalst, W. M. P., Verbeek, H. M.W., & Kumar, A.(2001). XRL/Woflan: Verification of an XML/Petri-net based language for inter-organisational workflows. In *Proceedings of the 6th Informs Conference on Information Systems and Technology (CIST-2001)* (p. 30-45).

Van Everdingen, Y., Hilsberg, J., & Waarts, E. (2000). ERP adoption by European midsize companies. *Communications of ACM, 43*(2), 27-31.

van Fenema, P. C., & van Baalen, P. J. (2005). *Strategies for Dealing with Drift during Implementation of ERP Systems.* Rotterdam: Erasmus Research Institute of Management.

Vaquez-Salceda, J., Dignum, V., & Dignum, F. (2005). Organizing multiagent systems. *Autonomous Agents and Multi-Agent Systems, 11*, 307–360.

Venkatesh, V., & Morris, M.G. (2000). Why Don't Men Ever Stop To Ask for Directions? Gender, Social Influence and Their Role in Technology Acceptance and Usage Behavior. *MIS Quarterly, 24*(1), 115-139.

Wadhwa, S., & Rao, K. S. (2003). Enterprise Modeling of Supply Chains Involving Multiple entity Flows: Role of Flexibility in Enhancing Lead Time Performance. *SIC Journal, 12*(1), 5-20.

Wadhwa, S., & Rao, K. S. (2004) A Unified Framework for Manufacturing and Supply Chain Flexibility. *Global Journal of Flexible Systems Management, 5*(1), 15-22.

Wagner, E. L., Scott, S. V., & Galliers, R. D. (2006). The creation of 'best practice' software: Myth, reality and ethics. *Information and Organization, 16*(3), 251-275.

Wah, L. (2000, March). Give ERP a Chance. *Management Review,* 20-24.

Walsham, G. (1993). *Interpreting Information Systems in Organizations.* Chichester: John Wiley & Sons.

Walsham, G. (1995). The Emergence of Interpretivism in IS Research. *Information Systems Research, 6*(4), 376-394.

Wang, F. H., & Shao, H. M. (2004). Effective personalized recommendation based on time-framed navigation clustering and association mining. *Expert Systems with Applications, 27*(3), 365-377.

Wang, R. (1998). A product perspective on total data quality management. *Communications of the ACM, 41*(2).

Wang, R., & Strong, D. (1996). Beyond accuracy: What data quality means to data consumers. *Journal of Management Information Systems, 12*(4).

Wautelet, Y., Kolp, M., & Achbany, Y. (2006). *S-tropos: An iterative spem-centric software project management process.* Technical Report IAG Working paper 06/01, IAGISYS Information Systems Research Unit, Catholic University of Louvain, Belgium. http://www.iag.ucl.ac.be/wp/.

Wegner, P., & Goldin, D. (1999). Interaction as a Framework for Modeling. In P. P. Chen, J. Akoka, H. Kangassalo, & B. Thalheim (Eds.), *Conceptual Modeling.* Berlin: Springer (LNCS 1565), pp. 100-114

Weiss, G., (ed.) (1997). *Learning in DAI Systems.* Springer Verlag.

Wenhong, L., & Strong, D. M. (2004). A framework for evaluating ERP implementation choices. *IEEE transactions on Engineering Management, 51*(3), 322-332.

WfMC (1999). *Workflow Management Coalition Interface 1: Process Definition Interchange Process Model* (Technical report No. WfMC TC-1016-P). Lighthouse Point, FL: Workflow Management Coalition.[gs1]

WfMC (2002). *Workflow Process Definition Interface - XML Process Definition Language* (Technical report No. WFMC-TC-1025). Lighthouse Point, FL: Workflow Management Coalition.

Wheatly, M. (2000). ERP Training Stinks. *CIO Magazine, 13*(June 1), 86-96.

Wiederhold, G. (1992). Mediators in the architecture of future information systems. *IEEE Computer, 25*(3).

Willcocks, L. P., & Stykes, R. (2000). The role of the CIO and IT function in ERP. Association for Computing Machinery. *Communications of the ACM, 43,* (4), 32-38.

Wilson, D. T. (1995). An Integrated Model of Buyer-Seller Relationships. *Journal of the Academy of Marketing Science, 23*(4), 335-345.

Winner, L. (1977). *Autonomous Technology. Technics-out-of-Control as a Theme in Political Thought.* London: MIT Press.

Woodie, A. (2006, January 25). AMR Sees 'Huge Surge' in ERP Spending, Most Likely at Microsoft. The Windows Observer. Retrieved on Feb. 9, 2006 from http://www.itjungle.com/two/two012506

Woods, S. G., & Barbacci, M. (1999). *Architectural evaluation of collaborative agent-based systems.* Technical Report SEI-99-TR-025, SEI, Carnegie Mellon University, Pittsburgh, USA.

Wooldridge, M., & Jennings, N. R. (1995). Intelligent agents: Theory and practice. *Knowledge Engineering Review, 2*(10).

Wright, S., & Wright, A. M. (2002). Information System Assurance for Enterprise Resource Planning Systems: Unique Risk Considerations. *Journal of Information Systems, 16* Supplement, 99-113.

WSMO Working Group (2005). *The Web Service Modeling Language WSML*. Retrieved Aug 20, 2005, from http://www.wsmo.org/wsml/wsml-syntax

Wu, J.-H., & Wang, Y.-M. (2007). Measuring ERP Success: The Key-Users' Viewpoint of the ERP to Produce a Viable IS in the Organization. *Computers in Human Behavior, 23*, 1582-1596.

Yamazaki, Y., Iwamida, H., & Watanabe, K. (2004). Technologies for voice portal platform. *Fujitsu Scientific and Technical Journal, 40*(1), 179-186.

Yoshino, M. Y., & Srinivasa Rangan, U. (1995). *Strategic alliances: An entrepreneurial approach to globalization.* Harvard Business School Press.

Young, G., & Fort, L. (1994). Household Responses to Economic Change: Migration and Maquiladora work in Ciudad Juarez, Mexico. *Social Science Quarterly, 75*(3), 656-670.

Yu, E. (1995). Modelling Strategic Relationships for Process Reengineering. PhD thesis, University of Toronto, Department of Computer Science.

Zadeh, L. A. (1973). Outline of a new approach to the analysis of complex systems and decision processes. *IEEE Transactions on Systems, Man and Cybernetics, 3*(1), 28-44.

Zhai, S., Kristensson, P.-O., Smith, B. A., (2005). In search of effective text input interfaces for off the desktop computing. *Interacting with Computers, 17*(3), 229–250.

Zrimsek, B. (2002). *ERPII: The Boxed Set.* Retrieved July 7, 2005, from http://www.gartner.com/pages/story.php.id.2376.s.8.jsp

Zuboff, S. (1988). *In the Age of the Smart Machine: The Future of Work and Power.* Oxford, UK: Heinemann Professional Publishing.

About the Contributors

Angappa Gunasekaran is a professor of Operations Management and the Chairperson of the Department of Decision and Information Sciences in the Charlton College of Business at the University of Massachusetts (North Dartmouth, USA). Previously, he has held academic positions in Canada, India, Finland, Australia and Great Britain. He has BE and ME from the University of Madras and a PhD from the Indian Institute of Technology. He teaches and conducts research in operations management and information systems. He serves on the editorial board of 20 journals and edits a journal. He has published about 200 articles in journals, 60 articles in conference proceedings and four edited books. In addition, he has organized several conferences in the emerging areas of operations management and information systems. He has extensive editorial experience that includes the guest editor of many high profile journals. He has received outstanding paper and excellence in teaching awards. His current areas of research include supply chain management, enterprise resource planning, e-commerce, and benchmarking. He is also the director of Business Innovation Research Center (BIRC).

* * *

Emad M. Kamhawi is an associate professor in the Efficient Productivity Institute Zagazig University. He received his PhD in management information systems from The University of North London. His previous research articles have been published in international journals such as: *Information Resources Management Journal; Business Process Management Journal; International Journal of Enterprise Information Systems*; and *Journal of Enterprise Information Management*, in subjects concerning: Business process reengineering; ERP systems, the adoption of e-commerce systems in the Arab countries IS requisite skills, and risk factors for IT projects in the Gulf area. His current research interests are in BPR, ERP systems, Knowledge management and IT infrastructures management.

Ronald E. McGaughey (PhD, Auburn University) is a professor of Management Information Systems at the University of Central Arkansas. His research appears in the *Journal of Systems Management, Information and Management, International Journal of Production Economics, International Journal of Computer Integrated Manufacturing, Journal of Information Technology Management, Production Control, Benchmarking: An International Journal, Journal of Electronic Commerce in Organizations,* the *European Journal of Operational Research* and more. He is the Internet editor for *Benchmarking: an International Journal* and serves on the editorial board of numerous journals. He has practical management experience in the textile, construction and logging industries. His current research interests include advanced manufacturing technology, e-commerce, m-commerce, and IT careers.

Mohan Rao is an associate professor of Computer Information Systems at the University of Texas Pan American. He holds a PhD in business administration from the University of Alabama. He received a master's degree in Management Sciences from the University of Waterloo, Canada. He is a certified fellow in production and inventory management. His research interests are in decision support systems, expert systems, IT evaluation and performance measurement. He has over 50 refereed journal publications and proceedings. Some of his articles have appeared in *Management Science, Expert Systems with Applications, Management Accounting Quarterly, International Journal of Operations & Production Management, Industrial Management & Data Systems, Journal of International Technology and Information Management,* and *Total Quality Management & Business Excellence.*

Purnendu Mandal is professor and chair at the Information Systems and Analysis Department, Lamar University, Beaumont, Texas. His teaching and research interests are in the areas of supply chain management with SAP, database management systems, e-commerce, strategic management information systems, and management information systems, system dynamics. He published over 150 journal and conference refereed articles. His research papers have appeared in *European Journal of Operational Research, International Journal of Production Economics, Management Decision, International Journal of Operations & Production Management, International Journal of Quality & Reliability Management, Logistics Information Management, Intelligent Automation and Soft Computing: An International Journal, International Journal of Technology Management, ASCE Journal of Management in Engineering, Decision, Applied Mathematical Modeling,* etc.

Henk Jonkers received an MSc degree in computer science from the University of Twente, The Netherlands, in 1990 and a PhD from Delft University of Technology in 1995. From 1995 until 2007, he was a member of Scientific Staff at Telematica Instituut, where he was involved in various research projects and advice trajectories in the areas of, among others, business process modelling and analysis, enterprise architecture, service-oriented architecture and model-driven development. Since October 2007 he has been employed as a senior research consultant at BiZZdesign, a company offering modelling and analysis tools, consultancy and training in the areas of business process management/engineering and enterprise architecture.

Maria-Eugenia Iacob is currently assistant professor at the University of Twente. Previously she worked as scientific researcher at Telematica Instituut (2000-2006). She holds a PhD degree in mathematical analysis from the University Babes-Bolyai of Cluj-Napoca, Romania, where she also worked (1990-2000), as an assistant professor at the Department of Computer Science. She has carried out research in the areas of business and e-business process (re)engineering, (enterprise) information systems architectures, service oriented architectures, model-driven development and e-government. She has also carried out consultancy work for Dutch financial and governmental institutions in the above-mentioned areas.

S. Parthasarathy is a lecturer in the Department of Computer Applications, Thiagarajar College of Engineering, Madurai, Tamil Nadu, India. He is a BSc, (Mathematics), MCA, (Master of Computer Applications), MPhil., (Computer Science), PGDBA., (Business Administration), PGDPM, (Planning and Project Management) professional. A habitual rank holder, he is now working for his PhD, in computer science in the Anna University, Chennai, India. He has been teaching at the post-graduate level from 2002. He has published 4 articles in peer reviewed international journals and 10 articles in the proceedings of national and international conferences. He has written a text book "Enterprise Resource Planning (ERP) – A Managerial and Technical Perspective" published by The New Age International Publishers (P), Ltd., New Delhi, India in the year 2007. His current research interests include enterprise information systems, enterprise resource planning and software engineering.

Manuel Kolp is a professor in Information Systems at the Université catholique de Louvain, Belgium where he is also head of the Information Systems Research Unit and Academic Secretary of Research for the Louvain School of Management. Dr. Kolp is also invited professor with the University of Brussels and the Universitary Faculties St. Louis of Brussels. His research work deals with agent-oriented and socio-technical architectures for e-business and ERP II systems. He was previously a post doctoral fellow and an adjunct professor at the University of Toronto. He has been involved in the organization committee of international conferences and has chaired different workshops. His publications include more than 60 international refereed journals or periodicals and proceedings papers as well as three books.

Yves Wautelet is an IT project manager and a postdoc fellow at the Université catholique de Louvain, Belgium. He completed a PhD thesis focusing on project and risk management issues in large enterprise software design. Dr. Wautelet also holds a bachelor and master in management sciences as well as a master in Information Systems. His research interests include aspects of software engineering such as requirements engineering, software project management, software development life cycles and CASE-Tools development as well as information systems strategy.

Stéphane Faulkner is an associate professor in Technologies and Information Systems at the University of Namur (FUNDP). Dr. Faulkner is also invited professor with the Universitary Faculties St. Louis of Brussels. His interests of research evolve around requirements engineering and the development of precise (formal) modeling notations, systematic methods and tool support for the development of multi-agent systems, database and information systems. His publications include more than 40 international refereed journals or periodicals and proceedings papers.

Piotr Soja is a senior lecturer in the Department of Computer Science at the Cracow University of Economics (Poland). He holds a PhD in economics from the Cracow University of Economics and an MBA from the School of Entrepreneurship and Management at the Cracow University of Economics in association with the University of Teeside (UK). He also holds an MSc in computer science and mathematics from Jagiellonian University of Cracow (Poland). Dr. Soja's current research focuses on enterprise systems, their impact and implementation issues. He has over eight years of industry experience as an ERP consultant, system analyst and software developer. Dr. Soja has published articles is *Business Process Management Journal, Information Technology for Development, International Journal of Enterprise Information Systems,* and *Journal of Enterprise Information Management.*

Dariusz Put is a senior lecturer in the Department of Computer Science at the Cracow University of Economics (Poland). He graduated from the Cracow University of Economics in 1992 and received PhD in economics in 2001. He has been working for the Cracow University of Economics for 14 years supervising master students and doing research in statistics and computer science. He has published more than thirty both academic and student papers and books. His research focuses mainly on statistics and computer science, especially data, information and knowledge management and integration of business proceses.

Shuchih Ernest Chang is an associate professor at the Institute of Electronic Commerce, National Chung Hsing University (NCHU) in Taiwan. He received his MSCS and PhD degrees from the University of Texas at Austin. Before joining the faculty at NCHU, Dr. Chang worked at UBS Financial Services Inc. in U.S.A. as a Divisional Vice President for about 5 years. He has 15 years of working experience in major computer companies and financial service firms in U.S.A., including Unisys, IBM, Sun Microsystems, JP Morgan, Bear Stearns, and UBS. His research interests are in information management, electronic commerce, enterprise application architecture, technology management, information security management, and voice-enabled web systems. His publications have appeared in *IEEE Pervasive Computing, Information and Software Technology, Expert Systems with Applications, International Journal on Artificial Intelligence Tools, Industrial Management & Data Systems, International Journal of Enterprise Information Systems, International Journal of Information Technology and Management, International Journal of Technology Management, and International Journal of Production Research.*

Dafid Agourram holds a doctorate in business administration (DBA) from the Université de Serbrooke. Before joining Bishop's University in 2001, Dr. Agourram taught at McGill University, École des Hautes Études Commerciales de Montréal, and Université du Québec à Montréal. Dr. Agourram has also worked in the industry for nine years. He was the dean of a private business school, human resource director in an insurance company, and software engineer in a bank. Dr. Agourram is a regular member of the Groupe de recherche en Geobusiness de l'Université de Sherbrooke.

John Krogstie has a PhD (1995) and a MSc (1991) in information systems, both from the Norwegian University of Science and Technology (NTNU). He is professor in Information, Systems at IDI, NTNU, Trondheim, Norway. He is also a senior advisor at SINTEF. He was employed as a manager in Accenture 1991-2000. John Krogstie is the Norwegian representative for IFIP TC8 and vice-chair of IFIP WG 8.1 on information systems design and evaluation, where he is the initiator and leader of the task group for Mobile Information Systems. He has published around 80 refereed papers in journals, books and archival proceedings since 1991.

Csaba Veres completed his PhD in 1997, in Tucson Arizona. In the successive years he held appointments at the Australian Department of Defence, and at the University of Melbourne. He has in 2003-2006 at the Norwegian University of Science and Technology, Trondheim, working on foundational issues in Ontology design for Semantic Web applications. He currently works as researcher and systems analyst at DSTO, Melbourne, Australia

Guttorm Sindre got his PhD in information systems from the NTH, Trondheim, Norway in 1990. He has been an associate professor at NTNU, Trondheim, Norway since 1999, and a full professor since 2003. His research interests are IS modeling and requirements engineering, recently with a particular focus on interoperability, security, privacy, and trust. He has been involved in several national and international research projects, currently participating in the EU Network of Excellence INTEROP. He has spent two sabbatical periods totaling 14 months at the Univ. Auckland, New Zealand.

Øyvind Skytøen is a master student at Norwegian University of Science and Technology (NTNU), Information Systems group

Vittaldas Prabhu received his PhD in Mechanical Engineering from the University of Wisconsin-Madison. He is currently an associate professor in Industrial and Manufacturing Engineering at Penn State University. His research interests include distributed control systems, sensing and control of machines, and high performance computing for manufacturing systems. He teaches courses in robotics, controls, and manufacturing systems. He is the founder and co-director of the Center for Manufacturing Enterprise Integration at Penn State University.

Docent Lea Kutvonen acts as a professor at the Department of Computer Science at the University of Helsinki, Finland. She leads the Collaborative and Interoperable Computing Group (CINCO) with interest to federated management of B2B collaboration lifecycle and interoperability. The themes emerging from the area include architecture issues, e-contracting, non-functional aspects such as trust management, and coordination and composition of Web Services. The CINCO group is a part of the Distributed Systems and Data Communication research area.

Toni Ruokolainen holds an MSc in computer science and he is currently a PhD student in the CINCO group at the University of Helsinki. His research interests include service-oriented software engineering and metainformation management facilities in the context of interoperability middleware.

Sini Ruohomaa holds an MSc in computer science and she is currently a PhD student in the CINCO group at the University of Helsinki. Her research interests include trust and reputation management in open collaboration systems and inter-enterprise computing, with a focus on automated trust decisions.

Janne Metso holds an MSc in Computer Science and he is currently a PhD student in the CINCO group at the University of Helsinki. His research is focused on runtime negotiation facilities and expert system support for establishing and maintaing inter-enterprise collaborations.

Joseph Bradley is an assistant professor of Accounting at the University of Idaho. He received his BA from Claremont McKenna College and his EMBA and PhD from Claremont Graduate University. His research focuses on ERP implementation issues. His research has been published in the *International Journal of Enterprise Information Systems, Issues in Information Systems and the International Journal of Accounting Information Systems.* He has presented his research at the Information Resource Management Association International Conference and Americas' Conference on Information Systems. His teaching interests include accounting information systems, management accounting, leadership, and strategy. Prior to his academic career, he spent 30 years in industry in various accounting and general management positions.

C. Christopher Lee is an associate professor of Business Administration at Pacific Lutheran University. He received his PhD and MBA at Saint Louis University. His research interests include information systems and finance. His research has been published in *Issues in Information Systems, E-Business Review,* the *International Journal of Enterprise Information System*s and the *Journal of Economic Studies.* His teaching interests include management information systems and finance.

Diego Milano earned his PhD in computer science at the Department of Computer and Systems Science of the University of Rome "La Sapienza", under the supervision of Prof. Tiziana Catarci, and he is currently a postdoctoral researcher at the Department of Computer Science of the University of Basel. His main research interests are in the areas of Data Quality and Data Cleaning, with a specific focus on the problem of Object Identification for semi-structured and XML Data. In this context, he has developed solutions based on novel, efficiently computable distance measures for tree-structured data. He is also active in the areas of data curation, digital libraries, and service oriented architectures. He has been involved in various EU funded research initiatives, including the Networks of Excellence INTEROP and DELOS.

Monica Scannapieco is a researcher at ISTAT and a lecturer at Università di Roma "La Sapienza", Dipartimento di Informatica e Sistemistica, where she earned a PhD in computer engineering with the thesis "DaQuinCIS: Exchanging and Improving Data Quality in Cooperative Information Systems", in which theoretical and application oriented aspects of data quality in distributed and heterogeneous systems were investigated. She is author of more than 30 papers mainly on the data quality, privacy preservation and data integration architectures. She published, amongst others, in the ACM SIGMOD Conference, IEEE International Conference on Data Engineering (ICDE), the International Conference on Information Quality (ICIQ), International Conference on Cooperative Information Systems (CoopIS), Journal of Data Semantics, Information Systems. She has been involved in several Europeans and Italian projects on quality of data and data integration.

Tiziana Catarci received her PhD in computer science from the University of Rome, where she is currently a full professor. Tiziana Catarci's main research interests are in theoretical and application oriented aspects of database design, cooperative information systems, data quality, visual formalisms for databases, user interfaces, usability, and Web access. On these topics she has published over 100 papers and 12 books. Tiziana Catarci has been often invited to give talks during important international conferences and is regularly in the program committees and editorial boards of the main conferences and journals in her areas of interest.

Vipul Jain is a researcher at INRIA (The French National Institute for Research in Computer Science and Control) since December 2006. He has received his PhD in Industrial Engineering from the Department of Mechanical Engineering at IIT-Delhi in 2006. At INRIA, in addition to the fundamental research, he is also involved in the European project I*PROMS (Innovative PROduction Machines and Systems). His primary research interests are supply chain management and mechanism design in supply chain settings. He is the editorial board member for seven international journals, including *International Journal of Industrial Engineering, International Journal of Intelligent Enterprise, International Journal of Information Systems and Supply Chain Management, International Journal of Management Development, International Journal of Agile and Extereme Software Develoment, International Journal of*

Information & Decision Sciences and Information Technology Management an official publication of Information Resources Management Association.

S. G. Deshmukh is a professor of Industrial Engineering at the Mechanical Engineering Department of IIT, Delhi. His areas of research interest include supply chain management, quality management, information systems, and systems optimization. He has been actively involved in sponsored research and consultancy projects. He is dedicated to the goal of bringing synergy between academics, industry and research.

Subhash Wadhawa (Eur. Ing., C. Emg.) received his PhD from NUI, Ireland, while working on an ESPRIT project at CIM Research Unit., Galwai. He extensively contributed to the development of generalized simulators and expert systems for flexible systems. He is currently professor at Indian Institute of Technology, New Delhi (IITD). He has originated novel research themes: decision and information delays involving decision-information synchronization (DIS) applications in CIM, supply chain, e-business; DRIS architecture for agile manufacturing; SAMIN architecture in IMS context, etc. He is an active contributor to EC projects in the IT&C domain and has coordinated several EU workshops. He has been a consultant/contributor/national-expert to many International bodies EC, UNIDO, CW, APO (Tokyo), etc.

Index

North American Free Trade Agreement (NAFTA) 34

O

ontologies 177
organizational drift from enterprise system use 331
organizational patterns, modeling 95
organization theory 92, 93
outbound transaction system 203
overseas competition 37
OWL 179
OWL-S 182

P

peer-to-peer architecture, data quality 261–287
PennDiConn 203
PeopleSoft Implementation survey 249
performance analysis model transformations 59
Pilarcos middleware services and elements 214
platform-specific models (PSMs) 53
prioritized fuzzy constraint 291
process automation with Web services (PAWS) 204
process modeling languages 184
public sector undertaking company (PSC) 82
pyramid pattern 93

Q

quality evaluator for XML data sources 271
quality factory 262
quality factory, generic architecture 267
quality improvement experiments 281
quality metrics, defining 273
quality storage for XML data 269
query processing steps 277
query processor 277

R

RDF schema 176
realisation layers 57
reference ontology 266
reorientation 37
requirements-driven methodology 109
resource description framework (RDF) 174
RFID-based manufacturing execution system 202
rollout plan for training 197

S

S2S simulation tool 199
sales force automation (SFA) 21
SecSys 325
seller agent 297
service-oriented enterprise architectures 49–73
service-oriented middleware 209–241
service-oriented software engineering (SOSE) tool chain 212
service layers 57
service offer repositories 220
service types 220
simple genetic algorithms (SGAs) 142
simulation tool 199
specifying software models with organizational styles 91–113
strategic alliances 94
structure-in-5 93, 95
structuring organizations 92
supervisor agent 303
supply chain management (SCM) 21
supply chain systems 290
system interoperability by semantic Web services 172

T

technology acceptance model 245
text to speech (TTS) engine 144
TransCom 324
transport engine 279

V

voice-enabled pervasive Web system 137–155
voice-enabled Web system (VWS) x, 137
VUI optimization, example 146
VUI optimization, experiment method 145
VUI optimization, genetic algorithm 148

W

Web service modeling ontology (WSMO) 181
Web services 179
workflow modeling 184

X

XML 174
XML data, quality storage 269